App. Alt.	OCT.–MAR. SUN APR.–SEPT.				STARS PLANETS
	Lower Limb	Upper Limb	Lower Limb	Upper Limb	
0 00	−18·2	−51·7	−18·4	−51·4	−34·5
03	17·5	51·0	17·8	50·8	33·8
06	16·9	50·4	17·1	50·1	33·2
09	16·3	49·8	16·5	49·5	32·6
12	15·7	49·2	15·9	48·9	32·0
15	15·1	48·6	15·3	48·3	31·4
0 18	−14·5	−48·0	−14·8	−47·8	−30·8
21	14·0	47·5	14·2	47·2	30·3
24	13·5	47·0	13·7	46·7	29·8
27	12·9	46·4	13·2	46·2	29·2
30	12·4	45·9	12·7	45·7	28·7
33	11·9	45·4	12·2	45·2	28·2
0 36	−11·5	−45·0	−11·7	−44·7	−27·8
39	11·0	44·5	11·2	44·2	27·3
42	10·5	44·0	10·8	43·8	26·8
45	10·1	43·6	10·3	43·3	26·4
48	9·6	43·1	9·9	42·9	25·9
51	9·2	42·7	9·5	42·5	25·5
0 54	−8·8	−42·3	−9·1	−42·1	−25·1
0 57	8·4	41·9	8·7	41·7	24·7
1 00	8·0	41·5	8·3	41·3	24·3
03	7·7	41·2	7·9	40·9	24·0
06	7·3	40·8	7·5	40·5	23·6
09	6·9	40·4	7·2	40·2	23·2
1 12	−6·6	−40·1	−6·8	−39·8	−22·9
15	6·2	39·7	6·5	39·5	22·5
18	5·9	39·4	6·2	39·2	22·2
21	5·6	39·1	5·8	38·8	21·9
24	5·3	38·8	5·5	38·5	21·6
27	4·9	38·4	5·2	38·2	21·2
1 30	−4·6	−38·1	−4·9	−37·9	−20·9
35	4·2	37·7	4·4	37·4	20·5
40	3·7	37·2	4·0	37·0	20·0
45	3·2	36·7	3·5	36·5	19·5
50	2·8	36·3	3·1	36·1	19·1
1 55	2·4	35·9	2·6	35·6	18·7
2 00	−2·0	−35·5	−2·2	−35·2	−18·3
05	1·6	35·1	1·8	34·8	17·9
10	1·2	34·7	1·5	34·5	17·5
15	0·9	34·4	1·1	34·1	17·2
20	0·5	34·0	0·8	33·8	16·8
25	−0·2	33·7	0·4	33·4	16·5
2 30	+0·2	−33·3	−0·1	−33·1	−16·1
35	0·5	33·0	+0·2	32·8	15·8
40	0·8	32·7	0·5	32·5	15·5
45	1·1	32·4	0·8	32·2	15·2
50	1·4	32·1	1·1	31·9	14·9
2 55	1·6	31·9	1·4	31·6	14·7
3 00	+1·9	−31·6	+1·7	−31·3	−14·4
05	2·2	31·3	1·9	31·1	14·1
10	2·4	31·1	2·1	30·9	13·9
15	2·6	30·9	2·4	30·6	13·7
20	2·9	30·6	2·6	30·4	13·4
25	3·1	30·4	2·9	30·1	13·2
3 30	+3·3	−30·2	+3·1	−29·9	−13·0

App. Alt.	OCT.–MAR. SUN APR.–SEPT.				STARS PLANETS
	Lower Limb	Upper Limb	Lower Limb	Upper Limb	
3 30	+3·3	−30·2	+3·1	−29·9	−13·0
35	3·6	29·9	3·3	29·7	12·7
40	3·8	29·7	3·5	29·5	12·5
45	4·0	29·5	3·7	29·3	12·3
50	4·2	29·3	3·9	29·1	12·1
3 55	4·4	29·1	4·1	28·9	11·9
4 00	+4·5	−29·0	+4·3	−28·7	−11·8
05	4·7	28·8	4·5	28·5	11·6
10	4·9	28·6	4·6	28·4	11·4
15	5·1	28·4	4·8	28·2	11·2
20	5·2	28·3	5·0	28·0	11·1
25	5·4	28·1	5·1	27·9	10·9
4 30	+5·6	−27·9	+5·3	−27·7	−10·7
35	5·7	27·8	5·5	27·5	10·6
40	5·9	27·6	5·6	27·4	10·4
45	6·0	27·5	5·8	27·2	10·3
50	6·2	27·3	5·9	27·1	10·1
4 55	6·3	27·2	6·0	27·0	10·0
5 00	+6·4	−27·1	+6·2	−26·8	−9·9
05	6·6	26·9	6·3	26·7	9·7
10	6·7	26·8	6·4	26·6	9·6
15	6·8	26·7	6·6	26·4	9·5
20	6·9	26·6	6·7	26·3	9·4
25	7·1	26·4	6·8	26·2	9·2
5 30	+7·2	−26·3	+6·9	−26·1	−9·1
35	7·3	26·2	7·0	26·0	9·0
40	7·4	26·1	7·2	25·8	8·9
45	7·5	26·0	7·3	25·7	8·8
50	7·6	25·9	7·4	25·6	8·7
5 55	7·7	25·8	7·5	25·5	8·6
6 00	+7·8	−25·7	+7·6	−25·4	−8·5
10	8·0	25·5	7·8	25·2	8·3
20	8·2	25·3	8·0	25·0	8·1
30	8·4	25·1	8·1	24·9	7·9
40	8·6	24·9	8·3	24·7	7·7
6 50	8·7	24·8	8·5	24·5	7·6
7 00	+8·9	−24·6	+8·6	−24·4	−7·4
10	9·1	24·4	8·8	24·2	7·2
20	9·2	24·3	9·0	24·0	7·1
30	9·3	24·2	9·1	23·9	7·0
40	9·5	24·0	9·2	23·8	6·8
7 50	9·6	23·9	9·4	23·6	6·7
8 00	+9·7	−23·8	+9·5	−23·5	−6·6
10	9·9	23·6	9·6	23·4	6·4
20	10·0	23·5	9·7	23·3	6·3
30	10·1	23·4	9·8	23·2	6·2
					6·1
					6·0
					5·9
					5·8
					5·7
					5·6
					5·5
10 00	+11·0	−22·5	+10·7	−22·3	5·3

Additional corrections for temperature and pressure are given on the following page.
For bubble sextant observations ignore dip and use the star corrections for Sun, planets, and stars.

A4 ALTITUDE CORRECTION TABLES—ADDITIONAL CORRECTIONS

ADDITIONAL REFRACTION CORRECTIONS FOR NON-STANDARD CONDITIONS

App. Alt.	A	B	C	D	E	F	G	H	J	K	L	M	N	App. Alt.
0 00	−6·9	−5·7	−4·6	−3·4	−2·3	−1·1	0·0	+1·1	+2·3	+3·4	+4·6	+5·7	+6·9	0 00
0 30	5·2	4·4	3·5	2·6	1·7	0·9	0·0	0·9	1·7	2·6	3·5	4·4	5·2	0 30
1 00	4·3	3·5	2·8	2·1	1·4	0·7	0·0	0·7	1·4	2·1	2·8	3·5	4·3	1 00
1 30	3·5	2·9	2·4	1·8	1·2	0·6	0·0	0·6	1·2	1·8	2·4	2·9	3·5	1 30
2 00	3·0	2·5	2·0	1·5	1·0	0·5	0·0	0·5	1·0	1·5	2·0	2·5	3·0	2 00
2 30	−2·5	−2·1	−1·6	−1·2	−0·8	−0·4	0·0	+0·4	+0·8	+1·2	+1·6	+2·1	+2·5	2 30
3 00	2·2	1·8	1·5	1·1	0·7	0·4	0·0	0·4	0·7	1·1	1·5	1·8	2·2	3 00
3 30	2·0	1·6	1·3	1·0	0·7	0·3	0·0	0·3	0·7	1·0	1·3	1·6	2·0	3 30
4 00	1·8	1·5	1·2	0·9	0·6	0·3	0·0	0·3	0·6	0·9	1·2	1·5	1·8	4 00
4 30	1·6	1·4	1·1	0·8	0·5	0·3	0·0	0·3	0·5	0·8	1·1	1·4	1·6	4 30
5 00	−1·5	−1·3	−1·0	−0·8	−0·5	−0·2	0·0	+0·2	+0·5	+0·8	+1·0	+1·3	+1·5	5 00
6	1·3	1·1	0·9	0·6	0·4	0·2	0·0	0·2	0·4	0·6	0·9	1·1	1·3	6
7	1·1	0·9	0·7	0·6	0·4	0·2	0·0	0·2	0·4	0·6	0·7	0·9	1·1	7
8	1·0	0·8	0·7	0·5	0·3	0·2	0·0	0·2	0·3	0·5	0·7	0·8	1·0	8
9	0·9	0·7	0·6	0·4	0·3	0·1	0·0	0·1	0·3	0·4	0·6	0·7	0·9	9
10 00	−0·8	−0·7	−0·5	−0·4	−0·3	−0·1	0·0	+0·1	+0·3	+0·4	+0·5	+0·7	+0·8	10 00
12	0·7	0·6	0·5	0·3	0·2	0·1	0·0	0·1	0·2	0·3	0·5	0·6	0·7	12
14	0·6	0·5	0·4	0·3	0·2	0·1	0·0	0·1	0·2	0·3	0·4	0·5	0·6	14
16	0·5	0·4	0·3	0·3	0·2	0·1	0·0	0·1	0·2	0·3	0·3	0·4	0·5	16
18	0·4	0·4	0·3	0·2	0·2	0·1	0·0	0·1	0·2	0·2	0·3	0·4	0·4	18
20 00	−0·4	−0·3	−0·3	−0·2	−0·1	−0·1	0·0	+0·1	+0·1	+0·2	+0·3	+0·3	+0·4	20 00
25	0·3	0·3	0·2	0·2	0·1	−0·1	0·0	+0·1	0·1	0·2	0·2	0·3	0·3	25
30	0·3	0·2	0·2	0·1	0·1	0·0	0·0	0·0	0·1	0·1	0·2	0·2	0·3	30
35	0·2	0·2	0·1	0·1	0·1	0·0	0·0	0·0	0·1	0·1	0·1	0·2	0·2	35
40	0·2	0·1	0·1	0·1	−0·1	0·0	0·0	0·0	+0·1	0·1	0·1	0·1	0·2	40
50 00	−0·1	−0·1	−0·1	−0·1	0·0	0·0	0·0	0·0	0·0	+0·1	+0·1	+0·1	+0·1	50 00

The graph is entered with arguments temperature and pressure to find a zone letter; using as arguments this zone letter and apparent altitude (sextant altitude corrected for dip), a correction is taken from the table. This correction is to be applied to the sextant altitude in addition to the corrections for standard conditions (for the Sun, planets and stars from the inside front cover and for the Moon from the inside back cover).

INDEX TO SELECTED STARS

Name	No.	Mag.	S.H.A.	Dec.
Acamar	7	3·1	316	S. 40°
Achernar	5	0·6	336	S. 57
Acrux	30	1·1	174	S. 63
Adhara	19	1·6	256	S. 29
Aldebaran	10	1·1	292	N. 16
Alioth	32	1·7	167	N. 56
Alkaid	34	1·9	153	N. 49
Al Na'ir	55	2·2	28	S. 47
Alnilam	15	1·8	276	S. 1
Alphard	25	2·2	219	S. 9
Alphecca	41	2·3	127	N. 27
Alpheratz	1	2·2	358	N. 29
Altair	51	0·9	63	N. 9
Ankaa	2	2·4	354	S. 42
Antares	42	1·2	113	S. 26
Arcturus	37	0·2	146	N. 19
Atria	43	1·9	109	S. 69
Avior	22	1·7	235	S. 59
Bellatrix	13	1·7	279	N. 6
Betelgeuse	16	Var.*	272	N. 7
Canopus	17	−0·9	264	S. 53
Capella	12	0·2	281	N. 46
Deneb	53	1·3	50	N. 45
Denebola	28	2·2	183	N. 15
Diphda	4	2·2	350	S. 18
Dubhe	27	2·0	195	N. 62
Elnath	14	1·8	279	N. 29
Eltanin	47	2·4	91	N. 51
Enif	54	2·5	34	N. 10
Fomalhaut	56	1·3	16	S. 30
Gacrux	31	1·6	173	S. 57
Gienah	29	2·8	176	S. 17
Hadar	35	0·9	150	S. 60
Hamal	6	2·2	329	N. 23
Kaus Australis	48	2·0	85	S. 34
Kochab	40	2·2	137	N. 74
Markab	57	2·6	14	N. 15
Menkar	8	2·8	315	N. 4
Menkent	36	2·3	149	S. 36
Miaplacidus	24	1·8	222	S. 70
Mirfak	9	1·9	310	N. 50
Nunki	50	2·1	77	S. 26
Peacock	52	2·1	54	S. 57
Pollux	21	1·2	244	N. 28
Procyon	20	0·5	246	N. 5
Rasalhague	46	2·1	97	N. 13
Regulus	26	1·3	208	N. 12
Rigel	11	0·3	282	S. 8
Rigil Kentaurus	38	0·1	141	S. 61
Sabik	44	2·6	103	S. 16
Schedar	3	2·5	350	N. 56
Shaula	45	1·7	97	S. 37
Sirius	18	−1·6	259	S. 17
Spica	33	1·2	159	S. 11
Suhail	23	2·2	223	S. 43
Vega	49	0·1	81	N. 39
Zubenelgenubi	39	2·9	138	S. 16

No.	Name	Mag.	S.H.A.	Dec.
1	Alpheratz	2·2	358	N. 29°
2	Ankaa	2·4	354	S. 42
3	Schedar	2·5	350	N. 56
4	Diphda	2·2	350	S. 18
5	Achernar	0·6	336	S. 57
6	Hamal	2·2	329	N. 23
7	Acamar	3·1	316	S. 40
8	Menkar	2·8	315	N. 4
9	Mirfak	1·9	310	N. 50
10	Aldebaran	1·1	292	N. 16
11	Rigel	0·3	282	S. 8
12	Capella	0·2	281	N. 46
13	Bellatrix	1·7	279	N. 6
14	Elnath	1·8	279	N. 29
15	Alnilam	1·8	276	S. 1
16	Betelgeuse	Var.*	272	N. 7
17	Canopus	−0·9	264	S. 53
18	Sirius	−1·6	259	S. 17
19	Adhara	1·6	256	S. 29
20	Procyon	0·5	246	N. 5
21	Pollux	1·2	244	N. 28
22	Avior	1·7	235	S. 59
23	Suhail	2·2	223	S. 43
24	Miaplacidus	1·8	222	S. 70
25	Alphard	2·2	219	S. 9
26	Regulus	1·3	208	N. 12
27	Dubhe	2·0	195	N. 62
28	Denebola	2·2	183	N. 15
29	Gienah	2·8	176	S. 17
30	Acrux	1·1	174	S. 63
31	Gacrux	1·6	173	S. 57
32	Alioth	1·7	167	N. 56
33	Spica	1·2	159	S. 11
34	Alkaid	1·9	153	N. 49
35	Hadar	0·9	150	S. 60
36	Menkent	2·3	149	S. 36
37	Arcturus	0·2	146	N. 19
38	Rigil Kentaurus	0·1	141	S. 61
39	Zubenelgenubi	2·9	138	S. 16
40	Kochab	2·2	137	N. 74
41	Alphecca	2·3	127	N. 27
42	Antares	1·2	113	S. 26
43	Atria	1·9	109	S. 69
44	Sabik	2·6	103	S. 16
45	Shaula	1·7	97	S. 37
46	Rasalhague	2·1	97	N. 13
47	Eltanin	2·4	91	N. 51
48	Kaus Australis	2·0	85	S. 34
49	Vega	0·1	81	N. 39
50	Nunki	2·1	77	S. 26
51	Altair	0·9	63	N. 9
52	Peacock	2·1	54	S. 57
53	Deneb	1·3	50	N. 45
54	Enif	2·5	34	N. 10
55	Al Na'ir	2·2	28	S. 47
56	Fomalhaut	1·3	16	S. 30
57	Markab	2·6	14	N. 15

* 0·1—1·2

"*You are being sent into a fraternity where men are closer to each other than they are to their own blood brothers, into a service whose only purpose and mission is to protect the common rights of men, into the comradeship of a group where there are no eight-hour days and no five-day weeks, where loyalty is the watchword and where 'well done' is duty's compensation; into the traditions of men like Jones, Porter, Farragut, Kidd.*"—Captain William N. Thomas (Ch.C.), Chaplain, U.S. Naval Academy, Annapolis, June 14, 1942.*

Primer *of* Navigation

EIGHT BELLS

From the Etching by Winslow Homer

Primer
of
Navigation

SIXTH EDITION

With Problems in Practical Work

AND

Complete Tables

By GEORGE W. MIXTER

Revised for Sixth Edition
By DONALD McCLENCH
Captain, USNR (Ret.)
and
DONALD B. MILLAR
Captain, USN (Ret.)

VAN NOSTRAND REINHOLD COMPANY
NEW YORK   CINCINNATI   ATLANTA   DALLAS   SAN FRANCISCO
LONDON   TORONTO   MELBOURNE

Van Nostrand Reinhold Company Regional Offices:
New York   Cincinnati   Chicago   Millbrae   Dallas

Van Nostrand Reinhold Company International Offices:
London   Toronto   Melbourne

Copyright © 1979 by Litton Educational Publishing, Inc.
Library of Congress Catalog Card Number 78-13932
ISBN: 0-442-25222-6

Published by Van Nostrand Reinhold Company
135 West 50th Street, New York, N.Y. 10020

Published simultaneously in Canada by
Van Nostrand Reinhold Ltd.

15 14 13 12 11 10 9 8 7 6 5 4 3

Library of Congress Cataloging in Publication Data

Mixter, George Webber, 1876-1947.
  Primer of navigation.

  Includes index.
  1. Navigation.   I.   McClench, Donald, joint author.
II.   Millar, Donald B., joint author.   III.   Title.
VK555.M58   1979   623.89   78-13932
ISBN 0-442-25222-6

Preface to the Fifth Edition

Whether regarded as an Art or as a Science, the "mystique" of the navigator continues to be nourished by progress in technology. Many of the advances occurring during the last few years have been included in this Fifth Edition. Without attempting to weigh their relative importance, the following developments may, perhaps, be of most interest to present-day navigators:

The new *Sight Reduction Tables for Marine Navigation* (H.O. 229) soon to be published in six volumes. This is the first, truly-universal table giving precomputed solutions of the navigational triangle for uniform, world-wide 1° intervals of latitude, declination, and hour angle.

A new method for defining visibility in the atmosphere as it affects the luminous range of navigational lights.

Certain changes in the shapes of buoys and the characteristics of lights.

A discussion of the new International Rules of the Road which, for the first time, clarify the role of radar in collision avoidance at sea.

Other refinements in this edition include illustrations of some new electronic gear, a restatement of the significance of the navigational triangle, and more examples of the use of loran and radiobeacons, particularly in the "Cruises." In addition, the few errors brought to light by letters from readers have been corrected. Such letters are always welcome.

Voice announcements of time signals from Bureau of Standards radio station WWV, formerly given in Eastern Standard Time (G.M.T. − 5 hours) are now, in January 1967, given in Mountain Standard Time (G.M.T. − 7 hours). Surface navigators may have difficulty in receiving transmissions from the new Colorado location on the frequency 2.5 mc. Radio equipment to be used for receiving time signals from WWV should be capable of tuning to one or more of the higher transmitted frequencies, 5, 10, 15, 20, and 25, mc.

Appreciation is expressed to the U. S. Coast Guard, particularly to LCdr. W. R. Fearn, USCG for much current information on the loran and radiobeacon systems; and to Mr. Charles Pearce for his help on aids to navigation. The kind permission of the Nautical Almanac Office, U. S. Naval Observatory, Mr. Ralph F. Haupt, Assistant Director, to reproduce the Navigational Star Chart and other material from the almanacs is gratefully acknowledged.

I am also indebted to Mr. John H. Blythe, Director of the Division of Navigational Science, U. S. Naval Oceanographic Office, and to Dr. Raynor L. Duncombe, Director of the Nautical Almanac Office, U. S. Naval Observatory, for permission to excerpt their article in *Navigation* on H. O. 229 which was co-authored with Dr. D. H. Sadler of H. M. Nautical Almanac Office, Royal Greenwich Observatory.

Since many of the illustrations and other matters have been carried forward into this edition, the previous acknowledgments are again extended where applicable. However, special thanks are due and offered to the suppliers of some of the navigational equipment mentioned in the text, particularly Raytheon Company, Radio Corporation of America, and Weems System of Navigation for furnishing illustrations of some of their devices.

I wish also to extend thanks to Captain and Mrs. Howard L. Peterson for their very great assistance and meticulous care in again verifying new examples and problems, and for typing and proofreading manuscript. And to my wife, a big "thank you" for her careful help in compiling the tabular excerpts and in proofreading the index.

'Annapolis, Maryland   D. M.

Preface to the Sixth Edition

The continued development of navigation since 1967 has brought several new tools for use by the marine navigator particularly in the area of precise positioning and communications by electronic means. The expansion of LORAN C as the planned future replacement of LORAN A as the U.S. coastal electronic positioning system and the steady development of the world wide OMEGA system are prime examples. Also the advancement of very high frequency—frequency modulated (VHF-FM) and single side band (SSB) radio telephone communication systems providing long-range reliable communication is a noteworthy aid to all mariners.

A further advance of great importance to navigators is the implementation of the new International Rules for Preventing Collisions at Sea, 1972—(72 COLREGS). This changed the rules governing certain lights, shapes and the actions required by all vessels navigating on the high seas.

In bringing the previous edition up to date, it has been necessary to modify or replace those portions of the text and related illustrations which have become obsolete. The Special Star Charts have been recomputed and replotted. Also they have been enclosed in a compass rose to assist in the determination of azimuth.

Simplicity, the outstanding feature of former editions, is continued and emphasis retained on how to navigate with available tables and almanacs. Every effort has been made to retain the original style and format which has proven to be clear and helpful to many students of navigation. Since many of the illustrations have been carried forward into this edition the previous acknowledgments are extended where applicable.

Thanks are due to Mr. C. H. Menke, Director of the Cartographic Department of the Defence Mapping Agency Hydrographic Center for his help in preparation of the new Star Charts and to Mr. Paul M. Anderton of Annapolis, Maryland, for his constructive criticism in pointing out areas requiring revision.

Although care has been exercised to insure accuracy, notification of any errors will be appreciated.

D.B.M.

G. W. Bunxter

GEORGE W. MIXTER

The following sketch of George W. Mixter was written by Mr. William
H. Taylor, now deceased. Because of its biographical interest, it is
repeated in this edition.

FOR a man whose career began in the farm machinery business, who
was later an industrial and consulting engineer, who served his country in the Army Air Force rather than in the Navy, and whose hobbies in
early life were canoeing, fishing and hunting in the Canadian North
Woods, to have produced the outstanding book of his time on nautical
piloting and celestial navigation may seem surprising. It is a field usually associated with retired shipmasters. But as George Mixter more
than once remarked, everything he had ever done from boyhood on
seemed to have contributed, in one way or another, to the production of
the *Primer of Navigation*. It was a work which became not only his absorbing hobby but a major contribution to the science of navigation and
to his country's training program in World War II.

George Webber Mixter was born in Rock Island, Illinois, May 21,
1876. His boyhood summers were spent in the West but he was educated
in private and public schools in New Haven, Connecticut, and in Yale
University where his father, William Gilbert Mixter, was professor of
chemistry. He studied electrical engineering and was graduated from
Yale's Sheffield Scientific School at nineteen; he tutored in mathematics
and physics and was assistant in physics during a year of graduate work
under Willard Gibbs, and then did additional graduate work at Johns
Hopkins, under Henry A. Rowland.

As a boy, with two friends, he got out a newspaper, setting the type—
this at the age of ten. With another friend, Harry Foote, he set up and
operated a private telegraph line and built a canoe in which they subse-
quently cruised down the Connecticut River from its headwaters to the
Sound. Fond of athletics, he played varsity football, but his favorite
pastimes were camping, canoeing, fishing and hunting. Surviving log
books of these trips demonstrate the same thorough preparation and efficient execution that were to characterize whatever he did through life.

These logs show the genesis of another hobby, photography, which he carried on throughout his later travels, thus illustrating his diaries. His early interest in ships and the water is indicated by two summer jobs during college years, one as cook aboard a Nova Scotia coasting schooner and another running a donkey engine in a Mississippi River towboat.

In the summer of 1896, George Mixter went to work for Deere & Webber Co. of Minneapolis, a distributing house of Deere & Company, and in 1897, as cost clerk, he entered the main plant of Deere & Company at Moline, Illinois. This farm implement company had developed from the original blacksmith shop in which George Mixter's maternal great-grandfather, John Deere, had invented the steel plow after he moved West from his native Vermont by canal boat and covered wagon in 1837. Besides setting up what was then an entirely new cost accounting system, young Mixter successively became master mechanic, foreman, assistant superintendent, superintendent of their Plow Works, and vice president in charge of manufacturing. His trips as field expert and to study farm conditions and requirements took him into most of the 48 States and to various foreign countries, especially South America and Russia. He played an important role in the financial and production operations of the company and in the design and development of some of its products. Until 1942 he remained a director of Deere & Company, making frequent trips West up to that time.

He left Deere & Company in 1917 to enter the U. S. Army's Air Service as a major, rising to colonel; became Chief of Aircraft Production and Inspection, and was head of the Air Service Claims Board in 1918.

After World War I he was a partner in the engineering firm of George W. Goethals & Company, New York, until that organization was dissolved. In 1923 George Mixter became a vice president and director of Day & Zimmermann, Inc., engineers and consultants, of Philadelphia. He was manager of their New York office until his death in 1947.

W. Findlay Downs, president of Day & Zimmermann and close personal friend of George Mixter, writes:

"Colonel Mixter brought with him a background of training and experience in the heavy manufacturing industry in which he had won signal success. For nearly a quarter of a century with Day & Zimmermann he made important contributions by reason of his strong personality, analytical and research abilities, firm convictions and sound judgment. His advice and counsel, invaluable to his associates, were sought in many fields of industrial activity, wherever large-scale factory layouts, production problems and the economic development and use of tools were involved.

"His unbounded energy and canny ability to search out and evaluate the essential facts of the problem before him were the basis of his rare judgment and wise advice. No essential detail was overlooked, even if it meant long hours burning midnight oil.

"During World War II his professional engineering talents were sought and used to great advantage in the execution of important contracts for the Army, Navy and Air Services."

A book, *Aircraft Production Facts;* a series of papers on problem study of industrial management presented at the University of Pennsylvania, and similar work, together with his writing of engineering reports, all contributed in a sense to the later writing of the *Primer,* as did his teaching experience at different periods, beside his early mathematical, drawing and drafting training. A lifelong habit of designing on his drawing board various things for his own use added to the foundation for the graphic portion of this final work. Making his home in New York in later life, he served that city on its Taxicab Commission in 1930 and Board of Taxicab Control in 1932.

Return to the seaboard permitted a resumption of his early interest in sailing, and he took part in the 1926 and 1928 Bermuda races in Findlay Downs' schooners *Black Goose* and *Malabar VIII.* In 1927 a yachting accident cost Colonel Mixter the sight of one eye which put an end to his hunting trips but failed to dim his enjoyment of sailing, and in the fall of 1928 he began the building of his own schooner, *Teragram.*

Teragram was designed by John G. Alden, but much of her detail, on deck and below, was her owner's own work, the result of his study of many other yachts' faults and virtues. Built to Colonel Mixter's specifications, she was one of the best constructed and equipped schooners of her day. Nothing that contributed to seaworthiness, safety or comfort was sacrificed to speed, so she was not inherently as fast as some of her lightly built and rigged rivals. Yet, thanks to her owner's constant and often inspired efforts, she won her share and more of prizes in the next decade's ocean and coastwise races.

He was constantly experimenting with and improving her rig, trim and gear, so the *Teragram* that won the New York Yacht Club's Vineyard-Marblehead Race in 1938 was a much faster boat than the *Teragram* we first sailed in the Gibson Island Race of 1929. Colonel Mixter signed on *Teragram's* amateur racing crews from among a group of crack sailors, young men mostly, who were intensely loyal to the ship and her well-loved skipper. As a member of *Teragram's* regular gang you felt a part of something special, and you had to prove it by getting the best out of her.

Characteristically, the skipper started organizing and preparing for the next June's Bermuda or Gibson Island race about the time *Teragram*

was laid up late in the previous fall.   Crews were lined up, lists of supplies made out, a few new sails usually ordered and every bit of gear
thoroughly inspected, replaced if at all doubtful.   *Teragram* was always
a boat you could crack sail onto and drive, no matter how tough the going
got, knowing there would be no mechanical failures.   Equally important
on a long, hard race, you were sure of three or four hot square meals a
day, for George was as able a culinary artist as he was a sailor and navigator; when rough weather put the professional cook in his bunk, the
skipper took over the galley and we ate better than ever.

Needless to say, *Teragram's* navigation, her skipper's specialty, was
always impeccable, and some of his first teaching of navigation was done
on board.   One of his first pupils, during the 1932 Bermuda Race, was
Chick Larkin, and when in 1946 George put up a trophy for the winning
navigator in the Cruising Club of America's Bermuda Race and Chick
won it that first year, it would be hard to say who was the prouder.

Teragram was Colonel Mixter's home for long periods of cruising during the years he owned her, and much of the work on the *Primer* was
done aboard her; or while traveling about on business since he went nowhere without his notes or manuscript.   After Pearl Harbor he presented
Teragram to the U. S. Coast Guard Academy at New London, where she
is still helping to make sailors out of future officers.

While it is on record that in 1895 the nineteen-year-old Mixter, when
working his way down the coast in the lumber schooner *Abby K. Bentley*,
took along a book on navigation, his special interest in the subject dated
from the Bermuda Race of 1926.   As cook in *Black Goose*, he was in-
trigued by the navigator's work of finding the ship's position by the sun,
moon and stars.   Learning to navigate was no great problem to a man of
George Mixter's mind and training, but in learning he found that the
existing books on this subject, as he expressed it, "lacked possible simplicity"; that their complexity discouraged the non-scientific-minded
amateur; that many were obsolete because of lately developed aids and
methods.   Most had been written by professional navigators who, having
learned the hard way, had long since lost touch with the beginner's difficulties; and many of whom apparently had the old-time shipmaster's
instinct to make navigation a mysterious art which only the chosen few
who were ship's officers could master.   This offended the sense of a man
whose work had involved simplification and clarification of engineering
matters.   He set his mind to "trying to make simple statements of scientific facts," to use his own words.

Colonel Mixter had practiced navigation not only aboard *Teragram*
but also on the bridges of ships in which he had traveled over the world
on business.   By 1930 he had put together notes from his own studies

which he called *Position from the Sun for Amateur Sailors,* bound copies of which he gave to friends. This was followed in 1932 by a set of *Position Tables and Work Forms.*

From that time on, as an increasingly absorbing hobby, he was engaged in work that culminated in the publication of the first edition of *Primer of Navigation* in 1940. His lecture *Lighthouses in the Sky* at the Franklin Institute in Philadelphia in 1938, later incorporated as a chapter in the *Primer,* was widely hailed as the greatest contribution yet made toward simplifying navigation for the layman. He also wrote helpful articles for the *U. S. Naval Institute Proceedings* and for *Yachting.*

His researches in navigation brought Colonel Mixter in touch with many navigators and astronomers here and abroad, leading to wide correspondence and discussion. His associates in the U. S. Navy, Naval Observatory, Coast Guard, and Hydrographic Office, and particularly Captain Robert E. Jasperson, USN (ret.), encouraged him to put his work into permanent book form. These men to whom he turned for information soon found that Colonel Mixter could be of great aid to them in their own work and was ready to give unstintingly of his time and effort. Few people except those immediately concerned realize the importance of the contributions that this amateur student of navigation made in the preparation of the present vastly improved Air and Nautical Almanacs, beginning with the Air Almanac of 1933.

The production of the original *Primer,* which was his own work from its broad conceptions to the detailed drawings and calculations, involved a tremendous amount of time and effort, and a great deal of expense. To Colonel Mixter it was purely a hobby, born of interest in a fascinating subject and carried through in the conviction that there was a great need, not only among yachtsmen but among officer candidates for all services, for a clearer textbook than was then available. No publisher could have envisioned it as a "best seller." Yet circumstances made it so, for by the time the *Primer* was published in 1940 Europe was ablaze and America arming. Men with an eye to possible future Naval, Merchant Marine or other service who wanted to learn navigation, quickly found in the *Primer* just the book they needed. It became a standard textbook for many training courses, and at a conservative estimate, more than 100,000 wartime navigators learned their trade primarily from the *Primer.*

A second, enlarged edition of the *Primer* and the *Primer of Navigation Key,* a book of problems, were brought out in 1943. But Colonel Mixter still found time not only for his profession, but to conduct, in his library at home, and elsewhere, classes for candidates for Navy and Coast Guard commissions; to give private instruction to many individuals—old friends and new ones alike; to lecture on navigation at Princeton University where many candidates for Naval Reserve commissions were under instruction.

At the time of Colonel Mixter's death in 1947, he and Ramon O. Williams, another enthusiastic amateur in the art of navigation, were planning a third edition to include the new developments in navigational aids and equipment which became available after World War II. Mr. Williams completed this edition shortly before his untimely death in 1952.

The lapse of time, the appearance of changes in the almanacs and other navigational publications, and the development of new and better methods justified a fourth—and now a fifth—edition. This work was undertaken by Captain Donald McClench, USNR (Ret.) who was associated with both Colonel Mixter and Mr. Williams in the preparation of the previous editions. Captain McClench has had a wide experience in navigation, having taught the subject for the U. S. Naval Academy and the U. S. Power Squadrons, and served as navigator at sea in the Navy and in several yacht races from Newport to Bermuda and Annapolis. For some years before retirement, he was Head of the Navigation Branch, Division of Navigational Science at the U.S. Naval Oceanographic Office.

CONTENTS

ABBREVIATIONS AND SYMBOLS

The abbreviations listed on the next page are commonly used by navigators. They need not be memorized; understanding of their meaning and use will develop automatically as the student progresses.

The symbols printed below are also in common use. The small letters of the Greek Alphabet are used when designating a star with the name of its constellation.

MATHEMATICAL		ARC AND TIME	
+	Plus, or add	°	Degrees
—	Minus, or subtract	′	Minutes of arc
±	Plus or minus	″	Seconds of arc
×	Times, or multiply by	d	Day
÷	Divide	h	Hours
~	Take difference	m	Minutes of time
Δ	Delta (as in H. O. 214)	s	Seconds of time

ASTRONOMICAL

☉	Sun, center	☿	Mercury
☉̲	Lower limb	♀	Venus
☉̅	Upper "	⊕	The earth
☽	Moon, center	♂	Mars
☽̲	Lower limb	♃	Jupiter
☽̅	Upper "	♄	Saturn
☆	Star	♆	Neptune

♈ Aries, the Vernal Equinox

SMALL LETTERS OF THE GREEK ALPHABET

α	Alpha	ι	Iota	ρ	Rho
β	Beta	κ	Kappa	σ or ς	Sigma
γ	Gamma	λ	Lambda	τ	Tau
δ	Delta	μ	Mu	υ	Upsilon
ϵ	Epsilon	ν	Nu	φ	Phi
ζ	Zēta	ξ	Xi	χ	Chi
η	Eta	ο	Omicron	ψ	Psi
ϑ or θ	Theta	π	Pi	ω	Omega

NOTE: The special symbols and abbreviations used on charts are explained thereon.

ABBREVIATIONS

A ....Away from assumed position

a ....Intercept or altitude difference

A.A. ....Air Almanac

AFC ....Automatic frequency control, loran

Alt. or h ....Altitude

A.M. ....Ante-meridian, before noon

A.P. ....Assumed position

Az or Z .....Azimuth angle

C ....Course

C or Chro. ..Chronometer or time by chronometer

C.E. ....Chronometer error or compass error

C. & G.S. ...U. S. Coast and Geodetic Survey

Corr. or C ..Correction

C.P. ....Computed point

C.P.A. ......Closest point of approach

C − W ....Chronometer minus watch

D ....Dip

Decl. or d ...Declination

Dev. ....Deviation

DLo. ....Difference in longitude

DMAHC ...Defence Mapping Agency Hydrographic Center

D.R. ....Dead reckoning or position by D.R.

DRT ....Dead reckoning tracer

e ....Guide or own ship's position—Maneuvering Board

E.P. ....Estimated position

Eq.T. ....Equation of time

ETA ......Estimated time of arrival

F ....Fast

G ....Greenwich or meridian of Greenwich

G.A.T. ......Greenwich apparent time

G.C.T. ......Greenwich civil time

G.H.A. .....Greenwich hour angle

G.M.T. .....Greenwich mean time

G.P. ....Geographic position

H ....High basic rate of loran

h or Alt. ....Altitude

H.A. ....Hour angle

Hc or H_c ...Computed altitude from assumed position

H.D. ....Hourly difference

H.O. ....Hydrographic Office

Ho or H_o ...Observed altitude as corrected

H.P. ....Horizontal parallax

Hs, H_s or h_s..Altitude as read from sextant

Ht. eye ......Height of eye

I.C. ....Index correction

kc ....Kilocycles

kt. ....Knot

L ....Low basic rate of loran

L.A.N. ......Local apparent noon

L.A.T. ......Local apparent time

Lat. or L ....Latitude

L.H.A. or *t*..Local hour angle or meridian angle

L.M.T. .....Local mean time

Long. or λ ..Longitude

LOP ....Line of position

M ....Meridian of ship

m ....Meridian lower branch

M_1 ....Target or maneuvering ship, 1st position

M_2 ....Target or maneuvering ship, 2nd position

min. ....Minute of time

ms. ....Microsecond

N.A. ....Nautical Almanac

NOS ....National Ocean Survey

Obs. ....Observed

p.g.c. ....Per gyro compass

P.M. ....Post meridian, after noon

P_n ....North Pole

PPI ....Plan position indicator, radar

P.R.R. ......Pulse recurrence rate, loran

P_s ....South Pole

p.s.c. ....Per standard compass

p.stg.c. ......Per steering compass

R.A. ....Right ascension

R Bn ......Radio beacon

R.D.F. ......Radio direction finder

Ref. ....Refraction

R. Fix ......Running fix

S ....Slow

S ....Speed

S.D. ....Semidiameter

S.H.A. ......Sidereal hour angle

T ....Time

T ....Toward assumed position

T ....Difference in time of arrival of loran signals

t ....Meridian angle or L.H.A.

Tab. ....Tabulated

Tg. ....Loran ground wave reading

Ts. ....Loran sky wave reading

Var. ....Variation

V.H.F. ......Very high frequency radio waves

W ....Watch

W.E. ....Watch error

W.T. ....Watch time

X ....Point of execution

Z ....Zenith

z ....Zenith distance

Z, Az ....Azimuth angle

Z.D. ....Zone description

Zn or Z_n ....Azimuth from north

Z.T. ....Zone time

Primer *of* Navigation

1. INTRODUCTION

FOR six centuries or more, the art of navigation has developed with the sciences of astronomy and mathematics, the work of the cartographer and of the instrument maker, and the expansion of governmental aids to navigation into the vast systems of today. This increasingly rapid development, spurred on by the demands of aviation, has greatly simplified the subject so far as it can be taught from books.

101. Navigation, as discussed herein, is the art of directing ships in any waters. The general working of the ship and the management of sails pertain to seamanship. Navigation is commonly divided into four elements: piloting, dead reckoning, electronic navigation, and celestial navigation.

Piloting includes conducting vessels along coasts and in and out of bays and harbors anywhere. Captain Dutton described piloting as requiring the greatest experience and the nicest judgment of any form of navigation. As used in this Primer, the term piloting implies an important element of navigation which has a much broader meaning than the work of a harbor pilot limited to familiar waters.

Dead reckoning, it is said, was originally called "deduced" reckoning, thence abbreviated D-E-D, or in the vernacular "dead" reckoning. It is an element both of piloting and of navigation at sea. In modern navigation, it is the process of finding the approximate position of the ship by plotting courses and distances from the last well-determined position, which may have been found from lighthouses or other marks along the coast, or from observations of the sun, moon, or stars. This task seems simple, but for various reasons such positions may be inaccurate.

Electronic navigation consists of the use of various electronic devices for fixing the position of the ship, both in piloting near land or among other ships, as well as at sea. The importance of electronic navigation is increasing rapidly with improvements in quality and availability of these

1

devices to the extent that it should be considered as a subject necessary for the navigator to understand.

Celestial navigation, sometimes called nautical astronomy, is the art of checking or fixing the position of the ship from observations of so-called navigational bodies which include the sun, the moon, four of the planets, and the principal stars.

102. Advances in the art. Since about 1910, in response to demand for greater safety at high speeds and, later, to necessities in the air, improvement in the equipment and methods available to navigators has been very rapid. Principles remain the same, but practice varies widely. Obviously, many of the devices used for piloting a great ship are not practical on smaller craft, although both vessels use the same charts and observe the same lighthouses and buoys. The divergence between the various methods of celestial navigation is even greater. Although some *old* navigation still continues to be used, the *new* navigation is practiced by the navies of the world, and is the usual method of yachtsmen. Most professional navigators have a general knowledge of both the old and the new, but wisely continue to practice the methods with which they are familiar.

Important advances are taking place, particularly in the application of electronics—and now the space sciences—to practical and theoretical navigation. Actual requirements vary according to the work to be undertaken. The student should seek to fit his study to his needs, as pointed out in the discussion of Study and Teaching, Appendix I.

103. Books on navigation. The major epitomes, which must serve all mariners, include a multiplicity of subjects and methods, old and new, which often overwhelm an unguided reader. The present Primer presents only the elements of piloting, the graphic methods of dead reckoning, a simple description of the basic uses of electronic navigation, and the principles and technique underlying all celestial navigation, together with the newer methods of working sights. Such matters as are discussed form a basis, and perhaps an incentive, for further study. In such cases, one or more of the following books are recommended:

CHAPMAN: *Piloting, Seamanship, and Small Boat Handling* (Motor Boating) deals with small boat problems; replete with illustrations, questions and answers.

KNIGHT: *Modern Seamanship.* This standard work on seamanship also includes a clear presentation of the complete rules of the road and contains several chapters on equipment used when piloting major ships.

FARWELL: *The Rules of the Nautical Road,* clear and complete, the accepted treatise on this subject. (5th Edition)

CUGLE: *Practical Navigation,* with many problems and their solutions, is of special value to those going up for licenses in the Merchant Marine.

DUTTON: *Navigation and Piloting;* 12th Edition. Written for use at the

U. S. Naval Academy, this volume has been the best known textbook of modern navigation.

BOWDITCH: *American Practical Navigator*, Pub. No. 9, the standard reference book on practical and theoretical navigation and nautical astronomy for over 150 years, is published by DMAHC. The 1977 edition was completely rewritten to include new developments and should be owned by every navigator because of the technical and historical information and tabular data it contains.

LECKY: *Wrinkles in Practical Navigation.* Greatest of all, but only for those with some knowledge of celestial navigation. The preface to the first edition (1881) states: "The particular aim of this treatise is to furnish seamen with thoroughly *practical* hints, such as are not found in the ordinary works on Navigation." Quaint and charming, *Wrinkles*, now revised, lives on after seventy years because it teaches navigators to think.

Many other excellent books on navigation are available, but books alone do not make a navigator. One must practice and practice, and learn to sense the import of everything one sees, hears, feels, or smells. Thus, from practice and from books, the observant navigator, ever mindful of possible errors, learns to conduct his ship in safety to the haven where he would be.

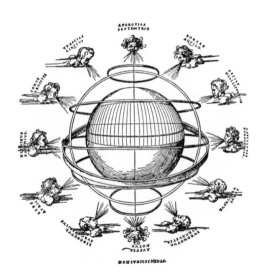

2. TOOLS OF THE TRADE

MARINERS, especially when near the coast, use various instruments, tools, and sources of information. Understanding these aids, and how to use them, together with experienced judgment of probable or possible errors, is the basis for the safe conduct of ships.

201. Equipment. The following tools and publications are necessary or convenient for piloting in strange waters. Fishermen omit some items, yachtsmen use more gadgets; big ships have additional equipment for observing and plotting bearings and for sounding in deep water.

TOOLS	PUBLICATIONS
Compass	Charts of the coast
Lead and line and/or echo sounder	*Light List*
Patent log and/or speed indicator	*Tide Tables*
Parallel rulers	*Current Tables*
Dividers	*Tidal Current Charts*
Binoculars	*Coast Pilot* with latest supplement
Watch or clock	*Pilot Rules,* 2 copies
Stop watch	Log Book
Barometer	RADIO
Pencils with erasers	Broadcast receiver
Deviation card	Direction finder
Flashlights	Radiobeacon chart

Navigators Note Book, with Work Forms

Even though no chart table is available, a bookcase can and should be provided exclusively for the volumes used by the navigator. A *Light List* lost in a bunk is of little use in an emergency.

202. Publications of the U. S. Government relating to navigation include charts and tables and present much of the best discussion of nautical matters. A summary of these publications, and how they may be obtained, will be found in Apx. IV. Those relating to piloting appear at the beginning of the list; an examination of these items will indicate their importance. When purchasing charts, the beginner is fortunate who can go directly to any of the principal instrument dealers in the great ports. They are authorized agents for the sale of government publications and are valuable sources of information.

203. Chart tools. The minimum equipment for chart work includes parallel rulers or air navigation plotter, dividers, and suitable pencils.

Parallel rulers are used to draw a line parallel to another line, as when transferring a course or bearing to or from the compass rose on a chart. The Field type, shown in Fig. 203*a* is most convenient, as it may be used to plot from any meridian or parallel of latitude as well as from the compass rose, thereby avoiding the chance of slipping error when moving the rulers across the chart or plotting sheet. This is particularly useful if a good chart table with a firm flat surface is not available.

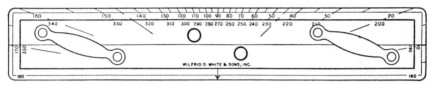

FIG. 203*a*. FIELD TYPE PARALLEL RULERS.

An aircraft navigational plotter even though developed for aircraft use, can easily be used by the surface navigator and is especially convenient for yachtsmen. Made of flexible, strong plastic material, one design is shown in Fig. 203*b*. The protractor on this *plotter* provides its own compass rose and the course followed by the straight edge can be determined by placing the pivot hole at the center on any convenient meridian line. The course is read where the meridian used cuts the outer edge of the protractor which is marked in degrees. Two directions are shown, one the reciprocal of the other, but there should be no difficulty picking out the one to use. With a little practice, lines of position can be plotted very quickly with this simple instrument.

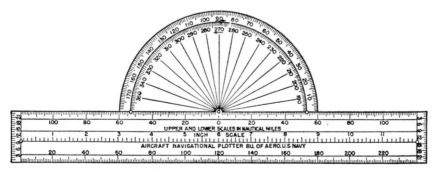

FIG. 203*b*. AIRCRAFT NAVIGATIONAL PLOTTER.

Dividers should be of the simpler sturdy type sold by nautical instrument dealers, as shown in Fig. 203c.

Keep the points clean and sharp. New dividers will open and close smoothly with sufficient friction to prevent movement when distances are transferred to or from the scale of miles. When the joint works loose, tighten with the two-point wrench which should accompany a new instrument and in some miraculous way be kept where it can be found once or twice a year. If the joint sticks, try a drop of oil; if need be, disassemble and clean the parts.

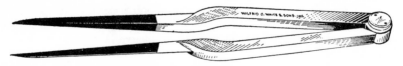

FIG. 203c. STURDY MARINE DIVIDERS.

Pencils. Avoid hard pencils that cut a permanent line. Softer hexagonal pencils with oversize erasers are best. Keep them sharp with a real pencil sharpener, the kind with a crank; when you like, wipe out the lines with an eraser of plastic rubber.

Other chart tools will be accumulated according to fancy or necessity. A good supply of masking tape to secure the chart to a flat surface comes first. A compass for drawing visibility and danger circles is convenient; if none is at hand, a pencil tied to one leg of the dividers may be used.

204. Charts of the coasts of the United States and its possessions are listed in the free *Catalog of U. S. National Ocean Survey* (NOS). This catalog also contains valuable discussions of charts and other NOS publications. One or more charts of familiar waters are the best aids to understanding their wonderful store of detailed information.

In the interest of mariners, most charts are constructed on Mercator's projection (§1102). The skeleton of a Mercator chart, as in Fig. 204, consists of: (1) Vertical, parallel lines (meridians of longitude) which run true north and south to longitude scales across top and bottom of chart; (2) horizontal lines (parallels of latitude) running true east and west to vertical scales of latitude at either side. Within the outline of the land, various legends and symbols give information for the pilot; figures over water areas give depths at frequent intervals; everywhere lighthouses and buoys are shown in their correct positions, together with much other information.

True north lies in the direction of the geographic north pole. *Magnetic north* is almost never the same as true north because the earth's magnetic poles are not the same as its true poles. On coastwise charts a combination compass rose indicates both true and magnetic directions. The outer 360° rose measures true directions counted clockwise from its zero which marks true north. The inner rose measures magnetic directions by quarter-points or degrees.

A straight line on a Mercator chart represents the course to steer continuously from one point to another. The *direction* of a course represented by such a line may be measured with parallel rulers from the rose on the chart either in degrees true or in points magnetic. When properly corrected, it is the course to steer by the compass card in order to follow the direction of the line. Similarly, the direction of a compass course already sailed may be corrected and plotted on the chart. The corrections referred to are discussed in a later chapter.

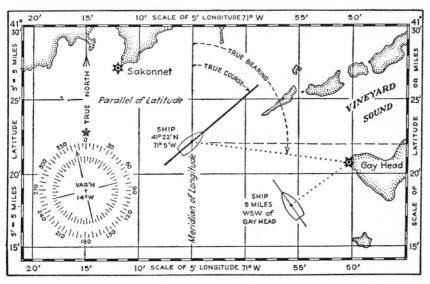

Fig. 204. Skeleton of a Mercator Chart.

Distance is measured in international nautical miles of 6076+ feet, very nearly the length of one minute (1′) of latitude. Thus, the vertical scale of minutes of latitude at the right and left of a chart may be used as a measure of miles. On Mercator charts of large areas, this scale varies somewhat as one moves up or down the chart, although minutes of latitude always represent miles of distance in that latitude. Therefore, *to measure distance* in miles between two points on a chart, *use the latitude scale* of minutes opposite the middle of the line between the points. This rule applies to any Mercator chart or plotting sheet, but, except as a matter of convenience, need not be followed when a scale of miles is printed on the chart. Harbor charts have such scales, as do the much-used NOS series of the Atlantic and Gulf Coasts. Those sailing these waters should note that all these charts have the same scale, 1/80,000 or 0.911 inch per nautical mile.

Position of a ship, or of any point on a coastwise chart, may be defined by its relation to landmarks or by its latitude and longitude as when at sea. On the skeleton chart (Fig. 204) the position of the vessel at lower right is given as 5 miles West Southwest (magnetic) from Gay Head. That of the vessel near the center of the chart is stated in terms of latitude and longitude. A horizontal line through the vessel meets the latitude scale at 41° 22′ N; a vertical line through the same point marks 71° 5′ W on the scale of longitude, and the vessel is said to be in 41° 22′ N and 71° 5′ W. Reversal of this process serves to plot a position of known latitude and longitude.

The preceding outline indicates how *position, direction,* and *distance,* the elements of all navigation, are handled on charts. One may project a voyage in advance by drawing the various courses (directions) and distances from the initial position to the desired destination. Or, from the point of departure, one may plot the courses and distances and thus find the dead reckoning position of the ship at any time. In either case, the chart work is simple. In practice, however, the accuracy with which the result reflects the ship's position depends on many factors which are matters of skill, experience, and judgment.

Soundings on charts are shown by numerous figures which indicate the depth of their various positions at low water. Depths are stated either in fathoms (1 fathom = 6 feet) or in feet, in accordance with the legend directly under the title of the chart. Offshore charts show depths in fathoms; in addition to the various figures, a 100 fathom curve and often 50, 40, 30, 20, 10, and 5 fathom curves indicate the shoaling of the water as one approaches from the sea. Large-scale charts of the coast and all harbor charts give soundings in feet. The shallower depths extending outward from the shore line are emphasized by gradient tints. Navigators should be aware that the international program to shift to the metric system applies to nautical charts. U. S. hydrographic agencies have a long-term program underway to change soundings to meters. Many foreign hydrographic agencies have always used meters for soundings. To be sure, always check the chart heading for the unit of measurement.

Character of bottom is indicated by various abbreviations which mean mud, sand, shells, rocky, etc., as explained in NOS Chart No. 1, *Nautical Chart Symbols and Abbreviations,* which also explains the vast amount of interesting information conveyed by the symbols, abbreviations, and typographical conventions shown on NOS charts.

Caution: For various reasons, tides (§209) are irregular, and under some conditions the minimum depth of water may be seriously LESS than that indicated by the printed soundings.

205. Depth measurement. The lead with its line is the time-honored device for measuring the depth of water at the ship. Next to the compass, it has been the most important tool of the coastwise mariner.

However, reliable and inexpensive electronic depth finders are now available to the navigator, permitting him to read the depth on a dial instead of listening to the "song" of the leadsman in the chains. But despite the convenience of the electronic depth finder, the careful navigator makes sure that an "old reliable" lead and line are stowed so that they can be put into use quickly if needed. The *anchor* is still an important navigational device!

The lead itself is a slightly conical lead casting with an eye at the top and with the bottom hollowed out so that it can be "armed" with tallow or grease to which a sample of the bottom will adhere. A *hand lead* of 3 or 4 pounds on 30 or 40 feet of line is convenient on a small motor boat. Larger craft should carry two hand leads weighing from 7 to 14 pounds on from 10 to 20 fathoms of line. For work offshore, a 25-pound lead with 100 fathoms of line is helpful when making a landfall in thick weather. In any case, there should be a definite place for stowing each lead with its line attached and coiled ready for use.

The marks on the line, which the leadsman must learn to recognize by feel in the dark as he hauls the line vertical from the lead on the bottom, are as follows:

FATHOMS	MARKINGS
2	Two strips of leather
3	Three strips of leather
5	White cotton rag
7	Red woolen bunting
10	Piece of leather with a hole in it
13	Same as 3
15	Same as 5
17	Same as 7
20	Cord with two knots
25	Cord with one knot
30	Cord with three knots

Markings on the line are called "marks" and the estimated whole fathoms between the marks are called "deeps." When the lead is on the bottom and the line is vertical, the mark or deep at the surface indicates the depth of water. A picturesque phraseology was often used by the leadsman to sing out the soundings, as, for example, "By the mark two" (formerly "Mark twain"!), "By the deep six," "Less a quarter seven," etc.

Modern technology has provided the mariner with the *echo sounder;* a device which (a) generates a pulse of energy, (b) directs it toward the bottom, and then (c) times the return of the echo. Since sound travels approximately 4,800 feet per second in water, one-half of the time interval between the start of the pulse and the return of the echo is proportional to the depth of water. This time interval is converted into feet or fathoms and presented to the navigator on an indicator, one type of which is shown in Fig. 205. Echo sounders are available in various configurations from the small, transistorized package powered by flashlight batteries, and suitable for depths of a hundred feet or so, to the complex recording devices which will automatically draw a profile of the ocean bottom even under several thousand feet of water.

Courtesy Raytheon Company, South San Francisco, Cal.

FIG. 205. A RECORDING DEPTH INDICATOR.

206. Speed measurement. Long ago mariners judged speed, and therefrom distance, by throwing a chunk of wood overboard from the bow and estimating the speed at which the ship passed the floating *log*, either by timing or by just walking along the deck. This came to be known as the "Dutchman's Log". Later, the chip-log, typical of the days of sail, was attached to a line having knots so spaced that the number of knots paid out in a given time measured the speed of the ship in nautical miles per hour (knots). Today, speed is usually obtained by a mechanical or electronic device. If the vessel is under power, the revolutions per minute (RPM) of the engine, obtained from a reliable tachometer, provide an excellent means for measuring speed through the water. It is only necessary to prepare a table or curve showing the relationship between ship speed and RPM.

For a vessel under sail, many types of indicator are available which are actuated by the flow of water streaming past the hull. Some devices, like that shown in Fig. 206a, not only indicate the vessel's speed in knots, but are also capable of being set to greatly increased sensitivity so as to reveal small speed changes of as little as perhaps 1/100 of a knot. Thus, the skipper of a sailing vessel can instantly determine the effect on speed of changes in the trim of sails, ballasting, and propellor position behind the deadwood; and how much speed is lost by coming up on the wind a few degrees, or gained by falling off.

Fig. 206a. A Speed Indicator.

The construction of a speed curve or the calibration of a speed indicator is easy on a power vessel or a sailing vessel with auxilliary power. A series of runs at a fixed engine speed (RPM) is made over a known distance such as a measured mile shown on a chart. At least two runs are made in opposite directions so as to minimize the effect of current; and the time required for each run is noted together with the reading of the speed indicator. Dividing the known distance by each of these times gives the speed over the bottom for each run. The average speed in still water (S) is found by adding the speed upstream (S_1) to the speed downstream (S_2) and dividing by two. Thus, $S = \frac{1}{2} (S_1 + S_2)$. If the distance is exactly one nautical mile, it is convenient to make use of Table 18 in Bowditch, which gives the speeds for various times over this distance. Note: It is the *speeds* that are averaged, not the times.

Any difference between the reading of the speed indicator and the speed just measured is assumed to be the error of the speed indicator at this speed. The RPM, the measured speed, and the error of the speed indicator are all recorded; and the process is repeated for other engine speeds. The results can be arranged in tabular form; however, it is customary to plot them on graph paper.

The navigator now knows that whenever his engine is running at a particular RPM, his vessel's speed in still water is so much. Also, for a sailing vessel, he knows whether the reading of his speed indicator is just right or a little high or a little low and how much.

The speed through the water of a vessel under sail alone is constantly varying; hence calibration of a speed indicator is more difficult. Howeve., by careful observation and some record keeping of distances, times, and indicated speeds, a pretty good idea can be obtained of any error existing in the speed indicator.

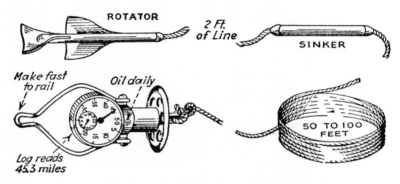

FIG. 206b. SMALL TAFFRAIL LOG.

The *taffrail* or *patent log* (Fig. 206b) is still in general use for measuring distance through the water. The rotator is towed by a line attached to the register located aft on the taffrail where it may be read conveniently and where the line will lead clear of the ship. As the rotator is towed, its spiral fins make it spin, and through the log line it drives the register, which is calibrated to indicate the run in miles and tenths of miles. Obviously, the distance run in any period is the difference between the log readings at the beginning and end of the period; if the interval is one hour, the difference is the speed in knots.

The accuracy of a log, particularly of a new one, should be tested on runs over known distances during periods of slack water (§210). Accuracy can be affected by such conditions as bent fins, seaweed or other matter afoul of the rotator, too short a line (causing the rotator to skip over the surface), heavy seas, or ship speed too slow to turn the rotator. The last condition is a common occurrence on a sailing vessel in light airs; in shoal water it is advisable to get the rotator aboard to avoid snagging it on the bottom and perhaps losing it. When hauling in the rotator, unhook the line from the register and pay this end overboard. The

line will untwist and can be properly coiled as it is hauled in again starting with the rotator.

Some of the other devices for measuring speed and distance are described in Bowditch. The revolutions of the propellor shaft, when corrected for "slip" also provide a measure of both speed and distance.
Slip is the percentage by which the advance of the ship falls short of
the theoretical amount determined by the pitch of the ship's screw. In
any case, remember it is speed or distance *through the water* that is
measured, which may not be the same as *over the bottom*.

207. The barometer and the weather. The earth is surrounded by
a mixture of gases, principally nitrogen and oxygen, which also contains
particles of dust and moisture. We live near the bottom of this sea of air
where the weight of the atmosphere creates pressures which, for sundry
reasons, vary from time to time and at different points on the earth's surface. The barometer is an instrument for measuring these pressures and
is almost a necessity for any prudent mariner.

The significance of changes in the atmospheric pressure and other
phenomena are given extensive treatment in Bowditch and in numerous
publications of the U. S. Weather Bureau.

FIG. 207. MERCURY
BAROMETER.

The mercury barometer, less often found at sea, is
the standard instrument for measuring atmospheric
pressure. The principle of this instrument is illustrated by Fig. 207. Since the weight of the column of
mercury in the tube is equal to the pressure of the
atmosphere which holds it in position, the height of
the column will vary with changes in atmospheric
pressure. With lower pressures, the height becomes
less and "the glass is falling"; with increasing pressures, "the glass is going up." The mean height of the
barometer at sea level is about 30 inches of mercury
or about 1013 millibars, a more modern unit.

The aneroid ("without fluid") barometer is the
round, clocklike instrument ordinarily used by mariners. Within is a circular metallic box, exhausted of
air, the ends of which are corrugated diaphragms kept
apart by springs. The varying pressure of the atmosphere causes a variation of the distance between the
diaphragms. This variation, multiplied through a
delicate mechanism, actuates the pointer which moves
over the scale of the instrument. The graduations on
the scale are obtained by comparison with the readings
of a standard mercury barometer under various pressures.

A good aneroid is easier to read than a mercury barometer and is affected less by changes in temperature. However, from time to time its readings should be compared with those of a standard mercury instrument and without moving or changing the position of the aneroid which may be either vertical or horizontal. The pressure of the atmosphere at sea level (barometer reading) is announced frequently by coastal broadcasting and other radio stations. Schedules for broadcasts of weather and marine information are listed and indexed in the *U. S. Coast Pilots* (§211). If substantial error exists, the reading of an aneroid may be adjusted by turning a screw reached with a small, long screw driver through a hole in the back of the instrument.

The Barograph ("weight writer") is an aneroid barometer which records its readings by a line weaving up and down along a properly graduated sheet of paper. The value of this relatively expensive instrument lies in the fact that it presents at a glance the preceding trends of the barometer, which are far more informative than any single reading. Contrary to common opinion, it is a practical instrument on smaller craft such as cruising yachts.

208. Binoculars or field glasses are almost a necessity when piloting and are often needed at sea. They not only enlarge distant objects, but also clarify details such as the numbers on buoys and, when wisely selected, greatly improve visibility at night. There are two general classes of binoculars, but the variety of such instruments offered by dealers, who often have little knowledge of the requirements, is confusing. One should remember that neither high magnifying power nor high price necessarily indicates a good marine glass. The types in general use for marine work are shown in Fig. 208 together with their principal characteristics.

Galilean or old-style field glasses are double-barreled telescopes with a common central focusing screw. Each tube has a more or less straight taper and contains only the ordinary lenses without any prisms. Magnifying power seldom is marked on these glasses but commonly ranges from two and one-half times (2.5×) to five times (5×) the size of an object when seen with the naked eye. The taller glasses have the greater power and the smaller field. Low price is the only advantage of the Galilean type, yet they have served sailormen for a hundred years and today these glasses are still widely used by mariners.

Modern prismatic binoculars have odd-shaped tubes or barrels with enlargements to accommodate a series of prisms in addition to a complete lens system. These prismatic instruments have a number of advantages over Galilean glasses:

(1) Higher magnification or power
(2) Field of view much wider for any given power
(3) Brightness and definition almost the same over the entire picture

(4) Superior for judging relative distances or relief of objects

(5) New types of glasses have coated lenses which allow a much greater amount of light to come through the lens to the eye

(6) For above reasons, superior as night glasses

Selection and purchase depend on both purpose and purse. Second-hand glasses or those low-priced for their type should be considered with caution. Avoid any glass which shows exposed metal which salt water corrodes.

Of the Galilean glasses, the small pilot or bell type, 2.5×, is most popular and is a useful glass for coastwise work; the tall, 5×, instrument, often found at sea, is the better night glass. In general, the big lenses, or objectives, of a Galilean glass should be as large as possible; higher price for a given type should assure better optical qualities:

A binocular is rated by its magnification (6×, 7×, etc.) and by the diameter of its objective lens, the lens farthest from the eyepiece (30mm, 50mm, etc.). Magnification (sometimes called "power") is equal to the diameter of the objective lens divided by the diameter of the exit pupil, the eyepiece lens. Relative brightness is the exit pupil diameter multiplied by itself. Thus, for a binocular rated 7× 35 mm, the exit pupil diameter is 5 mm and the relative brightness is 25.

GALILEAN FIELD GLASSES			PRISMATIC BINOCULARS		
PILOT	MEDIUM	TALL	6 x 30	7 x 35	7 x 50
MAGNIFICATION			MAGNIFICATION		
X 2.5	X 3.5	X 5	X 6	X 7	X 7
FIELD OF VIEW IN FEET AT 1,000 YARDS					
400	280	200	450	380	380
ILLUMINATION			RELATIVE BRIGHTNESS, ENTIRE FIELD		
Brilliant near Center of Image			25	25	50

FIG. 208. MARINE GLASSES.

The 7× 50 prismatic binocular with coated lens is generally considered the best all-around marine glass. It is the best night glass and is more effective in any condition of limited visibility than other glasses. However, on a clear day its relative brightness (50) results in more light than human eyes can use, although no discomfort results because the eyes' pupils are contracted. Under these conditions the 7× 35 glass, brightness 25, is almost equal to the larger glass, and is more convenient because of its smaller size and lighter weight. The 6× 30, also with a brightness of 25, has a wider field, is excellent for observing small boat racing, and is superior to a Galilean glass under any conditions.

16 *Primer of Navigation*

Care of marine glasses is often not understood and more often neglected.

(1) Have a definite place for the instrument and see that it is returned to its place when not in use. This may be a rack, box, or section of a drawer convenient to the navigator but must not be exposed to water or to direct sunlight.

(2) Avoid sudden changes in temperature. A common abuse is to leave the glasses in the sun, which is particularly bad for prismatic instruments.

(3) To clean the glasses, blow off loose dirt, breathe on the lenses and polish by a circular motion with lens paper or soft facial tissue. Chamois probably contains grit; cotton cloth or waste will leave lint. If necessary, first use a very little mild soap and water, then wash off with clean water. Do not use alcohol or other special solutions which may loosen the cement holding the lenses.

(4) Glasses should be periodically disassembled and cleaned, preferably by the maker, and especially if any moisture gets into a prismatic glass. Do not try to disassemble the instrument yourself.

(5) On yachts the abuse of glasses used by everybody is almost unlimited. At least insist that crew *and guests* always return the glasses to their proper place.

NEW YORK (THE BATTERY), N.Y.
TIMES AND HEIGHTS OF HIGH AND LOW WATERS

	APRIL						MAY						JUNE				
DAY	TIME H.M.	HT. FT.	DAY	TIME H.M.	HT. FT.	DAY	TIME H.M.	HT. FT.	DAY	TIME H.M.	HT. FT.	DAY	TIME H.M.	HT. FT.	DAY	TIME H.M.	HT. FT.
1 F	0430	4.5	16 SA	0524	4.0	1 SU	0512	4.7	16 M	0524	4.0	1 W	0036	-0.4	16 TH	0024	0.3
	1106	-0.1		1142	0.2		1130	-0.4		1142	0.2		0642	4.5		0618	3.9
	1712	4.2		1800	4.1		1748	5.1		1754	4.6		1242	-0.4		1218	0.3
	2324	-0.1											1900	5.7		1836	5.2
2 SA	0536	4.8	17 SU	0006	0.4	2 M	0000	-0.4	17 TU	0012	0.3	2 TH	0124	-0.5	17 F	0112	0.0
	1200	-0.5		0612	4.2		0612	4.9		0612	4.1		0612	4.5		0700	4.0
	1806	4.7		1224	0.0		1218	-0.6		1218	0.1		1330	-0.3		1306	0.2
				1836	4.4		1836	5.4		1836	4.8		1948	5.7		1918	5.4
3 SU	0630	5.1	18 M	0048	0.2	3 TU	0054	-0.7	18 W	0100	0.1	3 F	0218	-0.5	18 SA	0200	-0.2
	1248	-0.8		0654	4.3		0700	4.9		0654	4.2		0818	4.4		0748	4.1
	1900	5.1		1306	-0.1		1312	-0.7		1300	0.1		1418	-0.2		1354	0.1
				1912	4.6		1924	5.7		1912	5.1		2030	5.5		2000	5.5
4 M	0112	-0.9	19 TU	0130	-0.1	4 W	0142	-0.9	19 TH	0142	-0.1	4 SA	0300	-0.5	19 SU	0248	-0.4
	0718	5.2		0730	5.2		0748	4.9		0730	4.2		0906	4.2		0836	4.2
	1336	-1.0		1342	-0.1		1354	-0.7		1342	0.1		1500	0.0		1436	0.1
	1942	5.4		1948	4.8		2006	5.7		1942	5.2		2118	5.3		2042	5.5

FIG. 209*a*. TIDE TABLES, TABLE 1, REFERENCE STATIONS.

209. Tides. The word tide as used in navigation refers to the vertical rise and fall of the ocean resulting principally from the attraction of the moon and sun (§1720). Currents set up thereby are popularly called tides but technically are termed tidal currents. This section relates to tides as first defined.

In general, rise and fall of the tide takes place twice in a lunar day of about 24h 50m, the times of *high tide* or *high water* being about 50 minutes LATER each day. The intervening minimum level is called *low tide* or *low water.* At high water, and at low water, there is a period termed the *stand* when no change in the water level can be detected. The *range* of a tide is the difference in height between high and low water. *Spring tides,* which rise higher and fall lower than mean or average tides, occur about every two weeks at the time of a new moon or of a full moon. The term *spring,* as applied to tides, has no relation to the season of that name. *Neap tides* occur midway between springs, at the time of the first and last quarter of the moon when the range of the tide is less than the mean range. The dates of the various phases of the moon are given in back of the *Tide Tables.*

All sailors know that the tidal range differs widely at different ports. Around the Gulf of Mexico there is almost no tide, in New York Harbor the range is more or less 5 feet, with half this range at New London, and around 10 feet at Boston. In Minas Basin, up the Bay of Fundy, the range is about 40 feet. Less often is it understood that the range at a given station varies, sometimes to an important degree. Furthermore, the times of the tides may vary materially at relatively nearby points; for example, high tide at New London may be two hours later than at Newport. These vagaries of the tides, although sometimes of negligible magnitude, are found along all the coasts of the world.

Tide Tables, published annually in advance by the U. S. National Ocean Survey, are issued in four volumes: *Europe and West Coast of Africa (including the Mediterranean Sea); East Coast, North and South America (including Greenland); West Coast, North and South America (including*

TABLE 2.—TIDAL DIFFERENCES AND OTHER CONSTANTS

No.	PLACE	POSITION		DIFFERENCES				RANGES		
				Time		Height				Mean Tide Level
		Lat.	Long.	High water	Low water	High water	Low water	Mean	Spring	
		° ′ N.	° ′ W.	h. m.	h. m.	feet	feet	feet	feet	feet
	NEW YORK Long Island Sound, North Side			on WILLETS POINT, p.58						
				Time meridian, 75°W.						
1253	Port Chester-------------------	41 00	73 40	−0 09	−0 12	+0.1	0.0	7.2	8.5	3.6
1254	Rye Beach----------------------	40 58	73 40	−0 14	−0 07	+0.1	0.0	7.2	8.4	3.6
1255	Mamaroneck---------------------	40 56	73 44	−0 08	−0 11	+0.2	0.0	7.3	8.6	3.6
1257	New Rochelle-------------------	40 54	73 46	−0 13	−0 05	+0 05	0.0	7.2	8.6	3.6
1259	Davids Island------------------	40 53	73 46	−0 02	−0 07	+0.1	0.0	7.2	8.5	3.6
1261	City Island--------------------	40 51	73 47	−0 03	−0 03	+0.1	0.0	7.2	8.5	3.6
1263	Throgs Neck--------------------	40 48	73 48	+0 02	+0 14	−0.1	0.0	7.0	8.2	3.5
	East River									
1265	Whitestone---------------------	40 48	73 49	+0 02	+0 14	0.0	0.0	7.1	8.3	3.5
1267	Old Ferry Point----------------	40 48	73 50	+0 04	+0 16	0.0	0.0	·7.1	8.3	3.5
1269	College Point, Flushing Bay---------	40 47	73 51	+0 20	+0 28	−0.6	0.0	6.5	7.6	3.2
1271	Northern Blvd. Bridge, Flushing Cr--	40 46	73 50	+0 54	+0 37	−0.3	0.0	6.8	8.0	3.4
1273	Westchester, Westchester Creek------	40 50	73 50	+0 10	+0 16	−0.1	0.0	7.0	8.3	3.5
				on NEW YORK, p.62						
1287	Pot Cove, Astoria--------------	40 47	73 56	+2 20	+2 29	+0.8	0.0	5.3	6.3	2.6
1289	Hell Gate, Hallets Point------------	40 47	73 56	+2 00	+2 04	+0.6	0.0	5.1	6.1	2.5
1291	Horns Hook, E. 90th Street----------	40 47	73 57	+1 50	+1 30	+0.3	0.0	4.8	5.8	2.4
1293	Blackwells Island, north end--------	40 46	73 56	+1 45	+1 25	+0.3	0.0	4.8	5.8	2.4
1295	37th Avenue, Long Island City-------	40 46	73 57	+1 30	+1 10	0.0	0.0	4.5	5.5	2.2

FIG. 209*b*. TIDE TABLES, TABLE 2, SUBORDINATE STATIONS.

Hawaiian Islands); and *Central and Western Pacific and Indian Ocean.* Together, they contain daily predictions for reference points (Table 1) and differences and constants for subordinate stations (Table 2). Figures 209*a* and 209*b* show excerpts from these tables. In addition, these publications also include instructions for their use and present valuable information about tides.

Times of high and low tide at any reference station, such as New York (The Battery), may be read directly from Table 1, in Navy-style 24-hour time. For subordinate stations, apply the difference in time of tide from the appropriate column of Table 2 to the time at the reference station. The time so determined will be standard time for the subordinate station; daylight, or fast time, is not used in the *Tide Tables.*

Table 1 also shows, for each reference station, the predicted heights of the tide above the datum level of soundings used on the largest-scale chart of the locality. Table 2 gives, for each subordinate station, the difference in height to be added to or subtracted from the heights of high or low water at the stated reference station in order to find the height above or below the chart datum level at the subordinate station. These height differences are usually expressed in feet; but where unsatisfactory predictions would result, they are expressed as a ratio (indicated by an asterisk) by which the height at the reference station is to be multiplied. For some stations a further correction in feet is required.

The *height of tide* at any moment can be found by means of Table 3 of the *Tide Tables,* which gives the change in height for any time in-

RANGE OF TIDE IN FEET	HOURS BEFORE OR AFTER LOW WATER						RANGE OF TIDE IN FEET
	1	2	3	4	5	6	
	RISE OR FALL – FRACTIONS OF THE RANGE						
	1/16	3/16	4/16	4/16	3/16	1/16	
	FEET TO ADD TO LOW TIDE DEPTHS						
6	0.4	1.5	3	4.5	5.6	6	6
8	0.5	2	4	6	7.5	8	8
10	0.7	2.5	5	7.5	9.3	10	10
14	0.9	3.5	7	10.5	13.1	14	14
18	1.2	4.5	9	13.5	16.8	18	18
HRS.	1	2	3	4	5	6	HRS.

FIG. 209*c*. RISE AND FALL OF TIDES.

terval from the nearest high or low water. The table is entered with (1) the duration in hours and minutes of rise or fall between a high and low water next before and next after the required moment; and (2) the range or difference in height between the same high and low waters. A quick approximation of the height *above low water* at any time can be made by reference to Fig. 209c which assumes that the duration between high and low water is always 6 hours. The *depth of water* is the charted depth corrected for the height of tide; and for a minus correction, is *less* than the charted depth. In any case, remember that because of weather conditions, actual depths may be less than predicted depths.

Times of high and low water, derived from the *Tide Tables*, are sufficiently accurate for practical navigation, although, for unavoidable reasons, they are seldom exact. On the other hand, depths exactly computed from the same tables give a deceptive appearance of accuracy which seldom is warranted. The tabulated information is for points some distance apart, and in any case is subject to variable conditions which no table can take into account. Strong winds blowing toward the shore and a low barometer will increase high water heights, an extreme example being the hurricane which invaded New England in September, 1938. Similarly, an offshore wind and high barometer have the reverse effect. A typical legend, as on NOS chart No. 12367, reads as follows:

	New Rochelle	Great Captain Island Light
TIDES (referred to datum of soundings, M.L.W.)		
Mean high water	7.2 ft.	7.3 ft.
Mean tide level	3.6 ft.	3.6 ft.
Mean low water	0.0 ft.	0.0 ft.
Extreme low water	−3.5 ft.	−3.5 ft.

This means that (1) the high water depths at New Rochelle will probably be 7.2 ft. above those shown on the chart; (2) the mean or average

THE RACE, LONG ISLAND SOUND,

F—FLOOD, DIR. 315° TRUE   E—EBB, DIR. 120° TRUE

MAY

DAY	SLACK WATER TIME H.M.	MAXIMUM CURRENT TIME H.M.	VEL. KNOTS	DAY	SLACK WATER TIME H.M.	MAXIMUM CURRENT TIME H.M.	VEL. KNOTS
1 SU	0230 0812 1448 2042	0524 1136 1748	3.6F 4.6E 4.0F	16 M	0254 0818 1500 2048	0536 1142 1754	2.6F 3.7E 3.2F
2 M	0324 0906 1536 2136	0006 0612 1230 1836	5.1E 3.9F 4.8E 4.3F	17 TU	0336 0900 1536 2124	0012 0618 1224 1830	4.1E 2.9F 3.9E 3.4F
3 TU	0418 1000 1624 2224	0054 0706 1318 1924	5.4E 4.1F 5.0E 4.5F	18 W	0412 0942 1612 2206	0054 0700 1306 1912	4.3E 3.1F 4.0E 3.6F
4 W	0506 1048 1712 2306	0142 0754 1400 2012	5.5E 4.1F 5.0E 4.5F	19 TH	0454 1024 1648 2242	0130 0736 1348 1954	4.5E 3.2F 4.1E 3.7F

JUNE

DAY	SLACK WATER TIME H.M.	MAXIMUM CURRENT TIME H.M.	VEL. KNOTS	DAY	SLACK WATER TIME H.M.	MAXIMUM CURRENT TIME H.M.	VEL. KNOTS
1 W	0400 0936 1606 2206	0036 0642 1254 1906	5.0E 3.5F 4.5E 4.2F	16 TH	0342 0906 1536 2136	0018 0624 1236 1842	4.2E 2.8F 3.9E 3.5F
2 TH	0448 1024 1648 2248	0124 0730 1342 1948	5.0E 3.5F 4.5E 4.1F	17 F	0424 0954 1624 2218	0106 0712 1318 1924	4.4E 3.0F 4.0E 3.7F
3 F	0536 1106 1736 2336	0212 0818 1424 2036	5.0E 3.4F 4.4E 3.9F	18 SA	0506 1036 1706 2306	0148 0754 1400 2012	4.7E 3.2F 4.2E 3.9F
4 SA	0624 1154 1824	0300 0906 1512 2118	4.8E 3.3F 4.1E 3.6F	19 SU	0554 1124 1754 2348	0236 0842 1448 2100	4.8E 3.4F 4.3E 4.0F

FIG. 210a. TIDAL CURRENT TABLES, TABLE 1, REFERENCE STATIONS.

level will be 3.6 ft. above the charted figures; and (3) the depths of water at the lowest tide may be 3.5 ft. *below* those shown on the chart near New Rochelle.

Finding the times of high water from the time of the moon's transit, and without the use of tide tables, is discussed in §3211.

210. Currents.   A horizontal movement of the water, whether caused by meteorological conditions as in the case of ocean currents, or by the rise and fall of the tide, or by the flow of rivers, is called current.   This section deals with coastwise currents caused principally by the rise and fall of the tides. The *direction of a current* is that toward which the water moves, which is the reverse of the way winds are named. *Flood* direction of tidal currents is generally toward the land into bays and harbors; *ebb* is the reverse.

Tidal Current Tables, published annually in advance by the U. S. National Ocean Survey, are issued in two volumes: *Tidal Current Tables, Atlantic Coast, North America;* and a companion volume, *Tidal Current Tables, Pacific Coast, North America and Asia.* The *Tidal Current*

TABLE 2.—CURRENT DIFFERENCES AND OTHER CONSTANTS

No.	PLACE	POSITION		TIME DIF-FERENCES		VELOCITY RATIOS			MAXIMUM CURRENTS			
									Flood		Ebb	
		Lat.	Long.	Slack water	Maxi-mum current	Maxi-mum flood	Maxi-mum ebb		Direc-tion (true)	Aver-age veloc-ity	Direc-tion (true)	Aver-age veloc-ity
				h. m.	*h. m.*				*deg.*	*knots*	*deg.*	*knots*
	LONG ISLAND SOUND	N.	W.	on THE RACE, p.40								
	The Race			Time meridian, 75°W.								
579	0.3 mile SW. of Race Point-------	41 15	72 03	+0 40	-0 25	0.7	0.9		295	2.4	165	3.9
581	VALIANT ROCK, near-------------	41 13	72 04	Daily predictions					315	3.3	120	4.3
583	0.5 mile NE. of Little Gull I------	41 13	72 06	-0 20	-0 20	1.0	0.7		0	3.3	105	3.1
585	Between Great Gull I. and Plum I-----	41 12	72 08	+0 40	-0 40	0.6	0.5		305	2.1	125	2.3
587	Plum Gut-------------------------	41 10	72 13	-1 05	-1 10	1.1	0.9		320	3.5	120	3.9
589	Eastern Point, 1.5 miles south of-----	41 18	72 05	-1 30	-1 50	0.1	0.1		250	0.4	55	0.4
591	Thames River, Eastern Point to Norwich	-----	-----	(¹)	(¹)	(¹)	(¹)		(¹)	(¹)	(¹)	(¹)
593	Bartlett Reef, 0.2 mile south of------	41 16	72 08	-1 30	-1 10	0.3	0.3		255	1.4	90	1.3
595	Twotree Island Channel------------	41 18	72 09	-1 30	-1 00	0.4	0.3		290	1.3	110	1.3
597	Niantic, (Railroad Bridge)---------	41 19	72 11	-0 25	+0 05	0.5	0.5		35	2.1	215	1.3
599	Black Point, 0.5 mile south of------	41 17	72 13	-1 25	-1 00	0.5	0.3		255	1.6	95	1.5

Fig. 210b.   Tidal Current Tables, Table 2, Subordinate Stations.

Tables are arranged like the *Tide Tables*. As shown in Fig. 210a, Table 1 gives for each reference station the times of slack water and the times, directions, and velocities of maximum currents during flood (*f*) and ebb (*e*).   Table 2, shown in Fig. 210b, lists for the subordinate stations the geographical positions, time differences, velocity ratios, and the directions and average velocities of maximum currents.

Explanations and instructions printed with the *Tidal Current Tables* are unusually clear and require no amplification.   The mariner, however, is cautioned to remember:

(1) As predictions are for an average condition, the tabulated times and maximum velocities may be more or less in error because of the wind or of variations in the discharge of a river.

(2) The current runs at the tabulated maximum for only about the middle third of the period from slack to slack.

(3) The time of slack water generally does not coincide with the time the tide stands at high or low water, nor does the time of maximum velocity usually coincide with the time of the most rapid change in the vertical height of the tide. These differences may be as great as three hours.

(4) The direction of a current at a subordinate station is often different from that at the reference station; sometimes it is the reverse. Near and within the outline of the coast, where the tidal currents are most important and of the reversing type, it should be noted that the direction of ebb current may not be the reciprocal of the flood direction. These directions are given in Table 2.

Offshore the tidal current, not being confined to a definite channel, changes its direction continually and never comes to a slack, so that in a tidal cycle of about 12½ hours it will have set in all directions of the compass. This type of current, of relatively low velocity, is described and tabulated under the heading "Table 5.—Rotary Tidal Currents" in the *Tidal Current Tables*. Vagaries of the currents in Vineyard Sound are especially well developed in Eldridge's *Tide and Pilot Book,* which often is more convenient than Government tables for Long Island, Block Island, and Vineyard Sounds.

Tidal Current Charts, good for any year, are published for some of the busiest harbors and coastal waterways. These include New York Harbor, Boston Harbor, Narragansett Bay (in two parts), Block Island Sound, Long Island Sound, Delaware Bay and River, San Francisco Bay, and Puget Sound (in two parts). Each publication contains 12 charts showing the direction and speed of the tidal currents existing throughout the particular area. Charts are provided for intervals of one, two, and three hours before and after a reference time, which for most areas is a time of slack water before flood or ebb at a well-defined reference station listed in the *Tidal Current Tables*. The reference time of the charts for New York Harbor and for Narragansett Bay is a time of high or low water taken from the *Tide Tables*.

211. U. S. Coast Pilots are a series of books published by the U. S. National Ocean Survey. Each book furnishes information required by the navigator for the area indicated which cannot be shown conveniently on charts. They contain detailed information relative to the coast line, sailing directions for coasting and for entering harbors, port regulations, and general information concerning weather conditions, radio service, etc. New editions for each area are published about every five years. Interim corrections appear each week in the *Notice to Mariners* (§1110). At intervals of about one year supplements are issued, free on request, giving the more important corrections and additions to the text for the entire period since date of publication. The mariner's *Coast Pilot* should be corrected to date or, at least, the latest supplement should be at hand. When these corrections are lacking, caution is necessary in interpreting navigational statements concerning aids to navigation which are subject to change.

In addition to the information about local conditions, each volume includes a discussion of navigational aids and the use of charts and other piloting equipment, instructions in case of shipwreck, and the complete text of the laws and regulations applicable to navigation in the area.

Sailing Directions (*Pilots*), published by the U. S. Defence Mapping Agency Hydrographic Center (DMAHC), include more than fifty books which give information similar to that in *Coast Pilots*, but for foreign areas.

Coast Pilots and *Sailing Directions* are of special value to yachtsmen or other wanderers in strange waters. These guide books even may serve to direct a small motor boat, with fuel running low, to the nearest gas station.

212. The log book is the official record of the ship's cruise and is an important accessory to navigation. Among other things, it provides a record of courses and distances, and other data from which the ship's D.R. position is determined. In addition, readings of the barometer, direction and force of the wind, the nature of the sea and other weather conditions are recorded at regular intervals; and from time to time incidents of the voyage may be described. Except for periodic recording of the ship's position, the details of necessary celestial navigation go into the navigator's work book and not the log book. However, information from the log book is a necessary element of practical navigation both on the coast and at sea.

There are numerous printed forms of log books. The Maritime Commission form is common in the Merchant Marine. Others are specially printed for yachtsmen, often with too much detail and too little space. Although less convenient, a blank-book will serve the purpose. As a matter of interest, a double page from a yacht's log in the 1936 Bermuda Race is reproduced in Fig. 212. Whether at sea or near the land, keeping the log is a definite duty of the ship's officers in both Navy and Merchant Marine. Smaller coastwise craft too often neglect the log book, as do most yachtsmen.

213. Questions. Answer the following questions from the chart in Fig. 204 as accurately as the small scale of the drawing permits.

Q 1-2: *Position.* Find the Lat. and Long. of
(a) Sakonnet Lt. (b) Gay Head Lt. (c) Center of 360° rose.

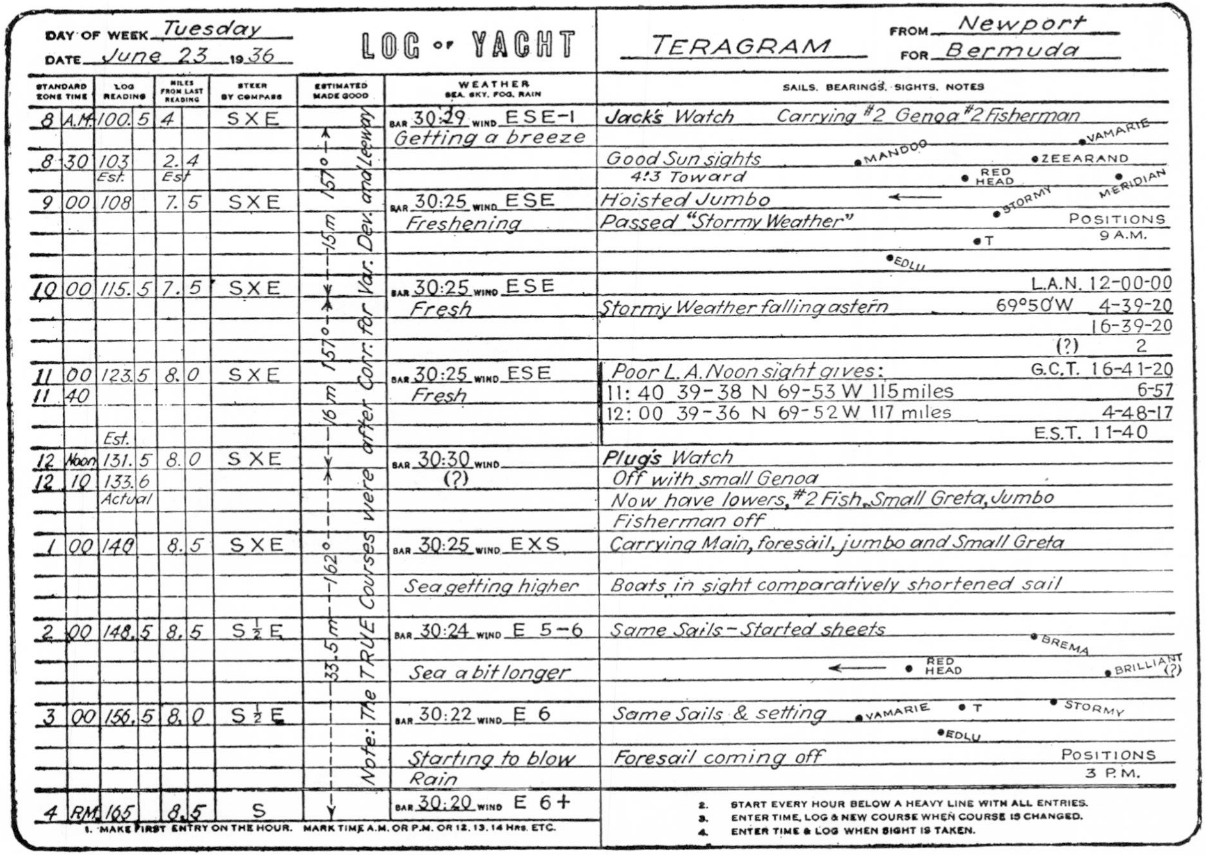

LOG of YACHT

TERAGRAM   FROM Newport   FOR Bermuda

DAY OF WEEK Tuesday   DATE June 23, 19_36_

STANDARD ZONE TIME	LOG READING	MILES FROM LAST READING	STEER BY COMPASS	ESTIMATED MADE GOOD	WEATHER (SEA, SKY, FOG, RAIN)	SAILS, BEARINGS, SIGHTS, NOTES
8 A.M.	100.5	4	SXE		BAR 30.29 WIND ESE-1 Getting a breeze	Jack's Watch Carrying #2 Genoa #2 Fisherman •VAMARIE
8:30	103	2.4 Est.				Good Sun sights •MANDOO 4:3 Toward •ZEEARAND •RED HEAD •MERIDIAN
9:00	108	7.5	SXE	← 0 157 →	BAR 30.25 WIND ESE Freshening	Hoisted Jumbo •STORMY POSITIONS 9 A.M. Passed "Stormy Weather" •T •EDW
10:00	115.5	7.5	SXE	← 15m 157 →	BAR 30.25 WIND ESE Fresh	Stormy Weather falling astern L.A.N. 12-00-00 69°50'W 4-39-20 16-39-20 (?) 2
11:00	123.5	8.0	SXE	← 16m 157 →	BAR 30.25 WIND ESE Fresh	Poor L.A. Noon sight gives: G.C.T. 16-41-20 6-57
11:40	Est.					11:40 39-38 N 69-53 W 115 miles 4-48-17 12:00 39-36 N 69-52 W 117 miles E.S.T. 11-40
12 Noon	151.5	8.0	SXE	← 0 162 →	BAR 30.30 WIND (?)	Plug's Watch Off with small Genoa
12:10	133.6 Actual					Now have lowers, #2 Fish, Small Greta, Jumbo Fisherman off
1:00	140	8.5	SXE	← 33.5m →	BAR 30.25 WIND EXS	Carrying Main, foresail jumbo and Small Greta Sea getting higher Boats in sight comparatively shortened sail
2:00	148.5	8.5	S½E		BAR 30.24 WIND E 5-6 Sea a bit longer	Same Sails – Started sheets •BREMA •RED HEAD •BRILLIANT (?)
3:00	156.5	8.0	S½E		BAR 30.22 WIND E 6 Starting to blow Rain	Same Sails & setting •VAMARIE •T •EDW •STORMY POSITIONS 3 P.M. Foresail coming off
4 P.M.	165	8.5	S		BAR 30.20 WIND E 6+	

Note: The TRUE Courses were after Corr. for Var. Dev. and Leeway

1. MAKE FIRST ENTRY ON THE HOUR. MARK TIME A.M. OR P.M. OR 12, 13, 14 HRS. ETC.
2. START EVERY HOUR BELOW A HEAVY LINE WITH ALL ENTRIES.
3. ENTER TIME, LOG & NEW COURSE WHEN COURSE IS CHANGED.
4. ENTER TIME & LOG WHEN SIGHT IS TAKEN.

FIG. 212. LOG BOOK PAGE, BERMUDA RACE, 1936.

Q 2-2: *Direction.* Find the following courses or bearings in degrees true from north. The ship referred to is that near the center of the chart.
(a) Course of ship. (b) Bearing of Sakonnet from ship. (c) Bearing of ship from Gay Head.

Q 3-2: *Distance.* Find the distance in nautical miles between,
(a) Top and bottom of chart. (b) Right and left sides of chart. (c) Ship and Gay Head.

Answers to the above questions:

	Q 1		Q 2	Q 3
	Lat.	Long.		Miles
(a)	41° 27′ N	71° 12′ W	050°	16
(b)	41° 21′ N	70° 50′ W	314°	27
(c)	41° 19′ N	71° 15′ W	276°	11

3. THE MAGNETIC COMPASS

THE compass is the most important instrument used by mariners. For many centuries it has been the principal source of that knowledge of direction upon which the navigation and the safety of ships depend. The origin of the magnetic compass and the time of its first use by navigators are uncertain. Its earliest form at sea included magnetized iron needles supported by floats on the surface of a liquid, the direction of the needles crudely indicating north and south. As the iron needles required frequent remagnetization, a magnetic stone for "touching the needle" was a necessary item of the pilot's equipment. These lodestones were an oxide of iron found along the Aegean Coast in the district of Magnesia; hence the word magnet.

Balancing the needle on a pivot, in a dry compass bowl, first appears as a European invention of the thirteenth century. When, and by whom, the compass card was added is a matter of conjecture. The *Rosa Ventorum,* or wind-rose, is older than the mariner's compass itself. Windroses on the earliest known Mediterranean charts had eight divisions marked with the initials of the winds, but in 1391 Chaucer wrote, ". . . ship men rikne thilke partiez in xxxii." Thus it is probable that in Chaucer's time compass cards were divided into the thirty-two points known to all sailors. The *fleur de lis* indicated north, just as the *fleur de lis* today marks, or often obscures, the north point of the card.

301. The magnetic compass, as now used at sea, consists of a bowl swinging level in gimbals but not free to rotate, a group of magnetized steel needles free to turn on a pivot at the center of the bowl, and a graduated circular card properly mounted on the needles and turning with them. Modern instruments have the bowl filled with a liquid to steady the card. A vertical line, called the *lubber's line,* is marked on the inner surface of the bowl, and the compass is so mounted that a line through its pivot and the lubber's line is parallel to the keel line of the vessel. The reading of the card opposite the lubber's line is then the ship's compass course. The compass bearing of a distant object is the reading where a line from center of compass to object observed intersects the edge of the card, as when one looks across a compass at a lighthouse. Sizes vary from a boat compass with a four-inch card to the nine- and ten-inch compasses found in the Merchant Marine. Binnacles for housing the compass, lighting facilities, and provisions for compensating magnets vary widely. Attachments for observing bearings range from a simple shadow pin to an azimuth circle with reflecting mirrors. Readings of the best magnetic compass are subject to corrections for *deviation,* caused by the magnetism of the ship, and for *variation,* resulting from the earth's magnetism. These errors and their correction are discussed in the next chapter.

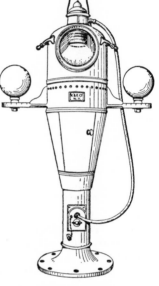

Two quite different systems for graduating the card of a magnetic compass are in common use; each has its place. And most navigators are familiar with both.

302. The quarter-point card, a development of several centuries, was used on all ships before the advent of steam and is preferable on any sailing vessel because it is easy to read and sufficiently accurate. For various reasons, most coastwise craft, even though they seldom sail, continue to steer by quarter points. A complete card of

FIG. 301. NAVY TYPE.

this type together with the designation of each of its 32 points is printed in Appendix VIII at the back of this book.

The circumference of the card is divided into 32 points, each point being equivalent to 11¼°. The *intercardinal points* are N E, S E, S W, and N W. An intermediate point, such as N ✕ E, is called North by East. N N E is simply North Northeast. N E ✕ N is Northeast by North, etc. The quarter points are named, according to Merchant Marine practice, as shown on page 541; N W ✕ N ¾ N is read as Northwest by North three-quarters North. Note how the ¼, ½, and ¾ divisions of each point are read away from a cardinal or intercardinal point, never from such points as N N E, E N E, etc. This usage is contrary to the old Navy custom, but is the actual practice of sailor men.

The mariner, steering by a quarter-point card, must be able to *box the compass.* First learn to name the points either way around from any point, and thereafter learn to name the quarter points. When able to name any point or quarter point and the reverse of such a direction, on the opposite side of the card, you have learned to box the compass.

303. The modern 360° card is divided into 360°, from 0° at the north point, to the right or clockwise, all the way around to 360° which is again the north point, 0°. The compass shown in Fig. 303 has such a card, with graduations every 2°. The glass (or plastic) cover containing the liquid allows the card to remain level without gimbals and also serves to magnify the area near the lubber's line.

Fig. 303. A Spherical Type Marine Compass.

304. The double card (Fig. 304), formerly in universal use, is now becoming of historical interest only. It is graduated in quarter points and degrees.

305. Roses on charts, similar to compass cards, facilitate measuring the direction of a course or bearing line. Although the roses on a chart may look like compass cards, they seldom point as does the compass because of the errors of that instrument. Ocean charts show only a 360° true rose graduated like a 360° compass card, but with its 0° point marking true north. Coastwise charts also show a magnetic rose inside the true rose, oriented in a manner to correct for the variation as in Fig. 305.

306. Compass equipment varies from a single small boat compass in a box up to the complete magnetic and gyro equipment of a great ship.

The minimum equipment for a seagoing vessel of the Merchant Marine is three magnetic compasses:

(1) *Standard compass,* on which the navigation of the ship is based, high up on the center line of the ship near the bridge and where the magnetic influence of the ship is least. The readings of this instrument are identified as *per standard compass,* or *p.s.c.*

Fig. 304. Double Card.

(2) *Steering compass,* at the wheel on the bridge in the center line of the ship. Its readings are labeled *per steering compass* or *p.stg.c.*

(3) *After compass,* or after steering station compass, which may be in the steering engine room.

To the above should be added one boat compass in a box stowed in each lifeboat. Gyro compasses, as discussed in Chapter 6, are not accepted as a substitute for any part of the minimum magnetic compass requirements.

The *accuracy* of any magnetic compass depends on various details. It must be installed with the lubber's line exactly forward of the pivot. The compass should be as far removed from the magnetic influence of masses of ferrous metal as is practicable. Electric circuits in or near the compass must have duplex cable or have their (+) and (−) leads twisted together to nullify their magnetic effect. The compass having been installed, and the ship's other equipment put in place, it should be adjusted by a competent compass adjuster, who will record the residual deviations on a deviation card. Thereafter, portable pieces of iron or steel must not be stowed or accidentally left near the compass.

A description of Compass Adjustment will be found in Chapter 5.

Another important instrument which is used to facilitate the observation of bearings of landmarks, other ships or celestial bodies, is described in the next section.

307. The pelorus has no magnets or other directive force, and is sometimes called a dumb compass.

As illustrated in Fig. 307, it includes a pair of gimbal rings like those of a compass but with a pendulum weight, so hung in a square box that the lubber's lines on the inner gimbal ring indicate fore and aft when the side of the box is parallel to the keel of the ship. Free to turn within the fixed ring is a dial, graduated like a compass card.

If the dial be turned so that its reading opposite the lubber's line is the same as the reading of the standard compass, bearings read from this dial will be identical with those read from that compass. The instrument also has devices for clamping the dial in any position and a more or less elaborate sight-vane bar which may be clamped on any desired bearing independently of the dial.

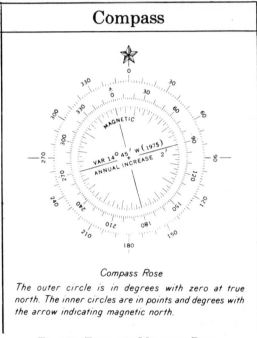

Compass

Compass Rose

The outer circle is in degrees with zero at true north. The inner circles are in points and degrees with the arrow indicating magnetic north.

FIG. 305. TRUE AND MAGNETIC ROSE.

A portable pelorus may be moved to any convenient position provided that care be taken to locate its lubber's line properly. More elaborate instruments are permanently mounted on vertical standards at points on the ship which afford a clear view for taking bearings. As ships with a gyro system may have bearing repeaters placed at any convenient point, the pelorus is less used than formerly.

The accuracy of bearings taken by pelorus depends, among other things, on how accurately the instrument is lined with the keel and whether or not the ship is on the course to which the pelorus is set. Best cry "Mark," "Mark," as the bearing is taken, letting the helmsman record the ship's heading at that instant.

FIG. 307. PORTABLE PELORUS.

308. Types of compasses vary from your pocket compass to the perfected instruments in elaborate binnacles found in the Navy and in the Merchant Marine.

Today, marine compasses are generally of the liquid type. A typical Merchant Marine binnacle is illustrated in Chapter 5, Fig. 506. The Navy service compass has a 7½-inch card and a bronze binnacle stand with many refinements for handling the compensating magnets (Fig. 301).

A type of compass and binnacle popular on sailing yachts is shown in Fig. 308. Questions of convenience are more important than on power vessels because the helmsman, in black night, exposed to storm and spray, must both watch the compass and sail his ship.

For this work a compass should have as large a card as is practical. A 4-inch card is the minimum; a 6-inch card is more than twice as easy to read. The graduations on the card adjacent to the lubber's line should be clearly printed for visibility under dim light. The so-called spherical compass steadies and advantageously magnifies the card. Magnifying glasses sometimes found opposite the lubber's line on steamers' compasses are not practical for rough-and-tumble sailing. The gimbals, and the entire compass bowl with its contents, except the card and the lubber's line, should be painted black to minimize reflections. Of the various attachments for observing bearings, those of the shadow-wire type are ordinarily sufficient and most practical on a sailing yacht. When not in use, they must be carefully stowed to avoid bending their somewhat delicate wires.

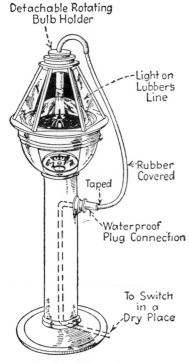

Detachable Rotating
Bulb Holder

Light on
Lubber's
Line

Rubber
Covered

Taped

Waterproof
Plug Connection

To Switch
in a
Dry Place

FIG. 308. YACHT COMPASS.

Practical results to be had from the best possible steering compass on a sailing craft depend on its location and on how it is housed and lighted. It should be as near to the eye and to the direct line of vision of the helms-man as may be. Compasses in the floor of the cockpit, or in a deck house remote from the wheel, are difficult for the helmsman to read and are almost useless for taking bearings. The so-called "skylight" type of binnacle, with six pieces of glass in a brass frame pyramided over the compass, is common on American yachts. Not less than two spare pieces of glass cut to replace those in the binnacle should be at hand.

The problem of lighting the steering compasses discussed above is especially important. The helmsman should be able to read the card easily without blinding his eyes which must watch the sails. The plan illustrated, which works well, includes black on all parts of the compass except the rim of the card, with only a spot of bright light on the lubber's line and adjacent card. Under-lighted cards blind the helmsman even with an irritating night hood over the compass.

* * *

There is a tendency among young officers on ships equipped with gyro systems to forget or neglect their study of the magnetic compass. This may spell disaster when the gyro fails, or in a steel lifeboat where any compass is erratic. Every student must realize that a working knowledge of the magnetic compass has been, and continues to be, the most important single element of the art of navigation.

4. ERRORS OF THE COMPASS

THE force which actuates the needles of a magnetic compass at sea is the resultant or combined effect of the earth's magnetism and the magnetism of the ship. The earth's magnetic poles unfortunately do not coincide with its geographic or true poles. The error caused by the irregularity of the earth's magnetism is called *variation*. It varies in amount and direction according to the locality. The magnetism of each ship differs, and the error caused thereby, known as *deviation*, differs for each compass of every ship, on every course, and may not be constant.

401. Direction. Because of the errors of the compass, there are three systems by which the direction of a course or bearing may be expressed.

(1) *True,* when measured from the earth's geographic meridians or true north; this is the *correct* direction.

(2) *Magnetic,* when measured from magnetic north. Magnetic differs from true by the variation in the locality.

(3) *Compass,* when measured from the north point of the compass card. Compass differs from magnetic by the compass' deviation for the particular heading of the ship. Of the three systems, a compass direction is *least correct*.

The importance of understanding compass errors and of learning how to convert a given course or bearing from one to another of the above systems cannot be overestimated. A compass course must be corrected before it can be plotted. Similar corrections must be applied in a reverse manner to a course taken from the chart to find the compass course to steer. So to do requires (1) that the corrections to be applied are known and (2) that you know how to apply them.

Variation may be taken from any chart that shows the position of the ship. It is the same on all courses and is the same on all ships in the same locality.

Deviation is taken from the compass' deviation card which tabulates its deviations when the ship heads on various courses.

The net total of *variation* and *deviation* is known as the *compass error*. Naming and applying the *compass error* is developed in the following sections. Thereafter, determination of the deviations, as recorded on each compass deviation card, will be discussed at length.

*   *   *

The general principles of compass work apply in all cases. Most coastwise mariners, however, wisely work directly from a magnetic rose already corrected for the variation. The simplicity of this method, where it can be used, is further explained in §416 and §417.

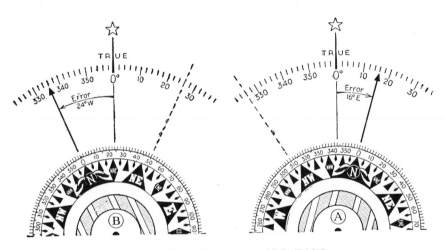

Fig. 402. When Correcting, ADD EAST.

402. Application of compass errors may be approached by rule, rhyme, or reason. Ability to visualize how the compass card turns to right or left, only because of variation or deviation, avoids the necessity for rules. The apparent movements of the lubber's line occur only when the ship turns around the card as it heads on different courses. If the last statement be hard to understand, take a boat compass in a box, place it on a level surface, and watch the lubber's line as you slowly turn the box. Remember that only variation or deviation turns the card.

Compass errors are named *East* or (+) when they turn the card to the right (clockwise), and *West* or (-) when the card is turned to the left (counter-clockwise), as viewed from the center of the card. Fig. 402 illustrates both E and W errors.

Easterly: With the situation as in (A) the card is turned with its north point 16° to the right of true north, and the error is 16° East or

+16°. To correct a compass course of 0° to true one must add 16° to
find the true heading of the ship. Furthermore, the error has turned
the whole card 16° to the right, and all true directions are 16° greater
than the same direction read from the card. Thus to correct any compass course for an easterly error, apply the correction to the right or
when correcting ADD EAST. For example, in the drawing (A) note
how the bearing line through 310° per compass meets the true rose at
326° or (310° + 16° E).

Westerly: Examine situation (B) where the north point of the compass is 24° to the left, or west, of true north, indicating an error of 24°
West or —24°. The card has been turned 24° to the left, and all true
directions are 24° less than the same direction read from the card. Situation (A) is reversed, and to correct a compass course for a westerly error apply the correction to the left or *when correcting Subtract West.*
Note how in (B) the bearing line through 50° per compass meets the true
rose at 26° or (50° — 24° W).

After considering and checking the following examples of applying a
compass error when correcting a compass reading to true, the student
should compute the answers to question Q 1-4 for himself.

WHEN CORRECTING

		(a)	(b)	(c)	(d)
From	Compass	137°	236°	357°	012°
	Error	13° E	12° W	10° E	20° W
To	True	150°	224°	007°	352°

Uncorrecting is the expressive Navy term for reversing the application of compass errors. Again observe situations (A) and (B) and consider how to uncorrect from a true direction to the course to steer by
compass. In (A), the error of 16° E must be applied to the left of the
true heading to find the compass course to steer, and all compass courses
read 16° less than the true direction of the course. With the situation
as in (B) where the error is 24° W, all compass courses read 24° greater
than the true direction of the course. Thus *when uncorrecting Subtract
East, Add West.*

Answers to question Q 2-4 may now be computed after checking the
following examples of uncorrecting a true course to a compass course
to steer.

WHEN UNCORRECTING

		(a)	(b)	(c)	(d)
From	True	290°	047°	349°	006°
	Error	11° W	6° E	22° W	16° E
To	Compass	301°	041°	011°	350°

*   *   *

The foregoing discussion affords a basis for handling all conversions of directions. The various problems of this kind include one or more steps of two opposite moves: (1) *Correcting* from compass to magnetic to true. (2) *Uncorrecting* from true to magnetic to compass. Thus a first consideration in any conversion is to sense which way you are moving. Or the problem may be that of finding the intervening error between two ways of stating the same direction. In any case, the most valuable aid is to visualize which way the card is turned by the error, and to remember not only how the North point swings to East or West, but also that the whole card turns to right or left, assuming you are at the center of the card. Experience also has proven the value of the thought ADD EAST, which automatically develops into the following rule:

Correcting, **ADD** **EAST**erly errors
Subtract Westerly

Uncorrecting, Subtract Easterly errors
Add Westerly

403. Variation is the difference between true north and magnetic north. It is measured by the angle through which it turns the card East (+) or West (−) from true north.

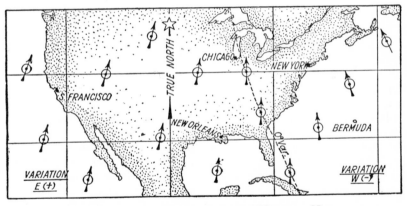

FIG. 403a. COMPASS NEEDLES POINTING MAGNETIC NORTH.

The variation of the magnetic compass results from the location of the earth's magnetic poles more than eight hundred miles from its geographic poles. The importance of this error is illustrated by Fig. 403a. Off New York, variation is about 11° W; off San Francisco it is about 18° E. At certain points on the steamer track from New York to the English Channel, variation exceeds 25° W. A line of 0° variation passes through South America, runs east of the coast of Florida and northward through Lake Michigan to the magnetic north pole which is north and west of Hudson Bay. The line of 0° variation which runs over Europe, Asia, and Australia is irregular. Variation in the Far East is generally small.

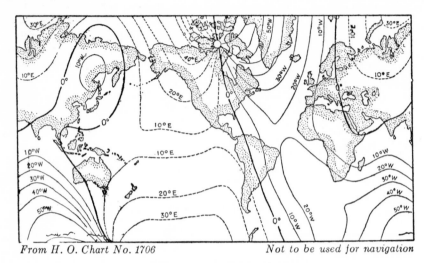

From H. O. Chart No. 1706   *Not to be used for navigation*

FIG. 403*b*.   LINES OF EQUAL VARIATION.

Although variation differs at different places on the earth's surface, it is the same for all courses of all ships near the same position; its amount and direction are marked on charts. Ocean charts show lines of equal variation, somewhat as in Fig. 403*b* but in detail sufficient for finding the variation in degrees E or W at the ship's position. The familiar combination rose (Fig. 305) on coastwise charts indicates the variation both in figures and graphically. Variation at any given place changes slightly from year to year and may have changed greatly throughout the ages. All charts show the date of the given variation and the rate of annual change, which should be taken into account if of evident importance. Due to the irregularity of the earth's magnetism, the direction of magnetic north seldom lies along a great circle toward the magnetic north pole. Nevertheless, the lines along which the earth's magnetism tends to hold the compass needle are known as magnetic meridians, crooked as they may be. Now answer question Q 3-4.

To apply the variation: The variation having been found from the chart, it is applied like any compass error. For example:

		CORRECTING				UNCORRECTING	
	(a)	(b)	(c)		(d)	(e)	(f)
From Mag.	141°	203°	354°	*From* True	013°	074°	349°
Var.	13° E	5° W	19° E	Var.	19° E	12° E	25° W
To True	154°	198°	013°	*To* Mag.	354°	062°	014°

To compute the variation: Assume a compass set up on land where there is no deviation, and further assume that the position of the compass and that of a distant landmark are accurately marked on a chart. The difference between the landmark's true bearing as taken from the chart and its magnetic bearing by compass is then the value of the variation. The name of the variation is E (+) when the true bearing is to the right of (greater than) the magnetic bearing. It is named W (—) when the true bearing is to the left of (less than) the magnetic bearing. *Examples*:

	(a)	(b)	(c)	(d)
True	290°	007°	096°	353°
Mag.	284°	353°	100°	007°
Var.	6° E	14° E	4° W	14° W

404. Deviation is the difference between magnetic north and north per compass. It is measured by the angle through which it turns the card East (+) or West (—) from magnetic north.

SKELETON
DEVIATION CARD
Standard COMPASS
S. S. *Primer*

Head by Comp.	Dev.	Head by Comp.	Dev.
000°	0°	180°	0°
030°	3°W	210°	3°E
060°	6°W	240°	6°E
090°	9°W	270°	9°E
120°	6°W	300°	6°E
150°	3°W	330°	3°E
180°	0°	360°	0°

Fig. 404.

Deviation is a tricky error caused by the ship's magnetism which plays strange pranks. The magnetic force of the earth draws the needle of the compass toward north, but that of the ship moves around the needle and turns the card to right or left of north as the ship heads on one course or another. The effect of the ship's magnetism may be demonstrated by slowly moving a magnet around any small compass and watching the needle move to and fro, its motion depending on the position, distance, and strength of the magnet. This experiment also suggests why deviations differ for compasses differently located in relation to the iron and steel of the ship.

Evidently the ship's magnetism will be greater in the case of a steel ship, but it is not always understood that even on the smallest wooden auxiliary or power boat, one cannot trust the compass unless its deviations be known and proper corrections be made for these errors. In the case of a steel lifeboat, the boat's compass may be useless unless it be located as far above the keel as is practical and its deviations approximated with care.

How the deviations of a compass are determined will be discussed later. For convenience they are listed on a deviation card which is usually more elaborate than Fig. 404. Note that the deviations are tabulated

38   *Primer of Navigation*

for various *compass headings*. When the ship's heading per compass is known, the deviation can be found from the table, interpolating if necessary. If deviations be small, the deviation when on a given magnetic heading may be assumed as that for the same heading per compass. If deviations be large, the problem of finding the deviation corresponding to a given magnetic course requires special consideration. Thus the Navy tabulates deviations for each 15° of heading per compass, or refers to a Napier diagram of deviations which may be entered with either the compass or magnetic heading.

Whether taken from a table or from a diagram, the deviation always must be selected according to the heading of the ship. *Never use the bearing of a light for entering a deviation table.* Enter the table with the ship's course per compass at the time the bearing was observed.

To apply the deviation: Having taken out the deviation from the table, it is applied like any compass error:

	CORRECTING				UNCORRECTING		
	(a)	(b)	(c)		(d)	(e)	(f)
From Comp.	139°	244°	358°	*From* Mag.	007°	049°	354°
Dev.	6° W	3° E	5° E	Dev.	12° E	4° W	9° W
To Mag.	133°	247°	003°	*To* Comp.	355°	053°	003°

To compute the deviation, take the difference between the magnetic bearing and the compass bearing of a distant object or other known direction. The name of the deviation is E (+) when the magnetic bearing is to the right of (greater than) the compass bearing. It is named W (−) when the magnetic bearing is to the left of (less than) the compass bearing.

Think for yourself as you check the following examples and then find the answers to questions from Q 6-4 to Q 11-4.

	(a)	(b)	(c)	(d)
Mag.	137°	219°	349°	007°
Comp.	133°	224°	002°	359°
Dev.	4° E	5° W	13° W	8° E

405. The compass error is a term used to designate the net total of the variation and the deviation. By arithmetic, it is the sum of the two errors when they are of the same name, or their difference when of different names, and is always named like the greater. Graphically the compass error is the angle between the true meridian and the north-south line of the compass needle. Both definitions are illustrated by Fig. 405.

The compass error is applied as in §402; it may be computed in either of two ways as illustrated by the following two groups of examples which are self-explanatory:

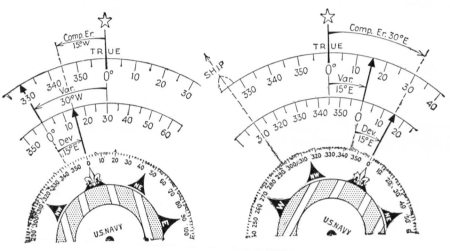

Fig. 405. The Compass Error.

I. *Given the Variation and the Deviation.*

	(a)	(b)	(c)	(d)
Variation	22° W	13° E	18° W	5° W
Deviation	2° W	7° E	5° E	18° E
Compass Error	24° W	20° E	13° W	13° E

II. *Given the True course and the Compass course.*

	(a)	(b)	(c)	(d)
True	045°	010°	129°	354°
Compass	056°	348°	121°	006°
Compass Error	11° W	22° E	8° E	12° W

406. To find the deviation one must find the difference between north per compass and magnetic north, or the difference between any compass reading and the corresponding magnetic direction which may be determined by any of the methods given later in this chapter.

A single difference of this kind serves to check the deviation when on the given heading. Should the resulting deviation differ materially from that found from the compass' deviation table, the situation must be investigated. To construct a complete table, the deviation must be determined when on not less than eight different headings, preferably the cardinal and intercardinal points.

If a motor boat were steered by eye on a course known to be North magnetic, the course per compass would at once indicate the deviation when headed north. If other known magnetic courses were available, as between buoys for example, a series of observations would furnish the basis for a table of deviations. This way of determining the deviation is often recommended as the best method for small craft.

On a ship it is customary to determine the deviations of the standard compass by observation, those of the steering and the after compasses being found by comparisons with the standard compass. The general method is to observe the compass bearing of some object whose magnetic or true bearing is known. In the latter case, the difference between the bearings is the compass error to which the variation is applied to find the deviation. For example, assume that the true bearing and the compass bearing of a distant object are known, and that the variation in the locality is 13° W. Deviation when on the given heading is then found as follows, computed figures being in *italics*:

TO FIND THE DEVIATION

Compass bearing	Dev.	Var.	Comp. Error	True bearing
196°	*7° W*	13° W	*20° W*	176°

Whether deviation be found by comparison with a magnetic bearing or with a true bearing, the common blunder is to give the difference the wrong name. That deviation is E(+) when the magnetic bearing is to the right (§404) is a simple rule, if one must have a rule. Nevertheless, a compass adjuster of long practice was recently disbarred because he habitually called his deviations the reverse of their proper names. The various kinds of bearings used for finding deviations are discussed in the following sections.

*   *   *

The above discussions further emphasize the importance of learning to handle compass errors. To assure a working knowledge of variation and deviation, go over the first group of questions in §418 day after day until they can be answered without hesitation or blunder.

407. Swinging ship, as a general term, means taking a round of observations for compass errors from which tables of deviations may be prepared or checked. Compass adjustment may or may not be included in the operation. As a matter of seamanship, it is the operation of turning and steadying the ship on the various desired headings. The study of swinging ship may be postponed until the student's general knowledge of navigation be further developed.

The vessel should be on an even keel with all movable iron or steel in the vicinity of the compass made fast as for sea. Calm water is essential to accuracy. Observations should be taken on headings at uniform intervals, but their number varies with the necessities and the service. Navy custom is to observe on every 15° or every 30° per compass. If the card is graduated in points, it is often the custom to observe deviation on every two points (22½°) or on the cardinal and intercardinal points, an interval of 45°.

Bearings of the sun are most often used for finding the deviation. Choice of the bearing or bearings to be used depends almost entirely on circumstances. In any case the ship must be steady on each heading.

408. Bearings of the sun. Azimuths, or true bearings, of the sun may be taken from azimuth tables for any given date, time, and latitude, as in §3005. Comparison of the sun's bearing per compass with its true bearing or azimuth gives the compass error and thence the deviation. This method is important, not only because it is preferred by compass adjusters near port, but because, in one form or another, it is the basis for finding the compass error at sea from any celestial body the bearing of which can be observed.

Swinging ship by the sun is further discussed in §3007 which also details the construction of a curve of its magnetic bearings.

409. Bearings of a distant object. From the chart and with the eye select a conspicuous object such as a lighthouse, tower, or mountain peak. With the ship handled so that it remains close to a known position, the true or the magnetic bearing of the mark may be taken from the chart. To eliminate the error in bearing due to the swing of the ship, the object observed should be not less than 6 miles distant from a ship at anchor. When the ship is swung under way, the distance must be greater, but may be less for a small craft kept near a buoy.

410. Ranges. Two objects in line mark a given direction known as a range (§903). When the objects can be identified on the chart, the direction of the range may be taken from the true rose, or from the quarter-point magnetic rose. If such a range be available, deviations are determined by sailing across the range on various headings. At each crossing, the compass bearing of the range is noted in degrees together with the heading of the vessel.

With the range method there is no question of distance off, and for this reason it is commonly used by compass adjusters when neither the sun nor a distant object can be used. It is important, however, that the objects marking the range be as far apart as may be to facilitate accurate observations.

411. Gyro compass readings. Gyro compasses, as described in Chapter 6, are subject to neither variation nor deviation. Thus, if the ship is gyro equipped, with the master gyro running true and the steering repeater in step, the deviation of the compass on any heading may be found by comparing the heading per steering repeater with the heading per compass. If the gyro has a known error, it must be applied to the gyro readings before making the comparisons.

When, for any reason, bearings of the sun or other body are to be observed by a bearing repeater of the gyro system, note: (1) The fore-and-aftness of the repeater's lubber's line must be assured before any azimuths therefrom have significance. (2) The ship must be steady on each heading when the bearing is observed. If the ship swings continuously, a torque is developed and bearings read from the repeater may be seriously in error.

412. Reciprocal bearings. A compass is sent ashore and set up where there is no deviation; readings of this compass are therefore magnetic bearings. A bearing of the ship taken from the shore, reversed by adding 180°, is then the magnetic bearing of the shore station from the ship. As the ship is steadied on a round of headings, simultaneous bearings are taken from the ship per compass and from the shore station. The differences between the bearings per compass and the reciprocals of the bearings from the shore are the deviations. Distance off is not important because a bearing from the shore is observed each time the shore station is observed from the ship. At best this is a method employing the inaccuracies of two people rather than of one.

413. Computed bearings of celestial bodies. The modern methods of working a sight include finding the computed bearing of the body. Navy practice is to have the sun's bearing per standard compass taken whenever the sun is observed for line of position, and thus get a check on the deviation by comparison with the azimuth found when computing the sight.

414. The Napier diagram, as devised by Admiral Sir Charles Napier (1786-1860) of the British Navy, serves to simplify the handling of large deviations.* The diagram provides (1) what is in effect a deviation table which may be entered with any compass course or magnetic heading and (2) for the interconversion of compass and magnetic headings without direct reference to the deviation. Thus it serves for making a complete table of deviations from observations made when on a few headings, and for putting the ship on magnetic headings when so desired.

---

* Study of the Napier diagram may be omitted from all junior courses.

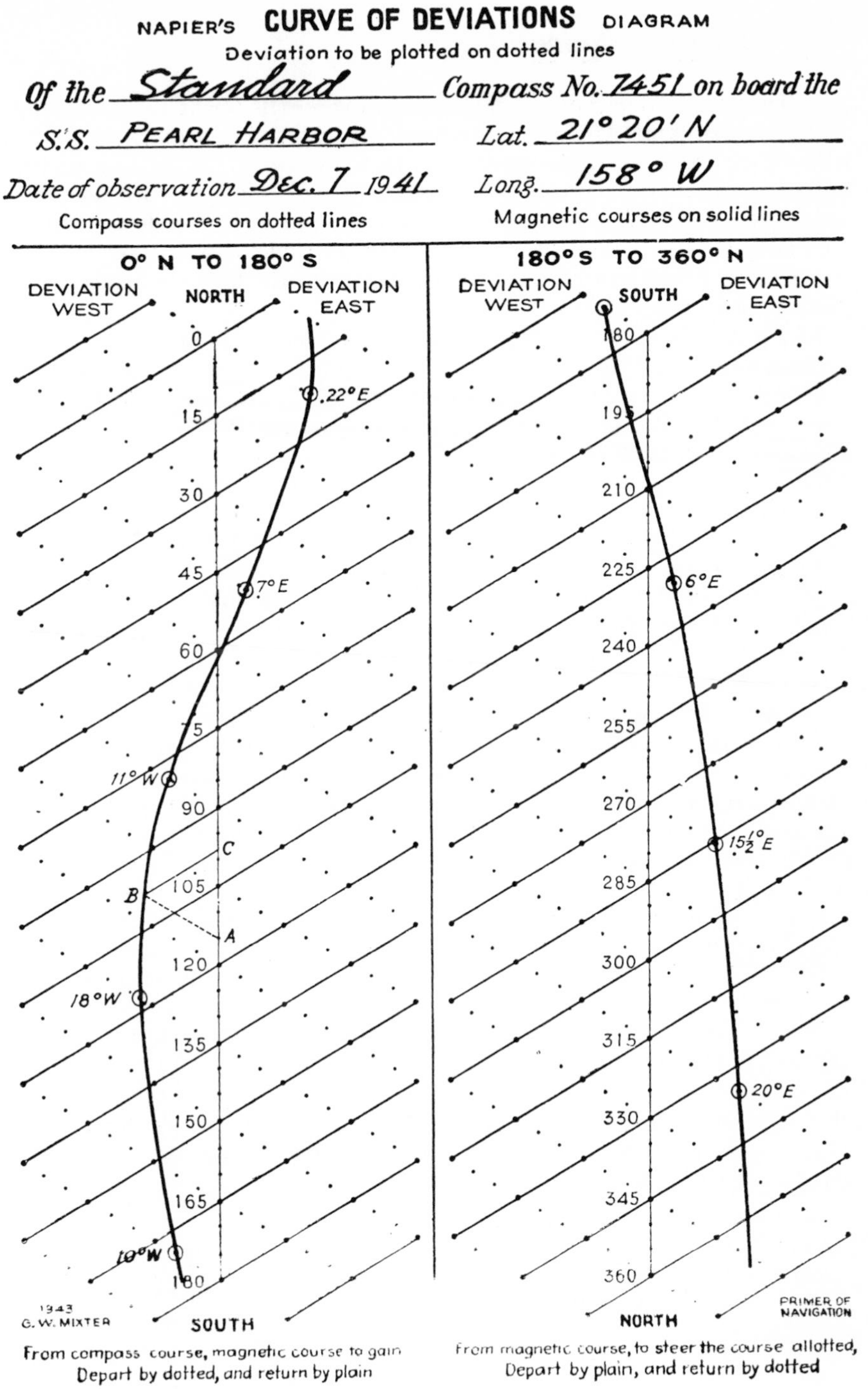

NAPIER'S **CURVE OF DEVIATIONS** DIAGRAM

Deviation to be plotted on dotted lines

Of the ___Standard___ Compass No. __7451__ on board the

S.S. __PEARL HARBOR__ Lat. __21° 20' N__

Date of observation __DEC. 7 1941__ Long. __158° W__

Compass courses on dotted lines   Magnetic courses on solid lines

0° N TO 180° S	180° S TO 360° N
DEVIATION WEST NORTH DEVIATION EAST	DEVIATION WEST SOUTH DEVIATION EAST

0
.22° E
15
30
45
7° E
60
75
11° W
90
C
B
105
A
120
18° W
135
150
165
10° W
180

180
195
210
225
6° E
240
255
270
285
15½° E
300
315
330
20° E
345
360

1943
G. W. MIXTER

SOUTH   NORTH

PRIMER OF NAVIGATION

From compass course, magnetic course to gain
Depart by dotted, and return by plain

From magnetic course, to steer the course allotted,
Depart by plain, and return by dotted

FIG. 414. NAPIER DIAGRAM.

The typical Napier diagram shown as Fig. 414 is about half the usual size but with large deviations plotted thereon the better to illustrate its use. Considered as if the right side were pasted at the bottom of the left, the center line represents the rim of a 360° compass card, cut and straightened out, the degrees of which form the scale for both vertical and diagonal measurements. A curve to either side of the center line indicates the deviations to right or left when on the various headings of the vertical scale.

At intervals of 15° down the center line two series of diagonals are so drawn that they form equilateral triangles with the center line. Dotted diagonal lines run downward from left to right. Solid lines slope down from right to left. Deviations when on various compass courses are laid off along, or parallel to, the dotted lines, to right (E) or left (W) of the center line. The deviation curve results from drawing a fair curve through the points so found.

For plotting the curve on the diagram (Fig. 414) deviations on the cardinal and intercardinal points per compass were assumed to be known. Each is shown plotted at the center of a small circle and labeled with its name and value. In practice the headings may not be spaced with perfect uniformity and with large and erratic deviations the interval between the known deviations should be less.

Having developed the diagram and plotted the curve, consider the logic and use of the equilateral triangles which are the essential characteristics of all Napier diagrams. Remember that the scale of deviations on the diagonal lines is always the same as the course scale on the vertical line. Assume the ship as on course 115° per compass, what is the ship's magnetic heading? Enter the diagram at 115° on the center line at (A). From this point draw a line parallel to the dotted lines to intersect the curve, and from the point of intersection (B) return parallel to the plain lines to (C) which marks the magnetic heading of 098°. Or reverse the process to find the compass course when the magnetic heading is given.

In the above example, the deviation when on a compass course of 115° is the number of degrees from 115° on the center line (A) out by the dotted line to the curve at (B) or 17° W. Had this figure been available from the deviation table, it would at once give the magnetic heading as (115° − 17° W) = 98°, and the convenience of the following table, constructed from the curve on the diagram is evident:

DEVIATION TABLE

Course	Dev.	Course	Dev.	Course	Dev.	Course	Dev.
0°	22° E	90°	11° W	180°	10° W	270°	15.5 E
15°	17.7 E	105°	15.4 W	195°	5.5 W	285°	17.5 E
30°	12.4 E	120°	17.2 W	210°	0.4 E	300°	19.3 E
45°	7.0 E	135°	18.0 W	225°	6.0 E	315°	20.0 E
60°	0.7 E	150°	16.5 W	240°	10.0 E	330°	20.7 E
75°	5.3 W	165°	14.0 W	255°	12.7 E	345°	22.5 E

Tabulating the above deviations to tenths of a degree is according to official custom although the tenths are, at best, only an approximation. The large deviations shown are those of a compass which has not been adjusted; in practice the card of the standard compass should look like that in Fig. 415. Sometimes, however, close compensation is impossible, as with an after compass in the steering-engine room or with the magnetic compass of a submarine, situations which indicate the use of a Napier diagram.

415. Accuracy and responsibility. The practical accuracy possible with a perfect magnetic compass properly installed depends on the accuracy with which bearings can be observed when determining the compass' deviations. Under favorable conditions, with the ship on an even keel in quiet water, the error in such observations may not exceed plus or minus $\frac{1}{2}°$. With the slightest roll the possible error either way approaches 1° and when observing the sun's azimuth at sea may be 2° or more. Thus a navigator should not put faith in fine figures. He must not blunder when handling compass errors. Many disasters attributed to "local magnetic influences" are, in all probability, due to such blunders. The seriousness of all of these matters is further emphasized by remembering that a 3° compass blunder means an error in position of 1 mile for every 20 miles run.

DEVIATION CARD

S. S. *British Tanker*

Date *1-1943* *Standard* COMPASS

COURSE	D.G. OFF	D.G. ON	COURSE	D.G. OFF	D.G. ON
NORTH	0	2° E	SOUTH	0	3° W
NNE	0	2° E	SSW	1° W	3° W
N. E.	0	2° E	S. W.	2° W	2° W
ENE	0	1° E	WSW	1° W	1° W
EAST	0	0	WEST	0	0
ESE	1° W	1° W	WNW	1° W	1° E
S. E.	3° W	2° W	N. W.	2° W	2° E
SSE	1° W	3° W	NNW	1° W	2° E
SOUTH	0	3° W	NORTH	0	2° E

Easterly Deviation takes Ship to the Right of Course
Westerly Deviation takes Ship to the Left of Course

FIG. 415. WAR II CARD.

The navigator has a continuing responsibility for the entire compass system of the ship. Proper precautions can be assured only by a daily and hourly routine of checks and comparisons recorded in the compass record book. The acid test of the system is the accuracy with which the readings of each and every compass can be converted to a true direction, and vice versa. The required routine may vary but commonly includes no less than the following steps which in each instance must be recorded for future reference:

Standard compass. Check the deviation every morning by a bearing of the sun or otherwise. Some services require a check during every watch when suitable bearings can be observed.

Steering compass is compared with the standard compass every watch or every hour.

After steering compass is compared with the standard compass at least once each day.

Master gyro compass, if the ship be so equipped, is checked every watch if conditions permit.

Steering repeater of the gyro system is compared with the magnetic steering compass every 30 minutes. At the same time, a word through the voice tube checks the steering repeater with the master gyro.

The checks and comparisons suggested above considered together with the deviation cards of the various compasses, are almost certain to bring to light any serious compass trouble.

In days of war, the compass problem is further complicated by the degaussing coils which, while protecting the ship in mined waters, create a new form of magnetic disturbance. Two sets of deviations must be determined and tabulated as in Fig. 415 which is a copy of a deviation card recently issued by a well-known compass adjuster.

416. Quarter-point sailing. Teachers of navigation often overlook the fact that thousands of mariners along the coasts of the world sail magnetic courses taken from the quarter-point magnetic roses found on coast and harbor charts (§305). This method of working from the nearest magnetic rose is used, and will continue to be used, because it is the best and simplest for the work in hand. Variation is eliminated from the mariner's problems. With a well adjusted compass, he pays little attention to deviation other than to remember that $2\frac{3}{4}$ or $3° = \frac{1}{4}$ point and that

> *Easterly Deviation takes Ship to the Right of Course*
> *Westerly Deviation takes Ship to the Left of Course*

Use of the magnetic rose is seldom referred to in Navy and Coast Guard teaching, probably because the method is not suitable for use at sea. With proper attention to the deviation, its practical accuracy for coastwise work equals that of more orthodox methods.

417. The circular deviation card, shown about half size in Fig. 417, is especially useful to those using the magnetic rose. It is widely used by motorboat men, and its use is the best way to handle large deviations when sailing coastwise. The deviations plotted in the illustration are those tabulated in §414.

The *outer* rose represents *magnetic* directions. The *inner* card represents the boat's *compass.* From each heading by compass for which the deviation is known, draw a line to the magnetic course when on that heading.

To find the compass course: Locate the magnetic course, as taken from the quarter-point rose on the chart, on the outer rose and follow the

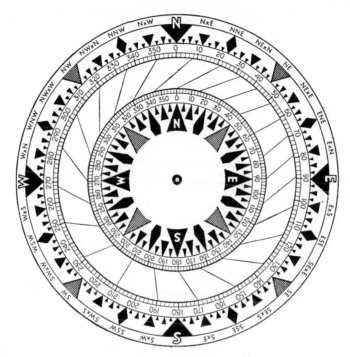

Fig. 417. Circular Deviation Card.

directions of the lines to the inner card from which the course to steer is read.

To correct a compass course to magnetic: Locate the course on the inner card and follow the direction of the lines to the outer rose from which take the magnetic course to plot on the chart.

Do not use the above methods for converting bearings of lights and the like. From the card find the deviation for the heading of the vessel at time bearing was observed and apply it to the bearings, right or left, in the usual manner. This is because deviation depends on the heading of the ship, and is probably quite different from that indicated by the lines at or near the direction of the bearing. Such a situation is avoided if time permits heading the ship directly toward the light.

418. Questions in compass arithmetic, as in the following groups, afford drill in the vital question of whether to add or to subtract. The first group is for all students. The second is an introduction to the compass work of finished navigators. For only coastwise work, include the Junior and the third or Quarter-point group.

JUNIOR GROUP

Q 1-4: *As in* §402. Correct the courses steered by *compass* to *true* courses to plot:

	Comp.	Error		Comp.	Error		Comp.	Error
(a)	085°	14° E	(c)	137°	6° W	(e)	019°	22° W
(b)	S	13° W	(d)	NE	9° E	(f)	356°	20° E

Q 2-4: *As in* §402. Convert the *true* course from the chart to the course to steer by *compass:*

	True	Error		True	Error		True	Error
(a)	018°	8° E	(c)	013°	23° E	(e)	048°	3° W
(b)	256°	14° W	(d)	349°	20° W	(f)	014°	37° W

Q 3-4: From Fig. 403*b* find approximate variation at the following locations:

(a) S.E. coast of Australia
(b) East tip of South America
(c) South end of Greenland
(d) Ireland
(e) Florida
(f) Alaska, West end

Q 4-4: Find the variation as of 1950 in each of the following cases:

		Var.	For year	Annual change
(a)	Cape Farewell	40° W	1943	−10′
(b)	New York	11° 15′ W	1939	+ 4′
(c)	Honolulu	11° E	1943	0′
(d)	Cape of Good Hope	24° W	1943	− 5′
(e)	Manila	30′ E	1943	+ 0′.5

Q 5-4: *As in* §403. Find the variation, given the bearing of a landmark in both *magnetic* and *true* directions:

	Mag.	True		Mag.	True		Mag.	True
(a)	347°	000°	(c)	000°	014°	(e)	135°	140°
(b)	049°	045°	(d)	273°	260°	(f)	197°	180°

Q 6-4: *As in* §403. Fill in the blanks in the following situations:

	Mag.	Var.	True		Mag.	Var.	True
(a)	193°	7° E	——	(d)	——	5° E	094°
(b)	——	19° W	352°	(e)	——	15° E	006°
(c)	189°	——	173°	(f)	357°	——	011°

Q 7-4: *As in* §404. Find the deviation in the following situations, given both the bearing per *compass* and the *magnetic* bearing of a distant object:

	Mag.	Comp.		Mag.	Comp.		Mag.	Comp.
(a)	319°	307°	(c)	345°	003°	(e)	010°	357°
(b)	095°	089°	(d)	192°	206°	(f)	033°	041°

Q 8-4: *As in* §404. Fill in the blanks in the following situations:

	Comp.	Dev.	Mag.		Comp.	Dev.	Mag.
(a)	349°	——	005°	(d)	179°	——	163°
(b)	——	3° E	003°	(e)	——	19° W	274°
(c)	——	9° E	078°	(f)	093°	7° E	——

Q 9-4: *As in* §405. Given the variation in the locality and the deviation for the course per compass, find the net compass error:

	(a)	(b)	(c)	(d)	(e)	(f)
Var.	3° E	17° E	13° W	22° W	11° E	29° W
Dev.	7° W	3° E	0°	11° E	22° W	4° E

Q 10-4: *As in §405.* Find the compass error by comparison with the gyro which is running true:

	(a)	(b)	(c)	(d)	(e)	(f)
Gyro	046°	306°	349°	014°	132°	216°
Comp.	056°	297°	009°	357°	149°	232°

Answers to Q 1 to Q 10 inclusive:

Question		(a)	(b)	(c)	(d)	(e)	(f)
Q 1	True	099°	167°	131°	054°	357°	016°
Q 2	Comp.	010°	270°	350°	009°	051°	051°
Q 3	Var.	10° E	20° W	40° W	16° W	0°	20° E
Q 4	Var.	38°	11°	11°	23°	0°	
		50' W	59' W	00' E	25' W	34' E	
Q 5	Var.	13° E	4° W	14° E	13° W	5° E	17° W
Q 6		200°	011°	16° W	089°	351°	14° E
Q 7	Dev.	12° E	6° E	18° W	14° W	13° E	8° W
Q 8		16° E	000°	069°	16° W	293°	100°
Q 9	Error	4° W	20° E	13° W	11° W	11° W	25° W
Q 10	Error	10° W	9° E	20° W	17° E	17° W	16° W

Q 11-4: Using the deviation given as Fig. 404, and assuming the variation in the locality to be 10° W, answer the following questions to the nearest whole degree:

	Ship's Course	Convert to		Ship's Course	Convert to
(a)	120° Comp.	True	(d)	340° True	Compass
(b)	310° Comp.	True	(e)	220° Mag.	True
(c)	240° True	Compass	(f)	040° Mag.	Compass

(g) Ship on compass course 100°. The compass bearing of a light is 180°. What is the true bearing of the light?

(h) Ship on compass course 320°. Two lights bear by compass 010° and 080° respectively. What are their true bearings?

(i) To put ship on magnetic North, what compass heading is required?

(j) What is the corresponding true heading?

(k) What is compass course to head ship on magnetic East?

(l) When heading magnetic East, how many degrees to the left must the ship turn to head magnetic North?

Answers:

(a)	104°	(d)	349°	(g)	162°	(j)	350°
(b)	305	(e)	210	(h)	004, 074	(k)	098
(c)	244	(f)	044	(i)	000	(l)	090

SECOND GROUP

Q 12-4: *As in §406.* Find the deviation of the compass given the *true* bearing of a distant light or celestial body, the variation in the locality, and the *compass* bearing of the distant object:

	True	Var.	Comp.		True	Var.	Comp.
(a)	135°	15° E	110°	(d)	201°	7° E	204°
(b)	278	8 W	293	(e)	009	19 E	339
(c)	047	5 W	041	(f)	358	3 E	006

Answers: (a) 10° E,   (b) 7° W,   (c) 11° E,   (d) 10° W,   (e) 11° E, (f) 11° W.

Q 13-4: *As in §409 (last paragraph).* Given the headings of the ship and bearings of a distant mountain peak, both per standard compass which has no constant error, find the deviation of that compass on each heading when the magnetic bearing of the peak is 253°:

Per Comp.		Per Comp.		Per Comp.		Per Comp.	
Head.	Bear.	Head.	Bear.	Head.	Bear.	Head.	Bear.
000°	262°	090°	236°	180°	246°	270°	265°
030	252	120	237	210	254	300	276
060	239	150	240	240	257	330	272

Answers:

Head.	Dev.	Head.	Dev.	Head.	Dev.	Head.	Dev.
000°	9° W	090°	17° E	180°	7° E	270°	12° W
030	1 E	120	16 E	210	1 W	300	23 W
060	14 E	150	13 E	240	4 W	330	19 W

Q 14-4: *As in §412.* Assume a compass set up on shore where there is no deviation, find the deviation in the following cases of simultaneously observed reciprocal bearings:

Bearing of	(a)	(b)	(c)	(d)
Ship from shore	082°	078°	086°	087°
Shore compass from ship	260°	264°	263°	263°

Ans: (a) 2° E,   (b) 6° W,   (c) 3° E,   (d) 4° E.

Q 15-4: *As in §411 and §414.* On March 29, 1942, navigator of U.S.S. *Canopus* swung ship to find the deviations of the standard compass by comparison with the gyro compass which had no error, i.e. gyro readings gave true headings. Ship swung in locality where the variation is 16° E. The headings observed were as follows:

Gyro	Std.	Gyro	Std.	Gyro	Std.	Gyro	Std.
016°	354°	106°	088°	196°	185°	286°	268°
046	025	136	121	226	214	316	296
076	056	166	154	256	242	346	324

(a) Find deviations of standard compass on above headings.

(b) With deviations found as in (a), plot a Napier diagram, joining the plotted points by straight lines.

(c) From the Napier diagram prepare a table of deviations, to nearest whole degree, for the standard compass for headings on every 30° p.s.c., commencing with 15°, then 45°, 75°, etc.

(d) Assume the same ship to be on course 315° true in a locality where the variation is 16° W. Using the deviation table prepared as in (c), find the course per standard compass.

Answers:
(a) Deviations on given headings per standard compass:

Head.	Dev.	Head.	Dev.	Head.	Dev.	Head.	Dev.
354°	6° E	088°	2° E	185°	5° W	268°	2° E
025	5 E	121	1 W	214	4 W	296	4 E
056	4 E	154	4 W	242	2 W	324	6 E

(b) If without a full size Napier diagram, trace the required curve over *Fig. 414,* which should give approximate answers to the next question.

(c) Deviation table:

Head.	Dev.	Head.	Dev.	Head.	Dev.	Head.	Dev.
015°	5° E	105°	0°	195°	5° W	285°	3° E
045	4 E	135	2 W	225	3 W	315	5 E
075	3 E	165	5 W	255	0 E	345	6 E

(d) Course 326° per standard compass.

*　　*　　*

QUARTER-POINT GROUP

These questions are only for those who know and use the quarter-point card.

All courses or bearings are assumed to be taken from or plotted by the quarter-point magnetic rose found on all coastwise charts. Where deviation is given in degrees, consider that 3° = ¼ point, and use the nearest quarter-point.

Q 16-4: *As in §402 and §410.* Correct the compass course to course to plot by the magnetic rose on the chart.

	(a)	(b)	(c)	(d)
Comp.	SE×E	E×N	NE	NW ¾ N
Dev.	14° W	5° E	½ E	¾ W

Q 17-4: *As in §402 and §416.* Given the course taken from magnetic rose on chart, find the compass course to steer.

	(a)	(b)	(c)	(d)
Mag.	SE	NNW	NE ½ E	SW ¼ W·
Dev.	11° E	7° W	½ E	¾ W

Q 18-4: Given the vessel's course per compass and the compass bearing of a light, find the magnetic bearing of the light, using the deviation table in *Fig. 404.*

	(a)	(b)	(c)	(d)
Compass Course	W	S	E	N
Bearing	S	W	N	E

Answers to Q 16 to Q 18 inclusive:

Question	(a)	(b)	(c)	(d)
Q 16	E×S ¾ S	E ½ N	NE ½ E	NW
Q 17	SE×E	N×W ½ W	NE	SW×W
Q 18	S ¾ W	W	N ¾ W	E

419. Adjusting the compass is the art of reducing its deviations by so placing compensating magnets and masses of soft iron as to counteract the effect of the ship's magnetism. The importance of this art, especially in the case of steel ships, is indicated by its exhaustive discussion in both Bowditch and Dutton. For many merchant vessels and for most fishermen and yachts, experienced professional compass adjustors are retained. Those readers who desire a description of compass adjusting will find a concise treatment of this subject in Chapter V.

5. COMPASS ADJUSTMENT

DEVIATION of the compass became a serious matter about one hundred years ago when iron ships were first built. Many men have contributed to developing the methods now used for its control but magnetism itself remains a mysterious force. Science does not know what magnetism is, although much is known of what it does. The earth's magnetism draws the compass needle toward the north; that of the ship deviates it to right or left. How to counteract the magnetism of the ship and thus reduce or eliminate the deviation is the subject of this chapter.

The first adjustment of the compasses of a new ship may well be left to an experienced compass adjuster. When necessary, any finished navigator should be able to readjust his compasses. The work may be done by rule, but is simplified if one understands how magnets act and the relative effects of the earth's and the ship's magnetism.

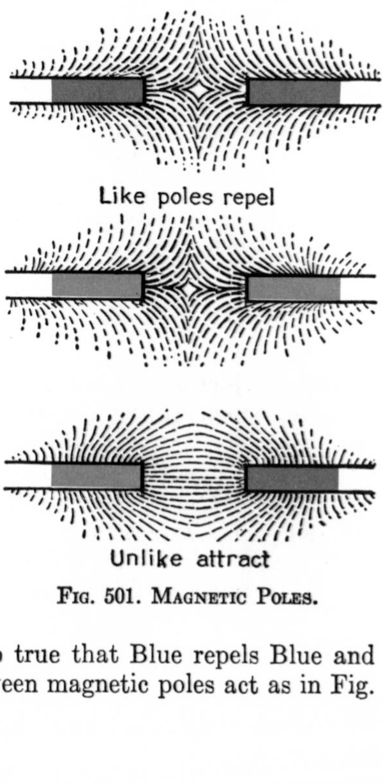

501. Magnetism for the mariner is of two kinds: RED, such as that at the north seeking end of a compass needle. BLUE, as at the north magnetic pole of the earth.

Like poles repel

Unlike attract

FIG. 501. MAGNETIC POLES.

Blue attracts Red and therefore the compass needle points north. It is also true that Blue repels Blue and Red repels Red and thus the forces between magnetic poles act as in Fig.

501: like poles repel, unlike attract. The magnetism of a ship is Red and Blue, hither and yon, and must be opposed by Blue and Red so placed as to compensate for the disturbing forces.

The north end of a compass needle is Red and its south end is Blue. The ends of the corrector magnets used when adjusting the compass are painted Red and Blue to indicate their polarity. Blue pulls the Red end of the needle and pushes the Blue; Red pulls Blue and pushes Red. This is the crux of compass adjustment.

502. A bar magnet, which may be any magnetized piece of iron or steel, has a Blue magnetic pole at one end and a Red pole at the other. These create lines of magnetic force, as in Fig. 502, and all around the magnet. Magnetic needles, balanced in such a magnetic field so that they may both turn and dip, behave in various ways, depending on their position. Always, however, the Red pole at the north seeking head of the arrow is attracted by the magnet's Blue pole and the Blue pole at the south seeking end of the arrow is drawn toward the Red end of the magnet.

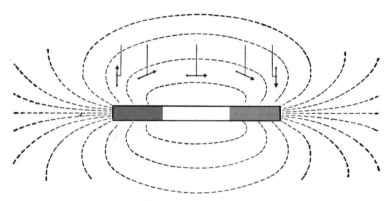

Fig. 502. Lines of Magnetic Force.

In the middle position, all of the force acts horizontally, to turn and direct the needle. Elsewhere only a part of the force acts horizontally, while the other part acts vertically and causes the needle to dip. Directly over the poles of the magnet, all of the force acts vertically.

503. The earth's magnetism is of uncertain origin and is somewhat irregular but for the purposes of this discussion may be considered as that of a magnet within the earth as in Fig. 503. This drawing also shows a series of magnetized needles freely suspended at various points around the earth. These needles point along the lines of the earth's magnetic force.

The irregular line around the middle of the earth is *the magnetic equator,* where all of the earth's magnetic force acts horizontally to direct the needles north and south. Away from this equator a part of the force becomes vertical and the horizontal force decreases. At the poles this north directing force becomes zero. Thus the proportion of the earth's magnetic force available for making the compass point north is greatest at the magnetic equator, half as great at 60° N or S, and becomes 0 at the magnetic poles.

In all discussions of the compass, the ship's magnetism, and compass adjustment, it is important to remember that the earth's force is partly horizontal and partly vertical, except at the poles or on the magnetic equator. This equator runs West across South America in about 15°S, bends up to the earth's equator in mid-Pacific, and crosses the Indian Ocean and Africa in about 10° N, thence down again to meet the earth's equator at about 30° W, and on down to 15° S.

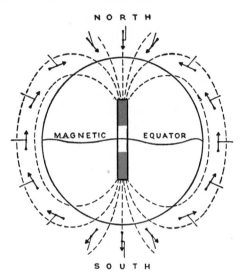

FIG. 503. THE EARTH'S MAGNETISM.

504. The making of a magnet. Magnets make magnets, or, stated otherwise, magnetism *induces* magnetism. In this way two kinds of magnets may be made:

(1) *Induced*, transient. Place a glass tube, filled with iron filings, lengthwise in a magnetic field. Give it a shake, or let the particles gradually turn end to end as the mass becomes magnetized. The tube of filings has become a bar magnet with Red and Blue poles, *opposite* in color to the poles of the field. A magnet has been made like a bar magnet of soft iron. However, soft iron does not retain magnetism and the bar becomes nonmagnetic when withdrawn from the field. The magnetism induced in soft iron comes and goes and is called *transient induced magnetism* or simply *induced magnetism*.

(2) *Subpermanent*. Place a bar of hard steel lengthwise in a magnetic field and pound it to jar its particles until they fall into line. It becomes a bar magnet but, unlike the soft iron bar, remains a magnet when withdrawn from the field. For some unknown reason, steel retains most of its magnetism. Such magnetism is called *subpermanent*.

Certain other characteristics of magnets and magnetism should be noted. Break a magnet into bits and each bit becomes a magnet. Or consider an irregular mass of ferrous metal of all kinds placed in a magnetic field. It becomes a magnet with Red and Blue poles, the axis of the magnet reaching from pole to pole. The forces it exerts are those of a bar magnet with the same poles and axis. Its magnetism may be transient *induced* or *subpermanent*, but in most cases is more or less of both.

505. The building of a ship of steel and iron, somewhere in the magnetic field of the earth, unconsciously includes the making of a subpermanent magnet destined always to cause deviation. As each plate, frame, or beam is hammered or bent and riveted in place, the earth's magnetism makes it a magnet. Thus the whole ship acquires magnetic characteristics, the result of which may be represented as a single subpermanent magnet somewhat as in Fig. 505.*

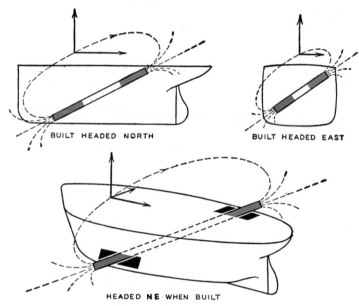

BUILT HEADED NORTH

BUILT HEADED EAST

HEADED **NE** WHEN BUILT

FIG. 505. SHIPS BUILT IN THE NORTHERN HEMISPHERE.

The polarity and position of the magnet through the ship depends on: (1) The direction of the lines of force of the earth's magnetic field at the place where the ship was built. These lines always run magnetic north and south but dip more or less at all shipyards not on the magnetic equator. (2) The heading of the hull during construction. The direction and intensity of the subpermanent magnetism acquired when building may change somewhat after launching. Thereafter, it becomes a permanent characteristic of the ship.

* These sketches were suggested by those in *Deviation and the Deviascope,* a British publication by Captain Charles H. Brown of the Royal Technical College, Glasgow. The book is recommended to those seeking a complete discussion of the magnetic compass and its adjustment.

The welding of plates and the war-time method of building assembled ships have introduced many new variables. The final result, however, appears to leave the subpermanent magnetism to be treated as heretofore.

506. The magnetism of a ship is that of a mass of innumerable magnets both permanent and temporary. The compass adjuster puts this chaos in order by dividing the ship's magnetism into three principal classes:

(1) *Subpermanent* magnetism, acquired by the ship when building as in the preceding section. In most cases, this magnetism is the predominant cause of deviation.

(2) *Vertical induced* magnetism, caused by the vertical part of the earth's force. This is the *Transient magnetism induced in vertical soft iron* mentioned in older editions of Bowditch.

(3) *Horizontal induced* magnetism, caused by the horizontal part of the earth's magnetism, or *Transient magnetism induced in horizontal soft iron.*

Other irregular magnetism is present in all ships, and the above classification is of necessity somewhat arbitrary and inexact. So also are the accepted methods of compass adjustment. Long experience, however, has proved that the general plan works well.

Deviation of the compass determined as in Chapter 4 is the net total effect of all of the different classes of the ship's magnetism. When discussing the principles of compass adjustment, that part of the deviation caused by each class of magnetism is treated separately. When actually adjusting a compass this demarkation becomes less exact and the order of applying the correctors may vary under differing conditions.

507. Subpermanent magnetism. The pole of the magnets in Fig. 505 nearest to the compass may be considered as representing the subpermanent magnetism. This pole, be it Red or Blue, is in a fixed position on the ship, which may be in any direction from the binnacle.

Semicircular deviation. The deviation caused by the subpermanent pole when it is opposite either end of the compass needle is 0. When this occurs, the ship may be on any heading. As the ship swings on other headings the subpermanent pole will deviate the needle. The deviation so caused is of like intensity but of different name on opposite headings. It is a maximum when the subpermanent pole is on a line at right angles to the needle.

How compensated. The force due to subpermanent magnetism which causes the so-called semicircular deviation is dealt with by considering it as divided into two forces, one acting in a fore-and-aft direction, the other acting athwartships. These forces are opposed by placing corrector magnets of opposing polarity in the fore-and-aft and athwartship pockets of the binnacle as in Fig. 506, or in the metal carriers of a Navy binnacle as in Fig. 301.

Adjustments are made with the ship headed East (or West) and also on North (or South). Examine Fig. 507, which explains the rule that corrector magnets are placed at right angles to the compass magnets. *On an East or West heading* use "forenaft" magnets. On a North or South heading, use "thwartship" magnets.

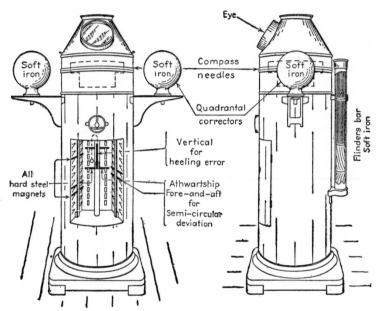

FIG. 506. MERCHANT MARINE BINNACLE.

With a little experience, the direction in which to place the Red end of the corrector magnets becomes instinctive. A simple rule of thumb is to place the Red end in the direction of the displacement of the North (Red) end of the compass magnet. Thus, when headed North, an easterly error (Red end displaced to the right) is corrected by placing the Red end of the corrector magnet to starboard. If heading East and the North (Red) end of the compass magnet is displaced to the left (westerly error), the Red end of the corrector magnet is placed aft.

Imagine yourself looking along the compass magnet from the Blue end to the Red end, and see which way the Red end of the corrector magnet should be placed in order to "push" the Red end of the compass magnet into place. Consult the *Compass Guide* in Apx. VIII which says the same thing in terms of the Blue ends. Several magnets low down are preferable to a lesser number higher up because they are less likely to affect the soft iron correctors on the binnacle.

It should be remembered that this discussion refers to a compass which is mounted in a standard binnacle on a vessel with a steel hull. The magnetic forces affecting a yacht compass are much smaller. The corrector magnets of some small, modern compasses are permanently mounted on perpendicular rods below the compass card. The position of these magnets can be adjusted by turning external screws with a non-magnetic screwdriver to achieve an approximate compensation on both East and North headings.

508. Vertical induced magnetism is that induced in vertical iron by the vertical part of the earth's force. This type of magnetism, like the force which creates it, is 0 at the magnetic equator and is a maximum at the poles. The single pole by which it may be represented is assumed to be on the center line of a symmetrically built ship. For example, the top of the funnel is always Blue in the northern hemisphere.

When the ship is headed North, the pole of the vertical magnetism is directly opposite the end of the compass needle, and will cause no deviation. As the ship swings to right or left, deviation due to the vertical induced magnetism appears, increases to a maximum on East or West, and again becomes 0 when on South.

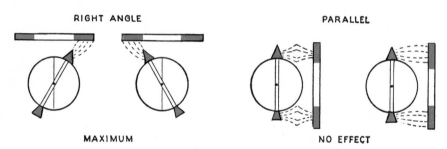

FIG. 507. FIXED MAGNETS AND THE PIVOTED NEEDLE.

How compensated. The deviating force due to the magnetism under discussion is opposed by the vertical induced magnetism in a soft iron bar, usually placed on the forward side of the binnacle. This is the Flinders bar. The top of the bar is level with or slightly higher than the compass needles. The polarity of the upper end of the bar, forward of the compass, is the same as that of the top of the funnel abaft the compass because both are induced by the same vertical force. Thus the Flinders bar affects the compass needles in a direction opposite to that of the force exerted by the vertical induced magnetism aft of the compass. Or the position of the compass relative to the vertical iron may be such that the Flinders bar must be placed abaft the binnacle. In either case, a perfectly adjusted Flinders bar reduces the deviation in question to 0, and the Flinders bar becomes a permanent part of the ship. To so adjust the bar, however, is often a difficult matter.

The Flinders bar is not a solid bar but is made up of varied lengths of soft iron cylinders. The desired length of bar, made up of one or more cylinders, is placed in the top of its brass tube case, supported from below by wooden blocks. The relative intensity of the magnetism at the top of the bar depends on its length, which must be altered when making this type of adjustment.

All of the sections of the Flinders bar should be strictly nonmagnetic soft iron. To check a section for magnetism, hold it in a horizontal position near the N or S point of the compass card. If the card deviates more than 1° the section should be demagnetized by reannealing.

Adjusting the Flinders bar. The compass adjuster in port can do no more than estimate the proper length of bar because he cannot distinguish the deviation for which it should compensate from other deviation.

The best method of adjusting the Flinders bar is available only if the ship cross the magnetic equator. There, the earth's vertical force is 0 and no vertical magnetism is induced in the ship or in the bar. While near the equator, let the semicircular deviation be adjusted with care by the forenaft and thwartship magnets. Thereafter, as the ship leaves the equator, any change in the deviation when on East or West is probably due to the increasing vertical induced magnetism. When and if such a change becomes well defined, it is reduced to 0 by varying the length of the bar. This adjustment is equally correct for all latitudes and the Flinders bar should not be further adjusted without good reason.

The same principle may be applied whenever a change of latitude causes a definite change in the deviation on East or West. As before, the change in deviation on either of these headings is reduced to 0 by varying the length of the Flinders bar. This is the practical form of the so-called mathematical method. It is useful on a new ship where the compass adjuster's estimate of the required Flinders bar has proved to be seriously in error.

509. Horizontal induced magnetism is that induced by the horizontal part of the earth's force, the same force which directs the compass needle. Like the force by which it is created, horizontal induced magnetism is greatest at the magnetic equator and reduces to 0 at the poles.

This class of magnetism occurs principally in the beams of the ship. For the most part, these beams are symmetrically arranged about any compass on the center line of the hull. Fore-and-aft beams are in the minority and their magnetic poles are relatively far from the compass. The athwartship beams are short and greatly predominate. Thus, for the purpose of compass adjustment, horizontal induced magnetism is considered as that of a soft iron beam across the ship, directly under the compass. This conception is illustrated in Fig. 509, which also illustrates how the effect of horizontal induced magnetism is opposed by the magnetism induced in soft iron spheres.

Quadrantal deviation. Observe the drawing at the left of Fig. 509. The magnetism induced in the beam, always Red toward the Blue north of the earth, whatever the heading of the ship, does not deviate the needle when the ship is headed North or East. Neither will it have any effect when on South or West. On North-East, however, the Red in the beam has moved to port and given the Red head of the needle a push to the right, i.e. the deviation is E. Exactly the same effect would be shown if the bow of the ship were sketched in the opposite direction from the compass as when on South-West, where the deviation also is E. On South-East and North-West the deviation is W. This is the so-called *quadrantal deviation* which is caused by the horizontal induced magnetism.

How compensated. At the right of Fig. 509 are shown the soft iron spheres as on the Navy and Merchant Marine binnacles. When headed on the cardinal points, the spheres have no effect on the needle. When on North-East the Blue of the port sphere has pulled the Red head of the needle to the left, aided by the other sphere pulling its tail. In this way the magnetism induced in the spherical corrector compensates for quadrantal deviation.

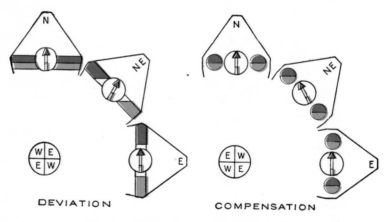

DEVIATION   COMPENSATION

FIG. 509. HORIZONTAL INDUCED MAGNETISM.

Adjustment is made by moving the sphere in or out at equal distances from the center of the compass. Once correctly adjusted they require no further attention and generally rust themselves into a fixed position. The direction to move the spheres, which should be evident, is tabulated at the lower right of the *Compass Guide.*

The spheres should be strictly nonmagnetic soft iron. To check for residual magnetism, steady the ship on North or South. Move one of the spheres all the way in. Watch the card as you slowly turn the sphere through 360°. If it deviates the card more than 1°, the sphere holds subpermanent magnetism and should be demagnetized. Repeat with the other sphere.

510. The heeling error is the deviation caused principally by the athwartship swing of vertical magnetism. The magnetism in question may be represented by a single pole vertically below or above the center of the compass. It causes no deviation so long as the ship remains on an even keel. The heeling error is 0 on East or West because the pole of the vertical magnetism swings athwartship in the plane of the compass needle. It is a maximum, for a given angle of heel, when on North or South where the vertical magnetism swings at right angles to the needle.

If uncompensated or not taken into account, the heeling error may cause two kinds of trouble:

(1) When the ship is rolling, the compass card may swing or oscillate.

(2) When heeled to port or starboard, the usual condition on a sailing vessel, the compass reading may be seriously misleading.

How compensated. The vertical magnetism of the ship is opposed by a vertical magnet or magnets exactly under the center of the compass. They are carried in a deep tubular bucket which may be raised or lowered. In the northern hemisphere place the Red painted ends of the magnets up, unless the compass is in a steel wheelhouse, in which case, Blue up is probably required. The effect of the magnets may be increased by raising their container or by increasing the number of magnets. More magnets low down are preferable to a lesser number higher up where they deaden the compass needle. Adjusted for a given list, the adjustment is equally correct for any angle of heel because the correcting magnets and the ship's magnetism swing equally.

Adjustment for the heeling error may be made in port by the compass adjuster or at sea by the navigator.

In port, the vertical force of the earth is the same on shore as through the center of a compass on a nearby ship. The compass adjuster uses a *Kelvin vertical force instrument* to separate this force from the vertical force due to the ship's magnetism which causes the heeling error. The instrument is a modified form of dipping needle so balanced on shore that the needle lies horizontal when subject only to the earth's vertical force. Thus adjusted, the instrument is placed so that its needle is in the position of the compass needle. Any dip that develops is then due only to the vertical force of the ship's magnetism and is reduced to 0 with the heeling magnet, which completes the adjustment without the ship being heeled.

As the heeling error is 0 on East or West, adjustments of the error itself, as at sea, must be made with the ship on a northerly or southerly course, preferably not far from North or South.

When rolling and the card swings to right and left, raise the heeling magnet until the card becomes steady. Do not mistake the yaw of the ship for the swing of the needle.

With a steady list, raise the heeling magnet and take out *only the difference in deviation caused by the list.* For example: The deviation card shows 1° W on North, as with the ship upright with no heel. If with a certain port list the deviation is 5° E when on North, move the heeling magnet until it corrects for the 6° change.

Sally the ship, by sending the crew to port or starboard, and proceed as when with a steady list. This method is useful with many of the smaller craft now being built for the Navy, especially for the first adjustment when no vertical force instrument is available.

511. Constant deviation, so called because it is the same on all headings, is a possible element in the net total deviation on all headings. It may be caused by unsymmetrical soft iron of the ship or by installation errors of the compass or binnacle, and is usually negligible. The point for the student to remember is that a constant deviation may exist, the visible effect of which is to upset the symmetry of the deviation card.

512. Review. The methods of compensating for each element of the deviation have been outlined in the preceding sections. In each case the adjuster must have simultaneous compass and magnetic bearings to indicate the error for which he is adjusting and his progress toward such reduction of the deviation as the situation requires. Any of the sources of magnetic bearings discussed in Chapter 4 may be used. Tables of the sun's azimuth and diagrams of magnetic azimuths are further discussed in Chapter 30.

Whether to put the ship on a *magnetic* heading or on a similar *compass heading* for making a given adjustment is, in most cases, immaterial because when the deviation in question is reduced to 0 the two headings are identical.

Magnetic. Bowditch and most textbooks direct that the ship be put on magnetic headings. This may be done with the aid of the gyro, an auxiliary compass, or a pelorus, and reflects Navy teaching.

Compass. The British Admiralty's *Notes on the Correction of the Magnetic Compass* (1943) directs that the ship be put on compass headings. Professional compass adjusters use this method because it requires less personnel and because they consider it shorter and more accurate for their work.

The question of putting the ship on a magnetic heading is not further discussed. The headings to which the ship should be swung as directed in the following sections may be considered as either compass or magnetic headings unless labeled otherwise.

513. To adjust the compass. The purpose of adjusting a compass is to eliminate large deviations and to reduce them to the lowest value consistent with good practice. This means that the reductions must be obtained so that the remaining deviations are subject to minimum change with latitude and without seriously reducing the directive force of the compass and thus deadening the needle. Beware of too many zeros on a deviation card.

The following plan reflects the accepted general order of procedure for the adjustment of a new standard compass but is subject to many variations. Alternate moves on other headings or in the southern hemiphere should be evident.

Preparation. The vessel must be on an even keel in smooth water, all movable iron or steel parts near the compass made fast as for sea. Examine the compass. See that all spare corrector magnets are at a safe distance. Decide what you propose to do and how to do it.

Before making any adjustments, the spheres, Flinders bar and heeling magnets should be in their approximate positions. If placed later, they may disturb the principal adjustments which are made with the forenaft and thwartship magnets.

Spheres should be equidistant from the compass in mid-position, unless better information is available from experience with like situations.

Flinders bar. The professional compass adjuster considers the probable location of the vertical induced magnetism in relation to the binnacle, recalls his experience with similar ships, and estimates the required length of Flinders bar accordingly.

Lacking experience on similar ships, it is considered better in Navy teaching to use no Flinders bar until sufficient data are obtained to estimate the amount of bar to use.

Heeling magnet or magnets. *After* the selected length of Flinders bar is in position, place and adjust the heeling magnets with the aid of a vertical force instrument. Remember to use a number of magnets in the lowest position rather than a lesser number higher up.

When no vertical force instrument is available, estimate the number of magnets to place in their container at its lowest position. Red up in the northern hemisphere, unless the binnacle be in a steel wheel house, in which case place Blue up. Lacking the necessary instrument, adjustment must wait until such time as the ship is heeled on a northerly or southerly course. A heeling magnet may not be needed on a nonmagnetic vessel such as a yacht with a wooden or fiberglass hull.

With the above correctors in their estimated positions, stand by to swing ship. The following instructions are simplified by assuming the ship is steadied on East first and then swung to the right. Preferably start on E or W. "A ship handles better with right rudder and it is bad luck to swing against the sun." However, the work of adjustment may start on any cardinal point and the ship may be swung in either direction.

Head East and reduce deviation to 0 with forenaft magnets.

Head South and reduce deviation to 0 with the thwartship magnets.

Head South-West and reduce deviation to 0 with the quadrantal spheres.

On a majority of vessels no further adjustments are required. It is customary, however, to halve the deviations on the next three headings if they are large enough to warrant further refinement.

Head West and observe the deviation. If the deviation be 2° or more, reduce it one-half with the forenaft magnets. Remember in so doing you have made an equal but opposite change in the deviation on E.

The reason for halving is based on the assumption that deviation found on W, after reducing to 0 on E, is caused by a constant error of the compass. If a constant error of 2° on E has been reduced to 0, the magnets which reduced it to 0 on E will increase it to 4° on W. The 4° on W is therefore halved, leaving 2° on W and 2° on E, which is preferable to 4° on either heading.

Head North-West and observe the deviation. If the deviation be large, reduce it one-half with the quadrantal spheres. This should have the same effect on the opposite heading but an opposite effect on the other two intercardinal points.

Head North and observe the deviation. If the deviation be 2° or more, reduce it one-half with the thwartship magnets, remembering that this adjustment has made an equal but opposite change in the deviation on S.

The work of adjusting the compass is now complete until circumstances permit and warrant an effort to perfect the Flinders bar or heeling magnet adjustments. Therefore, proceed and swing ship until the deviation remaining on the desired number of equally spaced headings is observed and recorded.

514. Readjustment. After a compass has been adjusted as above, and possibly readjusted after or during the ship's first six months at sea, it may continue in satisfactory adjustment for many years. This statement does not mean that deviations will not change. Rather that, as checked and revised from time to time, the deviations shown will not exceed about 5°. On the other hand, all magnetism is subject to change including that of the compass needles, the ship, and the correctors. Should readjustment be decided on, head the ship on two adjacent cardinal headings. On each heading reduce deviation to zero with the thwartship or forenaft magnets. Ordinarily nothing more will be required and the deviations, in most cases, will be small.

515. Cautions. The navigator should watch for changes in deviation with changes of 10° or more in latitude. If the Flinders bar is not perfectly adjusted, changes in deviation when on easterly or westerly courses in the higher latitudes are inevitable.

The so-called *Gaussin error* is the temporary change in deviation which may appear after a steel ship has long been on any heading, either at sea or in port. Or it may become serious after a short period during repair work or gunfire which pound or jar the metal of the ship. Some of the induced magnetism becomes temporarily "permanent," and when the ship suddenly heads toward North or South may cause a serious change in deviation. The tendency when altering a course that has been steered for several days is for the N point of the compass to want to return to the old course. For instance, after a ten-day trip heading E for England, when the ship turns N up the Irish Sea, the compass will take on E deviation for several hours.

The deviation table need not be revised for the Gaussin error because it presently disappears. The navigator, however, must not fail to check the deviation soon after such a change of course.

516. Electromagnetism is that developed by a current of electricity. A magnetic field surrounds any wire carrying an electric current. Thus a coil of wire carrying a current around an iron bar creates a magnet as in Fig. 516. Should the current be reversed in direction, the polarity of the magnet is reversed. Even without the iron core, such an electromagnetic field with its lines of force runs through the coil and acts like a magnet so long as the current flows. The Blue pole of the field is the end from which the current would appear to turn clockwise.

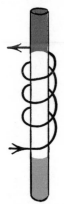

517. Degaussing effects. In time of war, degaussing coils, wrapped horizontally around the ship, are used to prevent the explosion of magnetic mines. Electric currents through the one, two, or three coils create a vertical magnetic field (§516) opposite to that of the ship. Thus compensated, the ship's magnetism does not set off the detonating devices of the mines.

FIG. 516.
ELECTROMAGNET.

When the current is switched through the degaussing coils, the magnetic field about the compass will be altered. The effect may be merely large and differing deviations, but the compass may tilt, stick, spin round and round, or stay 180° from the proper heading. For approximately maintaining the normal field, compensating coils, in circuit with the degaussing currents, are placed around and above the compass. This phase of compass adjustment is beyond the scope of this chapter. What every navigator must realize is that the compensating coils seldom exactly restore the normal field and that a special table of deviations must be determined for use when degaussing, a fact shown by the copy of an actual deviation card, as in Fig. 415 of the preceding chapter.

*   *   *

The magnetism of ships and how to compensate for it have been studied and analyzed by many scientists and mathematicians. The result of their work is the trial and error method of compass adjustment given in this chapter. Sometimes varied as occasion demands or embellished with a bit of mathematics, it is the method all but universally used. Each step is simple but all are inter-related, and the binnacle must be kept locked to make certain that correctors are not shifted by inexperienced hands. Once adjusted, a compass should not be disturbed without good reason.

Courtesy of the Metropolitan Museum of Art

"The stone has revealed to Flavio its secret love of
the pole, and he has revealed it to the mariner"

Old Legend

6. GYRO SYSTEMS*

THE gyro compass points true north. It is not subject to variation and deviation because it is neither directed nor affected by magnetism. The principles of the gyroscope, which are those of the gyro compass, were formulated by the French physicist Léon Foucault about 1852; its possibilities as a mariner's compass apparently were not recognized until many years later. In 1896 Whitehead torpedoes were gyro controlled, but Sperry's first installation of a gyro compass in 1910 marked the beginning of the modern gyro system.

601. The practical development of the gyroscope includes various instruments and devices related to navigation. They make blind flying

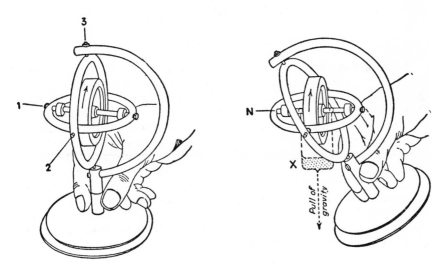

FIG. 601. GYROSCOPE AND GYRO COMPASS.

* The author is indebted to Mr. John J. Brierly of The Sperry Gyroscope Company for his review of this chapter.

possible and a gyro horizon for the sextant has been dreamed of for
many years. In this chapter, however, the word gyro means a gyro compass for marine work. During the first World War many naval vessels
were gyro equipped. Today all major ships of the Merchant Marine and
practically every vessel of the Navy and Coast Guard have complete
gyro systems.

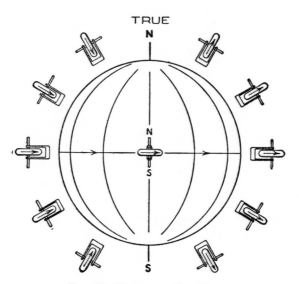

FIG. 602. GYROS AND THE EARTH.

602. Principles. A simple gyroscope is a rapidly spinning wheel
universally mounted so that its axis may point in any direction, like the
instrument at the left of Fig. 601. The first principle of the gyroscope
is that when it is spinning at high speed, its axis will continue to point in
the same direction regardless of how the instrument be held, unless disturbed by some other external force. This fact in itself is important to
physicists, but alone does not make a compass. However, if the axis be
maintained in a horizontal position by a weight (X), as in the drawing
at the right of Fig. 601, the pull of gravity and the forces resulting from
the rotation of the earth combine to cause the axis of the rapidly spinning wheel to *precess* or change its direction until it points true north
and south. This is the compass shown in various positions around the
earth in Fig. 602. The tendency to place itself north-south grows less
as the poles are approached.

603. The master gyro compass of today is a mechanism both complicated and reliable which gives little outward suggestion of the elemen-
tal compass described above. Built with great accuracy at every point, it
includes the ultra of mechanical and electrical devices to reduce friction
and to assure long life with little servicing. Many of the details are

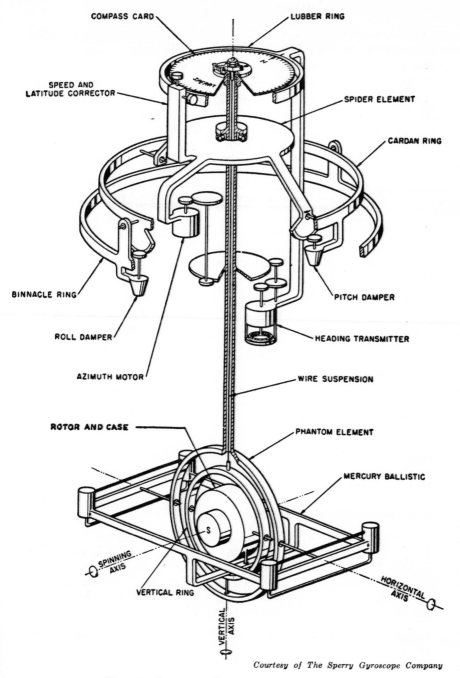

COMPASS CARD

LUBBER RING

SPEED AND
LATITUDE CORRECTOR

SPIDER ELEMENT

CARDAN RING

BINNACLE RING

PITCH DAMPER

ROLL DAMPER

HEADING TRANSMITTER

AZIMUTH MOTOR

WIRE SUSPENSION

ROTOR AND CASE

PHANTOM ELEMENT

MERCURY BALLISTIC

SPINNING
AXIS

HORIZONTAL
AXIS

VERTICAL RING

VERTICAL
AXIS

S

Courtesy of The Sperry Gyroscope Company

FIG. 603. SCHEMATIC DIAGRAM OF GYRO-COMPASS

omitted from the following description of the modern Sperry compass. Apart from other units of the gyro system, the compass consists of four elements:

(1) A solid frame, called *the spider,* hung in gimbals like any compass, on the top of which is a fixed flat lubber ring with the lubber's line on an adjustable plate.

(2) The so-called *phantom element,* supported by the spider but free to turn around the vertical axis of the instrument. Thus the compass card on the top of this unit may turn within the lubber ring on the frame, the reading of the card opposite the lubber's line indicating the heading of the ship.

(3) The gyroscope which finds true north, called the *sensitive element.* This unit is suspended by a steel wire from a point just above the center of the compass card on the phantom, and is steadied at the bottom by a lower vertical guide bearing.

(4) The *ballastic,* or weight, supported by the phantom but arranged to hold the axis of the gyroscope horizontal.

Before starting, the instrument is so adjusted that the gyro axis is approximately parallel to the meridian, i.e., points north. This is easily done when the operator knows the approximate heading of the ship. Or the adjustment to north may be made, after starting and without knowing the true heading, by observing the action of the bubble in the level. When running approximately on the meridian, the instrument then functions as follows:

The *sensitive element* is not only a gyroscope, but the gyro wheel with its casing forms an induction motor which is driven by a 3-phase alternating current. After the current is switched on and the rotor has started, the rotor will reach its assigned speed of 6000 R.P.M. in about 10 minutes. The gyro axis then will have started to level itself and to precess or seek true north. Although this directive force is 500 times that of a magnetic compass, it is not used to turn the heavy mechanism which carries the compass card.

A second motor, called an Azimuth Motor, is mounted on the spider frame, and is used to overcome the friction of gears and bearings, by keeping the phantom element which carries the compass card in alignment with the sensitive or North-seeking element. The Azimuth Motor, by keeping the phantom element in alignment with the sensitive element, prevents the suspension wires from becoming twisted.

Speed and Latitude Correctors on the master compass, when properly set, adjust errors inherent in the gyroscope and in the design of the compass itself.

604. Summary. The gyroscope within the *sensitive element,* kept level by the weight of the *ballastic,* causes the card on the *phantom* to turn to right or left of the lubber's line on *the spider* with the following results:

(1) Assuming the compass to be running without error, the north point of the card points true north.

(2) With the lubber's line exactly forward of the center of the card, the reading of the card opposite the lubber's line is then the true heading of the ship.

(3) If the compass be running with a slight constant error, the reading is corrected by moving the plate on the lubber ring on which the lubber's line is marked. The lubber's line reading on the card again becomes the true heading of the ship. The repeaters must then be readjusted to the master compass reading.

605. Repeater compasses, or simply repeaters, are the various instruments to which the indications of the master compass are transmitted by electric currents. Unlike other compasses, they may be placed at any angle, anywhere, except the bearing repeaters which must be hung in gimbals. When properly set to the master compass, the lubber's line reading of any repeater is subject only to the error, if any, in lubber's line reading of the master compass.

The *steering repeater* is mounted at the ship's wheel convenient to the helmsman. A voice tube to the master compass provides for setting and checking the lubber's line reading of this repeater.

Bearing repeaters are mounted on the wings of the bridge and elsewhere if required. These repeaters are hung in gimbals and are equipped to observe bearings, including azimuths of the sun or other celestial bodies. The lubber's line is fixed on a line parallel to the keel and cannot be adjusted.

The importance of the position of a bearing repeater's lubber line is sometimes overlooked. The reading of the repeater is set by the fixed lubber's line. If that line be in error, the bearing read from the repeater will be in error by a like amount.

Other repeaters are used with the radio direction finder, or as units of the gyro pilot and the course recorder, or as essential elements of the radar equipment and other special devices found on naval vessels.

606. To set the repeaters. Electrical connections keep the readings of properly set repeaters in agreement with the master compass so long as the current is on. There is no provision, however, for first bringing the repeaters to the master compass reading. Before starting the master compass, it is turned by hand so that its reading approximates the heading of the ship. While waiting for the gyro rotor to speed up, each repeater is set to the same reading before the repeater switch is closed. After the rotor is up to speed, the repeater switch is closed and the repeaters are automatically brought into exact adjustment.

607. The gyro system includes the master compass, steering repeaters, bearing repeaters, and all of the various instruments and devices which include repeaters. A gyro system for a well equipped merchantman is diagrammed in Fig. 607. Major naval vessels are equipped with two systems. The master compasses are below decks with repeaters at numerous stations.

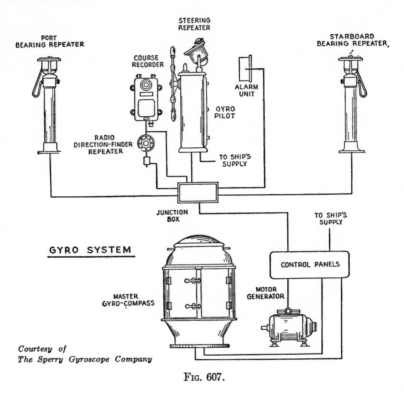

Fig. 607.

In merchant service, the navigating officer is ordinarily responsible for the gyro system and personally starts the system and sets the correctors on the master compass. Whatever the allocation of duties, the navigator should be competent to start the master compass, put the repeaters in step, and check both for possible compass error. To a young navigator, inexperienced in these matters, the maker's instruction books covering *each unit* of the system are invaluable.

608. Errors of the gyro compass. It is a mistake to think that there is no error in the gyro compass reading just because such compasses are said to point true north.

There are certain errors arising from the theory of the gyro compass and certain other errors which are inherent in its design. To practically eliminate these errors, the Speed and Latitude Correctors must be reset from time to time and always kept within 3 knots of the speed and within 3° of the latitude. If a permanent fixed error is proved to exist in the master compass, from causes known or unknown, it may be compensated for by adjusting its lubber's line.

Any of the methods used for finding the error of a magnetic compass may be used to determine the gyro error. Unlike a magnetic compass, the gyro error is the same for all courses and bearings. Thus when entering or leaving port, it is a simple matter to check whenever headed on a known range.

At sea, the bearing of the sun when not too high is the best check. The method of observing the compass bearing of the sun at the instant of its observation for a line of position is most simple.

The necessity of having the fixed lubber's lines of the bearing repeaters correctly located is evident. Otherwise an error determined with the aid of a bearing repeater may be far from the truth of the situation.

Regular comparison of the magnetic steering compass and the steering repeater is routine duty, as is the comparison of the repeater with the master gyro compass. The results should show if anything has gone wrong with the compass equipment and should indicate the steps required to right the situation.

*   *   *

The gyro compass points true north; it may be located without regard to magnetic conditions; its repeaters may be wherever needed. It is reliable but requires care *and electric current* which some day will fail. The moral is to take good care of the gyro but not to forget the magnetic compass.

7. LIGHTS, BUOYS, AND BEACONS

LIGHTS

THE United States Lighthouse Service, now operated by the Coast Guard, traces its ancestry back to 1715-16 when the first lighthouse on the American continent was built by the Province of Massachusetts at the entrance to Boston Harbor, where Boston Light flashes white every 30 seconds from sunset to sunrise. The jurisdiction of the Lighthouse Service today extends over all navigable waters of the United States except the Panama Canal Zone where the aids to navigation are maintained by the Canal authorities. The discussions in this chapter relate exclusively to the United States systems of lights and buoys; for other countries, see the *Sailing Directions* (*Pilots*), or the publications of the respective governments.

701. Light Lists. The U. S. Coast Guard publishes annually a series of five volumes (see Apx. IV) containing a complete listing of all aids to navigation on the Atlantic, Gulf, and Pacific Coasts of the United States, the Mississippi River, and the Great Lakes. Included are the aids maintained in Puerto Rico, the Virgin Islands and elsewhere in the West Indies, and the Pacific Islands. The lighted aids, fog signals, and radiobeacons maintained by British Columbia along that coast are also included as a convenience to mariners proceeding to and from Alaska.

Each volume contains an introduction of over 20 pages describing the arrangement of the listings, the meanings of the abbreviations and symbols, a map of the radiobeacons, coverage diagrams for the loran stations, and other information of value to the navigator. Fig. 701 is an excerpt from one of the *Light Lists;* however, the student may desire to procure a copy of the proper volume for study with his local charts and the remainder of this chapter.

The Defence Mapping Agency Hydrographic Center publishes a series of seven publications called List of Lights containing information on the location and characteristics of navigational lights not located in the United States or its possessions.

702. Characteristics of lights. All lighthouses, lightships, and buoys have distinctive characteristics by which they can be identified by

75

76 *Primer of Navigation*

day or by night, and certain of these characteristics, especially of buoys, have navigational significance. This is fully explained in the *Light Lists*, but the principal interest in lighted aids is centered in the color, period, and power of the light itself, by which the aid can be identified at night. Fig. 702 illustrates the phases found in lights and lighted buoys and de-

	LONG ISLAND SOUND		NEW YORK AND CONNECTICUT					THIRD DISTRICT
(1)	(2)		(3)	(4)	(5)	(6)		(7)
	Name		Location	Nominal	Ht.	Structure		
No.	Characteristic		Lat. N. Long. W.	Range	above Ht. above water ground		Daymark	Remarks Year
939	PLUM ISLAND HARBOR EAST DOLPHIN LIGHT. F. R.		In 15 feet	6	10	Dolphin		Maintained from sundown to 0130 daily. Maintained by U. S. Dept. of Agriculture. 1957
940	ORIENT POINT LIGHT . . . . F. R.		On outer end of Oyster Pound Reef. 41 09.8 72 13.4	10	64	Brown conical tower, on black pier.		HORN: 2 blasts ev 30ˢ (2ˢbl-2ˢsi-2ˢbl-24ˢsi). 1899
	(For Gardiners Bay, see No. 1319)							
	(For Long Island Sound, North Channel, see p. 155, 156)							
941	Hatchett Point Lighted Gong Buoy HP. Mo. (A) W.		In 106 feet 41 14.2 72 15.3	5	. . . .	Black and white vertical stripes.		Replaced by nun if endangered by ice.
941.10	HATCHETT POINT DOLPHIN LIGHT. Qk. Fl. W.		In 25 feet	. . . .	16	Dolphin		1973
	Hatchett Reef Buoy 6		In 24 feet, on south end of reef.	. . . .	. . . .	Red nun		Red reflector.
942	Saybrook Bar Lighted Bell Buoy 8 . Fl. W., 4ˢ		In 24 feet, on south point of shoal. 41 14.9 72 18.9	6	. . . .	Red		
	Long Sand Shoal East End Buoy. . .		In 24 feet	. . . .	. . . .	Red and black horizontal bands; nun.		Red reflector.
943 1040	SAYBROOK BREAKWATER LIGHT. Fl. G., 6ˢ		On south end of west jetty 41 15.8 72 20.6	11	58	White conical tower on brown cylindrical pier. 49		MKR RBN: 320 kHz. Antenna at light tower. HORN: 1 blast ev 30ˢ (3ˢbl). 1886
	(For Connecticut River, see No. 1040)							
	Orient Shoal Buoy 3		In 24 feet, on north-east side of shoal. 41 09.0 72 19.9	. . . .	. . . .	Black can		White reflector.
944	Long Sand Shoal Lighted Whistle Buoy 8A. Qk. Fl. R.		In 65 feet 41 13.7 72 22.0	3	. . . .	Red		Ra ref.
945	Cornfield Lighted Bell Buoy CF . . Mo. (A) W.		In 136 feet 41 11.3 72 22.3	8	. . . .	Black and white vertical stripes.		Ra ref.
946	Long Sand Shoal Lighted Gong Buoy 8B. Qk. Fl. R.		In 78 feet 41 13.8 72 22.0	4	. . . .	Red		Ra ref.
947	Long Sand Shoal West End Lighted Bell Buoy. I. Qk. Fl. W.		In 34 feet, at west point of shoal. 41 13.6 72 27.6	6	. . . .	Red and black horizontal bands.		
948	Horton Point Light . . . . Fl. G., 15ˢ		On northwest point of Horton Neck. 41 05.1 72 26.8	20	103	Black skeleton tower, small white house.		1857–1933
949	Sixmile Reef Lighted Whistle Buoy 8C. Fl. R., 4ˢ		In 100 feet, at south-erly edge of reef.	. . . .	. . . .	Red		Ra ref.
950	Twenty-Eight Foot Shoal Lighted Bell Buoy. I. Qk. Fl. W.		In 42 feet 41 09.3 72 30.5	7	. . . .	Red and black horizontal bands .		Ra ref.
951	Falkner Island Light . . . . Fl. W., 15ˢ		On island off Guilford Harbor. 41 12.7 72 39.2	15	94	White octagonal tower attached to dwelling. 46		RBN: 306 kHz (• ▬▬▬)II. Antenna at light tower. HORN: 2 blasts ev 20ˢ (2ˢbl-2ˢsi-2ˢbl-14ˢsi). 1802–1871
952	Goose Island Lighted Bell Buoy 10GI. Fl. R., 4ˢ		In 37 feet, off south end of shoal. 41 12.1 72 40.5	4	. . . .	Red		
952.50	SACHEM HEAD BREAKWATER LIGHT. Fl. R., 3ˢ		On rock 41 14.8 72 42.7	. . . .	. . . .	Pile		Private aid. Maintained from June 1 to Oct. 1. 1970

Fɪɢ. 701. Lɪɢʜᴛ Lɪsᴛ.

CHARACTERISTIC LIGHT PHASES

Illustration	Symbols and meaning		Phase description
	Lights which do not change color	Lights which show color variations	
	F.= Fixed...	Alt.= Alternating.	A continuous steady light.
	F.Fl.=Fixed and flashing	Alt. F.Fl.= Alternating fixed and flashing.	A fixed light varied at regular intervals by a flash of greater brilliance.
	F.Gp.Fl. = Fixed and group flashing.	Alt. F.Gp.Fl = Alternating fixed and group flashing.	A fixed light varied at regular intervals by groups of 2 or more flashes of greater brilliance.
	Fl.=Flashing	Alt.Fl.= Alternating flashing.	Showing a single flash at regular intervals, the duration of light always being less than the duration of darkness.
	Gp. Fl. = Group flashing.	Alt.Gp.Fl.= Alternating group flashing.	Showing at regular intervals groups of 2 or more flashes
	Gp.Fl.(1+2) = Composite group flashing.	....	Light flashes are combined in alternate groups of different numbers.
	Mo.(A) = Morse Code.	....	Light in which flashes of different duration are grouped in such a manner as to produce a Morse character or characters.
	Qk. Fl. = Quick Flashing.	....	Shows not less than 60 flashes per minute.
	I.Qk. Fl. = Interrupted quick flashing. *(Isophase)*	....	Shows quick flashes for about 4 seconds, followed by a dark period of about 4 seconds.
	E.Int.= Equal interval.	....	Light with all durations of light and darkness equal.
	Occ.=Occulting.	Alt.Occ. = Alternating occulting.	A light totally eclipsed at regular intervals, the duration of light always greater than the duration of darkness
	Gp. Occ. = Group Occulting.	.. ..	A light with a group of 2 or more eclipses at regular intervals
	Gp.Occ.(2+3) = Composite group occulting.	....	A light in which the occultations are combined in alternate groups of different numbers.

Light colors used and abbreviations: W = white, R = red, G = green.

FIG. 702. SYMBOLS FOR LIGHTS, THEIR MEANINGS AND DESCRIPTIONS.

scribes the symbols used to indicate them on charts and in the *Light Lists.* This list should be studied until, from the symbols, one can visualize the characteristics of a light expected to be raised over the horizon; and conversely, until one can name the phase and its symbol of a light already sighted.

The entire list should be memorized, but the following are some of the more important light characteristics:

A *flashing light* (Fl.) shows a flash whose duration is less than the duration of darkness.

An *occulting light* (Occ.) is wholly eclipsed at regular intervals; the duration of eclipse is less than the duration of light. An occulting light has been called colloquially "a light with black flashes."

An *equal interval* (isophase) *light* (E. Int.) is one in which the durations of light and darkness are equal.

A *group flashing light* (Gp. Fl.) shows groups of two or more flashes at regular intervals.

A *composite group flashing light* (Gp. Fl. 1 + 2) shows a single flash followed by a group of two flashes. A Gp. Fl. 2 + 1 light shows a group of two flashes followed by a single flash, etc.

A *Morse-code light* (Mo. A.) shows a short flash and a long flash (the letter *A* in Morse code). A light whose symbol is Mo. (U) shows two short flashes, and a long flash, (the letter *U* in Morse code).

Remember that the period of a light is the number of seconds required for the light to pass through a complete cycle including all flashes and eclipses.

703. Visibility of lights. Lighthouses—often called simply "lights" —range from the lowly post light of a few candlepower to the great lighthouse stations whose lanterns may be several hundred feet above the ground, enclosing lights of millions of candlepower. The distance at which a light can be seen in clear atmosphere depends upon several factors, chief of which are (*a*) height above the water and (*b*) candlepower. The height of the light above the water determines its *geographic range* regardless of its power, and the candlepower determines its *luminous range* regardless of its height. For example, Tantalus Light near Honolulu (height 1,345 ft.) has a geographic range of 46 miles and a luminous range of 14 miles.

Geographic range is defined as the maximum distance at which a light may be seen in perfect visibility by an observer whose eye level is at sea level.

Luminous range is the maximum distance at which a light may be seen under the existing meteorological visibility conditions.

Nominal range is a special case of the luminous range; it is defined as the maximum distance at which a light may be seen in clear weather. The nominal range for lights is given in column (4) of the light list.

Charted range is the range printed on the chart near the light symbol. On charts edited after June 1973 the charted range equals the nominal range. On previously issued charts the charted range is the maximum distance at which a light could be seen in perfect weather by an observer with a height of eye of 15 feet.

METEOROLOGICAL OPTICAL RANGE

Code No.	Weather	Nautical Miles	Kilometers
0	Dense fog	0.000 – 0.027	0.00 – 0.05
1	Thick fog	0.027 – 0.108	0.05 – 0.20
2	Moderate fog	0.108 – 0.27	0.20 – 0.50
3	Light fog	0.27 – 0.54	0.50 – 1.0
4	Thin fog	0.54 – 1.1	1 – 2
5	Haze	1.1 – 2.2	2 – 4
6	Light haze	2.2 – 5.4	4 – 10
7	Clear	5.4 – 11.0	10 – 20
8	Very clear	11.0 – 27.0	20 – 50
9	Exceptionally clear	over 27.0	over 50

FIG. 703*a*. OPTICAL RANGE CODE FOR LIGHTS, ADAPTED FROM INTERNATIONAL METEOROLOGICAL ORGANIZATION VISIBILITY CODE.

The *Light List* also gives a series of curves (Fig. 703*b* below) from which one can estimate the attenuation of a beam of light caused by unfavorable visibility conditions. The use of these curves is illustrated as follows:

Example: A light is listed as having a luminous range of 16 miles. How far should it be seen through haze which limits visibility to 1.5 miles (Code 5)?

Solution: Enter the Luminous Visibility Diagram at 16 on the bottom scale (point *A*), proceed vertically to the middle of the Code 5 area (point *B*), and horizontally to the scale at the left (point *C*).

Ans.: The light should be visible out to 3.8 miles.

Light sectors: An unobstructed light of constant character appears the same from all directions. In certain cases, however, lights show a different color, generally red, over dangerous areas (Fig. 703*c*). On charts, dotted lines radiating from the light, together with a suitable legend, indicate a light sector of this type. Similar lines sometimes indicate an area over which a light is obscured by intervening land.

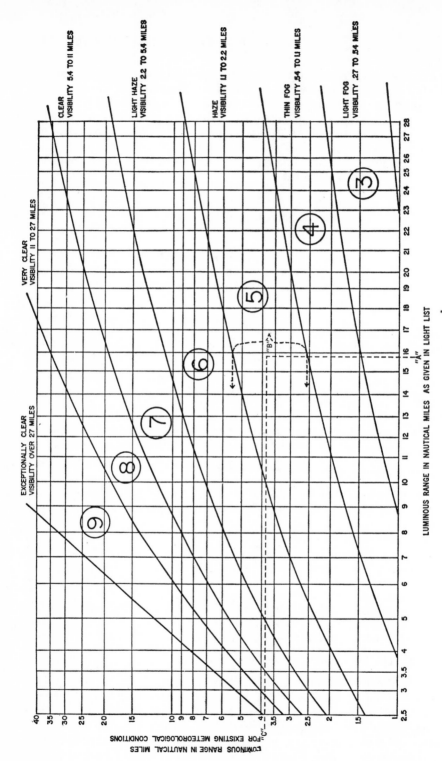

Fig. 703b. Luminous Range Visibility Diagram.

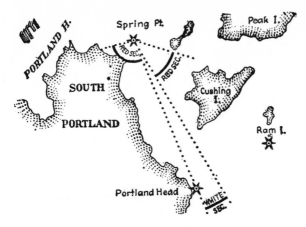

FIG. 703c. LIGHT SECTORS.

Bearings of lines limiting dangerous or obscured areas may be taken from the chart either in points magnetic or degrees true, and handled as in any coast piloting problem. In *Light Lists*, bearings relating to lights are as observed from a vessel when looking toward the light, and are always stated in terms of the 360° true rose. Lines of demarcation may be uncertain and the mariner should verify his position by taking a bearing of the light. Entry into a red sector is a warning of danger.

704. Lightships, sometimes called light vessels and abbreviated (LV), are floating lighthouses with all of the characteristics of light-houses. Their position is somewhat less accurate because they swing around their anchors. Information concerning lightships is obtained from charts and *Light Lists* as outlined in the preceding section. In general, their lights are of lower power than those found on major lighthouses and vary in height above the water from 40 to 65 feet. The name of the lightship, for example, NANTUCKET, is painted on both sides of the hull in large letters. If one cannot read the name, the description in the *Light List* will serve, in most cases, to identify the vessel, particularly if it be silhouetted broadside on. When a RELIEF ship is substituted, its appearance may not be the same as that of the regular ship, but every effort is made to maintain the regular light and sound signal characteristics.

705. Aeronautical lights are charted and listed in the *Light List* if they serve a useful navigational purpose and proper marine aids are lacking. Large airports and some smaller ones are marked by powerful rotating beacons which appear from a distance to be flashing lights, although their strongest beams are directed above the horizon. Also, tall radio and television towers are lighted with flashing red warning lights, some having over a million candlepower. When marked on the chart, these "aero" lights can be used with discretion by the surface navigator. Mariners are cautioned, however, that such lights are designed primarily for use from aircraft and that notice of change or discontinuance may not be received promptly by surface navigators.

706. Fixed fog signals which sound their warning at regular intervals are located, with few exceptions, in or near lighthouses or on lightships. They are indicated in the legends on charts by the addition of a single word or abbreviation, such as BELL or HORN or (F.S.), to the legend describing the light station; where such a word or abbreviation does not appear there is no fog signal.

All such signals at light stations sound at accurately timed intervals and an unfamiliar signal may be identified by its period and phase characteristics which, however, are given only in *Light Lists*. This accurate timing also differentiates such signals from the uncertain and irregular sounds of wave-operated bells and whistles on buoys.

The nature of the sound itself is a further aid to identification. In the following classification the descriptive names as printed in *Light Lists* are in capital letters; alternate names for the same signals, occasionally found on charts, are shown in small capitals:

BELL: Such signals are used inside the general coast line where a far-reaching blast is not necessary and may be confusing.

GONG: Usually four distinct tones. Used where it is necessary to distinguish between two or more bells in one locality.

WHISTLE: Occasionally used at light stations, and on lightships; not as sharply timed as more modern devices. A CHIME WHISTLE sounds a continuous chord of several notes and does not produce a rising and falling note.

Bells and whistles are used most often on buoys, as discussed in a later section.

HORN: This term is used throughout *Light Lists* to designate various devices, other than whistles, which produce a uniform sound throughout a timed blast or blasts. A reed horn is less sharply timed than a diaphragm horn; the term REED HORN is sometimes found on charts. The terms TYFON, NAUTAPHONE, and OSCILLATOR are occasionally used on charts to indicate special types of diaphragm horns which give precise, quick timing. Duplex or triplex horns of differing pitch produce a constant chord. No signal designated in *Light Lists* as a HORN gives blasts of rising and falling pitch.

DIAPHRAGM HORN: Here the sound is produced by a rapidly vibrating diaphragm which is actuated by compressed air, steam, or electricity.

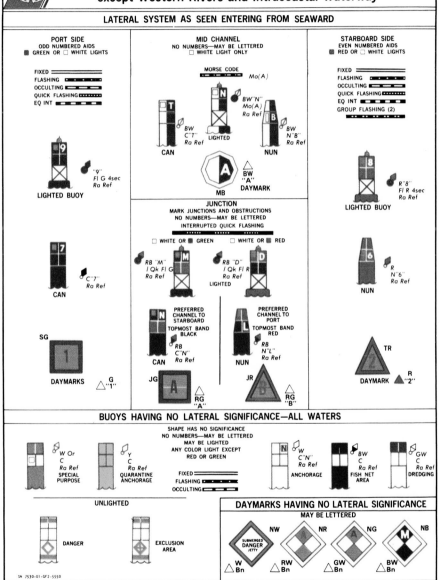

FIG. 708. THE BUOYAGE SYSTEM OF THE UNITED STATES.

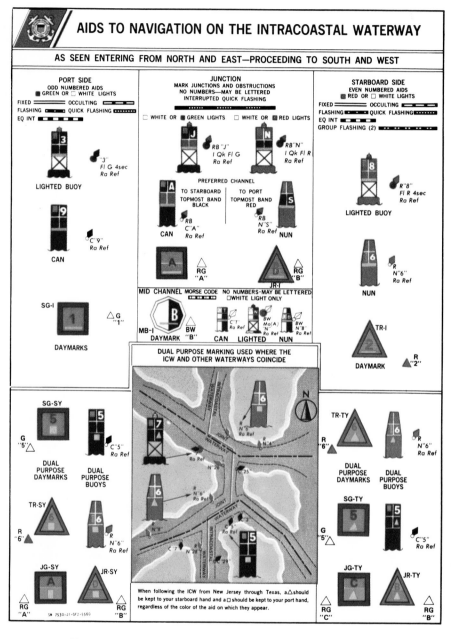

FIG. 709. AIDS TO NAVIGATION ON THE INTRACOASTAL WATERWAY.

SIREN: The pitch of each blast rises and falls and sounds like a yowl as does the siren on Race Rock.

Caution: There are various reasons why a fog signal sounded through the air may not be heard even though close aboard; when heard, it is always dangerous to attempt to estimate distance by the sound. Therefore, do not neglect the lead.

707. Radiobeacons are the most valuable fog signals, and are also available for navigation in clear weather. *Light Lists* contain explanatory charts of Loran and Radiobeacon systems; similar charts of a size suitable for posting near the radio direction finder are available at U.S. Coast Guard offices. The use of radiobeacons and direction finders is discussed in Chapter 10.

BUOYS

708. U. S. buoy system. *Introduction.* Buoys are the most important aids to navigation on the coasts of the United States. Buoys are used to mark shoals or other obstructions and dangers; to indicate the approaches, entrances, turns, and side limits of channels; as markers in the center of a fairway; and to define anchorage grounds and other special areas.

For the guidance of the navigator, buoys are given certain characteristics which indicate their purpose and serve to identify a buoy with the symbol by which it is represented on charts. One not only must understand the meaning of the buoy seen but must know what to look for when locating it on the chart; conversely, one must be able to picture the buoy represented by a given symbol and its legend. Fig. 708 illustrates all of these matters, including the manner in which each aid is shown on the chart. The black dot near the buoy symbol marks the geographical location. For lighted buoys, these dots are surrounded by a spot of magenta color which can be seen at night under red light which does not destroy one's visual adaptation to darkness.

Colors. The buoyage system of the United States is known as the "Lateral System," which is fully described in the Introduction to the *Light List.* In this system a buoy's color, shape, number, or light indicates *the side on which it is to be kept in passing.* Thus, when entering a channel and proceeding from seaward (the situation assumed in this text unless otherwise indicated):

A *red buoy* marks the right-hand side of a channel (Red Right Returning), or marks an obstruction which should be passed by keeping the buoy on the right (starboard) hand.

A *black buoy* marks the left side of a channel or an obstruction which should be passed by keeping the buoy on the left (port) hand.

A *red and black horizontally-banded buoy* (commonly called an "obstruction buoy") marks a junction or bifurcation in the channel, or an obstruction which can be passed on either side. The color of the uppermost band indicates the preferred side for passing the buoy, if any; red, keep it to starboard; black, keep it to port. Reference to the chart is advised when approaching an obstruction buoy.

A *black and white vertically-striped buoy* (often called a "mid-channel buoy") marks a fairway or the middle of a channel and should be passed close aboard on either side.

In some waterways and with offshore buoys, it is not always· easy to tell when one is "proceeding from seaward" in order to know on which side to pass a buoy. Hence, the buoyage system includes the arbitrary assumptions that one is "proceeding from seaward" when going southward along the Atlantic Coast, northward and westward along the Gulf coast, northward along the Pacific coast, westward and northward in the Great Lakes (except Lake Michigan), and southward in Lake Michigan.

Shapes. Under certain conditions it is difficult to make out the color of a distant, unlighted buoy; however, the shape of the buoy may be distinguishable, and shapes follow a consistent pattern. Referring to Fig. 708, it is seen that a nun buoy (conical top) is either a red buoy, an obstruction buoy with a red top, or a mid-channel buoy. Thus, a nun buoy is usually kept to starboard when proceeding from seaward. Similarly, a can buoy is usually a port-hand buoy, although can buoys serve a variety of purposes, as indicated in the figure. The shapes of lighted buoys, sound buoys (bell, whistle, etc.), and spar buoys have no significance, their purpose being indicated by their color, number, or light characteristic.

Numbers. All solid-red colored buoys bear even numbers (2, 4, 6, etc.) and all solid-black colored buoys bear odd numbers (1, 3, 5, etc.). Numbers increase from seaward, and the series is continued up the channel, omitting numbers if the corresponding buoys are not required. Multicolored buoys (obstruction, mid-channel, etc.) are not numbered but may bear letters for identification purposes.

Colored lights on buoys. A red light on a buoy is used only on a red buoy or a red and black horizontally-banded buoy with the red band topmost. A green light on a buoy is used only on a black buoy or a black and red horizontally-banded buoy with the black band topmost. A white light may be on a buoy of any color and carries no special significance; however, the phase characteristic (flashing, Morse code, etc.) is meaningful.

Phase characteristic of buoy lights. (a) Lights on buoys whose color is solid red or solid black, if not fixed lights, are regularly flashing or regularly occulting at not more than 30 flashes per minute (slow flashing). When it is desired that a light on a solid-colored buoy indicate caution, as at a sharp turn or constriction of the channel, or to mark a wreck or dangerous obstruction, the frequency of the flashes is not less than 60 per minute (quick flashing).

(b) Lights on buoys with red and black horizontal bands show a series of quick flashes interrupted by an eclipse about eight times a minute (interrupted quick flashing).

(c) Lights on buoys with black and white vertical stripes show the letter *"A"* in Morse code (short-long flashing) about eight times a minute.

Other features. Some lighted buoys are equipped with a device which turns the light on at dusk and turns it off at dawn. These buoys are marked with a white, circular spot bisected by a horizontal white line. Also, some unlighted buoys carry a reflector ("Ref") which lights up brightly in the rays of a searchlight. The reflectors are colored and have the same significance as lights. In addition, the major buoys of important ship channels are provided with radar reflectors ("RaRef") which increase the buoy's response to ship radars.

709. The Intracoastal Waterway (ICW) is an inland waterway providing a sheltered route for small craft proceeding between New Jersey and Florida, and along the Gulf Coast between Florida and New Orleans. Special NOS charts are available for most of the route except for Delaware Bay and Chesapeake Bay, where regular nautical charts are used.

The buoys and markers used along the ICW are shown in Fig. 709. ICW aids to navigation are distinguished from aids marking other waters by the inclusion of a characteristic yellow band or border. A red triangle with an even number is kept to starboard, and a black square with an odd number is kept to port when proceeding *southward* along the East Coast and *westward* along the Gulf Coast.

When the Intracoastal Waterway coincides with another waterway such as a river on which the aids to navigation conform to the lateral system (entering from seaward), special markings are used on such dual-purpose aids. A yellow triangle on an aid to navigation (regardless of its color, shape, or number) indicates that the aid to navigation is to be kept to starboard, and a yellow square indicates that the aid to navigation is to be kept to port by vessels following the ICW route southward along the East Coast or westward along the Gulf Coast.

BEACONS

710. Daybeacons (daymarks) are unlighted, fixed aids to navigation placed on shore or on marine sites. They are identified by their color and construction, which varies from an unpainted dolphin to great granite monuments, depending upon the locality and particularly upon the background against which they must be seen.

In general, they are painted and numbered under the same system as buoys. Some daybeacons carry reflectors or are painted with luminous paint which shines brilliantly in the beam of a searchlight and whose colors have the same significance as the colors of lights.

Gordon Grant

8. TO PREVENT COLLISION

E VERY master, officer or pilot in charge of a vessel, large or small, is assumed to have complete knowledge of the laws and regulations for the prevention of collision, the so called Rules of the Road which apply to the waters he navigates. Since important changes to these rules became effective on the high seas on July 15, 1977, the new rules should be thoroughly understood. Coast Guard publication (CG-169) Navigation Rules International-Inland dated May 1, 1977 contains the rules pertaining to navigation on the high seas and in the principal inland waters along the coasts of the United States. Also included in this publication are rules concerning boundary lines of inland waters, Pilot Rules for inland waters, vessel bridge to bridge radio-telephone regulations, excerpts from the Motorboat Act of 1940 and Federal Boat Safety Act of 1971, and regulations concerning regattas and marine parades. In applying the various rules the mariner should keep in mind the following: Rules apply to all vessels—Rules apply according to location of vessel—Rules are mandatory. Obedience must be timely. Copies of publication CG-169 may be obtained from Coast Guard Marine Inspection Offices or the U. S. Coast Guard Headquarters, 400 Seventh St. SW, Washington, D.C. 20590. Most chart agents also carry it in stock.

801. Rules of the road are arranged in distinct categories depending upon the scope of their applicability. Hence the mariner must have knowledge of the rules applicable to waters immediately surrounding his vessel; rules for other waters are, for the moment, irrelevant.

The principal rule categories are as follows:

(A) International Rules. The official title of these rules is "International Regulations For Preventing Collisions At Sea, 1972" (72 COLREGS). The 72 COLREGS are part of an international convention that was developed under the auspicies of the United Nations' Inter-Governmental Maritime Consultive Organization (IMCO) in 1972 and replace and abrogate the International Rules of 1960. 72 COLREGS is applicable to vessels (including seaplanes) while navigating on the high seas. The text of the rules are printed in a four column arrangement from left to right to assist

the reader who is just learning the rules and to help the seasoned mariner who is well versed in the 1960 International Rules as follows:

Column I: 72 COLREGS
Column II: Cross-reference index to the 1960 International Rules
Column III: Cross-reference index to Inland Rules of the Road.
Column IV: Comments discuss the significant differences between 1960 International Rule and 72 COLREGS.

(B) Inland Rules. These rules apply to all vessels while in harbors, rivers and other waters of the United States except:

1. The Great Lakes and their connecting and tributary waters as far east as Montreal.
2. The Mississippi River between its source and the Huey P. Long Bridge, and all tributaries emptying thereinto.
3. The Red River of the North (North Dakota and Minnesota).

The Inland Rules, created by U. S. statue, are declared to be "special rules duly made by local authority." They provide for establishing lines of demarcation between "high seas" and Inland Water area jurisdiction. They also authorize the establishment of Pilot Rules.

(C) Pilot Rules amplify the Inland Rules with respect to whistle signals, rights of way, lights and day signals for barges, dredges, pipelines, etc.

(D) Motorboat Act of 1940. These regulations classify by size those motorboats which are 65 feet long or less; and for each class, establish the lights and other equipment to be carried. The Act also prohibits negligent or reckless operation of a vessel and sets up enforcement procedures.

(E) Rules of the Road, Great Lakes (CG-172)

(F) Rules of the Road, Western Rivers (CG-184)

These regulations cover those United States waters which are exempted under the Inland Rules. Like the Inland Rules, they provide for the lights, fog signals and steering and sailing rules for their respective waters.

(G) Other categories of rules to which reference would be made include the Panama Canal Rules, St. Lawrence Seaway Regulations and Rules, and rules adopted by foreign nations concerning the navigation of their inland waters.

802. Notes on the International Rules.   The following is an outline of the format of the International Rules to assist in the study of the full text as layed out in CG-169. Changes or differences between the 72 COLREGS and the 1960 Rules are best studied from Column IV in the 72 COLREGS. It must be emphasized that the rules speak for themselves.

803.   Part A—General
RULE 1 —Application to governments.
RULE 2 —Responsibility. The "Rule of Good Seamanship" and the "General Prudential Rule."

Rule 3 —General Definitions. Defines types of vessels: power, sail, fishing, etc.

804. Part B—Steering and Sailing Rules

SECTION I—Conduct of Vessels in Any Condition of Visibility

Rule 4 —Application in any condition of visibility.
Rule 5 —Lookout. Specifies task of lookout and use of radar.
Rule 6 —Safe Speed. Specifies factors for determining safe speed.
Rule 7 —Risk of Collision. Use of all means to determine if risk exists.
Rule 8 —Action To Avoid Collision. Timely and substantial action.
Rule 9 —Narrow Channels. Proscribes procedures for transiting narrow channels.
Rule 10—Traffic Separation Schemes. Proscribes procedures in approaching, transiting, crossing and departing traffic separation zones.

SECTION II—Conduct of Vessels in Sight of One Another

Rule 11—Application. Specifies conditions of applicability.
Rule 12—Sailing Vessels. Action between approaching sailing vessels.
Rule 13—Overtaking. Designates when overtaking situation exists.
Rule 14—Head-on Situation. Covers situation of meeting vessels and action when doubt exists.
Rule 15—Crossing Situation. Duty of vessel which is to keep out of way and to avoid crossing ahead.
Rule 16—Action by Give-way Vessel. Burdened vessel is defined as give-way vessel.
Rule 17—Action by Stand-on Vessel. Privileged vessel is defined as stand-on vessel.
Rule 18—Responsibility between Vessels. Defines responsibilities between vessels of different status.

SECTION III—Conduct of Vessels in Restricted Visibility

Rule 19—Conduct of Vessels in Restricted Visibility. Covers speed, requirement of plot and alteration of course.

805. Part C—Lights and Shapes

Rule 20—Application. Covers time of display, size, color and shape.
Rule 21—Definitions. Specifies technical construction requirements lights must meet.
Rule 22—Visibility of Lights. Specifies visible range requirements.
Rule 23—Power-driven Vessels Underway. Specifies lights to be carried by all sizes of power-driven vessels.
Rule 24—Towing and Pushing. Specifies lights and shapes required of towing or towed vessels.

RULE 25—Sailing Vessel Underway and Vessels Under Oars. Specifies lights and shapes when sailing, rowing and combined sail with power.

RULE 26—Fishing Vessels. Specifies lights and shapes required by vessels engaged in the different types of fishing operations.

RULE 27—Vessels Not Under Command or Restricted in their Ability to Maneuver. Specifies lights and shapes for vessels not under command, minesweeping, dredging and conducting diving operations.

RULE 28—Vessels Constrained by their Draft. Special rule applying to very deep draft vessels.

RULE 29—Pilot Vessels. Specifies lights and shapes for all pilot vessels.

RULE 30—Anchored Vessels and Vessels Aground.

RULE 31—Seaplanes. Specifies seaplanes to comply as closely as possible to ship requirements in positioning lights.

806. Part D—Sound and Light Signals

RULE 32—Definitions. Defines whistle, short-blast and long-blast.

RULE 33—Equipment for Sound Signals. Technical specifications of whistles, bells and gongs.

RULE 34—Maneuvering and Warning Signals. Signals for altering course, passing, overtaking, danger and approaching a bend.

RULE 35—Sound Signals in Restricted Visibility. "Fog" signals for power vessels; vessels not under command, sailing, towing, towed, pushing, at anchor, aground and on pilot duty.

RULE 36—Signals to Attract Attention. Use of sound, light or searchlight.

RULE 37—Distress Signals. Describes sixteen methods of signalling distress.

807. Part E—Exemptions

RULE 38—Exemptions. Specifies exemptions caused by change of units from feet to meters for positioning lights and shapes and new technical requirements for light, shape and signalling appliances.

808. Annexes

ANNEX I —Positioning and Technical Details of Lights and Shapes

ANNEX II —Additional Signals for Fishing Vessels Fishing in Close Proximity

ANNEX III—Technical Details of Sound and Signal Appliances

ANNEX IV—Distress Signals

809. Study and Reference Source for the Rules. Many organizations such as the Coast Guard Auxilliary hold classes on the rules as part of boating safety programs. An excellent reference for the subject is *Farwell's Rule of the Nautical Road*, 5th Edition, by Bassett and Smith published by the Naval Institute.

INTERNATIONAL RULES

RULE 35

Sound Signals in Restricted Visibility

Situation—Underway	Signal	Interval
1. Power-driven vessel making way through water	—	2 Min.
2. Power-driven vessel underway but stopped not making way	— —	2 Min.
3. All vessels: Not under command Restricted in ability to maneuver Constrained by her draft Sailing vessel Fishing vessel Towing or pushing vessel	— - -	2 Min.
4. Towed vessel	— - - -	2 Min.
Situation—Not Underway		
1. Anchored vessel less than 100 meters in length	BBBBB	1 Min.
2. Anchored vessel more than 100 meters in length	BBBBB/GGGGG	1 Min.
3. Any vessel at anchor	- — -	As required
4. Vessel aground: Less than 100 meters in length More than 100 meters in length	SSS/BBBBB/SSS SSS/BBBBB/SSS/GGGGG	1 Min. 1 Min.
5. Pilot vessel	- - - -	As required

KEY:

—	Prolonged blast, 4-6 seconds
-	Short blast, about 1 second
S	Distinct stroke on bell
BBBBB	5 second ringing of bell forward
GGGGG	5 second sounding of gong aft

9. PILOTING

METHODS discussed in this chapter are those used to conduct a ship in strange waters along any coast and when within or near the land. The principles apply in all cases, but with different classes of vessels and under differing circumstances their practice may vary widely. The work is generally more difficult on sailing vessels, often of lesser draft and close in on a dangerous coast, but a relatively fast deep-draft ship may face problems seldom met with by smaller craft. Even on large ships practice differs. The following sections are arranged to give a general knowledge of the subject to be applied as experience dictates.

901. Terms. Dr. Worth, a distinguished English yachtsman, described piloting as plotting everything on the chart and taking every opportunity of verifying the positions thus found. An experienced navigator may not record as many details in the log book and on the chart as should the beginner, but in any case the record must serve to plot the position of the ship at any time.

A line of position, however determined, is a series of possible positions of the ship. It may be a straight line or a circle and should be considered as a series of points some one of which, not yet identified, is the ship's position. Every mariner uses lines of position although the term may be unknown to him.

A fix is an accurately known point which marks the ship's position at a given time. It is generally determined by the intersection of two lines of position. By definition, the ship could be on each line and therefore is probably at the point where they intersect. A fix is not always available, but, as circumstances permit, may be had by one or another theoretically correct method. The navigator must keep in mind the possible magnitude and direction of errors in the fix due to inaccurate observations or instruments.

The dead reckoning position, as the term is here used, is the position found by plotting courses steered and distances run from the last fix or other well determined position. Such a position should be regarded as inaccurate, for reasons presently developed. When two lines of position give a fix, plotting the D.R. is started anew from that point.

The course line is drawn in the direction of the course steered or to be steered, positions thereon being corrected, when necessary, for current and leeway. Sometimes the course is so drawn as to compensate for these errors. The direction of the desired course may be determined in two ways:

(1) For a power vessel or sailing craft that can lay the course, mark the ship's position on the chart. From that point draw a line to the point toward which it is desired to steer. With parallel rulers determine the direction of this line from a compass rose. When read from the 360° rose, it must be corrected to a compass course by applying variation and deviation, each in the opposite direction of its sign. Only deviation need be applied if the course is from the magnetic rose.

(2) A sailing vessel close-hauled on the wind sails the best course possible under the circumstances. This course is plotted either in the direction steered or in that believed made good. Such a course must be corrected to magnetic or true before plotting.

The D.R. at any time may be plotted on the course line by laying off the distance from the point of departure. The D.R. must be plotted whenever the course is changed and a new course line must be drawn from the D.R. at that time. Because of its uncertainties, it is not customary to regard the course line as a line of position, but in thick weather, without radio bearings, it is the only line available.

The estimated position is the point which represents the navigator's best judgment of the ship's position at a given time, no fix being available. It is found by applying corrections for tidal or ocean current, leeway, etc., to a D.R. position. The term is peculiar to Navy teaching. Many mariners call such a position the Corr. D.R. or simply the D.R.

Before going further, the subject of plotting should have attention. The habit of accurate plotting, neatly labeled in a consistent manner, is not only of value to the pilot, but is an essential of present-day celestial navigation. To avoid repetition in various chapters, plotting, labels and lettering have been discussed at length at the beginning of Appendix II. Study this discussion now, as a part of this chapter.

902. Graphic methods. The following sections deal with the simpler methods of checking or fixing a ship's position when near the coast. Landmarks on the drawings are lighthouses. Any mark identifiable on the chart may be used, such as water towers, spires, beacons, bold headlands, or light vessels and buoys. A Coast Guard station is useful provided it can be identified with certainty. This is sometimes difficult, as, for example, along the south shore of Long Island where a dozen or more stations are strung along the low lying beach. Tangents to the left and right sides (or ends) of an island often provide useful bearings. Bearings of radio stations obtained by a radio direction finder serve the same purpose as other bearings.

903. Ranges. When two fixed objects appear in line, one beyond the other, the ship must lie somewhere on the line of sight, or range line, which passes through both objects. If the marks observed can be identified and are shown on the chart, a line drawn through the two objects gives a line of position. Such lines are especially reliable, because observing when the ship is on the line involves neither taking compass bearings nor any possible compass errors. A range line may be had from lights, beacons, towers, bold headlands, and buoys. Two ranges are seldom available at the same time, but a single range line may be crossed with any other line of position for a fix. Two marks often are placed

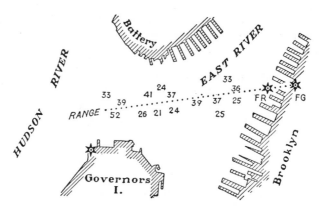

FIG. 903. EAST RIVER DEEP WATER CHANNEL RANGE.

to guide vessels through important channels. In Fig. 903 the line across the red light to the higher green light on the Brooklyn shore gives a range along the center of the deep water channel from the Hudson River to the East River.

904. Bearings of fixed known objects are the most common source of lines of position when on the coast. If the direction of a light be observed, the ship must be at some point on the line drawn through the light in the observed direction. A single bearing line does not give a fix but often gives valuable information which, in the case illustrated by Fig. 904, serves principally to correct the run.

Bearings measured by a magnetic compass either by sighting across the compass or with the aid of a pelorus, when corrected for deviation, may be plotted by the magnetic rose on the chart. Magnetic bearings are sometimes stated in quarter points. When so expressed in a *Coast*

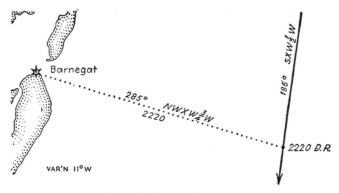

Fig. 904. Single Bearing.

Pilot or in other publications, consider the bearing as magnetic unless otherwise stated.

A bearing by magnetic compass when corrected both for deviation and variation is a true bearing to be plotted by the 360° true rose. Bearings stated in terms of degrees in a *Coast Pilot*, on charts, or in a *Light List* are true bearings as are those observed by gyro compass.

Unless otherwise noted all bearings are stated as from the sea. For example, if a light bears northeast from the ship, its bearing is N E although the ship lies southwest from the light. Bearings of radiobeacons (§ 1006) are also as from the ship. However, bearings transmitted in code from a radio direction-finder station ashore to a ship at sea, are as from the shore station.

905. Cross bearings. If two objects be observed at approximately the same time, the intersection of the resulting bearing lines gives a fix as in Fig. 905a. The minimum error in the position so found results from lines intersecting at a right angle. Sixty degrees is a good intersection, but with 30° or less, a slight error in either or both bearings may cause a serious error in position.

Fig. 905a. Fix by Cross Bearings.

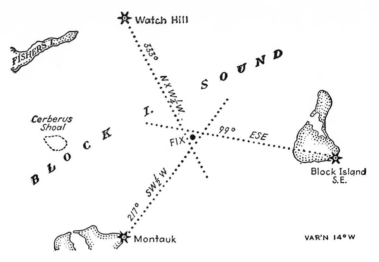

FIG. 905b. FIX BY THREE BEARINGS.

Three bearing lines, as in Fig. 905b, probably will not intersect in a point because the bearings are seldom exact, but whenever available a third bearing should be used as a check and the center of the resulting triangle used as a fix.

906. Advancing a bearing line. When bearings of two objects cannot be obtained simultaneously to cross for a fix, it is often possible to get a *running fix* from bearings of two objects observed at different times. In Fig. 906 a vessel from the eastward for Portland picks up Monhegan Light at 1:30 A.M. bearing N E ¾ N magnetic or 19° true. The D.R. is brought up to a point on the bearing line and labeled 0130 Corr. D.R., the distance of this point from Monhegan being unknown. The ship con-

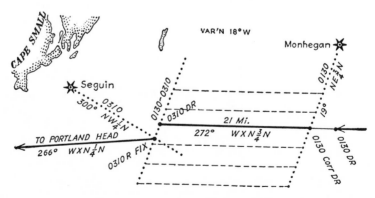

FIG. 906. ADVANCING A BEARING LINE.

tinues its course until 3:10 A.M. when the bearing of Seguin is observed and plotted.

To find the ship's position from the two bearings, consider the Monhegan line as a series of dots any one of which may have been the ship's position at 1:30 A.M. If each of these points be advanced by course and distance from 1:30 A.M. to 3:10 A.M. a new series of dots results which forms the line labeled **0130-0310** which is parallel to the **0130** line. In practice, only one point is advanced, the 0130-0310 line being drawn through the point so found parallel to the original line. *Provided that course and distance used are exactly what has been made good over the ground,* this advanced line is as accurate as its original and when crossed with the Seguin line gives what is known as a *running fix.*

Advancing a line of position is useful when near the coast and is a regular practice with navigators at sea, especially when working with the sun.

907. Distance off. If the distance from an object be determined, the ship must be somewhere on a circle of position as in Fig. 907a. If the

RADIUS OF CIRCLE
2½ MILES

FIG. 907a. CIRCLE OF POSITION.

bearing of the same object be observed, the intersection of its bearing line with the circle gives a fix, as in Fig. 907b. This is the geometry of defining a position by the eye. At a short distance off, such a procedure is generally sufficiently accurate. For example, position (1) in Fig. 1402 may be defined as 1 mile true south of Race Rock. A circle of position is of little value when far off a mark, unless the distance be determined accurately as by radar, or otherwise.

If the height of an object is known and the angle subtended by its height be measured with a sextant, the distance from the observer to the object may be taken from Bowditch (refer to Table 9). A small book by Captain Lecky, *The Danger Angle and Off-Shore Distance Tables,* presents a complete discussion of this subject.

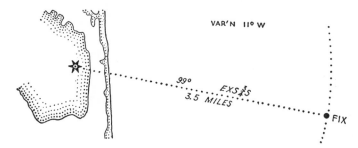

FIG. 907*b*. BEARING AND DISTANCE.

908. Two bearings of same object give information especially useful for determining distance off at which a single light or landmark will be or has been passed. The process is to observe a bearing of the mark and at the same moment read the log. After running a convenient distance, take a second bearing and again read the log. If the first bearing line be advanced by course and distance over the bottom, its inter-

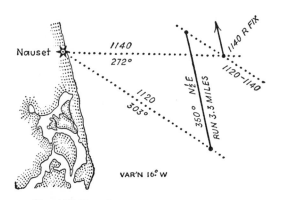

FIG. 908. TWO BEARINGS OF SAME OBJECT.

section with the second line gives a running fix, as in Fig. 908. A line through this point in the direction of the course is the ship's track as it will pass or has passed this mark. The effect of the procedure is to correct the distance off.

909. Bow and beam bearings. This method for determining distance off is known to all navigators. It is a special case of two bearings of one object that gives the distance at which the mark is passed abeam without plotting or mathematical solution. In Fig. 909 observer notes when Shinnecock bears 4 points or 45° off the bow and reads the log.

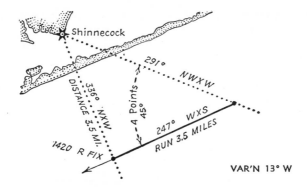

Fig. 909. Bow and Beam Bearing.

When the light comes abeam, at 90° to the course, he again reads the log. The distance run between the two observations is the distance off the light. This is evident on inspection of the isosceles right triangle formed by the course and the two bearing lines.

910. Danger bearings warn the navigator by a compass bearing when the course is leading into danger. Suppose a vessel to be steering 71° true, as in Fig. 910. Let the navigator draw a line through Little

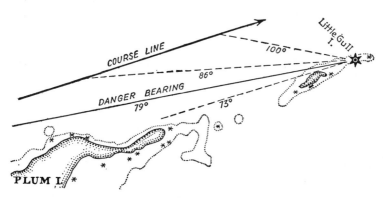

Fig. 910. Danger Bearing.

Gull Light clear of the rocks and shoals north of Plum Island and between that island and Little Gull, and note its direction, in this case 79°. Then if frequent bearings of the light, taken as the ship proceeds toward the Race, are greater or to the right of 79°, the ship is safe on the left side of the danger line. If, however, the bearing of the light is less than 79°, the ship is being drawn into trouble and the course must be altered at once.

Danger bearings are of greatest value in cases similar to the above where, with only one mark visible nearly ahead, it would be difficult to get precise positions if no radar is available. In any case, the method is more convenient than plotting several fixes.

911. Position by soundings. A single depth sounding may indicate that the ship is in danger. Even on a clear day there is no excuse for not knowing the depth when in unfamiliar waters near the land or in narrow channels. It is an important safeguard against blunders with buoys, bearings, and tidal currents known only to local watermen.

A series of soundings at regular intervals may serve to provide useful information as to the ship's position in a period of low visibility. These soundings are usually taken with the echo sounder if it is available. A lead and line can also be used and has the added advantage of bringing up a sample of the bottom which can be compared with the chart.

Advance the D.R. position along the course line on the chart for the run of the ship in regular intervals of, say, ten minutes depending upon the speed of the ship and the steepness of the bottom. Lay a strip of thin paper or tracing material over the course line, and with a pencil mark the D.R. position and the course line on the paper. At the times chosen for the advanced D.R. positions, obtain soundings and mark the depths and character of the bottom (if available) along the line.

Now, keeping the line on the paper parallel to the course line on the chart, move the paper over the chart until it is found that the series of soundings along the line agrees with the soundings at corresponding positions on the chart. Practical agreement between the tracing on the paper and the chart tends to confirm the D.R. Otherwise, it is probable that the ship is not on the D.R. line but is nearer to the position indicated by the tracing.

This method is most useful when approaching from off-soundings. It is dangerous over short distances in shoal water, especially when the rise and fall of the tide is important, and also in unfrequented areas where the chart may not show all variations in depth.

912. Plan in advance. Experience shows that the more thorough the preparation, the less hazardous the passage. Captain Dutton pointed out that the navigator, especially when piloting, deals not only with the present but with the future, and that preparation must be made in advance when at anchor. The navigator is always busy in pilot waters.

Courses should be laid out starting from the anchorage to some position favorable for fixing the point of departure from which to plot the D.R. From this point plot the desired courses to destination and see that they run clear of danger. Distances to be made good on the various courses may be stepped off from the chart. Assume the time of departure, estimate the times of arrival at various positions, and consult the *Tide Tables* and the *Tidal Current Tables*. It is possible that the time of departure or proposed courses should be reconsidered to avoid unfavorable conditions.

The general plan being determined, first study every detail of the harbor chart. Note depths of water, lights, landmarks, ranges, bearings, and buoys to be passed. Go on deck and identify every mark or aid to navigation that can be seen from the anchorage, especially those you propose to use when leaving the harbor. Then consider the various marks by which the ship's position may be checked or fixed after leaving port. Study the *Light List* and visualize not only the characteristics of the lights, but also the appearance of the lighthouses by day. These matters should be studied with the greatest of care when about to traverse strange waters.

Before setting forth see that the essential instruments and tools are available and in good order. The compass, or compasses, should be examined and their deviations should be known with reasonable accuracy. If in doubt, check the deviation card before leaving port or immediately thereafter. If the ship be so equipped, start the gyro compass four hours before sailing. When a portable pelorus is to be used, see that it is properly placed with its lubber's line axis parallel to the keel. Have necessary charts and data at hand. A pilot's notebook is convenient for recording courses, soundings, and bearings which later may be transcribed in the log book. Also check the radio direction finder and other equipment.

On a yacht with a numerous Corinthian crew, it should be definitely understood who is responsible for the piloting. Others may assist but what's everybody's business is nobody's business, a condition which sooner or later will put the ship aground.

Preliminary arrangements having been completed, note nearby buoys and landmarks, and have the leadsman ready for action when the hook comes up.

913. En route. Preferably, even within harbor limits, steer exact courses taken from the chart. This is not only good practice but serves to train the personnel in methods which must be used in thick weather. In a narrow, buoyed channel, however, with transverse tidal currents, steer by the buoys unless there be a range line for the center of a straight channel. If low visibility prevents taking bearings, courses should be laid from buoy to buoy. In either of these situations, every buoy should be identified by its number and if there be any question of depths or position, soundings should be taken continuously.

Having left port and having attained sufficient offing, define the vessel's position by the best available method. Mark this *point of departure* on the chart and label it with the time, stream the log, and record its reading and the time in the log book. Plot some miles of the course on the chart. Label this course line and record the course to steer.

Proceed and whenever the course is changed, note the time and read the log. On the course line lay off the distance from point of departure and label this D.R. with the time. Draw the new course line and label it. In the log book, note time, log reading, distance from last reading, and new course.

Check the D.R. position frequently by the best means at hand. In clear weather, identification on the chart of every buoy, light, or landmark which can be seen gives a rough check at all times. At night, particular care should be taken to identify every visible light. When you cannot see a light that should be seen, find out why.

A single line of position, whether a range or a bearing, serves to correct the D.R. in the direction of a perpendicular from that point to the line. Well crossed lines of position give a fix which is used as a new point of departure from which to plot succeeding D.R. positions and thus carry on the reckoning to destination.

The student seeking to acquire skill as a pilot should spend all his spare time observing and plotting bearings. An experienced man will take and record more bearings than he plots, but will not omit plotting a fix sufficiently often to check the errors which may affect the D.R.

Tidal currents, within the general line of the coast where the rise and fall of the tide is material, differ not only in velocity and direction at each hour of the tide but also because of wind and weather and the varying flow of rivers into bays and harbors. Often only local fishermen can judge the effect of such currents. If the average direction and velocity of a current be known for the time elapsed between two D.R. positions, the second D.R. may be corrected by plotting the current effect as a course and distance therefrom. Or the course from the first D.R. may be adjusted in advance to provide for the expected set.

Current tables and tidal current charts give accurate information when the weather is normal. It is just when one is in some out of the way spot and the weather is anything but normal that exact information is needed. In such cases, the navigator must use his wits and keep in mind the vagaries of tidal currents.

When approaching harbor, the look of the land seldom gives indication of the opening. The ship's position must be determined by a buoy identified by its number or some other fix. Then, with anchor cleared, steer predetermined courses and distances, watch the buoys, and keep the lead handy. Entering a strange harbor is more difficult than leaving a harbor where one has had time to look about while at anchor. Therefore, examine every detail of the harbor chart before making port. It is sometimes difficult to sense the change to the large scale of a harbor chart, which may be from four to twenty times that of the chart used outside, with the result that the "next buoy comes quicker."

914. Fog or loss of visibility from snow or rain puts a coastwise navigator to the supreme test and requires precautions at sea that are all too often neglected. It fills the most experienced seaman with uneasiness and may paralyze a beginner with unwarranted panic. A timorous navigator, confronted with a dirty situation, should remember that centuries of mariners have found their way through fog to safety and that he can and must do likewise. It is in fog that the radio direction finder and other electronic equipment pays off. The reader may judge for himself what parts of the text apply to regular runs along the coast or to ships at sea.

Fog may thicken gradually but it is more likely to approach as a low, gray bank of clouds which may blot out landmarks or other vessels before it envelops the ship. Sometimes foghorns are heard before the fog itself comes down, and at night the unexpected disappearance of previously visible lights may mean fog.

If oncoming fog be suspected, the first precaution is to check or fix the vessel's position by the best means available. This applies especially to yachtsmen who may be wandering about with no exact knowledge of where they are. Meanwhile, check the foghorn, have lead and line ready for action, and if anywhere near shoal water or the shore, clear an anchor. On a sailing yacht, consideration should be given to sending down such light sails as reduce ability to maneuver quickly.

When in the fog, place the lookout or lookouts where they can both see and hear. On a small vessel with one lookout, the best station may be a bit aft where the sound of the bow wave interferes less with the hearing. Sometimes a man at the masthead can both hear and see better than can those on deck. Cut out social chatter, sound the foghorn regularly, use the lead, keep the reckoning with the utmost care, and check it by any available radio bearings.

At first opportunity examine the chart for bell or whistle buoys that may be encountered and note the fog signals that may be heard from lighthouses or lightships. Mark on the chart their time characteristics, taken from the *Light List*, and have a stop watch handy. If without a watch and unaccustomed to counting seconds, tie a string to a small weight such as the nut off a bolt. Hold the string between the fingers so that the center of the weight is 9¾ inches below the point of suspension. The pendulum will then beat seconds.

Decision now must be made as to whether to continue the voyage, seek a nearby harbor, or anchor. Circumstances may dicate the answer but, if a choice be possible, almost innumerable conditions must be weighed. Fog involves grave risks and the safety of the ship must be the skipper's first consideration. Forget questions of convenience or of economy, and remember that the anchor is part of the navigator's equipment.

Danger of collision in fog is always present. When the whistle or horn of a vessel is heard, try to judge its bearing. If the bearings of successive blasts seem to change, you will probably pass in safety. If no change takes place, collision should be considered as imminent. The most dangerous situation is that of a small craft with a weak-voiced foghorn, which is unheard or unheeded by a fast-moving steamer. Lacking a good steam or compressed-air whistle, the best protection is a motor-driven horn that will make even a noisy steamer take notice. Gunfire may serve in an emergency or lights flashed on a yacht's sails may avoid a crash. When possible, small craft should keep clear of steamer lanes. One long and two short blasts indicate a tow; the barges and the hawsers between them are a danger to be guarded against. If no other vessels are heard, do not let a false sense of security lead to a violation of the rules which require sounding your foghorn at regular intervals. So doing is a deliberate neglect of the safety of your ship and the lives she carries.

Piloting in fog is a combination of careful dead reckoning, a variety of more or less inexact tricks for estimating one's position, and using the lead to keep out of trouble. When possible, it is better to make short runs from one buoy to another than to attempt long courses which offer

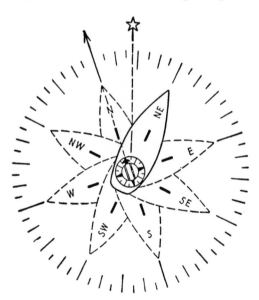

FIG. 914. THE SHIP TURNS AROUND THE COMPASS CARD.

less frequent checks. Make certain to identify each mark and observe any indications of current around it.

The beginner who sometimes develops false ideas of direction when fearful of being lost, must learn to believe in his compass. The compass points in one direction while *the ship revolves about the card.* The compass card does not turn as the ship swings its head on different courses. It is the ship that swings and not the card (Fig. 914). In fact, with a well-adjusted magnetic compass, the card is equivalent to a magnetic rose fixed on the chart at the ship's position.

It is a good practice in fog near shoal water to take soundings at regular intervals even though the course is supposed to lead clear of danger. The transducer (sound generator and receiver) of an echo sounder is usually near the keel; hence, the actual depth of water is somewhat greater than the indicator reading. If the ship has almost no motion through the water; with the lead on bottom, the action of the lead line will indicate the current. Near shore or shoals, or when entering harbor, soundings must be taken continuously while the navigator watches the chart as depths are reported. Locating the ship by soundings has been discussed in §911.

When seeking harbor in fog on a difficult coast, select some outlying mark which, once found, will give an accurate point of departure for port. This may be a lightship, an island without surrounding reefs, or a bold headland which can be approached until one sees the loom of the cliffs or hears the breakers.

Fog signals on or near lighthouses, which sound accurately timed blasts, and bells and whistles on buoys have been described in Chapter 7. Sound signals at light stations can be identified by their timing as given in the *Light Lists* and by the character of the sound. The irregular sounds from whistle, bell, and gong buoys operated by the action of the sea do not positively identify such buoys and sometimes a great whistle buoy to leeward cannot be heard until almost aboard.

Signals through the air are uncertain, therefore remember:

(1) Distance at which a signal may be heard varies.

(2) Do not judge distance by the power of the sound.

(3) Occasionally there are areas near a fog signal where it is inaudible.

(4) Fog may exist nearby a station and not be seen by the keeper, so that the fog signal may not be put in operation.

(5) After fog has been observed there may be delay in starting a signal.

(6) Under certain atmospheric conditions, one tone of a two-tone signal may be inaudible.

915. Examples and problems combining the many details of piloting discussed in this and preceding chapters require the use of one or more NOS charts, an appropriate *Light List,* and the necessary *Tide* and Tidal Current Tables. The nature of such problems and the details of their solution vary according to the draft of the vessel, the local experience of the master or pilot in charge, and the availability of radar and R.D.F. equipment.

Consider the problem of entering the harbor of Portland, Maine. A strange vessel, from off shore, especially in fog, will first pick up Portland Lightship which lies about 8 miles SSE from Portland Head. The skipper of a craft of 10 feet draft, coming up from Cape Ann, will probably try for the whistle buoy on Willard Rock, which is buoy "7"

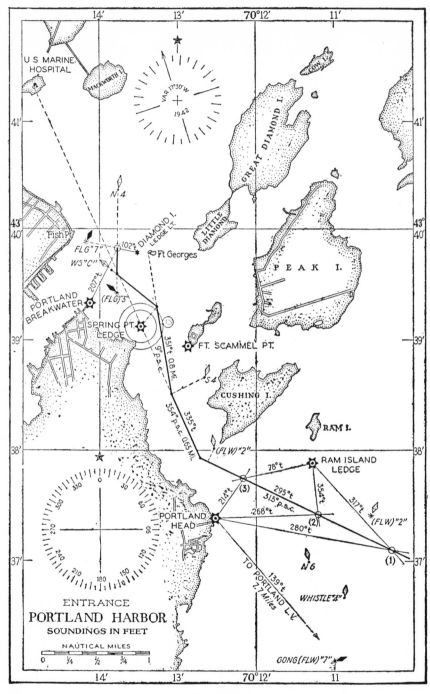

FIG. 915.

at the lower right of Fig. 915. From there he steers to clear Portland
Head, warned by the sound of the breakers when close in. To Spring
Point Ledge, weather thick, it is easy to follow the shore by sounding.
At night, in clear weather, the red sectors of Spring Point Ledge Light
(Fig. 703c) keep him out of trouble.

The pilot of a coastwise steamer, making Portland every other day,
may also pick up Willard Rock. In such service it is common practice
to keep a record of the course, as actually steered by the ship's steering
or gyro compass, which has proved correct for each leg of the trip
under various tidal conditions. Such a pilot, with Willard Rock close
on the port beam, gives the quartermaster 338° but adds "and crack
the light to port," orders which will surely take the vessel into the deep
water off Portland Head.

Navy teaching necessarily approaches the problem from a different
point of view. The navigator must be able to take a large deep draft
vessel into a strange harbor without the aid of a local pilot. The methods used are illustrated, in part, by the work plotted in Fig. 915.

The ship is for Portland on a course of 295° true. Charts and the
U. S Coast Pilot must be studied. Courses into the harbor are plotted
and each leg is labeled with true course, compass course, and distance
to run. The navigator also studies the lights, landmarks, ranges and
buoys he proposes to use, and notes the tidal conditions.*

As the coast is approached, assistants are placed at the bearing repeaters, and the navigator takes over the plotting. Cross bearings give
the ship's position at (1), (2), and (3). Leadsmen are at their stations.
Off buoy "2," at the south end of Cushing Island, the rudder is put over,
and the ship is steadied on course 335° with Spring Point Light in range
with the flagstaff on the U. S. Marine Hospital, near Martin Point, at
upper left of Fig. 915.

Off buoy S4 the course is changed to 351° true, with the west end
of Fort Georges dead ahead and Diamond Ledge Light about 5° off
the port bow. As Spring Point Light comes abeam, the position is
checked by vertical danger angles of the light, to assure clearing a 29
foot spot to the eastward.

The anchorage area is clear, and it is decided to anchor about 900
yards north of buoy "3" off Portland Breakwater, between that buoy
and buoy N4. The proper approach to the proposed anchorage is from
the south against the ebbing tide. Allowing for distance from the stem
to the bridge of the vessel, the position of the anchor is plotted so that
the bridge will be on the range between Diamond Ledge Light and buoy
"7" off Fish Point when letting go. As a guide to this position, the bearings of Diamond Ledge Light and Portland Breakwater Light from the
proposed anchorage point are noted.

* The author is indebted to Capt. Theo. Nelson, U.S.N.R., for the details of this
problem. Aids to navigation shown in Fig. 915 are illustrative only and may not
conform to the current *Light List*.

When Spring Point Light is broad on the quarter, the ship is put on 308° true toward buoy "C" until it is swung to the right on the range between buoys "3" and N4. Speed having been reduced, the anchor is let go when on the predetermined bearings of Diamond Ledge and Portland Breakwater.

916. Piloting with radar. While the availability of radar has greatly eased the burden of the pilot, it has not invalidated the principles of navigation discussed in this chapter; it has simply increased their importance. As described in Chapter 13, radar provides bearing and distance of prominent objects from the ship. This is the language of piloting, and information derived from radar is applied in the same manner as other piloting information. A radar bearing gives the direction of a line of position, and a radar range is the distance along that line as shown in Fig. 907b. With radar, the pilot obtains directly a succession of fixes without having to derive each fix by the manipulation of lines of position. The principles are the same, but the emphasis is changed.

917. Practice! Knowledge of all the matters discussed in this and preceding chapters is not sufficient to make a navigator competent as a coastwise pilot or to keep the reckoning when at sea. The beginner should navigate by rule and not sail by the look of the land. Then, whenever he can check his position, he may think out for himself the probable reason or reasons for the error therein, and learn to guard against similar errors when in thick weather. Exact practice is the only way to develop the necessary skill and judgment whereby to cope with difficult conditions when they arise.

10. RADIO ON BOARD SHIP*

A NEW era dawned at sea when Guglielmo Marconi first achieved the transmission of intelligible signals over long distances by Hertzian waves. Since about 1900 the development of radio has gone forward by leaps and bounds, and today it provides information and entertainment throughout the world. It is less well known that radio not only guards great liners but may play an important part in the safety of the smallest craft.

This chapter is limited to an outline of the radio services available to vessels that carry neither equipment nor operators for radio telegraphy. Technical radio engineering is beyond the scope of this Primer, and because of the daily advance in design, details of specific instruments are not discussed. Navigation by radiobeacons, an important radio aid to navigation, is treated at some length in the concluding sections.

1001. Emergency regulations. Under war conditions many radio aids to navigation are discontinued or altered, and new devices come into use, the knowledge of which is restricted to the armed forces. Presumably, in peace times all of the services discussed are available.

The acceptance of radio bearings as an essential element of navigation along the coast has become general. Other radio signals described in the Loran and Radar chapter extend to a range of a thousand miles or more and may be used for determining distance off. In any case, it seems certain that the use of radio signals, as an accepted part of the navigator's daily work, will increase with improvements in radio instruments.

1002. Waves and bands. Radio waves are commonly classified according to their frequency, which is the number of waves or cycles per second. For convenience, frequency is generally expressed in kilohertz (Khz) or megahertz (Mhz). A radio band gives the limits within which certain classes of signals are transmitted. The band for marine radiobeacon stations is from 285 Khz to 325 Khz. Marine radio sets are often

---

* Mariners are warned that many of the services listed in this chapter are modified or discontinued as wartime measures.

equipped with a switch for selecting appropriate frequencies in L.F., low frequency bands, extending from 30 Khz to 300 Khz, through the M.F., medium frequency band, 300 Khz to 3,000 Khz, to include some of the H.F., high frequency band 3,000 Khz to 30,000 Khz. Stations of interest to the navigator operate on frequencies within one or more of these bands.

Complete information about the various radio signals providing information to the navigator is contained in *Radio Navigational Aids*, H.O. 117A, (Atlantic and Mediterranean Area) and H.O. 117B (Pacific and Indian Ocean Area). Information about broadcasts of weather forecasts, storm warnings, etc., is given in *Radio Weather Aids, H.O.* 118A and 118B covering the same areas.

1003. Broadcast. As a strictly radio term, "broadcast" may mean any signal sent out in all directions. More often, the word is used as including the programs sent out by commercial stations on the so-called *standard broadcast* band from 535 Khz to 1,600 Khz. Among these broadcast programs are authentic weather reports in plain words, broadcast almost every hour from 7 A.M. to midnight, from one or another of the audible commercial stations. Often excellent reports are transmitted from minor stations, as listed in local newspapers. *Eldridge's Tide and Pilot Book,* for the current year, conveniently lists the sources and times or weather reports along the New England coasts. Many broadcast programs include a time signal of a single musical note. Such signals are not so accurate nor so easy to use as the regular Government signals.

Other broadcast signals of interest to the navigator are the time signals, weather reports, storm warnings, and notices concerning changes in buoys, lights, wrecks, etc. Most of these reports are transmitted on frequencies within the so-called marine band extending from about 2000 Khz to approximately 3000 Khz. The frequency 2182 Khz is known as the "calling frequency" and most vessels, including yachts, keep receivers tuned to this frequency at all times. It is the international radiotelephone distress frequency. Coast Guard broadcasts and much of the ship-to-ship traffic originates with a call-up on this frequency followed by a shift to the appropriate "working frequency" as 2670 Khz for Coast Guard marine information. The frequencies and schedules of weather and marine information broadcasts are contained in the *Coast Pilots* (§211). A general-purpose, radio communications receiver set up at home will assist the student in becoming familiar with the procedure for marine broadcasts and time signals.

1004. Time signals. As set forth in later chapters, celestial navigation requires an accurate knowledge of time. Today, radio time signals are the accepted source of exact time. Any signal broadcast at an exactly known time may be considered a time signal. The students' timekeeper may be checked accurately by one or another of the signals sometimes included in standard broadcast programs, but professional navigators

WWV AND WWVH BROADCAST FORMAT

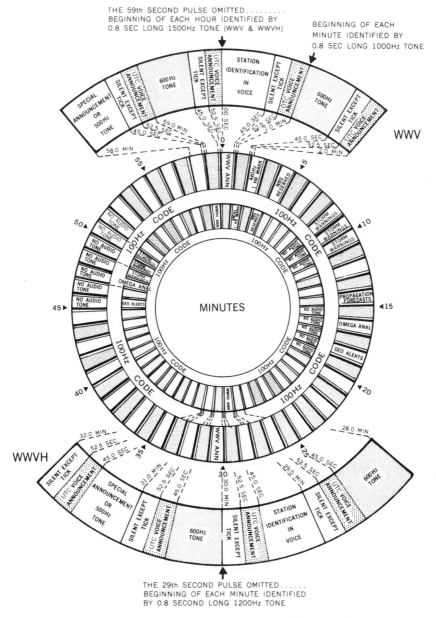

THE 59th SECOND PULSE OMITTED........
BEGINNING OF EACH HOUR IDENTIFIED BY
0.8 SEC LONG 1500Hz TONE (WWV & WWVH)

BEGINNING OF EACH
MINUTE IDENTIFIED BY
0.8 SEC LONG 1000Hz TONE

THE 29th SECOND PULSE OMITTED......
BEGINNING OF EACH MINUTE IDENTIFIED
BY 0.8 SECOND LONG 1200Hz TONE

Fig. 1004b. Structure of Time Signals from National Bureau of Standards.

prefer the more convenient and accurate special time signals. These are sent out from some two hundred stations throughout the world at various hours, and on a wide range of wave lengths, as given in *Radio Navigational Aids.*

WWV and WWVH broadcast stations. The National Bureau of Standards broadcast continuous signals from its high frequency radio stations WWV (Fort Collins, Colorado) and WWVH (Kauai, Hawaii). The radio frequencies used are 2.5, 5, 10, and 15 Mhz at radiated powers from 2.5 to 10 KW. All frequencies carry the same program. Except during times of severe magnetic disturbances, listeners should be able to receive the signal on at least one of the frequencies. As a general rule, frequencies above 10 Mhz provide the best daytime reception while the lower frequencies are best for night-time reception. Services provided by these stations are: Time Announcements, Standard Time Intervals, Standard Frequencies, Geophysical Alerts, Marine Storm Warnings, Universal Time Corrections and Binary Coded Decimal Time Code. The time announcement and marine warning service of the broadcast are of most interest to the navigator.

Time voice announcements are made from WWV and WWVH once every minute. To avoid confusion, a man's voice is used on WWV and a woman's voice on WWVH. The WWVH announcement occurs first—at 15 seconds before the minute, while WWV announcement occurs at 7½ seconds before the minute. The time referred to in the announcement is "Coordinated Universal Time" (UTC). This time may be considered the equivalent of "Greenwich Mean Time" (GMT).

Marine storm warnings in the Atlantic and eastern North Pacific are broadcast in voice from WWV at 8, 9 and 10 minutes after each hour. Similar storm warnings covering the eastern and central North Pacific are given from WWVH at 48, 49 and 50 minutes after each hour. The brief messages are designed to tell mariners of storm threats in their areas. If there are no warnings in the designated areas, the broadcast will so indicate.

CHU, Ottawa, Ontario. The Canadian government broadcasts a time signal continuously, with a voice announcement of Eastern Standard Time each minute. The beginning of each second is marked by a beat except for the 29th second and during the voice announcement. Each minute begins with a half-second beat, and each hour with a one-second beat. The beginning of the beats constitutes the time signal. Operating frequencies are 3330 kc., 7335 kc., and 14670 kc.

1005. Marine Telephones. The rapid development of the two-way telephone service within a few hundred miles of a coast has greatly improved safety at sea and enhanced the reliability and ease of communication between ship and shore. The licensing of radio installations aboard ship and the operators of the equipment are all regulated by the Federal Communications Commission (FCC) under Part 83 of FCC Rules and

Regulations. By following these rules and regulations your equipment and operators then become a part of an operational marine radiotelephone system.

This system is designed to do the following:

(A) Provide monitoring of distress, safety and calling frequencies.
(B) Provide frequencies for communication between vessels (Ship to Ship) and between vessels and Federal agencies such as the Coast Guard.
(C) Provide frequencies for communication related to vessel movement or management and navigation such as required by harbor and bar pilots.
(D) Provide frequencies for vessels and shore stations engaged in commercial operations.
(E) Provide non-commercial frequencies for special needs of recreational boating.
(F) Provide frequencies for vessels to communicate through shore telephone systems (Public Correspondence).

To provide the forgoing service, the marine telephone system is divided into three subsystems.

(A) A medium frequency (MF) band system operating in the single side band mode (SSB) between 2 and 3 Mhz.
(B) A high frequency (HF) band system operating in the single side band (SSB) mode between 4 and 23 Mhz.
(C) A very high frequency (VHF) band system operating in the frequency modulated (FM) mode between 156 and 162 Mhz. The MF band system has a medium to long-range capability (100—1000 miles). It has assigned frequencies for distress and calling, ship to ship, ship to shore and ship to Coast Guard. Examples of assigned frequencies are:

Ship/Coast   Use
2182/2182 Khz—Primary calling and distress frequency.
2670/2670 Khz—Coast Guard working frequency.
2406/2506 Khz—Public Correspondence, Boston Station WOU.
2009/2566 Khz—Public Correspondence, San Pedro Station KOU.

The HF band system has a long-range capability and is used primarily by the merchant marine on the high seas for communication to shore stations. It has assigned frequencies for ship to ship, ship to shore and public correspondence. Any of the public correspondence frequencies can be used for distress traffic. The VHF-FM system has a range of 10 to 30 miles depending on power output and antenna height. By use of the FM mode a total of 48 separate channels (paired transmit-receive frequencies) are fitted within the operating band of 156-162 Mhz. All VHF-FM stations must be equipped to operate on a minimum of three channels. They are: Channel 16—Calling and Distress, Channel 6—Intership Safety and at

least one other working channel. Examples of assigned frequencies are
as follows:

Channel	Ship Trans./Rec.	Use
16	156.8/156.8 Mhz—Distress, calling,	
06	156.3/156.3 Mhz—Intership safety	
22A	157.1/157.1 Mhz—Coast Guard	
12	156.6/156.6 Mhz—Port operations	
13	156.65/156.65 Mhz—Navigational (bridge to bridge)	
68	156.425/156.425 Mhz—Non-commercial. Internship and ship to shore.	
7A	156.35/156.35 Mhz—Commercial. Intership and ship to shore.	
86	157.2/161.8 Mhz—Public correspondence.	

All radio stations and operators must be licensed by the Federal Communications Commission (FCC). Application forms and information concerning station and operator licenses may be obtained from the FCC,
P.O. Box 1050, Gettysburg, Pennsylvania 17325.

Marine Radio Weather Service. The National Oceanic and Atmospheric Administration (NOAA) provides continuous 24-hour broadcast
of the latest weather information on taped messages repeated every 4 to
6 minutes, and revised frequently. These broadcasts are transmitted from
142 stations situated on the Atlantic-Pacific-Gulf coasts, Great Lakes,
Alaska, Hawaii, Porto Rico and Virgin Islands on one of the following
VHF-FM frequencies: WX-1 (162.55 Mhz), WX-2 (162.4 Mhz) and WX-3
(162.475 Mhz). The range of a station is about 40 miles.

Citizens Band Radio (CB) on 27 Mhz Band. Use of the popular CB
radio equipment is permitted aboard ships. However, the Coast Guard
does not officially monitor the CB system and it cannot be considered as
a substitute for the marine telephone system. CB equipment may have
23 channels or 40 channels with frequencies between 26.965 Mhz to 27.405
Mhz. Channel 9 (27.065 Mhz) is designated as the channel for emergency
communications.

1006. Radio bearings. The bearing of the source of any radio
signal received may be determined within close limits. This development
is of greatest value when near a coast in thick weather. At present,
experienced navigators regard radio bearings at sea as an aid to, rather
than a substitute for, celestial navigation. The use of a coil for determining the direction of radio waves was developed by Hertz in 1881. As
the transmission of such waves over long distances became practical, the
important possibilities of utilizing the directive element of radio signals
for navigation were recognized. Development of the general use of radio
bearings dates from about 1920 and has been especially rapid since.

Any radio bearing of a station or radiobeacon is a great circle bearing. Strictly speaking, all such bearings must be corrected by Table 1, Bowditch, before plotting on a Mercator chart. The correction is 0° when the bearing lies N or S and a maximum when it lies nearly E or W. The correction is greater for greater differences of longitude and in higher latitudes. Roughly speaking, this correction does not exceed 1° within latitudes not exceeding 45° and when the distance of the ship from the radio station does not exceed 150 miles. This means that for most coastwise work the correction may be neglected.

1007. Radiobeacons. For over two thousand years there have been lighthouses to guide ships, and for more than two hundred years fog warnings of some sort have aided the mariner in thick weather. Until recently he has not had a practicable method of taking accurate bearings on invisible objects. Today, radio supplies this need, and radiobeacons provide a reliable source of bearings, regardless of fog or storm.

A radiobeacon, as the term is used in *Light Lists*, is a radio station, of fixed and known position, especially equipped for sending out signals in all directions which may be easily identified as their bearings are observed from the ship. They are generally at lighthouses or on lightships. On May 1, 1921, radiobeacons were placed in regular operation on Ambrose, Fire Island, and Sea Girt lightships, all in the vicinity of New York. These were the first successful radiobeacons in the world. Today, hundreds of such beacons send out their signals from many coasts. They are the most valuable of all fog signals and are often useful in clear weather navigation.

No knowledge of radio telegraphy is required to use the radiobeacon system. Audible signals are heard on frequencies from 285 kc. to 325 kc., when a suitable receiver is tuned to the band. Simple combinations of dots and dashes are used to identify the station as shown in Fig. 1007. This identifying signal is sent for one minute except that the last ten seconds of each minute is devoted to a long dash to permit bearing refinement. At distance-finding stations (§1008), this ten-second dash is synchronized with the fog signal when operating.

Because of the limited number of frequencies available, most radiobeacons must share a single frequency with up to five other beacons. Each radiobeacon transmits, regardless of weather, for at least one minute of each six-minute period, in regular sequence (shown by a Roman numeral) with other beacons in the same general area. If no Roman numeral is shown, as at Scotland Lightship, the beacon transmits continuously. If a group consists of less than six beacons, one or more of them may transmit during two of the six one-minute periods.

During each beacon's transmitting period, a steady (continuous wave) carrier signal is sent out on the assigned frequency. This carrier is inaudible without special provision (beat frequency oscillator) in the receiver; but it does provide a one-minute signal for automatic direction finders to use. The radiobeacon's dot-dash identification is generated by transmitting a second continuous wave "on and off" at a frequency 1020 cycles per second above or below the carrier. The combination of these two continuous waves (known as dual carrier) produces a "beat note" which the receiver translates into the audible dot-dash signal. Numerous marker beacons are shown in Fig. 1007.

Charts of the marine radiobeacon system of the United States, similar to Fig. 1007, are shown in the various *Light Lists;* larger charts are issued for the Atlantic and Pacific Coasts respectively. These charts show the beacons and their characteristics, and are arranged especially for posting near the radio compass. Study of such a chart and the discussions in the *Light Lists* is the best way to learn about the operation of the system.

Many radio ranges and homing radiobeacons, provided primarily for airmen, are also available to the surface navigator and can often be used

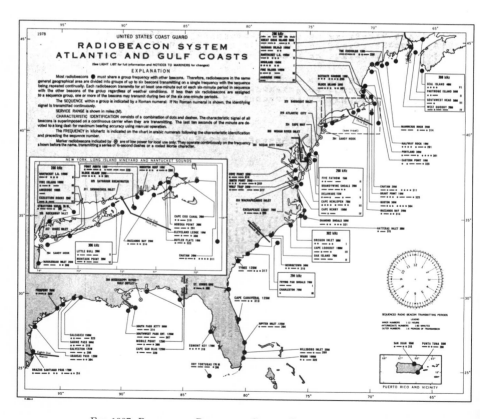

Fig. 1007. Position of Radiobeam System Chart, from Light List.

to advantage. Aviation beacons use frequencies from 200 Khz to 415 Khz. Frequencies allocated to the marine beacons are avoided for aviation use near the coast. At the present time little information about these air stations is provided on nautical charts. The surface navigator, however, can obtain station locations, frequencies, and identification signals from aeronautical charts. A catalogue of these charts is issued by the NOS.

1008. Distance-finding stations are radiobeacons which, when fog prevails, send out identical radio and sound signals at the same instant

DISTANCE FINDING — NAUTICAL MILES
BY INTERVALS BETWEEN RADIO AND AIR SIGNALS

INTERVAL SECONDS	DISTANCE MILES	INTERVAL SECONDS	DISTANCE MILES	INTERVAL SECONDS	DISTANCE MILES
1	0.2	6	1.1	20	3.6
2	0.4	7	1.3	30	5.4
3	0.5	8	1.4	40	7.2
4	0.7	9	1.6	50	9.0
5	0.9	10	1.8	60	10.8

FIG. 1008. DISTANCE SOUND TRAVELS PER SECOND.

of time. The radio signal is heard at practically the instant it is sent. The interval of time before the sound signal is heard is a measure of distance. When the sound signal of the station is operating, a group of two blasts, a one-second blast is followed after one second by a five-second blast. The beginning of the five-second blast is synchronized with the beginning of the long (ten-second) dash of the radio signal. When within audible range of the sound signal, navigators with any radio receiver capable of receiving the radiobeacon signals may determine their distance from the station by observing the time in seconds which elapses between hearing any part of the distinctive group of radio dashes, and the corresponding part of the group of sound blasts. Dividing the seconds by 5 (or, more exactly, multiplying the seconds by 0.18) gives the distance in nautical miles, or the conversion may be made by the table in Fig. 1008. The error of such observations should not exceed 10 per cent.

1009. Direction-finders on board ship are special radio instruments for observing the bearing of any radio station whose signals can be received by the direction-finder. This is accomplished by utilizing the directional characteristics of a loop antenna. The receiving and radiating pattern of a loop antenna takes the shape of a figure eight. When either end of the "8" (horizontal diameter of the loop) points toward the signal source, the output of the loop into the receiver is maximum. When the axis of the "8" is perpendicular to the signal source, the loop output is minimum, and a "null" is said to occur. The null is indicated aurally by the lowest sound level or visually by a minimum reading of a meter. The null is much sharper than the maximum and occurs in a direction perpendicular to the plane of the loop. Hence, the bearing of a transmitter is at a right angle (either direction) to the plane of the loop at a minimum or null point.

Antennas of the small, portable, battery-operated direction finders now in common use (Fig. 1009) operate on a somewhat different principle. The energy from the radio wave is concentrated by a slender (ferrite) rod which is inductively coupled to the input of the receiver. In this case, the signal is maximum when the rod is aligned with the signal and points toward or away from the transmitter. It is essentially the

Courtesy of the Raytheon Company, South San Francisco, Cal.

FIG. 1009. A THREE-BAND, BATTERY-OPERATED RADIO DIRECTION FINDER.

same figure-eight pattern as with the loop; the axis of the "8" is parallel to the plane of the loop but perpendicular to the ferrite rod.

A 180° ambiguity exists with the figure-eight pattern of either a loop or rod antenna; that is, the same response is received from directions 180° apart. Most of the modern radio direction finders contain a second (vertical) antenna called a "sense antenna" which resolves this ambiguity. The addition of the circular pattern from the vertical antenna distorts the figure-eight pattern into a "cardioid" or heart-shaped pattern having only one null. The direction of the null is now the direction of the transmitter.

Fig. 1009 shows a typical, three-band, battery-operated radio direction finder. The rod antenna forms a diameter of the bearing circle and the sense antenna is seen at the upper right. To take a bearing with such a direction finder, the bearing circle is oriented so that the 0° mark is dead ahead. All bearings taken in this position will be relative to the ship's head. After the signal from the desired beacon has been tuned in and identified, the antenna is rotated until the null is detected, and its relative bearing is read from the bearing circle. At the same time, the helmsman notes the compass heading. This is converted to true heading. The true bearing is the sum of the relative bearing with any calibration corrections applied, and the true heading.

Any radio signal arrives at the receiver along a great circle which would plot on a Mercator chart as a curve, convex toward the pole. Table 1, Bowditch gives the corrections which in theory should be applied to a radio bearing to convert the great circle to a straight line. Examination of this table, however, will show that for latitudes less than about 40° and for distances less than 150 miles or so, these corrections can be neglected. In plotting a radio bearing, remember that it is the direction *from* the ship *to* the beacon.

A ship's radio direction finder requires calibration to take account of bearing errors caused by structural features of the ship's hull and superstructure. Such calibration is usually accomplished by taking a round of radio bearings on a transmitting station that can be seen and comparing each radio bearing with that obtained visually.

The U. S. Coast Guard operates a number of calibration stations for this purpose. These are described in the *Light Lists;* and both these publications and Pub. 117A and B, *Radio Navigational Aids,* contain a discussion of errors which may affect a direction finder and much useful information on the practical handling of radio bearings.

Practice is all-important and may be had whenever the ship's position is known and a radiobeacon can be heard; it is even simpler when the beacon station is visible. Regular practice teaches facility in the use of the equipment, develops a knowledge of its errors, and checks its readiness for use when an emergency demands.

1010. Radio navigation. Having provided the equipment and the skill for observing radiobeacons, radio navigation is nothing more than the use of the bearings so obtained as lines of position. Thus radio bearings may be crossed with the bearings of visible landmarks or lines of position obtained by observing celestial bodies. It is customary, however, to give greater consideration to the probable accuracy of radio bearings and to consider positions determined thereby as estimated rather than as a new fix.

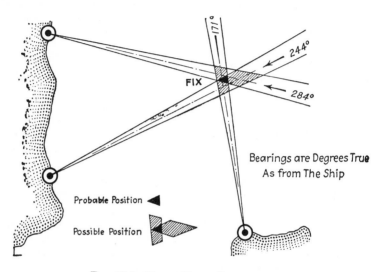

FIG. 1010a. FIX BY THREE RADIOBEACONS.

The question of probable and possible positions resulting from errors in bearing lines is illustrated in Fig. 1010a. Each radio bearing is assumed to have a possible error of plus or minus 2°. The 4° sectors from the two stations on the left give an area of position represented by the shaded diamond. The bearing of the station at lower right increases the possible area but indicates the small black diamond as the most probable position.

The graphic solution for an area of position by two bearings of the same radiobeacon, as shown in Fig. 1010b, also assumes a possible plus or minus 2° error in each bearing. Let the sides of the sector determined by the 301° bearing be advanced by course and distance, as represented by the direction and length of the lines from A to B, to the lines either side of the 332° bearing, they will intersect the sides of that sector at the four points labeled B which then mark the area of position.

All bearing lines, however determined, are subject to more or less error, although it is seldom necessary to plot sectors of position as in the last two illustrations. The practical effect of the error in any bearing, whether radio or otherwise, is best understood by remembering that a 2° error in the bearing of a station 30 miles from the ship means an error in position of 1 mile at right angles to the bearing line, or 10 miles when the distance from the station is 300 miles.

"Homing" means steering directly for a radiobeacon. In one sense it is the simplest use of a radio bearing, although in thick weather it has resulted in a number of disasters. The important point is to bear off at the proper time. Otherwise, the ship will run aground or crash the beacon as did the *S.S. Olympic* when she cut down Nantucket Lightship some years ago.

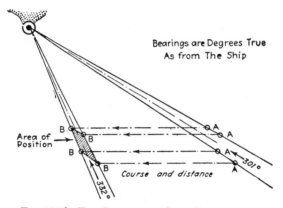

Fig. 1010*b*. Two Bearings of Same Radiobeacon.

An actual case of a ship, in thick weather, homing on Cape Cod station, which is not a distance-finding radiobeacon, is illustrated in Fig. 1010*c*. Soundings had been neglected and available cross bearings were distrusted. At 0700, the distance from the Cape Cod station being somewhat uncertain, the course was changed to 255° true, which was expected safely to clear the Cape. Bearings of the radiobeacon grew less. At 0730, having steamed 6 miles, the bearing was 200°. The 0700 line was moved forward to 0700-0730 and its intersection with the bearing line gave a running fix at 0730. This showed distance off from the beacon to be less than expected. As a precaution, the course was again changed, the new course being 265° true. At 0800 the bearing was 170° and indicated that the vessel was being advanced westward by the tidal current. A cross of the 0730 bearing as advanced to 0730-0800 with the 0800 bearing practically confirmed the distance of the vessel from the Cape. The course of 265° was continued until a bearing of 122° was reached, and it was considered safe to home on the radiobeacon on the breakwater of the Cape Cod canal.

CONSOL is a long-range (1000 miles) radio navigational system operating in the low frequency band (250-400 Khz) intended for use by a aircraft but useable by ships which cover the eastern and north eastern Atlantic

Ocean area. Its U.S.A. counterpart called COSOLAN has been disestablished.

To use the system a radio receiver capable of tuning the low frequency band and having a beat frequency oscillator (BFO) to sharpen the reception of dots and dashes is required. The CONSOL beacon transmits a radiation pattern of alternate dot and dash sectors separated by an equisignal (continuous note) formed by merging of the dots and dashes. A bearing line is determined by counting the number of dots and dashes (total of 60) which can then be translated into a great circle bearing from the CONSOL station by use of dot-dash count tables for the station or from special CONSOL charts. CONSOL tables for the various stations with complete instructions for use of the system are found in Chapter 7 of Radio Navigational Aids, Pub. 117A. CONSOL charts are published by the British Admiralty Hydrographic Service. CONSOL stations are situated at Stavanger, Norway; Andoya, Norway; Bear Island; Jan Mayen Island and Ploneis, France.

Radio is an established element of the art of navigation. The fitness of certain items of radio equipment is a direct responsibility of the navigator. Each unit should be used every day to assure that both apparatus and personnel are ready when emergency demands.

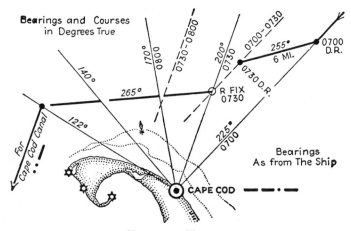

FIG. 1010c. HOMING.

11. MARINERS' MAPS

MAPS drawn on the surface of a globe correctly represent the curved surface of the earth; maps or charts on a flat surface, especially those of large areas, are necessarily distorted. The smallest globe, although impracticable for the daily work of the navigator, is an invaluable aid to understanding charts and various other matters with which navigators are concerned.

1101. Definitions on a globe. The drawing of the sphere of the earth illustrates certain definitions important to all mariners.

The *earth* is assumed to be a sphere with its *axis* passing through its *north pole* and its *south pole*.

Great circles. If a plane passes through the center of the earth, as when cutting an orange in half, its intersection with the earth's surface is a *great circle*. The plane must pass through the center or only smaller circles result. Arcs of great circles, often appearing as straight lines, are important elements of chart construction.

Angles, as measured from the center of the earth, are the principal basis for measurements on its surface. An angle is formed by the intersection of two lines and is measured by the divergence of the lines without regard to their length, as in Fig. 1101. The units of angular measurement result from dividing any circle, whose center is at the intersection of two lines, into 360°; each degree is further divided into 60′, and each minute into 60″. In practical navigation, it is sufficiently accurate to express seconds (″) of arc by the nearest tenth of a minute (′).

The *equator* is a great circle around the earth midway between the poles. Its distance from each pole is everywhere 90°, or one-fourth of a circle, but the equator, because it is a complete circle, is divided into 360°.

Meridians are best described as halves of great circles extending from pole to pole always at right angles to the equator. A line drawn through

123

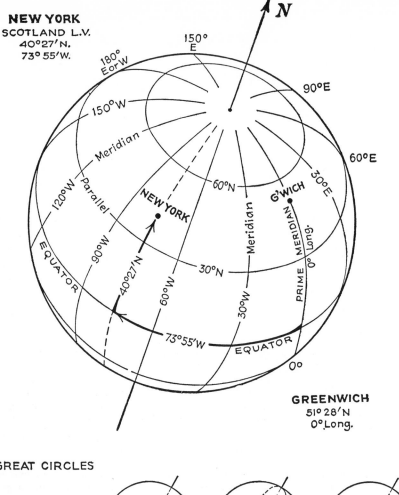

NEW YORK
SCOTLAND L.V.
40°27′N.
73°55′W.

N

180°
E or W

150°
E

150°W

90°E

Meridian

60°E

120°W Parallel

60°N

30°E

NEW YORK

G'WICH

0°Long.

EQUATOR

40°27′N

90°W

30°N

60°W

Meridian

30°W

PRIME MERIDIAN

73°55′W

EQUATOR

0°

GREENWICH
51°28′N
0°Long.

GREAT CIRCLES

HALF AN ORANGE

EQUATOR

MERIDIANS

COURSE

EQUATOR

MERIDIAN

COURSE

THE EARTH

Fɪɢ. 1100.

the ship, north and south to the poles, is the meridian of the ship. A similar line through Greenwich is called the *prime meridian* and is the zero line from which longitude is measured. Meridians on Mercator charts appear as vertical, parallel straight lines.

Parallels of latitude are smaller circles around the earth, parallel to the equator. On most charts, parallels of latitude appear as horizontal straight lines.

Latitude (*Lat. or L.*) defines position on the earth *north* or *south* from the equator. The latitude of a place on the surface of the earth is the arc of the meridian between the equator and that place. Latitude is 0° on the

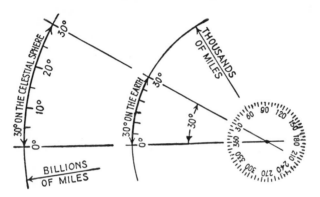

FIG. 1101. AN ANGLE MEASURED BY DEGREES OF ARC.

equator and never exceeds 90°, which is the latitude of either pole; it is marked N (+) or S (−). Observe how the latitude of Scotland Light-ship, off New York, is measured in Fig. 1100.

Longitude (*Long. or* λ) defines position on the earth *east* or *west* from the meridian of Greenwich, which is called the *prime meridian.* Longitude of a place on the earth's surface is the arc of the equator between the prime meridian and that of the place. It is measured East (E) or West (W) from the meridian of Greenwich (0° Long.), and therefore does not exceed 180° or halfway around the earth, where east meets west.

Position of any point at sea or on the land may be defined by its latitude and longitude. For example, the position of Scotland Lightship is in Lat. 40° 27′ N and Long. 73° 55′ W.

The true *direction* of a line on the surface of the earth at any point along the line is the angle the line makes with the meridian through that point. It is generally measured from 0° at true north around clockwise to 360°.

A *nautical mile* (6076 ft.) is the unit of distance used at sea. By international agreement, it is equal to exactly 1852 meters and is approximately equivalent to 1′ of latitude or to 1′ of arc of any great circle of the earth. A nautical mile is approximately one-seventh longer than the statute mile (5280 ft.).

1102. Mercator's projection. To represent approximately the spherical surface of the earth on a flat surface, maps are constructed in many different ways according to the purpose for which a particular type of map is devised. Mercator's projection, previously outlined in §204, is the system by which most maps used by mariners are constructed. Charts of this type have been in use since the publication about 1569 by Gerardus Mercator, a Flemish geographer, of his then excellent map of the world. The navigator may not be called on to construct a Mercator chart but a knowledge of how such charts are developed is an aid to understanding many things related to voyages at sea. The drawings in Fig. 1102 represent three stages in the development of a Mercator chart.

Imagine the true map of the earth's surface on a globe to be unfolded as if an orange were peeled. The segments shown in (*A*) everywhere represent 30° of longitude but are bounded by converging meridians as on the earth. The distance between these meridians at 60° N or 60° S is only 900 miles, whereas at the equator they were 1800 miles apart. The true length of 1′ of longitude continually decreases from 1 mile on the equator to ½ mile in 60° N or S and thence to 0 at the poles regardless of how it may appear on any chart. *Minutes of longitude are never a measure of nautical miles* except on the equator.

The horizontal lines drawn across the segments above and below the equator represent the parallels of 30°, 60°, and 80° N or S latitude. These are parallel lines; they do not converge as do the meridians of longitude, and the actual distance between any two such parallels of latitude is everywhere the same. The length of 1′ of latitude, which is measured on a great circle of the earth, is 1 mile according to one definition of a nautical mile. *Minutes of latitude are always a measure of nautical miles* in their latitude. For example, the distance between a parallel of 30° and that of 60° is 30° or

$$30 \times 60' = 1800' = 1800 \text{ nautical miles.}$$

In (*B*) the segments from the globe appear as expanded with their edges joined in vertical, parallel straight lines which represent the meridians on the Mercator chart shown as a cylinder wrapped around the earth. These apparently parallel meridians appear equally distant from one another, whereas on the earth the true distance between them constantly decreases as they converge from the equator to the poles. Except on the equator all of the east and west dimensions on the chart have been expanded, this expansion being greater the greater the latitude.

To avoid local distortion, the expansion of the longitude scale at any given distance from the equator is applied to the latitude scale in that area. The scale at the sides of the chart which represents a minute or a degree of latitude continually increases from the equator to north or south and becomes impossibly great when approaching the poles. This is

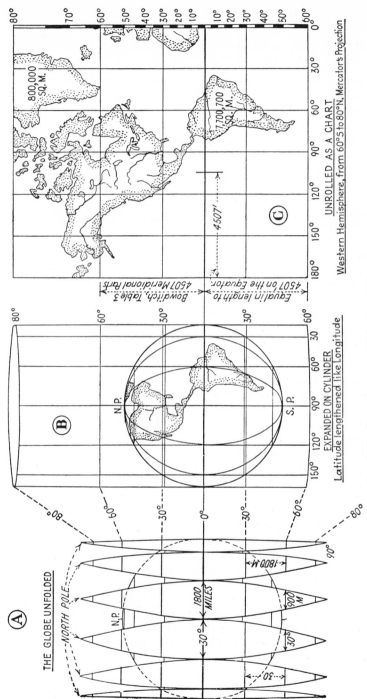

Fig. 1102. Development of Mercator's Projection.

Ⓐ THE GLOBE UNFOLDED

NORTH POLE

N.P.

1800 MILES

1800 M.

900 M.

80°

60°

30°

0°

30°

60°

80°

90°

30°

30°

Ⓑ EXPANDED ON CYLINDER
Latitude lengthened like Longitude

N.P.

S.P.

80°

60°

30°

0°

30°

60°

150° 120° 90° 60° 30° 30 60 80

Ⓒ UNROLLED AS A CHART
Western Hemisphere, from 60°S to 80°N, Mercator's Projection

800,000 SQ. M.

7,700,700 SQ. M.

450'

Equal in length to 450' on the Equator.

Bowditch, Table 3
450' Meridional Parts

80° 70° 60° 50° 40° 30° 20° 10° 10° 20° 30° 40° 50° 60°

0° 30° 60° 90° 120° 150° 180°

why drawings (*B*) and (*C*) reach only to 80° N; charts of the polar regions cannot be constructed on Mercator's projection.

The drawing (*C*) shows half of the cylinder unrolled as a flat chart of the Western Hemisphere, from 60° S to 80° N. Within these limits it represents a Mercator projection of the map shown on the globe (*B*). In practice charts of such large areas are seldom used. The drawing, however, illustrates an important characteristic of a Mercator chart. The scale of the chart increases as the latitude scale at the right of the drawing increases. If an area of the earth's surface be represented by a 1-inch square figure on the chart at the equator, an equal area at 60° N or S on the same chart will appear as a 2-inch square. On the drawing Greenland looks as large as South America. Actually, the area of our southern neighbor approximates ten times that of Greenland.

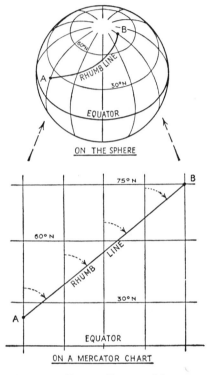

1103. Rhumb lines or Mercator tracks. Any straight line on a Mercator chart is a rhumb line as, for example, the line from *A* to *B* on the chart in Fig. 1103. Note the most important and useful property of a Mercator chart. A rhumb line between two points crosses each meridian at the same angle, which is the true course to steer continuously from one place to the other. All courses plotted on

Fig. 1103.   Rhumb Line, or Mercator Track.

coastwise charts are rhumb lines, and the course to steer remains unchanged all the way along the rhumb line or Mercator track from *A* to *B*.

Theoretically, a rhumb line is seldom the shortest track between two points because, with rare exceptions, it is actually a curved line on the earth's surface, be its curvature ever so small. Because a rhumb line may not be the shortest track, mariners sometimes follow a series of rhumb lines which approximate a great circle, along which lies the shortest course from one port to another.

1104. Great circle tracks. The coastwise man, dreaming of voyages to foreign climes, may easily understand the principles of great circle sailing.

Stretch a string or an elastic band between any two points on a globe; it will represent the great circle track which is the shortest distance between the points. On certain long voyages the distance saved by great circle sailing is of importance. This fact and one other characteristic of a great circle course may be illustrated, with a globe, by considering the somewhat extreme case of a voyage from Sydney, Australia, to Valparaiso, Chile. (See Fig. 1105.)

Hold a piece of string which does not stretch, in a straight line on the globe from Sydney to Valparaiso. This string will pass south of New Zealand and slightly below the parallel of 60° S. Cut the string so that its length measures the distance between the two ports. Place one end of this measuring string at Sydney, and apply it to the globe so as to "run down the latitude" toward Valparaiso on a rhumb line or Mercator track, about 3°.5 below and parallel to the line on the globe which represents 30° S latitude. The string will not reach Valparaiso by almost 800 miles, which represent the saving in distance by approximating the great circle track on which the length of the string was measured.

Again stretch a string, or better an elastic band, along the great circle from the one port to the other. Note that the initial course from Sydney will be toward the SE quarter but will continually change as the track crosses each meridian until, on approaching Valparaiso, the course will be toward the NE quarter. This is a radical illustration of the general fact that whenever great circle sailing is of practical advantage a ship must change its course from time to time in a manner to approximate the great circle track.

There are no practical advantages in great circle sailing under certain circumstances, which are:

For relatively short distances in any direction, as when sailing coastwise; since the rhumb line is almost coincident with the great circle track, the possible saving in distance is nil and great circles may be forgotten.

Along meridians which are themselves great circles extending north and south from pole to pole; when the course approximates N or S, there is no saving in distance between two places near the same meridian.

Within the tropics the true map as shown on a globe is almost a Mercator chart; the equator is both a great circle and a rhumb line as are the meridians; the parallels of latitude near the equator are almost rhumb lines. In these regions rhumb line sailing is very nearly as short as great circle sailing.

Summarized in a reverse manner: Great circle sailing is most advantageous when sailing a long voyage east or west in relatively high latitudes.

Atlantic coast yachtsmen are familiar with two such examples: (1) The track of 628 miles of 146° true from Newport to St. David's Head,

Bermuda, is only a hair shorter if measured on a great circle. (2) On the other hand, a great circle course across the North Atlantic to Europe is materially shorter than any rhumb line course. The victory of Olin Stephens' yawl *Dorade* in the transatlantic race of 1931 was partly due to the fortunate outcome of her owner's decision to approximate a great circle course.

1105. Great circle charts furnish a simple graphic method for determining a great circle track. They are so constructed that a straight line between any two points on the chart represents the great circle track. Such a line between two ports of departure and destination at once indicates whether it passes clear of danger or through latitudes which should be avoided at the time of a proposed voyage. Having considered the contingencies, one or more straight lines may be drawn to represent the desired track or tracks.

To attain these useful characteristics, a great circle chart is constructed on the so-called *gnomonic projection.* Neither meridians nor parallels of latitude appear as parallel lines, and neither courses nor distances can be taken directly from such a chart. However, the charts are arranged so that it is a simple matter to take off the latitude and longi-

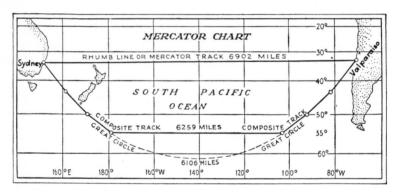

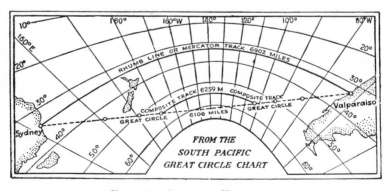

Fig. 1105. Sydney to Valparaiso.

tude of several intermediate points on a great circle. These points are then plotted on a Mercator chart and joined by straight lines which are a series of rhumb lines approximating the selected track. Course and distance represented by each rhumb line are determined as on any Mercator chart. The total distance via these rhumb lines will be only slightly greater than the distance along the great circle.

The nature and use of great circle charts and their relation to Mercator charts are illustrated in Fig. 1105, which diagrams various courses from Sydney to Valparaiso. It is assumed that the shipmaster, out of Sydney, desires to approximate a great circle track because it is shorter and because it takes the ship into the prevailing westerlies of the southern seas. On the great circle chart a straight line from Sydney to Valparaiso represents the great circle track and shows that it clears the southern end of New Zealand but passes below 60° S. To avoid the dangers of such a low latitude, it is decided not to go below 55° S, an assumption which serves the purpose of the illustration. A more probable course would be through Cook Strait between the New Zealand islands.

In the case illustrated, seven rhumb lines are assumed which approximate the great circle track except that the track does not go below 55° S. Each position where course is changed is marked in exactly the same latitude and longitude on either chart. The proposed track is correctly plotted on both charts, as are the great circle and Mercator tracks, although each track has an entirely different appearance when transferred from one chart to the other. The Mercator chart shows the great circle track as a much longer line than the rhumb because on such a chart one inch at 60° S measures only three-fifths as many miles as at 30° S.

Great circle charts have robbed great circle sailing of its mathematical mysteries. The initial great circle course and the great circle distance between any two points may be computed as in §2908, but for the practical business of great circle sailing the modern mariner uses great circle charts. The student who wishes to pursue this subject should procure one or more such charts and the corresponding Mercator charts.

1106. Various charts. Ocean charts and coastwise charts in general use are on Mercator's projection, and are scaled by nautical miles. Charts of the Great Lakes and other inland waters use a statute mile scale. *Ocean charts* are on small scales; they show lines of equal variation, steamer tracks, ocean currents, and other general information; only the true compass rose is printed on these charts. *Coastwise charts* show details on various larger scales and have a magnetic compass rose inside the true rose. There are a variety of special charts, mostly on Mercator's projection, whose titles as listed in the chart catalogs indicate their various purposes. *Pilot charts* for the different oceans contain an amazing variety of information, including the average weather conditions and other useful data. Nowhere can an oceangoing sailorman learn more than from a pilot chart.

1107. Small-craft charts. Of major interest to yachtsmen are the NOS small-craft charts now available. These charts are designated by the letters "SC" following the chart numbers.

The small-craft charts are issued already folded and are designed for ease of reference and plotting in cramped quarters. They stress the details appreciated by operators of small craft, such as large-scale insets of small-boat harbors, tide and tidal current tables, weather data, whistle signals, facilities at marinas, suitable anchorages, and often-used courses and distances.

Small-craft charts are available for many areas such as Long Island Sound and the Chesapeake Bay and rivers such as the Potomac and Rappahannock Rivers, commonly used by small boats. These charts are especially useful for craft cruising the important Intracoastal Waterway. See Apx. IV for catalogs of needed charts.

1108. Plotting sheets are blank charts for use instead of regular nautical charts. They are used when the scales of available ocean charts are too small for practical plotting or when it is desired to plot celestial lines of position without marking up the regular chart. Plotting sheets printed and issued by DMAHC show meridians and parallels drawn on the Mercator projection and include one or more compass roses. Apx. IV lists some of the plotting sheets currently on issue.

Homemade plotting sheets for limited areas are easily constructed with sufficient accuracy for plotting part of a day's work at sea or for plotting problems. Uniformly ruled paper facilitates their construction, although one, may rule the paper for himself.

The method of constructing a small area plotting sheet is shown in Fig. 1108 which represents the middle portion of the proposed layouts. Assume that the center of the work you expect to plot is in about 40° N and 70° W. Label a vertical line down the center of the sheet as 70° W. Draw a horizontal line across the middle and label it 40° N. In the drawing, each space between the vertical lines represents 1′ of longitude; therefore label each 10′ of longitude as shown.

To locate a 10′ parallel of latitude according to Mercator's projection, draw a line from the center at an angle to the horizontal equal to the middle latitude, in this case 40°. The length of this diagonal intercepted between two meridians 10′ apart is then the length of 10′ of latitude. With this distance, space, rule and label as many 10′ parallels as the problem requires or the paper permits. The graduations of the diagonal line marked by the 1′ meridians give the scale of miles to be used all over the plotting sheet.

There are numerous variations of the above procedure. In any case, the point to remember is to *draw the diagonal at an angle with the horizontal equal to the middle latitude* of the area to be represented and thus find the latitude scale. The method is not a mere school room fancy, and is often used to plot situations in the navigator's work book. The Problem Plotting Sheet designed for students and shown half-size with Appendix VIII further illustrates small area plotting sheets.

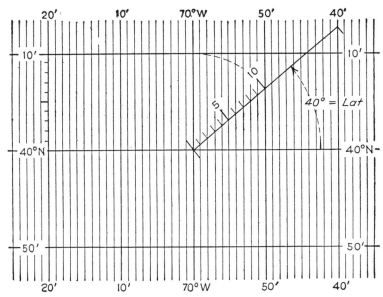

FIG. 1108. HOMEMADE PLOTTING SHEET.

To construct a Mercator chart. The above methods are theoretically correct at the equator and sufficiently accurate for all small plotting sheets. If the navigator ever should need to construct a Mercator chart of large areas beyond the Tropics, the method of meridional parts given in Bowditch should be used.

1109. Chart portfolios. Charts used by salt-water navigators are published by two branches of the United States government, (consult listing in Apx. IV):

(a) Charts of the coasts, harbors, and navigable rivers and waterways of the United States and its territories are published by the NOS. The price and area covered by each of these charts is listed in the *Catalog of Nautical Charts* along with information on related publications.

(b) Charts of the oceans and foreign waters are published by DMAHC. These are listed in Pub. No 1-N, *Catalog of Charts and Nautical Publications.*

All charts published as above are identified by number sometimes prefixed by letters; as "SC" for the small-craft charts (§1107).

1110. Notices to Mariners. *Notice to Mariners,* a weekly pamphlet prepared by DMAHC and the U. S. Coast Guard, contains notices of changes in lights, buoys, and other aids to navigation including radio which have occurred throughout the world. Notice to mariners is divided into three sections. Section I has corrections to charts, coast pilots, sailing directions, catalogs and paste on chartlet corrections. Also listed are new charts and publications, depth tabulations and hydrographic notes. Section II has corrections to light lists, radio navigational aids and other publications. Section III contains radio broadcast warnings and lists those warnings which are still effective from previous notices.

The DMAHC also publishes at intervals of about six months a summary of corrections in two volumes which assists the navigator in maintaining up-to-date charts, sailing directions and coast pilots. Volume 1 covers the Atlantic, Arctic and Mediterranean seas. Volume 2 covers the Pacific, Indian and Antarctic seas.

A listing of changes in local aids issued by the Commandant of each Coast Guard District on request is usually sufficient for many mariners who only operate locally. (See the Coast Guard and DMAHC listings in Apx. IV.)

Careless mariners may not record all of these changes on an extensive set of charts, but the arrangement of the *Notices* is simple and permits noting at a glance important changes in any particular area. All charts are stamped near the lower left-hand corner with the date to which they have been corrected before issue from Washington. Dealers do not correct charts and the purchaser should insist that the date of correction be reasonably recent.

1111. Care on small vessels. A good chart desk with drawers is desirable and, when possible, should be within speaking distance of the helmsman. Rolled charts are a nuisance but ideal conditions for filing charts flat without folding may be impracticable. A drawer $37 \times 25 \times 3$ inches, inside, will take the largest charts folded once, and will accommodate about 75 charts, assuming an average proportion of smaller charts that need not be folded. Fold the charts map side out. Mark the chart number on both sides at the right-hand corner next the folded edge, which should be toward the front of the drawer. File in numerical order; keep the chart catalogs handy and from their index maps select the required chart by number. A drawer of half the above size evidently will hold any chart folded twice, and if drawers are not available vertical files folded against a bulkhead or flat racks under the deck beams will avoid rolling. A plastic case about 25×21 inches with transparent sides is useful for protecting the chart on deck and keeping it from blowing away.

*　　*　　*

Charts are the most important tools of the navigator other than the compass itself. Present-day charts are the result of decades of work by the principal governments of the world, among which the United States and Great Britain have been the leaders. The meaning and use of the infinite detail appearing on modern charts has been discussed to a limited degree in other chapters of this book. It is not sufficient partially to understand a chart. The navigator must train himself to interpret the meaning of every mark on a chart and to convert every detail he observes along the coast or at sea into the symbols and the terms used on charts.

12. DEAD RECKONING

RECKONING the ship's position from the courses and distances sailed must have been an element of even prehistoric navigation. Today it enters into piloting, is the method depended on for most coastal voyages, and is at all times essential at sea. The older mathematical methods for keeping the reckoning and deducing the ship's position therefrom are known as the sailings. The newer graphic method is simpler and has many advantages, especially for use with the new navigation at sea. It is the method commonly used in the United States Navy, is becoming popular in the Merchant Marine, and is the principal subject of this chapter.

1201. Explanations. The expression *dead reckoning,* as used throughout navigation, has two meanings:

(1) The process by which the ship's position is carried forward by courses and distances from the last fix.

(2) The position so found, commonly called the D.R.

According to Navy teaching, dead reckoning is based on the courses steered and distances run through the water and is so carried forward until the next fix. The difference between the position so found and the fix is then the error in the reckoning. Positions where allowance has been made for probable errors in the reckoning are termed estimated positions. With few exceptions, this book follows the Navy custom in these matters.

Many navigators correct the D.R. from time to time so that it represents the navigator's best judgment of the ship's position, i.e. it is the estimated position. Under some circumstances this plan is the best. In any case there is no rule that dictates either custom. The important point is to remember what the D.R. as you plot it represents.

Air navigators never plot the D.R. on the course line. After drawing the wind triangle, they plot the D.R. on the track line and correct it whenever opportunity offers.

1202. Routine records are essential whether the resulting positions are to be computed or plotted. Good practice requires that necessary data be recorded at regular intervals, although the ship may continue on the same course for hours at a time. It must be recorded whenever the course is changed and whenever the D.R. is needed for use with celestial observations. The time and point of departure having been recorded, necessary entries include:

(1) *Time* of the entry, by ship's time, the same kind of time used to identify celestial observations.

(2) *Courses.* The course recorded is generally the course steered by compass which must be corrected before plotting.

(3) *Distance.* The entries must include whatever is necessary to determine the distance run from one time to another time. These may include the reading of the patent log, figures from the engine revolution counter, or the speed taken from the revolution table or as otherwise indicated.

The importance of regular entries at least every hour on the hour is sometimes overlooked. Such a series of entries tends to prevent blunders and permits quick work in an emergency.

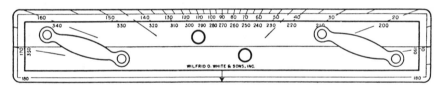

Fig. 1203. Field Type Parallel Rulers.

1203. Plotting the D.R. starts from a known or well determined position and is carried forward by plotting courses steered and distances run through the water.

The point of departure is the point from which the course line is first drawn. In the initial situation, as the ship puts to sea, this point should be fixed from landmarks. A nearby lightship or buoy will serve, but is less accurate than a fixed mark. An error in the point so fixed reappears in all D.R. positions until a new departure is taken from some future fix. Do not delay. It is important to record and plot the point of departure at the moment that point can be determined. On taking departure, stream the log and make any entries required later for finding the distance run. Then draw some miles of the course line and you are prepared to find the D.R. promptly if necessity arise.

The course to plot is the compass course steered, corrected to degrees true from north. This may be plotted, with any type of parallel rulers, from the 360° true rose on the chart or plotting sheet. Or the Field type of rulers, Fig. 1203, may be used to plot from any meridian or parallel of latitude, which can also be done by using the very efficient A.N. plotter described in Chapter 2.

If, perchance, the chart table is equipped with a universal drafting machine, so much the better. Take care that the plotting sheet is so placed that its meridians and parallels of latitude check with the 0° and 90° directions of the drafting machine.

The distance to plot is the distance run through the water. This distance is the difference between the patent log readings at the beginning and end of a period. Or it may be based on engine revolutions either directly or as indicating the speed in knots. In the latter case, compute the distance mentally or with a speed and distance table such as Table 7 (Apx. VIII) or Bowditch's Table 19. Table 7 is ordinarily sufficient as it may be used for speeds from 15 to 30 knots by multiplying the given speeds and distances by 2.

The time to plot the D.R. depends somewhat on circumstances but it must be plotted (1) whenever the course is changed and it should be plotted (2) when a fix is obtained. The necessity for plotting the D.R. at the time of a change in course is evident. Carrying forward the D.R. from hour to hour is often neglected except by navigators ever ready to give the ship's position when the SOS is sent or received. The D.R. also may be required when working sights of celestial bodies. Practically, it is always determined at the time of a new fix which is always used as a new point of departure. The difference between the old D.R. and the new fix is attributed to current since the last fix.

Cautions. When working on plotting sheets as at sea, it is necessary from time to time to transfer the ship's position to a new plotting sheet. A blunder, more common than most navigators will admit, is to plot the position on a new sheet with an error of 1° in latitude or longitude. Some years ago such a mistake cost a well-known yacht the Bermuda trophy, a victory dreamed of by all cruising yachtsmen. Only recently, and for the same reason, a convoy commodore for Canton was in the wrong place on the plotting sheet until the day before landfall. To assure the discovery of such a blunder, mark your position on the ocean chart at least once each day.

When approaching the land, transfer the ship's position to a chart of the coast at the first opportunity. This practice keeps the coastwise hazards ever before the navigator. Continue to transfer to larger scale charts as they become available.

The technique of plotting, the required labels and good lettering are summarized in Appendix II. The apparent simplicity of plotting the dead reckoning is such that two faults must be guarded against: (1) All too often, the work is permitted to lag contra the ideal of being kept up to the minute. (2) The possible errors in the seemingly exact D.R. position are overlooked.

1204. Errors in the D.R. The difference between a fix and the dead reckoning position at the time of the fix is the error of the D.R.

called *current*. The term is misleading because the error may have been caused by anything but current.

When determined as in the preceding section a D.R. position may be in error because of:

(1) Error in point of departure
(2) Deviation errors
(3) Bad steering
(4) Errors in distance
(5) Leeway
(6) Current

The navigator cannot estimate the effect of the first three possibilities. Errors in distance plotted may be due to errors of the patent log readings (§206). When distance is predicated on engine revolutions, a foul bottom or a list of a few degrees may cause errors. Proper allowance for these errors in distance may be made after a few days' experience with the ship. Estimating the effect either of leeway or of currents that may move the ship hither and yon is more difficult.

The error called *current* as defined above is the error accumulated during the time interval between fixes. The *set* of this "current" is the direction *toward* which it alters the ship's position, i.e. from the D.R. toward the fix. Its *drift* is its velocity in knots, i.e. the error of the D.R. in miles divided by the interval between fixes in hours.

After a fix, it is seldom safe to assume that the "current" just determined will continue until the next fix. If such an assumption leads the ship into danger, it must be considered, but ordinarily it is not taken into account in future plotting.

1205. Leeway is the leeward drift of the ship due to the pressure of the wind and the heave of the sea. It is not a fixed quantity but varies with the wind and sea and with the ship. Leeway, if any, is measured by the angle between the course steered and the direction made good through the water. If the wind is on the left, the ship will be set to the right of the course. Correction for estimated leeway to the right may be made by applying it as an easterly compass error. If the wind is on the right, the set will be to the left and leeway may be applied as a westerly compass error. Or the drift estimated to have taken place may be applied as a course and distance.

Estimating leeway is more difficult than applying the correction. A ship driving straight into wind and sea or with wind dead aft makes no leeway; wind abeam normally causes maximum leeway. A long, low, deep-laden ship will drift to leeward less than will a short, shallow craft. A motor boat may slip off like a balloon. The angle between the ship's wake or the log line and the line of the keel indicates the leeway, but in wild water and at slow speed such indications are of little value.

There are no rules for computing leeway. When conditions permit accurate observations, the navigator should observe the drift of his particu-

lar ship under various circumstances. He can then estimate leeway with
reasonable accuracy during long periods of dead reckoning.

Dr. Worth, a cruising sailor man of rare judgment, considered that a
yacht in ordinary weather will make little or no leeway unless the wind
is well forward of the beam. Also that, when close-hauled in smooth water, the leeway will probably not exceed a quarter point. To windward
under short canvas in rough weather, the leeway will be much greater.
If a yachtsman fails to find any leeway when it might be expected, it is
because the ship goes to windward in the puffs and because of the natural
tendency of the helmsman to point high of the course when he can.

1206. Ocean currents, clear of the land, flow continuously in more
or less the same direction in contrast to the reversing characteristic of
tidal currents. The principal causes of ocean currents are twofold, (1)
the wind and (2) the tendency of heavier cold water to flow toward the
lighter warm water of the equatorial areas. Of these two causes, the
wind predominates. The direction of a current is that toward which it
flows and is termed the *set* of the current. Its speed is the *drift* of the
current.

Given its set and drift during an interval of time, the effect of an
ocean current may be plotted as a course and distance from the D.R. to
the estimated position. Or it may be plotted in advance and the navigator may adjust his course to meet the current effect. All this is simple
enough if the average set and drift are known, a situation seldom encountered in strange waters, especially when near the land.

The velocity or drift varies with the wind and with some currents it
varies greatly, according to the season of the year. Often, when far at
sea, the direction and velocity of a current along its axis or center may be
estimated with some accuracy. Observe, however, that the proper allowance for drift when crossing a current is less than its velocity along its
axis. For example, as the Gulf Stream flows through the Straits of Florida its velocity near the middle of the stream may be almost 4 knots, but
the average drift to be allowed when crossing the Straits at that point is
little more than 2 knots.

The flow of an ocean current cannot be observed by the eye except as
it may change the character of the sea, but its motions are not unlike the
motions of the water in a river. On the straight reaches of a river the
fastest water runs down the center, but on a curve the velocity is greatest
along the outer shore of the curve. There may be a reverse current on
the inside of the curve, and an eddy in a reverse direction is almost certain to be found in a cove. Below a rock there is a quiet spot where the
big fish lie. The velocity of the current increases as the river narrows,
but is hardly to be observed in the wide quiet reaches below some wild
rapid.

When influenced by the land and possibly combined with coastwise tidal currents, both the set and drift of any current are most uncertain. Or a countercurrent at one side or the other of the principal current may be encountered. When dealing with such conditions the navigator plotting his D.R. by courses steered and distances run through the water must take special precautions. Plot broken lines to represent your best estimate of the movements of the ship over the bottom and proceed on the assumption that the ship is in the estimated position of the greatest dangers.

The ocean currents of the world are exceptionally well described in Bowditch. Specific information, essential for navigating the ship, may be had from a number of sources. Many charts show the set and drift of currents. *Pilot Charts* are often the most valuable because they are published for various seasons of the year. All *Coast Pilots*, and the *Sailing Directions (Pilots)* for foreign waters give information about currents, and the *Tidal Current Tables* include valuable chapters on the ocean currents touching the shores of the United States.

1207. The sailings are the mathematical methods formerly used by all navigators for keeping the reckoning at sea. They are used to compute the changes in the dead reckoning position resulting from courses and distances sailed. Some of these methods continue to be used in the Merchant Marine but, as previously stated, only the graphic methods of the new navigation are taught in this book.

Traverse Tables, like Bowditch's Table 3, are the tables generally used when working the sailings by inspection. They are the tabulated solution for any right triangle like the one formed in Fig. 1103 by the rhumb line, a meridian, and a parallel. Bowditch's Table 5, which gives the increase of the latitude scale on a Mercator chart, is also used.

The sailings as commonly listed include five methods, *all dealing with rhumb line courses*. The general problem is, given the course and distance, to find the change in latitude and the change in longitude. Or any two of these four quantities may be given to find the other two.

(1) *Plane sailing* is nothing more than the solution of a right triangle taken from Bowditch's Table 3 by inspection.

(2) *Traverse sailing*. This is a relic of the days of sail. A traverse is an irregular track made by a vessel on several different courses. Working a traverse means to combine the results of the various legs of the track so that a single solution by plane sailing gives the answer.

(3) *Parallel sailing* applies when the course is E or W, i.e. on a parallel of latitude. Miles may be converted into longitude by inspection of Bowditch's Table 3.

(4) *Middle latitude sailing*. When sailing between two points of different latitude, the mean of the latitudes is determined. With this middle

latitude substituted for the single latitude, the solution is identical with that of parallel sailing.

(5) *Mercator sailing.* Used principally to find the course and distances between two points on a Mercator chart by taking into account the expansion of the latitude scale which is characteristic of such charts. The method is important in high latitudes or when the differences in latitude and longitude are so large that neither of the preceding methods is sufficiently exact. For this method a table of Meridional Parts or Increased Latitudes like Bowditch's Table 5 must be at hand, and Table 3 is required for solutions by inspection.

Great circle sailing, in practice, is *composite sailing* carried on graphically as in §1105. However, the simplest way for a celestial navigator to find the total great circle distance between two points is to compute it as in §2908.

1208. The experienced judgment required to estimate the ship's position by the reckoning, after days of bad weather without sights, cannot be taught in books. It is difficult for a student who has not been tossed about for days on a wild grey sea to understand why navigating by the sun and stars is relatively simple. In midocean, an error in position of many miles may be unimportant, and with a few hours of visibility it may be corrected. Landfall from an uncertain position may involve grave danger. On a ship with a sonic depth finder or a Kelvin sounding machine, depth of water generally gives definite warning of approaching land before any lights or landmarks can be seen. Sometimes a hundred-fathom lead will serve to warn a yacht navigator. Even so, review the possible errors in your position, the character of the coast and its currents, and the weather conditions. If the weather be thick, hesitate to attempt a dangerous landfall until the weather clears.

The young navigator, seeking to develop his judgment in these matters, must study the sea itself. So to do, determine with care your estimate of the ship's position at the time of every fix. Then consider the possible reasons for the error in the E.P. so found.

1209. Two problems given below are simple exercises in dead reckoning by graphic methods. In both cases it is assumed that courses and distances are actually made good over the bottom with no disturbing factors. All of the practical work problems given with Chapters 30 and 33 afford practice in plotting the D.R. as a part of the general problem of plotting the work at sea.

If available, use standard plotting sheets; those fitting either problem include: *Large*, 3000-8, Lats. 40° to 46°; *Small*, 3000 14-Z, Lats. 41° to 45°. Otherwise, small area plotting sheets may be constructed for 4° of Lat. and 4° of Long.*

---

* The author is indebted to Dutton's *Navigation and Nautical Astronomy* for the patterns of the two problems used herein by permission of the United States Naval Institute.

P 1-12. U.S.S. Flagship, on maneuvers, took departure from Lat. 42° 10′ N, Long. 42° 45′ W (D.R. No. 1), variation 28° W, and steamed the following courses and distances:

From D.R. No.	Standard Compass	Dev.	Distance Miles	From D.R. No.	Standard Compass	Dev.	Distance Miles
(1)	096°	2° E	100	(4)	359°	1° W	80
(2)	028°	0	60	(5)	198°	0	90
(3)	299°	1° W	30				

Required: Plot and label the situation and record D.R. position at each change of course. Find course and distance from D.R. No. 6 to point of departure (D.R. No. 1).

Answers:

D.R. positions	D.R. positions
(2) 42° 44′.2 N, 40° 38′.0 W	(5) 44° 53′.5 N, 42° 15′.1 W
(3) 43° 44′.1 N, 40° 38′.0 W	(6) 43° 25′.0 N, 41° 53′.4 W
(4) 43° 44′.1 N, 41° 19′.4 W	

Course from D.R. No. 6 to point of departure (D.R. No. 1) 206°.8, distance 84 miles.

P 2-12. U.S.S. Concord, engaged in maneuvers, fixes her position at 0400 in Lat. 41° 50′.0 N, Long. 178° 09′.0 W. From each of the times listed below, the given course and speed was continued until the next given time.

0400, C 312°, S 15 kts.	1700, C 040°, S 20 kts.
0800, C 328°, S 12 kts.	1745, C 040°, S 10 kts.
1300, C 009°, S 12 kts.	1915, C 194°, S 12.6 kts.
1500, C 009°, S 18 kts.	0426, to rendezvous

Required: Plot and label the situation and record D.R. position at each of the given times. Find course and speed from 0426 D.R. to rendezvous at 0608 in Lat. 42° 10′.0 N, Long. 179° 46′.0 E.

Answers:

D.R. at 0800, 42° 30′.3 N, 179° 09′.4 W	1745, 44° 32′.0 N, 179° 26′.9 W
1300, 43° 21′.0 N, 179° 53′.0 W	1915, 44° 43′.3 N, 179° 13′.6 W
1500, 43° 44′.8 N, 179° 48′.0 W	0426, 42° 51′.0 N, 179° 52′.2 W
1700, 44° 20′.5 N, 179° 40′.1 W	

Course from 0426 to rendezvous 201°.5, speed 26 knots.

1210. The maneuvering board. A single ship is concerned with plotting its own position as it moves across the ocean, but when it is in the presence of other ships, the ability to maneuver efficiently to avoid collision or to take station in formation, requires that the relative movements of the ship be plotted, as related to the other vessels.

The accepted method to this end is to plot on a Maneuvering Board.

Plots of this kind are used in many phases of Naval operations. A good beginning toward learning the use of this type of plotting can be found in *Appendix III, Radar Plotting.*

13. LORAN, RADAR AND
SATELLITE NAVIGATION

1301. Loran, developed during World War II, is an electronic *long-range navigation* system by means of which a navigator can determine accurately one or more lines of position in all weathers and at great distances from shore. The system makes use of many special, shore-based *loran transmitting stations* operating in pairs; and a shipboard *receiver-indicator* capable of measuring small time differences electrically. Special charts and tables show the geographical coordinates where these time differences exist.

1302. Two loran systems are in operation (1966); Loran-A, the original system (formerly called "standard loran"), and Loran-C, a new system capable of extraordinary accuracy at extreme range. The mobile receiver-indicator of Loran-A (Fig. 1310) is relatively inexpensive, and the range and accuracy of the system are sufficient for ordinary navigation. To achieve fully the very accurate, very long-range results of which Loran-C is capable requires an automatic, high-precision receiver. However, manually operated receiver-indicators have been designed with which it is claimed that an experienced operator using great care may be able to obtain accuracies as good or perhaps slightly better than with Loran-A and over a somewhat larger area. It is possible to modify a Loran-A receiver-indicator so as to receive Loran-C signals.

The following table compares the pertinent characteristics of the two systems:

	Loran-A	Loran-C
Frequency	3 channels in 1850 to 1950 Khz band	90-110 Khz
Approximate range	700 miles day (groundwave), 1,400 miles night (groundwave and skywave).	1,200–1,500 miles groundwave.
Time difference measurement technique.	Envelope superposition, manual	Automatic, electronic, envelope (coarse) and cycle (fine).
Transmission	Single pulse from each station	Multipulse.

	Loran-A	Loran-C
Indication of malfunction	Yes	Yes.
Accuracy	1 mile groundwave, 6 miles skywave, most accurate near baseline; degrades as distance between loran lines increases, poor in baseline extension areas.	1,500 feet at 1,000 miles.
Position determination	Intersection of separate LOP from each pair.	Continuous fix from chain.

1302. A loran line of position is obtained by measuring time differences between radio signals from two different known sources. Loran transmitting stations operate in pairs and are located throughout the world in a network that provides practically universal loran coverage over the main travelled routes. The operation of the U.S.-controlled stations is one of the many functions of the U.S. Coast Guard Service. Fig. 1302 shows the world areas covered by Loran-A.

Each pair of stations consists of a master station and a slave station. The distance between any two usually varies from 200 to 400 miles. A master station is often located, where possible, between two slave stations and by means of "double pulsing" controls the signals of both adjacent slave stations, using different recurrence rates for each one. Slave stations can also be "double pulsed" to serve more than one master station. In this way more loran transmitting units can be established with the use of fewer stations.

Carefully synchronized electrical signals are sent out from both the master station and the slave station. These are short power bursts or *pulses* of radio energy broadcast in all directions.

The *pulses* recur at regular intervals and provide precise references for use in time measurements. The radio *pulses* travel out from the transmitter at a constant, known velocity of 162,000 nautical miles per second, or 983 feet per millionth of a second, commonly referred to as a microsecond. One nautical mile is covered in 6.18 microseconds. Therefore, distance can be measured in radio wave travel time as easily as in miles or feet, given a suitable measuring device.

1303. The loran principle is as follows:

(1) Radio signals consisting of short timed *pulses* are broadcast from a pair of shore-based loran transmitting stations.

(2) These signals are received aboard ship on a specially designed radio receiver.

(3) The difference in time of arrival (T) of the signals from the two stations is measured on a special indicator. The difference between

LORAN-A COVERAGE DIAGRAM

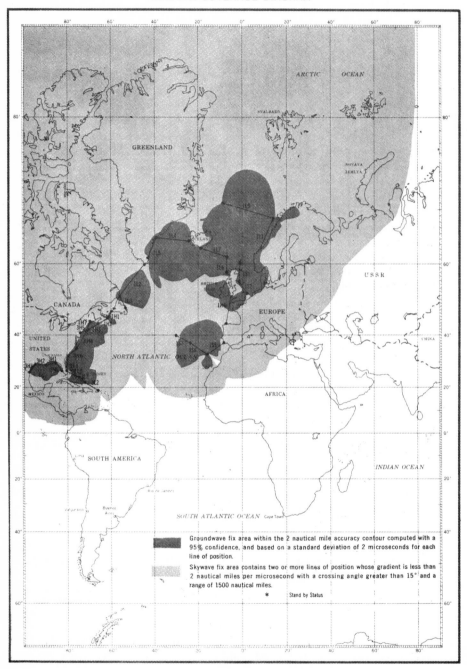

Groundwave fix area within the 2 nautical mile accuracy contour computed with a 95% confidence, and based on a standard deviation of 2 microseconds for each line of position.

Skywave fix area contains two or more lines of position whose gradient is less than 2 nautical miles per microsecond with a crossing angle greater than 15° and a range of 1500 nautical miles.

＊   Stand by Status

FIGURE 1302

LORAN-C COVERAGE DIAGRAM

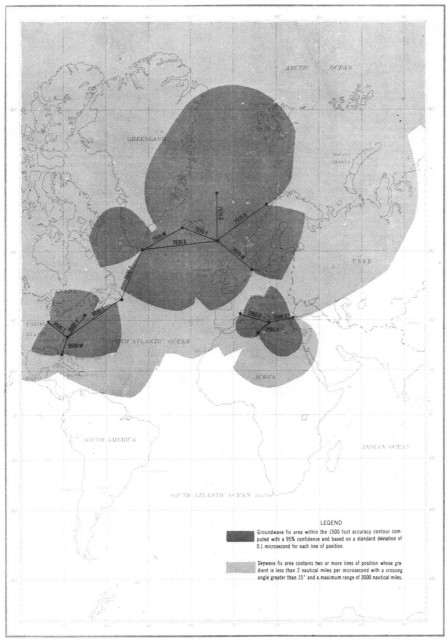

FIGURE 1302a

LORAN-A COVERAGE DIAGRAM

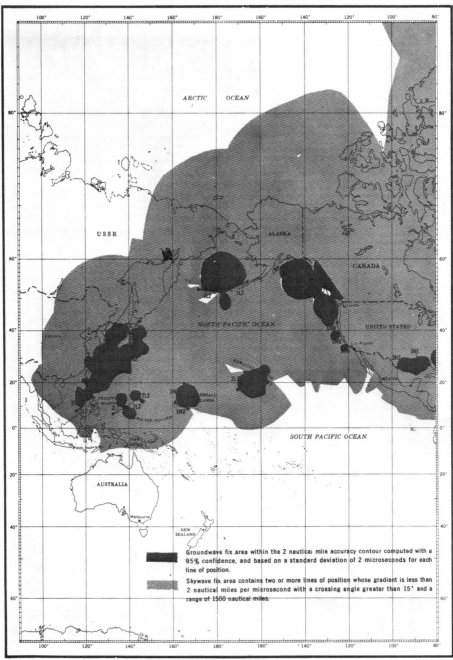

Figure 1302b

LORAN-C COVERAGE DIAGRAM

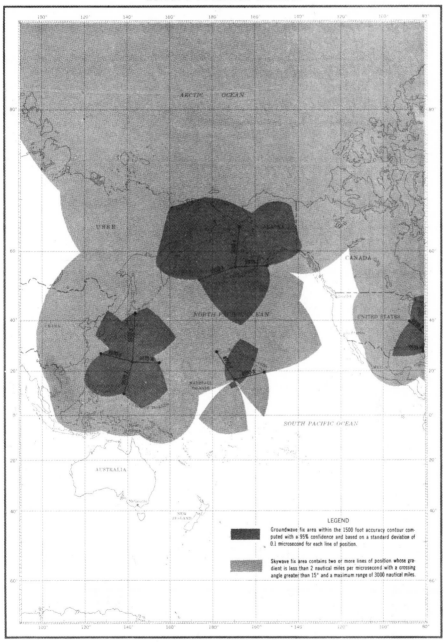

LEGEND

Groundwave fix area within the 1500 foot accuracy contour computed with a 95% confidence and based on a standard deviation of 0.1 microsecond for each line of position.

Skywave fix area contains two or more lines of position whose gradient is less than 2 nautical miles per microsecond with a crossing angle greater than 15° and a maximum range of 3000 nautical miles.

FIGURE 1302c

Loran-A and Loran-C lies mainly in the method used for measuring the time differences.

(4) This measured time difference (T) is used to determine from loran tables or charts, the loran line of position on the earth's surface.

(5) Two or more lines of position, determined from two or more pairs of stations, are crossed to obtain a loran fix. Loran lines can also be crossed with celestial or any other lines of position.

1304. Identification of a loran station depends entirely on the *radio frequency* and *pulse repetition rate* (P.R.R.) assigned to that station.

Different pairs of loran stations operate on different radio frequencies. The Channel switch on the receiver, Fig. 1310, is used to select the desired frequency channel. For Loran-A, there are four channels: (1) 1950 kc., (2) 1850 kc., (3) 1900 kc., and (4, not now used) 1750 kc. The Loran-C channel is 100 kc.

Each loran pair is further identified by its pulse repetition rate; that is, the rate at which its pulses are transmitted. These rates fall into three broad groups as follows:

BASIC RATE	PULSES PER SECOND	INTERVAL (MICROSECONDS)
Special (S)	20	50,000
Low (L)	25	40,000
High (H)	$33\frac{1}{3}$	30,000

Specific repetition rates are allocated within these groups in eight *decreasing* increments of 100 microseconds from 0 (no decrease in interval) to 7 (700 microsecond shorter interval). Thus, for example, the 3H 0 loran rate for the Gulf of Mexico is transmitted at 1900 kc. with 30,000 microseconds between pulses. The 2L 2 rate in the West Indies is transmitted at 1850 kc. with 39,800 microseconds between pulses.

The desired P.R.R. is selected by the Rate switch shown in Fig. 1310.

An extremely accurate timing device in both master and slave stations regulates the pulse repetition rate (P.R.R.), and properly synchronizes the signals from the two stations of the pair. The master and slave pulses are not transmitted simultaneously. Each slave pulse is delayed by a carefully controlled amount which makes the *constant time difference* lines increase continuously from a minimum value at the slave station to a maximum at the master station. This timing delay also provides a means of identifying which signal is from each station even though the signals look exactly alike.

Constant vigilance at both master and slave stations safeguards the accuracy of timing the signals. Electrical failure or mechanical troubles can temporarily cause incorrect signals from a pair of stations, but when this happens an easily recognizable *trouble blinking signal* warns the navigator that the signals are not to be used until the blinking ceases.

1305. Loran lines of position have been carefully precomputed and can be selected on a series of *Loran Charts* covering various parts of the world, on which are printed the computed loran lines from transmitting stations whose signals are within range. *Loran Tables* can also be used to plot loran lines of position on an ordinary chart or plotting sheet.

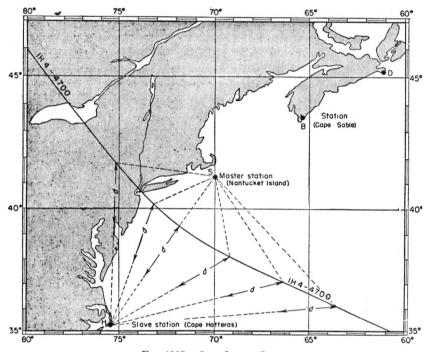

FIG. 1305.   ONE LORAN LINE.

The same time difference measurement will be obtained at all points on this loran line of position due to the uniform difference in distance labelled (d) between solid arrows.

The various loran lines of position are based on the time difference between the arrival of the signal from the master station and the time of arrival of the synchronized signal from its slave station. Loran lines have been precomputed by plotting a series of points at which the *same* time difference exists, and connecting these points to provide a *line of constant time difference*. Fig. 1305 shows one loran line. The same time difference measurement will be obtained at all points on this loran line of position, due to the constant difference in distance labelled (d), between solid arrows.

The difference in time of arrival at the ship of signals from a known pair of transmitting stations is measured by the loran receiving equipment. With this difference your loran line of position is identified on a *Loran Chart* and the ship is somewhere along that line.

Readings from a second pair of stations identifies another loran line on which the ship's position lies. Where the two or more lines found in this way intersect is the ship's position, and reference to the chart provides the latitude and longitude.

1306. Loran Navigation Charts are issued by DMAHC and the NOS. The scales used vary with the requirements of the navigator. Publication No. 1-N, issued by the DMAHC, catalogues the nautical Loran Charts.

Loran lines of position are printed on the *Charts* for convenient units of time difference from various pairs of stations within range, as in Fig. 1306. Lines are separated by time difference varying from 5 to 100 microseconds, depending on the scale of the chart. Each line is marked with the station identification *(frequency channel* and *pulse repetition rate)* and the *constant time difference* for that line. Lines from various station pairs are printed in different colors for further identification.

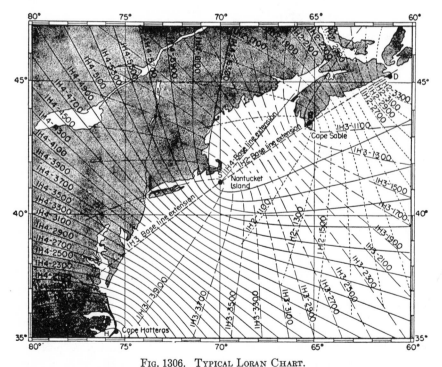

FIG. 1306. TYPICAL LORAN CHART.

Showing lines of position for three pairs of stations.

At this point do the two following examples, using Fig. 1306 as your *Loran Chart.*

Example I. Your ship's 1120 D.R. position is Lat. 41° 40′ N, Long. 66° 27′ W. Using your loran Receiver-Indicator you obtain readings from two pairs of stations as follows:

TIME	STATION PAIR	TIME DIFFERENCE
1120	1H 3	2100
1122	1H 4	6300

What is latitude and longitude of 1120 loran fix?
Ans. 1120 loran fix; Lat. 41° 41′.3 N, Long. 66° 11′.2 W.

In Example I find the loran line of position for a time difference of 2100 in the family of lines labelled 1H 3. Follow it until.it crosses the 1H 4 line labelled 6300. The loran fix is at the intersection. Latitude and longitude are then read from their scales on the chart.

Example II. Ship's 1500 D.R. position is Lat. 41° 29′ N, Long. 65° 23′ W. Time difference readings obtained from three pairs of stations were as follows:

TIME	STATION PAIR	TIME DIFFERENCE
1458	1H 3	1900
1500	1H 4	6200
1502	1H 2	1300

What is latitude and longitude of 1500 loran fix?
Ans. 1500 loran fix; Lat. 41° 26′.2 N, Long. 65° 11′ W.

The same method of selecting the properly labelled loran lines is used as in Example I, following them to their intersection. As there is no 1H 4-6200 line printed on the chart in Fig. 1306, the navigator must draw a line interpolated between the 1H 4-6100 line and 1H 4-6300 line, in this case halfway between.

In some areas where signals from five or six stations overlap, only lines from the three or four more useful ones are shown on the *Charts.* Lines of other stations can be obtained from the *Tables.* The *Tables* provide complete ocean coverage for each pair of stations.

1307. Ground waves or sky waves. The ground wave is that portion of the radio signal that travels from the transmitter parallel to the surface of the earth directly to the receiving set. Another portion of the radio energy travels upward and outward, and is reflected by the electrified layers of atmosphere called the ionosphere, back to the receiver. These reflected pulses are known as sky waves.

Loran Charts and *Tables* provide *ground-wave* lines of position. *Sky-wave* corrections, included with both Charts and Tables, reduce a *sky-*

wave time difference reading to its equivalent ground-wave reading. In this way the same lines of position in Charts and Tables can be used for sky waves.

In recording, time difference readings from ground waves are referred to as (T_G) and those from sky waves (T_S).

The ability to differentiate between ground waves or sky waves involves an understanding of the paths of the signals and experience in interpreting their appearance and relative position on the screen.

1308. Loran Tables provide information from which small segments of a loran line of position can be plotted on a chart or plotting sheet.

T	1H 2-1300	
Lat	Lo	Δ
° ′	° ′	
42 30 N	64 51. 1W	-20
42 N	64 59. 1W	-25
41 30 N	65 09. 0W	-30
41 N	65 20. 1W	-35

1H 3-2100		T
L	Δ	Long
° ′		° ′
42 12.7N	-14	66 45W
41 58.3N	-14	66 30W
41 44.8N	-15	66 15W
41 31.8N	-15	66 W

T	1H 3-3600	
Lat.	Lo	Δ
° ′	° ′	
41 30 N	69 24. 2W	+13
41 15 N	69 14. 5W	+12
41 N	69 09. 2W	+13
40 45 N	69 06. 8W	+14

1H 3-1900		T
L	Δ	Long
° ′		° ′
41 49.4N	-14	65 45W
41 38.8N	-15	65 30W
41 28.6N	-16	65 15W
41 18.7N	-17	65 W

1H 4-6200		T
L	Δ	Long
° ′		° ′
40 55.4N	+20	67 30W
41 01.6N	+22	67 W
41 15.0N	+27	66 W
41 29.3N	+31	65 W

1H 4-6300		T
L	Δ	Long
° ′		° ′
41 17.5N	+25	67 30W
41 26.3N	+28	67 W
41 35.6N	+31	66 30W
41 45.0N	+34	66 W

FIG. 1309a. EXCERPTS FROM LORAN TABLES.

The segment of a loran line in the area of the ship's dead reckoning position is all that is necessary to plot.

Several volumes of tables have been prepared by DMAHC and are arranged to provide plotting information divided into particular areas of coverage. Information for each pair of stations is listed in its separate section of the tables.

The tables provide latitude and longitude of points at which the constant time difference reading of a pair of stations would be obtained. After plotting two or three of these points, the line connecting them becomes a loran line of position.

All changes for both *Tables* or *Charts* are published in *Notice to Mariners*.

1309. When using the Loran Tables, enter the section marked with the station identification and turn to the column headed by a time difference reading (T) nearest the one obtained. On the top and bottom line of each page, labelled T, are found the *time difference* designations for each column. Refer to Fig. 1309*a*.

Follow the column headed by this time difference to the point where the combination of latitude (Lat. or L.) and longitude (Long. or Lo.) approximates the latitude and longitude of the ship's dead reckoning position. Take out two or three combinations of latitude and longitude from the lines that show these points surrounding the ship's position.

Locate these points on a chart or plotting sheet and connect with a line. This line will be a segment of a loran line of position (Fig. 1309*b*).

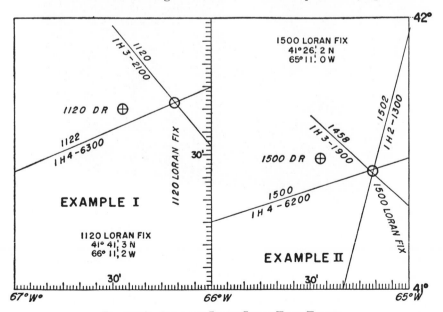

Fig. 1309*b*. Plotting Loran Lines From Tables.

The actual time difference reading will seldom correspond to the tabulated lines; therefore an interpolation must be made to obtain the exact line required. The directions in *Loran Tables* give a simple explanation of this interpolation.

With a second observation of another pair of stations, a second line is obtained and plotted. The point of intersection of the two lines is the loran fix.

As in the case of any line of position, if observed substantially before the time of the fix, it is necessary to advance the line by course and distance covered in the intervening time, if the speed of the vessel warrants this advance. Advanced lines of position are discussed in Chapter 16, §1605, and Chapter 31, §3113.

Examples:

Obtain or construct a plotting sheet covering 2° of latitude and 2° of longitude. Label center lines 41° N and 66° W.

Proceed to plot the necessary segments of the loran lines of position as just described, using the *excerpts* from *Loran Tables* found in Fig. 1309a. Plot lines for Examples I and II stated in §1306. Label lines as

Courtesy of the Radio Corporation of America

FIG. 1310. A DIRECT-READING LORAN RECEIVER-INDICATOR.

indicated in Fig. 1309b with the time above the line. Below the line write the station identification and time difference reading.

1310. Loran receiving equipment varies slightly in design depending on the manufacturer, but each set has the same essential features.

The Receiver-Indicator, Fig. 1310, is a superheterodyne radio set which receives *pulse* signals from loran transmitting stations within range. These *pulses* are displayed in the fluorescent screen of a cathode-ray tube as in television. Modern sets include motor-driven phase shifters and time difference indicators which speed up the operation of matching the signals.

1311. Obtaining a loran reading. The process of finding the line of position on which the ship is located consists of measuring very accurately the time interval between receipt of radio signals from the "master" and "slave" stations. This is accomplished electronically by manipulating the controls of a receiver-indicator, one type of which is shown in Fig. 1310.

The actual operation depends upon the design of the particular receiver-indicator in use, but the principle is the same. The incoming signals appear on the cathode-ray tube as many "pips" moving at various speeds along the two traces. When the switches are set to receive a particular rate such as 1H 5, two of the pips become stationary as shown in Fig. 1311-A. The horizontal distance between these two pips is in fact the electrical equivalent of the desired time difference and can now be measured. By means of the controls, it is possible to adjust the height

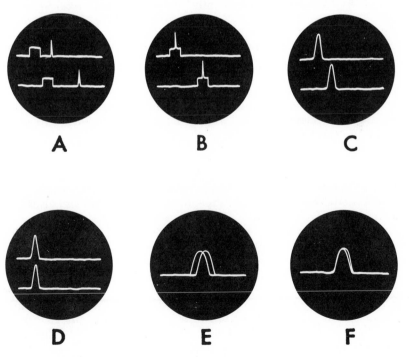

Fig. 1311. Matching Master and Slave Signals to Obtain Loran Reading.

of the two pips either separately or together, to cause them to drift slowly left or right, and to move the raised portion ("pedestal") of the *lower* trace either left or right. The objective is to mount the two pips on the pedestals, master on the left and slave on the right, as in Fig. 1311-B.

It is now possible to expand the tops of the pedestals (Fig. 1311-C), to move the slave pip under the master (Fig. 1311-D), to bring the two traces together (Fig. 1311-E), and to match the *left* sides of the two pips (Fig. 1311-F). This completes the match, and the loran reading is obtained from the dial on the face of the receiver-indicator which registers in microseconds the time interval between the pips.

The shape of ground-wave pips is usually quite stable, and little difficulty is experienced in making a match. Pips from sky waves are often very unstable, resulting in considerable distortion in shape and size of the pips and lessened confidence in the loran reading.

1312. Identification and matching of signals requires actual practice with a loran receiver.

If ground waves can be received from any pair of stations, use them. Weak ground waves are preferable to strong sky waves.

If only sky waves can be received, it is necessary to match the first sky wave from the master station with the first sky wave from the slave station.

As loran lines of position in *Charts* and *Tables* are computed for ground wave signals, the corrections provided with both Charts and Tables must be applied to sky wave readings before using the charts or entering the tables.

It must be clearly understood that loran is an additional aid to navigation and supplements information the navigator obtains from other sources. Loran lines frequently can and should be crossed with other lines to best establish the position of the ship.

*   *   *

1313. Omega. A new electronic hyperbolic navigational system similar to LORAN. It is a long-range phase difference system operating on a frequency of 10 to 14 Khz. It is a worldwide all-weather system for use by ships, aircraft and submarines. Its accuracy is about 1 mile during the day and 2 miles at night. Its operation is based on making phase difference measurements of continuous wave transmissions. Like LORAN, shore transmission stations are used. These stations are situated as follows: Norway, Liberia, Hawaii, North Dakota, Reunion Island, Argentina, Australia, and Japan. In the Omega system, the phase-difference measurement of a 10.2 Khz signal transmitted from two stations provides a hyperbolic line of position. The long base lines, 5000 to 6000 miles as indicated by the position of the stations, low frequency and high power serves to give worldwide coverage and accuracy. Special charts are produced by DMAHC for plotting positions. Although Omega receivers are relatively expensive, they are widely used by the merchant marine as well as the navy. The following chart shows the relative characteristics of radio navigational systems:

System	Frequency Khz	Type Operation	Range (Miles) Day/Night
Omega	10-14	CW phase difference	Worldwide
LORAN C	90-110	Pulse time difference and phase comparison	1200/2400
LORAN A	1850-1950	Pulse time difference	800/1400
Radio Beacon	30-3000	CW transmission	20/200

1314. Radar is another very important electronic device developed for practical use since 1941. With its many and varied applications it is often considered the outstanding technical development of the World War II period. For the navigator, it has become an important aid in piloting, determining position, and preventing collision. The name RADAR is a contraction of Radio Detection and Ranging.

1315. Radar has an advantage over ordinary eyesight as it is not blinded by darkness, fog, rain or snow.

Radar usually can pick up images at greater distances than by direct sight.

It furnishes the navigator with a picture of all objects surrounding the ship at every angle, showing a 360° field of vision at one time.

The bearing and distance of any object from the ship, can be determined simultaneously.

A fix can be plotted from a single object whose position is known, using the bearing and distance obtained by radar.

Radar can also be used in either bad or good visibility to locate and track the courses of individual vessels, or ships in formation.

The pattern on the radar scope maintains continuous relative positions of all reflecting objects.

True motion radar distinguishes moving from stationary objects.

1316. The principle of marine radar is as follows:

(1) Short bursts of radio energy are transmitted in a concentrated beam from a continuously rotating antenna that scans the area surrounding the ship.

(2) Any object in the path of this beam reflects some of this energy back to the antenna.

(3) The reflected energy returning to the antenna is amplified in the receiver and provides a visual indication of the reflecting object.

(4) As the transmitted pulses and their echoes from a reflecting object travel in a straight line, at a uniform speed, the bearing and range of reflecting objects can be determined.

1317. Radar equipment consists of three main units, as shown in Fig. 1317: scanner, transceiver, and indicator.

The *scanner* is usually placed high on the mast or at some other un-

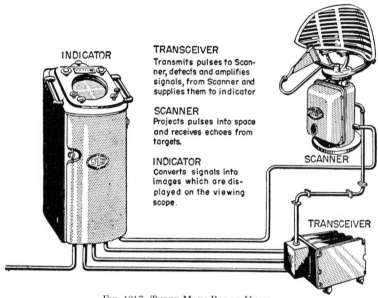

INDICATOR

TRANSCEIVER
Transmits pulses to Scanner, detects and amplifies signals, from Scanner and supplies them to indicator

SCANNER
Projects pulses into space and receives echoes from targets.

INDICATOR
Converts signals into images which are displayed on the viewing scope.

SCANNER

TRANSCEIVER

FIG. 1317. THREE MAIN RADAR UNITS.

obstructed place on the ship where it can rotate and scan the horizon. It sends out a directional beam of energy and receives the echoes from objects visible above the water.

The *transceiver* generates the energy pulses in the beam, and also accepts the returning waves from the scanner. It then converts these into signals which can be used in the indicator.

The *indicator* presents the returning signals on a scope similar to a television screen, in the form of a radar pattern that can be interpreted by the operator.

1318. The scope, as in television, is a cathode-ray tube with its screen surface showing a dark background. This screen is brightened when struck by electrons. A narrow electron beam, synchronized with the rotation of the scanner, travels from the center of the scope to its edge. When reflected energy is received from an object, it causes this rotating electron beam to "paint" bright spots on the dark background of the scope. Because the fluorescent screen retains this picture until it is renewed on each turn of the beam, a chart-like pattern of the surrounding area is formed, together with images of all other reflecting objects. This type of scope is known as a PPI or plan position indicator.

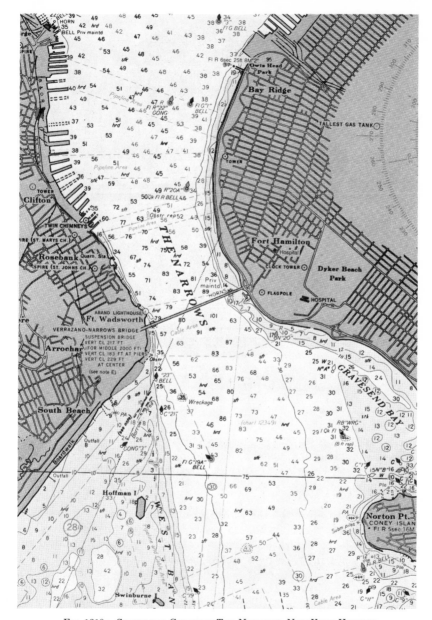

FIG. 1318*a*. SIMPLIFIED CHART OF THE NARROWS, NEW YORK HARBOR.

Fig. 1318*a* is a simplified chart of The Narrows, New York Harbor. Fig. 1318*b* is a radar presentation of the same area. Reflections from several vessels are to be seen on the scope pattern.

162*Primer of Navigation*

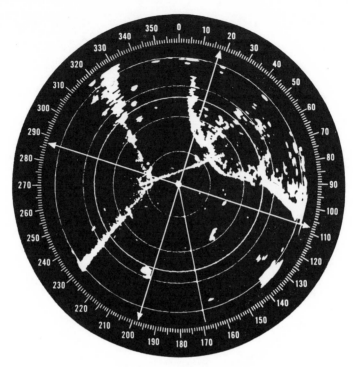

FIG. 1318*b*. RADAR PATTERN OF THE NARROWS, NEW YORK HARBOR. INSTRUMENT SET FOR TRUE BEARING PRESENTATION.

1319. Bearing: As the radio energy has been transmitted in a narrow directional beam controlled by the rotation of the scanner, and as the sweeping electron beam of the tube is synchronized with the same rotation, the reflected images appear on the screen at their actual bearing from the ship.

As in Figs. 1318*b* and 1318*c*, an azimuth scale surrounds the scope. A heading marker indicates the course of the ship. Sighting lines, extending from the center to the azimuth scale, can be directed toward any image and its bearing then read on the azimuth circle.

Some sets provide a choice of *true* or *relative* bearing presentation. If the switch is set at TRUE, the heading marker will appear on the ship's true course, and true North will appear at the top of the scope (0° on the circle), the picture being oriented by the gyro compass. All other bearings will be read from the azimuth scale as true bearings.

When turned to REL, the heading marker of the ship points to 0°, and "dead ahead" will always be at the top of the scope. All other bearings will be relative to the ship's heading.

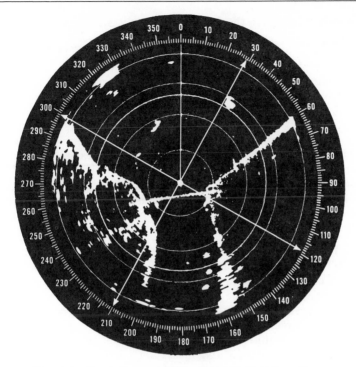

Fig. 1318c. Radar Pattern of The Narrows, New York Harbor.
Instrument Set for Relative Bearing Presentation.

The pattern on Fig. 1318*b* presents the true bearing position. The heading marker shows the ship's course of 169° as it leaves the harbor. One of the adjustable sighting lines is directed toward Hoffman Island, showing a true bearing of 198° (or 029° to the right of the ship's heading).

The pattern on Fig. 1318*c* presents the relative bearing position. The heading marker points to 0° at the top of the scope, or "dead ahead." The sighting line toward Hoffman Island shows a relative bearing of 029° to the right of the ship's heading.

1320. Range is determined by measuring the distance from the center of the scope to the particular image of the reflecting object. The concentric range marker circles appear on the scope at definite known intervals, representing specific ranges. A comparison of the position of the image to the range circles approximates its range.

Radar sets provide a selection of over-all range scales. Since all range scales use the same effective viewing area on the scope, the shorter the range scale selected the larger each image will appear, with resulting improvement in definition. A typical set provides a selection of 1, 2, 6, 15, and 30-mile over-all range scales. Choice depends on the requirements of the navigator, for clarity or distance. The space between the fixed range marker circles on such a radar would be ½ mile for the 1 and

2-mile ranges, 2 miles for the 6-mile range, and 5 miles for the 15 and 30-mile ranges.

Turn to Figs. 1318*a* and 1318*b*. From the chart of The Narrows locate the image of Hoffman Island on the radar pattern. Estimate the range of Hoffman Island from the ship. The instrument in this Figure was set for an over-all range of 2 miles, and the distance between marker circles is ½ mile. Hoffman Island is seen to be about 1⅓ miles away from the ship.

On some radars a variable range marker circle measures ranges with more accuracy than can be estimated from the fixed range circles. The variable circle can be manually changed in radius to intersect any target image for which range is to be measured. This range measurement is read from a meter on the instrument panel, showing the distance in miles and tenths of miles. Figs. 1318*b* and 1318*c* show the variable range marker line touching the image of Hoffman Island.

1321. **Radar scope interpretation** requires considerable training and practice. The operator must know how to use the controls, varying in type and arrangement with each make of instrument, in such a way as to obtain a clear pattern on the scope under varying conditions of weather and sea. He must select the most practical scale for his requirements as well as the true or relative pattern presentation.

He must become familiar with the capabilities of the particular radar he uses, such as its minimum and maximum ranges, also the distances indicated between the fixed range marker circles of his set, at each over-all range setting. The obstruction of his ship's own mast or stack in the path of the transmitted energy will reduce the maximum range or may entirely obscure small targets in that particular direction.

The operator must understand the general limitations of radar. A high shore line or large reflecting object will prevent the radar beam from travelling further in that direction and will create a shadow obscuring the area beyond it. A low coastline with hills in the immediate background may only present the reflection of the hills on the scope, and give a false impression of the distance off shore. The echo from a ship near shore may be masked out by the larger and stronger echo from the shore line itself. Vessels or other objects located on the same bearing, or at the same distance from the antenna, may appear on the screen as only one echo, if the reflecting objects are close together. Choppy seas may cause sufficient interference to obscure some targets. Several other conditions can exist where reflections may cause false echoes to appear on the scope.

1322. Radar fixes can be obtained when the bearing and range of one or more objects, having known fixed positions, is determined from the pattern on the radar scope.

Return to Chapter 9, Piloting, which discusses plotting fixes from *cross bearings*, as well as *bearing and distance*, of fixed known objects.

1323. Radar plotting. To utilize fully the great potentialities of radar, a plot of successive ranges and bearings is required. A description of radar plotting and interpretation of relative movement is contained in Annex III. DMAHC issues a Radar Plotting Manual (Pub. 257) and a Radar Navigation Manual (Pub. 1310) which explain with illustrations the use of radar in meeting, crossing, overtaking and positioning situations.

1324. Satellite Navigation. The navigation satellite system is based on the principle of the measurement of the doppler shift of a radio signal transmitted from a satellite in a known position in its orbit by a receiver on the earth's surface. The measurement of doppler shift at a given moment is unique to the relative position of the receiver to the satellite, Accordingly, by knowing the position of the satellite, the approximate position of the receiver and having the capability of measuring the doppler shift transmitted by the satellite the navigator can determine his relative position to the satellite and therefore his own precise latitude and longitude.

Doppler shift is the apparent change in frequency observed at a ship of a fixed frequency transmitted from a satellite when the distance between the ship and the satellite is changing. When the satellite is approaching the ship the frequency is slightly higher and when going away from the ship slightly lower. When the received signal frequency is the same as the satellite fixed frequency the satellite is at its closest point of approach to the ship.

The U. S. Navy Satellite System (NAVSAT) consists of an integration of three components: the satellite orbiting the earth, the ground support network and the receiver aboard the ship.

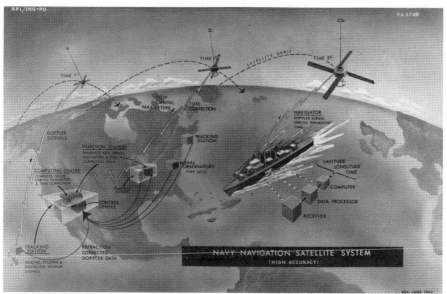

Fig. 1324. (Courtesy Applied Physics Lab, The Johns Hopkins University)

The satellite is in circular polar orbit at about 600 miles above the earth and makes a complete orbit every 107 minutes. Six satellites have been placed in orbit separated by approximately 45 degrees of longitude. The constellation of orbits forms a "birdcage" within which the earth rotates and thereby carries the ship receiver past each orbit in turn making it possible to take a fix at intervals of 35 to 100 minutes of time. Each satellite can be considered as a self-contained navigation beacon transmitting two stable radio frequencies (150 and 400 Mhz), timing marks and a navigational message describing its position as a function of time.

The ground support network consists of four tracking stations, a computing center and two injection stations. By tracking the satellites the tracing stations provide information to the computing center to determine the parameters of the orbit of the satellite. The computing center in turn computes the predicted orbital parameters and transmits this plus time corrections to the injection station in the form of a navigational message. The injection station in turn transmits the navigational message and time correction to the orbiting satellite.

The navigation receiver aboard ship receives the stable radio frequency as affected by the doppler effect, the navigational message and time and makes the doppler measurement from the satellite. Combined with the receiver is a small digital computer for processing the doppler measurement and the navigational message. A typical satellite pass will be above the horizon for 10 to 18 minutes during which time 20 to 40 doppler measurements can be collected. Using the doppler measurements, navigational message information, ships estimated position and ships speed and course the computer determines a precise position thus reading out to the navigator latitude, longitude and time.

Compared to celestial navigation fixes, NAVSAT positions are very accurate. The system is capable of producing accuracies to 0.10 of a nautical mile.

1325. Global Positioning System.   The Department of Defense is developing a satellite navigation system called NAVSTAR or GPS (Global Positioning System) which operates on the same principle as NAVSAT but is extended to permit world-wide, all weather use on a 24 hour basis for marine, air and land navigators. The GPS will have a configuration of 24 satellites arranged in 3 orbital planes with 8 satellites in each plane. Each orbital plane is inclined 63° to the equatorial plane and offset one from the other by 120° of longitude. The satellite trace is at an altitude of about 11,000 nautical miles. As the earth rotates under the orbital traces of satellites the navigator is thereby within range to take measurements on at least six of the satellites simultaneously or in quick succession to determine time, latitude, longitude and altitude. It is expected that positional accuracies will be 10 meters or less in three dimensions. The system is presently in the development stage, the first satellite having been launched in 1978. Full operational status is not expected until the 1987-90 time frame if operational implementation is approved. If its potential applications to marine, air and land navigation are realized, its use is limited only by the imagination.

14. OUTWARD BOUND

BEFORE proceeding to sea and the problems of a navigator long out of sight of land, it is well to summarize certain matters with which the student is assumed to be familiar.

1401. Review. The *earth* is practically a sphere whose axis intersects its surface at the true north and true south poles. The equator is a great circle around the earth midway between the poles. Meridians are halves of great circles from pole to pole and therefore at right angles to the equator. Latitude is the arc of a meridian, north or south, from equator to ship. Longitude is the arc of the equator east or west from meridian of Greenwich to meridian of ship.

The *position* of any point on the earth's surface may be defined by its latitude, N or S, and its longitude, E or W. True *direction* is the angle a line makes with a meridian. The principal source of the mariner's knowledge of direction is the compass. The magnetic compass is subject to two errors, deviation and variation. The navigator must understand correcting a compass reading to true, and reversing a true course to a compass course. *Distance* is measured in nautical miles, the length of a nautical mile being the length of 1′ of latitude or 1′ of any great circle of the earth.

A *Mercator chart* is so constructed that vertical parallel lines represent meridians, which on a globe converge toward the poles. On such a chart a straight line represents the course to steer continuously from one point to another, which may be a curved line when plotted on a globe. Latitude is measured by the scales at the sides of the chart; 1′ of the latitude scale measures 1 mile in that latitude. Longitude is measured by scales across the top and the bottom, but the longitude scales must never be used as a measure of distance. Plotting sheets also are constructed on Mercator's projection.

Dead reckoning is the process of finding the ship's position by plotting courses steered and distances run, and checking and correcting the D.R.

167

whenever opportunity offers. It requires accurate chart work, good judgment, and much experience best gained from careful work along the coast.

Although a competent deep-sea navigator may not have practiced intricate coastwise piloting, lack of a thorough working knowledge of the compass, charts, and keeping the reckoning is an almost insurmountable handicap to the study and successful practice of celestial navigation.

1402. From coast to sea. The transition from coastwise piloting to navigation at sea is illustrated in Fig. 1402 by an example of a vessel outward bound from the eastern entrance to Long Island Sound. The vagaries of courses and distances used to facilitate the illustration may be accounted for by assuming the vessel to be a sailing craft subject to shifting winds or calms and to tidal currents which play the devil in these waters. Cerberus Shoal is well named.

As a coastwise pilot, the navigator observes that his ship is 1 mile true south of Race Rock Light and marks this position at (1) on the chart. From this point of departure the ship proceeds on a 118° true course, 20.5 miles, when the D.R. position is plotted at (2). This may be in error; the safe assumption is that the ship may not be at the D.R. point but elsewhere. Under unfavorable conditions it may be miles away.

Fortunately, especially at night, it is easy to check and correct this D.R. position at (2). The great light known as Block Island Southeast flashes green every few seconds, and with aid of ship's compass the navigator notes the bearing of the light as 18°. The position of the ship may be uncertain but the position of this man-made lighthouse is known to be exactly where it is shown on the chart. Thus a line drawn in the direction of 18° through the lighthouse is a *line of position,* shown by dots, any one of which may be the position of the ship. Observe that this single observation of the light gives only a line of position and does not locate the ship on that line; the best estimate of the ship's position would be at (3) where the perpendicular from the D.R. intersects the Block Island line.

However, Montauk is flashing white every 5 seconds and bears 283° from the ship. A line in this direction through Montauk is also a line of position and the ship must be somewhere along this line. Assuming the two bearings to have been taken simultaneously, one knows that the ship is somewhere on the Block Island line and somewhere on the Montauk line and therefore must be at that point where the two lines of position intersect. In this way the D.R. position at (2) has been corrected to the *fix* at (4) from which ship proceeds, 228° true, 13.5 miles, to the D.R. marked (5). Block Island Southeast is no longer visible, but Montauk can be seen bearing almost exactly true north. With this information, a single line of position is drawn; but no other land-lighthouse is visible from which a second line of position can be had for a fix.

As a navigator at sea, one must turn to the *Lighthouses in the Sky* which are: the sun and moon, four planets, and the brighter stars. Whenever an accurately timed altitude of any one of these navigational bodies

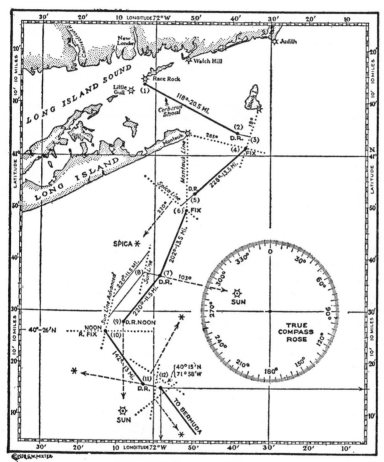

FIG. 1402. OUTWARD BOUND.

can be had, a line of position may be plotted with considerable accuracy. Navigating by lines of position so found is the very essence of modern practice. This so-called new navigation had its genesis on December 17, 1837, in the discovery by Captain Thomas H. Sumner, an American shipmaster, that a single observation, taken at any time, sufficed for determining a line on the chart somewhere on which the ship must be.

Sumner lines are at right angles to the bearing of the body observed, and in this way differ from lines representing bearings of land-lighthouses. In either case a single observation gives only a line of position and does not give a ship's position other than at some undetermined point on the line. Methods for finding Sumner lines are dealt with in later chapters; their use will be understood by continuing the outward bound voyage.

The bearing of Montauk from the D.R. position (5) has been noted and plotted as a line of position. Immediately thereafter, at morning twilight, the navigator observes the star Spica, bearing 220°, and computes and plots the Spica line at right angles to the star's bearing. The intersection of this Sumner line with the Montauk line gives the fix at (6). From this point, the ship sails to (7) and the sun is observed to the eastward, the resulting sun line indicating the ship to be somewhat west of its D.R. position which, however, was not moved west until noon. Thereafter conditions dictate a change in course, along which the ship sails until the traditional noon sight of the sun bearing true south gives a line of position which is the parallel of latitude of 40° 26′ N.

To obtain the customary noon fix the navigator, with parallel rulers, moves forward the morning sun line marked (8) by the course and distance estimated to have been made good from D.R. (7) to D.R. (9). Thus, in effect, each possible position marked by dots on the morning line has been advanced by the course, and the distance made good from the time of the morning sight to time of the noon sight and, assuming no errors, the ship is somewhere on this sun line as advanced. The intersection of such a line with a later line is called a running fix and in the case on the chart marks the ship's noon position at (10), Lat. 40° 26′ N, Long. 72° 13′ W.

In the afternoon a shift of wind and light air results in a course of 142° for a distance of only 13 miles to the D.R. marked (11) at evening twilight, when the skillful navigator, knowing in advance those stars which best will serve his purpose, observes three stars at almost the same time. The resulting three lines of position give a fix within a triangle. Theoretically, three or more lines of position, determined from observations taken simultaneously, should intersect at a point. Practically, results as shown are excellent and the resulting fix may be considered accurate.

The preceding discussion and the chart indicate that plotting the reckoning and correcting the D.R. by lines of position are important elements of both coastwise and deep-sea navigation. The next step is to develop the methods of determining necessary position lines, or Sumner lines, when out of sight of land.

15. LIGHTHOUSES IN THE SKY

THE title of this chapter suggests both the mystery which seems always to have surrounded the work of the navigator and the simplicity of the modern conception of the old principles which guide oceangoing vessels. The text, based on a lecture before The Franklin Institute of the State of Pennsylvania, presents a picture of celestial navigation as a background for further study of the art as practiced at sea or in the air.

1501. The celestial sphere and the earth. The celestial bodies, of which there are a vast and unknown number, are distributed throughout an infinitely great universe and include the earth, the sun, and the various other bodies observed by mariners. The earth is assumed to be at the center of the universe, and all other celestial bodies, regardless of their enormously varying distances from the earth, appear as upon the great dome of the heavens, or as upon the inner surface of the hollow ball called the celestial sphere.

The relation of this imaginary sphere to the earth is suggested by Fig. 1501, which necessarily shows the earth as too large and the surrounding celestial sphere as far too small. Poles and equator of the celestial sphere are always directly over those of the earth, and the axes of the spheres coincide. The earth's center is the center of the astronomical universe. The ship is on the surface of the earth; sun, moon, and stars all appear as on the celestial sphere, although only five stars are shown in the picture.

1502. A rotating chart. On a clear, dark night, look carefully at the stars directly overhead and also at those near the eastern and western horizons. An hour or two later the stars that were overhead will appear to have moved westward; new stars will have risen in the east; and the stars first seen near the western horizon will have set. The entire celestial sphere, on which the heavenly bodies are seen, appears to rotate from east to west around the earth although the stars become invisible as the sun rises, moves westward, and sets.

A further illustration of this apparent westward motion may be obtained by examining the succession of charts of the fixed stars in Chapter 31, remembering that the stars are always overhead although unseen in daylight. The charts are drawn as if one were looking down from outside the celestial sphere at some point on the earth in 40° N latitude. Each chart pictures the heavens two hours later than the preceding

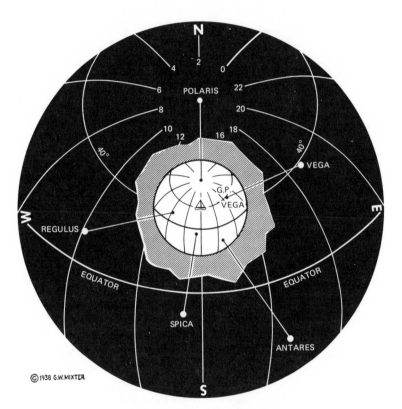

**THE CELESTIAL SPHERE
AND THE EARTH**

Fig. 1501.

chart. Thus, as one turns the pages and watches succeeding positions of various stars, the celestial sphere will seem to move westward. Sun, moon, and planets, ever present, are not shown on these charts because they gradually change their positions among the fixed stars.

The rotation of the earth on its axis is the principal cause of the apparent motion of the heavenly bodies but it is simpler to think of the earth as stationary with all of the other bodies revolving around and about the earth. The stars remain in almost fixed positions on the celestial sphere, and thus the apparent motion of the stars is most simple, although the stars approximately overhead at a given hour of the evening change from month to month. The sun, slowly falling back, takes about 4 minutes longer to appear to move around the earth than do the stars, and, unlike the stars, the sun is seen to move from north to south and back again once each year. The moon changes its position more rapidly than any of the other bodies. The apparent position of planets is most irregular. Were one further to amplify this sketch of the universe and discuss the actual motions of heavenly bodies, it would emphasize that the navigator deals with four quite different types of Lighthouses in the Sky, sun, moon, stars, and planets, whose varying apparent positions over the earth are caused by their own motion and the motions of the earth.

1503. Geographic position of an observed body. A lighthouse or other landmark serves as a guide when piloting only because its fixed position is shown on the chart. For the purposes of the navigator it is equally necessary to define the apparent position of the sun, for example, at the instant it is observed.

An easy way to understand the sun's position as related to the earth at any moment is to imagine one's self at the center of the earth, which is the common center of both spheres. Then, thinking of the earth as only a cellophane globe, the sun will be seen at a point on its surface, called the geographic position (G.P.) of the sun. Or a plumb line from sun to earth will mark the same point, sometimes termed the sub-solar point. Fig. 1501 illustrates the sub-stellar point or geographic position of the star Vega which marks its momentary position for the navigator. Such positions are always moving, but, if the time of an observation is known by chronometer or other exact timekeeper, the latitude (declination) and longitude (Greenwich hour angle) of any navigational body at the instant it is observed may be taken from the Almanac.

Thinking of the apparent position of a celestial body at any moment as a point on the earth is an old conception often neglected in the teaching of navigation. It is far simpler to bring sun, moon, and stars to earth than to deal with their positions as on another sphere. So doing with chronometer and Almanac, which is a part of the technique of practical navigation, will be discussed in later chapters. For the moment it is sufficient to remember that each navigational body, at any instant of time, is directly over a point on the earth and that the position of such a point may be determined with almost the accuracy of the position of a land-lighthouse on a chart. It will be shown how, with such information available, a line of position may be had whenever a timed altitude of sun, moon, or star can be observed.

1504. Altitudes. Before going further with the principles which underlie modern navigation it is essential to understand the nature of the altitude figures used in the navigator's final computations.

Altitudes as observed with the sextant are necessarily taken from varying heights of eye above the spherical surface of the sea, and, in the case of the sun, usually are measured to its lower edge as in Fig. 1504. Succeeding drawings will indicate that the corrected or so-called true altitude of the center of the observed body above the celestial horizon must be used when determining lines of position. Correcting a sextant altitude (Chap. 19) involves only the addition or subtraction of a few figures, but the altitude must be corrected, otherwise serious errors in position may result. An altitude observed by bubble sextant from a plane in the air must also be corrected to true. In either case correcting an altitude has the effect of placing *the observer at the center of the earth.*

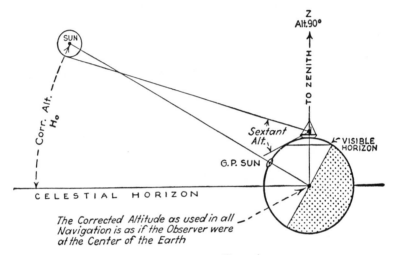

FIG. 1504. CORRECTED OR TRUE ALTITUDE.

1505. Use of true altitudes. The next step is to develop how altitudes so corrected are used for checking the ship's position. Figure 1505 shows a line from the center of the earth through the ship on the earth's surface and continuing upward to the zenith, which is the point on the celestial sphere directly over the ship. The imaginary celestial horizon is drawn at right angles to this line, and therefore the altitude of the zenith above the celestial horizon is always 90°. The sun is shown with a corrected altitude of 50°, leaving 40° from sun to zenith, or 40° from G.P. sun to a ship which is directly under the zenith.

Thus, coming down to earth, the distance from ship to G.P. sun is found to be 40°. This may be expressed in miles because by definition a nautical mile is the length of 1′ of arc of any great circle of the earth. As there are 60′ of arc in each degree, 40° would equal 60′ × 40, or 2400′ of arc, or 2400 nautical miles. This distance was determined with the aid of the sextant. When conditions are favorable for observing altitudes, distances so determined may be considered as accurate within one-half mile.

1506. Circle of equal altitudes. Assume the navigator has determined the true altitude of the sun at an accurately known time. With this information one may find:

(1) *Position* of the G.P. *Sun,* as taken from the Almanac for date and time of observation.

(2) *Distance from Ship to G.P. Sun,* which is 90° less the true altitude as determined by correcting the sextant reading.

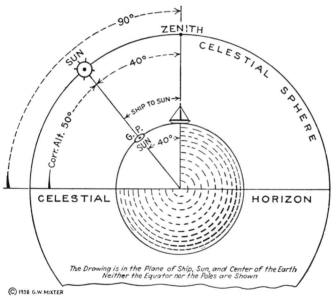

USE OF ALTITUDES
To find Distance, Ship to G.P. Sun

Fig. 1505.

Any observer who finds the same altitude, whether he be north, south, east, or west, or in any other direction from the sun, will be the same distance from the sun. The navigator may be any one of these observers. Therefore, all that is known from a single timed observation of any celestial body is that the ship is *somewhere on a circle of equal altitudes* whose center is the G.P. of the body, and whose radius is the distance from that position to the ship.

The circle of equal altitudes may be drawn on a globe or projected on a chart as in Fig. 1506. The G.P. sun, on the Atlantic Ocean, is 5° S of the equator and in 15° W longitude. The corrected altitude is 50°, and therefore the radius of the circle, or distance from ship to sun, is 40°, which, when reduced to minutes of arc, represents 2400 nautical miles. The peculiar, somewhat elliptical shape results from plotting the circle on a Mercator chart. The only definite knowledge obtained from the timed altitude of the sun is that the ship is somewhere on this circle: off Gibraltar, off the Cape of Good Hope, or in any one of an infinite number of other positions in the South or North Atlantic Oceans.

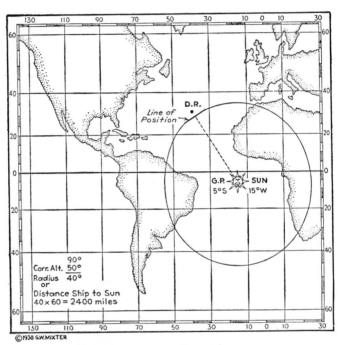

FIG. 1506. CIRCLE OF EQUAL ALTITUDES.

By dead reckoning from the last fix, however, the navigator knows his approximate position, which may be any point within a relatively small area. With this added knowledge, he is justified in assuming that the ship is somewhere on a nearby arc of the circle, which arc is generally so short that it may be represented by a straight line tangent to the circle and therefore at right angles to the direction or bearing of the sun. *This is the Sumner line* or line of position. The ship must be on this line and the D.R. position may be partially corrected, although the navigator does not know exactly at what point on the line is the position of the ship.

Remember that the somewhat distorted curves on this and the succeeding chart represent true circles, and note that if you draw a line from the center of a circle to any point on its circumference, such a line will always meet the circumference at right angles. The important point is that the line of position, or Sumner line, which represents a short arc of the circle of equal altitudes, is always at right angles to the direction or azimuth of the observed body.

1507. Two circles. From the single observation plotted on the preceding chart, only a single line of position was obtained. This is not sufficient to fix the ship's position. If, however, the navigator observes two bodies at approximately the same time, two circles of equal altitude can

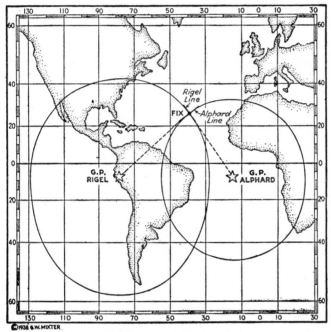

FIG. 1507. FIX FROM TWO STARS.

be had. The ship is somewhere on each circle and therefore must be at one of the two points where the circles intersect. On the chart, Fig. 1507, it is assumed that the navigator has observed two stars, Alphard being in about the same position as the sun on the previous chart, with Rigel almost on the boundary between Peru and Ecuador. Thus two circles of equal altitude result. The ship is known to be near the northern intersection of the circles, and two lines of position are shown crossed at that point for a fix.

*　　*　　*

The drawings and charts in the preceding sections present the principles discovered by Captain Sumner in 1837 which underlie the work of all navigators whether at sea or in the air. In practice, it is difficult to plot the line of position accurately on a globe or on charts which represent almost half the world on a flat surface. Sumner's method for over-coming this difficulty was somewhat burdensome, and for this and other reasons navigation by lines of position made little progress for almost a century. The first major step in advance occurred nearly forty years after Sumner's time.

1508. Method of Marcq Saint-Hilaire. In 1875 Marcq Saint-Hilaire of the French Navy published a method for laying down a Sumner line which is the basis for all of today's so-called new methods.*

The general plan is to assume a trial position at or near the D.R., correct this position to the true distance of the ship from the body observed, and through the point so found draw the line of position at right angles to the bearing of the body. Turn forward to Fig. 1510 and note the assumed position at (1), the 11′ correction toward the sun, and the Sumner line drawn through the point (6) at right angles to the sun's bearing. This is the line of position, although it has not been necessary to plot either the circle of equal altitudes or the geographic position of the body at its center.

The principle of altitude differences, used by Marcq Saint-Hilaire to determine the correction to the assumed position, is developed in Fig. 1508. Assume two stars as shown, the one directly below the other, as observed from the ship at the same instant of time. Note that the *difference in altitude* of the stars, 10°, *measures* the *difference in distance* from the ship to their respective geographic positions. When the altitude is 10° *less,* the ship is 10° farther *away.* When 10° *greater,* the ship is 10° or 600′ or 600 miles nearer or *toward* the observed body.

Reverse the situation pictured, and consider the case of two simultaneous altitudes of a single body such as the sun, the one computed from the trial position, the other observed from the ship. As before, *difference in altitude* will be *difference in distance* from the trial position to the line of position of the ship. Return to Fig. 1510 and note the use of the altitude difference, or intercept as it is called, in this case 11′, to locate the Sumner line. In practice these differences range from a few minutes of arc or miles of distance up to about 40 miles at sea or 100 miles or more in the air.

The *azimuth* or bearing of the body, in this case 135° true, serves to draw a short line through the trial position running in the direction of the center of the circle of equal altitudes which is the geographic position of the observed body. The intercept or altitude difference is laid off on this line from the assumed trial position. The direction in which to apply the intercept may be summarized as follows:

---

* Mathematically, Sumner's line is a chord of the circle of equal altitudes; Saint-Hilaire's line of position is a tangent. As used by navigators they are considered as identical for all practical purposes.

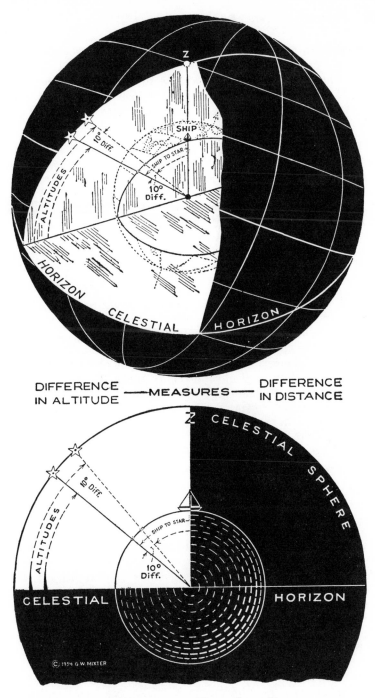

DIFFERENCE IN ALTITUDE — MEASURES — DIFFERENCE IN DISTANCE

Fig. 1508. Principle of Marcq Saint-Hilaire.

If observed altitude be *greater,* lay off the altitude difference *toward* the body from the trial position. If *less,* measure *away* from the trial point. The correctness of these statements should be evident from Fig. 1508. If this seems difficult to remember, look at the top of a telegraph pole; walk *toward* it and the altitude grows *greater;* back *away* and it becomes *less.*

The *computed altitude* (Hc) referred to above is the corrected altitude which would have been found by an observer at the assumed trial position at the instant the body was actually observed from the ship. The position of the body at that instant as taken from the Almanac and the latitude and longitude of the assumed point furnish the data for finding both the *computed altitude* (Hc) and the *azimuth* (Z). In recent years new methods and short tables have greatly simplified the determination of these quantities. The methods commonly known as H.O. 211 and H.O. 214 will be developed later. In this chapter it is assumed that the quantities in question may be readily determined.

1509. Principles repeated. Celestial navigation consists of locating the ship from the geographic position of one or more of the heavenly bodies. The distance of the observer from these geographic positions is determined with the sextant. The geographic position itself is found by entering the Almanac with the exact time of the observation. This position may be plotted on a globe or chart and a circle drawn around it, using as a radius the observer's distance from the geographic position. The observer is somewhere on this circle. If two bodies be observed at the same time, two circles of position may be drawn on the globe. The observer, on both circles, can be at only one of these two points of intersection. First recognized by Captain Sumner, these are the principles of all celestial navigation.

1510. Practicalities reviewed. The accepted method of putting Sumner's principles to practical use is illustrated by the example plotted in Fig. 1510 to which previous reference has been made.

With his sextant the navigator observes the altitude of the sun's lower limb and notes the exact time of the observation.

Correction of the sextant reading gives a corrected altitude of 55° 21′.

A trial position is assumed such as that marked (1) on the plotting sheet. This may be the dead reckoning position or some nearby point within not more than 40 miles of the D.R. selected to permit the use of certain tables. In either case, *the same Sumner line would result.* Whatever trial position be selected, its latitude and longitude are noted, in this case, 36° 44′ N and 47° 40′ W.

The sun's geographic position at the instant it was observed from the ship is found from the Almanac to be 9° 38′ N (Decl) and 23° 29′ W (G.H.A.).

With the Lat. and Long. of the assumed position, and the Lat. and

Long. of the sun's position as data, the navigator determines the *computed altitude* to be 55° 10′, as if observed from the assumed position at the instant actually observed from ship.

Similarly, the computed *azimuth* or bearing of the sun is found to be 135° true.

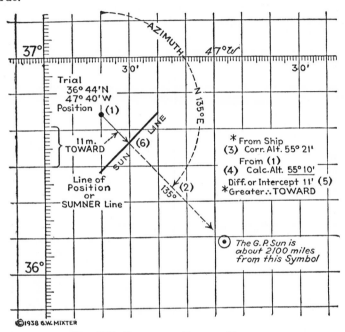

FIG. 1510. PLOTTING A LINE OF POSITION.

After proceeding as above the data listed below, numbered as on the drawing, are available for plotting the Sumner line,

(1) *Assumed position,* Lat. 36° 44′ N, Long. 47° 40′ W
(2) *Azimuth,* or sun's bearing, as computed, Zn 135°
(3) *Altitude, observed* from ship and corrected   55° 21′
(4) *Altitude, computed* as from assumed position   55° 10′
(5) And thus *Altitude Difference*   11′ Toward

With this information, the Sumner line is plotted in this manner:

From the trial position (1), draw a line 135° true, which will then point in the direction of the G.P. sun, which is the center of a circle of equal altitudes.

Because the altitude from the ship is 11′ *greater* than the computed altitude from the trial position, the line of position of the ship is 11 miles nearer or *toward* the sun. Therefore, step off 11 miles from the trial position toward the sun to the point marked (6).

Through the point thus obtained, draw a line at right angles to the bearing or azimuth of the sun. This is the line of position or Sumner line and is, in fact, a short arc of a circle of equal altitudes, although it has not been necessary to plot either the circle or the geographic position of the sun at its center.

A fix from two Sumner lines and many details of their use will be discussed in the next chapter.

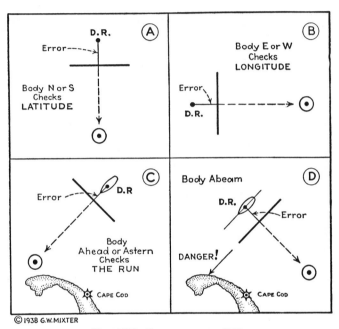

© 1938 G.W.MIXTER

FIG. 1511. CHECKING THE D.R.

1511. Checking the D.R. Sumner lines are like the line across the top of the capital letter T, the vertical leg of which then points toward the body observed. Evidently the value of a Sumner line in any given situation depends on the bearing or azimuth of the body. The sketches (Fig. 1511) illustrate several situations.

In case (A), the sun lies true south and the sketch represents the traditional noon sight for latitude. The same general result would be had by observing any body either north or south of the ship; for example, the North Star (Polaris), which bears almost true north.

In case (B), the sun is to the eastward and the resulting Sumner line checks the *longitude* which measures the east-west position of the ship.

However, a line of position may be had from a body bearing in any direction, and in case (C) the sun, bearing ahead of a ship steering to clear Cape Cod, furnishes a position line which checks the distance of the ship from the Cape. Aviators call this a "speed line."

Case (D) shows the same ship with the sun abeam. The "old man" thinks he is where the ship is shown on the chart on a course to clear the Cape. In fact, he is on the sun line, running parallel to his course, and if weather comes thick, the ship may pile up on Peaked Hill Bar. For obvious reasons, this sometimes is called a "course line."

The Outward Bound chart (Fig. 1402) further illustrates how the navigator proceeds with his work from day to day, through night after night, always keeping his dead reckoning, which may be his only resource through days of thick weather, until the moment the horizon and the sun or a star can be seen. He may take the stars at morning twilight, the sun in the forenoon, at noon, and again in the afternoon, and at evening twilight he may again take the stars. How much work he actually does will depend upon requirements of his service, upon the necessities of a particular situation, and upon the man himself.

1512. Questions. Without some technical training or knowledge of these subjects, this brief presentation of the principles of modern navigation may seem somewhat difficult. If so, reread and thus be better fitted to understand the succeeding chapters. Whether or not their practical meaning is understood may be determined by one's ability to answer the following questions:

Q 1-15: Given the following corrected altitudes:

(a) Sun	39° 29′		(d) ☆Vega	54° 10′
(b) Moon	47° 53′		(e) Sun	73° 49′
(c) Jupiter	72° 33′		(f) ☆Polaris	62° 17′

Req: In each case, find the distance in nautical miles from the observer to the geographic position of the body.

Q 2-15: Sun's altitude, as observed from the ship and corrected, 54° 40′. From a trial position the altitude was computed and found to be 54° 17′ at the instant the sun was actually observed from the ship.

Required:
(a) Radius of circle of equal altitudes on which lies the ship (nautical miles).
(b) Radius of the circle of equal altitudes through the trial position (nautical miles).
(c) Difference between distance from ship to G.P. sun and distance from trial position to G.P. sun (nautical miles).
(d) Difference between corrected altitude of the sun as observed and its altitude as computed from the trial position.

Q 3-15: Given the observed altitude properly corrected (Ho), and the altitude computed (Hc) as if taken at the same time from an assumed position, as in the following cases:

	Ho	Hc			Ho	Hc
(a)	32° 07′	32° 27′		(d)	26° 02′	25° 46′
(b)	67° 29′	66° 53′		(e)	51° 16′	51° 24′
(c)	44° 53′	44° 50′		(f)	72° 54′	73° 05′

Req. In each case: Distance in nautical miles to be laid off from the assumed position, along the azimuth line, toward (T) or away (A) from the observed body, to locate the Sumner line. Print T or A after each answer.

Q 4-15: Given the computed azimuth or bearing of various bodies, expressed in terms of the 360° true rose, as follows:

(a) Jupiter	141°		(d) Moon	280°
(b) Sun	220°		(e) ☆Polaris	0°
(c) ☆Sirius	29°		(f) Sun	93°

Req. In each case: The direction of the Sumner line, expressed by the lesser reading of the 360° true rose.

Answers to the above questions:

Q 1	Q 2	Q 3	Q 4
(a) 3031	2120 miles	20 A	051°
(b) 2527	2143 miles	36 T	130
(c) 1047	23 miles	3 T	119
(d) 2150	23′	16 T	010
(e) 971		8 A	090
(f) 1663		11 A	003

16. SUMNER LINES

NAVIGATION by lines of position determined as in the last chapter is the general method today universally taught both surface and air navigators. It requires that the navigator plot his results correctly and that he understand the meaning and use of Sumner lines on charts and plotting sheets. Without such ability and knowledge the most accurate computations are of little value. The importance of these matters is evident. Along with his study of the art, the student should not fail to plot all of the problems given in §1604, and whenever possible he should discuss with others any questions which may arise.

1601. Use of Sumner lines. Before going forward with drawings and details, it is well to have before one the purposes served by Sumner lines, although complete understanding of these purposes and how they are accomplished requires further study.

The value of a single line of position is not always appreciated, and marine navigators trained for air work seem to agree that more emphasis should be put on the use of such lines for surface navigation. When possible to observe a body of suitable bearing, a single Sumner line serves:

(1) To check the navigator's estimate of the ship's position, but only in a direction toward or away from the body observed. Review §1511 which discusses and illustrates latitude, longitude, speed, and course lines.

(2) For a running fix either by a cross with a previous line advanced or by advancing the line to a later time and crossing it with a new line. Universally used at sea and essential when seeking position from the sun.

(3) For a fix by crossing the line with the bearing of a landmark, a simple trick too often forgotten.

(4) For a fix by crossing the line with a radio bearing or loran line of position. Standard practice with airmen.

(5) To find the true bearing of the land as did the line of position discovered by Captain Sumner 17 December 1837.

A

NEW AND ACCURATE METHOD

OF

FINDING A SHIP'S POSITION AT SEA,

BY PROJECTION ON MERCATOR'S CHART.

———

WHEN THE LATITUDE, LONGITUDE, AND APPARENT TIME AT THE SHIP ARE
UNCERTAIN ; ONE ALTITUDE OF THE SUN, WITH THE TRUE
GREENWICH TIME, DETERMINES,

FIRST,

THE TRUE BEARING OF THE LAND;

SECONDLY,

THE ERRORS OF LONGITUDE BY CHRONOMETER,
CONSEQUENT TO ANY ERROR IN THE LATITUDE;

THIRDLY,

THE SUN'S TRUE AZIMUTH.

———

WHEN TWO ALTITUDES ARE OBSERVED, AND THE ELAPSED TIME NOTED, THE
TRUE LATITUDE IS PROJECTED ; AND IF THE TIMES BE NOTED BY
CHRONOMETER, THE TRUE LONGITUDE IS ALSO
PROJECTED AT THE SAME OPERATION.

———

The Principles of the Method being fully explained and illustrated
by Problems, Examples, and Plates,

WITH RULES FOR PRACTICE AND EXAMPLES FROM ACTUAL OBSERVATION.

———

BY CAPT. THOMAS H. SUMNER.

———

BOSTON:
PUBLISHED BY THOMAS GROOM & CO., 82 STATE STREET.
1843.

(Title page of Captain Sumner's book)

The intersection of two lines of position established by simultaneous observations of two stars or other bodies is a theoretically perfect fix. This use of Sumner lines is generally understood but is subject to numerous variations and possible errors presently discussed.

Consideration of all the above further emphasizes the importance of considering when to observe the sun or moon, or what stars to observe, to obtain lines which give the particular information desired. Remember that a Sumner line is always at right angles to the bearing of the observed body.

1602. Review. A line of position (LOP) is a series of possible positions of the ship. It is a locus of the possible positions of the ship and may be considered as a series of points marking each of these positions. Bearings of landmarks give a line of position. At sea LOP may be established from a single timed observation of a celestial body, the procedure being:

(1) Observe and correct a timed altitude of the body.

(2) Assume a trial position at or near the D.R.

(3) Correct the assumed position, toward or away from the body observed, by the method of altitude differences.

(4) Through the point so found draw the LOP at right angles to the azimuth line or bearing of the body.

These four steps are the crux of celestial navigation. Use of the resulting LOP is the subject of this chapter.

1603. The assumed position (A.P.) may be any nearby point from which it is convenient to determine the line of position. Marine practice is to use an A.P. within 40 miles; a similar figure in the air is 100 miles or more. The altitude observed from the ship is, of course, the same wherever the A.P. may be. Computed altitudes, and therefore altitude differences, will differ when computed from different A.P., but the variation of the azimuths so computed is practically immaterial. In any case the same line of position results from using any trial position reasonably near the ship. Theoretically questionable, this is a practical fact. Of all the possible assumed positions three classes are in common use.

(1) *D.R. positions.* Use of the D.R. as an assumed position is the older custom. Plotting is simpler for the novice; only a single simple table is required for the necessary computations which, however, are slightly longer than with some of the latest methods. At this point it is well to remember that the D.R. is seldom the exact position of the ship and is itself an assumed position.

(2) With the special Aircraft Plotting Sheets, which are ruled for every 10' of latitude and longitude, the navigator may assume a position at an intersection of these lines, and read off the L and λ of the A.P. without any plotting work. With an A.P. determined in this manner the sight must be computed by the methods used when working from the D.R.

(3) *Assumed positions.* As used today, the label "A.P." generally applies to positions selected by the navigator to permit the use of the shorter methods for finding Hc and Zn. Such positions are of a whole degree of latitude and an especially selected longitude and may be many miles from the D.R. After selection the A.P. must be plotted, and the intercepts are often longer than when working from the D.R.

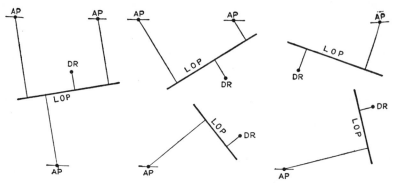

FIG. 1603. ANY NEARBY A.P. GIVES SAME LOP.

There is no rule dictating what type of assumed position must be used. The prevailing custom is first to teach students to work all sights from the D.R. Final choice rests with the navigator and on the tables available. For a number of reasons, it seems probable that working from an especially assumed A.P. ultimately will become all but universal.

The question is often asked how any method which depends on the assumption of a nearby position can be used when the ship's position is unknown. A ship is never completely lost. If, after checking, intercepts are excessive, rework the sight from a more suitable A.P.

1604. Interpretations. The details of plotting a Sumner line have been illustrated in §1510 and problem P1-16 requires the student to practice plotting single LOP. Having learned to plot a single line, consider the most probable position of the ship on the line, as developed in Fig. 1604. In the upper sketches the LOP are plotted from the D.R. as an assumed position; the lower group show the same LOP plotted from an especially assumed A.P. Each small sketch outlines the plotting of a problem of similar number.

Example P2 shows a 1000 sun line plotted from the 1000 D.R. The ship is somewhere on the line and the most probable position is the point on the line nearest to the D.R. This point is the foot of the perpendicular from the D.R., *at time of sight,* to the line and is called the computed point (C.P.).

The reasonableness of the above statement of the most probable position may be proved by circumscribing an area of position around the D.R. using as a radius the possible error in that position. Whatever D.R. error be assumed, the probable position of the ship, which must be somewhere on the LOP, is then on the dotted portion of that line within the circle. The average of such positions is the dot at the center of the line, which again is the foot of the perpendicular from the D.R. and is the computed point (C.P.).

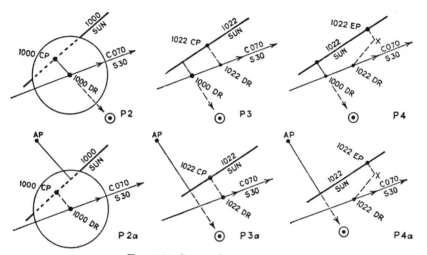

Fig. 1604. Single Sumner Lines.

Stated in another way, the C.P. is where the azimuth line from the D.R. *at time of sight* intersects the LOP. This leads to the error of thinking of the point so found as a fix. It is not a fix because the azimuth line is drawn from a more or less uncertain D.R. which may be miles from the ship. It is an even greater mistake to think of the foot of the perpendicular from some A.P. far from the D.R. as any kind of a point of position, a fact illustrated by the lower sketch, P2-*a*.

Example P3 is that of a similar sight computed and plotted from the same 1000 D.R. as an assumed position. Time of sight, however, was 1022 and the resulting LOP was therefore a 1022 line, correct only at that time. In such a case, plot 1022 D.R. from which a perpendicular to LOP gives 1022 C.P. The fallacy of dropping a perpendicular from a 1000 D.R. to a 1022 LOP is shown by the sketches.

Example P4. By Navy definition a D.R. position is determined by course and distance through the water and may be subject to correction for current. In the sketch P4 the 1022 D.R. is corrected for current to X from which a perpendicular to the 1022 line gives the most probable position and is labeled 1022 E.P. The reason for this lies in the definition of an estimated position as the best position obtainable short of a fix or running fix. Without the sun line, X was this point; given the line of position the E.P. is the point on that line nearest to X.

1605. Advanced lines of the Sumner type are similar to the advanced LOP discussed in §906 which should be reviewed at this point. The time interval from a Sumner line to the line as advanced may be from a few minutes to several hours. Such advanced lines are in constant use at sea and in the air, and the student must grasp their meaning and learn to plot them.

With a ship under way, an original Sumner line can be correct only at the instant of the observation by which the line was determined. This is true because the ship, somewhere on the line at that instant, immediately moves off the line and goes her way, unless, indeed, ship's course and direction of LOP coincide. To make the Sumner line useful at a later time it must be advanced with the ship.

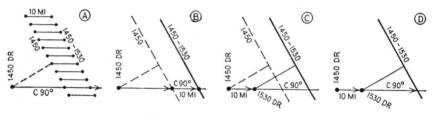

Fig. 1605. Advanced LOP.

An advanced line may be plotted from a Sumner line in several ways as in Fig. 1605 where dot or dash lines represent a 1450 Sumner line. The navigator required a similar line correct at 1530. For the 40-minute interval, course was 090° true, distance 10 miles.

The sketch (A) shows the 1450 Sumner line as a series of points, any one of which might have been the ship's position at 1450, with each point advanced 10 miles 90° true to form the 1450-1530 advanced line.

In (B) a single point, any point, on the 1450 line, is advanced by course and distance, and through the point so found the 1450-1530 advanced line is drawn parallel to the Sumner line. This is common practice, especially where the distance is stepped off from the point where the first line intersects the course line.

The (C) method is quite different in that the 1450 point from which the 1450 Sumner line was plotted is first advanced and then used as a point from which to plot the advanced line with same intercept and Zn as used to plot the Sumner line.

(D) shows the practical application of (C). Only the advanced line is plotted from the 1450 point advanced by course and distance to 1530. This is the simplest way to plot an advanced LOP when the Sumner line itself is not required; a confusion of lines is avoided, and the method is in general use by all experienced navigators.

The use of advanced LOP is outlined later in this chapter.

1606. Summary. The terminology used when interpreting the most probable position of the ship on LOP is that used at Annapolis. Old timers and airmen know nothing of C.P. and E.P. but use only the term D.R. or DRP to represent their best judgment of the ship's position until a fix or running fix be had. These are minor differences and do not affect certain facts about a single Sumner line which must be remembered:

(1) *Same Sumner line results from the use of any suitable assumed position.*

(2) *The only time at which an original Sumner line is correct is the time when the body was observed.* For use at a later time the line must be advanced.

(3) *An advanced line is correct only at the time to which it was advanced.*

(4) *Most probable position of ship on a LOP is foot of perpendicular from "best" position at time for which line is correct.*

The moral of the above is that points or lines with different time labels must not be combined.

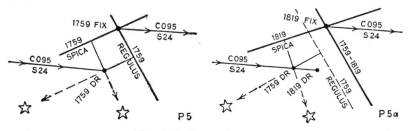

Fig. 1607. Fix by Two LOP.

1607. Fix by intersection of two Sumner lines is illustrated in Fig. 1607.

Example P5 shows Regulus and Spica lines, resulting from simultaneous observations of the two stars, intersecting almost at right angles. The ship, on the Regulus line and on the Spica line, can only be at their intersection, the latitude and longitude of this point being a perfect fix except for possible errors in the LOP.

Observing two bodies at the same instant is seldom practicable. A brief interval between sights may be overlooked on slow moving craft, but on a fast ship the change in position between sights must be allowed for.

Example P5a. In this case Regulus was observed at 1759 as in P5, but Spica was not observed until 20 minutes later at 1819. The ship, somewhere on the 1759 Regulus line at that time, advanced 8 miles 095° true during the interval between sights. Accordingly the Regulus line was advanced to 1759-1819 and this advanced line is shown crossed with the 1819 Spica line for the 1819 Fix. This is, in truth, a running fix, but is called a fix because of the short interval between sights. In the interest of uniformity, 30 minutes is the accepted maximum interval which warrants the label "Fix." Both sights worked from 1759 D.R.

Three stars for a fix is common practice. With simultaneous observations, and no errors, the three LOP should intersect at a common point. Practically the lines form a triangle or cocked hat, and in most cases the first and second lines are advanced to time of last observation. Fixes of this type are illustrated in Chapter 31.

* * *

1608. A running fix is a position determined by the intersection of two LOP established at different times. The earlier line is advanced for course and distance during the interval between the sights. The intersection of this advanced line with the line established from the later sight is a running fix as of the time of that sight. A position so determined is less accurate than a good fix because of possible errors in the intervening dead reckoning. Running fixes most often result from two sun sights at an interval sufficient to give a good cross as the sun changes its bearing. Two such cases are illustrated in Fig. 1608.

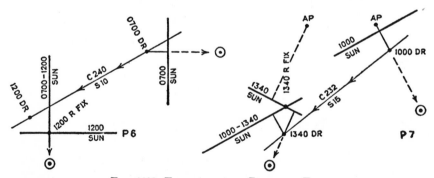

FIG. 1608. EXAMPLES OF A RUNNING FIX.

Example P6 is symbolic of the old navigation in that it combines a morning sun sight for longitude and the noon sight for latitude to find the ship's position at noon, by what is now called a running fix.

Example P7 is a modern version of a running fix from two sun sights when for one reason or another no noon sight had been had.

Cases P6 and P7 are typical of work done every day by every navigator at sea. In the air this type of position from the sun is seldom of practical value.

1609. Errors? When dealing with Sumner lines one must again remember that navigation is not an exact science. The accuracy of these lines of position may be affected by errors in the observed altitude

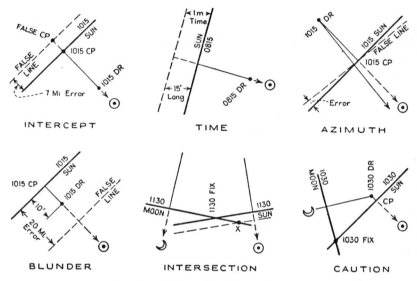

Fig. 1609. Errors, Blunders, Caution.

due to faulty observation, improper sextant adjustments, questionable horizon and abnormal refraction, to chronometer errors, and to the unavoidable errors inherent in the computations, forgetting for the moment the possibility of blunders. Bowditch suggests 2 miles either side of a Sumner line as a reasonable allowance for possible errors. Under the conditions of air navigation, 5 to 10 miles either side of the line is the usual estimate. In any case, regard a line of position as a strip of position rather than as an infallible line. Several different types of errors which may affect lines of position are shown in Fig. 1609. The errors assumed in the sketches are excessive but any one or all of them may be encountered at one time or another. The first two errors discussed below are always present in a greater or lesser degree.

Intercept errors, caused by an error in either the observed altitude or the computed altitude or both, displace a line of position toward or away from the observed body by the amount of the error. "A minute's a mile."

An error in the time of the instant when the altitude was observed displaces a line of position eastward if the time be slow, and westward when the error is fast. This is because the geographic position of every celestial body, with its circles of equal altitudes, of which the LOP is a part, is always moving westward at a rate of about 900' of longitude per hour, or 1° in 4 minutes! In the sketch, a time error of 1 minute fast has moved the sun line 15' of longitude to the west, or almost 8 miles in the latitude of New York, 40° N.

Azimuth errors tip the line of position, the difference in direction equaling the error in the azimuth. The sketch pictures the effect of a 10° blunder in Zn. Accurate plotting of a 1° error in the azimuth would show an error of only ½ mile toward or away from the LOP at a point 30 miles from its intersection with the azimuth line (30 × tan 1° = 0.52).

Blunders with Toward or Away displace a line of position toward or away from the observed body by a distance equal to double the intercept. If this is not clear, examine the sketch which shows the result of plotting *a* 10' A as *a* 10' T. With long intercepts such blunders may be discovered before the line is used, but with the short intercepts which often occur when working from the D.R. the line may be plotted without recognizing the mistake.

Poor intersections increase the possible error in a fix. In the sketch a moon line and a sun line are crossed at an angle of 20° and a 4' error in the 1130 sun intercept is shown as moving the fix to X, 12 miles to the eastward.

Caution should be used when interpreting a single line which runs close to the D.R. especially when such a line has been established by a short intercept computed from the D.R. as an assumed position. This is illustrated by the sketch where *a* 3' T for the sun line gives the C.P. distant only 3 miles from the D.R. This suggests that all's well with the D.R. The possible fallacy of such a conclusion is shown by the 1030 fix, where a moon line crosses the sun line, 25 miles 235° true from the C.P.

When the sun is almost overhead, as is possible within the Tropics, the circle of equal altitudes may become very small as the ship nears the G.P. sun. In such a case, draw the circle itself, and avoid the error of using a straight line to represent the arc of a small circle. Two such circles within a few minutes of time may give a fix as in §3008.

1610. Areas of position result from a habit of thought which promotes safety. A possible error of 2 miles toward or away from the LOP expands the LOP to a strip of position 4 miles wide. Similar assumptions when two lines intersect at right angles for a fix give an area 4 miles square as in Fig. 1610. With a 30° cut the area becomes 16 miles long. These sketches show why, when near the land, the situation must be reviewed on the assumption that the ship is in the possible position nearest to danger.

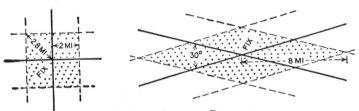

FIG. 1610. AREAS OF POSITION.

1611. To find 'The True Bearing of the Land' is both an old and a new use of a Sumner line.

Example, 1837. The first of all such LOP gave Captain Sumner the bearing of Small's Light on the coast of Wales one stormy December day in 1837. His plotting of that event is reproduced in Fig. 1611a, unaltered other than to emphasize important points.

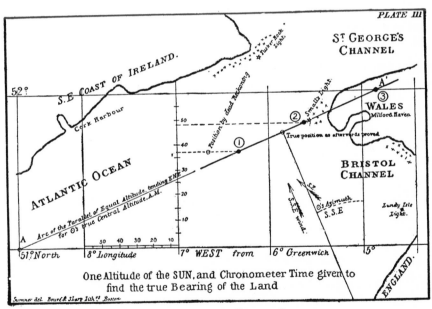

FIG. 1611a. PLOTTED BY CAPTAIN SUMNER.

Without sights for several days, the ship's position was uncertain and, the wind having hauled SE, the Irish coast was a lee shore. Weather boisterous, visibility poor, but about 10 A.M. an altitude of the sun was obtained. Three time-sight solutions of the observation, assuming three different latitudes, gave the positions (1), (2), and (3). These were seen to be in a straight line which passed through Small's Light. It thus appeared that the observed altitude must have occurred at the same instant of time at all three points, and at Small's Light, and at the ship.

Then followed the conclusion that, although the absolute position of the ship was uncertain, she must be somewhere on that first Sumner line. The true bearing of the land had been found, the ship, kept on E N E, made Small's Light in less than an hour, and the circle of equal altitudes had been discovered.

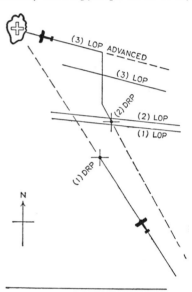

FIG. 1611*b*. ISLAND LANDFALL.

Example 1950. A recent daylight over-water flight on a mission to an island landfall illustrates how a Sumner line found the land from the air in 1950.

Ship's heading, adjusted for wind forecast to be out of the northeast, gave a course to the center of the island as in Fig. 1611*b*. Early part of trip was made above an overcast with no drift sights available, sun lines of no value for course. From DRP (1) sun sight was taken and a large intercept resulted which was at once checked by sight (2). Speed required to be on course line at point indicated by LOP exceeded the probable speed. It was more probable that the position lay to the right. If the wind, instead of being northeast, had switched to southeast, a better than expected ground speed would be explained as well as a track to the right of intended course. Later this was found to be the case.

However, for the proposed method of making the landfall it was necessary to be sure of being to the right and a course was flown due north up to an advanced LOP passing through the island, then down the line to destination. This again illustrates the use of Sumner's method for finding the true bearing of the land.

1612. Sumner lines to plot. Students of this chapter have learned certain facts about Sumner lines, but have found few rules and no formulae to memorize. The more thoughtful have also increased their ability to think straight in a pinch. Even the most casual reader must have sensed the importance of skillful plotting as he goes forward with the use of Sumner's lines. In fact, the art of modern navigation cannot be mastered unless and until one has learned to plot. To this end the following problems are provided.

Before plotting, review the sections in Chapter 11 and Appendix II which discuss small area plotting sheets, plotting, and labeling.

PLOTTING SUMNER LINES FROM GIVEN DATA

ALL courses and bearings are given in degrees true from north unless otherwise stated.

P 1-16. *Single lines.* Given, the results of eight sights as tabulated below. The first five illustrate a day's swing of the sun. The three star sights are as of various dates.

		Assumed Position		Ho	Hc	Zn
(a)	Sun	40° 12′ N	51° 36′ W	35° 29′	35° 33′	103°
(b)	Sun	40° 20′ N	52° 07′ W	54° 41′	54° 22′	135°
(c)	Sun	40° 12′ N	52° 01′ W	62° 04′	62° 00′	180°
(d)	Sun	40° 06′ N	52° 14′ W	56° 23′	56° 26′	219°
(e)	Sun	40° 15′ N	52° 12′ W	29° 58′	29° 48′	260°
(f)	Star	40° 00′ N	51° 50′ W	57° 34′	57° 18′	150°
(g)	Polaris	39° 38′ N	52° 01′ W	39° 45′	39° 39′	000°
(h)	Venus	39° 50′ N	52° 30′ W	25° 19′	25° 13′	122°

Req: (1) Compute intercepts and record figures prefixed by *a* for intercept and followed by T or A to indicate *toward* or *away*. (2) Construct small plotting sheet, label center lines 40° N and 52° W; use large scale. (3) Plot each LOP on the one plotting sheet so constructed.

Ans: (1)

(a) *a* 4′ A	(c) *a* 4′ T	(e) *a* 10′ T	(g) *a* 6′ T
(b) *a* 19′ T	(d) *a* 3′ A	(f) *a* 16′ T	(h) *a* 6′ T

Construct 3 small plotting sheets for the following 6 problems, label center lines 36° 40′ N and 64° 20′ W; use large scale. Each of the 6 problems is separately plotted in miniature in the figure titled "Single Sumner Lines."

P 2-16. *Probable positions.* Observed ☉ at 1000 when on C 070, S 30. 1000 D.R. 36° 35′ N, 64° 30′ W. Correcting the sextant reading gave Ho as 38° 32′.5. By computation, using 1000 D.R. as assumed position, found Hc 38° 40′.5, Zn 140°.

Req: (1) Find the intercept. (2) Plot 1000 sun line. (3) There being no known current or other correction to D.R., what is L and λ of most probable position of ship at 1000?

Ans: (1) *a* 8′ A. (3) 1000 C.P. 36° 41′.2 N, 64° 36′.4 W.

P 2a-16. This is the same sight as P 2 except that it is not worked from the D.R. but from an especially assumed position (37° N, 64° 45′ W), which gave Ho 38° 32′.5, Hc 38° 13′.5, Zn 139°.8.

Req: (1) Find the intercept. (2) On P 2 sheet, in red pencil, plot LOP from the especially assumed position. The LOP so plotted should coincide with that of P 2. (3) Plot and record most probable position of ship at 1000.

Ans: (1) *a* 19′ T. (3) C.P. at 1000, 36° 41′.2 N, 64° 36′.4 W.

P 3-16. *Computed position.* Course 070° true, S 30. Observed ☉ at 1022. Worked sight using as an assumed position 1000 D.R. 36° 35′ N, 64° 30′ W, and found *a* 6′ A, Zn 148°.

Req: (1) With S 30 on C 070 plot most probable position of ship at time of sight. (2) Record L and λ of C.P.

Ans: C.P. at 1022, 36° 45′.9 N, 64° 22′.7 W.

P 3a-16. Same sight as P 3 but worked from assumed position (37° N, 64° 45' W), which resulted in intercept *a* 21'.7 T and Zn 148°.
Req: (1) Plot new lines in red on P 3 sheet. (2) Record C.P. at time of sight.
Ans: C.P. at 1022, 36° 45'.9 N, 64° 22'.7 W.

P 4-16. *Correcting for current.* Same as P 3 except: Plot possible current estimated as 13 miles 045° true from 1022 D.R. This represents total error in D.R. considered to have accrued since last Fix.
Req: Plot and record estimated position of ship.
Ans: E.P. at 1022, 36° 52'.6 N, 64° 09'.1 W.

P 4a-16. Same as P 3 except: Establish sun line from assumed position (37° N. 64° 46' W) with intercept *a* 22' T, Zn 148°. Use red pencil.
Req: Plot and record estimated position of ship.
Ans: E.P. at 1022, 36° 52'.6 N, 64° 09'.1 W.

P 5-16. *Two stars for a Fix.* At 1759 on C 095, S 24, navigator observed ☆ Regulus and at the same instant his assistant observed ☆ Spica. Using 1759 D.R. 36° 20' N, 64° 35' W as an assumed position, the results of the sights were

1759, Regulus *a* 11' A, Zn 243°
1759, Spica   *a* 12' A, Zn 157°

Req: (1) Construct small plotting sheet, label center lines 36° 20' N, 64° 30' W; use large scale. (2) Plot the 1759 Fix and record L and λ of ship.
Ans: Fix at 1759, 36° 35' N, 64° 29'.1 W.

P 5a-16. *Star line advanced.* Navigator observed ☆ Regulus at 1759, D.R. 36° 20' N, 64° 35' W, and 20 minutes later observed ☆ Spica. Ship on C 095, S 24. Computing both sights from 1759 D.R. results were:

1759 ☆ Regulus *a* 11' A, Zn 243°
1819 ☆ Spica   *a* 12' A, Zn 157°

Req: (1) Construct small plotting sheet, label center lines 36° 20' N, 64° 30' W; use large scale. (2) Plot LOP and record 1819 Fix.
Ans: Fix at 1819, 36° 37'.8 N, 64° 21'.6 W.

P 6-16. *R. Fix at Noon.* Observed ☉ at 0700; D.R. 36° 40' N, 63° 32' W. With this D.R. as the assumed position the 0700 sight gave *a* 8' T, Zn 090°. Ship on C 240, S 10. Noon latitude was found to be 36° 10' N.
Req: (1) Construct small plotting sheet, label center lines 36° 30' N, 64° W; use small scale. (2) Plot 0700 LOP. From 0700 D.R. plot course and distance to 1200. Plot parallel of latitude at noon. Advance 0700 sun line to 1200 and record 1200 R. Fix.
Ans: Noon R. Fix, 36° 10' N, 64° 16' W.

P 7-16. *Two sun lines for R. Fix.* Observed ☉ at 1000, D.R. 36° 41' N, 63° 10' W. Using 1000 D.R. as an assumed position, found *a* 8' A, Zn 155°.

Proceeded on Course 232° at a speed of 15 knots.

Again observed ☉ at 1340, D.R. 36° 07' N, 64° 03'.7 W. With this D.R as an assumed position found *a* 9' A, Zn 205°.
Req: (1) Construct small plotting sheet, label center lines 36° 30' N, 63° 40' W; use small scale. (2) Plot 1000 D.R. and 1000 LOP. (3) Plot 1340 D.R. Advance 1000 sun line to 1340. Record R. Fix.
Ans: R. Fix at 1340, 36° 16'.3 N, 64° 02'.3 W.

P 7a-16. Same sight as P 7 except: Establish 1000 sun line from assumed position (37° N, 63° 20' W) with intercept *a* 13' T, Zn 155°. Establish 1340 sun line from assumed position (37° N, 63° 50' W), *a* 44'.0 T, Zn 205°.

P8-16. New London for Bermuda by sail.
Construct small plotting sheet for 2° L and 1° λ, label center lines 40° 40′ N
and 72° W; use large scale.

(a) Plot and label positions of the following lights:

Race Rock	Block Island S.E.	Montauk Point
41° 15′ N	41° 09′ N	41° 04′ N
72° 03′ W	71° 33′ W	71° 51′ W

(b) *Took departure* from point estimated to be 1 Mi. south of Race Rock. Plot
and label this point No. 1 D.R.

(c) *Fix by two lights.* Sailed 20.5 Mi. by log, Course 118° to No. 2 D.R. and
took bearings of Block Island S.E. 018° and Montauk Point 283° for a Fix.
Req: Plot No. 2 D.R. and record No. 2 Fix.
Ans: Fix, 41° 01′.4 N, 71° 36′.3 W.

(d) *Fix by one light and a star.* From No. 2 Fix sailed 13.5 Mi. Course 228°
to No. 3 D.R. At time of this D.R. navigator took bearing of Montauk Point, 000°
and ☆ Spica was observed for LOP. The sight, using No. 3 D.R. as an assumed
position, gave *a* 3′.4 T, Zn 220°.
Req: Plot No. 3 D.R. and No. 3 Fix, and record, the Fix.
Ans: Fix, 40° 49′.1 N, 71° 51′ W.

(e) *Sun line.* From No. 3 Fix sailed 13.5 Mi. Course 202° to No. 4 D.R. and
observed ⊙ for LOP. Using No. 4 D.R. as an assumed position, computation of
sight gave *a* 3′.8 A, Zn 103°.
Req: Plot No. 4 D.R. Plot LOP for use later.

(f) *Noon R. Fix.* From No. 4 D.R. changed course and sailed 11.5 Mi. on C 220°
to No. 5 D.R. at time when a noon sight of the sun gave the latitude as 40° 26′ N.
Req: Plot No. 5 D.R., plot noon latitude line, and cross with No. 4 LOP advanced for R. Fix. Record L and λ of No. 5 R. Fix.
Ans: R. Fix, 40° 26′ N, 72° 13′ W.

Use noon R. Fix as new point of departure for D.R.

(g) *Evening twilight.* From No. 5 R. Fix, during the afternoon with little or
no wind, navigator estimated 13 Mi. on C 142° to No. 6 D.R. and observed three
stars * almost simultaneously. Sights worked from No. 6 D.R. gave:

Vega	Betelgeuse	Arcturus
a 2′.7 T	*a* 2′.5 A	*a* 3′.6 T
Zn 030°	Zn 280°	Zn 142°

Req: Plot No. 6 D.R. Plot the three star LOP. Record L and λ of center of
resulting triangle as No. 6 Fix.
Ans: Fix, 40° 15′ N, 71° 58′ W.
Plot Bermuda course 142° true from the Fix.

P 9-16. East of Cape Hatteras.
Construct small plotting sheet for 2° L and 4° λ, label center lines 35° 30′ N
and 73° W; use small scale.

---

* The stars in P 8 and P 9 have been given well known names but are in imaginary positions.

(a) *Morning sun.* At 0730, D.R. 36° 00′ N, 75° 00′ W, course 120°, S 15, navigator observed ☉. Using 0730 D.R. as an assumed position, the sight gave Ho 15° 20′.0, Hc 15° 15′.0, Zn 095°.

Req: (1) Plot 0730 D.R. (2) Compute intercept. (3) Plot 0730 sun line for future use.

Ans: a 5′ T.

(b) *Noon sight.* At local apparent noon (1220) observed sun's meridian altitude and found Lat. to be 35° 28′.2 N.

Req: (1) Plot and label 1220 parallel of latitude. (2) Advance 0730 sun line for the run from 0730 to 1220 (4h 50m, 72.5 miles), for cross with 1220 line and record the R. Fix.

Ans: R. Fix at 1220, 35° 28′.2 N, 73° 36′.3 W.

(c) With the above information, and assuming that there has been no current, make best estimate of ship's position at 1200 as follows. From 1220 R. Fix plot back on the reverse of C 120, S 15, for the run since 1200 and record E.P. so found.

Ans: E.P. at 1200, 35° 31′.0 N, 73° 41′.7 W.

Continue D.R. line from 1200 D.R. In this case, do not use R. Fix or E.P. as a new point of departure.

(d) *Sun and moon for a Fix.* At 1700, simultaneous observations of sun and moon resulted in: ☉ a 11′.4 A, Zn 272°, ☾ a 0′.9 T, Zn 185°.

Req: (1) Plot 1700 D.R. (2) Plot both lines from 1700 D.R. (3) Record L and λ of 1700 Fix.

Ans: Fix at 1700, 34° 47′.2 N, 72° 15′.0 W.

At 1700, course was altered to 050° and S 15 was continued.

(e) *Round of stars.* At 1930 three stars were observed simultaneously with the following results; using 1930 D.R. as assumed position:

	Vega	Arcturus	Dubhe
Ho	34° 22′.7	75° 39′.4	17° 59′.1
Hc	34° 16′.7	75° 32′.6	17° 59′.1
Zn	050°	130°	180°

Req: (1) Plot 1930 D.R. (2) Plot 1930 Fix, labeling all lines and points. (3) Record L and λ of 1930 Fix.

Ans: Fix at 1930, 35° 11′.1 N, 71° 30′ W.

* * *

Additional and more advanced work in the use and plotting of Summer lines is to be found among the Problems following Chapters 30 to 33 inclusive. All of this work may be used as given data problems in plotting without solving the sights.

A L   D V S

17. NAUTICAL ASTRONOMY

AT SEA or in the air celestial navigation is based on the science of astronomy. The elements of this science necessary to navigators are called *nautical astronomy*, a term sometimes used to include the entire art of celestial navigation. The navigator need not be an astronomer, but he must understand certain terms and the general nature of the universe with which he deals. The several definitions in the following sections have been arranged to show the similarity and interchangeability of angular measurements on the earth and on the celestial sphere. Therefore the repetition and expansion of those relating to the earth. Fig. 1704 illustrates each term presently defined.

1701. The two spheres. The *earth* is assumed to be a sphere rotating eastward on its axis which passes through its north pole and its south pole. The center of the imaginary *celestial sphere* on which the heavenly bodies appear is at center of earth; its axis is that of the earth extended to the celestial poles. Because of the earth's easterly rotation, the celestial sphere always appears to be turning westward around the earth. Whenever the westward movement of a celestial body is referred to, it should be understood to mean the apparent movement.

1702. Zenith and G.P. The *zenith* of an observer on the earth's surface is the point on the celestial sphere vertically overhead. A line from the center of the earth through the ship will meet the celestial sphere at the zenith of the ship. Points directly over other points on the earth are the zeniths of those points.

The geographic position, or sub-solar, sub-stellar, or sub-lunar point, of a heavenly body is the point on the earth vertically below the body. A line from the body to the center of the earth intersects the earth's surface at the G.P. of the body.

1703. Great circles. If a plane passes through the center of a sphere, as when cutting an orange in half, its intersection with the sphere's surface is a great circle. The plane must pass through the center, or only smaller circles result. Since the center of the earth is the center of the celestial sphere, a plane in any direction through that center will

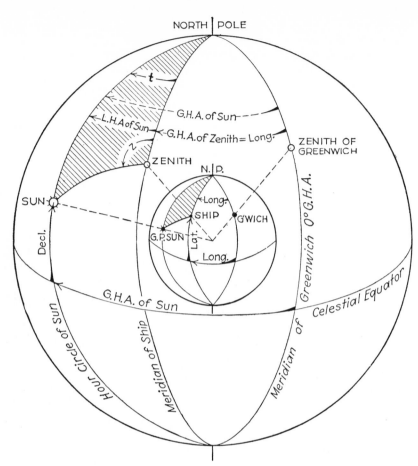

DEFINITIONS OF NAVIGATION

Identical Positions						
On the Earth			On the Celestial Sphere			
	Lat.	Long.			Decl.	G.H.A.
Greenwich	51°28'N	0°	Zenith of G'wich.		51°28'N	0°
CORNERS OF THE ASTRONOMICAL TRIANGLE AS ON DRAWING						
NORTH POLE	90°N	—	NORTH POLE		90°N	—
SHIP	45°N	55°W	ZENITH OF SHIP		45°N	55°W
G. P. SUN	20°N	90°W	SUN		20°N	90°W

FIG. 1704.

cut great circles on both spheres, the one in the sky being directly over that on the earth. A plane may pass through any three points. Therefore a great circle may be drawn through any two points on either sphere, the center of the sphere being the third point. Furthermore, the arc of this circle from point to point will measure the angular distance between them as from the center of the earth.

1704. Two equators. The earth's equator, as before defined, is a great circle around the earth midway between the poles. It is formed by the intersection with the earth's surface of a plane perpendicular to its axis.

The celestial equator is the great circle formed by extending the plane of the earth's equator until it intersects the celestial sphere and is, therefore, directly above the equator of the earth. It is sometimes called the *equinoctial* because when the sun appears on the equator, "crossing the line," about March 21 and again about September 21, night and day are of equal duration over all the earth.

1705. Meridians are halves of great circles extending from pole to pole and therefore are at right angles to the equator. In navigation, various meridians have special names, often with a double meaning, which generally refer to only one half of the great circle.

ON THE EARTH:

Meridian of Greenwich (Long. 0°) is the half of a great circle from pole to pole through Greenwich. It is called the *prime meridian* because it is the zero line from which longitude is reckoned.

Lower meridian of Greenwich (180° E or W) is the other half of the great circle, on the opposite side of the earth.

Meridian of the ship, or that of any observer, is the half of a great circle between the poles which passes through the ship or the position of the observer; it is sometimes called *the local meridian.* The opposite half of the same great circle is the *lower meridian of the ship.*

ON THE CELESTIAL SPHERE:

Celestial meridians may be formed by extending the planes of terrestrial meridians to intersect the celestial sphere.

Celestial meridian of Greenwich is the half of a great circle of the celestial sphere directly above the meridian of Greenwich. It is the zero line from which Greenwich hour angles of navigational bodies are measured. *The lower celestial meridian of Greenwich* is the opposite half of the same great circle. It is the meridian from which Greenwich time is measured.

Celestial meridian of the ship is similar to that of Greenwich. It is the zero line from which local hour angles are measured. The opposite half of the same great circle is the ship's *lower celestial meridian.*

Hour circles. The hour circle of a star or other celestial body is that half of a great circle of the celestial sphere which passes through the poles and the body; it is nothing more than the upper celestial meridian of the body, but with one important difference:

The celestial meridians of Greenwich or of the observer remain fixed over Greenwich or over the ship. Hour circles of sun, moon, or stars on the apparently revolving celestial sphere always appear to be moving westward at a rate of about 15° per hour. Therefore for clarity, the term *celestial meridian* for those over terrestrial points and *hour circle* for the meridians of the heavenly bodies.

In Practice:

The meridian means the upper meridian of the ship on either sphere. *Meridian of Greenwich* means its upper meridian on either sphere. Although the prefix *upper* may be omitted, it is essential that a *lower* meridian always be so designated. Every meridian runs from pole to pole and the terms *upper* and *lower* are in no way related to the latitude of the observer above or below the equator. Whatever they be called, meridians and hour circles appear as vertical straight lines on Mercator charts and on rectangular star charts.

1706. Latitude (Lat. or L) and declination (Decl. or *d*). *Latitude* defines position on the earth north or south from the equator. The latitude of a place on the surface of the earth is the arc of the meridian between the equator and that place. Latitude is 0° on the equator and never exceeds 90°, which is the latitude of either pole; it is marked N (+) or S (−).

Declination on the celestial sphere is identical with latitude on the earth. It defines the position of a body north or south from the celestial equator and is the latitude of the geographic position (G.P.) of the body. Declination of any star remains almost fixed; that of sun, moon, or planet is variable.

1707. Longitude (Long. or λ) and Greenwich hour angle (G.H.A.). *Longitude* defines position on the earth east or west from the meridian of Greenwich. The longitude of a place on the surface of the earth is the arc of the equator between the meridian of Greenwich from which longitude is reckoned and the meridian of the place. It also may be defined as the angle between the meridian of Greenwich and the meridian of the place where the two intersect at either pole. The latter definition is an aid to visualizing the problems of celestial navigation. Longitude is measured to 180° east (E) and to 180° west (W) from the meridian of Greenwich (0° Long.).

Greenwich hour angle (G.H.A.) of sun, moon, or star defines its position on the celestial sphere westward from the celestial meridian over Greenwich. It is the angle at the pole between the celestial meridian of

Greenwich (0° G.H.A.) and the hour circle through the body. It may also be regarded as the arc of the celestial equator between these meridians. According to definition, G.H.A. is measured westward in a positive direction from 0° to 360° and is so tabulated in the Almanac. However, it may be expressed in an easterly or negative manner; for example, a G.H.A. of 350° W (+) may also be stated as 10° E (−). When the Greenwich hour angle is measured from 0° to 180° W and from 0° to 180° E it becomes identical with the longitude of the geographic position (G.P.) of the body.

The term *hour* angle reflects the fact that such angles measure time and are expressed by astronomers in time units rather than in units of arc.

1708. Local hour angles (L.H.A.) are like Greenwich hour angles, except that they are measured from any local meridian. They define the momentary position of the sun or other navigational body westward from the celestial meridian over the ship. Stated in another way, the local hour angle of an observed body is the angle at the pole between the meridian of the ship and the hour circle through the body. Such an angle may be imagined as drawn on either sphere.

Although the L.H.A. as defined is measured westward from 0° to 360° (0h to 24h), the term has long been used, and often continues to be used, as meaning the local hour angle expressed from 0° to 180° east or west.

1709. The meridian angle (*t*) is a new term for the local hour angle when measured east or west from 0° to 180° (0h to 12h). The hour angle so expressed is used whenever a sight is worked for line of position by any of the modern methods. The label *t* reflects the fact that the meridian angle of the sun is the measure of local apparent time. Obviously *t* is measured by the shorter arc of either equator between the two meridians.

1710. Hour angles on earth. The three preceding sections have discussed four interrelated quantities with which the navigator must deal when working any sight. The circular diagrams across the center of Fig. 1710 summarize how each of the quantities is measured. The illustration also indicates the relations between longitude, Greenwich hour angle, local hour angles, and the meridian angle, by plotting the geographic position of several celestial bodies and various positions of the ship on rectangular charts of the world.

The scale at the top of the upper chart shows how the G.H.A. of a celestial body, as determined from the Almanac for any instant of time, may be plotted. The longitude scale across the bottom of the same diagram indicates where to mark the east-west position of the ship. The lower chart assumes the same positions for the ship and the celestial bodies and illustrates the nature of the meridian angle, *t*. On both charts, Greenwich, the ships, and the bodies observed are plotted in their respective latitudes or declinations.

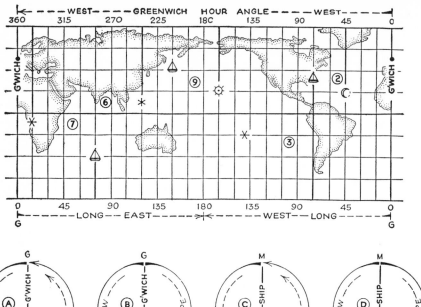

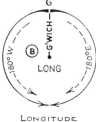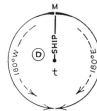

G.H.A. from ALMANAC
MEASURED
FROM (G), 360° W TO (G)

LONGITUDE
MEASURED
FROM (G), 180° E OR W

LOCAL HOUR ANGLE
MEASURED
FROM (M), 360° W TO (M)

MERIDIAN ANGLE, t
MEASURED
FROM (M), 180° E OR W

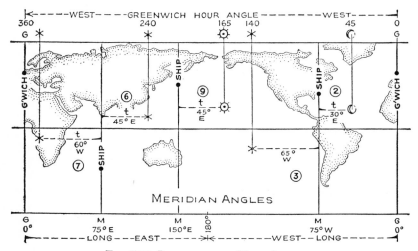

FIG. 1710. LONGITUDE AND HOUR ANGLES.

1711. The azimuth (Az, Z, or Zn) of the sun or other celestial body is its true bearing as seen from the ship. It is measured by the arc of the horizon from the pole to the point directly under the body. Mathematically, the azimuth is the angle of the astronomical triangle at the corner marked by the ship on the earth or by its zenith on the celestial sphere. Chapter 28 further defines azimuths and illustrates how they are named and measured to best serve the navigator.

1712. Review. If the observer again assumes himself to be at center of the earth he will see, as on one sphere, various points and lines from which positions on either sphere are measured, including the poles, the equator, and the meridian of Greenwich.

The ship will appear in its proper latitude and longitude. On earth, latitude is measured from the equator, longitude from the meridian of Greenwich. The equator and the meridian of Greenwich are fixed zero lines, and the positions of fixed landmarks, measured therefrom by latitude and longitude, remain unchanged throughout the ages.

The observed body also will appear as on the one sphere. Its declination is measured from the equator, like latitude, and its Greenwich hour angle is measured from the meridian of Greenwich as is longitude. However, celestial bodies always are moving westward over the meridian of Greenwich, and, for this and other reasons, their apparent position, as defined by their declination and hour angle, is continually changing.

If the observer remains at the center of the earth until, for example, a sight of the sun be taken from the ship, he will see, among other things, three points apparently *all on one sphere*:

(1) *Sun,* on the celestial sphere.
(2) *Ship,* on the earth's surface.
(3) The *pole* nearest the ship, called the *elevated pole.*

These points mark the astronomical triangle or triangle of navigation, which, although its corners be on different spheres, may be considered as projected either on the celestial sphere or on the earth. Contrary to the older custom, it seems simpler to imagine the triangle as drawn on the earth, using the G.P. sun as one corner.

The side of the triangle from ship to the G.P. sun is the same arc of a great circle as those marked "Ship to Sun" in Fig. 1505 and "Ship to Star" in Fig. 1508. The azimuth or bearing of the sun is the angle at the corner marked by the ship or its zenith. The computed altitude and azimuth, as required when laying down a line of position, result from a solution of this spherical triangle by the methods of trigonometry and the use of logarithms. In practice the triangle is apparently solved by simple arithmetic, or needed data are taken from tabulated solutions.

*   *   *

The remainder of this chapter discusses various astronomical facts and phenomena so that the nature and characteristics of the navigational bodies, and why they appear to move about in various ways, may be understood.

1713. The universe of the astronomer includes an endless number of luminous and nonluminous bodies scattered irregularly throughout space. Among these are the earth and the bodies observed by navigators which are: sun, moon, four planets, and a limited number of the brighter stars. In order to deal with the apparent motions of these bodies, and their resulting apparent positions from which the position of the ship is determined, astronomers assume the earth to be at the center of the universe and all the celestial bodies as on the inside of the celestial sphere, a conception previously illustrated and discussed.

Stars seem infinite in number and, because of their vast distances from the earth, their relative position on the apparently revolving celestial sphere remains almost constant. Therefore, they are sometimes called *fixed stars* to distinguish them from the planets which appear to move about among the stars. Each star, unlike the planets and the moon, is a self-luminous sun, but all are so far away that the visible stars appear only as points of light twinkling in the sky. Of the brightest, 57 are listed in the Almanacs as principal navigational stars, of which a dozen or more are sufficient for simple star navigation in mid-northern latitudes.

A proper conception of the astronomical universe cannot be formed without realizing the relatively infinite distance of the stars from the solar system. Light, traveling at a constant velocity, reaches the earth from our nearby sun in 8 minutes; but light requires more than 4 years to reach the earth from the nearest fixed star, and about 38 years from the star Arcturus, beyond which distances are uncertain.

The solar system includes the sun at its center, the planets revolving about the sun, of which the earth is one, and the satellites of the planets. Satellite means "attendant" and our moon is a satellite of the earth. The distance from sun to earth is about 93,000,000 miles. Certain planets are much farther away, but the whole solar system is indeed only a pin point in the universe. The navigational elements of the solar system are diagrammed in Fig. 1713.

The sun is self-luminous and is in truth a fixed star, but relatively so near the earth that it appears as a blazing disk of light whose brilliance makes the stars invisible in daytime. If the stars were visible when the sun is shining its position among them would be seen to vary greatly throughout the year. Actually, it annually traces the same path through the unseen star map on the celestial sphere, this path being known as *the ecliptic*.

The earth is a planet which revolves around the sun once each year. Although the earth is nonluminous and a relatively minor body, its center is assumed to be the center of the universe.

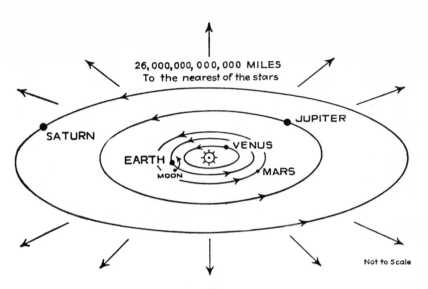

26,000,000,000,000 MILES
To the nearest of the stars

Not to Scale

THE SOLAR SYSTEM

Only a pin point in the Universe

Navigational Bodies only	Mean Diameter MILES	YEARS to revolve about Sun	Mean distance from the Sun MILES
SUN	866,400	———	———
VENUS	7,700	0.6	67,200,000
EARTH	7,918	1.0*	92,900,000
MARS	4,230	1.9	141,500,000
JUPITER	86,500	11.9	483,300,000
SATURN	73,000	29.5	886,000,000
MOON	2,163	New moon to new moon, about 29.5 Days	Mean distance from the Earth 238,840

*Also rotates constantly eastward on its axis in 23 h. 56 m 3.4 s of Mean Time

1951 G.W. MIXTER

Fig. 1713.

The moon, a satellite of the earth, is the smallest visible celestial body and shines only by reflected light, but appears as large as the sun because its distance away from the earth is relatively minute.

Planets, other than the earth which is itself a planet, are well described as "wanderers," which is the Greek meaning of the word. The nine major planets include the earth and four planets used by navigators, namely, Venus, Mars, Jupiter, and Saturn. Planets are not self-luminous and shine only by reflected sunlight. For practical navigation they are considered as points of light as are the stars, although their form often may be seen and they lack the twinkle of stars.

Venus is so brilliant as to be visible frequently in daylight, and is called the morning star or the evening star because the apparent position of Venus is never more than 48° away from the sun. Mars is strikingly red. Jupiter is at times the brightest planet and is the largest body of the solar system except the sun. Saturn, at its brightest, appears like a first magnitude star, and its color is almost white. A planet varies in brilliancy mainly because of its widely varying distance from the earth as suggested by the diagram of the solar system.

1714. Cause of apparent motions. The apparent motions of navigational bodies, as seen from the earth, are caused by one or more of the *actual* motions of the earth, the planets, or the moon, which include:

(1) Earth's *regular* rotation on its axis once in 23h 56m 3.4s of civil time. This affects the apparent motion of all celestial bodies; it is the principal cause of their apparent motions from east to west.

(2) Earth's annual revolution around the sun, which is always completed in exactly the same period of time, although, for various reasons, the angular velocity of this motion is *irregular.* This motion affects apparent positions of sun and planets but does not affect apparent positions of stars or moon.

(3) Planets' motion around the sun, which differs for each planet. The motion of Venus affects only Venus' apparent position, etc.

(4) Moon's *irregular* revolution around the earth, once each lunar month, which affects only the apparent position of the moon.

All of these *actual* motions are suggested in the sketch of the solar system (Fig. 1713). They cause stars, sun, planets, and moon to appear to move in quite different ways. However, because of the rotation of the earth on its axis, all of the celestial bodies, except the circumpolar stars, are seen to rise in the east, move westward across the heavens, and set below the western horizon.

1715. Stars' apparent motion results only from the earth's *regular* rotation on its axis. Therefore the celestial sphere with the fixed stars appears to revolve at a constant rate westward around the earth, slightly faster than does the mean sun. Because of the relatively infinite distances of the stars away from the earth, neither their own motions nor the earth's annual motion around the sun have any substantial effect on their positions as seen on the constantly revolving celestial sphere. Thus as the stars appear to move westward their G.H.A. *increases at a constant rate;* their declinations remain almost fixed, as does the relative position of one star to another. Of all navigational bodies, the apparent motion of the stars is the most simple.

1716. Sun's apparent motion is caused by the two motions of the earth. The resulting position of the sun over the earth is the greatest factor affecting the character and mode of existence of the human race. It determines the heat of the tropics, the cold and long arctic nights, the

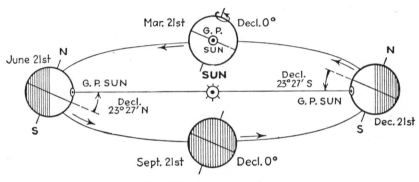

FIG. 1716. EARTH AND SUN.

calendar, the seasons, and day and night throughout the world. Also it is the most important element of nautical astronomy because its average position measures mean time and because it is most often observed by navigators. The earth's movements are shown in Fig. 1716 by arrows indicating *actual* motions; the sun's *apparent* position is illustrated by the G.P. sun.

The net apparent westward motion of the sun around the earth, which causes day and night, results from both motions of the earth:

(1) The regular rotation of the earth on its axis would cause the sun to appear to move *westward* around it in slightly less than one day as do fixed stars.

(2) But if only its annual revolution around the sun be considered, then the sun would appear to move *eastward* around the earth once each year.

Thus the earth's annual motion slows the apparent westward motion of the sun, an effect which is not uniform, principally because of the varying angular velocity of the earth's motion around the sun. The net result is that the G.H.A. of the sun *increases irregularly*. However, the *average* time for the sun to appear to move westward once around the earth is exactly 24 hours of civil time.

The apparent movement of the sun from north to south and return each year is caused by the earth's annual revolution about the sun with its axis inclined to the plane of revolution. The drawing (Fig. 1716) offers a visual explanation of these matters. For an instant about March 21 the sun is directly on the equator but moving northward as it "crosses the line." This is the time of the vernal equinox, or spring equal night, and the point on the celestial sphere where the sun crosses the equator at this time is called the *vernal equinox*. As shown by the changing position of the G.P. sun, its declination now increases northward until about June 21 when it reaches its northerly limit of 23° 27′ N or (+), and thereafter decreases. About September 21 it again "crosses the line" at the time of the autumnal equinox, and about December 21 reaches its southerly limit of 23° 27′ S or (−) and begins to move northward.

These phenomena cause the seasons and longer or shorter days. In the northern hemisphere, June 21 is the longest day and is the first day of summer, and December 21 is the shortest day and is the first day of winter, although maximum and minimum average temperatures are reached about six weeks later. While changes in the sun's declination are vital to navigators, the maximum daily change is not great, and to casual observers the sun will seem to follow the same path for days together.

1717. Planets' apparent motion is quite different from that of fixed stars and each planet moves after its own fashion. Because they are comparatively near to earth, their apparent positions are the combined result of both motions of the earth and the motions of the planets themselves. The result differs for each planet because their motions differ. All appear to move about among the fixed stars. Of the navigational planets, Venus' position on a star map changes most rapidly, and that of Saturn least rapidly. Their movements across the heavens are irregular and their declination varies but they are always near the ecliptic. A little imagination applied to Fig. 1713 will partially explain these doings of planets.

1718. Moon's apparent motion, actually somewhat slower than that of the other navigational bodies, is characterized by its extremely rapid change of position among the stars. This results from the earth's regular rotation on its axis and the moon's journey around the earth, with varying velocity and declination, in about four weeks (Fig. 1718).

Its apparent westward motion, principally caused by the earth's rotation, is slowed by the actual motion of the moon to the eastward. The angular velocity of the moon eastward around the earth is notably irregular, and therefore its net apparent westward motion is erratic. Although on an average the moon will rise about 51m later each day, in the latitude of New York this retardation varies from 13m to 80m. The fact for a navigator to remember is that the rate of increase of the moon's G.H.A. may be changing rapidly.

The changing declination of the moon is caused by its monthly revolution about the earth, the plane of this revolution being inclined at a varying angle to the plane of the earth's equator somewhat as shown on the drawing in Fig. 1718. Thus the moon completes its journey from north to south and back again in about one month, in contrast to the annual period required for the sun to complete a similar cycle. This rapid

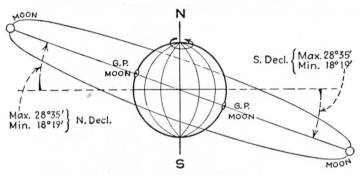

FIG. 1718. EARTH AND MOON.

change in declination causes no inconvenience when observing the moon, although the rate of change may be fifteen times that of the sun and may vary greatly in a single day.

Astronomers have found the moon's motions an intricate problem and many older navigators are prejudiced against its use because, until recently, little or no effort had been made to tabulate its declination and hour angle in a way to avoid difficult interpolations. These difficulties have been overcome. The moon is easy to observe, and its observation often gives a much needed line of position obtainable from no other body.

1719. Phases of the moon. This expression refers to the varying shapes of the luminous portion of the moon as seen from the earth. Light from the moon is reflected sunlight and the sun always shines on half of the moon's sphere, as indicated by the inner group of sketches of the moon in Fig. 1719. If one always looked at the moon from the same direction as that from which come the sun's rays, one would always see the illuminated circular disk called the full moon. But the observer on earth looks at the moon's bright hemisphere from various angles because the moon is always revolving about the earth. Except at full moon, one cannot see all the bright hemisphere, and the illuminated part visible from the earth gradually changes its shape during each lunar month, as shown by the outer sketches.   The shadow of the earth has nothing to do with the varying visible shape of the moon.

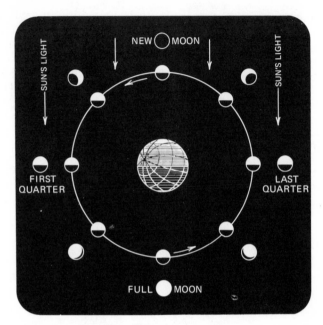

FIG. 1719.   PHASES OF THE MOON.

1720. Causes of tides.   The waters of the spinning earth are held to its surface by the force of gravity which acts uniformly at all points and always toward the earth's center.   The causes of the tides are the varying modifications of this force by the attraction of the moon and the sun (Fig. 1720).

Since the earth and the moon are not actually drawn together it is

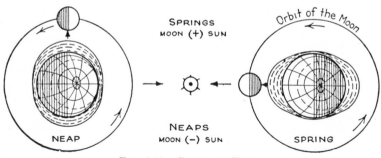

FIG. 1720.   CAUSES OF TIDES.

evident that the attraction of the moon for the earth as a whole, namely for its center, is balanced by other forces. This balance, however, does not apply to units of mass not at the earth's center. Particles of water nearer the moon will be attracted to a greater degree and tend to move toward the moon. On the opposite side of the earth, farther from the moon, the attraction is less and the water particles tend to move away. The sun's attraction has a similar but lesser effect.

Spring tides, which rise higher and fall lower than mean tides, occur about every two weeks near the time of a new moon or a full moon, when the attraction of the moon is augmented by that of the sun. *Neap tides* occur midway between springs, near the time of the first and last quarter of the moon, when the range of the tide is reduced by the effect of the sun. The sources of tidal information and practical matters relating thereto have been discussed in §209.

1721. Eclipses. The preceding discussions, together with Fig. 1721, explain the nature of these phenomena which are of interest although not an element of celestial navigation.

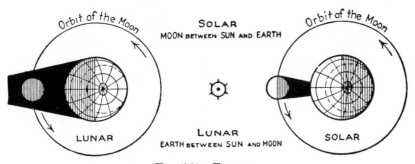

FIG. 1721. ECLIPSES.

A *solar eclipse* takes place when the moon comes between earth and sun and totally or partially covers the sun as seen from certain places on the earth. There may be from two to five solar eclipses in a year, always at the time of a new moon. A total eclipse of the sun lasts not more than seven minutes.

A *lunar eclipse* occurs when the earth comes between moon and sun and may be total or partial as seen by terrestrial observers. Such eclipses take place at times of full moon, are visible from great and varying areas, but seldom occur more than twice a year. A total eclipse of the moon, however, may continue from two to three hours.

The definitions at the beginning of this chapter are essential to the practice of navigation and facilitate reviewing the picture presented in "Lighthouses in the Sky." Such a review will indicate that one must have practical knowledge of the sextant and the observation and corrections of altitudes, time and timekeeping, and how to use the Almanacs, in order to go forward with a navigator's work at sea. These subjects and the working of sights with the knowledge so developed are discussed in the following chapters.

Mariner with Cross-Staff 1676

18. THE SEXTANT AND ITS USE

THE sextant is an instrument which measures the angle between two objects. The most important function of the sextant is the measurement of altitudes above the sea horizon. Because of its small dimensions and its accuracy, and because it does not require a stable mounting, it is peculiarly suited for use at sea. The sextant shares with the compass and the chronometer the honor of being one of the three instruments that have made modern ocean navigation possible.

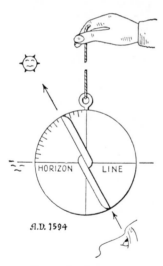

A.D. 1594

Fig. 1800. Astrolabe.

Until the advent of Hadley's sextant in 1731, all instruments in use at sea for measuring angles either depended on a plumb line, as does the astrolabe (Fig. 1800), or required the observer to look in two directions at once as when using a cross-staff. Hadley's name is that most often connected with the sextant, although at the same time Godfrey, at Philadelphia, constructed a similar instrument. It also appears from notes of Sir Isaac Newton (1642-1727), published some time after his death, that he had conceived the principle of the sextant well in advance of either Hadley or Godfrey.

This chapter discusses principally the *horizon sextant* used by surface navigators. *Quintants* and *octants* are similar to sextants in principle and use and do not require specific discussion. The sextant is so named because its arc approximates one-sixth of a circle although, on account of the principle of double reflection, the instrument measures angles of about 120°. The descriptions in the ensuing sections should, if possible, be read with a sextant in one's hand; they will then be more easily understood and not readily forgotten.

217

1801. Elements of a sextant. Various makes of sextants differ in details of design and in auxiliary equipment; all include the same principal elements. The drawing (Fig. 1801) shows a modern sextant as when a 45° sextant altitude of the sun's lower limb be observed.

On the frame is fixed the graduated *arc*, or limb, at whose exact center is pivoted the *index arm*. The *index mirror*, fixed on the upper end

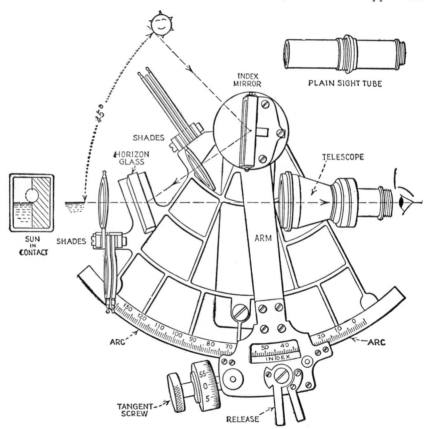

FIG. 1801. ELEMENTS OF A MODERN SEXTANT.

of the arm, moves when the arm is moved; it reflects the sun to the *horizon glass*, which is fixed to the frame and does not move. The half of the horizon glass next to the frame is a mirror which reflects the sun toward the eye; the outer, or left-hand half, is clear glass through which the horizon is seen. A *telescope* is attached to the frame and directs the line of sight, magnifies the observed body, and clarifies the horizon. Various *shades* are provided, principally for use when observing the sun.

The visible horizon will appear through the clear half of the horizon glass. By moving the arm, the sun, reflected from the index mirror, is brought on the horizon glass and thence reflected back through the telescope to the eye; *contact* is attained by minutely moving the arm with the *tangent screw*. The ideal picture in the horizon glass at the instant of contact with the sun's lower limb is shown by the sketch at the left of the sextant.

The arc in the figure reads to degrees and the reading of the sextant is the reading of the arc exactly opposite the *index* which is usually marked by an arrow on the arm. An altitude may be observed to 0′.5 or closer, but if such divisions could be cut on the arc they could not be read. The older device for reading the arc is the vernier which will be discussed first. Thereafter the micrometer shown in the drawing will be easily understood.

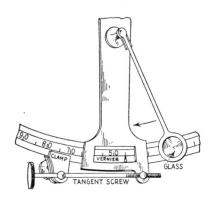

FIG. 1802a. ARM ASSEMBLY WITH VERNIER.

1802. Vernier sextants utilize the device of Pierre Vernier (1631) for measuring a fractional part of the equal divisions of a fixed scale. Figure 1802a shows the position of the vernier on the index arm, and the clamp and the tangent screw with which contact is perfected. When observing, the clamp is loosened and the arm is moved until the body is seen in the horizon glass. The clamp is then made fast and the arm is minutely adjusted by turning the tangent screw until contact is made. The vernier scale is built into the arm and the reading of the arc opposite the arrow which marks the 0 of the vernier is the sextant altitude. A magnifying glass is provided for reading the angles on the arc and on the vernier.

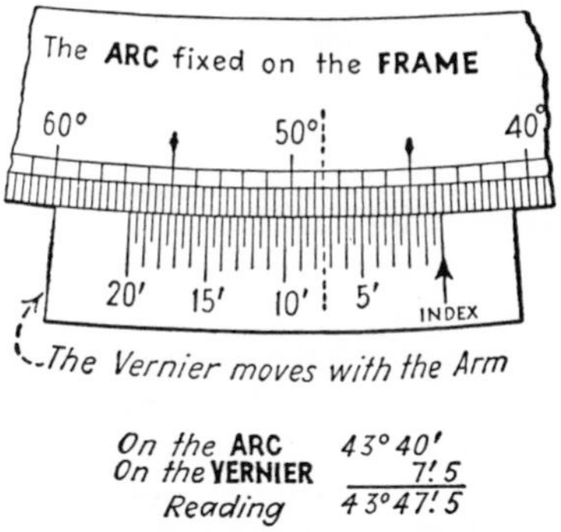

Reading a sextant equipped with a vernier is illustrated by Fig. 1802b. In this case, the scale on the arc shows

FIG. 1802b. READING THE VERNIER.

20′ divisions. The vernier scale as shown is marked from 0′ to 20′ by 0′.5 divisions and serves to read fractional parts of the divisions on the arc to an accuracy of 0′.5. The reading of the sextant is the sum of a reading from the scale on the arc and another reading from the scale of the vernier. First, the reading of the division on the arc next to the right of the zero mark on the vernier is noted as 43° 40′. The eye then moves to the left until some division of the scale on the arc appears exactly opposite one of the divisions of the vernier scale. The reading of this division on the vernier scale, marked on the drawing with a dotted line is noted as 7′.5. The sextant reading is the total of 43° 40′ and 7′.5 or 43° 47′.5, the fractional interval of 7′.5 having been read by the aid of the vernier.

The above example illustrates the general method of reading any scale with a vernier, but the divisions on the arcs and on the verniers of sextants often differ from those shown in the drawing. For this reason the beginner should secure expert advice on reading any vernier sextant he proposes to use. The theory of the vernier is discussed on page 43 of Bowditch (1943).

1803. Micrometer sextants are so named because of the device used to read the fractional parts of the divisions of the arc. Figure 1803 shows the assembly on the arm of the tangent screw with its micrometer head

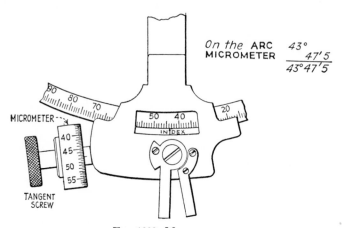

FIG. 1803. MICROMETER.

and release latch. The arc is graduated only into a scale of degrees. Gear teeth, not visible in the drawings, are cut in the outer or lower edge of the arc, one tooth exactly corresponding to one degree of the scale. These teeth engage a hidden thread on the end of the tangent screw, so that one revolution of the tangent screw moves the index mark exactly 1° on the scale of the arc. Fractional revolutions of the tangent screw measure the fractions of a degree by a division of the micrometer head which reads to 0′.5. The reading of the sextant is the sum of the whole degree reading of the arc next to the right of the index mark, which in the figure reads 43°, and the reading of the micrometer head which is 47′.5, or a total of 43° 47′.5.

1804. Choice. The micrometer type is preferable because it is easy to read even when moist and because it eliminates the chance of blunders with a vernier. New sextants issued to the U. S. Navy are of this type, have an arc with a radius of about 7 inches, and weigh slightly over 4 pounds. Smaller, lighter instruments are more difficult to hold steady.

New vernier sextants represent the refinement of the type used by navigators for two hundred years. Although a nuisance to a beginner, verniers do the work. Practically all instruments of this type read to 10″, a degree of accuracy seldom obtained in actual practice.

Obviously a new sextant will be purchased from a regular dealer who should be able to assist in its selection. A few good second-hand instruments are available; but should not be considered, however new they appear, unless their accuracy and condition be vouched for by an expert. A slight blow may have done irreparable damage.

Not less than two sextants should be on every ship at sea. There is always a chance that by some accident one will be ruined or lost.

1805. Care. Once you have a good sextant, properly adjusted, remember that it is a delicate instrument and must not be knocked around. It should be kept in its box, accessible to the deck, with the box arranged so that it cannot jump out of position and slide about in a seaway. The instrument should be removable without moving the box and should be returned thereto immediately after taking sights. It must not be dropped and should not be long in the direct rays of the sun. When shelter is not available, a towel will protect it while waiting to get a sight. Moisture must not remain on the mirrors and glass surfaces, which are best dried with old, clean, soft linen. Silk or chamois may scratch the mirrors; cotton cloth or waste leaves lint. A 50 per cent alcohol solution helps clean glass and is safe to use on a sextant. Never polish the arc or the vernier; when necessary clean with ammonia. A touch of thin oil and lampblack will bring out their divisions. A few drops of oil are needed occasionally on the sextant's working parts.

Adjustments of the sextant are fully described and illustrated in Bowditch. The amateur should remember Raper's advice, "The adjusting screws are *never to be touched except from necessity*, and then with the greatest possible caution." Better leave all adjustments to your instrument dealer rather than risk upsetting the sextant on which your landfall depends.

1806. Index correction (I.C.). Let the sextant be held vertically with the telescope pointed at the horizon and with the index mark on the arm about opposite the 0° division of the arc. With the tangent screw bring the direct and reflected horizon lines exactly in line as in Fig. 1806a. Evidently an altitude of 0° is being measured. Examine the reading of the instrument which will probably be slightly different from zero. This difference is the index error in the instrument, known as the *index correction*. A somewhat more accurate method of determining the index correction is to bring the direct and reflected images of a star into coincidence.

The index correction must always be applied to any altitude as read from the sextant; thus, adding or subtracting the I.C. is an element of correcting every altitude. This is the practice of sea navigators, because any attempt to reduce the index error to zero may upset other adjustments which the theory of the sextant requires to be exact. The index error is not necessarily constant and should be verified from time to time.

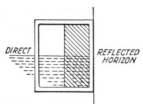

The Altitude of the Horizon = 0

Fig. 1806a. OBSERVING FOR I.C.

If the index, or zero of the vernier, lies to the left of the 0° mark, or on the arc, the I.C. is marked (−) and must be subtracted from all readings; if the index appears to the right of 0°, or off the arc, the I.C. is (+) and must be added to the reading. The old rule is: "When it's on it's off and when it's off it's on."

Reading the I.C. is no different from reading any other angle except when the zero of the vernier is off the arc to the right of the 0° mark. In this case the left-hand division of the vernier must be considered as its zero and its divisions must be counted from that point to the right. See Fig. 1806b, which also suggests that the same result is obtained by subtracting the usual vernier reading from its highest reading. To illustrate the principle, the figure reads 1° 26′ off the arc, which far exceeds any ordinary index correction.

1807. Observing the sun. It is customary to observe the angle between the horizon and the lower edge of the sun's disk which navigators call the sun's *lower limb*. The beginner well may take his first sights without any telescope or sight tube because he can see what he is doing. Thereafter he should use the plain sight tube, or the low-power telescope.

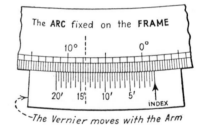

The ARC fixed on the FRAME

10°   0°

20′   15′   10′   5′   INDEX

~The Vernier moves with the Arm

Off the ARC   1° 20′
VERNIER, 20′ to 14′   6′
Reading   1° 26′

Fig. 1806b. READING OFF THE ARC.

Select the desired telescope or sight tube and screw it in place. See that all glass surfaces are clean and that all shades are thrown back. Go on deck and choose a comfortable steady position from which the sun and the horizon under it can be seen. Focus the telescope on the horizon and, if necessary, turn a shade before the horizon glass to limit the glare of the sun's reflection from the water. Turn one or more shades before the index glass according to the estimated brightness of the sun.

Hold the instrument vertically in the right hand, both eyes open, and direct the line of sight to the horizon directly under the sun. While continuing to hold the horizon on the direct line of vision, move the index arm out from 0°, away from the observer, until the reflected image of

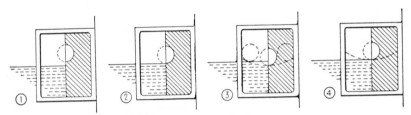

FIG. 1807. WHEN OBSERVING THE SUN.

the sun is seen in the horizon glass, with its lower edge preferably near the horizon, as in (1), Fig. 1807. Pushing the arm out lowers the sun as it appears on the glass. If the student finds difficulty in getting the reflected sun on the horizon glass, first find its approximate altitude as in §1811. When the sun is approximately on the horizon, vernier sextants of the older type require that the arm be clamped. With the tangent screw, perfect the contact of the sun's lower limb with the horizon as in (2). The beginner may forget which way to turn the tangent screw to move the sun up or down on the horizon glass. On most sextants, if the right-hand edge of the tangent screw be moved down, the sun will appear to move down. Having made contact, determine whether the instrument has been held vertically by rotating it slightly about the line of sight. The sun will appear to move in a small arc as in sketch (3). The instrument is vertical when the sun appears lowest, therefore again perfect the contact as in (4). The instant of contact is the time of the observation. The reading of the instrument is the sextant altitude.

The observation just described may be simple from the bridge of a steamer in fine weather but it is seldom easy to get an accurate altitude from a small sailing craft at sea. Beginners often are more at fault with their altitudes than with figures or theory.

When taking a sight from a small craft, stand where there is the least motion, braced against some vertical support or a companion's shoulders, with arms and upper body flexible. Take the sights when near the top of a sea and avoid the top of a nearby wave as a horizon. When spray is flying use a plain sight tube, or no tube or telescope. Let an assistant take time and record the figures, and use the average of several sights like an airman.

1808. Evaluation of altitudes. An experienced navigator forms a judgment of the probable accuracy of every altitude he observes. From a big ship and under perfect conditions the error, plus or minus, may not exceed 0′.2; a more probable assumption, under favorable circumstances, is 0'.5. It may be much greater on a small craft in foul weather where 5', plus or minus, is nearer the truth.

The observer may check his skill with the sextant under various conditions by taking a series of altitudes of the sun at regular intervals. Have an assistant, with a watch, prepared to record the sextant's readings. Observe a few altitudes; thereafter take the sun's altitude each minute or half-minute, as warned by your assistant, and let him record the sextant readings. The difference between such altitudes, observed at regular intervals, should be constant during any few minutes of time. Otherwise consider the observations as possibly in error by plus or minus the variations in the differences.

It is often desirable to take several altitudes in succession or, if possible, at regular intervals. Comparison of their difference with the difference in time between the sights will give some indication of the most accurate altitudes. Some navigators average the altitudes and times of several sights. Others prefer to choose the sight which is considered most accurate. Sometimes the best three sights are worked separately. The extra arithmetic required by the last suggestion is a good check for the beginner and further indicates the probable limits of error in the observations.

Notwithstanding the difficulties of getting an accurate, properly timed altitude, a skilled observer, seeing a chance to catch the sun through a hole in the clouds, may pick up his sextant and stop watch and quickly get a single valuable observation.

1809. The moon's altitude is often easier to observe than is that of the sun. Probably because of an old prejudice against moon sights the subject is hardly mentioned in most books on navigation. The moon may be observed while the sun shines, or in twilight and sometimes during the night when the light from the moon itself makes the horizon visible. Shade glasses are seldom required, otherwise the sight is taken as when observing the sun. It is often necessary to observe the moon's upper limb because of the varying shape of the visible portion of the moon's disk, in which case the image in the horizon glass may look somewhat as in Fig. 1809. When in bright sunlight and the moon is pale, or when the horizon is difficult to see as at night, it is helpful to approximate the altitude as in §1811.

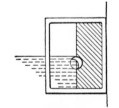

Fig. 1809. Moon's Upper Limb.

1810. Altitudes of stars and planets. The most favorable time for observing these bodies is during twilight when the horizon is at its best. However, with a sextant that has a good star telescope and well silvered mirrors, there is little difficulty at any time on a clear night, especially with moonlight, in obtaining reliable star sights. Whenever stars are to be observed one should go on deck several minutes before taking the sights and let the eyes become adjusted to the semi-darkness.

Methods for taking the altitude of a star or planet differ somewhat from those used when observing the sun or the moon. Stars are only points of light and many such twinkling points may be visible. If the line of vision be held on the horizon, as when observing the sun, and if one attempts to bring the desired star to the horizon in the usual way, several other stars may appear in the mirror, among which the observer cannot identify the star he proposes to use. Therefore different methods are used to bring the star down to the horizon.

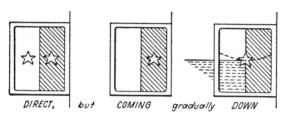

DIRECT, | but | COMING | gradually | DOWN

FIG. 1810. WHEN OBSERVING A STAR.

Select the low-power telescope or the high-power erecting star telescope, if you have one. Do not use the inverting telescope, found with some sextants, because it confuses a beginner. Focus the telescope on the horizon and fix it to the sextant; turn back all shades. With the sextant set at zero, and both eyes open, point the line of vision at the star; the direct view will be seen approximately coincident with the star as reflected from the horizon mirror. Slowly lower the line of vision and at the same time move the index arm out and away from the zero on the arc, *always keeping the image of the star visible in the horizon mirror.* When the reading of the arc approximates the altitude of the star, the horizon will appear and the star is said to have been "brought down," as in Fig. 1810. Perfect the contact so that the point of light which is the image of the star is on the horizon line, and test the vertical position of the sextant as when observing the sun. The reading of the instrument is the sextant altitude of the star at the instant of contact. Avoid bright light until star observations are completed and, if possible, have an assistant take the time.

An unexpected opportunity to observe a single star may give a valuable line of position. It is usual, however, to select two or three stars to be observed at about the same time for a fix. Preparation for a round of stars, including estimating altitudes for setting the sextant in advance, is discussed at length, in Chapter 31.

1811. Upside down! When observing a star some navigators prefer the method shown in Fig. 1811. With the index arrow at zero, turn the sextant upside down and direct the line of sight through the telescope to the star itself as seen through the clear half of the horizon glass. Hold the instrument in this position and push out the arm until the reflected line of the horizon appears across the horizon glass through which the star is also seen. With the arm thus fixed at the approximate altitude, reverse the sextant and perfect the contact in the usual way.

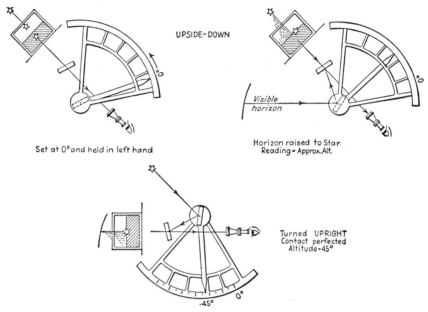

FIG. 1811. THE SEXTANT UPSIDE DOWN.

The advantage of the above method is that the desired star remains constantly in view while the approximate altitude is obtained with the inverted sextant, and immediately appears in the horizon glass when the sextant is righted, without the star's being "brought down." The bright stars are far enough apart to eliminate the chance of picking up the wrong star with the righted sextant. This method may also be used when it is difficult to get a faint, daylight image of the moon, or the sun, onto the horizon glass.

19. ALTITUDES AND THEIR CORRECTION

THE principles of celestial navigation require the use of the true altitude of the center of an observed body above the celestial horizon when determining lines of position. Every altitude read from the sextant must be corrected, otherwise errors may occur ranging from a few miles to upward of fifty miles when the moon be observed. Remember that the practical result of correcting an altitude is to place the observer at the earth's center.

1901. Altitudes and horizons are illustrated on the next page (Fig. 1901), the flat surface of the drawings representing a plane passing through the center of the earth, the ship, and the body observed. Because the position of the ship and that of the body may be anywhere, such a plane may cut through the center of the earth in any direction, and the circles may represent any great circle of the earth. Neither equator, meridians, nor poles appear in the drawings.

The altitude of a celestial body is its angular distance measured vertically above the horizon.

The visible horizon, sometimes called *the sea horizon* or *the natural horizon*, is where the sky appears to intersect the sea. In clear weather it is a circle around the ship the angular level of which depends on the height of the observer's eye above the water.

The sextant altitude, (Hs), is the altitude of a body as read from the sextant without correction of any kind.

The celestial horizon is where a plane through the center of the earth, at right angles to a line from the earth's center through the ship to its zenith, intersects the celestial sphere.

The true altitude, (Ho), sometimes called the *corrected altitude*, is the altitude of the center of the observed body above the celestial horizon, as if measured by an observer at the earth's center.

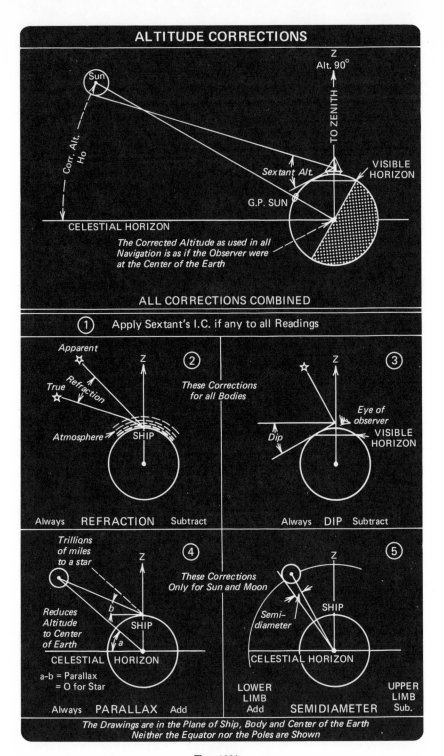

Fig. 1901.

The computed altitude, (Hc), as used when determining a Sumner line, is as from the center of the earth and does not require correction.

The total corrections to be applied to a sextant reading to find the true altitude is the net total of several separate altitude corrections, some of which are (+) and some (−). Bowditch lists 19 different corrections applicable to sextant observations. However, some of these apply only to artificial-horizon type sextants, and others are so small that they can be safely neglected for ordinary navigation. Generally, only 5 or 6 corrections have to be considered; and of these only 3 (index, refraction, and dip) are always required for observations taken with a marine type sextant.

1902. Index correction (+) or (−). This is the correction for the instrumental error of the sextant determined as in §1806. The I.C. must be added to, or subtracted from, all sextant readings if any index error exists.

1903. Refraction (−) is the downward bending of a ray of light as it passes obliquely through the earth's atmosphere to the sextant. The measure of the correction for refraction is the angular difference between the apparent direction and the true direction of an observed body. The drawing indicates that refraction is always a subtractive correction. It applies to all bodies.

Refraction is 0 for an altitude of 90° because the rays from the observed body do not enter the earth's atmosphere at an oblique angle. It increases with decreasing altitudes and, to an observer on the earth's surface, is about 3′ for a body 18° above the horizon, and approximates 35′ for an apparent altitude of 0°. Refraction varies with atmospheric conditions, the effect of which cannot be estimated with complete accuracy, particularly at low altitudes. Therefore observations of a body below 10° should be regarded with suspicion, although the new correction tables for extremes of temperature and pressure in the 1966 *Nautical Almanac* improve the accuracy of low-altitude observations.

The refraction correction for any given altitude decreases as the observer rises to less dense atmospheres far above the earth, and for that reason air navigators use corrections adjusted for such differences.

1904. Dip (−). An observer above the surface of the water must lower his line of vision in order to see the horizon, and the required dip of the eye becomes greater as the height of eye increases. This is why all altitudes measured from the horizon must be corrected for height of eye. The sketch shows that dip is always a subtractive correction. When the observer's height of eye is about 10 feet, failure to correct for dip would result in an error of about 3 miles in the line of position. From the bridge of a steamer, the error would be more or less 6 miles.

1905. Parallax (+) is the difference between the altitude of a body as observed from the ship (corrected for refraction and dip), and its altitude as from the earth's center. It is zero for a body directly over-head and reaches a maximum at an altitude of 0° when it is known as the *horizontal parallax* (H.P.). Altitudes as from the center of the earth are greater than from a ship on its surface, and therefore the correction for parallax, if any, is always additive.

Parallax of a star or planet is counted as 0 by navigators. That of most stars is too minute to be measured; a planet's parallax, at most, is small and variable. For the sun the H.P. is 0'.15 and the parallax correction is included in the altitude corrections tabulated for that body.

The moon's H.P. is about 400 times that of the sun and varies from 54' to 61' every two weeks. This is because the moon is relatively very near the earth and because its distance from us varies from about 222,000 to 253,000 miles in about 14 days.

For many years most correction tables have combined the correction for parallax of the Sun into a single correction which also includes correction for refraction and an average semidiameter. In the *Nautical Almanac* tables beginning in the 1950 Almanac, the parallax correction for the moon is included in the two corrections to the observed altitude of the moon. These are found on the inside back cover for altitudes of 35° to 90° and on the facing page for altitudes of 0° to 35°. The table on each page is divided into two parts which, when added together, give a moon correction that includes refraction, parallax, semidiameter, and augmentation. The latter is a minor correction which is fully explained in Bowditch.

1906. Semidiameter (+) or (−). The required true altitude is that of the center of the body, but it is customary, when using a horizon sextant, to observe the sun's lower limb. In such case the semidiameter always must be added. Altitudes of the moon's lower limb are similarly corrected, but when its upper limb is observed the semidiameter is subtractive. These corrections are important because the apparent semidiameter of both the faraway big sun and the nearby little moon is about 16'. Stars and planets are considered as points of light without diameter.

Semidiameter of sun and moon varies with the varying distances of these bodies from the earth. That of the sun varies within + 0'.6 of the assumed constant minimum semidiameter of 15'.7, and the variation is the same for similar dates in any year. The moon's semidiameter changes about 2' within 2 weeks and the dates of its maxima and minima differ from year to year.

1907. Tables of altitude corrections are so arranged that a few simple figures from them may be combined to give the net correction which must be applied to the sextant reading. Tables printed on the inside cover pages of this Primer, are similar to the tables of the *Nautical Almanac,* and give the corrections applicable to altitudes as measured with a marine type sextant from the sea horizon.

The index correction, peculiar to each sextant, cannot be accounted for in such tables, and the I.C. *should always be recorded,* even though it be 0; preferably before listing the tabulated corrections.

Beginning with 1958, the altitude correction tables in the *Nautical Almanac* provide corrections for altitudes as low as 0°. Corrections for the sun, stars, and planets for altitudes of 10° to 90° are given on the inside front cover, and for altitudes of 0° to 10° are on the facing page. Corrections for the moon for altitudes of 35° to 90° are given on the inside back cover, and for altitudes of 0° to 35° are on the facing page. These tables have been inserted in the corresponding places in this book.

Before 1958, altitude correction tables were entered with "observed altitude" which mariners generally interpreted to mean the uncorrected sextant altitude (Hs). This was not strictly accurate because the index correction peculiar to each sextant and the dip correction for the height of the eye of each observer cannot be accounted for in such tables. In most cases, the error introduced was small for altitudes commonly observed. However, at low altitudes, large changes of refraction occur for small changes of altitude. For these sights, failure to correct for index error and dip might result in an error of several minutes because the table would be entered with the wrong value. Before entering the new tables, the sextant altitude should be corrected for index error and dip if maximum accuracy is to be obtained. The corrected sextant altitude is named "apparent altitude" in the almanac and "rectified altitude" in Bowditch—two names for the same quantity. The *Nautical Almanac* terminology will be followed in this book to avoid confusion for the reader. Furthermore, the examples and problems involving the correction of sextant altitudes will consistently use "apparent altitude" for entering the tables for all altitude corrections, even though such refinement is frequently unnecessary in practice.

Some of the tables are of the "critical" or "turning-point" type in which a range of altitudes (or of heights) correspond to one value of the correction. No interpolation is necessary for tables of this type; but if the entering altitude happens to be one that is tabulated, the correction next higher on the page is taken. For correction tables not of the critical type, interpolation wherever possible is recommended for greatest accuracy. This will be done in the examples, and problems in this book.

In addition to providing corrections for altitudes down to 0°, the 1958 *Nautical Almanac* also introduced a table of corrections for changes of refraction due to abnormal conditions of temperature and pressure of the atmosphere. This table is found on page A4 in the front of the almanac and on page iv of this book. Application of this correction is omitted in the problems of this book unless temperature and pressure are given in the statement of the problem. The altitude correction tables in the *Air Almanac* are explained in Chapter 24.

Corrections for the lower and upper limbs of the sun are found in the column for the appropriate month and are applied to apparent altitude in accordance with the tabulated sign. Except for extremes of temperature and/or pressure, no other correction is required. The tabulated quantity includes the correction for mean refraction, semidiameter, and parallax.

Corrections for stars and planets are found in the "Stars and Planets" columns. For all stars, and all planets except Venus and Mars, the correction is for refraction only and is always subtracted from apparent altitude. For Venus and Mars, a small additional correction is for the effect of parallax because they are near, and for phase because their illumination varies somewhat like the moon. Again excepting abnormal temperature and pressure conditions no other correction to the apparent altitude of a star or planet is required.

Corrections for the lower and upper limbs of the moon are taken in two parts from the table in the back of the almanac. The main corrections in the upper half of the table are tabulated for each 10′ (right and left margins) of each whole degree (boldface type) of apparent altitude. The second correction is found for the lower limb (L) or upper limb (U) in the same column below the main correction opposite the horizontal parallax (H.P.) of the moon. The H.P. is found on the daily page for the time observation. The second altitude correction is always to be *added* to the main correction for either lower or upper limb. However, for *upper-limb sights, 30′ is always to be subtracted from the sum.* The moon corrections include the effects of semidiameter, parallax, mean refraction, and augmentation. Augmentation is the apparent increase of the moon's semidiameter resulting from the fact that one is closer to the moon by the radius of the earth when the moon is in the zenith than when it is on the horizon.

1908. Rules for using the altitude correction tables become a matter of habit. Each following rule is illustrated by an example showing how the various corrections are found and recorded. Since the order of applying the corrections is important, the same procedure will be followed in the examples illustrating each rule as obtains in the forms illustrated in Chapter 29. As noted above, the correction tables are entered with apparent altitude which is sextant reading corrected for index error and dip; therefore apparent altitude is always found first. The correction for air temperature and pressure is shown only for the stars and planets but i. applicable to the sextant altitude of any body if conditions require. All examples in this chapter are for altitudes measured from the sea horizon by a marine type sextant.

1909. Star or planet, to correct the altitude by horizon sextant: (1) Record sextant reading. (2) Record I.C. as (+) or (−). (3) Enter the "Dip" table with "Ht. of Eye" and record the dip (−) correction.

(4) Apply the net total of the I.C. and dip corrections to obtain altitude (Ha). (5) Enter the "Stars and Planets" column (inside front cover) and record the main correction. (6) For Venus or Mars only, record the correction for the appropriate date. (7) Enter the temperature-pressure correction table with the given air temperature (in degrees C or F) across the top and the given air pressure in millibars (left margin) or inches of mercury (right margin), and find the slanting column (A, B, C, etc.). Follow down this column to the line opposite the apparent altitude and record the correction (+ or −). (8) Find the net total of these corrections and apply this total to apparent altitude in accordance with its sign.

Example: Find the true altitudes (Ho) for Sirius and Venus observed on February 5, 1966; I.C. − 2′.5, Ht. Eye 39 ft., temperature 10° F, barometer 30.32 in.: Sirius, Hs 40° 16′.6, Venus, Hs 2° 27′.7.

	Sirius		Venus	
Hs	40°	16′.6	2°	27′.7
	(+)	(−)	(+)	(−)
I.C.		2′.5		2′.5
Dip		6′.1		6′.1
Ha	40°	08′.0	2°	19′.1
Main		1′.2		16′.9
Venus-Mars	—	—	0′.5	
Temp.-Press.		0′.1		2′.2
Totals		1′.3	0′.5	19′.1
Net		− 1′.3		− 18′.6
Ho	40°	06′.7	2°	00′.5

Note that the Ho of a star is always less than its Hs, except where there is an excessive (+) I.C. Note also that the main correction for Venus will be in error by 0′.6 if the table is entered with sextant altitude.

1910. Sun, lower limb and upper limb, to correct the altitude by horizon sextant: (1) Find apparent altitude. (2) Enter the "Sun" table (front of the book) for the appropriate month and record the main corrections found in "Lower Limb" (Upper Limb) column opposite the interval of "App. Alt" which includes the given value of apparent altitude. Do not interpolate; but if the given Ha happens to be one that is tabulated, record the correction next higher on the page. (3) Record the temperature-pressure correction if any. (4) Find the net total of the corrections and apply this total to apparent altitude in accordance with its sign.

Example: Find the true altitudes (Ho) for the sun observed on November 25, 1966; I.C. + 1′.2, Ht. Eye 24 ft.: lower limb Hs 56° 13′.4, upper limb Hs 9° 36′.7.

	☉		☉	
Hs	56° 13′.4		9° 36′.7	
	(+)	(−)	(+)	(−)
I.C.	1′.2		1′.2	
Dip		4′.8		4′.8
Ha	56° 09′.8		9° 33′.1	
Main	15′.6			22′.8
Temp.-Press.	—	—	—	—
Totals	15′.6			22′.8
Net		+ 15′.6		− 22′.8
Ho	56° 25′.4		9° 10′.3	

1911. Moon, upper or lower limb, to correct the altitude by horizon sextant: (1) Find apparent altitude. (2) Record the moon's horizontal parallax (H.P.) for the given date and time found on the daily page (right). (3) Enter the top half of the "Moon" table (back of book) with the whole degrees of Ha (vertical columns) and the minutes of Ha (right or left margins) and record the main correction (always +) interpolating where possible. (4) In the lower half of the same column, find opposite the H.P. the correction for the lower limb under "L" or (as appropriate) the correction for the upper limb under "U" and record this correction. Both of these corrections are always (+). (5) For an upper limb observation, record − 30′, a quantity which does not change. (6) Record the temperature-pressure correction of any. (7) Apply the net total to apparent altitude in accordance with its sign.

Example: Find the true altitudes (Ho) for the moon observed at G.M.T. 1900 on September 29, 1966; I.C. − 2′.5, Ht. Eye 47 ft.; lower limb Hs 21° 29′.6, upper limb Hs 21° 59′.1.

	☽		☽	
	21° 29′.6		21° 59′.1	
Hs				
I.C.	(+)	(−)	(+)	(−)
Dip		2′.5		2′.5
Ha		6′.6		6′.6
	21° 20′.5		21° 50′.0	
Main	61′.9		61′.8	
Temp.-Press.	—	—	—	—
H.P. 54′.1 ☽̲̅	0′.7		—	—
☽	—	—	1′.3	
(−) 30′	—	—		30′.0
Totals	62′.6		63′.1	30′.0
Net	(+)	62′.6	(+)	33′.1
Ho	22° 23′.1		22° 23′.1	

1912. With the 1958 *Nautical Almanac,* the correction of upper limb observations of both the sun and the moon has been greatly simplified over the procedure required by previous almanacs. In fact, the navigator can now use either limb with equal convenience, since the method of correcting the observations are essentially the same for both limbs.

1913. Altitudes in retrospect. The accuracy of a line of position resulting from an observation of a heavenly body, assuming the body's position exactly known, depends only on the accuracy of the true altitude. A difference of 1′ in Ho places the line of position 1 mile toward or away from the body. Inaccuracy of true altitudes may result from several causes, among which are:

(1) Questionable sextant observation
(2) Poor horizon
(3) Abnormal refraction
(4) Errors in correcting the altitude

The magnitude of the errors from the first three depends on the navigator's skill with the sextant and conditions beyond his control. At best, he only can form a judgment as to the reliability of each altitude he observes. *Correcting* an altitude is a more exact process wherein blunders are inexcusable.

Q 1-19: The altitudes listed below were measured from the horizon with a marine type sextant. *Req:* In each case, the true corrected altitude (Ho).

Body observed	1966 Date		G.M.T. h m	Ht. Eye Ft.	I.C.	Sextant reading
(a) ☆ Regulus	Oct.	5	08 26	40	+ 0′.5	34° 28′.7
(b) Venus	April	28	23 15	60	+ 2′.0	21° 31′.5
(c) Sun ☉	May	19	19 43	39	0′.0	35° 33′.3
(d) Sun ☉	July	22	04 18	35	+ 1′.0	38° 30′.0
(e) Moon ☽	July	2	17 00	27	+ 2′.5	40° 38′.1
(f) Moon ☽	March	7	09 31	20	− 2′.0	33° 20′.4
(g) Jupiter	Aug.	4	07 27	30	− 1′.5	24° 18′.9
(h) Sun ☉	June	1	00 14	53	+ 1′.5	8° 39′.6

(In the following, correct also for temperature and pressure.)

Body observed	1966 Date	G.M.T. h m	Ht. Eye Ft.	I.C.	Temp.	Press.	Sextant reading
(i) Mars	Dec. 22	13 46	30	+ 2′.5	40° F	30.12 in.	19° 55′.7
(j) Sun ☉	July 22	18 20	35	+ 1′.0	80° F	29.86 in.	1° 54′.5
(k) Moon ☽	June 3	16 26	60	+ 2′.0	24° C	993 mb.	33° 37′.4
(l) ☆ Capella	July 22	02 22	35	+ 1′.0	−5° C	1013 mb.	30° 34′.1

Answers to Q 1-19. The true altitudes (Ho) are:

(a) 34° 21′.7   (d) 38° 07′.1   (g) 24° 10′.0   (j) 1° 48′.3
(b) 21° 23′.7   (e) 41° 32′.0   (h) 8° 43′.9   (k) 34° 02′.5
(c) 35° 41′.9   (f) 33° 47′.1   (i) 19° 50′.2   (l) 30° 27′.7

20. THE BUBBLE SEXTANT*

VISIBILITY of the sea horizon is essential to the measurement of altitudes with the type of sextant used by mariners. When the horizon cannot be seen altitudes cannot be observed, and even when visible the horizon line may be blurred or inaccurate. Efforts to overcome these limitations are as old as the sextant itself, but the modern bubble sextant has been a recent development brought about by the necessities of aviation. Most of these instruments are in truth octants although called sextants, a term which has become a synonym for any instrument used by navigators to observe altitudes. Bubble sextants are principally used by air navigators, but are also essential to submarines seeking a fix at night. The following discussion affords the mariner, who may be interested, a brief introduction to a subject of growing importance.

2001. Bubble horizons. An artificial horizon, or its equivalent, must be embodied in any instrument for measuring altitudes from ships or aircraft without reference to the natural horizon. The device for this purpose in general use is a spirit level with its bubble, although several satisfactory gyro sextants have been developed. By watching the bubble the observer holds the base plane of the instrument level. Where this plane intersects the celestial sphere is the bubble horizon. It is always parallel to the celestial or true horizon, although it may be at different heights above the earth, depending on the height of eye or altitude of the observer.

To illustrate the bubble method of providing an artificial horizon, imagine an empty watch case, with its crystal in place, to be completely filled with water except for a small bubble of air. When the case is laid on a level surface the bubble will rise to the center of the curved crystal. Conversely, if the surface is not level the bubble will be at one side or the other of the crystal but may be brought to center by leveling the surface. A bubble sextant is leveled in the same way.

2002. Bubble sextants. All instruments of this kind include certain basic elements but, unlike marine sextants, optical systems vary widely,

---

* Except as a matter of general interest, this chapter may be omitted from courses in surface navigation.

as do details of design and equipment. With all types, the bubble marks the horizon. When it is in the center of the field the instrument is level. When the image of the observed body and the bubble are seen together at the center, the reading of the instrument is the altitude of the body.

The drawing in Fig. 2002, scale one-half, outlines a well-known aircraft octant. To simplify the sketch, the lenses of the optical system and the fixed horizon prism have been omitted, as well as an automatic recording device. In use, the octant is held in the position shown. The principal elements of the instrument and how they are used to find the altitude of the sun or any celestial body may be summarized as in the following paragraphs.

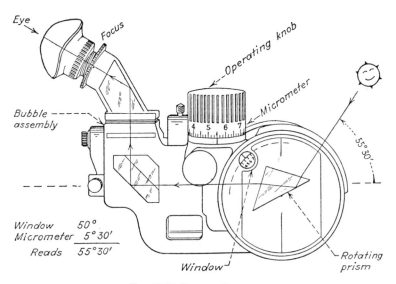

Fig. 2002. Bubble Sextant.

(1) The beam of light from the sun passes down into the instrument, then back and up through the bubble assembly and out at an angle to the observer, who looks down into the eyepiece. In some instruments the bubble assembly is not in the direct line of vision, the image of the bubble being reflected into the field. In either case the bubble and the sun may be seen at the center of the field at the time the altitude is measured.

(2) The sun is reflected back from the mirrored surface of a prism mounted on a worm wheel, the rim of which is seen through the window. The wheel with the prism is rotated by a tangent screw or worm on the spindle of the operating knob, which also serves as a micrometer head.

(3) With the octant turned toward the sun and held level as indicated by the bubble, the image of the sun is brought into the field by turning the operating knob. When the bubble and the image of the body coin-

cide, or nearly so, the reading of the instrument is the altitude of the body above the bubble horizon.

(4) The edge of the worm wheel seen through the window is graduated in units of 10°. The micrometer head on the tangent screw is divided into ten units of 1° with 5′ divisions, although only 10′ divisions are shown on the drawing. The reading of the octant is the window reading plus the micrometer reading.

(5) Like most bubble sextants, the instrument provides for observing altitude from the natural horizon. At the option of the observer the horizon line is shown across the field and altitudes may be measured as with a marine sextant.

There are many other small but important details of design and operation which differ with the make and mark of various models. The novice should seek personal instruction concerning any bubble sextant he proposes to use before attempting to adjust or practice with the instrument. Lacking such assistance, study and follow the maker's printed instructions. Several of the best types of these instruments may be seriously injured by ignorant handling. The following discussion touches on matters related to all bubble sextants.

2003. Practice. To the student first undertaking to use a bubble sextant, its principal characteristic is the elusiveness of the bubble. Unlike a horizon line it is almost always moving about over the field of the instrument. When it appears stuck at one point or another around the field, the instrument is far from level. The bubble must be free and when free it always tends to move. It moves because of an unsteady hand, the motion of the ship or the roll and pitch of a plane. In some instruments the size of the bubble is adjustable; others provide a choice of two sizes. A large bubble moves faster than a small bubble and the smaller size is preferable for the beginner's first practice.

Initial practice should be from a stable position on the ground, from the top of a building or from a window. The sextant is held in both hands with elbows against the chest and the body free from the waist up. Set, rigid muscles are unfavorable to accuracy and speed.

The first step is to learn to center the bubble in the field, sometimes a difficult trick, but with practice one can throw the sextant to his eye and have the bubble centered almost instantly. This is essential to the use of a bubble sextant for a number of reasons presently developed.

Having learned to control the bubble, practice bringing the sun to the center of the bubble. After a little practice, lower the sextant after each sight. As your skill increases, record each altitude and reduce the intervals between the sights. Plenty of practice of this kind is the best preparation for taking and timing the altitudes needed for a line of position.

2004. Averaging for accuracy. The almost invariable method is to take the average of a number of sights. Generally speaking, the greater the number of sights, the greater accuracy. For various reasons, sights taken in rapid succession at regular intervals are preferable to a studied effort to perfect each sight.

In response to the necessity of averaging, a number of devices have been developed for recording a series of altitudes taken in rapid succession. When so recorded, the average altitude is selected by inspection. A similar result may be had by marking each altitude with a pencil on the micrometer scale of the operating knob shown in Fig. 2002.

With sights taken rapidly, it is neither practical nor necessary to time each sight. Time the first and last sights and use the average.

The above remarks indicate little more than the general approach to the problem of getting an accurate timed altitude. They do make clear the necessity for skillful and rapid handling of the instrument. The resulting accuracy in the air with a skilled observer is within 5 to 10 miles, errors which may increase with unfavorable conditions. These results may be bettered from a surface craft in quiet waters, but the quick roll of a submarine is as troublesome as bumpy air.

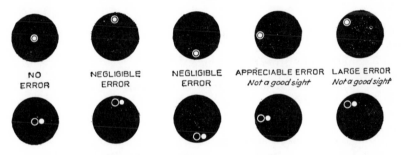

| NO ERROR | NEGLIGIBLE ERROR | NEGLIGIBLE ERROR | APPRECIABLE ERROR *Not a good sight* | LARGE ERROR *Not a good sight* |

FIG. 2004. THE BUBBLE AND THE BODY.

Matching the bubble and the body exactly in the center of the field is not necessary although desirable. This matter is illustrated in Fig. 2004. Roughly speaking, there will be no substantial error when the bubble and the body are nearby on a horizontal line with the bubble not far from the vertical center of the field. The least favorable positions for the bubble are on the intercardinal points near the edge of the field.

2005. To correct the altitude as measured from the bubble horizon, two or three corrections may be required:

(1) *The index correction* (*I.C.*) is similar to the I.C. of a marine sextant and is similarly applied. The index error may be determined in several ways. A simple method is to squat down at the edge of the water when it is not too rough and observe the sea horizon, the altitude of which should then read zero if there be no I.C. Or observe a distant

mark known to be at the exact level of the observer's eye. The accuracy of the instrument also may be tested by taking and working a number of sights from a known fixed position. This method will develop differences in the I.C. at different altitudes.

(2) *Refraction,* other than the I.C. if any, is the only correction to be applied, always (−), to altitudes of the sun, a star or a planet. Altitudes of the moon must be further corrected for parallax.

The ordinary correction for refraction may be taken from the Primer *excerpts.* Use the the top line of the *Air Almanac's* refraction table as in Appendix VI. As the observer's height above the surface of the earth increases, the refraction decreases as shown in the *Air Almanac* table.

When taking the bubble sight from a surface vessel the refraction correction can also be taken from the *Star and Planets* column of the Altitude Correction Tables on the front cover of *Nautical Almanac* or Primer.

(3) *Moon's parallax,* always (+), must be taken into account. It may be read directly from the daily sheet of the *Air Almanac* by inspection and applied together with the refraction correction just mentioned.

To correct a bubble sextant observation of the moon using the *Nautical Almanac,* proceed as with a marine sextant except:

1. Ignore the dip correction.
2. Use the mean of the upper and lower limb corrections in the lower half of the moon table.
3. Subtract 15′ from the altitude.

The Z correction, or displacement of the zenith, discussed and tabulated in the *Air Almanac,* is not strictly an altitude correction, and is applicable only in air navigation.

2006. As a horizon sextant. Most bubble sextants provide for observing altitudes from the natural or sea horizon. Such altitudes are not as accurate as might be determined with a standard sextant but are more accurate than altitudes observed with the bubble.

The I.C. is not the same as for bubble altitudes, and the index error must be determined in the same way as is that of a marine type of instrument.

The other altitude corrections also are quite different from the corrections applicable to bubble altitudes. When the altitude is observed from the horizon the corrections are the same as those applied to altitudes taken with a regular sextant.

2007. Cautions. From the moment you first handle any sextant with an adjustable bubble, take care never to put excessive pressure on the diaphragm which controls the size of the bubble. After using, turn the adjusting knob in the direction of least resistance until it feels free, and thus avoid useless strain on the diaphragm. Remove lighting batteries before putting away.

Otherwise treat your octant like any other delicate and valuable instrument. Keep it in its case, stowed so it cannot bang about. Never touch the optical surfaces with your fingers, which are always greasy. If necessary, first dust with a soft brush, and then clean the glass with soft tissue or lens paper possibly moistened with a few drops of alcohol. Do not oil. Never leave any optical instrument in hot sun.

*   *   *

There appears to be little place for the bubble sextant in surface navigation except as an emergency tool. For reasonably accurate results it requires the rapid and skillful handling of a string of approximations, something new for an old navigator.

21. TIME

THE subject of time, always difficult for students of navigation, has been greatly simplified since 1933. Today, with the same kind of time used in civil life, the position of the sun, the moon, or any of the navigational stars or planets may be taken from the Almanacs without the use of apparent or sidereal time. This simplification does not eliminate the necessity for determining the exact instant of an observation; chronometers and timekeeping are discussed in the next chapter.

2101. The natural measure of time is the sun's apparent motion over the earth which causes the periods of darkness and light, as well as the seasons. It does not provide a practical measure, however, because the apparent motion of the true sun is not uniform (§1716) and units of time measured thereby are of varying duration. The variation is slight but clocks cannot be regulated by apparent time (§2116).

To retain the advantage of a time based on the sun, an imaginary sun, called the mean sun, is used. *The mean sun* is an imaginary body which would appear to move westward around the earth at a uniform rate equal to the average rate of the true sun. If both suns were seen in the sky, following the same track, their positions would coincide at only four instants during the year but would never appear far apart.

2102. Mean time, sometimes called civil mean time or civil time, is time as measured by the motion of the mean sun. Under various names, it is the time we live by and is the only kind of time essential to present-day navigation.

A civil day is the interval of time required for the mean sun to make one revolution about the earth. It is divided into 24 hours of 60 minutes of 60 seconds always of the same duration. The day begins at midnight (0h) at the instant the mean sun crosses the lower meridian of the observer. As the sun moves westward around the earth, the time increases. The instant of the upper transit of the mean sun across the meridian marks noon (12h) mean time for that meridian. The sun then continues westward until it again crosses the lower meridian, and a civil day of 24 hours, always of the same duration, is ended never to return.

242

For most purposes of civil life the day is divided into two periods of 12 hours each. Time before noon is marked A.M. which means *ante* or before the sun has crossed the meridian. After noon, time to midnight is marked P.M. indicating time *post* or after the sun crosses the meridian. In the Almanacs the hours are numbered from 0 to 24 without special designations.

Although the duration of a civil day is the same for all places, the time of day is common only to points on the meridian of longitude from which the momentary east-west position of the mean sun is measured. The sun's transit westward over that meridian marks the instant of noon, 12h, mean time, but the sun already will have crossed meridians to the eastward where time is therefore after noon or later; for points westward the time is before noon or earlier.

Listeners to international broadcasts know that standard time at London (75° to the eastward) is five hours later than New York standard time, just as the football fan knows that time on our Pacific Coast (45° to the westward) is three hours earlier than at New York. Minor differences in exact civil time are less well understood. If one walks across Manhattan Island on 42nd Street, New York City, the exact local time will have changed about 9 seconds. To the eastward of New York at Boston, local time is about 12.5 minutes faster; westward, at Philadelphia, the local time is about 5 minutes slower than at New York.

Local Mean Time (*L.M.T.*). An infinite number of different mean times is possible, each being L.M.T. for the meridian on which the time is based. Comparatively few are in standard use and these are given special designations, the most important to navigators being Greenwich mean time (G.M.T.).

The term L.M.T. as used in navigation generally means local mean time for the meridian of longitude of the ship, although it may mean local time at any place.

2103. Greenwich mean time is the local mean time for all points on the meridian of Greenwich, England. The reason for its importance is that some place had to be chosen as a base for the tabulations in the almanacs. Since Greenwich historically is on the prime meridian for the measurement of longitude, the Greenwich meridian became also the meridian of reference for the predicted time of occurrence of astronomical events.

Greenwich mean time, sometimes called Coordinated Universal Time (UTC), is the standard for civil time keeping and for navigation. It is not strictly uniform, but when corrected by a few milliseconds for variations in the earth's motion, it gives UT1 for use by geophysicists and others requiring a more uniform measure of time.

Greenwich mean time is the same throughout the world. Hence, activities of world-wide scope keep their clocks and watches set to Greenwich mean time. Military communications and other operations are regulated by this time.

The lower, circular drawing of Fig. 2103 is the sphere of the earth as viewed from above its south pole. Around it is shown the apparent progress of the mean sun around the earth and how its position measures G.M.T. The upper, rectangular diagram illustrates the same facts by plotting succeeding geographic positions of the mean sun on a map of the world. For convenience the sun is shown as moving westward along the equator (0° Decl.), a permissible assumption because the westward motion of the mean sun, which is the measure of civil time, is not affected by the sun's varying declination.

As always in the measurement of mean time, the day begins at midnight (0h), the instant the center of the mean sun, marked (0) in the drawing, crosses the lower meridian, 180° E or W, at the time of its *lower transit.* As the mean sun moves westward at the rate of 15° per hour the time grows later and at (3), having moved westward 45° to the meridian 135° E of Greenwich, G.M.T. is 3h 00m A.M. or simply 0300 when stated in accordance with Navy practice. When the mean sun crosses the meridian of Greenwich at the time of *upper transit,* or simply transit, G.M.T. is 12 M. or 1200. For reasons stated later, this instant is almost never the exact time of transit of the true sun. After noon the mean sun continues to travel westward, always at a constant rate of 15° of longitude per hour. When it is 45° west of Greenwich it is 3 P.M. or 1500 G.M.T. and thus onward until its succeeding lower transit marks the end of the day (24h) and a new day begins.

In a similar manner, local mean time for any meridian is measured by the relative position of the mean sun to that meridian.

2104. Time and longitude. Either quantity may be expressed in units of arc or in units of time. Understanding this relation between time and longitude is facilitated by the following considerations:

Longitude is measured in degrees (°) and minutes (′) of angular measure. Arcs representing time, however, are often expressed in units of time as a measure of arc. As 24 hours of time are required for the mean sun to traverse a circle of 360° at a uniform rate of 15° per hour, the circle may be divided into 24 hours with each arc further divided into minutes and seconds of time. When an arc is so divided time units may be used as a measure of arc. Useful equivalents of identical arcs measured in degrees and minutes of arc or by units of time may be expressed in these ways:

$$360° = 24 \text{ hours}$$
$$15° = 1 \text{ hour}$$
$$1° = 4 \text{ minutes}$$
$$15' = 1 \text{ minute}$$
$$1' = 4 \text{ seconds}$$

GREENWICH MEAN TIME

MEASURED by the MEAN SUN

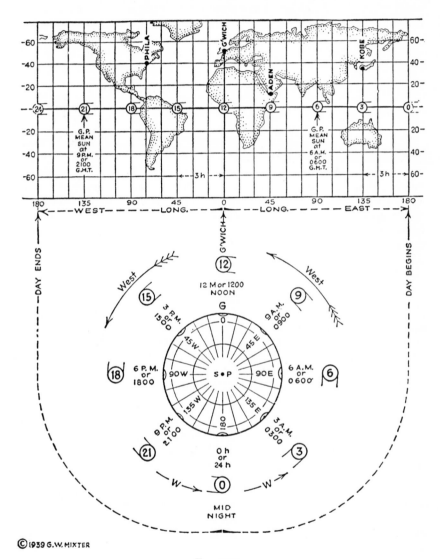

© 1939 G.W. MIXTER

Fig. 2103.

2105. Converting time into arc, or vice versa, is often necessary. With the above figures in mind, conversions may be computed or determined with the aid of CONVERSION OF ARC TO TIME Table I, on page 484, or with any similar table. For example:

<table>
<tr><td colspan="2" align="center">CONVERSION OF
123° 46'.5 INTO TIME</td><td colspan="2" align="center">CONVERSION OF
8h 15m 06s INTO ARC</td></tr>
<tr><td>123°</td><td>= 8h 12m</td><td>8h 12m = 123°</td><td></td></tr>
<tr><td>46'</td><td>=   3m 04s</td><td>3m 4s =   46'</td><td></td></tr>
<tr><td>0'.5 =</td><td>2s</td><td>2s =   0'.5</td><td></td></tr>
<tr><td>*Ans.*</td><td>8h 15m 06s</td><td>*Ans.*   123° 46'.5</td><td></td></tr>
</table>

Conversions in full detail as above are less often required than with the old navigation. Conversions of a rounded figure to another rounded figure are necessary at almost every turn. These become almost instinctive with practice. Begin this practice at once by computing the answers to Q 1, Q 2, and Q 3 found at the close of this chapter. The basic fact to remember is that 15° = 1 hour. Picture the 60 minutes of this hour as they appear on the face of a watch. 4 minutes = 1°, and one of those minutes is equivalent to 15' of arc. For many purposes, this is all that is necessary.

2106. Time diagrams consist of a circle representing the equator as viewed from above the pole at the center. Radii of the circle represent the meridians of two or more places and the relative east-west position of the sun or other body. In this Primer *westward* is assumed to be counter-clockwise, as if the time diagram were viewed from above the south pole. Typical time diagrams which may be drawn free hand to fit any situation are like those shown with the solutions of numerous problems in later chapters.

Westward counter-clockwise is in current accord with Bowditch, the Almanacs, Dutton, and all modern textbooks of surface navigation. The student should avoid confusion with the old custom which assumes westward as clockwise, although either assumption is permissible.

2107. Time at another place. The basic relations between time and longitude, as demonstrated in Fig. 2107, are important.

At the center of the drawing is a time diagram. The four radii of the circle shown by solid lines are the meridians of Kobe (135° E), Aden (45° E), Greenwich (0° Long.), and Philadelphia (75° W). The dotted extensions of these radii to the opposite side of the circle are their lower meridians from which time is measured. The outer circles graduated in hours of time show the local mean time for each place when the mean sun is in a given position. On the circle marked Kobe, 0h is when the sun is on the lower or dotted meridian of that place; noon (12h) is marked by the sun's transit of the meridian above Kobe. The 0h and 12h points are similarly fixed for each of the other places.

The drawing offers a graphic illustration of the relations between time and longitude and the differences in local time when measured from various meridians. For example, the instant the mean sun is in longitude 135° E, the extension of this meridian to the outer circles indicates local mean time at Kobe as 12h (noon), 6h at Aden, 3h at Greenwich, and 22h (previous day) at Philadelphia.

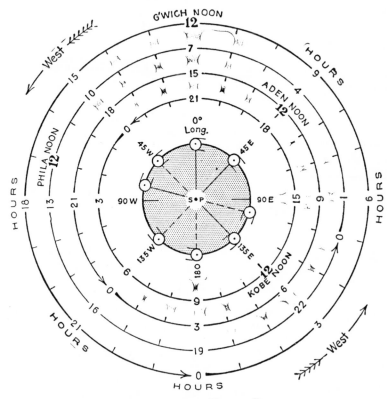

FIG. 2107. TIME AT VARIOUS PLACES.

Remembering that an arc of the equator may be measured by units of arc or units of time, a further examination of Fig. 2107 will confirm the following theorems:

(1) *At any two places the local mean times differ by the longitude difference between the places.*

(2) *The place east has the later time; at places west time is earlier.*

(3) *To find the time at another place: Add longitude difference east, subtract west.*

As used in navigation, the term *longitude difference* of two places is the smaller arc of the equator intercepted between the meridians of the places. This may be: (*a*) Difference between two longitudes of like name, the longitude of both places being E or both W. (*b*) Sum of two longitudes when of different names, one place E, the other W. (*c*) If the total of *b* exceeds 180°, 360° minus such total is the smaller arc between the meridians of the places.

The three theorems stated above are as instinctive to the experienced navigator as is time-arc conversion. Let the student prove each for himself, again and again, with the aid of Fig. 2107. Then compute the answers to questions Q 4 to Q 7 inclusive before going further.

2108. Standard time. It is impracticable to carry on the affairs of modern civilization with a different local time for every city, village, and farm, therefore:

Standard time zones have been established for the operation of railroads and the business of the world. Standard time is the L.M.T. for some selected standard meridian. In the United States four kinds of standard time are in use:

Eastern	(E.S.T.)	L.M.T. for 75° W.
Central	(C.S.T.)	L.M.T. for 90° W.
Mountain	(M.S.T.)	L.M.T. for 105° W.
Pacific	(P.S.T.)	L.M.T. for 120° W.

The longitude differences of 15° between the governing meridians indicate a time difference of one hour from zone to zone, Pacific time being three hours slow of Eastern time. The dividing lines between areas which use these times are somewhat arbitrary.

Daylight saving time or *fast time* is one hour fast of standard time for a community. *War time* is daylight saving time when used throughout the entire calendar year. *Double daylight saving time* is two hours fast of standard time, as used during the summer in England for the period of World War II.

2109. Ship time. In the old days, the clock was set at 12 when the captain, taking the sun, cried "Noon." The custom of using local time, sometimes adjusted more often than once each day, continued to be the general practice at sea until shortly after World War I, and today is that of many merchantmen. This kind of ship time is of little interest to the celestial navigator.

2110. Zone time was established in the U.S. Navy in 1920. It provides for the keeping of standard time at sea over all the oceans of the world. This system of timekeeping is more than an official convenience. It has so simplified the handling of time that it should be understood and used by all students.

The miniature chart, Fig. 2110, shows the water areas divided into **24** zones, each reaching from pole to pole, 15° of longitude in width, the

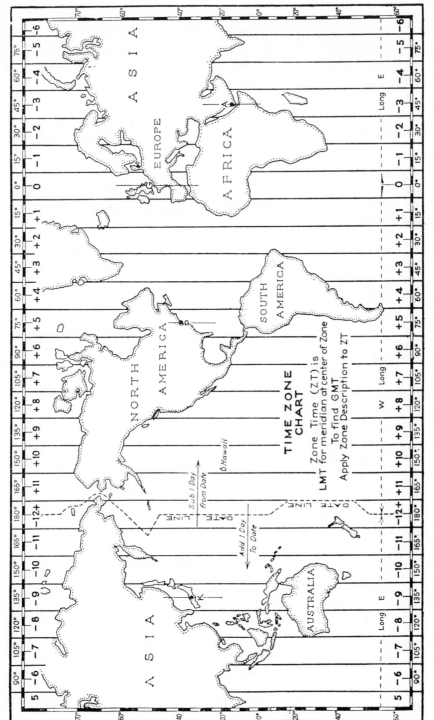

Fig. 2110.

meridians through the center of the zones being 15° or 1h apart. Zone time over the entire width of any zone is L.M.T. for the central meridian of that zone.

Zone descriptions are so named as to indicate the hours to be added to or subtracted from the zone's time to find Greenwich mean time. The central meridian of Zone 0 is the meridian of Greenwich (0° Long.), the time difference is zero and the zone is named accordingly.

First west of Greenwich, where time is 1 hour earlier, comes Zone +1, the zone description indicating that 1 hour must be added to Zone +1 time to find G.M.T. The plus zones continue westward at 1h intervals of 15° to Zone +12 which includes only the area between 172½° W and 180°.

Eastward of Zone 0, where time is later, the descriptions Zone −1, Zone −2, etc., to Zone −12 indicate the whole hours of time to be subtracted from Z.T. to find G.M.T. Note that the twelfth zone is divided into Zone +12 and Zone −12 because the dates either side of the meridian of 180° differ by one day or 24 hours.

To find the zone description for any given longitude: Practice counting from 0 to 180 by 15° intervals, 0, 15, 30, etc., to 105, 120, 135, etc. Each count is the longitude of the center of a zone which extends 7½° east and west from that longitude. With these stop points in mind, the zone description of any longitude is at once identified. The formal rule is to divide the ship's longitude by 15 to the nearest whole number and prefix the appropriate (+) or (−) sign.

Ships' clocks keeping zone time must be reset after leaving a time zone. Exactly when is immaterial, but the change is generally made on the hour following entry into the new zone, or one or two hours later. When using zone time for timing sights, the navigator need only remember the zone description of the time to which his watch is set.

The zone time system and some of its local modifications are given in Bowditch. The standard times kept by several hundred places over the world are given in the *Nautical Almanac.*

2111. Conversions of L.M.T. to Z.T. and vice versa are often required for one or another special purpose.

Zone time is local mean time only for points on the central meridian of the zone. From that meridian *eastward L.M.T. is later* because the sun gets there first; to the *westward L.M.T. is earlier.* The maximum difference between zone time of the correct description and L.M.T. is ½ hour (7½° of Long.) or 30 minutes, a figure which will be increased if the navigator's watch is not yet set to the zone of the ship's longitude.

The interconversion of Z.T. and L.M.T. is a simple case of finding the time at another place. The longitude difference is that from the zone center to the actual longitude of the ship. The steps in the conversion are (1) find the longitude difference, (2) convert it into time, and (3) apply the difference, and when so doing reason for yourself. East from the zone center, L.M.T. is greater than Z.T. West of the zone center, L.M.T. is less than Z.T. As a matter of instruction, rather than for trained navigators, the rules and corrections to whole minutes of time are shown in Table 3, Fig. 2111. To compute the same figures it is only necessary to note the longitude difference and remember that 1° = 4 minutes and that 15′ = 1 minute.

TABLE 3	To convert **L. M. T.** TO **Z. T.** Corr in minutes																		
	ADD										SUBTRACT								
	For Long Diff. WEST of Zone Center										For Long Diff. EAST of Zone Center								
	8°	7°	6°	5°	4°	3°	2°	1°	0°		0°	1°	2°	3°	4°	5°	6°.	7°	8°
0′	32	28	24	20	16	12	8	4	0	0′	0	4	8	12	16	20	24	28	32	0′
15′	33	29	25	21	17	13	9	5	1	15′	1	5	9	13	17	21	25	29	33	15′
30′	34	30	26	22	18	14	10	6	2	30′	2	6	10	14	18	22	26	30	34	30′
45′	35	31	27	23	19	15	11	7	3	45′	3	7	11	15	19	23	27	31	35	45′
60′	36	32	28	24	20	16	12	8	4	60′	4	8	12	16	20	24	28	32	36	60′

SUBTRACT   ADD

To convert **Z. T.** TO **L. M. T.** Corr. in minutes

TABLE 4	Centers of **TIME ZONES** and Zone Description											
			LONGITUDES EAST →									
0	15°	30°	45°	60°	75°	90°	105°	120°	135°	150°	165°	180°
0	−1	−2	−3	−4	−5	−6	−7	−8	−9	−10	−11	−12+
			← WEST LONGITUDES									
180°	165°	150°	135°	120°	105°	90°	75°	60°	45°	30°	15°	0
−12+	+11	+10	+9	+8	+7	+6	+5	+4	+3	+2	+1	0

FIG. 2111. ZONE TIME DATA.

Example: Ship in longitude 137° 45′ E, clocks keeping Zone −9 time. Find L.M.T. at 1123 ship's time. The longitude difference from 135° E is 2° 45′ East where time is later. 2° 45′ = 11 minutes to be added to the zone time. *Ans.* At 1123 Z.T. the L.M.T. is 1134.

2112. Navigator's time. Sights may be timed by any kind of time handled in any way that results in the G.M.T. and date required for entering the Almanacs. For this purpose time must be stated with hours reading from 0h to 24h. The date must be that at Greenwich which may be tomorrow or yesterday. The date is important. An error of one day (24h) in the Greenwich time of a sight means an error in longitude which may exceed 7′ when the sun is observed, about 1° for a star sight, and more or less 12° for the moon. The ideal method would be to time a sight by a watch with hours reading from 0 to 24 and keeping exact G.M.T. This is seldom practical at sea where either of the methods given in the next two sections may be used.

2113. G.M.T. and date by zone time are almost self-evident, as may be understood after noting the following steps:

A sight is timed by the navigator's watch set to zone time. Let the time be recorded with P.M. time reading from 12h to 24h. This is Z.T. of sight as of the date at the ship.

Add a (+) zone description to the zone time to find G.M.T. Unless the total exceed 24h, the Greenwich date will be the same as at the ship If the total exceed 24h and 24h must be deducted, the time at Greenwich has passed into the next day, and the Greenwich date is one day later.

For example: If you live in Zone +5, as in New York or Boston, when the time is 7 A.M. (0700), it is noon (1200) of the same day at Greenwich, London. Or if you observe a star from Zone +5 at 8 P.M. (2000) it is 5 hours later at Greenwich (2500) or 1 A.M. (0100) of the next day.

Subtract a (−) zone description from the zone time to find G.M.T. If the zone time is greater than the hours to be subtracted, the date at Greenwich is the same as at the ship. If 24h must be borrowed from the oncoming day, the Greenwich date is one day earlier.

For example: You are in Melbourne, Australia, Zone −10. At 7 P.M. (1900) it is 9 A.M. (1900 − 10h = 0900) of the same day in Greenwich. At 7 A.M. (0700), however, your day has not begun at Greenwich where it is 9 P.M. or (7 + 24) − 10h = 2100 of the previous day.

2114. G.M.T. and date by chronometer. When the method of timing gives the chronometer time of the sight, care must be exercised to determine G.M.T. and date.

Checked by radio time ticks, chronometers are depended on for accurate time at sea whether it be G.M.T. or zone time. Set to Greenwich time, the face of a chronometer, like that of any clock, reads only from 0h to 12h and its reading is 12h slow when G.M.T. is from 13h to 24h. The navigator knows when to add 12h to the chronometer reading by approximating G.M.T. from his longitude and local time as in question Q 6. The Greenwich date then becomes evident as when working from zone time. It is helpful to remember that when it is noon in Greenwich, the same date exists all over the world.

2115. To check the G.M.T. and date. At the United States Naval Academy a time diagram is required in the solution of all time problems. The use of such diagrams for checking the G.M.T. and date and for indicating the handling of the chronometer reading is illustrated in Fig. 2115.

If the beginner cannot understand these conventional diagrams, let him proceed in this manner: Trace one of the diagrams and place it over the center of the diagram in Fig. 2107 so that G on the tracing coincides

Ship in **WEST** Longitude	Ship in **EAST** Longitude
Greenwich east of ship where Time is later	*Greenwich west of ship where Time is earlier*
ADD *Long. to L.M.T.*	**SUBTRACT** *Long. from L.M.T.*

Ship's Long. about 75° W
L.M.T. about 10 A.M. Nov. 8
Chro. reads 3h 15 m

Approx. L.M.T.	8d 10h
Long. 75° W (+)	5h
Approx. G.M.T.	8d 15h

Same date but add 12h to Chro.

Chro.	3h 15m
Add	12
G.M.T.	15h 15m, Nov. 8

Ship's Long. about 45° E
L.M.T. about 9A.M. Nov. 8
Chro. reads 5h 29m

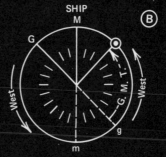

Approx. L.M.T.	8d 09h
Long. 45° E (−)	03h
Approx. G.M.T.	8d 06h

Same date and Chro. face is correct

Chro.	5h 29m
G.M.T.	5h 29m, Nov. 8

Ship's Long. about 75° W
L.M.T. about 10 P.M. Nov. 8
Chro. reads 2h 49 m

Approx. L.M.T.	8d 22h
Long. 75° W (+)	5h
Approx. G.M.T.	9d 03h

One day later, Chro. face correct

Chro.	2h 49m
G.M.T.	2h 49m, Nov. 9

Ship's Long. about 135° E
L.M.T. about 6 A.M. Nov. 8
Chro. reads 9h 29m

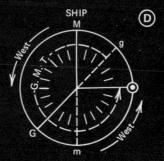

Approx. L.M.T.	8d 06h
Long. 135° E (−)	9h
Approx. G.M.T.	7d 21h

One day earlier but add 12h to Chro.

Chro.	9h 29m
Add	12
G.M.T.	21h 29m, Nov. 7

M = Ship   **G** = Greenwich   ◉ = Sun

Fig. 2115. To Check G.M.T. and Date.

with the meridian of Greenwich. The extension of the meridian of the sun on the tracing will then mark L.M.T. on the time circle for the place whose name is on the meridian of the ship and G.M.T. on the Greenwich time circle.

Four examples are given in Fig. 2115, together with their respective time diagrams. Observe examples (C) and (D), which are when G.M.T. is one day later and one day earlier than the local date. In such cases the sun's position always lies between the lower meridian of Greenwich and the lower meridian of the ship, and gives warning of a different Greenwich date.

To lay out a time diagram requires practice, particularly to acquire the knack of estimating angles. In so doing, it is helpful to remember that a quarter of a circle is 90° or 6h and one-third of this quadrant is 30° or 2h.

The upper half of the vertical diameter is assumed as the meridian (M) of the ship; the dotted half of this diameter represents the lower meridian (m). Westward, counter-clockwise, is to the left across the top of the diagram but to the right across the bottom. The ship's approximate longitude serves to locate the meridian of Greenwich. For example, in case (A) of Fig. 2115, longitude is 75° W which means that Greenwich is 75° east of the ship and that the end of an arc of 75° to the right of M indicates where the upper meridian of Greenwich (G) should be drawn; its lower meridian is marked (g).

In problems of finding approximate G.M.T. and date the meridian of the sun is located by an arc equivalent to local time at the ship measured westward from its lower meridian (m). In case (A) this is an arc of 10h or 150°.

2116. Apparent time is almost the same as mean time but is measured by the apparent motion of the *true* sun which is the sun we see.

The duration of 1 year of apparent time is exactly the same as 1 year of mean time but during the year apparent time is irregular because of the varying angular velocity of the sun as it appears to move around the earth (§1716). In two periods of the year the true sun is ahead of the imaginary mean sun and apparent time is greater than mean time; during the two intervening periods the reverse is true.

The position of the mean sun is almost always slightly different from that of the sun itself but its substitution for the true sun scarcely would be noticed except when observing azimuths. Tables of the sun's azimuth always must be entered with apparent time or its equivalent.

2117. Equation of time (Eq.T.) is the minutes and seconds of time to be added to or subtracted from the mean time at any instant to find the apparent time at the same instant. It has a maximum value of 16 minutes which reduces to zero four times a year as in Fig. 2117.

The *Nautical Almanac,* on the right-hand daily pages, tabulates the equation of time at intervals of twelve hours of Greenwich mean time.

In previous almanacs, it was marked (+) or (−) to indicate whether apparent time was fast or slow of mean time, respectively. In the current almanac the signs are omitted and the sign is determined by noting the time of meridian passage in an adjacent column. If the time of meridian passage is earlier than 12h 00m, the apparent sun is ahead of the mean sun and the sign of the equation of time is (+) (see excerpt for May 11, 1966). If the time of meridian passage is later than 12h 00m, the sign is (−) (see excerpt for Feb. 5, 1966). Days when the equation of time changes from (+) to (−) or vice versa are underscored.

Another method of determining the sign is to note the G.H.A. of the sun. If the G.H.A. of the sun at 1200 G.M.T. is from 0° to 4° the time equivalent obtained in the Arc to Time conversion table is a (+) equation of time. If the G.H.A. at 1200 is between 356° to 0° the converted equation of time is (−). This method is used for the *Air Almanac.*

In one instance a reverse conversion is a convenience for any navigator: Local apparent noon (12h 00m L.A.T.) is the time of the traditional noon sight for the sun's maximum altitude from which latitude is determined by the same method Bowditch used. Local mean time, when this observation must be made, may be anywhere from about 11:45 to 12:15, according to the date. To find this time a (+) Eq.T. must be subtracted from, or a (−) Eq.T. added to, the 12h 00m of apparent time which marks apparent noon. This is because the conversion is from apparent to mean time whereas the signs before the Eq.T. in the Almanac indicate its application when converting mean time to apparent time.

2118. Sidereal time, the time used by astronomers, is measured by the stars and is quite different from time measured by the sun. The stars appear to move around the earth in only 23h 56m 3.4s of mean time (§1715). The mean sun requires 24h and sidereal time is faster than mean time by about 4 minutes per day.

When working any sight it is necessary to find the hour angle (geographic longitude) of the observed body. Previous to 1933, finding the hour angle of a star

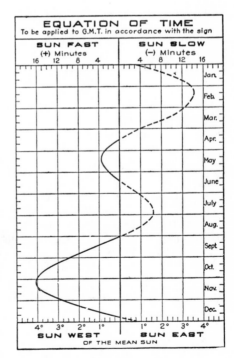

Fig. 2117.

or planet or the moon involved the use of sidereal time and a quantity known as the right ascension of the body. This use of these quantities is not essential with the Almanacs as now arranged. Discussion of older methods which use sidereal time is omitted from this book as unnecessary and confusing.

2119. Questions about time. The following exercises relate to mean time as used daily by navigators at sea. Answers should be computed mentally wherever possible. Do all necessary paper work in your notebook; use no scratch paper. Record the results for all of the questions in a group before comparing with the given answers.

CONVERSION OF TIME AND ARC

Q 1-21: *As in §2105.* Convert the following arcs into time units:

(a)	165°	(d)	12°	(g)	11'
(b)	35°	(e)	7° 30'	(h)	7'.5
(c)	190°	(f)	10° 15'	(i)	12'.5

Q 2-21: *As in §2105.* Convert the following times into arc units:

(a)	11h	(d)	80m	(g)	24s
(b)	3h	(e)	10m	(h)	48s
(c)	6h	(f)	56m	(i)	74s

Q 3-21: *As in §2105.* Convert the following quantities from time to arc or vice versa:

(a)	9h	(d)	44s	(g)	150°
(b)	9'	(e)	56m	(h)	6m
(c)	75°	(f)	11'	(i)	45'

GREENWICH TIME

Q 4-21: *As in §2107.* How fast or slow of Greenwich (0° Long.) time is the time on the following meridians? Mark your answers (F) or (S).

(a)	75° W	(d)	40° E	(g)	179° E
(b)	135° E	(e)	155° W	(h)	13° E
(c)	165° W	(f)	62° W	(i)	17° W

Q 5-21. *As in §2107.* Given Greenwich time (G.M.T.) and the observer's longitude, find the local time (L.M.T.) on that meridian.

	G.M.T.	Long.		G.M.T.	Long.		G.M.T.	Long.
(a)	0823	45° E	(d)	1902	105° 30' W	(g)	1400	60° W
(b)	1204	76° W	(e)	1000	20° 45' E	(h)	0700	165° E
(c)	0900	152° E	(f)	0703	109° 15' E	(i)	1900	105° W

Q 6-21: *As in §2107.* Given the observer's longitude and the local time (L.M.T.) for that meridian, find the Greenwich time (G.M.T.).

	Long.	L.M.T.		Long.	L.M.T.		Long.	L.M.T.
(a)	60° E	1100	(d)	89° E	1056	(g)	150° 30' E	2004
(b)	90° W	1600	(e)	117° W	1000	(h)	16° 45' W	0503
(c)	135° E	1100	(f)	33° W	0300	(i)	49° 15' E	0317

TIME AT ANOTHER PLACE

Q 7-21: *As in* §*2107.* Given the longitude and local time (L.M.T.) at A and the longitude of B. What is the local time (L.M.T.) at B?

	Place A Long.	Place A L.M.T.	Place B Long.			Place A Long.	Place A L.M.T.	Place B Long.
(a)	75° W	1745	135° W		(f)	49° E	2136	101° W
(b)	105° W	1022	90° W		(g)	53° E	1642	85° E
(c)	45° E	1022	105° E		(h)	159° W	0812	67° W
(d)	133° E	1529	103° E		(i)	62° E	1648	40° W
(e)	60° W	1249	15° E					

Answers to Q 1-21 to Q 7-21 inclusive:

	Q-1	Q-2	Q-3	Q-4	Q-5	Q-6	Q-7	
(a)	11h	165°	135°	5h S	1123	0700	1345	(a)
(b)	2h 20m	45°	36s	9h F	0700	2200	1122	(b)
(c)	12h 40m	90°	5h	11h S	1908	0200	1422	(c)
(d)	48m	20°	11′	2h 40m F	1200	0500	1329	(d)
(e)	30m	2° 30′	14°	10h 20m S	1123	1748	1749	(e)
(f)	41m	14°	44s	4h 8m S	1420	0512	1136	(f)
(g)	44s	6′	10h	11h 56m F	1000	1002	1850	(g)
(h)	30s	12′	90′	52m F	1800	0610	1420	(h)
(i)	50s	18′.5	3m	1h 08m S	1200	0000	1000	(i)

The conversion of arc into time required in the following four problems may be made with the aid of the tables on page 484.

Q 8-21: The local mean time is 3h 06m 00s at Philadelphia, longitude 75° 00′ W. What is the local mean time in Rio, longitude 43° 09′ W?
Ans: 5h 13m 24s in Rio.

Q 9-21: The local mean time is 16h 00m 00s in Cairo, longitude 31° 15′ E. What is the local mean time in Manila, longitude 120° 58′ E?
Ans: 21h 58m 52s in Manila.

Q 10-21: The local mean time is 8h 15m 20s in Tokyo, longitude 139° 45′ E. What is the local mean time in Canton, longitude 113° 16′ E?
Ans: 6h 29m 24s in Canton.

Q 11-21: The local mean time is 10h 47m 02s in Aden, longitude 45° 00′ E. What is the local mean time in New York, longitude 74° W?
Ans: 2h 51m 02s in New York.

ZONE TIME

Q 12-21: *As in* §*2110.* Find the time zone description for each of the following longitudes:

(a) 165° E		(d) 173° E		(g) 3° W	
(b) 19° E		(e) 169° W		(h) 178° W	
(c) 172° W		(f) 37° E		(i) 82° W	

Q 13-21: *As in* §*2111.* In each case, find L.M.T. given the ship's longitude and the zone time:

	Long.	Z.T.		Long.	Z.T.		Long.	Z.T.
(a)	65° W	1432	(d)	75° 30′ W	0345	(g)	6° 30′ E	0900
(b)	65° E	1432	(e)	117° 45′ W	1349	(h)	82° 15′ W	1729
(c)	55° E	1432	(f)	131° 15′ E	1000	(i)	126° 45′ E	0600

Q 14-21: *As in §2111.* In each case, find Z.T., given the ship's longitude and the L.M.T.:

	Long.	L.M.T.		Long.	L.M.T.		Long.	L.M.T.
(a)	65° W	1432	(d)	75° 30′ W	0345	(g)	6° 30′ E	0900
(b)	65° E	1432	(e)	117° 45′ W	1349	(h)	82° 15′ W	1729
(c)	55° E	1432	(f)	131° 15′ E	1000	(i)	126° 45′ E	0600

GREENWICH TIME AND DATE

Q 15-21: *As in §2113.* Determine the zone description and find G.M.T. and date, given longitude of ship, zone time of a sight and the date at the ship:

	Long.	Z.T. of sight	Date		Long.	Z.T. of sight	Date
(a)	70° W	3h 46m 29s	Dec. 5	(f)	112° E	12h 14m 43s	May 2
(b)	115° E	18h 37m 10s	Oct. 5	(g)	163° W	20h 19m 09s	Feb. 8
(c)	106° W	21h 19m 03s	Apr. 7	(h)	135° E	7h 45m 36s	Aug. 3
(d)	7° W	14h 24m 58s	Mar. 4	(i)	33° E	1h 46m 37s	Nov. 5
(e)	155° E	8h 53m 16s	Jan. 7				

Q 16-21: *As in §2114 or §2115.* Find G.M.T. and date, given the date and the approximate longitude and local time at the ship, and the time of a sight by chronometer reading which may be 12h slow of G.M.T.

	Chronometer time of sight	Long.	Local time	Date
(a)	5h 13m 26s	112° E	1245	Apr. 5
(b)	8h 20m 10s	163° W	2140	Feb. 7
(c)	10h 42m 37s	135° E	0745	May 5
(d)	11h 45m 29s	33° E	0200	Jan. 4
(e)	8h 47m 30s	70° W	0400	Mar. 7
(f)	8h 38m 13s	115° E	1620	Oct. 2
(g)	4h 18m 53s	106° W	2115	Apr. 8
(h)	2h 25m 01s	7° W	1445	Nov. 3
(i)	10h 52m 59s	155° E	0910	Dec. 6

Answers to Q 12-21 to Q 16-21 inclusive:

	Q 12 Z.D.	Q 13 L.M.T.	Q 14 Z.T.	Q 15 G.M.T. h m s	Date	Q 16 G.M.T. h m s	Date	
(a)	−11	1412	1452	8 46 29	Dec. 5	5 13 26	Apr. 5	(a)
(b)	− 1	1452	1412	10 37 10	Oct. 5	8 20 10	Feb. 8	(b)
(c)	+11	1412	1452	4 19 03	Apr. 8	22 42 37	May 4	(c)
(d)	−12	0343	0347	14 24 58	Mar. 4	23 45 29	Jan. 3	(d)
(e)	+11	1358	1340	22 53 16	Jan. 6	8 47 30	Mar. 7	(e)
(f)	− 2	0945	1015	5 14 43	May 2	8 38 13	Oct. 2	(f)
(g)	0	0926	0834	7 19 09	Feb. 9	4 18 53	Apr. 9	(g)
(h)	+12	1700	1758	22 45 36	Aug. 2	14 25 01	Nov. 3	(h)
(i)	+ 5	0627	0533	23 46 37	Nov. 4	22 52 59	Dec. 5	(i)

22. THE CHRONOMETER AND TIMEKEEPING

THE determination of longitude at sea requires an accurate knowledge of the time at some standard meridian such as that of Greenwich, England. This fact was understood even before the days of Columbus, but practical solutions of the problem were not developed until about one hundred and fifty years ago. Previously few navigators could approximate longitude except by dead reckoning. Two possibilities of finding the needed time were recognized. The changing position of the moon among the fixed stars offered a measure of Greenwich time but for various reasons the so-called method of *lunar distances* was not practicable. The employment of a timekeeper for determining longitude was proposed about 1530, but the watches of that time, called "Nuremberg eggs," could not be relied on within some fifteen minutes per day. For more than one hundred years, however, accurate shipboard timekeepers have been available. Today they may be checked frequently by radio time signals and the problem of timekeeping at sea has become relatively simple. The development of the marine chronometer presents an interesting bit of history.

Constituted in England in 1714, the "Commissioners for the Discovery of Longitude at Sea" offered a prize of £20,000 for the solution of the problem. Maskelyne, the Astronomer-Royal, contended for the method of lunar distances but the practical solution proved to be a little ticking thing in a box, the work of a Yorkshire carpenter, John Harrison, to whom the payment of £20,000 was ultimately completed about 1773. Thus the chronometer was created and longitude was "discovered." During the last century Harrison's principles were further refined and the care and checking of chronometers was developed until an astonishing degree of accuracy was attained. Although the universal development of radio has modified chronometer requirements, good timekeepers continue to be a necessity of the navigator.

2201. Timekeeping at sea has for its principal object the determination of the exact Greenwich times of celestial observations. Without this information wherewith to enter the Almanacs, a sight is useless except in a few special cases. Any error in the G.M.T. of a sight will at once reappear in the longitude of the resulting line of position. An error of 4 seconds means an error in longitude of 1′ in any latitude.

The details, from the time of marking the altitude to the G.M.T. of a sight, vary widely. This chapter deals with chronometers, watches, errors, rates, records and their use. The navigator may work as he prefers or as circumstances dictate. There are few fixed rules of procedure. The objective is the correct G.M.T.

2202. Error and rate defined. When a chronometer is delivered to a ship it is set to approximate Greenwich mean time and is gaining or losing more or less a second each day. Such a condition is shown by the typical rate certificate shown in Fig. 2202. It is not customary to set chronometers while in service because so doing would probably change the amount they gain or lose. These facts require the definition of two terms used throughout all discussions of timekeeping at sea.

The *error* is the difference between the time indicated by the chronometer and Greenwich mean time. When the chronometer reading is greater than G.M.T. the error is called *fast* and represents a correction to be deducted from the reading. When the error is *slow* add the correction. The magnitude of the error is not important if it be accurately known.

RATE CERTIFICATE   38 Water Street,

To be wound daily at 8 o'clock, a. m.   New York, May 13th 1936

2 day Chronometer No. 13246 by Mercer

Is this day Fast *of Greenwich Mean Time*

0 *hours* 7 *minutes* 35 *seconds* 0 *tenths*

and Losing *per day*

0 *seconds* 8 *tenths*

HOURS	MIN.	SEC	TENTHS
0	7	35	0 Fast
0	0	0	8 Losing

Captain Geo W Uitar

Ship

Kelvin & Wilfrid O. White Co
Geo Aiken

All Chronometers are liable to change their rates. The average rate given above can be verified by means of the daily comparisons which are regularly filed by us for references.

(# 115)

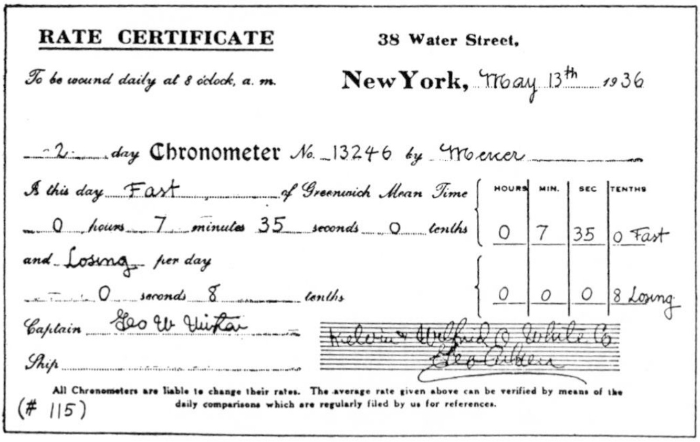

Fig. 2202. Rate Certificate.

The *rate* of a chronometer is the amount it is gaining or losing each day. It is more important that a chronometer have a uniform rate than the rate be small. To find the rate, divide the gain or loss for the period between two dates when the error is known by the number of intervening days, and name the rate *gaining* or *losing*.

To find the *computed error* the rate is accumulated and added to or subtracted from the last known error. This work involves: (1) Multiplying the known rate by the number of days since the last check, and marking the product *loss* or *gain* according to the nature of the rate. (2) A gain must be added to a fast error or subtracted from a slow error. The reverse is true if the accumulated rate be a loss.

Marking errors and rates with the signs plus or minus is confusing because such signs do not always indicate whether to add or to subtract. Therefore in this book *errors* are marked *fast*(*F*) or *slow*(*S*) and rates are márked *gaining* or *losing*.

2203. Finding the Greenwich time of an observation may be resolved into six elements:

(1) One or more chronometers, which indicate G.M.T. with a known error and whose most valuable characteristic is a constant rate.

(2) Sources of exact time, such as radio time ticks, for checking the error of the chronometer.

(3) A record book of the chronometer's performance including its known errors on certain dates, the computation of its rates and therefrom its computed error at the time of an observation.

(4) The timing of the observation by a watch.

(5) Comparison of the watch with the chronometer to determine its error on chronometer or on zone time.

(6) Computing the G.M.T. by properly applying the errors or differences to the watch time of sight.

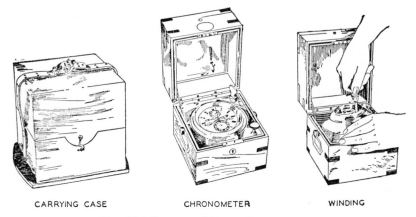

CARRYING CASE   CHRONOMETER   WINDING

Fig. 2204. Standard Marine Chronometer.

2204. The marine chronometer is a large watch, about 5 inches in diameter, hung in gimbals in a case of about $7 \times 7 \times 7$ inches, which also contains the winding key and a device for clamping the instrument rigidly in its gimbals (Fig. 2204). A larger outer case is provided for transportation. Whether new or old, they should be certified by a responsible dealer.

Chronometers are not only larger than watches but differ in other ways. The power of the mainspring is made uniform throughout the period between windings by a variable lever device called the fusee; the balance is especially compensated for temperature variations. The escapement is not self-starting as is that of a watch. To start a chronometer, place it on a flat surface and turn it gently to right and left. The chronometer continues to be the standard timekeeper at sea, although many of its characteristics are incorporated in modern watches.

The term chronometer is often used as meaning the navigator's source of Greenwich time. This may be a good watch or a bank of three standard chronometers, the minimum equipment for major ships prior to the advent of radio time ticks.

With the development of electrical battery operated chronometers using a quartz crystal oscillator the problem of chronometer error due to chronometer rate is greatly reduced. However even with their great accuracy, they must still be checked against a time standard.

2205. Installation and care. Chronometers must be intelligently installed and constantly cared for, as otherwise the results will be unsatisfactory. These precautions are well understood in the Navy and on ships of the Merchant Marine but are often neglected on yachts when carrying a chronometer for a single voyage.

A chronometer must be transported with care, with the instrument clamped in its gimbals. Dropping the instrument a few inches or a quick, sharp twist may destroy its reliability though without its showing any outward sign of injury. With the most careful handling the rate during transfer to a ship almost certainly will differ from that given in the certificate. Thereafter the rate may be as certified, or the instrument, after several days, may settle down to a new rate. It is dangerous to trust chronometers put on board a few hours before departure.

Chronometers should be wedged or packed in a fixed position and located to assure their best performance as timekeepers. This requires the least practicable change in temperature, a minimum of ship's motion, freedom from shock and vibration, and a reasonable distance from magnetic and electrical influences. Convenience is a secondary consideration but should be considered when locating these instruments.

Timekeepers must be wound not only to make them run but in a way to steady their rate. Standard chronometers will run for 56 hours, but should be wound gently in the same manner every day at the same hour. On a yacht, whose radio equipment may fail, it is of vital importance that the single chronometer does not run down and that it be wound regularly. This is a routine duty with ship's officers in regular service but presents a serious problem which every amateur navigator must solve in his own way.

When a ship goes out of commission, its chronometers are delivered to a nautical instrument dealer to be kept running while their errors and rates are recorded preparatory to delivery with a new certificate. Standard chronometers should be cleaned every three years, otherwise the rates tend to become slower and irregular as the oil is used or becomes sticky.

2206. Watches as timekeepers. Aviators use second-setting watches set to Greenwich time. An Air Corps type of such a watch is shown in Fig. 2206 in its outer case, and again in Fig. 2209. This use of watches assumes that they are set accurately at relatively short intervals.

The use of watches at sea in place of chronometers is a different matter. Selection for such service must eliminate wrist watches, small or thin watches, or any cheap watch movement. Watches serving as timekeepers must be stowed, protected, and cared for as are chronometers. Regular winding every 24 hours is especially important, because thereafter the rate of a watch becomes slower. Unlike chronometers, watches must be cleaned at least once a year.

FIG. 2206. WATCH BOX.

Dr. Worth considered three good watches the best timekeeping equipment for small vessels without radio time signals or where the radio set may fail. The author's experience with single mechanical watches over periods of months, carefully stowed near the chronometer and wound at the same time, has been unsatisfactory.

2207. Whence the time? The U. S. Naval Observatory at Washington, the Royal Observatory at Greenwich, and those of other nations maintain clocks of great accuracy regulated by the transits of the heavenly bodies. Such clocks are the source of the time signals transmitted to navigators.

With the advent of telegraphy and the submarine cable, time signals from the observatories were displayed at some defined instant each day in all important ports, often by dropping a time ball. Today, radio time signals furnish the best check on the error of the chronometer.

Chronometers may be checked without time signals. Let an observer at any exactly known position determine longitude by the methods of celestial navigation, the assumed G.M.T. of the observations being derived from the chronometer. The difference between the longitude so found and the true longitude of the known position, converted into time, is the error of the assumed G.M.T. If the longitude by observation is west of the true longitude, the time used in the computation was too fast and vice versa.

2208. The chronometer record.   The navigator must keep an orderly record of the performance of the ship's timekeepers from the date of the certificates with which they were delivered.   Such a record is not only the basis for computing the error of the chronometer but also gives an indication of the reliability, or otherwise, of the ship's timekeeping equipment.   However elaborate the record, it must include basic entries similar to those in Fig. 2208.   This old record also shows examples of finding the error, rate, and the accumulated error.

Practice in handling the various elements of the timekeeping problem is too often neglected.   The required arithmetic is simple enough, but experience indicates that blunders are abundant.   In a classroom, when working a sight the given watch and chronometer errors are accepted without question.   At sea, a serious blunder in these quantities nullifies the results of the most accurate computation.   Thus practice with the questions at the close of this chapter is important.

The ready availability of time by radio does not eliminate blunders. It has, however, reduced the importance of a bank of three chronometers and their comparison and care as fully discussed in Bowditch.   These were major matters in the days of long voyages without time signals of any kind.

2209. Timing a sight.   The navigator cannot see the chronometer at the instant he marks an altitude with the sextant.   He may walk to the chronometer as he counts seconds or he may have an assistant at that instrument who can hear his cry of "mark" and take the chronometer time.   More often a watch is used in the hand of the navigator or his assistant.

Pocket watches or wrist watches will serve provided they have a second hand.   A full sweep second hand is preferable, especially for a navigator taking the time without an assistant.

Chronograph watches are more convenient.   That at the right of Fig. 2209 is both a standard watch and a stop watch.   If regulated with its full sweep second setting hand running, it may be set to G.M.T. and so used for several hours without practical error

Stop watches are best for the beginner timing his own sights.   When so used, they are stopped or started at a convenient reading of the chronometer to which the stop watch reading at time of sight is applied to find the chronometer time of sight.

Stop watches are also convenient for observing the period of lights and fog signals, and one such watch is almost a necessity.   They are relatively inexpensive but sometimes are badly regulated or become so

134th. Day   WEDNESDAY, MAY 13, 1964

Received from K. & W.

Certificate reads:
Error   0 - 7 - 35.0   FAST
Rate   0.8   LOSING

Carried to ship next day.
Moved several times before
May 30 a/c changes in cabin.

178th Day   FRIDAY, JUNE 26, 1964

Cannot get radio time signal.

Computed Error:
Fast, 6/22   6 - 57.5
4 ds. X .06 losing   2.4
Error: 6 - 55   FAST

The true error by radio
as of July 3 suggests that
the rate during the blow
exceeded 3 sec. LOSING.

151st. Day   SATURDAY, MAY 30, 1964

By Radio at 12 E.S.T.
Error   0 - 7 - 14.0 FAST

5/13 Error   7 - 35.0 FAST
5/30   7 - 14.0
17 days   21.0
Rate 1 day   1.23 LOSING
Result of moving - expect change

181st. Day   MONDAY, JUNE 29, 1964

Being without other sources
of time, but at anchor in a
known position, the navigator
should have checked the
chronometer by observations

164th. Day   FRIDAY, JUNE 12, 1964

By Radio at 12 E.S.T.
Error   3. at 58^m
            3.5   59^m
    FAST   7 - 03.5   12:00

5/30 Error   7 - 14.0 FAST
6/12   7 - 03.5
13 days   10.5
Rate 1 day   0.8 LOSING

185th Day   FRIDAY, JULY, 3, 1964

Time signals working O.K.

By Radio at 12 E.S.T.
Error   6 - 36   FAST
6/22 Error   6 - 57.5 FAST
7/3   6 - 36
11 days   21.5
Rate 1 day   2.0 LOSING

174th. Day   MONDAY, JUNE 22, 1964

By Radio at 12 E.S.T.
Error   6 - 57.5 FAST

6/12 Error   7 - 03.5 FAST
6/22   6 - 57.5
10 days   6.0
Rate 1 day   0.6 LOSING

NOTE: Heavy weather next 4 days

214th. Day   SATURDAY, AUGUST 1, 1964

By Radio at 12 E.S.T.
Error   6 - 01 FAST

7/3 Error   6 - 36 FAST
8/1   6 - 01
29 days   35
1 day   1.2 LOSING

Rate remained 1.0 to 1.5
losing until close of season

FIG. 2208. CHRONOMETER RECORD OF A YACHT.

with idleness.   Check the rate of a new stop watch and occasionally check old stop watches against a 30-minute run of the chronometer.   If the error exceeds 2 seconds the watch should be regulated and, if necessary, cleaned.   When you pick up a stop watch for quick action make sure that the hands have been returned to zero and that the watch is wound.   When you read the recorded time note the way the minute dial is divided, because its circumference generally represents only 30 minutes, the numbered divisions being marked 3, 6, 9, etc.

PLAIN STOP WATCH	SPLIT SECOND STOP WATCH	ARMY AIR CORPS TYPE	SECOND SETTING CHRONOGRAPH
For lights, Fog signals and sights	Same uses but better for a series of Sights	For use as small chronometer. Second Setting	May be set exactly to Time-tick or chronometer

Fig. 2209. Navigators' Watches.

Two typical stop watches are shown at the left of Fig. 2209.   The plain type is much better than none at all, but a split-second stop watch is more useful.   With this type of watch, depressing the pin in the crown simultaneously starts the two long second hands and the upper small hand which registers up to 30 minutes.   For taking the time of the first of a series of sights, depress the pin on the left which stops one of the long second hands.   Record the reading and again depress the same pin; the stopped hand will at once catch up with the other long hand.   Time the succeeding sights in the same way.   Again depressing the pin in the crown will stop or return the minute hand and both long second hands together.   The "comparing watch" of the U.S. Navy is similar to the chronograph shown above.   The crown is retracted and the watch is set to the time of next time tick.   Pressing the crown at the exact instant restarts the watch.

2210. Comparison of one timekeeper with another is a continuing element of time keeping at sea.   This is principally because the observer cannot see the chronometer, and the watch time of sight must be reduced to zone time or to chronometer time.   In either case the error of the watch on the chronometer must be determined.

To compare a watch with the chronometer, select an even minute or half minute of chronometer time for the comparison.   Ten seconds in advance, with eyes on the chronometer's second hand which ticks half seeonds, count "half, one, half, two, half, three, etc." A few seconds before the end of the minute or half minute, turn your eyes to the watch, but continue counting in cadence. On the count of ten note the seconds of time shown by the watch. The difference between the readings of the watch and that of the chronometer at this time gives the desired comparison.

C − W is the correction to be added to watch time to obtain chronometer time. It is the chronometer time, increased by 12 hours if necessary, minus the watch time. Handled in this way, the C−W correction is always additive. It will at once be evident if the G.M.T. found when using the C−W correction is 12 hours in error.

Examples. To find C−W: Assuming simultaneous readings of chronometer and watch, proceed as in either example:

Chro.	9h	57m	00s		Chro.	5h	57m	00s	(+12)
Watch	6	36	42		Watch	6	36	42	
C−W	3h	20m	18s		C−W	11h	20m	18s	

W.E. on Z.T. is the correction to be added to or subtracted from watch time to find zone time. With the navigator's watch set to approximate zone time, the correction is seldom more than a minute or two and some seconds.

To find the W.E. on Z.T.: Take simultaneous readings of the watch and the chronometer and correct the chronometer reading to G.M.T. If the watch has no error on Z.T. its minute and second figures will exactly agree with the minutes and seconds of G.M.T. If the watch's minutes and seconds are the greater, the watch is fast of Z.T. by the difference, and vice versa. The reason is that the true difference between Z.T. and G.M.T. is always one or more integral hours.

Examples. To find W.E. on Z.T.: Assuming simultaneous readings of chronometer and watch, proceed as in either example:

Long. 75° W, (Zone +5)				*Long. 90° E, (Zone −6)*			
Chro. reads	10h	*16m*	00s	Chro. reads 11h	*23m*	00s	(+12)
Chro. slow	(+)	*4m*	*13s*	Chro. fast	(−)	*16m*	*11s*
G.M.T.	10h	*20m*	*13s*	G.M.T.	23h	*06m*	*49s*
Z.D. (rev.)	5	(−)		Z.D. (rev.)	6	(+)	
Z.T.	5h	*20m*	*13s*	Z.T.	5h	*06m*	*49s* (next day)
Watch reads	5	*20*	*03*	Watch reads 5	*07*	*16*	
W.E. on Z.T.		Slow	*10s*	W.E. on Z.T.	Fast	*27s*	

Observe the figures in *italic*. With only these figures, or even without the minute figures, a navigator who understands the situation determines his W.E. on Z.T. with little more than a look at the chronometer. Or a radio time signal also indicates W.E. on Z.T. without any figures.

2211. Computing G.M.T. The procedure necessarily differs according to the kind of time used to time the sight. If timed with a watch set to G.M.T. no correction is required. If time of sight is chronometer time, it requires correction only for the error of the chronometer. The zone time method and the C−W method are illustrated as follows:

With W.E. on Z.T.   Watch set to approximate zone time.

		April 8				*June 1*			
		Longitude 47° W				*Longitude 60° E*			
		h	m	s			h	m	s
Watch, A.M.	W	4	13	52	W, A.M.		3	12	05
W.E. on Z.T.	F	(−)	1	04	S		(+)	1	05
Zone Time	Z.T.	4	12	48	Z.T.		3	13	10 (add
Zone Diff.	Z.D.	(+) 3			Z.D.	(−) 4			24)
G.M.T.	G.M.T.	7	12	48	G.M.T.		23	13	10
G'wich date		April 8				May 31			

With *C−W and Chro. Corr.*   Watch may be set to any kind of time. For this illustration the same watch times are used as above.

		April 8				*June 1*		
		h	m	s		h	m	s
Watch A.M.	W	4	13	52	W	3	12	05
Chro.−Watch	C−W	3	12	25	C−W	7	51	18
Chro. time	Chro.	7	26	17	Chro.	11	03	23 (+12)
Chro. Corr.	Fast	(−)	13	29	Slow	(+) 9	47	
G.M.T.	G.M.T.	7	12	48	G.M.T.	23	13	10
G'wich date		April 8			May 31			

With the improvement of radio communications and accurate time signals, the "C−W method" has fallen into disuse. Most navigators express time either as zone time or as G.M.T. and keep their watches set to either of these times within known errors. Use of a stop watch has much to recommend it. Such a watch can be *started* on a time signal, either zone time or G.M.T. The reading of the watch at time of sight gives the amount of time to be *added* to the time the watch was started; this remains constant during the round of sights.

2212. Time keeping questions. The following questions provide exercises in the daily details of time keeping. Do the work by mental arithmetic wherever possible. Record all of the answers to a group of questions before comparison with the given answers. Make necessary computations in your notebook. Use no scratch paper. Do not use (+) or (−) to characterize an error or a rate. Label an error *fast* (F) or *slow* (S). Mark a rate *gain* or *loss*.

Q 1-22: *As in §2208.* Find the error of the chronometer on G.M.T. in each of the following cases. Chronometer's face reads from 1h to 12h. Assume that the time tick used was the beginning of the final dash of the 1200, zone (+)5, Arlington signal, and that the chronometer was read at that time.

Chro. reads	Chro. reads	Chro. reads
(a) 5h 06m 16s	(c) 4h 06m 16s	(e) 4h 58m 24s
(b) 4h 49m 10s	(d) 5h 49m 10s	(f) 5h 01m 36s

Q 2-22: *As in §2208.* Find the rate of the chronometer, assuming that the given errors in each case were determined at the same hour of the day:

	Date	Error	Date	Error
(a)	Apr. 10	F 12m 32s	Apr. 20	F 12m 47s
(b)	May 13	S 2m 40s	May 20	S 2m 12s
(c)	Mar. 25	S 21m 19s	Apr. 5	S 21m 52s
(d)	Nov. 3	S 13m 49s	Nov. 23	S 14m 25s
(e)	Jan. 1	S 1m 46s	Jan. 21	F 6s
(f)	May 29	F 22m 14s	June 22	F 21m 42s

Q 3-22: *As in §2208.* Find the accumulated error of the chronometer on the given current date in each of the following situations:

	Date	Previous Error	Rate	Current Date
(a)	Jan. 3	F 2m 42s	Gain 0.5s	Jan. 23
(b)	May 25	S 11m 05s	Loss 0.8s	June 15
(c)	Nov. 1	S 21m 59s	Gain 1.2s	Dec. 1
(d)	Mar. 13	F 17m 05s	Loss 0.7s	Mar. 27
(e)	Jan. 1	S 1m 40s	Gain 7.4s	Jan. 31
(f)	Mar. 23	F 0m 29s	Loss 4.1s	Apr. 2

Q 4-22: *As in §2210.* Find C-W in each of the following cases, assuming simultaneous reading of chronometer and watch:

	Chro.	Watch		Chro.	Watch
(a)	11h 49m 36s	3h 19m 24s	(d)	3h 40m 20s	2h 14m 14s
(b)	8h 19m·02s	5h 47m 23s	(e)	6h 19m 37s	10h 53m 17s
(c)	3h 40m 20s	7h 14m 14s	(f)	9h 18m 40s	11h 15m 30s

Q 5-22: *As in §2210.* Find the error of your watch on zone time, W.E. on Z.T., in each of the following cases of simultaneous readings of chronometer and watch:

	Chronometer Read.	Error	Watch Read.	Zone
(a)	12h 10m 00s	F 26m 34s	23h 44m 16s	(0)
(b)	11h 14m 00s	S 11m 54s	15h 26m 14s	(+8)
(c)	3h 26m 00s	F 9m 41s	17h 17m 22s	(−2)
(d)	1h 05m 00s	F 8m 43s	11h 56m 32s	(+1)
(e)	5h 49m 00s	S 19m 17s	19h 07m 56s	(+11)
(f)	8h 57m 00s	S 28m 02s	6h 24m 43s	(−9)

Q 6-22: *As in §2211.* Find G.M.T. and date of each of the sights listed, using zone time method:

	Ship Date	Watch reads	Time zone	W.E. on Z.T.
(a)	Sept. 1	15h 50m 30s	(+2)	F 20s
(b)	Jan. 6	4h 25m 26s	(+3)	S 49s
(c)	Aug. 5	4h 45m 38s	(−11)	S 1m 42s
(d)	Nov. 3	3h 12m 05s	(−4)	S 1m 05s
(e)	Apr. 8	17h 17m 14s	(+6)	S 23s
(f)	June 9	4h 00m 30s	(−10)	S 1m 30s

Answers to Q 1-22 to Q 6-22 inclusive:

	Q 1 Chro. Error m s	Q 2 Chro. Rate s	Q 3 Chro. Error m s	Q 4 C-W h m s	Q 5 W.E. on Z.T. m s	Q 6 G.M.T. h m s	Date	
(a)	F 6 16	Gain 1.5	F 2 52	8 30 12	F 50	17 50 10	Sept. 1	(a)
(b)	S 10 50	Gain 4.0	S 11 22	2 31 39	F 20	7 26 15	Jan. 6	(b)
(c)	S 53 44	Loss 3.0	S 21 23	8 26 06	F 1 03	17 47 20	Aug. 4	(c)
(d)	F 49 10	Loss 1.8	F 16 55	1 26 06	F 15	23 13 10	Nov. 2	(d)
(e)	S 1 36	Gain 5.6	F 2 02	7 26 20	S 21	23 17 37	Apr. 8	(e)
(f)	F 1 36	Loss 1.3	S 12	10 03 10	S 19	18 02 00	June 8	(f)

23. THE ALMANAC AND ITS USE

THE principal purpose of any nautical almanac is to supply convenient data for finding the apparent or geographic position of an observed body. Such information is an essential adjunct to the sextant and the chronometer.

Almanac, the Arabic word for "calendar" has been the descriptive title of this collection of information. Nautical almanacs for each year are published and issued some months in advance by the United States, Great Britain, and other nations. Such almanacs have been compiled and published in one form or another by many different countries, both ancient and modern, whose interest in trading, shipping, and navigation justified their preparation and publication.

According to the Naval Observatory, the first known nautical almanac material was compiled by the Egyptians in 467 A.D.. There were other later findings of occasional almanac data, but the first regular Almanac was published in medieval times in Germany, from 1475 to 1531. France provided the first Almanac regularly published by a national government, beginning in 1679. Should it be necessary to use an unfamiliar foreign almanac, care must be exercised to understand the varied forms in which the data may be presented.

2301. The American Nautical Almanac, the subject of this chapter, was first published in 1855, for the year 1858. Beginning with the 1958 edition, it is issued jointly by the United States Naval Observatory and Her Majesty's Stationery Office. It is for sale in the United States by navigational supply dealers, and by the Superintendent of Documents, Washington, D.C. 20402.

For 75 years there was little change in its arrangement, but in 1934 the presentation of data was simplified for the navigator by tabulating Greenwich hour angle in units of arc instead of in units of time. In 1950, the *Nautical Almanac* was again redesigned following the popular approval of the *Air Almanac* issued in 1941. The 1958 edition of *The*

American Nautical Almanac, which began a new series, common to both American and British navigators, contains several new features and has been rearranged further to simplify its use and to reduce the chance of error. Beginning in 1960, its title became *The Nautical Almanac.*

2302. Contents of the newly designed almanac. In this single volume the navigator can find the necessary astronomical data for the entire year. The book is divided into two main sections. The first section, printed on white paper, provides the daily positions, G.H.A. and Declination of sun, moon, four planets and 57 stars, tabulated for each hour of the day. Each two facing pages provide complete hourly data for three full days. In the second main section of the book, printed on yellow paper, there are sixty correction tables, one for each minute of the hour, printed on thirty pages. (See excerpts in Apx. V.)

Entering these correction tables with the minutes and seconds of the time of sight, one can find the correction for both Greenwich Hour Angle and Declination. These are to be applied to the hourly listing at time of sight, which is obtained from the daily page in the first section.

Other Useful Tables:

On the inside front cover and the facing page are Altitude Correction Tables for the stars and planets, and the sun's upper and lower limbs. Separate tables are provided for altitudes above and below 10°. A correction table for Height of Eye is also given. A table of additional corrections allowing for abnormal conditions of temperature and pressure is carried on page A4. Convenient civil and religious calendars, eclipse data, and a useful planet diagram precede the daily pages.

Sunrise, sunset, twilight, moonrise and moonset tables are included in the daily data section. The daily page also provides the equation of time at 12-hour intervals; the G.M.T. of the upper transit and semidiameter of the sun; the S.H.A. of the four planets; the G.M.T. of upper transit of the planets and the Vernal equinox; the G.M.T. of the upper and lower transit of the moon; and the semidiameter, age, and phase of the moon.

On the inside back cover and the facing page are Altitude Correction Tables for the moon's upper and lower limbs. The correction in the upper half of each page applies to both upper and lower limbs. Separate corrections for the two limbs are given in the lower half of the page. All corrections are to be added, but 30' is always to be *subtracted* from the total corrections for the moon's *upper limb.*

Three pages provide corrections for an Altitude of Polaris and for obtaining the Azimuth of Polaris. There is a Conversion of Arc to Time table.

The *Nautical Almanac* also includes a supplementary list of additional stars giving for each its constellation name, proper name, magnitude, S.H.A., and declination for each month. Any of these stars may be used in navigation and are utilized in the same way as the selected stars shown on the daily pages. Also contained in the Almanac are star charts to assist in identification and a list of time standards in use in several hundred places throughout the world.

With this new arrangement, the Greenwich Hour Angle and Declination of sun, moon, planets and stars can always be found with two openings of the book, and each final result is obtained as the sum of only two or three quantities, without interpolation.

Excerpts from the *Nautical Almanac* for 1966, sufficient for working all of the problems given in this book, are printed in Appendix V. Although reproduced from actual clippings, the various excerpts present only a limited picture of the *Nautical Almanac* for 1966. The student should obtain and examine a copy of the edition for the current year.

2303. To use an Almanac to find the position, G.H.A. and Declination of an observed body, at time of sight, requires the use of both the daily page tables and the minute correction tables. The construction of the newly designed *Nautical Almanac* is now such that the methods for correcting the tabulated declination and G.H.A. are essentially the *same* for the sun, a star, the moon, or a planet. The following discussion of these matters refers to the use of the tables in the *Nautical Almanac* as illustrated by excerpts from that publication which may be found in Appendix V. Methods applicable to the *Air Almanac* are outlined in the next chapter. There are certain facts, however, which are true of all bodies when working with either Almanac:

(1) *Values of G.H.A. and declination* are tabulated only for particular instants of time; e.g., for each hour, in the *Nautical Almanac*. Since observations are rarely made exactly on the hour, it is usually necessary to correct the tabulated values for the minutes and seconds which elapse between the preceding full hour and the time of observation. This correction is done visually, or by tables whose use is explained below.

(2) *Declination* of any body may be increasing or decreasing in value. Whether to add or to subtract a correction, if correction be required, can best be determined by noting the trend of the tabulated figures. Always label the declination N or S as designated in the *Nautical Almanac*.

(3) *Greenwich hour* angle is always increasing. Corrections for the minutes and seconds, beyond the hourly listing, are always added to the tabulated G.H.A. If the total exceeds 360°, deduct 360° to find the required G.H.A. There is an occasional exception to be found in the usual "*v*" correction for Venus which is sometimes subtractive, the reasons for which will be explained in Chap. 32.

(4) *Interpolation by inspection* is not recommended until experience has been acquired. However, where tabulated values are changing slowly, as with the declination of the sun and planets, the inspection method is convenient and rapid as explained in Appendix II-6. Even if correction tables are employed, it is advisable to make an approximate

visual interpolation to be sure that the correction is correctly applied. An interpolated quantity falls between two adjacent tabulated quantities.

2304. Sun's declination is tabulated on the right-hand side of the "Sun" column on the daily data pages. The tabulated figures are for each hour of G.M.T., i.e., the sun's declination is given at hourly intervals. Northerly declination is indicated by an N in front of the declination figure; southerly declination is indicated by an S in front of the declination figure. Review definition of *declination* in §1706.

At the foot of each page, below the "Sun's declination" column, is a small letter *d* followed by a number. This figure represents the average hourly change in the sun's declination for the three days listed. While an experienced navigator can visually correct the tabulated declination for the time interval over the proper hourly listing, entering this corrected figure directly on the work form as N or S, it is better for a beginner to make use of the yellow correction tables in the back of the almanac. The yellow pages headed "Increments and Corrections" give the corrections to be applied to the values on the daily pages for the minutes and seconds between the tabulated hours. To use these pages, find the page for the desired minute; and in the "d corr ⁿ" column opposite the "*d*" number given under the declination column of the daily page, find the desired correction. If the declination (either N or S) is increasing, add the correction; if it is decreasing, subtract the correction.

The four daily tables of the sun's declination brought together in Fig. 2304 illustrate the different situations met with in the following examples.

FEBRUARY 27

G.M.T. d h	G.H.A. ° '	Dec. ° '
27 00	176 45·7	S 8 36·6
01	191 45·8	35·7
02	206 45·9	34·8
03	221 46·0	·· 33·8
04	236 46·1	32·9
05	251 46·2	31·9
06	266 46·3	S 8 31·0
T 07	281 46·4	30·1
H 08	296 46·5·	29·1
U 09	311 46·6	·· 28·2
R 10	326 46·7	27·3
11	341 46·8	26·3
S 12	356 47·0	S 8 25·4
D 13	11 47·1	24·4
A 14	26 47·2	23·5
Y 15	41 47·3	·· 22·6
16	56 47·4	21·6
17	71 47·5	20·7
18	86 47·6	S 8 19·7
19	101 47·7	18·8
20	116 47·8	17·9
21	131 48·0	·· 16·9
22	146 48·1	16·0
23	161 48·2	15·0
	S.D. 16·2	d 0·9

SOUTH
Decreasing

MAY 16

G.M.T. d h	G.H.A. ° '	Dec. ° '
16 00	180 56·1	N18 55·7
01	195 56·0	56·3
02	210 56·0	56·9
03	225 56·0	·· 57·5
04	240 56·0	58·1
05	255 56·0	58·6
06	270 56·0	N18 59·2
07	285 56·0	18 59·8
F 08	300 56·0	19 00·4
R 09	315 56·0	·· 01·0
I 10	330 56·0	01·6
11	345 56·0	02·1
D 12	0 55·9	N19 02·7
A 13	15 55·9	03·3
Y 14	30 55·9	03·9
15	45 55·9	·· 04·5
16	60 55·9	05·0
17	75 55·9	05·6
18	90 55·9	N19 06·2
19	105 55·9	06·8
20	120 55·9	07·3
21	135 55·8	·· 07·9
22	150 55·8	08·5
23	165 55·8	09·1
	S.D. 15·8	d 0·6

NORTH
Increasing

AUGUST 16

G.M.T. d h	G.H.A. ° '	Dec. ° '
16 00	178 54·1	N13 58·4
01	193 54·3	57·6
02	208 54·4	56·8
03	223 54·5	·· 56·1
04	238 54·6	55·3
05	253 54·8	54·5
06	268 54·9	N13 53·7
S 07	283 55·0	52·9
08	298 55·1	52·1
A 09	313 55·3	·· 51·3
T 10	328 55·4	50·6
U 11	343 55·5	49·8
R 12	358 55·6	N13 49·0
D 13	13 55·8	48·2
A 14	28 55·9	47·4
Y 15	43 56·0	·· 46·6
16	58 56·1	45·8
17	73 56·3	45·0
18	88 56·4	N13 44·2
19	103 56·5	43·5
20	118 56·6	42·7
21	133 56·8	·· 41·9
22	148 56·9	41·1
23	163 57·0	40·3
	S.D. 15·8	d 0·8

NORTH
Decreasing

OCTOBER 8

G.M.T. d h	G.H.A. ° '	Dec. ° '
8 00	183 02·8	S 5 36·1
01	198 03·0	37·1
02	213 03·2	38·0
03	228 03·4	·· 39·0
04	243 03·6	40·0
05	258 03·7	·40·9
06	273 03·9	S 5 41·9
W 07	288 04·1	42·8
E 08	303 04·3	43·8
D 09	318 04·4	·· 44·7
N 10	333 04·6	45·7
E 11	348 04·8	·46·6
S 12	3 05·0	S 5 47·6
D 13	18 05·1	48·6
A 14	33 05·3	49·5
Y 15	48 05·5	·· 50·5
16	63 05·7	51·4
17	78 05·8	52·4
18	93 06·0	S 5 53·3
19	108 06·2	54·3
20	123 06·4	55·2
21	138 06·5	·· 56·2
22	153 06·7	57·1
23	168 06·9	·58·1
	S.D. 16·0	d 1·0

SOUTH
Increasing

Fig. 2304. Excerpts of Sun's Declination and G.H.A.

Example: Using the declination tables in Fig. 2304 and the "Increments and Corrections" tables in Appendix V of this book, find the sun's declination at the following Greenwich mean times and dates:

Date	G.M.T.
(A). 27 February	8h 20m 31s
(B). 16 May	4h 41m 23s
(C). 16 August	15h 20m 20s
(D). 8 October	13h 50m 10s

	27 Feb.	
(A). Tabulated decl. for 8h	8° 29'.1 S	$d - 0'.9$
Correction for 20m 31s	− 0'.3	
Decl. at 8h 20m 31s	8° 28'.8 S	

South declination and *decreasing*, so the correction is *subtracted.*

	16 May	
(B). Tabulated decl. for 4h	18° 58'.1 N	$d + 0'.6$
Correction for 41m 23s	+ 0'.3	
Decl. at 4h 41m 23s	18° 58'.4 N	

North declination and *increasing*, so the correction is *added*. Note that the *d* correction is 0.6 while the actual hourly difference is 0'.5. Either value is considered correct although the actual value is preferred for precise work.

	16 Aug.	
(C). Tabulated decl. for 15	13° 46'.6 N	$d - 0'.8$
Correction for 20m 20s	− 0'.3	
Decl. at 15h 20m 20s	13° 46'.3 N	

North declination and *decreasing*, so the correction is *subtracted.*

	8 Oct.	
(D). Tabulated decl. for 13h	5° 48'.6 S	$d + 1'.0$
Correction for 50m 10s	+ 0'.8	
Decl. at 13h 50m 10s	5° 49'.4 S	

South declination and *increasing*, so the correction is *added*.

The hourly difference of the Sun's declination is 0 about June 21 and December 21, and reaches a maximum of 1' in March and September. Correcting the Sun's declination may seem unimportant, but one must remember that an error in declination creates a similar error in the north-south position of the ship. An error of 1' in declination, when computing latitude from a noon sight, means an avoidable error of 1 mile in position.

A more serious error may occur when the novice, first working a noon sight, fails to enter the Almanac with G.M.T. Off the Atlantic Coast of the United States, use of E.S.T. will cause an error of 5 miles when the hourly difference of declination is 1'.

2305. Sun's Greenwich hour angle is tabulated on the left-hand side of the "Sun" column on the daily pages for each hour of G.M.T.

Greenwich hour angle of the Sun is always increasing at the approximate rate of 15° per hour. There is only one correction to be added to the hourly tabulation of the Sun. This correction is obtained from the minute correction pages, which are entered with the minutes and seconds of the time of sight. The correction is obtained from the column marked "Sun-Planets." If the sight is taken on an even minute, the correction is obtained on the page applying to that exact number of minutes, on the top line marked 0 seconds. If the time of sight includes seconds, the correction is found down the same column opposite the number of seconds of the time of sight. *Repeating, only one correction is necessary for the Sun's G.H.A., and it is always added to the tabulated G.H.A. taken from the daily page.*

To find G.H.A. of the sun. From the daily page, proper date, record the tabulated figure immediately preceding the time of observation. Obtain correction for minutes and seconds in the "Sun-Planets" column on minute correction page corresponding to the minutes and seconds of sight. The total of the tabulated hourly figure and this correction, is the required G.H.A. In the following examples, use Fig. 2304 and the minute correction tables in Appendix V.

Example: Observed the sun on 8 October at 9h 41m 39s G.M.T. Find G.H.A.

G.H.A. at 9h	318°	04′.4
Correction for 41m 39s	+ 10°	24′.8
G.H.A. at 9h 41m 39s	328°	29′.2

Example: Observed the sun on 16 August at 12h 20m 53s G.M.T. Find G.H.A.

G.H.A. at 12h	358°	55′.6
Correction for 20m 53s	+ 5°	13′.3
	364°	08′.9
Subtract 360°	360°	00′.0
G.H.A. at 12h 20m 53s	4°	08′.9

There is no additional correction for the G.H.A. sun, as the "Sun-Planets" columns in the minute correction pages are computed at the rate of 15° increase in G.H.A. per hour, which for all practical purposes equals the speed of the sun's apparent westerly travel.

2306. Planets' Decl. and G.H.A. have ways of their own, peculiar to each planet and without regard to the seasons of the year.

The G.H.A. and Decl. of the four navigational planets, Venus, Mars, Jupiter and Saturn are tabulated for each G.M.T. hour of the day on the left-hand daily data pages in separate columns under the name of each planet.

Declination of a planet, as in the case of the sun, may be increasing or decreasing in value and the trend can easily be observed by following along the column of tabulated declinations. In most cases, the hourly change is so small that Decl. at time of sight can be taken out by inspection. However, the "*d* corr^{n}" can be taken from the correction tables in the same way as for the sun. This will be done in all appropriate examples and problems in this book.

G.H.A. of a planet, different from the sun, requires two corrections to the exact time of sight. The first or "main" correction, like that of the sun, is the increment for the minutes and seconds beyond the hour tabulated on the daily page, based upon an increase in G.H.A. of 15° per hour as with the sun. In general, the G.H.A. of planets increases faster than G.H.A. of the sun; and the second correction adjusts for this faster rate. The average hourly rate above 15° is given by a "*v* correction" found at the bottom of the planet's G.H.A. column as the "*d* correction" for the sun. The "*v* correction" is always to be *added* except occasionally for Venus when, as in Fig. 2308, a negative value is indicated. In the following examples, use Fig. 2308 and the Appendix V tables.

Example: Observed the planet Mars on 7 October at 13h 11m 28s G.M.T. Find G.H.A. and decl.

G.H.A. at 13h	149°	57′.4	$v + 2'.4$
Correction for 11m 28s	2°	52′.0	
v correction		+ 0′.5	
G.H.A. at 13h 11m 28s	152°	49′.9	
Decl. at 13h	19°	12′.2 N	$d + 0'.1$
d correction		0′.0	
Decl. at 13h 11m 28s	19°	12′.2 N	

2307. The Moon's Decl. and G.H.A. are peculiar in that their change in one hour may vary materially during a single day. Both Decl. and G.H.A. of moon are found in the same manner as for a planet, except that the *v* and *d* corrections are found alongside the respective hourly entries. The G.H.A. increments are always *added* and the corrections to declination are added or subtracted depending upon whether the declination (north or south) is increasing or decreasing respectively.

Example: Observed moon's lower limb on 7 October at 17h 10m 18s G.M.T. Find G.H.A. and declination, using Fig. 2308 for hourly data.

G.H.A. at 17h	145°	45′.8	$v + 9'.5$
Correction for 10m 18s	2°	27′.5	
v correction		1′.7	
G.H.A. at 17h 10m 18s	148°	15′.0	
Decl. at 17h	14°	12′.6 N	$d - 7'.1$
d correction		− 1′.2	
Decl. at 17h 10m 18s	14°	11′.4 N	

2308. Star's Decl. and G.H.A. at the time of sight are obtained by a slightly different method than for Sun, Moon, and Planets, although it is equally easy to obtain the necessary information. The stars are listed alphabetically on each left-hand daily page in a table which gives each star's sidereal hour angle (S.H.A.) and declination (Dec.) as shown in Fig. 2308.

OCTOBER 7

G.M.T.	ARIES	VENUS -3.4		MARS -1.3		MOON					STARS		
d h	G.H.A.	G.H.A.	Dec.	G.H.A.	Dec.	G.H.A.	v	Dec.	d	H.P.	Name	S.H.A.	Dec.
7 00	15 08.1	190 46.9 S 0 18.9		314 26.7 N19 10.9		259 38.0	9.8	N16 00.1	5.6	57.1	Acamar	315 49.2	S 40 28.0
01	30 10.5	205 46.5	20.2	329 29.0	11.0	274 06.8	9.8	15 54.5	5.7	57.2	Achernar	335 56.8	S 57 26.6
02	45 13.0	220 46.1	21.4	344 31.4	11.1	288 35.6	9.8	15 48.8	5.7	57.2	Acrux	173 55.9	S 62 52.2
03	60 15.4	235 45.7 ··	22.7	359 33.7 ··	11.2	303 04.4	9.7	15 43.1	5.9	57.2	Adhara	255 44.8	S 28 54.8
04	75 17.9	250 45.4	23.9	14 36.1	11.3	317 33.1	9.8	15 37.2	5.9	57.3	Aldebaran	291 36.4	N 16 25.6
05	90 20.4	265 45.0	25.2	29 38.5	11.4	332 01.9	9.7	15 31.3	6.1	57.3			
06	105 22.8	280 44.6 S 0 25.4		44 40.8 N19 11.5		346 30.6	9.7	N15 25.2	6.1	57.4	Alioth	166 57.4	N 56 11.1
07	120 25.3	295 44.2	27.7	59 43.2	11.6	0 59.3	9.7	15 19.1	6.3	57.4	Alkaid	153 31.8	N 49 31.3
T 08	135 27.8	310 43.8	28.9	74 45.5	11.7	15 28.0	9.7	15 12.8	6.3	57.4	Al Na'ir	28 35.0	S 47 09.7
U 09	150 30.2	325 43.4 ··	30.2	89 47.9 ··	11.8	29 56.7	9.7	15 06.5	6.4	57.5	Alnilam	276 28.0	S 1 13.6
E 10	165 32.7	340 43.0	31.4	104 50.3	11.9	44 25.4	9.7	15 00.1	6.5	57.5	Alphard	218 36.7	S 8 28.7
S 11	180 35.2	355 42.6	32.7	119 52.6	12.0	58 54.1	9.6	14 53.6	6.6	57.5			
D 12	195 37.6	10 42.2 S 0 33.9		134 55.0 N19 12.1		73 22.7	9.7	N14 47.0	6.7	57.6	Alphecca	126 46.1	N 26 51.4
A 13	210 40.1	25 41.8	35.2	149 57.4	12.2	87 51.4	9.6	14 40.3	6.8	57.6	Alpheratz	358 25.7	N 28 52.0
Y 14	225 42.6	40 41.4	36.4	164 59.8	12.3	102 20.0	9.6	14 33.5	6.9	57.7	Altair	62 48.3	N 8 45.8
15	240 45.0	55 41.0 ··	37.7	180 02.1 ··	12.4	116 48.6	9.6	14 26.6	6.9	57.7	Ankaa	353 55.9	S 42 31.7
16	255 47.5	70 40.6	38.9	195 04.5	12.6	131 17.2	9.6	14 19.7	7.1	57.7	Antares	112 17.0	S 26 20.4
17	270 49.9	85 40.2	40.2	210 06.9	12.7	145 45.8	9.5	14 12.6	7.1	57.8			
18	285 52.4	100 39.8 S 0 41.4		225 09.3 N19 12.8		160 14.3	9.6	N14 05.5	7.3	57.8	Arcturus	146 33.6	N 19 24.0
19	300 54.9	115 39.4	42.7	240 11.6	12.9	174 42.9	9.6	13 58.2	7.3	57.9	Atria	108 56.0	S 68 57.4
20	315 57.3	130 39.0	43.9	255 14.0	13.0	189 11.5	9.5	13 50.9	7.4	57.9	Avior	234 35.0	S 59 22.4
21	330 59.8	145 38.6 ··	45.2	270 16.4 ··	13.1	203 40.0	9.5	13 43.5	7.5	57.9	Bellatrix	279 16.0	N 6 18.8
22	346 02.3	160 38.2	46.4	285 18.8	13.2	218 08.5	9.5	13 36.0	7.6	58.0	Betelgeuse	271 45.7	N 7 24.0
23	1 04.7	175 37.9	47.7	300 21.2	13.3	232 37.0	9.5	13 28.4	7.7	58.0			
Mer. Pass. 22 51.8		v -0.4	d 1.2	v 2.4	d 0.1	S.D.	15.7		16.0	16.2			

FIG. 2308. EXCERPTS FROM DAILY DATA PAGE, NAUTICAL ALMANAC

Whereas the G.H.A. of Sun, Moon, and Planets is tabulated on the daily pages in their respective columns, the 57 stars would require too much space to list their G.H.A.'s individually. The first column on the daily page, therefore, lists the G.H.A. of the first point of Aries (♈) sometimes called Vernal (or March) equinox. This is the zero point on the celestial equator from which the westward distance of the stars is measured. This angular distance is called sidereal hour angle (S.H.A.). It is listed for each star in the star table of the daily pages.

The G.H.A. of a star is obtained as follows:

G.H.A. ☆ = G.H.A. ♈ + S.H.A. ☆

Turn to daily page, proper date, and record the tabulated figure in the G.H.A. ♈ column immediately preceding the time of observation. Obtain correction for minutes and seconds in the ♈ column on the minute correction page corresponding to the minutes and seconds of sight. Add to these two the S.H.A. of the star sighted, obtained from the Star data on the daily page. If the sum of these three exceeds 360°, subtract 360° from it until the final G.H.A. is below 360°.

Declination of the stars is tabulated on each three-day page of daily data, and changes so slowly that the tabulated declination on the page containing date of sight can be recorded and used *with no correction.* The declinations are marked (N), meaning north declination, and (S), meaning south declination.

Example: Observed star Altair on 7 October at 10h 21m 39s G.M.T. Find G.H.A. and declination using Fig. 2308.

G.H.A. ♈ at 10h	165°	32'.7
Correction for 21m 39s	5°	25'.6
S.H.A. Altair	62°	48'.3
G.H.A. Altair at 10h 21m 39s	233°	46'.6
Declination	8°	45'.8 N

Example: Observed star Alpheratz on 7 October at 22h 51m 57s G.M.T. Find G.H.A. and declination using Fig. 2308.

G.H.A. ♈ at 22h	346°	02'.3
Correction for 51m 57s	13°	01'.4
S.H.A. Alpheratz	358°	25'.7
	717°	29'.4
Subtract	360°	
G.H.A. Alpheratz at 22h 51m 57s	357°	29'.4
Declination	28°	52'.0 N

2309. To find the meridian angle (*t*). The Greenwich hour angle having been found, it is used to find the meridian angle (*t*) as required when seeking the computed altitude (Hc) and the azimuth. Finding *t* is an element of working a sight for line of position by any method. This important angle has been defined in Chapter 17 and is further illustrated in Fig. 2901. Briefly stated, it is the longitude difference between the ship and the G.P. of observed body, i.e., the degrees and minutes of longitude the body is E or W of the observer.

The G.H.A. of the body, as taken from the Almanac, is measured from 0° to 360° westward from Greenwich (0° Long.). The longitude of the assumed position of the ship is measured 180° E or W from Greenwich. The two quantities must be combined in a manner to give *t* as measured E or W of the ship from 0° to 180°. Should the hour angle found by applying the Long. to the G.H.A. exceed 180° it must be subtracted from 360° to give *t*, the shorter arc of the equator from the ship's meridian to that of the body observed.

The simplest approach to the question of finding the meridian angle varies with different students. The orthodox method is to draw a time diagram which at once indicates how to handle Long. and G.H.A. Another approach is to think of the position of the ship and the G.P. of the observed body as on a chart or globe, a practice which also indicates what to do with the Long. and the G.H.A. At sea, under most circumstances, the navigator knows whether the body was east or west of his meridian and can make a rough guess of the designation of *t* before doing any paper work. Or a rule may be derived from the definitions of Long. G.H.A. and *t*.

TO FIND THE MERIDIAN ANGLE *(t):* Apply the Long. of the observer to the G.H.A. of the body as follows:

Add East Long. to G.H.A., if sum exceeds 360°, subtract 360°.

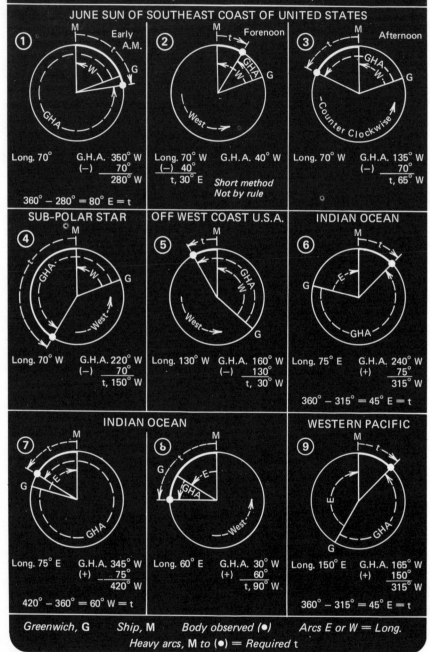

Given Longitude and the Greenwich Hour Angle measured W up to 360°
To find Meridian Angle measured either E or W up to 180°

JUNE SUN OF SOUTHEAST COAST OF UNITED STATES

① Early A.M.

Long. 70°   G.H.A. 350° W
(−)   70°
       280° W

360° − 280° = 80° E = t

② Forenoon

Long. 70° W   G.H.A. 40° W
(−)   40°
t, 30° E

Short method
Not by rule

③ Afternoon

Long. 70° W   G.H.A. 135° W
(−)   70°
t, 65° W

SUB-POLAR STAR

④

Long. 70° W   G.H.A. 220° W
(−)   70°
t, 150° W

OFF WEST COAST U.S.A.

⑤

Long. 130° W   G.H.A. 160° W
(−)   130°
t, 30° W

INDIAN OCEAN

⑥

Long. 75° E   G.H.A. 240° W
(+)   75°
       315° W

360° − 315° = 45° E = t

INDIAN OCEAN

⑦

Long. 75° E   G.H.A. 345° W
(+)   75°
       420° W

420° − 360° = 60° W = t

⑧

Long. 60° E   G.H.A. 30° W
(+)   60°
t, 90° W

WESTERN PACIFIC

⑨

Long. 150° E   G.H.A. 165° W
(+)   150°
       315° W

360° − 315° = 45° E = t

Greenwich, **G**   Ship, **M**   Body observed (●)   Arcs E or W = Long.
Heavy arcs, **M** to (●) = Required t

Fig. 2309a.

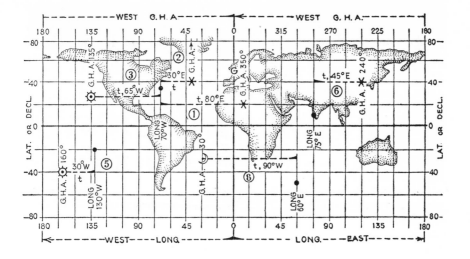

Upper diagram – Center 0° Long.

MERIDIAN ANGLES

Lower diagram – Center 180° E or W

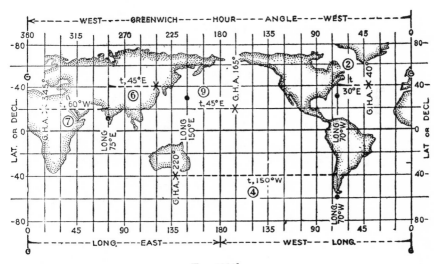

Fɪɢ. 2309b.

Subtract West Long. from G.H.A., if necessary having added 360° to G.H.A. to permit the subtraction.

If either result be less than 180°, it is the value of t (W).
If it exceeds 180°, subtract from 360° to find the value of t (E).

Nine examples of finding t are arranged in Fig. 2309a under their time diagrams. With one exception, they are computed according to the above rule. In (2), t is found by an obvious short cut. The same examples marked with their respective numbers are plotted on rectangular charts of the world in Fig. 2309b.

The student should note the application of the rule to each example. Study the time diagrams until you can draw them without reference to the illustrations. Note the plotting of each example on the world charts and sense the meaning of t. Then think for yourself in your own way as you compute the answers to Q4-23 and Q5-23.

2310. Other tables and schedules in the *Nautical Almanac,* not described in this chapter, are of two classes: (1) Tables of sunrise, sunset, moonrise, moonset discussed in later chapters; (2) Tables of altitude corrections which are the basis for those at the front and back of this book, described in Chap. 19.

2311. Questions. All of the following questions may be answered from the *Nautical Almanac excerpts* for 1966, as reproduced in *Apx. V.* Exercises in finding the Decl. and G.H.A. of planets and the moon will also be found at the close of Chapter 32.

Q 1-23: *As in §2304.* Find the sun's declination in each of the following situations. Local dates are as of 1966. Watch set to approximate zone time. The usual small W.E. on Z.T. need not be considered when taking Decl. of the sun.

Local Date	Watch reads	Time zone	Local Date	Watch reads	Time zone
(a) July 2	8h 20m A.M.	+3	(d) Mar. 6	4h 11m P.M.	+10
(b) Feb. 5	1h 41m P.M.	+7	(e) Dec. 28	7h 20m A.M.	−10
(c) Sept. 29	9h 21m A.M.	−4	(f) Oct. 29	4h 51m P.M.	+2

Q 2-23: *As in §2305.* Given the 1966 Greenwich date and G.M.T., find the Greenwich hour angle of the sun in each of the following cases:

Date	G.M.T.	Date	G.M.T.
(a) Feb. 5	6h 40m 00s	(d) July 2	0h 50m 45s
(b) Apr. 5	17h 50m 10s	(e) Dec. 27	7h 11m 36s
(c) Mar. 7	12h 20m 20s	(f) Oct. 29	22h 21m 32s

Q 3-23: *As in §2306.* Given the 1966 Greenwich date and G.M.T., find the Greenwich hour angle of the following planets:

Planet	Date	G.M.T. h m s	Planet	Date	G.M.T. h m s
(a) Venus	Feb. 5	5 31 47	(c) Jupiter	Oct. 29	0 10 18
(b) Mars	Dec. 27	15 50 02	(d) Venus	July 2	22 51 53

Q 4-23: *As in §2307.* Given the 1966 Greenwich date and G.M.T., find the Greenwich hour angle and declination of the moon in each of the following cases:

Date	G.M.T		Date	G.M.T.
(a) March 7	12h 41m 04s		(c) July 2	10h 31m 23s
(b) Dec. 27	0h 40m 18s		(d) Dec. 27	20h 41m 09s

Q 5-23: *As in §2308.* Given the 1966 Greenwich date and G.M.T., find the Greenwich hour angle and declination of the following stars:

Star	Date	G.M.T. h m s		Star	Date	G.M.T. h m s
(a) Regulus	Dec. 27	1 10 33		(d) Capella	July 2	7 20 04
(b) Sirius	Oct. 29	23 41 28		(e) Altair	Sept. 29	14 21 18
(c) Deneb	Mar. 7	18 50 50		(f) Arcturus	Feb. 5	11 30 47

Q 6-23: *As in §2309.* Draw the time diagrams and find the meridian angle (t) of the sun in each of the following situations. The case number refers to a similar situation illustrated in Figs. 2309a and 2309b.

⊙ G.H.A.	Ship's Long.	Case No.		⊙ G.H.A.	Ship's Long.	Case No.
(a) 87° 31′	29° 24′ W	(3) (5)		(d) 21° 21′	63° 41′ W	(2)
(b) 265° 09′	135° 13′ E	(7)		(e) 43° 54′	15° 19′ E	(8)
(c) 349° 51′	44° 34′ W	(1)		(f) 245° 45′	85° 15′ E	(6)

Q 7-23: *As in §2309.* Draw the time diagrams and find the meridian angle (t) in the following situations. The case number refers to a similar situation illustrated in Figs. 2309a and 2309b.

	Body	G.H.A.	Ship's Long.	Case No.
(a)	☆Capella	63° 36′	32° 36′ W	(3)
(b)	Moon	52° 30′	92° 14′ W	(2)
(c)	Venus	344° 07′	56° 11′ E	(7)
(d)	☆Spica	166° 22′	179° 13′ E	(9)
(e)	Moon	233° 52′	164° 48′ E	(7)
(f)	Jupiter	116° 01′	168° 11′ E	(9)

Answers: Q 1-23 to Q 7-23 inclusive:

	Q 1 Decl.	Q 2 G.H.A.	Q 3 G.H.A.
(a)	23° 03′.4 N	276° 29′.5	276° 51′.3
(b)	15° 51′.8 S	86° 51′.3	141° 18′.7
(c)	2° 14′.1 S	2° 17′.6	273° 28′.7
(d)	5° 30′.1 S	191° 44′.7	197° 22′.4
(e)	23° 19′.4 S	287° 41′.3	
(f)	13° 29′.5 S	159° 26′.7	

	Q 4 G.H.A.	Decl.	Q 5 G.H.A.	Decl.
(a)	179° 40′.9	6° 58′.3 N	321° 03′.6	12° 07′.8 N
(b)	19° 43′.1	26° 43′.2 N	292° 17′.7	16° 39′.9 S
(c)	161° 31′.9	26° 41′.7 S	137° 41′.1	45° 09′.2 N
(d)	308° 03′.4	27° 16′.5 N	311° 21′.6	45° 57′.9 N
(e)			285° 55′.9	8° 46′.8 N
(f)			94° 20′.1	19° 21′.3 S

24. THE AIR ALMANAC

CHILD of necessity, the air almanac of today marks a great forward step in the art of navigation. *The Air Almanac,* published for the year 1933 by the U. S. Naval Observatory, tabulated the G.H.A. of the moon for each 10 minutes of time directly in units of arc, together with the declination at similar intervals. Supported by a false sense of economy, the spirit of the dead past prevailed and *The Air Almanac,* as such, was not continued. The arrangement of the *Nautical Almanac* did not meet the exigencies of the air, and the opportunity and importance of providing a simplified almanac to facilitate the training of all navigators in an emergency was overlooked. Others sensed the situation, and the *British Air Almanac,* initiated in 1937, was used by all American airmen prior to the advent of *The American Air Almanac* for 1941. Since January, 1953, it has been prepared jointly by the U. S. Naval Observatory and Her Majesty's Stationery Office. Many navigators prefer to use the *Air Almanac,* although recent changes in the *Nautical Almanac* have narrowed the choice.

2401. Outline of the *Air Almanac*. Published in advance for six-month periods of each year, the principal features of *The American Air Almanac* are illustrated by the excerpts from that publication printed in *Apx. VI.*

Daily Sheets give the necessary astronomical data for each day. The G.H.A. is tabulated at 10-minute intervals for the sun, vernal equinox (♈), the three planets most suitable for observation at that time, and for the moon. Declination is tabulated at 10-minute intervals for the moon and at hourly intervals for sun and planets.

The G.H.A. and declination of the sun and the G.H.A. of Aries are tabulated to 0'.1. This is to accommodate some types of astrotracker (automatic star tracker); a special interpolation table is also provided for this purpose. However, for general use, the tabulated quantities should be rounded off to the nearest minute (*even* minute if the tabulation is 0'.5). This will be the consistent practice of this book when these quantities are taken from the *Air Almanac*.

The A.M. side of the daily sheet also carries tables giving the time of moonrise (§3210) and its parallax in altitude (§2404), the semidiameters of the sun and moon, and the age of the moon in days since the previous new moon. The P.M. side of the daily page carries the same data except that the time of moonset is tabulated instead of moonrise. It should be remarked that corrections should be taken from the side corresponding to G.M.T. as they are not always the same on both sides.

Altitude correction tables, and the S.H.A. and declination of each navigational star are given on the cover pages and the linen-backed flap which carries the star chart. Some 82 pages of explanations, additional tables, and diagrams, to which the reader is referred, include various items of special interest to air navigators. Also included are convenient sky diagrams and a very useful planet location diagram from which one can read the relative daily positions of the sun, moon, ♈, five planets, four first magnitude stars near the ecliptic, and the point on the ecliptic which is just north of the brightest star, Sirius.

Also included in the explanations are a table of symbols and abbreviations with their equivalents in English, French, and Spanish; and a table of standard times used by various countries of the world.

2402. Simplicity in use of the *Air Almanac* results principally from the short time interval between the tabulated figures. This arrangement permits finding Decl. and G.H.A. at time of sight by the same general method for all bodies.

Declination of sun, moon, or planet is taken directly from the daily sheet without interpolation. That for a star is taken from the Stars table on the inside front cover page which is duplicated on the flap.

G.H.A. of sun or planet is the last tabulated figure before G.M.T. of sight plus a single G.H.A. correction from *Interpolation of G.H.A.* table *for the interval to time of sight.*

The *Interpolation of G.H.A.* table for sun, planets and ♈ is correct for the sun and sufficiently correct for the planets and for ♈, because the required correction is never for an interval exceeding 10 minutes. Observe that the tabulated corrections are nothing more than the time interval ÷ 4. *Caution:* When seeking these corrections, keep out of the moon table.

G.H.A. of the moon is that tabulated on the daily sheet plus a correction to time of sight taken from the Moon side at the right of the *Inter-*

polation of G.H.A. table. The values given on the daily page are adjusted slightly so that the fixed increments of the interpolation table can be used with negligible error.

Observe that the *Interpolation of G.H.A.* tables are of the so-called *critical* or *turning point* type, which means that the times given in the tables are those when the correction changes from one unit to the next. If the time for which the correction is required be one of the tabulated times, the upper of the two adjacent values of the correction should be taken. The several other tables of this type found in the *Air Almanac* should be used in the same way.

Examples: For April 12, 1966, at 9h 14m 26s G.M.T., find G.H.A. and declination of the sun, Venus, and the moon using *A.A. excerpts* in *Apx. VI:*

	Sun	Venus	Moon
G.H.A. at 9h 10m	317° 17′	0° 17′	47° 21′
Corr. for 4m 26s	1° 07′	1° 07′	1° 04′
G.H.A. at 9h 14m 26s	318° 24′	1° 24′	48° 25m
Declination	8° 34′ N	8° 59′ S	26° 17′ S

Examples: For April 12, 1966, at 22h 48m 09s G.M.T. find G.H.A. and declination of the sun, Jupiter and the moon using *A.A. excerpts* in *Apx. VI:*

	Sun	Jupiter	Moon
G.H.A. at 22h 40m	159° 49′	94° 58′	242° 53′
Corr. for 8m 09s	2° 02′	2° 02′	1° 58′
G.H.A. at 22h 48m 09s	161° 51′	97° 00′	244° 51′
Declination	8° 47′ N	23° 18′ N	25° 31′ S

2403. The G.H.A. of a star, as taken from the *Air Almanac*, is the G.H.A. of ♈, found as for the sun, plus the sidereal hour angle of the star taken from the inside front cover page, or flap:

$$\text{G.H.A.} \,✩ = \text{G.H.A.} \,♈ + \text{S.H.A.} \,✩$$

The reasons for the above rule lie in the definitions of the quantities. ♈ is the zero point on the celestial equator from which sidereal hour angles are measured westward. It is called the first point of Aries, the Ram, symbolized by its horns as ♈.

(1) The G.H.A. of ♈ is the longitude (hour angle) of this zero point **west** of Greenwich.

(2) The Sidereal Hour Angle (S.H.A.) of a star is its longitude (hour angle) west of ♈.

Thus, the hour angle of the star west of Greenwich or G.H.A.✩ is the **total of (1) and (2).**

Example: On April 12, 1966, observed ☆ Vega at 10h 23m 19s G.M.T. From *A.A. excerpts* in *Apx. VI* find G.H.A. and declination at time of sight.

G.H.A. ♈ at 10h 20m	355° 10′
Corr. for 3m 19s	50′
S.H.A. ☆ Vega	81° 03′
	437° 03′
subtract	360°
G.H.A. ☆ Vega	77° 03′
Declination	38° 45′ N

The star tables of the *Air Almanac* list all of the navigational stars included in the *Nautical Almanac*. These are arranged both in alphabetical order and in order of the S.H.A. of the stars. Star numbers followed by an asterisk indicate the stars used in H.O. 249, Vol. 1. A dagger after the name indicates those stars whose declinations are such that they can be used with H.O. 249, Vol. II and III.

2404. The altitude correction tables of the *Air Almanac* are of course designed primarily for air navigation with a bubble octant in which the bubble replaces the natural horizon (Chap. 20). However, tables are provided for correcting altitudes taken with a marine type sextant. As explained in Chap. 19, the four principal corrections are for dip, refraction, semidiameter, and parallax. These are in addition to the index correction, if any, which is normally applied first.

The dip correction is given on the back cover in a critical type table similar to the *Nautical Almanac* table but extended to heights of over 2,600 feet. The correction is always *subtracted* from the sextant altitude of all bodies (§1904).

The refraction correction is found by the table on the inside back cover. This table accommodates the special conditions experienced in high-altitude flight in polar regions where observations may be required of bodies below the celestial horizon. For marine use with the natural horizon, enter with the altitude, the column at the left, headed 0, and find the refraction correction in the extreme left column, headed *Ro*. For extremes of temperature, this correction can be adjusted by applying the factor (*f*) found below *Ro* and opposite the temperature range which includes the existing temperature in °C. The refraction correction is always *subtracted* from the sextant altitude of all bodies (§1903).

The semidiameter of the sun and moon is found at the right of the A.M. daily page near the bottom. It is applied to the sextant altitudes of the sun and moon only, *adding* for a lower limb observation, and subtracting for an upper limb observation (§1906).

Parallax in altitude for the moon is given on both the A.M. and P.M.

sides of the daily page, and may not be the same in both places. The correction taken from the critical-type table is *added* to the sextant altitude of either the moon's upper or lower limb. (§1905.)

Example: Find the true altitudes (Ho) for the following sights taken with a marine sextant on April 12, 1966 at about 0530 G.M.T.; I.C. + 2′, Ht. Eye 36 ft., using *A.A. excerpts* in *Apx. VI:*

Body	Hs		Body	Hs
Sun ☉	19° 17′		Moon ☾	33° 46′
Altair	54° 06′		Moon ☾̄	34° 16′

	☉		☆		☾		☾̄	
Hs	19° 17′		54° 06′		33° 46′		34° 16′	
	(+)	(−)	(+)	(−)	(+)	(−)	(+)	(−)
I.C.	2′		2′		2′		2′	
Dip		6′		6′		6′		6′
Ref.		3′		1′		1′		1′
S.D.	16′		—	—	15′			15′
Par'lx	—	—	—	—	46′		45′	
Tot'ls	18′	9′	2′	7′	63′	7′	47′	22′
Net		+9′		−5′		+56′		+25′
Ho	19° 26′		54° 01′		34° 42′		34° 41′	

Other tables and graphs relating principally to air navigation are fully discussed in every edition of the *Air Almanac.* The use of the *Polaris table* for finding latitude by Polaris is reviewed in Chapter 27.

2405. The accuracy of the *Air Almanac,* while somewhat less than that of the *Nautical Almanac,* is nevertheless adequate for practical work at sea. The maximum error in G.H.A., after interpolation, is always less than 1′.4 for the Sun, 2′.0 for the moon, 1′.6 for the planets, and 1′.3 for Aries. Except for high declination stars, the *average* error is approximately 0′.5. In declination, the error cannot be greater then 2′ for the moon, or 0′.8 for the Sun, planets, or stars.

If these possible errors are transferred to a line of position, the maximum error in a single intercept resulting from inaccuracies of tabular values is 3′ for the moon and 2′ for other bodies. The positional error of a two-body fix attributable to the *Air Almanac* will rarely exceed 5 miles and on average will be less.

When the full precision of the table is utilized (0′, 1 for the sun, Aries, and the stars taken from the special table on pages A76–78), the maximum errors in altitude difference are 0′.3 for the sun, and 0′.5 for the stars. The resulting positional error in a two-body fix will rarely exceed 1′.0.

*   *   *

As a joint American and British publication, the *Air Almanac* is exclusively used by military and commercial air navigators of both countries. It is widely used by mariners because of its simplicity and adequate accuracy, although the improved arrangement of the modern *Nautical Almanac* has reduced its former advantage in convenience.

25. METHODS

B OWDITCH, in the first edition of *The American Practical Navigator,*
printed in 1802, provided for the work of the navigator at sea by
the then known methods which included *lunars* and *time sights* for
longitude and *noon* or *meridian altitude sights* for latitude. Since the
time of Bowditch there has been a gradual, but increasingly rapid,
development of the science of navigation. Some thirty methods for finding the solution of the astronomical triangle have been published, and
the required computations have been greatly simplified.

2501. Principles. Experienced navigators may, and do, differ as
to the method they prefer to use, but one should remember that *with
any method:*

(1) A single observation gives only a line of position at right angles
to the bearing of the body. There are as yet no practical methods for
obtaining a fix from a single sight.

(2) To determine a line of position, the navigator must first observe,
time, and correct the altitude; must determine from the Almanac the
declination and the Greenwich hour angle of the observed body: and
thereafter must find its meridian angle. There is no "short" method
which eliminates this part of the work, wherein many errors and blunders
occur. It has been greatly simplified, however, by the redesigned
Nautical Almanac or use of the *Air Almanac* for marine work.

The methods for computing the results of celestial observations taught
in this Primer are the simplest and best at present available and accept-
able, and are sufficient under all circumstances. Mention of other
methods is for the information of the student when in contact with older
navigators or when reading other books.

2502. The old navigation, the system which reached its zenith
shortly after 1900, computed the D.R. by the sailings, used time sights

for longitude, and depended on numerous variations of the meridian altitude sight for latitude. There was little or no plotting, and the navigator delved the depths of trigonometry. As this system developed into the new, several of its well known methods have lost their former importance, among which are:

The sailings, which are the mathematical methods for handling course and distance, are often taught but seldom used.

Time sight (1763). This was the standard method for longitude of the old navigation and continues to be widely used in the Merchant Marine. The body should be observed when near E or W. Latitude is assumed as that of the D.R. The difference between the local time, as computed from the observation, and the Greenwich time, as determined from the chronometer, gives the longitude, hence the name "time sight." Without any plotting the D.R. latitude and the computed longitude define a point of position. Such a point is correct only if the assumed latitude is correct. If two different latitudes are assumed and two points are computed, a line through the points is a line of position as accurate as that found by any method. The time sight method is fairly long, must not be used within an hour or more of the meridian, and, although it may be used for laying down a line of position, should be avoided by the student.

Latitude by meridian altitude, other than the noon sight of the sun, is no longer important because of the ease with which a line of position may be worked at any time without bothering with the time of transit.

Ex-meridians are sights for latitude taken when a body is near the meridian and worked like a noon sight after correcting the observed altitude to the meridian. This *reduction to the meridian* was an important element of the old navigation but is practically obsolete for the same reason as are meridian altitudes of bodies other than the sun; i.e. the ease of computing a line of position from any observation.

2503. The new navigation, as taught today, may be described as a graphic system. Continuous plotting of course and distance gives the D.R. Lines of position, available whenever sun, moon or stars can be observed, serve to check the D.R. and from time to time give a fix. Skillful plotting is an essential adjunct to every phase of the navigator's work.

Two sights of the old navigation, solved by the old methods, continue in daily use because they are short cuts for finding latitude.

Noon sight for latitude by the meridian altitude of the sun is so simple that it is used by all mariners. However worked, it results in a line of position which is the parallel of latitude of the ship.

Latitude by Polaris, a method used by Columbus, is used more than ever before by both mariners and air navigators. Like the noon sight, it gives a line of position which is the parallel of latitude.

2504. New methods to facilitate finding the computed altitude and azimuth were developed as the use of Sumner lines determined by altitude differences increased. The tables of Aquino (1910) and Ogura (1920) and the bulky H.O. No. 203 (1923) marked steps in advance. The methods most often taught in 1930 included:

Marcq Saint-Hilaire or cosine-haversine. Strictly speaking, all the methods of the new navigation which plot a line of position by any process of altitude differences with the corresponding azimuth are Marcq Saint-Hilaire methods.

In the more common use of the term, a navigator saying he uses Marcq Saint-Hilaire means that he computes the altitude by the *cosine-haversine* formula of Saint-Hilaire. This gives the intercept but the azimuth must be taken from azimuth tables or found by an additional computation.

This method came into general use in the Navy about 1910, was taught during World War I, and today remains in common use by navigators so trained. The method has been popular for many years, plots from the D.R. position, and requires few rules or precepts. However, it is somewhat long and is being supplanted by new methods which give both altitude and azimuth with less work.

Line of Position Book, Weems (1927), is a small book of Japanese tables by Ogura which provide a short method for computing the altitude from an especially assumed position. It has received considerable publicity for air work and was used by Colonel Lindbergh. Rust's diagram at the back of the book gives the azimuth. Although not now in general use, this thin red book marked a step in Weems' bold and successful efforts to simplify navigation.

H.O. No. 208, Dreisonstok (1928), is a small book of about 90 pages. The tables provide for computing altitude and azimuth from an especially assumed position with a minimum of figures and without interpolation. These *Navigation Tables for Mariners and Aviators,* with their accompanying instructions and examples, remain popular in the Navy and the Merchant Marine and with other navigators who adopted this method when first published.

Since 1930 several important new tables for altitude and azimuth have been published, two of which were completed in 1942. In view of these developments, the older methods can be omitted if desired.

2505. H.O. 211, *Dead Reckoning Altitude and Azimuth Tables, Ageton.* This table has provided one of the most popular of the "short methods" of computing. The method is of universal application and gives both altitude and azimuth from *any* geographical position. The single table, requiring only 36 pages of A and B columns, is printed in Appendix

VII. Since the development of precomputed methods described below, interest in the H.O. 211 method has waned; however, many navigators find it useful as a standby method because of its compactness and universal applicability. A later chapter outlines the construction of the table and gives instructions for its use.

Ageton (1942), sometimes called the *A.A.A. method* to distinguish it from Ageton's H.O. 211, results from a new arrangement of tables devised by Rear Admiral Ageton, first published in 1942 with the title *Manual of Celestial Navigation*. This method is the best yet devised for computing altitude and azimuth from an especially assumed position. The method is preferable for such solutions because (1) it is uniform under all conditions, (2) requires no interpolation, (3) covers all latitudes, and (4) when working a round of star sights requires fewer openings than do other tables.

2506. H.O. 214. Probably the most widely used of the modern methods for finding Hc and Z is that contained in H.O. 214, *Tables of Computed Altitude and Azimuth*. These tables consist of a set of nine volumes, each applicable to 10° of latitude. Only those volumes serving the latitudes of interest need be acquired.

Figures 2904*a* and 2904*b* each show across the top an excerpt from these tables for latitudes 36° and 39°. As noted in the headings, the portion used in Fig. 2904*a* can be used for either north or south latitude, provided the declination of the observed body is of the same name. Other pages, as in Fig. 2904*b*, are used for declinations of contrary name to the latitude.

It will be seen that each vertical column is headed by a declination and contains the values for altitude (Alt.) and Azimuth (Az.) determined by a particular meridian angle (H.A.). For the angles tabulated, the values obtained are exact. For intervening values of declination and hour angle, interpolation is accomplished by means of the tabulated "$\triangle$d" and "$\triangle$t."

When using H.O. 214, it is customary to select an assumed position near the D.R. but resting on a whole degree of latitude and having a longitude such that the meridian angle also is a whole degree. When this is done, it is only necessary to interpolate "Alt." between adjacent declination columns for the exact declination of the body observed. Mental interpolation of azimuth also is feasible but rarely required.

2507. H.O. 229, *Sight Reduction Tables for Marine Navigation.*[1] These new tables are the first truly universal tables of precomputed solutions of the navigational triangle. They accommodate all latitudes, dec-

---

[1] The reader is referred to an article entitled *Sight Reduction Tables for Marine Navigation*, by John H. Blythe, R. L. Duncombe, and D. H. Sadler, published in *NAVIGATION* Journal of the Institute of Navigation, Summer 1966. Much of the information contained in §2507 and §2903 has been taken from this article by permission.

linations, and hour angles in equal intervals on 1°. The tables are the result of the joint efforts of the U.S. Naval Oceanographic Office, the Nautical Almanac Office of the U.S. Naval Observatory, and H.M. Nautical Almanac Office of the Royal Greenwich Observatory.

The tables consist of six volumes, each covering 16° of latitude with an overlap of 1° between volumes, as follows:

	Latitude	
Volume	First Zone	Second Zone
1	0°– 7°	8°– 15°
2	15°– 22°	23°– 30°
3	30°– 37°	38°– 45°
4	45°– 52°	53°– 60°
5	60°– 67°	68°– 75°
6	75°– 82°	83°– 90°

Volume 6 for latitudes 75° to 90°, north or south, is being issued first, to be followed by the other volumes.

Like H.O. 214, the new tables provide precomputed solutions of navigational triangles where latitude and hour angle are in integral degrees, with provision for interpolating declination. However, unlike the earlier table, H.O. 229 gives altitudes from the horizon to 90°, and includes every integral degree of declination from 0° to 90° north and 90° south without the gaps found in H.O. 214.

Thus, the immediate solution of a navigational triangle having any combination of hour angle, latitude, and declination, when measured in whole degrees from 0° to 90°, is obtained at one opening of the table without interpolation. The provisions for interpolating altitude for the exact declination to a precision of 0′.1 is straightforward and uniformly proceeds in the same direction—downward on the page—with signs to indicate whether the correction is to be added or subtracted. A two-step interpolation table facilitates this process. The 0′.1 precision in altitude is maintained through critical areas of declination by means of a simple additional correction based on "double second differences" for which short, critical-type tables are provided.

Azimuth angle is tabulated for each set of entering arguments to a precision of 0°.1, and usually can be taken from the table without interpolation, for which no provision is made.

Examples of the use of H.O. 229, together with proforma excerpts from the tables are contained in §2903.

2508. H.O. No. 249, *Sight Reduction Tables for Air Navigation,* comprise three volumes which provide world-wide coverage. Volume I gives computed altitude and azimuth (not azimuth angle) for seven selected stars for every whole degree of latitude from 0° to 89° north or south and for every whole degree of L.H.A. ♈ (every 2° polewards of latitude 69°). Volumes II and III provide computed altitude and azimuth angle for each whole degree of latitude from 0° to 89° north or south, each whole degree of declination 0° to 29° north or south, and each degree of L.H.A. Provision is made for sextant angles having negative values (zenith distance more than 90°), a condition encountered in high altitude flight. Volumes II and III are permanent in character, but Volume I is issued at 5-year intervals.

2509. What is the shortest method? Often asked, this question is difficult or impossible to answer to everyone's satisfaction. Almost any method can be shortened if less accuracy can be tolerated. Accordingly, from a practical standpoint, it is probable that H.O. 249 with data taken from the modern *Nautical Almanac* provides the fastest, easiest, and most trouble-free method in use today. Substitution of the *Air Almanac* reduces slightly the number of figures required to be written down but results are expressed to one less decimal point.

2510. Mechanical and graphic methods for computing or laying down a line of position, or getting a fix, have been devised in wide variety. Thus far, such methods are little used by surface navigators. Because of the brevity of other present-day solutions, the cost of the required devices, and the fact that no permanent record is made of the work, it seems unlikely that they will come into general use at sea.

*   *   *

The methods above discussed are a few of many which have been developed for obtaining the desired elements of the astronomical triangle. All are sufficiently accurate and all result in identical Sumner lines. Not one can fix the position of the ship from a single observation. The newer tables facilitate and shorten a part of the work but in no case do they eliminate the necessity of understanding basic principles.

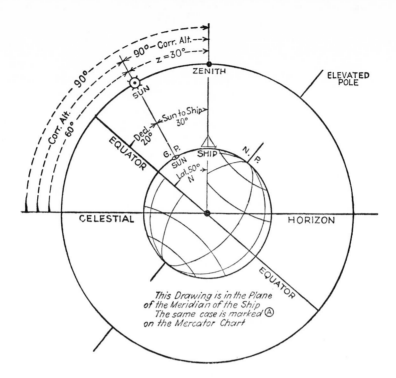

THE NOON SIGHT

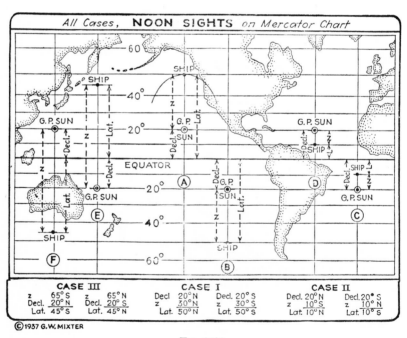

CASE III		CASE I		CASE II	
z 65°S	z 65°N	Decl 20°N	Decl. 20°S	Decl. 20°N	Decl.20°S
Decl. 20°N	Decl. 20°S	z 30°N	z 30°S	z 10°S	z 10°N
Lat. 45°S	Lat. 45°N	Lat. 50°N	Lat. 50°S	Lat. 10°N	Lat.10°S

Fig. 2601.

26. THE NOON SIGHT

CENTURIES old, the noon sight is a convenient and simple element of both the old and the new navigation. It results in a line of position which is the parallel of latitude of the ship. Accuracy of the latitude determined depends only on the accuracy of the sun's maximum altitude as observed at noon and the accuracy with which its declination at that time is known. Exact time is useful but not essential. With the sextant one determines how far the ship is north or south of the sun; the Almanac tells how far the sun is north or south of the equator; the sum or difference of these quantities is the latitude of the ship. These facts suggest that, in an emergency, latitude not only may be determined without exact time but may be found by any intelligent person who can use the sextant. Thus the ship can make port by running down the latitude of the desired landfall as did many shipmasters before methods for finding longitude came into general use. Although less important than formerly, the noon sight continues in wide use and is considered as one of the principal observations of the day's work at sea.

2601. Outline of the sight. The sun appears to move across the heavens each day in an arc at the top of which it attains the maximum altitude wherewith latitude is computed. This occurs when the sun, on the meridian, bears true south or true north at the time of local apparent noon, hence the term *noon sight*. This momentary collapse of the astronomical triangle makes possible the ages-old solution used by all mariners.

The upper drawing on the opposite page illustrates finding latitude by a noon sight from mid-northern latitudes in summer. The same situation is plotted on the meridian (A) of the Mercator chart. The sun is on the meridian and the required latitude is the arc of the meridian from the equator to the ship. The length of this arc is then the declination of the sun plus the arc from the sun to the ship, or:

Declination,   *d* 20° N from equator to sun
90° — Corr. Alt., *z* 30° N from sun to ship
————————— (add)
Latitude,   L 50° N from equator to ship

Declination is taken from the Almanac (§2304). The distance from the G.P. sun to the ship is found with the sextant. The total of the two quantities is the latitude of the observer.

The drawing of the various arcs and angles gives the conventional geometrical demonstration of Case I. A simpler conception of the noon sight results from thinking of the G.P. sun and the ship as plotted on a chart. Such sketches for each case show at once, without reference to rules or formulae, whether to add Decl. and $(90° - Ho)$ or take their difference to find the latitude.

2602. Solutions of the different cases of the noon sight further illustrate how to sense the rule for each case from the positions of sun and ship on the meridian which may be that of any longitude.

The following examples are grouped according to the various cases, which are encountered in practice at sea. Except for correcting the altitude to Ho, each example is a complete solution for latitude. The capital letter designations (A), (B), etc., indicate the label of a similar situation plotted on the chart in Fig. 2601. The chart is too small for plotting the examples to exact scale. The rule and formula for each case are given according to custom. They are of little importance to one who thinks in terms of the relative positions of the ship and the sun as when at sea.

CASE I. *When latitude is greater than declination and of the same name, both N or both S:* Add zenith distance to declination and give resulting latitude their common name. *(Lat. = Decl. + z)*.

Example (A). D.R. Lat. 51° 00′ N, Ho at L.A.N. 62° 34′.5, Decl. 23° 26′.7 N. Latitude?
The sun is north of the equator and the ship is north of the sun, therefore add Decl. and z:

89° 60′	Decl.	d 23° 26′.7 N, from equator to sun
Ho 62° 34′.5	Z. Dist	z 27° 25′.5 N, from sun to ship
		——— (add)
z 27° 25′.5	Latitude,	L 50° 52′.2 N, from equator to ship

Example (B). D.R. Lat. 59° 28′ S, Ho at L.A.N. 44° 23′.6, Decl. 13° 54′.7 S. Latitude?
The sun is south of the equator and the ship is south of the sun, therefore add Decl. and z:

89° 60′	Decl.	d 13° 54′.7 S, from equator to sun
Ho 44° 23′.6	Z. Dist.	z 45° 36′.4 S, from sun to ship
		——— (add)
z 45° 36′.4	Latitude,	L 59° 31′.1 S, from equator to ship

CASE II. *When declination is greater than latitude but of the same name, both N or both S:* Subtract zenith distance from declination and name resulting latitude like Decl. (*Lat.* = *Decl.* − *z*).

Example (C). D.R. Lat. 11° 45′ S, Ho at L.A.N. 78° 17′.4, Decl. 23° 26′.7 S. Latitude?
The ship is between the sun and the equator, therefore subtract *z* from Decl.:

89° 60′	Decl.	*d* 23° 26′.7 S, from equator to sun
Ho 78° 17′.4	Z. Dist.	*z* 11° 42′.6 N, from sun to ship
		—————— (sub)
z 11° 42′.6	Latitude,	L 11° 44′.1 S, from equator to ship

A similar situation occurs in north latitude when the ship is between the sun and the equator. Such an example of Case II is plotted as (D) on the chart.

CASE III. *When latitude and declination are of opposite names:* Subtract declination from zenith distance and name resulting latitude like *z*. The formula in this case becomes (*Lat.* = *z* − *Decl.*).

Example (E). D.R. Lat. 55° 02′ N, Ho 21° 11′, Decl. 13° 48′.4 S. Latitude?
The sun is on the opposite side of the equator from the ship, therefore subtract Decl. from *z*:

89° 60′	Z. Dist.	*z* 68° 49′.0 N, from sun to ship
Ho 21° 11′	Decl.	*d* 13° 48′.4 S, from equator to sun
		—————— (sub)
z 68° 49′	Latitude, L	55° 00′.6 N, from equator to ship

An example of Case III in south latitude is labeled (F) on the chart.

The midnight sight of the sun as seen below the pole from high latitudes is sometimes considered as a fourth case but is not discussed in this Primer.

To review the above situations effectively, do each example in this way: On ruled paper draw and label a meridian like that at the right of Fig. 2609. On the meridian plot the ship by its D.R. Lat. and the sun by its given Decl. Remember that the distance from the sun to the ship is (90° − Ho), think for yourself and solve for latitude. Do the examples over again until they can be done without hesitation with only a picture in mind of the ship and the sun on the meridian. Thereafter answer the questions in Q 1-26, locating the sun by its declination and the ship by its distance from the sun, 90° − Ho.

2603. Practicalities. The noon sight is a tradition of the past when it was depended on for latitude and was the only sight available during the middle of the day. With the new navigation, a line of position may be had whenever visibility permits and the navigator need not worry if he misses "sun time." The very good reasons for the continued use of the noon sight are its accuracy and simplicity.

Accuracy of the declination is practically assured. The Almanacs may be entered within comparatively wide limits of G.M.T. of sight without appreciable error in the Decl. because its hourly change does not exceed 1'.

Ease of observing the maximum altitude and often the accuracy of the result depend on an estimate of when the sun will be on the meridian, the time of local apparent noon (L.A.N.). This may vary from the noon of the ship's clocks by more than 45 minutes.

Useful accuracy in an estimate of the time of L.A.N. in turn depends on the method to be used for taking the sight and on how long the sun's altitude will appear unchanged at the top of its daily journey from east to west.

The duration of this "hang" period under various conditions may be approximated from the table in Fig. 2603. When above 80° the change in altitude is comparatively rapid and there is practically no hang above 85°. On the optimistic assumption that changes of more than 0'.2 (12″) can be observed, from 80° down the sun will appear to hang for from 2 to 4 minutes. With the average observer these periods will materially increase.

BEFORE L.A.N.	ALTITUDES								AFTER L.A.N.
	30°	40°	50°	60°	70°	75°	80°	85°	
1 m	0′	0′	0′	.1′	.1′	.1′	.2′	.4′	1 m
2 m	.1	.1	.2	.2	.4	.5	.7	1.5	2 m
3 m	.3	.3	.4	.6	.8	1.1	1.7	3.4	3 m
4 m	.5	.6	.7	1.0	1.5	2.0	3.0	6.0	4 m

MAXIMUM CHANGE OF ALTITUDE FROM MERIDIAN
Not to be used for at²

FIG. 2603. THE HANG OF THE SUN.

2604. Taking the sight. There are several ways of observing the meridian altitude of the sun. Choice depends on conditions and on how the navigator prefers to do his work.

(1) *Following the sun to its maximum altitude* is the old and most widely practiced method. It does not require an accurate knowledge of the time of transit and is recommended for the beginner because it is suited to many conditions.

At about ten minutes in advance of apparent noon, the observer, with his sextant, makes contact between the sun's lower limb and the horizon. Tilt the sextant from side to side and adjust until the sun, seen moving in an arc, just touches the horizon at the lowest part of the arc. As the sun rises, a widening space is seen between its lower limb and the horizon. Turn the tangent screw and close up the slightest streak of sky whenever it appears and keep the lower limb in contact. The change in altitude becomes slower and slower as the sun approaches the meridian. As the sun hangs, swing the instrument and make certain of accurate contact. Continue the observation, *without turning the tangent screw,* until the sun is seen to dip into the horizon. This loss of altitude gives assurance that the reading of the sextant was the sun's maximum altitude.

(2) *Numerous sights near noon* offer a modification of the method first described which is useful under certain conditions. On a small vessel in a heavy, confused sea, violent motion and flying water make sextant work uncertain. It is difficult to follow the sun to its maximum altitude and a single altitude at the estimated time of L.A.N. might be materially in error. In such a situation the following plan is recommended:

Well before expected noon begin taking a series of sights. Continue to read off altitudes to an assistant, preferably at uniform intervals of time, practically whenever they may be had. Turn the tangent screw slightly after each observation to assure that the next altitude will be an independent sight. Discontinue only when the run of altitudes is definitely lower. After such sights as are radically different from the preceding or succeeding series of readings have been eliminated, the hang becomes evident and one may form a judgment of the maximum altitude. This plan, although not orthodox, has served small craft well in times of stress. In a mess of weather the result is more dependable than that of either of the more common methods.

(3) *At the instant of transit* a single sight gives the maximum altitude. To follow this plan the time of transit must be estimated in advance, a precaution often omitted with the older method. Although thought of as an element of the new navigation, seventy years ago Captain Lecky wrote: "There is then no fear of missing 'sun time,' and the plan for many reasons is preferable to the usual one of making eight bells by the sun."

The older method of following the sun is somewhat tedious. It is a strain on the eyes, and in many ways a single altitude at the time of L.A.N. is more convenient. On the other hand, a single altitude should be regarded with suspicion unless the navigator be certain that the estimated time of L.A.N. is sufficiently accurate to assure a maximum altitude.

2605. The time of noon in workaday life is when the whistle blows or when the clock shows 12 at midday. This is almost never the time when the sun is seen on the meridian and, with daylight saving time, it may differ from "sun time" by almost 2 hours. Even with standard or zone time the difference may exceed 45 minutes. Estimating in advance the time of the sun's transit is not an academic question found only in books. Every navigator must predict apparent noon every day or he **may** miss "high noon." The method to use depends on circumstances and on how the sight is to be taken.

The approach of the sun to a bearing of true south or true north **warns** of when its altitude should be followed up and taken at its maximum. Formerly, ships clocks were set at noon each day to local mean time and

FIG. 2605. TIME OF L.A.N. BY EQUATION OF TIME METHOD.

the skipper mentally corrected the clock for the change of longitude **to** the next noon, thus knowing when to begin observing the sun. This method for estimating L.A.N. is as useful today as it was in the days of sail and is in common use whatever be the time kept by the clock.

With faster ships and when only a single sight is to be used, the estimate of the time of L.A.N. requires more care. The local apparent time when the sun crosses the meridian is always 1200 L.A.T. The problem is to predict this instant of time in terms of *the time the navigator is using*. Given the longitude of the observer, the exact time of L.A.N. may be computed in a number of ways, two of which are illustrated in Fig. 2605. Both arrangements show that there are two reasons for the varying times of L.A.N.:

(1) The Eq. Time which varies between 0 and 16 minutes during the year although its rate of change is seldom as great as 1 second per hour.

(2) The difference between the observer's longitude at L.A.N. and the longitude by which the clock was set. For this reason no estimate of the time of L.A.N. can be more accurate than the longitude used for making the estimate.

2606. Primer's Tables 2 and 3 provide for taking out the time of L.A.N. by inspection with sufficient accuracy for all practical purposes. The possible exceptions occur with very high altitudes and when steaming at high speeds. Table 2 is nothing more than 1200 L.A.T. plus or minus the Eq. Time and is never more than 1 minute in error. The corrections in Table 3 are exact for the given longitude differences.

The zone time of apparent noon is its L.M.T. taken from Table 2 plus or minus the correction found in Table 3. The result seldom varies by more than 1 minute from that of the most meticulous computations. The principal possibility for blunders when using the tables lies in the Long. Diff. with which to enter the correction table. This is the difference between the governing zone meridian and the expected longitude at 1200 zone time. It is named East or West according to the position of the ship east or west of the zone meridian. The example given below has been computed by two methods in Fig. 2605 for June 21 of any year using Table X, which should be compared with the following solution by Tables 2 and 3.

Example: June 21, any year, predicted "best" longitude at 1200 (Z − 11) time 160° 09′ E. Estimate zone time of L.A.N.

Longitude			Time of L.A.N.		
Zone − 11	165°	E	Table 2, June 21,	**1202**	L.M.T.
"Best" at 1200 Z.T.	160° 09′E		Table 3, Corr. (+)	**19**	Long. Diff.
Long. Diff.	4° 51′West		Time of L.A.N.	**1221**	Zone − 11

The estimate of the "best" longitude at 1200 is important with any method for predicting the time of L.A.N. When predicated on the projected 1200 D.R. correction should be made for probable errors in the D.R. before estimating the "best" longitude. A longitude line from an earlier sight, advanced to 1200, often gives the preferable "best."

2607. The G.H.A. method, as taught in the Navy for estimating the time of L.A.N. accurately and conveniently, is based on the following facts:

(1) When the sun is on the meridian its G.H.A. is the same as the longitude W of that meridian. In east longitude, 360° − Long. E. = Long. W.

(2) Thus the longitude of the observer is the G.H.A. of the sun at L.A.N. in west longitude.

(3) The time when this G.H.A. occurs, found from the Almanac, is then the G.M.T. of L.A.N. which may be converted into zone or watch time of L.A.N. as desired.

The above method is illustrated by the following *Examples* and Fig. 2607 *A.*

Example: At sea on February 5, 1966, the best estimate of the longitude at 1200 Z.T. (zone + 7) is 104° 20′ W, W.E. on Z.T. fast 30s. Find the watch time of L.A.N. by first estimate only.

Answer: W.T. of L.A.N. 12h 11m 54s.

FIG. 2607. TIME OF L.A.N. BY G.H.A. METHOD.

A, west longitude, first estimate only; *B* and *C,* east longitude, first estimate-second estimate.

Solution: (1) Refer to Fig. 2607 *A.* Establish an estimated longitude at or about noon from the best information available (104° 20′ W.). If the ship is in east longitude, subtract the longitude from 360°, as in Fig. 2607 *B.*

(2) Take from the Almanac sun tables for the day the tabulated G.H.A. nearest to, but less than, the "best" longitude, and note the corresponding G.M.T. (101° 29′ at G.M.T. 19h). In other words, at longitude 101° 29′ W. the G.M.T. of L.A.N. is 19h. For a meridian farther *west,* the time of L.A.N. will be *later* (earlier if east) by the interval required for the sun to traverse the intervening longitude.

(3) Subtract the selected G.H.A. from the "best" longitude west. The resulting difference (2° 51′) is the difference in longitude which the sun must traverse from its position at 19h G.M.T. to reach 104° 20′ W.

(4) Convert the difference found in (3) into time (§2105). The "Increments and Corrections" table in the yellow pages of the *Nautical Almanac* is convenient for this purpose; be careful to enter the appropriate column. The DLO 2° 51′ found in (3) is equivalent to 11m 24s of time.

(5) Add this time difference to the time of the Almanac entry (19h) to find the G.M.T. of L.A.N. at longitude 104° 20′ W., and convert to zone time or watch time by applying in *reverse* the zone description and watch error on zone time. The time of L.A.N. so found is known as the "first estimate" and in most cases is sufficiently accurate for a meridian altitude.

Example: At sea on October 29, 1966, the best estimate of the noon longitude (1200 zone − 6) is 95° 56′ E, W.E. on Z.T. slow 30s. The ship is changing longitude to the eastward at the rate of 36′ per hour. Find the W.T. of L.A.N. by first estimate-second estimate method.
Answer: W.T. of L.A.N. 11h 21m 10s.

Solution: (Fig. 2607 *B* and *C*.) Since the longitude is east, subtract it from 360° and proceed as in the previous example. The first estimate is an approximation and is subject to an error which may be important. This error is the time required for the sun to make up any difference in longitude traversed by the ship in the interval between the time of the "best" longitude, usually 1200 zone time, and the time of L.A.N. The magnitude of the error is 20s for 5′ of longitude and if circumstances indicate the necessity a second estimate may be made as in the next paragraph. In any case the navigator must determine whether his change of longitude between the position for which he computed L.A.N. and his D.R. position for *that* time will result in a significant change in L.A.N.

In this example, the first estimate (Fig. 2607 *B*) shows that the change of longitude is significant and a second estimate is desirable. The first estimate of approximately 1120 shows that L.A.N. will occur 40m earlier than 1200; at L.A.N. the ship will not have reached the 1200 longitude. Since longitude is changing at the rate of 36′ per hour (= 0′.6 per minute), at 1120, the ship will be 24′ *west* of the 1200 longitude or 95° 32′ E. Working the second estimate as in Fig. 2607 *C* gives a new Z.T. of L.A.N. 11h 21m 40s. If the navigator had relied upon the first estimate only for his meridian altitude, he would have missed it by over a minute and a half. Applying the watch error gives a W.T. of L.A.N. 11h 21m 10s. In theory, a third estimate could be made, but in view of the uncertainty of the actual longitude more than two estimates are unrealistic.

A short method to arrive at the second estimate Z.T. of L.A.N. is to multiply the DLO by 4 and apply this figure as a correction to the first Z.T.; later if west (as in this example), or earlier if east.

$$24' \times 4 = 96s = 1m\ 36s.$$

2608. Supplementary. There are a number of matters related to noon sights which do not directly concern the business of finding the latitude.

Predicted altitude at the time of local apparent noon may be computed with an accuracy limited only by the accuracy of the expected D.R. or "best" latitude. An approximate setting of the sextant in advance is helpful when the sun is partially obscured by thin or fleeting clouds. The computation, the reverse of that for latitude, is shown at the right in Fig. 2609. As the figures used are those required for working the sight, little additional time is needed for predicting the altitude when one so desires. Practice with the questions in Q 2-26 and develop the habit of approximating the altitude in advance.

Many navigators, knowing approximate expected altitude and Greenwich time of sight, record altitude corrections and declination before observing the sun, thus expediting final computation of latitude.

Noon constant: The data for a noon sight may be so arranged that all computations, except application of the sextant reading, are completed in advance. The result of the preliminary computation is known as the *noon constant*, to which one need only apply the altitude read from the sextant to find the latitude. Thus latitude is known a few seconds sooner than with the procedure previously described.

89° 48′ Rule is based on the assumption that the altitude correction is (+) 12′ under all circumstances, regardless of height of eye or sun's altitude. The sextant altitude is always subtracted from 89° 48′ which evidently gives the same distance from sun to ship (*z*) as if the altitude had been corrected by adding 12′ and then subtracting from 90°. Lati-

FIG. 2609. THE STORY OF THE NOON SIGHT.

tude computed by this device is in error by the amount that proper correction differs from 12′. Captain Lecky dismisses the method by saying, "... the man who does such a lazy trick, to save himself at most half-a-dozen figures, is not fit for command."

2609. The complete solution of the following noon sight problem shown in Fig. 2609 consolidates the different elements of the work previously discussed.

Latitude may be found by the single computation down the center of the work form without any of the figures at left or right. Sextant reading is corrected to true. The approximate G.M.T. for taking the declination from the Almanac sun tables is always 12 hours plus or minus the value of the zone description. Or, as illustrated, the G.M.T. of L.A.N. may be read from the scale across the bottom of the form. Positions of sun and ship are plotted at the right. They show that the ship is north of the sun; and hence the zenith distance (angular distance from sun to ship) is named north. In solving meridian-altitude problems, the student should ask himself what needs to be done to *zenith distance* to find the latitude. From the diagram, it is seen that declination is to be added to zenith distance.

Example A-26: En route, Seattle to Yokahama. On April 5, 1966, a navigator expected to observe the sun at L.A.N. He ran the D.R. up to the approximate time of L.A.N. taken from Tables 2 and 3, *Apx. VIII*, and recorded the 1211 D.R. L 45° 00′ N, λ 163° 05′ E. At L.A.N. he observed the sun Hs 50° 47′.3, W.E. on Z.T. 34s fast, I.C. −1′.5, Ht. Eye 28 ft.

Required: (a) First estimate of Z.T. and W.T. of L.A.N. by G.H.A. method. (b) Predicted altitude for setting sextant in advance. (c) Latitude at L.A.N.

Answers: (a) Z.T. 12h 10m 36s, W.T. 12h 11m 10s.; (b) Predicted Hs 50° 41′.5, Lat. 44° 54′.2 N.

2610. Precaution for small craft. On a long voyage with only one navigator, teach a second man to use the sextant and find the latitude. Let him follow the sun until it dips and subtract the sextant reading from 89° 48′ which, with altitudes of from 30° to 70° from a low height of eye, gives distance from sun to ship with reasonable accuracy. Watch time of sight or 12h when without a timekeeper plus or minus the zone description gives G.M.T. for finding the declination. In most cases the crudest knowledge of the D.R. latitude will indicate whether to add zenith distance and declination or take the difference. The result will serve for running down the latitude of the nearest port when in distress.

2611. Questions and problems, as given below, cover a variety of noon sight work. The questions are of special importance because they afford drill in basic conceptions related to all navigation.

Q 1-26. What is latitude of ship in the following cases of noon sight?

Ship	Decl.	Corr. Alt.		Ship	Decl.	Corr. Alt.
(a) N of ⊙	+15°	60°		(d) N of ⊙	−15°	80°
(b) S of ⊙	−20°	70°		(e) S of ⊙	+10°	50°
(c) S of ⊙	+20°	75°		(f) N of ⊙	−20°	40°

Ans: (a) 45° N, (b) 40° S, (c) 5° N, (d) 5° S, (e) 30° S, (f) 30° N.

Q 2-26. Predict the corrected altitude of ⊙, given expected D.R. Lat. of ship and Decl. of sun at L.A.N. as follows:

At L.A.N Lat.	Decl.		At L.A.N Lat.	Decl.
(g) 40° N	+10°		(j) 10° S	−15°
(h) 45° S	−20°		(k) 30° S	+ 5°
(i) 5° N	+20°		(l) 45° N	−20°

Ans: (g) 60°, (h) 65°, (i) 75°, (j) 85°, (k) 55°, (l) 25°.

The following two groups of questions are to be answered with the aid of Tab. 2 and Tab. 3.

Q 3-26. Tabulate L.M.T. and Z.T. of L.A.N. to nearest minute for each of the following dates and longitudes:

Date	Long.		Date	Long.		Date	Long.
(a) 3 Dec.	60° E		(e) 12 Nov.	73° 15′ W		(i) 28 Nov.	157° 29′.8 E
(b) 28 Jan.	75° W		(f) 17 Jan.	65° 45′ W		(j) 17 Sept.	157° 30′.1 E
(c) 2 Apr.	175° W		(g) 22 Mar.	170° 30′ E		(k) 3 Mar.	16° 13′ W
(d) 2 Apr.	105° E		(h) 6 Oct.	177° 15′ E		(l) 16 Feb.	134° 36′ W

	L.M.T.	Z.T.		L.M.T.	Z.T.		L.M.T.	Z.T.		L.M.T.	Z.T.
Ans: (a)	1150	1150	(d)	1204	1204	(g)	1207	1145	(j)	1155	1225
(b)	1213	1213	(e)	1144	1137	(h)	1148	1159	(k)	1212	1217
(c)	1204	1144	(f)	1210	1233	(i)	1148	1118	(l)	1214	1212

Q 4-26. Tabulate Z.T. of L.A.N. to nearest minute in the cases of problems P 1-26 through P 12-26.

	Z.T.		Z.T.		Z.T.		Z.T.
Ans: P 1	1210	P 4	1206	P 7	1212	P 10	1151
P 2	1204	P 5	1211	P 8	1141	P 11	1211
P 3	1241	P 6	1150	P 9	1140	P 12	1231

* * *

NOON SIGHTS

Three answers are printed below each of the succeeding twelve problems.
(a) Estimate Z.T. and W.T. of L.A.N. by the G.H.A. method.
(b) Predicted altitude for setting sextant in advance. Seldom required in actual practice, but should be computed by all students as training in the principles of noon sights.
(c) Latitude at L.A.N. to be computed by all students.

P 1-26. In the Gulf of Alaska.
July 2, 1966, expected 1200 D.R. 55° N, 151° 37′ W, observed ⊙ at L.A.N. Hs 58° 05′.4, W.E. on Z.T. 8s slow, I.C. − 2′.0, Ht. Eye 20 ft.
Ans: (a) Z.T. 12h 10m 24s, W.T. 12h 10m 16s; (b) 57° 52′.4; (c) 54° 47′.0 N.

P 2-26. From east of Clipperton Island off the Mexican coast.
July 2, 1966, expected 1200 D.R. 9° 50′ N, 105° 04′ W, observed ☉ at L.A.N. Hs 76° 34′.9, W.E. on Z.T. 36s fast, I.C. − 1′.5, Ht. Eye 30 ft.
Ans: (a) Z.T. 12h 04m 12s, W.T. 12h 04m 48s; (b) 76° 39′.0; (c) 9° 45′.9 N.

P 3-26. From a C.G. Cutter just east of Georges.
Feb. 5, 1966, expected 1200 D.R. 43° 17′.5 N, 66° 46′ W, observed ☉ at L.A.N. Hs 30° 38′.5, W.E. on Z.T. 1m 30s slow, I.C. 0′.0, Ht. Eye 25 ft.
Ans: (a) Z.T. 12h 41m 08s, W.T. 12h 39m 38s; (b) 30° 38′.0; (c) 43° 17′.0 N.

P 4-26. Ship off Cape Lopatka in the North Pacific.
Sept. 29, 1966, expected 1200 D.R. 51° N, 161° 14′ E, observed ☉ at L.A.N. Hs 36° 44′.8, W.E. on Z.T. 30s fast, I.C. + 2′.0, Ht. Eye 15 ft.
Ans: (a) Z.T. 12h 05m 40s, W.T. 12h 06m 10s; (b) 36° 37′.2; (c) 50° 52′.4 N.

P 5-26. In the heat of the Arabian Sea.
July 2, 1966, expected 1200 D.R. 10° 14′.8 N, 58° 14′.0 E, observed ☉ at L.A.N. Hs 77° 01′.4, W.E. on Z.T. 30s slow, I.C. − 1′.0, Ht. Eye 20 ft.
Ans: (a) Z.T. 12h 10m 56s, W.T. 12h 10m 26s; (b) 77° 00′.3; (c) 10° 15′.9 N.

P 6-26. On patrol in the North Sea.
Feb. 5, 1966, expected 1200 D.R. 55° 02′ N, 5° 59′ E, observed ☉ at L.A.N. Hs 18° 53′.6, W.E. on Z.T. 2m 20s fast, I.C. − 0′.5, Ht. Eye 35 ft.
Ans: (a) Z.T. 11h 50m 08s; W.T. 11h 52m 28s; (b) 18° 52′.2; (c) 55° 00′.6 N.

P 7-26. From far south of Australia.
Feb. 5, 1966, expected 1200 D.R. 59° 28′ S, 120° 37′ E, observed ☉ at L.A.N. Hs 46° 22′.7, W.E. on Z.T. 1m 15s fast, I.C. + 0′.5, Ht. Eye 30 ft.
Ans: (a) Z.T. 12h 11m 32s, W.T. 12h 12m 47s; (b) 46° 25′.8; (c) 59° 31′.1 S.

P 8-26. In the Indian Ocean, Sunda Strait for Cape Town.
July 2, 1966, expected 1200 D.R. 11° 45′ S, 80° 43′ E, observed ☉ at L.A.N. Hs 55° 02′.6, W.E. on Z.T. 20s slow, I.C. − 1′.5, Ht. Eye 25 ft.
Ans: (a) Z.T. 11h 40m 56s, W.T. 11h 40m 36s; (b) 55° 01′.7; (c) 11° 44′.1 S.

P 9-26. Away down in the South Atlantic.
Sept. 29, 1966, expected 1200 D.R. 51° 10′ S, 2° 35′ E, observed ☉ at L.A.N. Hs 40° 59′.6, W.E. on Z.T. 2m 20s fast, I.C. 0′.0, Ht. Eye 35 ft.
Ans: (a) Z.T. 11h 40m 08s, W.T. 11h 42m 28s; (b) 41° 01′.0; (c) 51° 11′.4 S.

P 10-26. From east of Cape Horn.
Feb. 5, 1966, expected 1200 D.R. 57° 00′.0 S, 54° 08′ W, observed ☉ at L.A.N. Hs 48° 41′.3, W.E. on Z.T. 30s slow, I.C. + 1′.0, Ht. Eye 30 ft.
Ans: (a) Z.T. 11h 50m 36s, W.T. 11h 50m 06s; (b) 48° 44′.4; (c) 57° 03′.1 S.

P 11-26. Below the equator, west of the Galapagos Islands.
Feb. 5, 1966, expected 1200 D.R. 5° 14′ S, 104° 07′ W, observed ☉ at L.A.N. Hs 79° 10′.2, W.E. on Z.T. 30s fast, I.C. − 2′.0, Ht. Eye 25 ft.
Ans: (a) Z.T. 12h 10m 32s, W.T. 12h 11m 02s; (b) 79° 12′.0; (c) 5° 12′.2 S.

P 12-26. Halfway from Punta Arenas to Cape Town.
July 2, 1966, expected 1200 D.R. 44° 30′ S, 21° 40′ W, observed ☉ at L.A.N. Hs 22° 17′.7, W.E. on Z.T. 3m 20s slow, I.C. + 1′.0, Ht. Eye 35 ft.
Ans: (a) Z.T. 12h 30m 32s, W.T. 12h 27m 12s; (b) 22° 17′.9; (c) 44° 30′.2 S.

27. POLARIS

COLUMBUS depended on the North Star and it served him well as he sailed, returned, and again found San Salvador. Today, of all the stars, Polaris is most often observed, marking north for half the world, and giving latitude to both mariners and aviators.

2701. Polaris, or the North Star as it is often called, is about 1° from the celestial north pole. Although an isolated second magnitude star, it is easy to identify by following a line across the end of the Dipper through the pointers, as indicated in Fig. 2701. The relation of Polaris to the Dipper as the Dipper rotates around Polaris through the night, is shown on the Special Star Charts at the end of Chapter 31. Rectangular

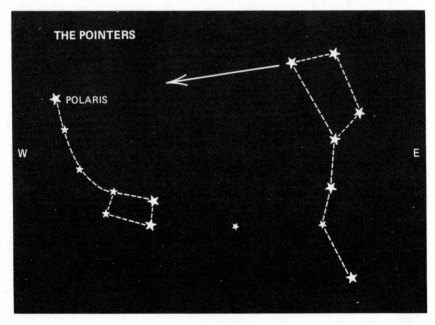

THE POINTERS

POLARIS

W

E

FIG. 2701,

310

star charts, such as those in the Almanacs or like the Universal Star Chart of this Primer, are in this case misleading because of their distortion near the poles. Since long ago Polaris has served two purposes:

(1) From wherever it can be seen, it marks north with sufficient accuracy to guide any wanderer. With a slight correction, its bearing gives the true north which navigators sometimes use for finding compass errors.

(2) The altitude of Polaris, again with a slight correction, is the latitude of the observer. Latitude by Polaris is the principal subject of this chapter.

Polaris cannot be used by observers in the southern hemisphere because it is never visible from points below the equator. There is no star near the south celestial pole to serve similar purposes.

2702. The principle of the Polaris sight lies in the fact that the altitude of the celestial pole equals the latitude of the observer.

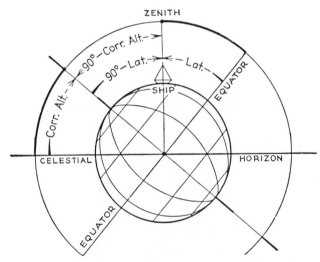

This Drawing in the Plane of the Meridian of the Ship

FIG. 2702. ALTITUDE OF POLE = LATITUDE OF OBSERVER.

Imagine a bright star exactly at the north pole of the heavens and assume that its altitude has been observed and corrected. The star will be on the meridian of the ship because all meridians pass through the pole. Its altitude is an arc of the same meridian continued to the horizon. Examine Fig. 2702 and note that

(1) The arc of the celestial meridian from the zenith of the ship to the imaginary star at the pole is (90° − Corr. Alt.), and that

(2) On earth the arc of the meridian from ship to pole is (90° − Lat. of Ship).

Thus (90° − Corr. Alt.) is the same arc as (90° − Lat.) and the corrected altitude of the celestial pole equals the latitude of the observer. With this principle accepted as a fact, it is easy to understand Polaris sights.

2703. Latitude by Polaris, the oldest of all sights, is again in common use because it is a convenient element of the star fixes required by fast ships and aviators. The general method of finding the true altitude of the star and applying a correction to find latitude is the same as that used by Columbus. Computing the sight is simple, but details vary somewhat, according to the Almanac used. It results in a line of position which is the parallel of latitude of observer.

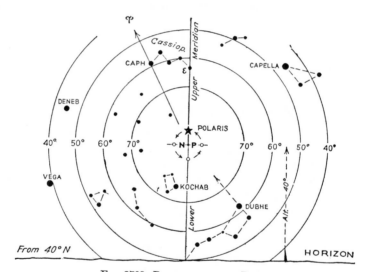

FIG. 2703. POLARIS AND THE POLE.

Unfortunately Polaris is not exactly at the north celestial pole. Its declination of about 89° N indicates that it is about 1° from the center around which the northern heavens appear to revolve counterclockwise. The effect of this fact is emphasized in Fig. 2703 by exaggerating the distance of Polaris from the pole.

With Polaris above the pole, the true altitude of the pole will be approximately 1° less than that of the star, and 1° must be subtracted from the Corr. Alt. of Polaris to find the observer's latitude.

When below the pole about 1° must be added. If to left or right the correction is more or less zero. In practice the proper correction is taken directly from Almanac tables.

2704. Nautical Almanac corrections are divided into three separate terms: a_0, a_1, and a_2. These are always to be added, and 60′ is always to be subtracted from the sum. The latitude is found by applying the net correction to Ho in accordance with its sign.

(1) Set sextant to D.R. latitude, observe a timed altitude of Polaris, correct sextant reading to true as for any other star, using altitude correction tables.

(2) Obtain G.M.T. of sight in the usual way.

(3) Take G.H.A. of ♈ at G.M.T. of sight from the daily data page of the *Nautical Almanac* for date of sight, and add the correction for minutes and seconds over the hourly listing. This is found in the ARIES column on the minute correction page corresponding to minutes of sight.

(4) Apply D.R. longitude to G.H.A. of ♈ to find L.H.A. ♈ with which to enter Polaris correction to altitude tables of the *Almanac*.

(5) With this L.H.A. ♈, mentally expressed in tenths of a degree, enter "POLARIS (POLE STAR) TABLES" (see excerpts) and take out a_0 opposite L.H.A. ♈, a_1 opposite the D.R. latitude, and a_2 opposite the month, all from the same column.

(6) Add a_0, a_1, and a_2.

(7) *Subtract* 60′ from the sum.

(8) Apply the net total in accordance with its sign to the corrected altitude (Ho) to find the ship's latitude.

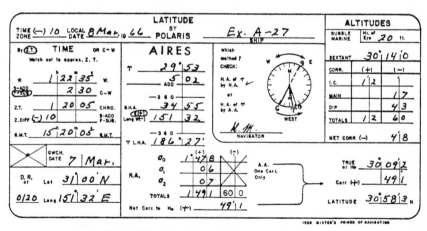

FIG. 2704. POLARIS BY NAUTICAL ALMANAC.

Details of the above computation are illustrated in Fig. 2704 which is a solution of the following problem using the N.A. excerpts found in the Appendix.

Example A-27: March 8, 1966, about 0120, D.R. 31° 00′ N, 151° 32′ E, moonlight horizon, navigator of submarine observed Polaris. Hs 30° 14′.0 at W.T. 1h 22m 35s. W.E. on Z.T. 2m 30s fast, I.C. + 1′.2,

Height Eye 20 ft. *Req:* Latitude by *Nautical Almanac.* *Ans:* 30° 58′.3 N.

In practice, a skilled man makes quick work of a Polaris sight. A watch within one minute of Z.T. plus or minus Z. Diff. gives G.M.T. with all useful accuracy, and only the G.M.T. need be recorded. Tenths of minutes (0′.1) are of no value in the H.A. column. All this is because the final correction varies at most 1′ for 1° difference in L.H.A. ♈.

2705. By Air Almanac. The method of finding latitude by Polaris with the *Air Almanac* is basically the same as with the *Nautical Almanac.* The Polaris (Q) correction table is also entered with the L.H.A. of ♈. The nearest 10-minute tabulation of G.H.A. ♈ to G.M.T. of sight is sufficient. To that is applied D.R. longitude to obtain L.H.A. ♈ with which to enter the correction table facing the back cover of the *A.A.* This table is in rounded minutes of arc. There is no interpolation necessary and no other corrections.

Given an equally correct Ho, the results of working a Polaris sight with the *A.A.* are practically as accurate as when using the *N.A.*

2706. Adrift in a boat. If one has a sextant but no watch or almanac, he can still determine his latitude within 20 or 30 miles. In the upper part of Fig. 2703, note the constellation Cassiopeiae. As this constellation moves counterclockwise around the pole, the leading star, Caph (no longer included among the navigational stars), is on the hour circle of the first point of Aries, ♈ (0° S.H.A.). The trailing star, E Cassiop., is on the hour circle of Polaris. One can tell from the position of this small star whether Polaris is above or below the pole and approximately how much to correct the sextant altitude of Polaris. (See Star Chart, §3105.)

2707. North by Polaris. Further consideration of Fig. 2703 shows that Polaris will only bear true north when it is directly above or below the pole. At any other time the azimuth is different from 0°. The true azimuth is found in the *Nautical Almanac* at the bottom of the same page as the Polaris altitude corrections. Enter the azimuth table with the approximate L.H.A. ♈ at the top and the D.R. latitude at the side.

Practically the azimuth of Polaris is seldom used for finding compass errors because it is difficult to observe with sufficient accuracy.

There may be readers of this chapter who will never turn a sextant toward Polaris. Even so, know the North Star, teach others how to find it and to enjoy the friendly guidance of this lonely bit of the universe.

2708. Polaris problems, as given below, may be solved with the Almanac data in Appendix V. Try to answer the questions without reference to the given answers.

Q 1-27: What is the approximate correction (sign and value) to be applied to Ho of Polaris to find the latitude,

(a) When ☆ ε *Cassiopeiae,* the small star at the other end of the Chair from Caph, is below Polaris?
(b) When same star is E of the North Star?
(c) When same star is above Polaris?
Ans: (a) + 1°, (b) 0°, (c) — 1°.

With Nautical Almanac Excerpts as in Apx. V:

P 1-27. North and east of Newfoundland.
Morning twilight, 29 Sept. 1966, D.R. 49° 51′ N, 48° 04′ W, observed Polaris. Hs 50° 24′.4, at W.T. 5h 40m 25s. W.E. on Z.T. 20s fast, I.C. — 1′.0, Ht. Eye 20 ft. Latitude?
Ans: 49° 51′.4 N.

P 2-27. Norfolk for the Azores.
About 1810, 7 Mar. 1966, D.R. 37° 48′.5 N, 70° 13′ W, observed Polaris. Hs 38° 27′.9 at W.T. 6h 05m 20s P.M. W.E. on Z.T. 5m 12s slow, I.C. + 1′.0, Ht. Eye 20 ft. Latitude?
Ans: 37° 51′.4 N.

P 3-27. North of Luzon, entering South China Sea.
About 1910, 2 July 1966, D.R. 19° 15′ N, 120° 38′ E, observed Polaris. Hs 18° 30′.9 at W.T. 19h 10m 00s. W.E. on Z.T. 25s slow, I.C. + 1′.5, Ht. Eye 35 ft. Latitude?
Ans: 19° 17′.6 N.

P 4-27. On patrol, west of the Faroe Islands.
About 1920, 5 April 1966, D.R. 62° 03′ N, 8° 09′ W, observed Polaris. Hs 62° 00′.0 at W.T. 7h 20m 15s P.M. C — W 0h 06m 32s, Chro. 5m 40s fast, I.C. + 1′.5, Ht. Eye 33 ft. Latitude?
Ans: 61° 52′.6 N.

P 5-27. Eastern end of Mediterranean.
5 April 1966, navigator of a destroyer steaming true N to a patrol station decides to check the run by two sights of Polaris about two hours apart.
1st sight: D.R. 31° 51′ N, 30° 44′ E, Hs 32° 00′.0, W.T. 18h 47m 30s. W.E. on Z.T. 3m 42s slow, I.C. + 1′.5, Ht. Eye 26 ft.
2nd sight: D.R. 33° 05′ N, 30° 44′ E, Hs 32° 41′.6, W.T. 20h 47m 15s. Other data same as 1st sight. (a) Latitude at 1st sight? (b) Latitude at 2nd sight? (c) Distance made good between sights?
Ans: (a) 31° 52′.9 N; (b) 33° 01′.6 N; (c) 68.7 miles.

P 6-27. West and north of the Golden Gate.
About 1921, 4 April 1966, D.R. 39° 40′ N, 126° 16′ W, observed Polaris. Hs 39° 51′.7 at W.T. 19h 21m 05s. C — W 8h 01m 15s, Chro. 1m 10s fast, I.C. + 1′.5, Ht. Eye 25 ft. Latitude?
Ans: 39° 45′.0 N.

P 7-27. On the North Atlantic well off the Jersey beach.
About 1850, 12 April 1966, D.R. 40° 22′ N, 65° 11′ W, observed Polaris. Corrected altitude, Ho 40° 22′ at 22h 51m 10s G.M.T. Latitude by *Air Almanac?*
Ans: 40° 21′ N.

P 8-27. Over the island of Luzon.
About 1835, 31 March 1966, D.R. 15° 50′ N, 120° 35′ E, observed Polaris. Bubble octant average altitudes corrected, Ho 15° 55′ at W.T. 10h 34m 32s. Watch set to G.M.T., G.H.A. ♈ 346° 59′. Latitude by *Air Almanac?*
Ans: 15° 44′ N.

P 9-27.   Off the California coast.

Evening twilight, 11 April 1966, D.R. 35° 47′ N, 125° 01′ W, observed Polaris. Corrected altitude, Ho 35° 42′ at W.T. 18h 48m 30s. W.E. on Z.T. 20s fast. Latitude by *Air Almanac?*

Ans: 35° 40′ N.

P 10-27.   North Pacific, south of Dutch Harbor.

11 April 1966, about 2222, D.R. 52° 36′ N, 165° 58′ W, observed Polaris. Bubble octant corrected altitude, Ho 52° 09′ at W.T. 22h 18m 22s. W.E. on Z.T. 3m 48s slow. Latitude by *Air Almanac?*

Ans: 52° 53′ N.

P 11-27.   From north of Wake Island in the Pacific, a Polaris sight.

13 April 1966, about 0525, D.R. 23° 23′ N, 165° 08′ E. Corrected altitude, Ho 23° 06′ at W.T. 5h 20m 29s. W.E. on Z.T. 4m 30s slow. Latitude by *Air Almanac?*

Ans: 23° 23′ N.

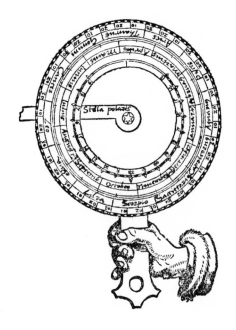

28. AZIMUTHS

A CERTAIN officer of the Navy once recounted his youthful relief when he found that the azimuth of the sun was nothing more than its bearing. Another meaning of the Arabic *alsumut* is direction. Either word solves the mystery and finding the azimuth of any observed body is most simple. Rather, the student blunders in the use of the figures.

2801. Azimuths, defined. Consideration of several definitions is helpful to a complete understanding of the azimuth angle. It may be defined in various ways:

(1) *From the ship*: Bearing of body observed.

(2) *On earth*: Angle at ship between meridian and line to geographic position (G.P.) of body.

(3) *On celestial sphere*: Angle at zenith between celestial meridian and arc from zenith to body.

(4) *Per Bowditch*: ". . . . angle at the zenith between the meridian of the observer and the vertical circle passing through the point."

(5) *Mathematically*: The angle of the astronomical triangle at the corner marked by the ship on earth or by the zenith on the celestial sphere. (See Fig. 2901.)

2802. How found and used. Consider the case of the sun. Its bearing will vary with the time of day, its declination, and the observer's latitude. With these factors the azimuth may be computed. However, since the publication of Burdwood's Tables (1866), these and other tables and azimuth diagrams have made special computations for azimuth unnecessary.

Azimuth tables are now used principally as a source of true bearings of the sun for use when swinging ship for compass errors. They are also useful for indicating when the sun's bearing will have changed sufficiently to give a good running fix, or otherwise give a needed line of position. The standard tables and their use for these purposes are discussed in Chapter 30.

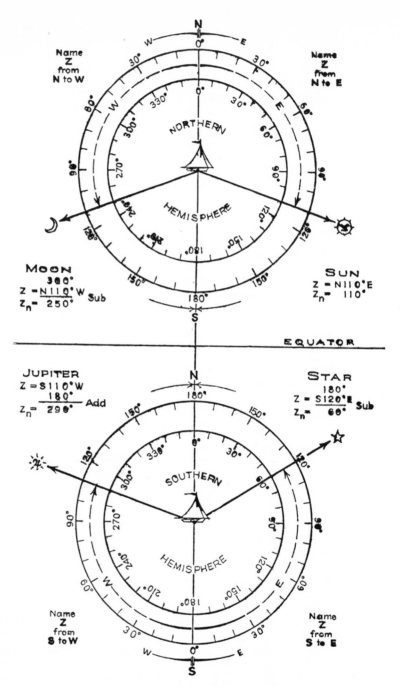

FIG. 2804. AZIMUTHS AS IN MODERN NAVIGATION.

Computed azimuths are used for plotting the lines of position of celestial navigation. The required azimuths result from the solution of the sights or are taken from tables of computed solutions.

2803. Azimuths are measured by the arc of the horizon from north or from south to the point on the horizon directly below the body. This point is where a vertical circle from the zenith through the body meets the horizon.

The azimuth of an observed body may be expressed in various ways. However, all azimuth tables in common use and the different methods of computing the azimuth when working sights give the azimuth as from 0° to 180°, and it is assumed that the navigator knows how to use the figures. This simple question perplexes many students.

The beginner should avoid the confusing older method of expressing the azimuth only up to 90°, as with the quadrant card, although it is required with certain azimuth diagrams and with Lecky's famous A.B.C. tables.

2804. Naming the azimuth. Tabulated or computed azimuth values must be named to indicate how they are measured. Examine Fig. 2804 and observe that:

(1) Azimuths are measured from N or S, 180° through E or W.

(2) In the *northern hemisphere,* azimuths are measured from N through E when the body observed lies east of the meridian; from N through W when the body is west of the meridian. In the drawing, the 110° azimuth of the sun is measured from N through E, and named N 110° E. That of the moon, west of observer's meridian, is named N 110° W.

(3) When in the *southern hemisphere,* azimuths are measured from S through E when the body is east of the meridian and from S through W when the body lies west of the meridian. Thus the 120° azimuth of the pictured star is named S 120° E, and Jupiter's azimuth is named S 110° W.

How to name azimuth values of the 0° to 180° variety is summarized in this rule: *Put the name of the latitude (N or S) in front of the value and the name of the meridian angle (E or W) after it.*

The azimuth angle named as above, (Z), may be used without further modification for plotting Sumner lines. Navy teaching is to convert Z to Zn, which is the azimuth measured from the north point clockwise to 360°, as most convenient for plotting lines of position and for compass work. No name need be given to the value of Zn because Zn means azimuth measured from north.

2805. Converting Z into Zn. The 0° point of what may be called the azimuth rose of the northern hemisphere is true north, 0° on the

360° rose. In the southern hemisphere, however, 0° for azimuths is true south or 180° on the 360° rose. Study Fig. 2804 and determine for yourself how N to E, N to W, S to E, or S to W azimuths must be handled to find Zn. Or if this be difficult, observe the following rule for converting Z to Zn, azimuth from north. 0° to 360°.

> When N to E, no change in value
> N to W, *subtract* from 360°
> S to E, *subtract* from 180°
> S to W, *add* to 180°

It is difficult to understand the ever-present classroom difficulties with naming an azimuth and converting it to Zn. The azimuth of a body is its bearing. At sea a man knows where the body was that he observed. Try to think in the same way, and avoid mistakes when naming, converting, and plotting azimuths.

2806. Questions. Every line of position problem given with later chapters presents the question of naming the azimuth and converting it to Zn. Prepare to do this part of the work without blunders by answering the following questions. The given azimuths (Az) are unnamed values from 0° to 180° such as found from azimuth tables or when working a sight.

Q1-28. The following situations occurred when observing the sun. The latitude given is that of the observer. In each case, name Z and find Zn.

	Lat.	Time	Az.		Lat.	Time	Az.
(a)	36° N	A.M.	146°	(e)	52° N	P.M.	73°
(b)	42° N	P.M.	127°	(f)	46° N	A.M.	162°
(c)	29° S	A.M.	83°	(g)	17° S	P.M.	115°
(d)	16° S	P.M.	112°	(h)	31° S	A.M.	73°

Q2-28. Various navigational bodies were observed as noted below. The local hour angle, *t*, indicates whether the body is east or west of the observer. In each case, name Z expressed to minutes (′) of arc and find Zn expressed to nearest tenth of a degree

	Lat.	*t*	Az.		Lat.	*t*	Az.
(a)	37° S	73° E	118° 22′	(e)	19° S	35° W	140° 40′
(b)	23° S	69° W	36° 24′	(f)	32° S	40° E	126° 52′
(c)	44° N	29° E	122° 36′	(g)	47° N	57° W	118° 12′
(d)	57° N	77° W	100° 55′	(h)	39° N	6° E	169° 54′

Answers to questions Q1-28 and Q2-28:

	Z	Zn		Z	Zn
(a)	N 146° E	146°	(a)	S 118° 22′ E	061°.6
(b)	N 127° W	233°	(b)	S 36° 24′ W	216°.4
(c)	S 83° E	097°	(c)	N 122° 36′ E	122°.6
(d)	S 112° W	292°	(d)	N 100° 55′ W	259°.1
(e)	N 73° W	287°	(e)	S 140° 40′ W	320°.7
(f)	N 162° E	162°	(f)	S 126° 52′ E	053°.1
(g)	S 115° W	295°	(g)	N 118° 12′ W	241°.8
(h)	S 73° E	107°	(h)	N 169° 54′ E	169°.9

29. SOLUTIONS FOR LOP

W HENEVER the navigator works a sight for line of position he must first prepare certain data and thereafter find the computed altitude and azimuth from the solution of a spherical triangle. The corners of this triangle are the assumed position of the ship, the nearest pole, and the geographic position of the body observed. Greek trigonometry, with John Napier's logarithms, is the basis for all such solutions, although in modern practice the required elements of the triangle are found without using the terms of mathematics. Several methods for working a sight will be given. Each has its place in both surface and air navigation.

2901. Objectives. Consider the spherical triangle (Fig. 2901) formed by the nearer pole, P, the position of the *ship*, and the projection (commonly known as the geographical position, *G.P.*) of a celestial body as the *sun* upon the earth. The distance from the equator to the ship is its latitude, and the side of the triangle from the ship to the pole is $90° - L$. The distance from the equator to the G.P. is equal to the declination of the body, and the side of the triangle from the G.P. to the pole is $90° -$ Decl. The distance from the G.P. to the ship, the third side of the triangle, is equal to the zenith distance of the body or $90° -$ Hc.

The angle of the triangle at the pole is the meridian angle, t, and the angle at the ship is the azimuth angle, Z. The angle at the G.P., often called the "position angle," X, is not used in navigation.

Thus, the navigational triangle, like any other spherical triangle, consists of three sides and three angles. If any three of these six parts are known, all of the other three parts can be determined.

In the usual navigational problem, the declination of the celestial body (hence, the length of the side $90° -$ Decl.) is known quite accurately. The latitude and longitude of the assumed position are known exactly; hence, the length of the side $90° - L$ and the magnitude of the angle t are both fixed. Thus, two sides and the included angle of a particular navigational triangle are defined.

The objective of the solution is to find the length of the third side, 90° − Hc and the magnitude of the azimuth angle, Z. Navigational tables are usually arranged so that the computed altitude of the body above the horizon, Hc, is derived directly, instead of its complement 90° − Hc. The LOP is measured off from the assumed position toward or away from the G.P. at a distance equal to the difference between the calculated altitude, Hc, and the observed altitude, Ho, in a direction determined by the azimuth angle, Z.

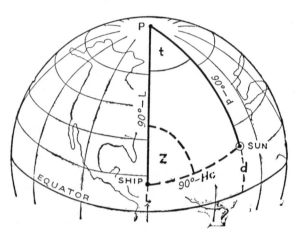

FIG. 2901. THE NAVIGATIONAL TRIANGLE.

2902. Initial steps for all methods. The following data should be recorded whichever reduction method is to be used:

1. Local date, watch error and time zone description (or C − W and chronometer error), and index correction of the sextant.

2. Name of each body observed, time of sight, and sextant reading.

3. Height of eye, and D.R. position near time of sight.

The preliminary computations for all methods include:

1. Find G.M.T. and date. Draw time diagram if necessary.

2. Extract from the Almanac the G.H.A.'s and declinations of all the bodies observed, corrected to the times of the individual sights. Avoid repeated openings of the Almanac.

3. Correct the sextant readings of all sights to find Ho.

4. Apply longitude to G.H.A. and compute L.H.A. and t. Be sure that correct values of t, Decl., and assumed latitude and longitude are recorded on each sight. Remember that an error in these preliminary steps invalidates the remainder of the work.

2903. LOP by H.O. 229. As stated in §2507, the new *Sight Reduction Tables for Marine Navigation* will provide the first, truly universal tables of precomputed solutions of the navigational triangle. Portions of the H.O. 229 tables are illustrated in Figs. 2903*a* and 2903*b*.

In the actual tables, each page serves for two values of hour angle. For values of *t* less than 90°, all hour angles equal to *t* and 360° − *t* are given on facing pages; declination and latitude of the same name on the left-hand pages, contrary name on the right-hand pages above the dividing lines where altitude becomes 0°. The right-hand pages below the dividing lines give solutions for the supplementary values of *t* (180° − *t*, and 180° + *t*) and for declinations of the same name as latitude.

Figs. 2903*a* and 2903*b* show portions of a left-hand page for *t* = 29°, and a right-hand page for *t* = 46°. Fig. 2903*c* shows an excerpt from the Interpolation Table and part of a sight reduction form (modified for H.O. 229) containing a sample solution.

Notes on the use of H.O. 229:

1. Enter the main table with the whole degree of declination next smaller than the actual value. Corrections for exact declination can then be applied according to the tabulated sign of "*d*". The "declination increment" is simply the excess of minutes in the declination.

2. Rules for converting Z to Zn are given at the top and bottom of the table.

3. Interpolation for exact declination is carried out in two (or three) steps. (a) Enter the interpolation table with the declination increment in the column at the left and pick out the first correction from the column for the largest multiple of ten in "*d*". (b) The correction for the remainder of "*d*" is found in the block at the right; units in the vertical column, and decimals across the top.

4. For altitudes above 60°, Hc increases at an excessive and nonuniform rate. In these critical areas, the tabulated "*d*" (numerical difference between tabulated values of Hc) is printed in italics and marked by a black dot (see bottom of Fig. 2903*a*) whenever the "double, second difference" is 4'.0 or greater. The double second difference is the numerical difference between the "*d*" values on the line *preceding* and the line *following* the entering value of declination.

Thus, suppose the actual declination is 76° 52'.6 N. In Fig. 2903*a*, the column for latitude 78° N reads:

Dec.	d
°	'
75	+ *33.8* ·
76	*27.2* ·
77	*19.2* ·

LATITUDE SAME NAME AS DECLINATION

N. Lat. { LHA greater than 180°...Zn=Z
{ LHA less than 180°........Zn=360°−Z

Dec.	76° Hc	d	Z	77° Hc	d	Z	78° Hc	d	Z	79° Hc	d	Z	80° Hc	d	Z	Dec.
0	12 12.9	+59.6	150.3	11 20.8	+59.6	150.4	10 28.6	+59.7	150.5	9 36.4	+59.7	150.5	8 44.1	+59.8	150.6	0
1	13 12.5	59.6	150.1	12 20.4	59.7	150.3	11 28.3	59.7	150.4	10 36.1	59.8	150.5	9 43.9	59.8	150.5	1
2	14 12.1	59.5	150.0	13 20.1	59.6	150.1	12 28.0	59.7	150.3	11 35.9	59.7	150.4	10 43.7	59.8	150.5	2
3	15 11.6	59.6	149.9	14 19.7	59.6	150.0	13 27.7	59.6	150.1	12 35.6	59.7	150.3	11 43.5	59.8	150.4	3
4	16 11.2	59.5	149.8	15 19.3	59.6	149.9	14 27.3	59.7	150.0	13 35.3	59.8	150.2	12 43.3	59.7	150.3	4
35	46 52.5	+59.1	144.5	46 03.5	+59.2	145.1	45 14.1	+59.4	145.7	44 24.4	+59.5	146.2	43 34.4	+59.5	146.8	35
36	47 51.6	59.0	144.2	47 02.7	59.2	144.9	46 13.5	59.3	145.5	45 23.9	59.4	146.0	44 33.9	59.6	146.6	36
37	48 50.6	59.1	144.0	48 01.9	59.2	144.6	47 12.8	59.3	145.2	46 23.3	59.5	145.9	45 33.5	59.6	146.4	37
38	49 49.7	58.9	143.7	49 01.1	59.2	144.4	48 12.1	59.3	145.0	47 22.8	59.4	145.7	46 33.1	59.6	146.3	38
39	50 48.6	59.0	143.4	50 00.3	59.1	144.1	49 11.4	59.3	144.8	48 22.2	59.4	145.4	47 32.6	59.5	146.1	39
75	82 44.8	+18.5	83.6	82 47.3	+26.4	91.5	82 41.7	+33.8	99.3	82 28.1	+40.3	106.8	82 07.3	+45.7	113.7	75
76	83 03.3	10.4	75.9	83 13.7	18.8	84.1	83 15.5	27.2	92.6	83 08.4	35.1	100.9	82 53.0	41.9	108.8	76
77	83 13.7	1.8	67.7	83 32.5	10.2	75.9	83 42.7	19.2	84.7	83 43.5	28.3	93.8	83 34.9	36.5	102.7	77
78	83 15.5	−7.1	59.2	83 42.7	0.8	67.0	84 01.9	9.9	75.8	84 11.8	19.6	85.4	84 11.4	29.4	95.2	78
79	83 08.4	15.4	50.8	83 43.5	−8.6	57.8	84 11.8	−0.4	66.2	84 31.4	9.4	75.8	84 40.8	20.2	86.2	79
80	82 53.0	−22.9	42.8	83 34.9	−17.5	48.9	84 11.4	−10.4	56.3	84 40.8	−1.6	65.2	85 01.0	+8.9	75.7	80
81	82 30.1	29.3	35.5	83 17.4	25.1	40.5	84 01.0	19.8	46.7	84 39.2	12.6	54.5	85 09.9	−3.3	64.1	81
82	82 00.8	34.7	29.1	82 52.3	31.7	32.9	83 41.2	27.7	37.9	84 26.6	22.4	44.2	85 06.6	15.1	52.3	82
83	81 26.1	38.9	23.4	82 20.6	36.9	26.3	83 13.5	34.1	30.1	84 04.2	30.5	34.9	84 51.5	25.3	41.2	83
84	80 47.2	42.5	18.5	81 43.7	41.0	20.6	82 39.4	39.2	23.4	83 33.7	36.8	26.9	84 26.2	33.5	31.5	84

| | 76° | | | 77° | | | 78° | | | 79° | | | 80° | | | |

29°, 331° LATITUDE SAME NAME AS DECLINATION

S. Lat. { LHA greater than 180°........Zn=180−Z
{ LHA less than 180°............Zn=180+Z

Fig. 2903a. H.O. 229. Portion of Left-Hand Page.

LATITUDE CONTRARY NAME TO DECLINATION

N. Lat. { LHA greater than 180°........ Zn=Z
{ LHA less than 180°............Zn=360−Z.

Dec.	76° Hc	d	Z	77° Hc	d	Z	78° Hc	d	Z	79° Hc	d	Z	80° Hc	d	Z	Dec.
0	9 40.5	−59.1	133.1	8 59.4	−59.2	133.3	8 18.2	−59.3	133.4	7 37.0	−59.4	133.5	6 55.7	−59.5	133.6	0
1	8 41.4	59.0	133.3	8 00.2	59.2	133.4	7 18.9	59.3	133.5	6 37.6	59.4	133.6	5 56.2	59.6	133.7	1
2	7 42.4	59.1	133.5	7 01.0	59.2	133.6	6 19.6	59.3	133.7	5 38.2	59.5	133.7	4 56.6	59.5	133.8	2
3	6 43.3	59.1	133.7	6 01.8	59.2	133.8	5 20.3	59.3	133.8	4 38.7	59.4	133.9	3 57.1	59.5	133.9	3
4	5 44.2	59.1	133.8	5 02.6	59.2	133.9	4 21.0	59.3	134.0	3 39.3	59.4	134.0	2 57.6	59.5	134.1	4
5	4 45.1	−59.0	134.0	4 03.4	−59.2	134.1	3 21.7	−59.4	134.1	2 39.9	−59.5	134.2	1 58.1	−59.6	134.2	5
6	3 46.1	59.1	134.2	3 04.2	59.2	134.2	2 22.3	59.3	134.3	1 40.4	59.4	134.3	0 58.5	−59.5	134.3	6
7	2 47.0	59.1	134.4	2 05.0	59.2	134.4	1 23.0	59.3	134.4	0 41.0	−59.4	134.4	0 01.0	+59.5	45.6	7
8	1 47.9	59.1	134.5	1 05.8	59.2	134.6	0 23.7	−59.3	134.6	0 18.4	+59.5	45.4	1 00.5	59.6	45.4	8
9	0 48.8	59.1	134.7	0 06.6	59.2	134.7	0 35.6	+59.4	45.3	1 17.9	59.4	45.3	2 00.1	59.6	45.3	9
25	14 56.2	+59.0	42.4	15 40.4	+59.2	42.6	16 24.5	+59.3	42.8	17 08.5	+59.3	43.0	17 52.3	+59.4	43.2	25
26	15 55.2	59.0	42.2	16 39.6	59.1	42.4	17 23.8	59.2	42.7	18 07.8	59.4	42.9	18 51.7	59.5	43.1	26
27	16 54.2	59.0	42.1	17 38.7	59.2	42.3	18 23.0	59.3	42.5	19 07.2	59.4	42.7	19 51.2	59.5	43.0	27
28	17 53.2	59.0	41.9	18 37.8	59.2	42.1	19 22.3	59.2	42.3	20 06.6	59.3	42.6	20 50.7	59.4	42.8	28
29	18 52.2	59.0	41.7	19 37.0	59.1	41.9	20 21.5	59.2	42.1	21 05.9	59.4	42.4	21 50.1	59.5	42.7	29
85	72 10.1	+48.8	11.8	73 08.7	+49.2	12.5	74 07.2	+49.7	13.2	75 05.5	+50.2	14.1	76 03.6	+50.7	15.1	85
86	72 58.9	47.6	9.9	73 57.9	48.0	10.5	74 56.9	48.3	11.1	75 55.7	48.8	11.9	76 54.3	49.3	12.8	86
87	73 46.5	46.2	7.7	74 45.9	46.5	8.2	75 45.2	46.9	8.8	76 44.5	47.2	9.4	77 43.6	47.7	10.2	87
88	74 32.7	44.6	5.4	75 32.4	44.8	5.8	76 32.1	45.0	6.2	77 31.7	45.3	6.7	78 31.3	45.6	7.2	88
89	75 17.3	42.7	2.8	76 17.2	42.8	3.0	77 17.1	42.9	3.3	78 17.0	43.0	3.5	79 16.9	43.1	3.9	89
90	76 00.0		0.0	77 00.0		0.0	78 00.0		0.0	79 00.0		0.0	80 00.0		0.0	90

| | 76° | | | 77° | | | 78° | | | 79° | | | 80° | | | |

134°, 226° LATITUDE SAME NAME AS DECLINATION

S. Lat. { LHA greater than 180°........Zn=180−Z
{ LHA less than 180°............Zn=180+Z

Fig. 2903b. H.O. 229. Portion of Right-Hand Page.

The table is entered with 76°, the "*d*" value is 27'.2 (in italics and dotted), and the double, second difference is 14'.6 (33'.8 − 19'.2). The correction (0'.4) is found in the small critical-type table at the right of the "Dec. Inc." range. The correction for the double, second difference is always *added to the altitude*. The maximum error caused by neglecting the double, second-difference corrections for "*d*" values *not italicized* is 0'.25.

INTERPOLATION TABLE

Dec. Inc.	Altitude difference (d)					Units	Decimals										Double Second Diff. and Corr.
	10'	20'	Tens 30'	40'	50'		'.0	'.1	'.2	'.3	'.4	'.5	'.6	'.7	'.8	'.9	
52.0	8.6	17.3	26.0	34.6	43.3	0	0.0	0.1	0.2	0.3	0.3	0.4	0.5	0.6	0.7	0.9	1.8
52.1	8.7	17.3	26.0	34.7	43.4	1	0.9	1.0	1.0	1.1	1.2	1.3	1.4	1.5	1.6	1.7	5.5 0.1
52.2	8.7	17.4	26.1	34.8	43.5	2	1.7	1.8	1.9	2.0	2.1	2.2	2.3	2.4	2.4	2.5	9.1 0.2
52.3	8.7	17.4	26.1	34.9	43.6	3	2.6	2.7	2.8	2.9	3.0	3.1	3.1	3.2	3.3	3.4	12.8 0.3
52.4	8.7	17.5	26.2	34.9	43.7	4	3.5	3.6	3.7	3.8	3.8	3.9	4.0	4.1	4.2	4.3	16.5 0.4
																	20.1 0.5
52.5	8.8	17.5	26.3	35.0	43.8	5	4.4	4.5	4.5	4.6	4.7	4.8	4.9	5.0	5.1	5.2	23.8 0.6
52.6	8.8	17.5	26.3	35.1	43.8	6	5.2	5.3	5.4	5.5	5.6	5.7	5.8	5.9	5.9	6.0	27.4 0.7
52.7	8.8	17.6	26.4	35.2	43.9	7	6.1	6.2	6.3	6.4	6.5	6.6	6.6	6.7	6.8	6.9	31.1 0.8
52.8	8.8	17.6	26.4	35.2	44.0	8	7.0	7.1	7.2	7.3	7.3	7.4	7.5	7.6	7.7	7.9	34.7 0.9
52.9	8.9	17.7	26.5	35.3	44.1	9	7.9	8.0	8.0	8.1	8.2	8.3	8.4	8.5	8.6	8.7	38.4 1.0
53.0	8.8	17.6	26.5	35.3	44.1	0	0.0	0.1	0.2	0.3	0.4	0.4	0.5	0.6	0.7	0.8	2.1
53.1	8.8	17.7	26.5	35.4	44.2	1	0.9	1.0	1.1	1.2	1.2	1.3	1.4	1.5	1.6	1.7	6.2 0.1
53.2	8.8	17.7	26.6	35.4	44.3	2	1.8	1.9	2.0	2.1	2.1	2.2	2.3	2.4	2.5	2.6	10.4 0.2
53.3	8.9	17.8	26.6	35.5	44.4	3	2.7	2.8	2.9	2.9	3.0	3.1	3.2	3.3	3.4	3.5	14.5 0.3
53.4	8.9	17.8	26.7	35.6	44.5	4	3.6	3.7	3.7	3.8	3.9	4.0	4.1	4.2	4.3	4.4	18.6 0.4
																	22.8 0.5
53.5	8.9	17.8	26.8	35.7	44.6	5	4.5	4.5	4.6	4.7	4.8	4.9	5.0	5.1	5.2	5.3	26.9 0.6
53.6	8.9	17.9	26.8	35.7	44.7	6	5.3	5.4	5.5	5.6	5.7	5.8	5.9	6.0	6.1	6.2	31.1 0.7
53.7	9.0	17.9	26.9	35.8	44.8	7	6.2	6.3	6.4	6.5	6.6	6.7	6.8	6.9	7.0	7.0	35.2 0.8
53.8	9.0	18.0	26.9	35.9	44.9	8	7.1	7.2	7.3	7.4	7.5	7.6	7.7	7.8	7.8	7.9	
53.9	9.0	18.0	27.0	36.0	45.0	9	8.0	8.1	8.2	8.3	8.4	8.5	8.6	8.6	8.7	8.8	

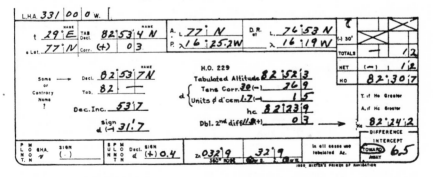

Fig. 2903c. H.O. 229. Portion of Interpolation Table and Sample Solution for Latitude 77° N, Declination 82° 53'.7 N, and L.H.A. 331°.

Example: Given L.H.A. 29°, latitude 78° N, and declination 76° 52′.6 N.

Required: Hc and Zn by H.O. 229 using Figs. 2903*a* and 2903*c*.

Tabulated altitude	83° 15′.5	*d* + *27′.2*· Z 92°.6
Correction 20′ (+)	17′.5	dbl. 2nd diff. 14′.6
Correction 7′.2(+)	6′.3	
hc	83° 39′.3	
Corr. dbl. 2nd diff.	(+) 0′.4	
Hc	83° 39′.7	

2904. LOP by H.O. 214. The procedure for using this table is best illustrated by examples. In *Example I,* latitude and declination have the same name; in *Example II,* they have contrary names. Students should be careful to select the correct "same name" or "contrary name" pages, as in the excerpt shown above the form.

DECLINATION SAME NAME AS LATITUDE

Lat. 36°

H.A.	20° 30′ Alt. ° ′	Δd Δt	Az. °	21° 00′ Alt. ° ′	Δd Δt	Az. °	21° 30′ Alt. ° ′	Δd Δt	Az. °	22° 00′ Alt. ° ′	Δd Δt	Az. °
25	63 12.4	65 71	118.6	63 31.8	64 72	117.7	63 50.8	63 73	116.9	64 09.6	62 73	116.0
6	62 29.5	64 72	117.3	62 48.5	63 73	116.4	63 07.3	62 73	115.6	63 25.7	61 74	114.7
7	61 46.1	63 73	116.0	62 04.8	62 74	115.2	62 23.3	61 74	114.3	62 41.4	60 74	113.4
8	61 02.2	62 74	114.8	61 20.7	61 74	113.9	61 38.8	60 75	113.1	61 56.7	59 75	112.3
9	60 17.9	61 74	113.6	60 36.1	60 75	112.8	60 54.0	59 75	112.0	61 11.6	58 76	111.1

H.A.	22° 30′ Alt. ° ′	Δd Δt	Az. °	23° 00′ Alt. ° ′	Δd Δt	Az. °	23° 30′ Alt. ° ′	Δd Δt	Az. °
25	64 28.0	61 74	115.1	64 46.1	60 74	114.1	65 03.9	59 75	113.2
6	63 43.9	60 74	113.8	64 01.6	59 75	112.9	64 19.1	57 75	111.9
7	62 59.2	59 75	112.6	63 16.7	58 76	111.7	63 33.8	57 76	110.7
8	62 14.2	58 76	111.4	62 31.4	57 76	110.5	62 48.3	56 76	109.6
9	61 28.8	57 76	110.3	61 45.8	56 76	109.4	62 02.4	55 77	108.5

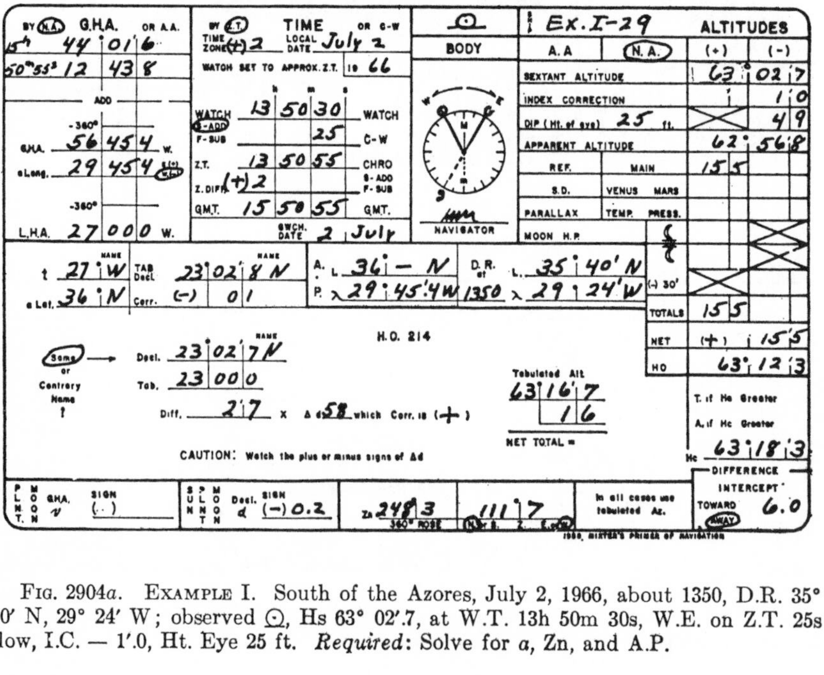

FIG. 2904*a*. EXAMPLE I. South of the Azores, July 2, 1966, about 1350, D.R. 35° 40′ N, 29° 24′ W; observed ☉, Hs 63° 02′.7, at W.T. 13h 50m 30s, W.E. on Z.T. 25s slow, I.C. — 1′.0, Ht. Eye 25 ft. *Required*: Solve for *a*, Zn, and A.P.

Solution: (1) Perform the initial steps listed in §2902. The assumed position is the D.R. adjusted to the *nearest* whole degree of latitude and an assumed longitude such that L.H.A. and *t* are also whole degrees. (See §2309.).

(2) Find the page in the table for the correct latitude and declination as shown in the figures.

(3) Select the declination column *nearest* to the actual declination of the body.

(4) In the selected declination column and opposite the value in the "H.A." column corresponding to the computed value of *t*, pick out and record the following quantities: "Alt.", "Az.", and "△d".

(5) The figure for △d is the change in altitude (in hundredths of a minute) corresponding to a change of 1'.0 in declination. In *Example I,*

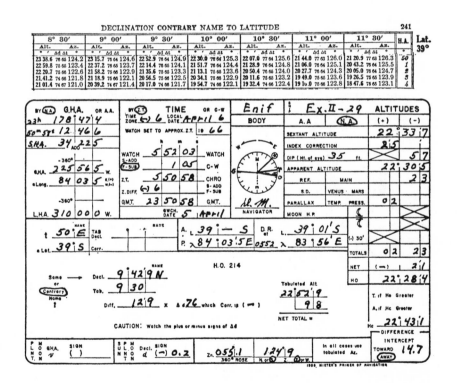

DECLINATION CONTRARY NAME TO LATITUDE												241	
8° 30'		9° 00'		9° 30'		10° 00'		10° 30'		11° 00'		11° 30'		H.A.	Lat. 39°
Alt.	Az.	Alt.	Az.	Alt.	Az.	Alt.	Az.	Alt.	Az.	Alt.	Az.	Alt.	Az.		
° ' △d △t	°	° ' △d △t	°	° ' △d △t	°	° ' △d △t	°	° ' △d △t	°	° ' △d △t	°	° ' △d △t	°		
23 38.6 76 65 124.2	23 15.7 76 64 124.6	22 52.9 76 64 124.9	22 30.0 76 64 125.3	22 07.0 77 64 125.6	21 44.0 77 63 126.0	21 20.9 77 63 126.3	50
22 59.8 75 65 123.4	22 37.2 76 65 123.7	22 14.4 76 65 124.1	21 51.7 76 64 124.4	21 28.9 76 64 124.8	21 06.0 76 64 125.1	20 43.2 76 64 125.5	1
22 20.7 75 66 122.6	21 58.2 75 66 122.9	21 35.6 75 65 123.3	21 13.1 75 65 123.6	20 50.4 76 65 124.0	20 27.7 76 64 124.3	20 05.0 76 64 124.7	2
21 41.2 74 66 121.8	21 18.9 75 66 122.1	20 56.5 75 66 122.5	20 34.1 75 66 122.9	20 11.6 75 65 123.2	19 49.0 75 65 123.6	19 26.5 75 65 123.9	3
21 01.4 74 67 121.0	20 39.2 74 67 121.4	20 17.0 74 66 121.7	19 54.7 74 66 122.1	19 32.4 74 66 122.4	19 10.0 75 66 122.8	18 47.6 75 65 123.1	4

FIG. 2904b. EXAMPLE II. Cape Town for Melbourne, about 0552 on April 6, 1966, D.R. 39° 01' S, 83° 56' E; observed star Enif, Hs 22° 33'.7, at W.T. 5h 52m 03s, W.E. on Z.T. 1m 05s fast, I.C. + 2'.5, Ht. Eye 35 ft., temperature 31°C, pressure 29.59 inches. *Required:* Solve for *a*, Zn, and A.P.

the actual declination is 2'.6 greater than the 23° for which the column was computed; hence the altitude is corrected for this difference by multiplying 2'.7 by $\triangle$d (or 2'.7 $\times$ 0.58 = 1'.5). This multiplication is facilitated by the multiplication table in the back of H.O. 214 and in Appendix VII of this book. The sign of the altitude correction is found by a comparison of the two declination columns which bracket the actual declination. The sign is plus in Example I and minus in Example II. Be sure to select the *nearest* declination column. The comparison is made horizontally between two adjacent columns, *not* vertically in the same column.

(6) Convert "Az" to Zn as in §2805.

(7) Determine the altitude difference (*a*) as in §1510.

(8) Record *a*, Zn, and A.P.

In these examples, the tabulated altitude required correction only for declination, since latitude and hour angle were selected to make whole degrees. If the D.R. longitude is applied to G.H.A., the hour angle for entering the table will probably not be a whole degree (like the H.O. 211 solution). In this case, enter with the *nearest* hour angle and interpolate vertically using $\triangle t$. One can also interpolate latitude using the table in the back of each volume. Full instructions for these interpolations are contained in the front of each volume of H.O. 214.

2905. LOP by H.O. 211. As previously stated, H.O. 211 is one of the best of the short computational methods. Use of this table is illustrated in Fig. 2905 by again solving *Example I* but using H.O. 211 instead of H.O. 214. Note that the altitude difference (*a*) and azimuth are slightly different from the H.O. 214 solution. This is mainly because they are computed for different positions; the D.R. in H.O. 211 and the A.P. in H.O. 214. However, as shown in Fig. 1603, both solutions result in essentially the same LOP.

Having made the necessary identifying entries, record sextant reading and time of sight, correct the altitude, determine *t* and *d*, and check the work, all as previously directed. With *t*, *d*, and L properly recorded, the problem is to compute Hc and Zn from the assumed or trial position which, in the example under discussion, is the D.R. at time of sight.

Examine the H.O. 211 tables in Appendix VII, and note that functions called A and B are tabulated for every half minute of arc from 0° to 180°. These are the functions to be used for solving the triangle. The tables are entered with an angle such as *t* or *d* to find A and B or they are entered with A or B to find unknown angles such as Hc and Z. If without experience in taking figures from tables of this kind, read the suggestions on the page preceding the tables.

Fig. 2905. Example I (by H.O. 211). South of the Azores, July 2, 1966, about 1350, D.R. 35° 40′ N, 29° 24′ W; observed ☉, Hs 63° 02′.7, at W.T. 13h 50m 30s, W.E. on Z.T. 25s slow, I.C. — 1′.0, Ht. Eye 25 ft. *Required:* Solve for *a* and Zn.

Interpolation can usually be omitted when using H.O. 211 in practical navigation. Slightly greater accuracy is achieved by interpolating when extracting Hc from the table. (See H.O. 211, page 6.)

With Hc and Zn found as above, the LOP is plotted from the assumed position which in this case was the D.R. at time of sight. Remember that the LOP is correct only for time of sight regardless of any time associated with some previous D.R. from which the line may have been worked and plotted.

2906. Learning to work a sight by H.O. 211, or by any method, is a matter of practice rather than rule. Begin by checking the printed solution of Example I. Follow the numbered rules, check every figure *back* to its source, and check every bit of arithmetic, until Hc and Z are finally taken from the H.O. 211 tables. Thereafter solve the same example for yourself with the aid of the rules but without unnecessary reference to the given solution. With a clean slate repeat the solution of Example I until it can be carried through rapidly without error. Repeat the checking and solving process with the examples found in the next two chapters.

As an exercise in the use of H.O. 211, the student can substitute the star Achernar for the star Enif in Example II and solve for Hc and Zn for the same time and D.R. position. Various details will be found to be different: *t* exceeds 90° and the bottom of the table is used for both *t* and K. The value of K is greater than the latitude and has the same name; hence, following the rules in the front of H.O. 211 and the form in Fig. 2905, Z is taken from the top of the table. As a check, the solution should give Hc 23° 23'.5, Zn 146°.2.

When working a sight by H.O. 214, there are two common blunders which may cause serious errors unless quickly recognized:

Same or Contrary name? With only the numerical values of L, *d*, and *t* one may enter either of two tables. DECLINATION SAME NAME AS LATITUDE OR DECLINATION CONTRARY NAME TO LATITUDE. Generally SAME is the page at left with CONTRARY on the right, but this is not always true. Watch the N or S or L and *d* and then see that the proper table is entered.

Watch the plus or minus signs of △ *d.* Examine the tabulated altitudes in the two columns between which the exact declination lies, and note whether the tabulated altitude which has been taken from the tables is increasing, △*d* being (+), or decreasing, △*d* being (−), as the exact declination is approached. Look sidewise to determine the sign of △*d*, not up or down the column.

BODY			LOCAL DATE	
Ω			12 July	
NAV W.W.M.			HT EYE 25	FT
Hs	51°	01 4		
AA (+)		(−)		NA
IC		1 0		IC
REF	15 2			MAIN
DIP		4 9		DIP
PAR'X				
SD				DAILY PAGE CORR
TOTALS	15 2	5 9		
NET CORR	(+)	9 3		
Hₒ	51°	10 7		

W	14	50	30	W
S-ADD F-SUB			20	C-W
ZT	14	50	10	CHRO
ZD + 2				S-ADD F-SUB
GMT	16	50	10	GMT

G'WICH DATE	12 July			
GHA		DECL d (−)	0!4	
SHA (Σ)				SHA GHA
GHA	58	37 8		CORR
CORR	12	32 5		CODE CORR
GHA	−3 6 0 71	10 3		W
A.R. LONG	29	10. 3		W(−)
L.H.A.	−3 6 0 42	00 0		W
t	42°	W		NAME
A.R. LAT	36°	N		NAME
TAB DECL	21°	59 0 N		NAME
CORR	−	0 3		
DECL	21	58 7 N		NAME
DECL COLUMN	22	00	Ad 51	
DIFF		1 3	SIGN (−)	

Tabulated Alt		T if Hc Greater A if Hc Greater	
51° 02 6		Hc 51° 10 7	
Ad Corr (−) 0 7		Hc 51 01 9	
Z N 99.3 w		DIFFERENCE	
Zn 260 9 7		TOWARD 8'8	

1960 MINTER'S PRIMER OF NAVIGATION Revised by R. O. WILLIAMS

FIG. 2907. VERTICAL FORM FOR H.O. 214 SOLUTIONS

Never interpolate $\triangle d$. When seeking the total altitude correction, it is helpful to remember that a $\triangle d$ tabulated as 61 means 0'.61 of altitude for each 1' difference in declination. Azimuths need not be interpolated for LOP, but should be interpolated for compass error work, the interpolation lying between the columns and not up and down.

The H.O. 214 tables have other uses than solutions for LOP. They are wonderfully complete azimuth tables, and include the simplest mathematical star identification tables. In one form or another the use of tables of this type may be expected to increase throughout all of the various fields of celestial navigation.

2907. A columnar work form for use with H.O. 214 is shown in Fig. 2907 with data from a typical sun sight. The vertical form, which can be used with the *Nautical* or *Air Almanac*, makes an orderly arrangement in the navigator's notebook.

2908. Great circle solutions. With few exceptions navigators do their great circle sailing with great circle charts, as in Chapter 11. It is often convenient, however, to compute the great circle distance from a point of departure to a far-distant destination. Turn back to Fig. 2901 and consider the triangle as drawn on the earth. Let the ship's corner be the point of departure and assume the far-distant destination to be at the corner marked "Sun." The azimuth angle Z is then the initial great circle course and the length of the side labeled 90° − Hc is the great circle distance from departure to destination.

The precomputed solution of the triangle by H.O. 214 is best suited for finding the great circle course and distance. For *t* substitute the difference in longitude between departure and destination. For Decl. substitute latitude of the destination. For Lat. use the latitude of the point of departure. Then select Z and Hc as for any sight. Z is the great circle course. 90° − Hc reduced to minutes (') is the great circle distance in nautical miles.

2909. Use of Pocket Calculators. In recent years small handy pocket size calculators of varying degree of sophistication have become very useful in solving arithmetical and trigonometric problems. Capabilities and technique of operation of given calculators varies with the sophistication of the circuitry. Basically all can add, subtract, multiply and divide. More elaborate calculators are marketed to include trigonometric functions, memory stacks and the capability of being programmed for rapid solving of special equations.

Since the degree of sophistication of the navigators' calculator cannot be assumed, the following material is intended to assist in solving the navigational triangle for Computed Altitude (Hc) and Azimuth (Zn).

Sine-Cosine Formulae. The classic spherical and trigonometry formulae may be used to compute the altitude (Hc) with specified rules for application of the $(\pm)$ symbol.

Sin Hc = (Sin Lat. × Sin Decl.) ± (Cos Lat. × Cos Decl. × Cos *t*)

Rules for sign of symbol ±:
1. If *t* is less than 90 degrees;
    a. Lat. and Decl. have SAME name, sign is +, (add).
    b. Lat. and Decl. have OPPOSITE name, sign is ∼, (take difference).
2. If *t* is greater than 90 degrees;
    a. Lat. and Decl. have SAME name, sign is ∼, (take difference).
    b. Lat. and Decl. have OPPOSITE name, sign is +, (add).

Versine-Cosine Formulae. By use of the versine (Ver ϕ = 1 − Cos ϕ) which is positive in all quadrants, a formulae for Hc is devised which requires only one rule for the sign of the ± symbol.

Sin Hc = 1 − [Ver *t* × Cos Lat. × Cos Decl.] + [Ver (Lat. ± Decl.)]

Rule for sign of symbol ±:
If Lat. and Decl. have OPPOSITE name, sign is +, (add).
If Lat. and Decl. have SAME name, sign is ∼, (take difference).
To calculate Zn the azimuth angle *Z* must first be determined then converted to Zn as explained in paragraph 2805. The formulae for determining azimuth angle *Z* is:

$$Z = \frac{\text{Sin } t \times \text{Cos Decl.}}{\text{Cos Hc}}.$$

To convert *Z* to Zn the navigator must note the compass quadrant in which the sight was taken and apply the following:

If sight is in: NE Quadrant, Zn = *Z*
SE Quadrant, Zn = 180 − *Z*
SW Quadrant, Zn = 180 + *Z*
NW Quadrant, Zn = 360 − *Z*

Other useful formulae which may be solved easily with the hand computer are:
Distance to Horizon: D(miles) = 1.15 $\sqrt{\text{Ht of Eye in Feet}}$
Dip of Horizon: Dip(minutes of arc) = .984 × $\sqrt{\text{Ht of Eye in Feet}}$
Mean Refraction: R(minutes of arc) = .94 × CoTangent of H_o.

Distance Off by Vertical Angle: D(miles) = $\dfrac{\text{Ht of Object in Feet} \times .565}{\text{Vertical Angle in minutes}}$

2910. Problems to solve. All of the problems given in this book which require the working of a sight for line of position may be solved by either of the methods of this chapter with the tables in the appendixes. Either of these methods suffices at sea when and if the necessary tables are available.

The generally accepted plan at the present time is to master H.O. 214 first and thereafter take up H.O. 211. To this end work the following problems and those following other chapters by H.O. 214. Keep the solution of each problem, marked with its number, for future reference. The Ho and G.H.A. of such solutions may be used for solutions by H.O. 211 method, without repeating the almanac and altitude correction part of the work.

The problems given below are to be solved by H.O. 214 using for an assumed position the latitude and longitude nearest to the D.R. from the computation (A.P. shown for each example). For *alternate* solutions, solve from the D.R. by H.O. 211.

Ex. 1-29. From south of the Azores. (See Figs. 2904a and 2905.)
July 2, 1966, about 1350, D.R. 35° 40′ N, 29° 24′ W, observed ☉. Hs 63° 02′.7 at W.T. 13h 50m 30s. W.E. on Z.T. 25s slow, I.C. − 1′.0, Ht. Eye 25 ft. *Req:* Solve for LOP.
Ans: A.P. 36° N, 29° 45′.4 W, a 6′.0 A, Zn 248°.3.
Alternate: Solve from D.R.
Ans: a 3′.3 T, Zn 249°.4.

Ex. 2-29. Cape Town for Melbourne. (See Fig. 2904b.)
April 6, 1966, about 0552, early morning, D.R. 39° 01′ S, 83° 56′ E, observed star Enif. Hs 22° 33′.7 at W.T. 5h 52m 03s. W.E. on Z.T. 1m 05s fast, I.C. + 2′.5, Ht. Eye 35 ft., temperature 31° C, pressure 29.59 inches. *Req:* Solve for LOP.
Ans: A.P. 39° S, 84° 03′.5 E, a 14′.7 A, Zn 055°.1.
Alternate: Solve from D.R.
Ans: a 9′.6 A, Zn 055°.0.

P 3-29. From afar in the Mid-Atlantic.
August 22, 1966, about 1450, D.R. 35° 02′ N, 47° 00′ W, observed ☾. Hs 22° 19′.7 at W.T. 2h 49m 39s P.M. C − W 2h 58m 57s, Chro. 2m 07s slow, I.C. + 2′.0, Ht. Eye 28 ft. *Req:* Solve for LOP.
Ans: A.P. 35° N, 47° 18′.1 W, a 9′.9 T, Zn 137°.8.
Alternate: Solve from D.R.
Ans: a 1′.5 T, Zn 137°.9.

P 4-29. Pacific Ocean, west and north of San Francisco.
May 10, 1966, about 1510, D.R. 39° 06′ N, 134° 58′ W, observed ☉. Hs 42° 44′.7 at W.T. 15h 12m 58s. W.E. on Z.T. 2m 07s fast, I.C. − 2′.5, Ht. Eye 37 ft. *Req:* Solve for LOP.
Ans: A.P. 39° N, 134° 38′.1 W, a 14′.1 T, Zn 257°.5.
Alternate: Solve from D.R.
Ans: a 0′.3 T, Zn 257°.3.

P 5-29. At sea, east of Savannah.
July 2, 1966, about 1038, D.R. 31° 22′ N, 75° 15′ W, observed sun's *upper limb*. Hs 69° 48′.4 at W.T. 10h 38m 12s, W.E. on Z.T. 2m 27s slow, I.C. + 3′.0, Ht. Eye 26 ft. *Req:* Solve for LOP.
Ans: A.P. 31° N, 75° 11′.4 W, a 13′.8 A, Zn 108°.1.
Alternate: Solve from D.R.
Ans: a 3′.9 A, Zn 108°.8.

P 6-29. Mid-Atlantic, south and west of the Azores.

May 11, 1966, about 0420 morning twilight, D.R. 30° 46′ N, 39° 32′ W, observed star Altair. Hs 68° 03′.6 at W.T. 4h 20m 26s. W.E. on Z.T. 49s slow, I.C. — 1′.0, Ht. Eye 33 ft. *Req:* Solve for LOP.

Ans: A.P. 31° N, 39° 39′.6 W, *a* 14′.9 T, Zn 185°.3.

Alternate: Solve from D.R.

Ans: a 1′.1 T, Zn 185°.6.

P 7-29. In the Sea of Japan.

March 7, 1966, about 1440, D.R. 38° 59′ N, 135° 13′ E, observed ☉. Hs 31° 54′.3 at W.T. 2h 40m 07s P.M. C — W 3h 08m 51s, Chro. 2m 01s slow, I.C. — 0′.5, Ht. Eye 16 ft. *Req:* Solve for LOP.

Ans: A.P. 39° N, 135° 03′.6 E, *a* 7′.6 **A, Zn** 229°.1.

Alternate: Solve from D.R.

Ans: a 2′.9 A, Zn 229°.3.

P 8-29. Between Bermuda and the Azores.

July 2, 1966, about 0820, D.R. 36° 57′ N, 44° 34′ W, observed sun's *upper limb.* Hs 41° 12′.9 at W.T. 8h 22m 33s, W.E. on Z.T. 1m 27s fast, I.C. 0, Ht. Eye 25 ft. *Req:* Solve for LOP.

Ans: A.P. 37° N, 44° 18′.6 W, *a* 15′.3 A, Zn 090°.4.

Alternate: Solve from D.R.

Ans: a 3′.1 A, Zn 090°.0.

P 9-29. South of Flores Island, the Azores.

April 5, 1966, about 1912, evening twilight, D.R. 39° 02′ N, 31° 09′ W, observed planet Jupiter. Hs 55° 53′.2 at W.T. 19h 12m 20s. W.E. on Z.T. 30s fast, I.C. — 2′.0, Ht. Eye 20 ft. *Req:* Solve for LOP.

Ans: A.P. 39° N, 31° 06′.3 W, *a* 4′.1 T, Zn 253°.8.

Alternate: Solve from D.R.

Ans: a 3′.2 T, Zn 253°.3.

P 10-29. In the South Pacific, west of Juan Fernandez.

May 10, 1966, about 1740, evening twilight, D.R. 34° 11′ S, 98° 12′ W, observed star Canopus. Hs 53° 33′.1 at W.T. 17h 40m 14s, W.E. on Z.T. 23s slow, I.C. + 2′.0, Ht. Eye 27 ft. *Req:* Solve for LOP.

Ans: A.P. 34° S, 97° 43′.0 W, *a* 20′.9 T, Zn 225°.9.

Alternate: Solve from D.R.

Ans: a 4′.1 A, 225°.7.

P 11-29. South Pacific, on satellite tracking station.

June 3, 1966, about 0650, morning twilight, D.R. 35° 02′ S, 142° 28′ W, observed planet Venus. Hs 27° 49′.4 at W.T. 6h 51m 14s. W.E. on Z.T. 27s fast, I.C. — 3′.0, Ht. Eye 27 ft., temperature 74° F, pressure 29.44 inches. *Req:* Solve for LOP.

Ans: A.P. 35° S, 142° 29′.1 W, *a* 3′.8 T, Zn 051°.8.

Alternate: Solve from D.R.

Ans: a 4′.3 T, Zn 051°.6.

P 12-29. Due east of Cape Hatteras.

July 2, 1966, about 0413, morning twilight, D.R. 34° 45′ N, 47° 50′ W, observed star Deneb. Hs 65° 11′.5 at W.T. 4h 13m 52s. W.E. on Z.T. 2m 04s fast, I.C. + 3′.0, Ht. Eye 30 ft. *Req:* Solve for LOP.

Ans: A.P. 35° N, 47° 45′.1 W, *a* 3′.7 T, Zn 302°.8.

Alternate: Solve from D.R.

Ans: a 8′.8 T, Zn 303°.7.

30. DAYS WITH THE SUN

THE daily return of the sun to outshine the stars during half the hours of the year makes it the most often observed navigational body. Throughout each day it gives lines of position when visibility permits. It is the best of bodies for finding the compass error and is the natural measure of time. The navigator in turn must not only be able to determine a line of position from the sun but should understand the when and where of the sun's position and how best to utilize the various services of this great luminary.

Sun sights today give a line of position whenever the sun can be observed, in contrast to the limitations of the old navigation with its time sights for longitude and the noon sight for latitude. One method serves to work all sights, although surface navigators using the noon sight generally work it as a meridian altitude. Observing altitudes, the methods for working sights and plotting lines of position have been discussed in previous chapters. The purpose of this chapter is to further develop the various uses of the sun.

3001. A day at sea. In the absence of electronic aids, a "day's work" for a navigator at sea starts with a round of star sights at morning twilight, and ends with another round of star sights at evening twilight. During the morning, he obtains a sun line from which a running fix can be developed by advancing one or more of the morning star lines. The morning sun line also enables him to estimate his noon longitude, from which he can determine the time of local apparent noon. At L.A.N., a sun line runs east and west and provides an accurate latitude; it can also be used for a running fix by advancing the morning sun line. During the afternoon, the navigator will often take another sun sight from which he can obtain an estimated position. Moreover, he will be glad to have a late afternoon sun line in case clouds prevent obtaining evening star sights.

Such a day with the sun is illustrated in Fig. 3001a, which shows the plotting of Problem P1-30 at the close of this chapter. Solutions of all sights are also shown. The ship's D.R. position is given for shortly before six in the morning when a Polaris line is obtained (Fig. 3001b). This

POSITION PLOTTING SHEET

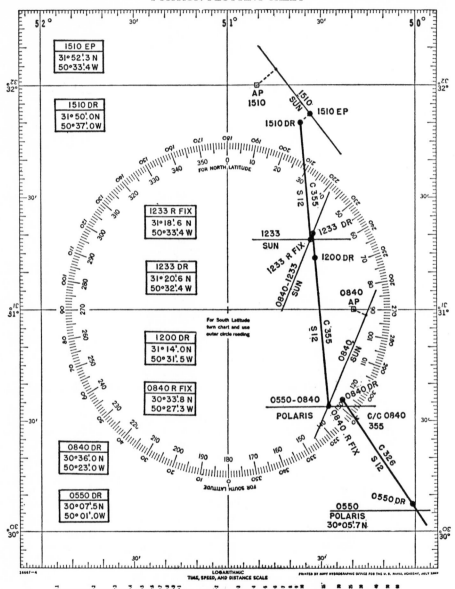

Fig. 3001a. A Day with the Sun (Problem P1-30).

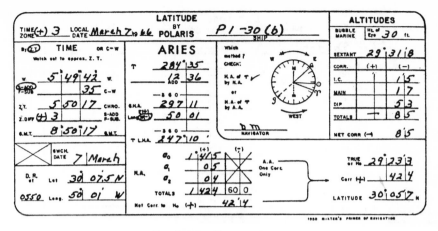

FIG. 3001b.   POLARIS SIGHT.

4° 30'			5° 00'			5° 30'			6° 00'			6° 30'			7° 00'			7° 30'			H.A. Lat. 31°
Alt.	Δd Δt	Az.	Alt.	Δd Δt	Az.	Alt.	Δd Δt	Az.	Alt.	Δd Δt	Az.	Alt.	Δd Δt	Az.	Alt.	Δd Δt	Az.	Alt.	Δd Δt	Az.	
25 43.6	65 79	113.9	25 25.0	65 79	114.3	25 06.3	65 79	114.8	25 47.6	65 78	115.2	25 28.8	65 78	115.6	25 09.9	65 77	116.1	24 50.9	65 77	116.5	65
25 56.4	64 79	113.2	25 38.0	63 79	113.6	25 19.5	65 79	114.1	25 00.9	64 78	114.5	24 42.3	65 78	114.9	24 23.5	63 78	115.4	24 04.7	63 77	115.8	6
25 09.0	62 79	112.5	24 50.8	61 79	113.0	24 32.4	63 79	113.4	24 14.0	63 79	113.8	23 55.5	62 78	114.3	24 36.9	62 78	114.7	23 18.3	62 78	115.1	7
24 21.4	60 80	111.9	24 03.3	61 80	112.3	23 45.1	62 80	112.7	23 26.8	61 79	113.2	23 08.5	62 79	113.6	22 50.1	61 79	114.0	22 31.6	61 79	114.5	8
23 33.6	60 80	111.2	23 15.6	60 80	111.7	22 57.6	60 80	112.1	22 39.4	61 79	112.5	22 21.3	61 79	112.9	22 03.0	61 79	113.4	21 44.7	61 79	113.8	9

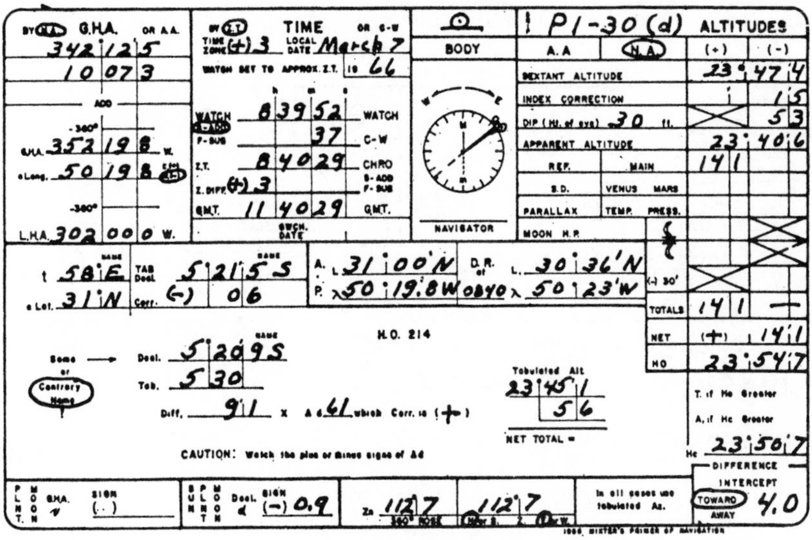

FIG. 3001c.   MORNING SUN.

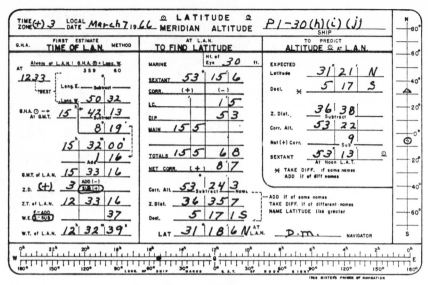

FIG. 3001d.   MERIDIAN ALTITUDE.

DECLINATION CONTRARY NAME TO LATITUDE

4° 30'			5° 00'			5° 30'			6° 00'			6° 30'			7° 00'			7° 30'			H.A.	Lat. 32°
Alt.	Δd Δt	Az.	Alt.	Δd Δt	Az.	Alt.	Δd Δt	Az.	Alt.	Δd Δt	Az.	Alt.	Δd Δt	Az.	Alt.	Δd Δt	Az.	Alt.	Δd Δt	Az.		
49 36.8	77 64	131.1	40 13.6	77 64	131.5	39 50.6	77 64	132.0	39 27.4	78 63	132.4	39 04.0	78 63	132.8	38 40.6	78 62	133.2	38 17.1	78 62	133.6	35	
39 58.2	76 65	130.1	39 35.4	77 64	131.0	39 12.5	77 64	131.0	38 49.5	77 64	131.4	38 26.4	77 64	131.8	38 03.2	77 63	132.2	37 39.9	78 63	132.6	6	
39 19.0	76 66	129.2	38 56.5	78 66	129.6	38 33.8	76 66	130.0	38 11.0	76 66	130.4	37 48.1	76 65	130.8	37 25.2	77 64	131.2	37 02.2	77 64	131.6	7	
38 39.3	74 67	128.2	38 17.0	78 67	128.6	37 54.5	76 66	129.0	37 32.0	76 66	129.4	37 09.4	76 66	129.9	36 46.6	76 65	130.3	36 23.9	76 65	130.7	8	
37 59.1	74 68	127.3	37 36.9	74 68	127.7	37 14.7	74 67	128.1	36 52.4	74 67	128.5	36 30.0	75 66	128.9	36 07.6	75 66	129.3	35 45.0	75 66	129.8	9	

FIG. 3001e.   AFTERNOON SUN.

line is advanced to give a running fix with the morning sun line (Fig. 3001c) at 0840. At this time a change of course is made.

To advance or retire an LOP from time A to time B, move any point on the LOP (such as its intersection with the course line) the same distance and direction as between the D.R.'s at the two times. This automatically allows for any intervening course changes.

The 1200 D.R. gives a fair idea of the noon longitude, and the navigator finds from Tables 2 and 3 in Appendix VIII that L.A.N. will occur at about 1233. From the longitude of the 1233 D.R., he computes the time of L.A.N. (Fig. 3001d), and at that instant observes the sun for a meridian altitude. The 1233 sun line, when crossed with the 0840 sun line, gives a running fix from which the navigator elects to start a new course line. At 1510, another sun line is obtained (Fig. 3001e). The point on this line nearest to the 1510 D.R. is the most probable position of the ship at that time; and if no star sights are taken during the evening, the 1510 E.P. will become quite important.

While no two navigators would take exactly the same steps, the work required in the detailed statement of Problem P1-30 should be regarded as the minimum for a day with the sun. In addition to this work, an alert navigator can also utilize his knowledge of the sun to check the deviation of his compass and also to obtain a good fix by crossing a sun line with another line from a daylight sight of the moon or—with luck—Venus.

3002. To best use the sun one should have some understanding of the altitudes and azimuths of that body to be expected during the coming day. Often the navigator must consider the time when the sun's altitude will afford a good first sight or when the sun will bear true east, the possibilities for a running fix, the maximum altitude at noon, and when conditions are favorable for swinging ship by the sun.

At sea, the navigator's knowledge of what the sun did yesterday is often sufficient to answer such questions as may arise. More exact answers require consideration of both the altitude and the azimuth of the sun. These quantities vary according to the sun's declination as determined by the date, the observer's latitude, and the local time of day.*

Altitudes of the sun. Observed from the equator when its declination is 0, the sun will rise at six o'clock and increase its altitude 15° each hour to a maximum of 90° at noon. Practically, this exact situation never occurs and the rise per hour, never exceeding 15°, will be greatest immediately after sunrise and least around noon. The difference in rate of rise is slight within the tropics, but from high latitudes while the sun hangs low at noon there is almost no change in altitude. If seen from

---

* Many of the broad statements in this and following sections are made without reference to the effects of refraction, the equation of time, hourly change in declination, the sun's semidiameter, and differing definition of the exact time of sunrise, sunset, and twilight.

either pole the sun would be visible throughout the entire 24 hours of the day with no perceptible change in altitude.

The sun's azimuth behaves in a reverse manner. To an observer at either pole, the sun, when visible, would appear to swing westward at a rate of 15° each hour. As one moves toward the equator it swings slower at sunrise and faster in midday. In the tropics the change in the sun's bearing may be slight until long after sunrise but may change very rapidly at noontime. The bearing of the sun is important to navigators for several reasons. It is used every day for compass correction and for plotting Sumner lines. It determines whether a line of position checks longitude, latitude, course, or speed (§1511). Less well understood are the opportunities for a running fix, or possibly a fix, which results from changes in the sun's azimuth as it swings westward.

Both the altitude and azimuth of the sun for any given declination, latitude and time may be read directly from H.O. 214. The H.A. column of the tables is entered with the hours and minutes of apparent time before or after noon, converted into arc, i.e. with the sun's meridian angle (*t*). Mariners, however, more often use a regular azimuth table when seeking a picture of prospective changes in the sun's azimuth or when swinging ship by the sun.

3003. Sunrise and sunset, as presently discussed, are the instants when the upper edge of the sun appears above or disappears below the sea horizon. The approximate times of these events may be taken from the almanacs.

In the *Nautical Almanac*, daily data section, is found Sunrise and Sunset *in various latitudes* for each day of the year. Simple interpolation between the latitude listings gives the minute of sunrise or sunset from 0° to 72° N or 60° S. Thus little more than an inspection of the tables gives L.M.T. of sunrise or sunset. For excerpts from these tables see Fig. 3210.

The air navigator is not dependent upon the visibility of the horizon because his sextant contains an artificial horizon. Hence, the times of sunrise and sunset are not as important to him as they are to the surface navigator. For this reason, such data and others of interest to the aviator are contained in the white pages in back of the *Air Almanac*.

3004. The sun does not rise true east except when its declination is 0 as when on the equator about March 21 and September 21. When the sun is north of the equator it will rise north of east in any latitude. When south of the equator it rises south of east. From a latitude of 60° the sun will rise 51° north of east about June 21 and 51° south of east about December 21. On the same dates, to an observer in latitude 40° the bearings of sunrise will be 31° from east, a figure which becomes 27° when the observer is in 30° N or S.

To check a small boat's compass by the bearing of sunrise or sunset requires an azimuth table except in the tropics. When within 30° of the equator, the bearing of the rising sun N or S of true east equals the sun's declination N or S of the equator, with a possible error of about ¼ point or less than 4° in extreme cases. Note that this gives a true bearing which must be corrected to magnetic by applying the local variation before comparison with the compass reading.

3005. Azimuth tables are the customary source of the true azimuths of the sun used for finding the deviation of the compass, and also are a principal source of information for determining when best to take sun sights. They are entered with observer's latitude, sun's declination, and the local apparent time either in time or arc units.

Burdwood's Tables, sometimes called *Davis 1* (Decl. 0°-24°, Lats. 0°-30°) and *Davis 2* (Decl. 0°-24°, Lats. 30°-64°), British publications, are the best of azimuth tables for the sun and are in general use in the Merchant Marine. This is principally because the azimuth is given for each 4 minutes of time, or at 2-minute intervals when it is changing rapidly, and because minutes of arc, useless with azimuths, are expressed by tenths of degrees which makes for easy and accurate interpolation.

The Red azimuth tables (Decl. 0°-23°, Lats. 0°-70°), officially Pub. No. 260, *Azimuths of the Sun,* are used by the U. S. Navy and the U. S. Coast Guard, and by some merchant officers. Azimuths are tabulated for each whole degree of latitude and declination, and for each 10 minutes of local apparent time. The arrangement of the tables, when latitude and declination are of the same name, is shown in Fig. 3005.

The Blue azimuth tables, Pub. No. 261, *Azimuths of Celestial Bodies* (Decl. 24°-70°, Lats. 0°-70°), and British publications similar to *Burdwood's,* give the azimuths of bodies whose declination exceeds the sun's maximum.

Although seldom referred to as such, the various volumes of H.O. 214 are perfect azimuth tables. In effect they tabulate all azimuths for each 4 minutes of time and every ½° of declination. With the necessary volumes at hand, no other azimuth tables are essential.

In practice the navigator must use whatever tables are available. Skill with Pub. 260 assures equal skill with *Burdwood's.* To avoid volumes of four times the present size all azimuth tables give the azimuth as from 0° to 180° which must be named from N or S to E or W or converted to 0° to 360° from north as in Chapter **28.**

3006. The compass and the sun. The true bearing of the sun is the basis for the method most often used for finding the deviations of the compass. The sun's bearing may be computed but for compass work it is more often taken from azimuth tables.

TRUE BEARING OR AZIMUTH.

LATITUDE 36°.

DECLINATION—SAME NAME AS—LATITUDE.

Dec.	15°	16°	17°	18°	19°	20°	21°	22°	23°	Dec.
				May.				June.		
	1	5	8	12	16	21	26	1	10	
Apparent Time. A.M.		August.					July.			Apparent Time. P.M.
	12	9	5	2	28	24	19	12	3	
				November.				December.		
	3	6	10	14	17	22	27	3	11	
		February.				January.				
	9	5	2	29	25	21	16	10	2	
h. m.	o ′	o ′	o ′	o ′	o ′	o ′	o ′	o ′	o ′	h. m.
IV 50	......	......	......	......	......	......	......	......	61 24	10
V 00	......	......	......	......	......	65 11	64 24	63 37	62 50	VII 00
V 10	......	......	69 01	68 13	67 26	66 38	65 51	65 03	64 16	50
V 20	72 04	71 16	70 28	69 40	68 52	68 04	67 16	66 28	65 40	40
V 30	73 31	72 42	71 54	71 06	70 17	69 28	68 40	67 51	67 02	30
V 40	74 57	74 08	73 19	72 30	71 41	70 52	70 02	69 13	68 23	20
V 50	76 22	75 32	74 43	73 54	73 04	72 14	71 24	70 34	69 44	10
VI 00	77 46	76 56	76 06	75 16	74 26	73 36	72 45	71 54	71 03	VI 00
VI 10	79 10	78 20	77 29	76 39	75 48	74 56	74 05	73 13	72 21	50
VI 20	80 34	79 43	78 52	78 00	77 09	76 16	75 24	74 32	73 39	40
VI 30	81 58	81 06	80 14	79 22	78 30	77 37	76 44	75 50	74 57	30
VI 40	83 21	82 29	81 37	80 44	79 50	78 56	78 02	77 08	76 14	20
VI 50	84 46	83 53	82 59	82 05	81 11	80 17	79 22	78 27	77 31	10
VII 00	86 10	85 16	84 22	83 28	82 32	81 37	80 41	79 45	78 48	V 00
VII 10	87 36	86 41	85 46	84 50	83 54	82 58	82 01	81 03	80 05	50
VII 20	89 02	88 07	87 11	86 14	85 17	84 19	83 21	82 22	81 23	40
VII 30	90 30	89 34	88 37	87 39	86 41	85 42	84 42	83 42	82 42	30
VII 40	92 00	91 02	90 04	89 05	88 05	87 05	86 04	85 03	84 01	20
VII 50	93 31	92 33	91 33	90 33	89 32	88 31	87 28	86 25	85 22	10
VIII 00	95 05	94 05	93 05	92 03	91 01	89 58	88 54	87 49	86 44	IV 00
VIII 10	96 42	95 41	94 38	93 36	92 32	91 27	90 21	89 15	88 08	50
VIII 20	98 22	97 19	96 15	95 11	94 05	92 59	91 52	90 43	89 34	40
VIII 30	100 05	99 01	97 56	96 49	95 42	94 34	93 25	92 14	91 02	30
VIII 40	101 52	100 47	99 40	98 32	97 23	96 13	95 01	93 48	92 34	20
VIII 50	103 45	102 37	101 29	100 19	99 08	97 56	96 42	95 27	94 10	10
IX 00	105 42	104 34	103 23	102 11	100 58	99 43	98 27	97 09	95 50	III 00
IX 10	107 47	106 36	105 24	104 10	102 54	101 37	100 18	98 57	97 35	50
IX 20	109 58	108 45	107 31	106 15	104 57	103 38	102 16	100 52	99 26	40
IX 30	112 17	111 03	109 47	108 29	107 08	105 46	104 21	102 54	101 25	30
IX 40	114 46	113 30	112 12	110 52	109 29	108 03	106 36	105 05	103 32	20
IX 50	117 26	116 09	114 49	113 26	112 00	110 32	109 01	107 27	105 50	II 10
XI 00	143 36	142 22	141 04	139 40	138 10	136 34	134 49	132 57	130 55	I 00
XI 10	148 47	147 40	146 28	145 10	143 46	142 14	140 35	138 46	136 48	50
XI 20	154 23	153 24	152 21	151 13	149 58	148 36	147 05	145 26	143 35	40
XI 30	160 23	159 35	158 44	157 48	156 47	155 39	154 23	152 58	151 24	30
XI 40	166 42	166 09	165 33	164 53	164 09	163 20	162 25	161 23	160 12	20
XI 50	173 17	173 00	172 41	172 21	171 57	171 32	171 02	170 29	169 51	XII 10
Sun rises. Sun sets.	h. m. 5 15 6 45	h. m. 5 12 6 48	h. m. 5 09 6 51	h. m. 5 05 6 55	h. m. 5 02 6 58	h. m. 4 59 7 01	h. m. 4 55 7 05	h. m. 4 52 7 08	h. m. 4 48 7 12	Sun rises. Sun sets.
Azimuth.	o ′ 71 21	o ′ 70 05	o ′ 68 49	o ′ 67 33	o ′ 66 16	o ′ 64 59	o ′ 63 42	o ′ 62 25	o ′ 61 07	Azimuth.

FIG. 3005. EXCERPTS FROM H.O. 260.

The tables must be entered with the approximate latitude and declination, and with the local apparent time. When an Almanac is not at hand, the declination and the equation of time may be taken from Primer's Tables 9 and 10 (Apx. VIII) with sufficient accuracy for this purpose.

To check the standard compass on a single heading, it is routine practice on many ships to observe a timed bearing of the sun p.s.c. during the forenoon watch, preferably shortly after eight bells. The time of the bearing, converted into L.A.T., serves to enter the azimuth tables. The true bearing so found compared with the bearing p.s.c. gives the compass error on the given heading.

To check by a computed azimuth, or true bearing determined when working a sight, the compass bearing must be observed at time of sight. This requires neither azimuth table nor the use of apparent time.

Before swinging ship for a round of deviations, follow Captain Lecky's advice and set a hack watch to local apparent time. To do this, set the watch to whatever standard or zone time is available. Apply the longitude difference by turning the hands of the watch and then apply the equation of time in the same way. The sun's azimuth when on each heading may then be taken from *Burdwood's* by inspection.

Compass adjustment. For the expected period of the swing make a list of magnetic bearings of the sun to be entered at the L.A.T. from the hack watch. This plan serves the purpose of the diagram next described.

3007. A diagram of magnetic azimuths, which gives the magnetic bearings of the sun at any given time during the swing is convenient for

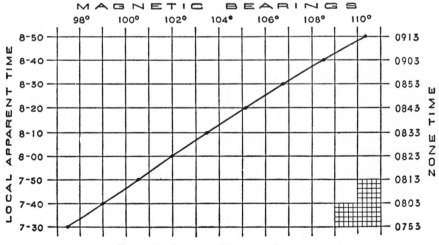

Fig. 3007. Curve of Magnetic Bearings.

compass adjustment. The development of such a diagram in the following paragraphs illustrates both interpolation from azimuth tables and the construction of the diagram. The page from H.O. 260 in Fig. 3005 serves as the azimuth table. Eq.T. and Decl. are taken from Primer's Tables 9 and 10.

Situation: At sea, 4 August to swing ship between 0800 and 0900 Zone + 4 time. Approximate position of ship during the swing 36° 41′ N, 64° 15′ W. Variation 8°.6 W. Decl. of sun 17°.3 N. Eq.T. (−)6m 02s.

Required: Construct a diagram of magnetic azimuth of the sun for the period of the swing, tabulated azimuths to be corrected as at time of mid-swing.

L.A.T. of mid-swing: Zone + 4 time of mid-swing, 0830. Long. Diff. (64° 15′ W − 60° W), (−)17m. Eq.T. = (−)6m. L.A.T. of mid-swing 0807 or 8h 07m A.M.

H.O. 260, first part, Declination Same Name as Latitude. Enter the page for Latitude 36° in Decl. 17° column on line for Apparent Time A.M. VIII-10 which is the tabulated time nearest to the L.A.T. of mid-swing.

To find the correction to be applied to the tabulated true azimuths to find the magnetic bearing of the sun at 10-minute intervals during the swing:

		Declination			
Lat.	17°	17°.3	18°		
36°	94°.6	94°.3	93°.6	94°.6	
36°.7		94°.9		94°.9	
37°	95°.4	95°.1	94°.3		

Correction   (+) 0°.3 + 8°.6 Var. W = (+)8°.9

To find the magnetic bearings to plot on the diagram of magnetic azimuths:

L.A.T.	7–30	7–40	7–50	8–00	8–10	8–20	8–30	8–40	8–50
From H.O. 71	88°.6	90°.1	91°.6	93°.1	94°.6	96°.3	97°.9	99°.7	101°.5
Corr. (+)	8°.9	8°.9	8°.9	8°.9	8°.9	8°.9	8°.9	8°.9	8°.9
Magnetic	97°.5	99°.0	100°.5	102°.0	103°.5	105°.2	106°.8	108°.6	110°.4

Plot the diagram of magnetic azimuths as in Fig. 3007. The exact arrangement will depend on the cross-section paper available.

The above example sets forth the use of H.O. 260 in great detail. In practice, mentally compute both the L.A.T. and the correction. Plot the true azimuths from the tables, move these points by the amount of the correction, and thus complete the diagram without other paper work. H.O. 214 or *Burdwood's* 4-minute tables simplify the work or may eliminate the need for any diagram.

Yacht CHIVA, from Galapagos to The Marquesas, March 4, 1937

GEORGE F. ADAMS, NAVIGATOR

NOON FIX BY ARCS OF POSITION

D.R. Lat. 4° 29'S Long. 107°40 W

Predicted L.A.N. 12h 03m by watch

	1st SIGHT	2nd SIGHT
Watch	11–57–21	12– 08-50
CENTER		
G.H.A or Long.W	106°14.8	109°07.1
Decl. or Lat. S	6° 22.1	6° 22.1
Sextant	87° 36'2	87°41.5
Index Corr.	(−) 04.5	(−) 04.5
Corr.	(+) 12.8	(+) 12.8
TRUE, H_o	87° 44.5	87° 49.8
Subtract from	89° 60.0	89° 60.0
Zenith Distance	2° 15.5	2° 10.2
RADIUS, Miles	135. 5	130.2

FIX Lat 4°41'S, Long.107°45'W

1st. SIGHT

Watch	11 h 57 m 21 s
Slow of C	7 09 26
Chro.	19 06 47
C. Slow	10 03
G.M.T.	19 16 50
G. H.A. 18h	87° 02.3
Corr.	19 00.0
Corr.	12.5
G.H.A. 1st.	106° 14.8

2nd. SIGHT

Watch	12 h 08 m 50 s
1st. Sight	11 57 21
Increase	11 29
Into Arc	2° 52.3
1st. G.H.A.	106° 14.8
G.H.A. 2nd.	109° 07.1

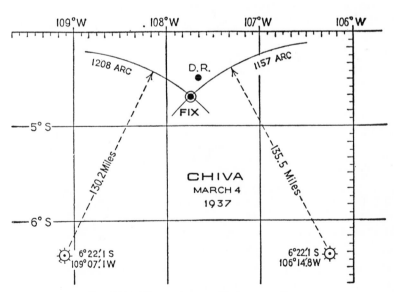

FIG. 3008. WHEN ALMOST UNDER THE SUN.

3008. Almost under the sun. The usual observation of the sun's maximum altitude for latitude at apparent noon becomes somewhat difficult when the sun is near the zenith because of its rapidly changing azimuth and altitude. Under these circumstances, a single timed observation near noon gives an arc of position which may be crossed with an earlier line or arc advanced for a running fix.

Or, under similar conditions, a fix may be had by crossing two or more arcs of position resulting from observations within a few minutes of noon. Lieutenant Commander George F. Adams' experience when skipper of the schooner *Chiva* illustrates such a case (Fig. 3008). Note at the right of the work sheet that G.H.A. of second sight is found simply by adding difference in times of sights, converted into arc, to G.H.A. of first sight. On a faster vessel the earlier arc should be advanced by course and distance to time of last sight. Arcs of position afford the shortest and best method for a fix around noon when latitude and declination are almost identical.

*   *   *

A principal purpose of this chapter has been to interest the student in the multiple uses of the sun. Think what a bearing line through his hoped-for landfall might have meant to Captain Rickenbacker.

3009. Work with the sun. The scope of the first three problems in practical work as given below is similar to that of final examinations for junior courses in celestial navigation. Problems 4 and 5 are simple exercises in the use of circles of position when the sun is almost overhead but may be omitted by junior students.

All courses and bearings are given in degrees true from north unless otherwise stated. In advancing Lines of Position (LOP), use the LOP of H.O. 214 Solution instead of LOP from D.R.

P 1-30. At sea Mar. 7, 1966, 0550 D.R. 30° 07'.5 N, 50° 01'.0 W, course 326°, speed 12 knots.

(a) To conform best with key plotting of problem, use Position Plotting Sheet No. 3000-10z, Latitudes 30° to 33°, issued by DMAHC, and label center meridian 51° W, or construct small plotting sheet for 2° L and 2° λ, label center lines 31° N, 51° W. Plot 0550 D.R.

(b) *Lat. by Polaris.* Mar. 7, 1966, observed Polaris. Hs 29° 31'.8 at W.T. 5h 49m 42s, W.E. on Z.T. 35s slow, I.C. − 1'.5; Ht. Eye 30 ft. *Req:* Latitude.
Ans: Lat. at 0550, 30° 05'.7 N.

(c) Plot 0550 Polaris line. Advance 0550 D.R. until 0840; C 326°, speed 12 knots. Plot 0840 D.R. (30° 36' N, 50° 23' W).

(d) *Morning sun.* About 0840, observed ☉; Hs 23° 47'.4 at W.T. 8h 39m 52s, W.E. on Z.T. 37s slow, I.C. − 1'.5, Ht. Eye 30 ft. *Req:* Solve for LOP.
Ans: A.P., 31° N, 50° 19'.8 W, a 4'.0 T, Zn 112°.7.

(e) Plot 0840 LOP and advance 0550 Polaris line for course and speed. Record 0840 R. Fix.
Ans: 0840 R. Fix, 30° 33'.8 N, 50° 27'.3 W.

(f) Start new D.R. course line at 0840 R. Fix. At 0840, change course to 355°, S 12 knots. Plot and record 1200 D.R.
Ans: 1200 D.R., 31° 14′.0 N, 50° 31′.5 W.

(g) Using Tables 2 and 3, Apx. VIII, estimate L.M.T. and Z.T. of L.A.N. at longitude of 1200 D.R.
Ans: L.M.T. of L.A.N. on Mar. 7 of any year, 1211; Z.T. at 1200 D.R. 1233.

(h) Using Table 7, Apx. VIII, plot and record 1233 D.R.
Ans: 1233 D.R., 31° 20′.6 N, 50° 32′.4 W.

(i) By G.H.A. method, estimate Z.T. and W.T. of L.A.N. at the ship. W.E. on Z.T. 37s slow.
Ans: Z.T. 12h 33m 16s, W.T. 12h 32m 39s.

(j) Predict Hs ☉ at L.A.N., using 1233 D.R., Ht. Eye 30 ft., I.C. − 1′.5.
Ans: Predicted Hs ☉ at L.A.N., 53° 13′.

(k) At L.A.N., observed ☉; Hs 53° 15′.6, Ht. Eye 30 ft., I.C. − 1′.5. *Req:* Latitude.
Ans: 1233 Lat., 31° 18′.6 N.

(l) Plot the 1233 latitude line, and advance the 0840 sun line. Plot and record the 1233 R. Fix.
Ans: 1233 R. Fix, 31° 18′.6 N, 50° 33′.4 W.

(m) Transfer the course line to the 1233 R. Fix and continue C 355°, S 12 knots. Plot and record the 1510 D.R.
Ans: 1510 D.R., 31° 50′ N, 50° 37′ W.

(n) About 1510, observed ☉; W.T. 15h 09m 47s, W.E. on Z.T. 41s slow. Hs 37° 11′.1, Ht. Eye 30 ft., I.C. − 1′.5. *Req:* Solve for LOP; plot 1510 sun line; plot and record 1510 estimated position.
Ans: 1510 Sun; A.P., 32° N, 50° 50′.5 W
a 6′.8 A, Zn 232°.3
1510 E.P.; 31° 52′.3 N, 50° 33′.4 W.

P 2-30. At sea June 3, 1966, clocks keeping Zone + 5 time, 0720 D.R. 34° 45′ N, 72° 05′ W. Course 333° true; speed 12 knots.

(a) To conform best with key plotting of problem, use Position Plotting Sheet No. 3000-11z, Latitudes 33° to 37°, issued by DMAHC, and label center meridian 73° W. Or construct small plotting sheet for 4° L and 4° λ, and label center lines 36° N, 73° W. Plot 0720 D.R.

(b) *Morning sun.* June 3, 1966, about 0720, D.R. 34° 45′ N, 72° 05′ W, observed ☉. Hs 31° 11′.9 at W.T. 7h 20m 00s, W.E. on Z.T. 20s slow, I.C. − 10″, Ht. Eye 20 ft. *Req:* Solve for LOP.
Ans: A.P., 35° N, 71° 35′.4 W, a 22′.0 A, Zn 083°.4.

(c) Plot 0720 LOP. Without adjustment for LOP, plot and record 0800 D.R.
Ans: D.R. at 0800, 34° 52′ N, 72° 09′.5 W.

(d) From Tables 2 and 3 in Apx. VIII, estimate Z.T. of L.A.N. to be at approximately 1150. Plot and record the 1150 D.R.
Ans: D.R. at 1150, 35° 33′ N, 72° 35′ W.

(e) *Noon sight.* June 3, 1966, about 1150, D.R. 35° 33′ N, 72° 35′ W, observed ☉. Hs 76° 30′.9 at W.T. of L.A.N. 11h 48m 00s, W.E. on Z.T. 20s slow, I.C. − 10″, Ht. Eye 20 ft. *Req:* Lat. by meridian altitude.
Ans: Lat. at 1148, 35° 37′.0 N.

(f) Plot 1148 latitude line. Advance 0720 line to 1148. Record R. Fix.
Ans: R. Fix at 1148, 35° 37'.0 N, 72° 30'.6 W.
Continue C 333° and S 12 from 1150 D.R., *not* from R. Fix.

(g) *Afternoon sun.* June 3, 1966, about 1450, observed ☉. Hs 48° 24'.4, W.T.
14h 50m 12s, W.E. on Z.T. 20s slow, I.C. − 10″, Ht. Eye 20 ft. Plot 1450 D.R.
(36° 05' N, 72° 55' W). *Req:* Solve for LOP.
Ans: A.P., 36° N, 73° 07'.6 W, *a* 13'.6 A, Zn 263°.5.
From 1450 D.R., continue course 333° true, S 12.

(h) *Latitude by Polaris.* June 3, 1966, about 1940, D.R. 36° 57' N, 73° 28' W,
observed Polaris for latitude, Hs 36° 03'.2 at W.T. 19h 40m 15s, W.E. on Z.T. 20s
slow, I.C. − 10″, Ht. Eye 20 ft. *Req:* Latitude.
Ans: Lat. at 1940, 36° 47'.6 N.
(i) Plot 1940 Polaris line, advance 1450 sun line, and record R. Fix.
Ans: R. Fix at 1940, 36° 47'.6 N, 73° 22'.3 W.

P 3-30. Cape Town for Rio, Saturday, Feb. 5, 1966, clocks keeping Zone − 1
time, at 0310 took departure from two lights whose L and λ were taken from Bowditch's Maritime Positions.

Green Point	33° 54' S, 18° 24' E,	bearing 065° true
Cape of Good Hope	34° 21' S, 18° 29' E,	bearing 126° true

(a) To conform best with key plotting of problem, use Position Plotting Sheet
No. 3000-11z, Latitudes 33° to 37', issued by DMAHC. (Plotting sheet used for
P 2-30 may be used for P 3-30 by inverting for South latitude.) Label center meridian
17° E, and use outer circle reading on compass rose. Or construct small plotting
sheet for 2° L and 4° λ, labeling center lines 34° S, 17° E. Use small scale. Plot
lights, bearings, and 0310 departure Fix. *Req:* L and λ of point of departure.
Ans: Departure Fix at 0310, 34° 03'.5 S, 18° 00'.0 E.

Ship proceeded on first leg of great circle course for Rio (22° 54' S, 43° 13' W),
course 264°, speed 10 knots.

(b) *Morning sun.* Feb. 5, 1966, about 0740, observed ☉. Hs 28° 09'.7 at W.T.
7h 40m 38s. W.E. 22s fast on Z.T., I.C. − 2'.5, Ht. Eye 30 ft. Plot 0740 D.R. (34°
08' S, 17° 06' E). *Req:* Solve for LOP.
Ans: A.P., 34° S, 17° 26'.5 E, *a* 19'.2 A, Zn 090°.6.

(c) Plot 0740 LOP. Disregard this line at this time.
Continue C 264°, S 10. In mid-morning, navigator decided to observe sun again
to check for current.

(d) *Mid-morning sun.* Feb. 5, 1966, about 1020 observed ☉. Hs 59° 35'.2 at
W.T. 10h 20m 42s, W.E. on Z.T. 22s fast, I.C. − 2'.5, Ht. Eye 30 ft. Plot 1020 D.R.
(34° 11' S, 16° 34' E). *Req:* Solve for LOP.
Ans: A.P., 34° S, 16° 25'.6 E, *a* 4'.7 A, Zn 060°.2.

(e) Plot 1020 line and advance 0740 line to 1020. *Req:* (1) Record 1020 R. Fix.
(2) What can be learned about current from the 1020 R. Fix?
Ans: (1) R. Fix at 1020, 34° 17'.3 S, 16° 30'.9 E. (2) Running fix is not a good
current indicator; however, 1020 sun line suggests southwesterly set of current.
Continue C 264°, S 10 from 1020 D.R.

(f) Advance 1020 R. Fix to 1200 and with λ 16° 10' E so found as 'best,' make
first estimate of watch time of L.A.N. by G.H.A. method Assume W.E. on Z.T.
22s fast.
Ans: 12h 09m 46s W.T.

(g) Advance D.R. from 1020 to 1209 and record that position.
Ans: D.R. at 1209, 34° 13′ S, 16° 12′ E.

(h) Using 1209 D.R. Lat., predict Hs at L.A.N. I.C. — 2′.5, Ht. Eye 30 ft.
Ans: 71° 37′.9.

(i) *Noon sight.* Feb. 5, 1966, observed ☉ at L.A.N. W.T. 12h 09m 46s, W.E. 22s fast on Z.T. Hs 71° 32′.9, I.C. — 2′.5, Ht. Eye 30 ft. *Req:* Latitude by meridian altitude.

Ans: Lat. at 1209, 34° 18′.0 S.

(j) Plot 1209 latitude line, advance 1020 line, and record 1209 R. Fix.
Ans: R. Fix at 1209, 34° 18′.0 S, 16° 08′.4 E.

After considering 1020 and 1209 R. Fixes, D.R. was transferred to 1209 R. Fix, and at 1300, course was changed from 264° to 267° true, speed continued at S 10.

(k) *Afternoon sun.* Feb. 5, 1966, about 1610, observed ☉. Hs 34° 01′.3 at 4h 10m 23s P.M. by watch. W.T. 22s fast on Z.T., I.C. — 2′.5, Ht. Eye 30 ft. *Req:* (1) Plot and record 1610 D.R. (2) Solve for LOP.

Ans: (1) 1610 D.R., 34° 21′ S, 15° 20′ E. (2) A.P., 34° S, 15° 00′.6 E, *a* 12′.1 A, Zn 273°.4.

A fix from a round of stars at twilight confirmed the 1610 indication that ship was overrunning her logged distance.

P 4-30. From Lecky. Rewritten for 1966 from the 1900 work book of Capt. T. S. Angus, P. & O. S.S. "CHINA" as in *Wrinkles.*

(a) Small plotting sheet for 2° L and 2° λ; use small scale, label center lines 18° N and 116° E.

In the South China Sea out of Singapore bound for Yokohama July 31, 1966, course 063°, speed 15 knots, clocks keeping Zone — 8 time, it appeared that at noon the G.P. sun would pass within less than 2° of the ship, and observations were taken for a fix by arcs of position. Expected D.R. at 1200 was 18° 05′ N, 116° 02′ E.

(b) Estimate G.M.T. of L.A.N.
Ans: 4h 22m 12s, or 1222 Zone — 8 time.

(c) Observed ☉, Hs 88° 54′.8 at 4h 24m 40s by Chro. which was 5m 28s fast. I.C. + 1′.5, Ht. Eye 55 ft.

Req: L and λ of G.P. sun, which is center of circle of equal altitudes.
Ans: G.P. sun at time of sight; 18° 23′.7 N, 116° 47′.2 E.
Req: Zenith distance converted to miles which is radius of circle of equal altitudes.
Ans: Radius of this circle, 55.0 miles.

(d) Same as in (c) except: About 6m later observed ☉, Hs 89° 08′.0 at 4h 30m 40s by Chro. which was 5m 28s fast.

Req: L and λ of G.P. sun and radius of circle of equal altitudes for second sight.
Ans: G.P. sun at time of second sight; 18° 23′.7 N, 115° 17′.2 E. Radius of 2nd circle, 41.8 miles.

(e) Plot the 1219 G.P. Convert time interval between sights into arc units and move the 1219 G.P. westward by that amount.

(f) Plot the 1225 G.P.

(g) Plot arcs of position from (e) and (f) and record Fix.
Ans: Noon Fix; 18° 02′.5 N, 115° 55′.5 E.

P 5-30. Off Madagascar, Dec. 27, 1966, navigator of a destroyer considered noon sight conditions and decided on a fix by arcs of position.

(a) Construct a small plotting sheet, label center lines 23° S and 69° E; use small scale.
Course 125° true, S 30, expected best D.R. at 1200 (Zone − 5) 22° 32′.4 S, 69° 20′ E.

(b) Estimate watch time of L.A.N. at λ 69° 20′ E, watch error 14s slow of Z.T.
Ans: 12h 23m 18s.

(c) Record change in ship's longitude between 1200 and L.A.N. found in (b).
Ans: 11′.0 east.

(d) Converting longitude difference to time, correct W.T. Record second estimate of W.T. of L.A.N.
Ans: 12h 22m 34s.

(e) Navigator observed two sights of ⊙ at about 1220 and 1225 W.T.
For both sights: W.E. on Z.T. 14s slow, I.C. − 2′.5, Ht. Eye 28 ft.

	1st sight	2nd sight
W.T.	12h 20m 04s	12h 24m 52s
Hs	88° 43′.0	88° 58′.0

Use excerpts for hourly G.H.A. of sun at 1st sight. Compute time interval between sights, convert to arc units, and move G.P. of 1st sight westward by that amount.
Req: For each sight: L and λ of G.P. sun and radius of circle of equal altitudes.
Ans: 1st sight: G.P. sun at 1220, 23° 20′.9 S, 70° 08′.2 E. Radius of 1220 circle, 68.5 miles.

2nd sight: G.P. sun at 1225, 23° 20′.9 S, 68° 56′.2 E. Radius of 1225 circle, 53.5 miles.

(f) 'Plot 1st arc advanced for 5m run. Plot 2nd arc, and record 1225 Fix.
Ans: Fix at 1225, 22° 32′.0 S, 69° 20′.4 E.

31. THE STARS

IN THE days of sail many navigators worked principally with the sun, although star sights were well understood. In this era of high speed, star sights are an important element of every navigator's work at sea. They may be worked and used as are other sights, with the added advantage that observations of two or more stars give a fix. In the air with bubble sextants, star fixes throughout the night are of major importance, and it is in this field that recent developments in celestial navigation have been most rapid. Both the *Nautical Almanac* and the *Air Almanac* list fifty-seven of the principal navigational stars. These stars are easily identified and are distributed so that good fixes are usually obtainable anywhere on earth.

3101. Names. From ancient times the brighter stars have been grouped in constellations named for objects they were supposed to resemble. Each constellation has its Latin name which, whether spelled in old or modern manner, identifies the constellation on star charts and elsewhere. Many of the constellations have common English names such as Big Dipper, Chair, Southern Cross, etc. The stars themselves are named in two ways.

By constellations, a star is given the family name of its constellation prefixed by a letter of the Greek alphabet, the first letter of that alphabet generally being given to the brightest star in the constellation. Thus the stars of *Ursa Major*, translated Great Bear, but called the Big Dipper, are marked α *Ursae Majoris*, β *Ursae Majoris*, γ *Ursae Majoris*, and so on to include the seven stars which make up the constellation. This is the type of name used in most books on astronomy.

Individual names also are given to the principal navigational stars. The *Nautical Almanac* uses the individual star names in the Star lists. They are the easiest to remember and will be used in this book. A few such names with their corresponding identifications by constellations are:

POLARIS (α *Ursae Minoris*)   SIRIUS (α *Canis Majoris*)
RIGEL (β *Orionis*)   ARCTURUS (α *Boötis*)
CAPELLA (α *Aurigae*)   VEGA (α *Lyrae*)

351

3102. Magnitudes (Mag.) of stars indicate their relative bright-ness, the lower numbers being assigned to the brighter stars. That of Sirius, the brightest star, is − 1.6, Vega 0.1, Altair 0.9, Polaris 2.1, and Acamar 3.1 which is the least bright of the so-called principal naviga-tional stars. Those with a magnitude of less than 1.5 are called stars of the first magnitude. Less bright stars, with magnitudes of 1.5 or more but less than 2.5, are known as second magnitude stars. A so-called sixth magnitude star is the least bright star visible to the naked eye under fa-vorable conditions. In addition to the visual magnitude, the *Air Al-manac* lists the photo-electric magnitude corresponding to photo-sensi-tive response S-4.

3103. Positions on the celestial sphere. A skilled observer recog-nizes a star by its relative position among other stars. Its exact position, however, is defined in much the same way that latitude and longitude define position on the earth.

Declination of a star defines its position north or south from the celestial equator exactly as latitude defines position north or south from the earth's equator. The equators are the zero lines.

Longitude on the earth is measured from a zero meridian arbitrarily selected as that through Greenwich. A similar zero line on the celestial sphere is the hour circle through the Vernal Equinox (V.E.), which is the point where the sun crosses the celestial equator each spring. Naviga-tors call this point the First Point of Aries, the Ram, symbolized by its horns as ♈.

Sidereal hour angle (S.H.A.) of a star defines its position on the celestial sphere westward from ♈ (0° S.H.A.). It is the arc of the celestial equator measured *westward* from ♈ to the hour circle (meridian) through the star. It is expressed from 0° to 360°, *always westward*, whereas longitude is measured to 180° east or west.

The position of a star's hour circle may also be defined in a reverse manner after the fashion of astronomers:

Right ascension (R.A.) of a star or other point on the celestial sphere is the arc of the celestial equator measured *eastward* from ♈ to the hour circle (meridian) through the star. It is measured in time units from 0h to 24h, *always eastward*. The right ascension is not used when working star sights as taught in this book.

Either of the above quantities defines the east-west position of the hour circle (celestial meridian) of a star. Both are measured from the same zero line but in opposite directions, and their relations are such that:

$$\text{S.H.A.} = 360° - \text{R.A. (in degress)}$$
$$= 360° - \text{R.A. (in hours)} \times 15$$

Thus the position of a point on the celestial sphere, such as that of Vega, may be stated in two ways:

(1) Decl. 38° 44′ N, S.H.A. 81° 11′   (81° 11′ *west* of ♈)
(2) Decl. 38° 44′ N, R.A. 18h 35m 16s (278° 49′ *east* of ♈)

Caution: A star's fixed position on the celestial sphere should not be confused with its apparent position as used when working a sight. The latter is defined, as for any other body, by the star's declination and its Greenwich hour angle, which are the latitude and longitude of its momentary geographic position.

3104. Star charts. It is customary to observe two or more stars at almost the same time for a fix. To do this effectively the navigator must know the stars, a knowledge best perfected through many night watches at sea. Star charts and star finders, however, are a convenient aid to any navigator, and are a necessity for the student undertaking to learn the stars from books.

A true map of the world can be drawn only on a globe which represents the sphere of the earth. Likewise, a true chart of the stars as we see them must be drawn on a globe representing the celestial sphere. As with maps and charts of the world, various different projections are used for constructing useful star charts on a flat surface. Neither sun, moon, nor planets can be shown in a fixed position on such charts, or on a star globe, because they appear to move about among the stars.

Before one can use any star chart, it is necessary to determine what part of the heavens is visible (above the horizon) at the date and time of intended observation. This is done in two steps. Refer to Fig. 3105.

First—and easiest—remember that your latitude is equal to the declination of stars which will pass over head. For example, if your latitude is 38° N, all of the stars whose declination is near 38° N (e.g., Vega) will pass near your zenith sometime during the next 24 hours.

Second, locate the position of your meridian on the star chart for the time of observation. This is done by remembering that the angular distance westward of any point from the meridian of the March equinox (♈) is its sidereal hour angle (§3103). Thus, the S.H.A. of the meridian containing your zenith is the distance west of ♈ on the star chart.

The upper part of Table 8 in Appendix VIII gives the approximate S.H.A. of the sun for each day of the year, plus 180°. (One can not see the stars at noon.) The lower part of Table 8 gives the correction for every four minutes after 0 hour L.M.T. at 15° per hour. This correction is *subtracted* because the stars seem to be moving westward and the distance to ♈ is thus decreasing.

Table 1 in Appendix VIII gives the same information in reverse. It gives the Local Hour Angle of ♈ which is the angular distance, measured westward, from your meridian to ♈ at 0h L.M.T. The lower part of Table 1, identical with that of Table 8, gives the correction for every 4m after 0h L.M.T. The correction is *added* because the local hour angle of anything continually increases westward.

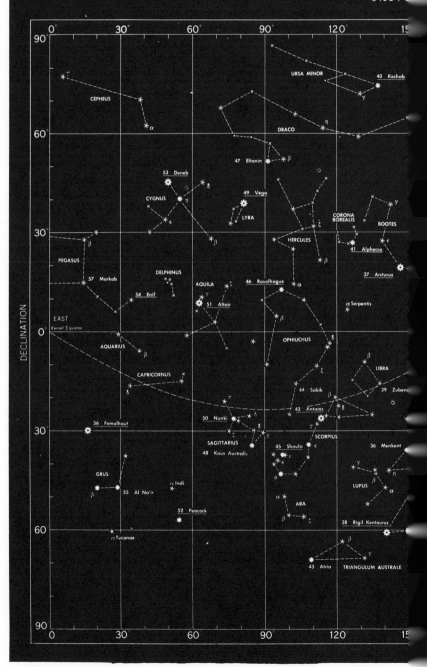

The Air Almanac—5

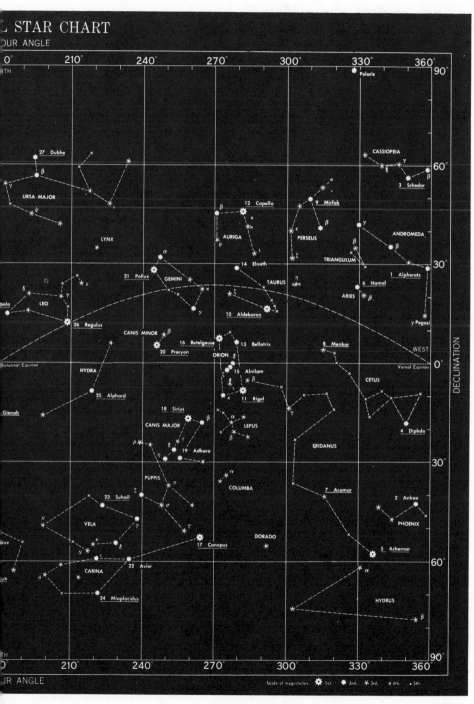

FIG. 3105. NAVIGATIONAL STAR CHART.
To locate one's meridian at any instant, consult Table 8, Apx. VIII.

The L.H.A. of ♈ is equal to 360° minus the S.H.A. of your zenith. Thus, for March 9 of any year at 18h 24m (about the time for star sights):

	Table 8			Table 1
March 9		March 9		
S.H.A. Z at 0h	194°	L.H.A. ♈)		166°
add	360°	corr. 18h 28m	(+)	278°
	554°			444°
corr. 18h 28m	(−) 278°	subtract		360°
S.H.A. zenith	276°	L.H.A. ♈)		84°

Note that 360° − 276° = 84°

Figure 3105 shows that for this date and time (S.H.A. 276°), the Orion group of navigational stars will be nearly on your meridian.

Out-of-door folk also know that the evening stars seen in winter are not the evening stars seen in summer and that different stars are seen overhead each month. This is because, as we see them, the stars move faster around the earth than does the sun. The result is that a star over Boston this evening will be about 1° west of that meridian tomorrow night. One month later at the same hour it will be 30° west of Boston. Conversely, the point on a star chart which marks the zenith of Boston at a given hour is 30° east of where it was one month earlier.

The above paragraphs may now be summarized, assuming for this purpose that the stars be observed from a fixed position on the earth. Briefly stated, the zenith of the observer moves eastward on the celestial sphere 30° during each two hours of time and in addition it moves eastward 30° during each month. These figures are subject to minor qualifications but are a practical guide when considering what stars may be overhead at a given time and date.

3105. The *Navigational Star Chart*, Fig. 3105, appearing on pages 354-355 is reproduced from *The Air Almanac* produced jointly by the Nautical Almanac Offices of the U. S. Naval Observatory and the Royal Greenwich Observatory. The stars are arranged as they appear to one facing *south;* those bearing numbers are included in the list of 57 navigational stars.

3106. Special charts of the Navigational Stars, developed for this Primer and shown at the close of the present chapter, have been constructed for the use of observers in mid-northern latitudes. The charts show the principal stars seen from 40° N at the given local times and dates. At such times the proper chart, face up and oriented to true north, reflects the visible stars. Each star is on its true bearing as from the observer at the center and in its true altitude above the horizon at the edge of the chart.

There are twelve special charts, one for each 2 hours of the given date, or one for each month at the given time, all as from 40° N. Properly selected, however, they serve for any time and date within latitudes from 30° N to 50° N. Their accuracy when so used is increased by shifting the zenith of the observer a few degrees from the center to its true position. In many ways these are the best small charts available for studying the navigational stars from mid-northern latitudes.

For selecting one of the special charts shown at the end of this chapter, Table 1 should be used as it gives L.H.A. ♈ directly. On these charts, each star is shown at its true azimuth as measured by a straight line from "Z" through the star symbol to the compass rose. The star's altitude can also be measured by scaling the distance to the star symbol from the dark edge marked "Horizon." A star's altitude is, of course, 0° at the horizon and 90° at the zenith.

Using the data from the above illustration, (March 9, 18h 28m, L.H.A. ♈ 84°), the chart for L.H.A. ♈ 90° is selected. Then, assuming your latitude is within a few degrees of 40° N, the following first-magnitude stars will be available for observation:

Star	Azimuth	Altitude
Regulus	099°	29°
Pollux	111°	66°
Procyon	141°	49°
Sirius	167°	32°
Betelgeuse	183°	57°
Rigel	195°	41°
Aldebaran	224°	60°
Capella	310°	too high
Deneb	333°	too low

3107. How know the stars? The navigator must learn to identify the principal stars by their relative position to each other. The discussion in this section, together with the star charts, gives information for so doing.

Four constellations are recommended for locating the other constellations and identifying individual stars in one's memory:

I. THE DIPPER (*Ursa Major*) for stars well to the north. It appears on all of the Special Charts. The two stars at the outer corners of the Dipper's bowl are known as *the pointers*. Fig. 3107a.

II. ORION (*Orion*) for stars in the region of the celestial equator. This great constellation may be located by its stars Rigel and Betelgeuse between which lies the belt of Orion the Hunter. Fig. 3107c.

III. THE SCORPION (*Scorpius*) for stars somewhat south of the celestial equator. It is about 180° from Orion and thus can be used when Orion is not visible. As on the Navigational Star Chart, Antares is its head while Shaula marks the stinger in its tail. Fig. 3105.

IV. THE SOUTHERN CROSS (*Crucis*) for stars far to the south. It is the most conspicuous constellation of the southern hemisphere but is never visible from mid-northern latitudes. It may be located at lower center of the Navigational Star Chart. Fig. 3105.

Stars should be studied at sea or where the heavens may be seen to the horizon with a brilliancy undiminished by the lights of a great city. The beginner, turning from a star chart or description, may find the stars as seen in the sky surprisingly far apart. Remember that one-third of the arc from horizon to zenith is 30°, a unit useful when visualizing intervals in any direction on the celestial sphere. With this thought as a yardstick, the celestial equator may be located where it crosses the meridian, always at an altitude equal to 90° − Lat. of the observer. The following list of stars and how to identify them begins with the so-called circumpolar stars visible from more or less 40° N, continues irregularly south and concludes with the stars that are useful only from below the equator.

The data given for each star, as an aid to identification, are rounded figures and should not be used for working a sight. Where a number precedes the name of a star, it corresponds to similar numbers in the *Nautical Almanac* and the *Air Almanac*.

POLARIS, α *Ursae Minoris,* Mag. 2.1, Decl. 89° N, S.H.A. 327°. On a line through the pointers across the end of the Dipper. Always bears true north at an altitude equal to the latitude of the observer. (Fig. 3107*a*)

(27) DUBHE, α *Ursae Majoris,* Mag. 2, Decl. 62° N, S.H.A. 194°. Marks the outer corner of the rim of the Dipper, and is the pointer nearest Polaris. (Fig. 3107*a*)

CAPH, β *Cassiopeiae,* Mag. 2.4, Decl. 59° N, S.H.A. 358°. A bright star of Cassiopeia, the Chair, which is about the same distance

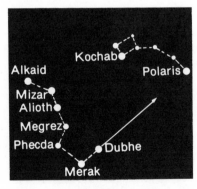

FIG. 3107*a*.

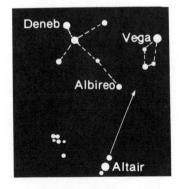

FIG. 3107*b*.

from Polaris as the Dipper but on the opposite side of the pole in the Milky Way. When below the pole, the five principal stars of the Chair represent a straggling W, but when above Polaris they suggest an indifferent M. Caph is at the bright end of the chair and leads this constellation towards the west. It is nearest the Northern Cross. (Figs. 3105, 3107c)

(3) SCHEDAR, α *Cassiopeiae*, Mag. 2.5, Decl. 56° N, S.H.A. 350°. This star is next to Caph in the Chair and of almost the same magnitude. (Fig. 3107d)

(49) VEGA, α *Lyrae*, Mag. 0.1, Decl. 39° N, S.H.A. 81°. On a line from its lower outer corner diagonally across the bowl of the Dipper to the eastward at the edge of the Milky Way. The most brilliant star in this part of the sky with a decided blue tint. Easily recognized, Vega is seldom forgotten. (Figs. 3105 and 3107b)

(53) DENEB, α *Cygni*, Mag. 1.3, Decl. 45° N, S.H.A. 50°. About 24° east and north of Vega and in the midst of the Milky Way. It is at the top of the Northern Cross and is the brightest star of that constellation. (Fig. 3107b)

(51) ALTAIR, α *Aquilae*, Mag. 0.9, Decl. 9° N, S.H.A. 63°. On a line from Polaris midway between Vega and Deneb, about 81° south of the pole, is attended by a lesser star on either side. Altair, Vega, and Deneb form a vast triangle, right-angled at Vega. Close to the eastward of Altair is a group of five stars, shaped like a diamond with a handle, known as the Dolphin or Job's Coffin. (Fig. 3107b)

(1) ALPHERATZ, α *Andromedae*, Mag. 2.2, Decl. 29° N, S.H.A. 358°. On a line from Polaris through Caph, 30° south of Caph. Alpheratz is at one corner of the Square of Pegasus, the Winged Horse, with Markab at the diagonally opposite corner. (Fig. 3107d)

It is well to remember that Caph and Alpheratz are almost on, and therefore mark, the 0 hour circle through ♈.

(12) CAPELLA, α *Aurigae*, Mag. 02, Decl. 46° N, S.H.A. 281°. On a line from the heel of the Dipper between the pointers and westward about 49° where Capella is halfway between Orion and Polaris. It is a very bright star of a yellow tinge attended by a small triangle of three stars to the southward called the Kids. (Fig. 3107c)

(21) POLLUX, β *Geminorum*, Mag. 1.2, Decl. 28° N, S.H.A. 244°. A line drawn between the pointers from the star where the handle meets the bowl of the Dipper (Megrez, Fig. 3107a) leads to the Twins, Castor and Pollux. The brightest twin is Pollux, nearest to Procyon. Castor is nearest Capella. Pollux, Betelgeuse, and Procyon form a triangle right-angled at Procyon. (Fig. 3107c)

(26) REGULUS, α *Leonis*, Mag. 1.3, Decl. 12° N, S.H.A. 208°. The brightest star of Leo, the Lion. Follow the pointers backward, away

FIG. 3107c.

from Polaris, to Leo where Regulus is at the base of the handle of the Sickle. (Fig. 3105)

(37) ARCTURUS, α *Boötis*, Mag. 0.2, Decl. 19° N, S.H.A. 146°, may be found by following the curve of the handle of the Dipper southward. It is a brilliant star with a reddish tint and forms great triangles with Spica and Regulus and with Spica and Antares. (Fig. 3105)

(33) SPICA, α *Virginis*, Mag. 1.2, Decl. 11° S, S.H.A. 159°. Continue the curve of the Dipper handle (Fig. 3105) through Arcturus and about 35° down to Spica, a bright white star. The gaff of the nearby Colvus, the "Gaff Mainsail," points to Spica.

(11) RIGEL, β *Orionis*, Mag. 0.3, Decl. 8° S, S.H.A. 282°. The bright star at the southwest corner of Orion, opposite the Belt from Betelgeuse. (Fig. 3107c)

(16) BETELGEUSE α *Orionis*, Mag. from 0.1 to 1.2, Decl. 7° N, S.H.A. 272°, is at the northeast corner of Orion opposite the Belt from Rigel. (Fig. 3107c)

(20) PROCYON, α *Canis Minoris*, Mag. 0.5, Decl. 5° N, S.H.A. 245°, is the bright star about 33° east of Orion. It forms an equilateral triangle with Sirius and Betelgeuse. (Fig. 3107c)

(18) SIRIUS, α *Canis Majoris*, Mag. − 1.6, Decl. 17° S, S.H.A. 259°. The Dog Star, brightest of all, shines with a scintillating white light. The three stars of Orion's Belt point southeastward to Sirius, distant about 23°. (Fig. 3107c)

(10) ALDEBARAN, α *Tauri*, Mag. 1.1, Decl. 16° N, S.H.A. 291°. Follow

the direction of Orion's Belt about 20° in the opposite direction from Sirius to find Aldebaran the Bull. (Fig. 3107c)

Beyond Aldebaran are the Pleiades, a tiny cluster of stars known to all who study the heavens. (Fig. 3105)

(42) ANTARES, α *Scorpii*, Mag. 1.2, Decl. 26° S, S.H.A. 113°. On an hour circle about halfway between Vega and Arcturus, but well south of the equator, Antares may be seen about 46° east and south of Spica. This red tinted head of the Scorpion is easily identified by three small stars at the ends of its whiskers. (Fig. 3105)

(56) FOMALHAUT, α *Piscis Austrini*, Mag. 1.3, Decl. 30° S, S.H.A. 16°. Follow the western side of the Square of Pegasus south through Markab to the isolated bright star in the eyes of the Southern Fish. (Fig. 3105)

(38) RIGIL KENT., α *Centauri*, Mag. 0.1, Decl. 61° S, S.H.A. 140°. A brilliant star about 30° directly east of the Southern Cross. Rigil Kent. and (35) Hadar nearer the Southern Cross serve as pointers aimed at the top of the Cross. The two stars suggest Castor and Pollux. (Fig. 3105)

(30) ACRUX, α *Crucis*, Mag. 1.1, Decl. 63° S, S.H.A. 174°. The bright star at the foot of the Southern Cross, Acrux is the star of that constellation nearest to the south celestial pole. The pointers from Rigil Kent., through Hadar indicate the true Cross contra the false Cross, a similar formation farther west. (Fig. 3105)

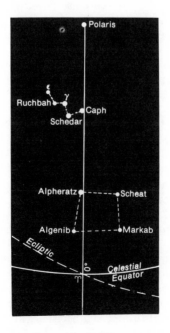

FIG. 3107d.

(17) CANOPUS, α *Carinae*, Mag. − 0.9, Decl. 53° S, S.H.A. 264°. Second brightest of all stars, 36° due south of Sirius, on a line through the Magellanic clouds to the westward. (Fig. 3105)

(5) ACHERNAR, α *Eridani*, Mag. 0.6, Decl. 57° S, S.H.A. 336°. A brilliant isolated star, north of and forms a right-angled triangle with the two Magellanic clouds. (Fig. 3105)

(52) PEACOCK, α *Pavonis*, Mag. 2.1, Decl. 57° S, S.H.A. 54°. A line from Antares through Shaula, the stinger in the Scorpion's tail, leads to Peacock. It is the northwestern star of four in a peculiar four-sided group. (Fig. 3105)

3108. Star Finder and Identifier, H.O. 2102-D, Fig. 3108a, is a simple and convenient device for finding the approximate altitude and azimuth of the 57 navigational stars. It consists of a star base, nine transparent, altitude-azimuth templates (one for each 10° of latitude from 5° to 85°), and a meridian-angle diagram. To locate any of the navigational stars, select the template nearest to the D.R. latitude and place it over the pin at the center of the star base. Be careful that the latitude name on the template and the letter indicating the pole are *both* N (north) or S (south), as appropriate. Compute L.H.A. ♈ as explained in §2704 and §2705 or by Table 1 of Apx. VIII, and set the blue index arrow of the template to this value on the peripheral scale of the star base. The closed curves on the template now indicate the altitude; and the radial curves, the azimuth of all of the navigational stars in the almanac list which are above the horizon. The zenith is indicated by a cross.

The meridian-angle diagram printed in magenta has three principal uses: (1) to plot the celestial bodies whose positions are variable, as the planets, moon, or sun; (2) to provide a means for identifying an unknown body (§3110); and (3) to indicate the approximate meridian angle and declination of any celestial body. The following explanations will be clarified by remembering that L.H.A. ♈ is equal to the right ascension of the meridian. Thus, the scale on both sides of the base plate represents the equivalent of right ascension, 360° − S.H.A. The concentric circles on the magenta template represent declination north or south of the celestial equator shown on the base plate.

Suppose it is desired to plot for north latitude, a celestial body whose S.H.A. is 75° and whose declination is 13° S. Subtract the S.H.A. from 360° to find the body's right ascension (285°). Place the magenta template on the central pin on the "N" side and set the index arrow to 285° on the base plate scale. Plot the body's position in the slot of the template opposite 13° S by eye interpolation as shown in Fig. 3108b. In Fig. 3108a, several planets have been plotted by this method.

It is sometimes helpful to plot the positions of the sun and moon. If the sun is plotted, a fair approximation of the configuration of the celestial bodies at dawn and dusk can be obtained by turning the altitude-azimuth template until the sun is just below the eastern or western horizon. If the moon is also plotted, one can judge from its relationship to the sun whether it will be suitable for a daytime fix and its approximate time of rising and setting with respect to sunrise and sunset.

Right ascension of any body is equal to G.H.A. ♈ minus G.H.A. of the body; or for a body on the meridian, it is equal to the hour angle of Aries. Therefore, right ascension is easily found for the sun, moon, or planets from the data in the almanacs. Look down the G.H.A. column of the body until the value is found which is nearest 0°. The adjacent value in the G.H.A. ♈ column is the approximate right ascension after adjusting mentally for the fact that the value in the body's G.H.A.

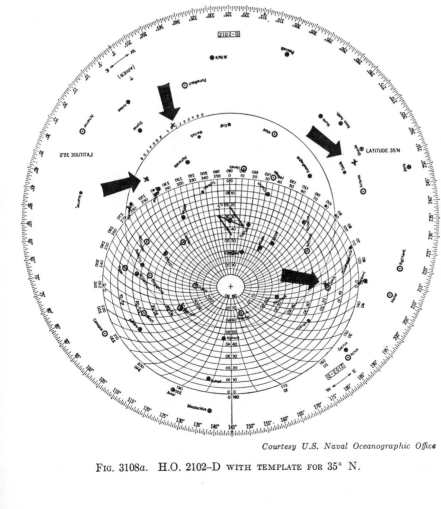

Courtesy U.S. Naval Oceanographic Office

FIG. 3108a. H.O. 2102–D WITH TEMPLATE FOR 35° N.

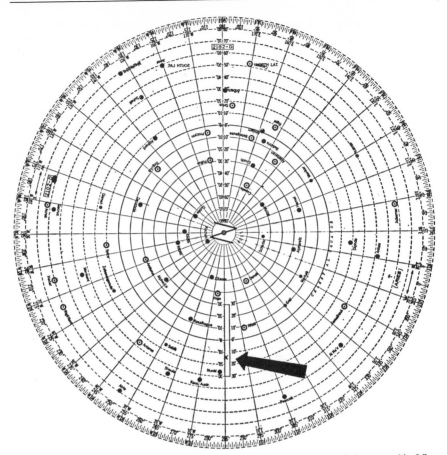

Courtesy U.S. Naval Oceanographic Office

Fig. 3108b. H.O. 2102–D with meridian angle diagram.

column is usually not exactly 0°. Thus, on July 2, R.A. Venus is 65° and R.A.⊙ is 100° approximately. A small box at the bottom of the almanac page gives for the four planets, the time of meridian passage at Greenwich on the middle day and the S.H.A. at that time. The value 360° − S.H.A. can also be used to plot the planets on the star base.

To find the approximate meridian angle of a body, set the index of the magenta template to L.H.A. ♈, making sure that the side of the template for the correct latitude is uppermost. The radius through the body now indicates the meridian angle on the peripheral scale of the template, and the declination (N) or (S) is indicated by the circles.

The required L.H.A. of Aries (♈) for the given date and L.M.T. may be approximated with all useful accuracy from a number of tables, including:

Primer's Table 1, L.H.A. of Aries. Enter the table with the date and to the figure so found add the correction for L.M.T. taken from the lower table.

3109. Sky Diagrams in the *Air Almanac,* as described in §2401, Air Almanac chapter, provide an excellent means of selecting the most prominent navigational stars for observations. The diagrams also include the positions of Moon and Planets as well.

3110. Identification of an unknown star. An unknown star can be identified if you know its altitude, its compass bearing, and the time of observation. For example, you observed a star through a break in the overcast and obtained the following data:

Altitude		50°
Azimuth		126°
L.H.A. ♈		122°
Latitude	about	40°

The star can be identified by various methods.

One quick method is to look at one of the charts at the end of this chapter. The chart for L.H.A. ♈ 120° is nearest to your data. Look for a star whose azimuth is about 126° and whose altitude scales at about 50°. Obviously, the star is Regulus.

Many navigators use H.O. 2102-D to identify stars. (See §3108). Orient the appropriate template (Lat. 35° N) to L.H.A. ♈ 122°, and again the star nearest to Ho 50°, Zn 126° is Regulus.

H.O. 229 provides a convenient method of identification. It can be used in two ways.

1. *By inspection:* Look through the columns for your latitude until you find the combination of altitude and azimuth corresponding to your measurements. Note the star's declination in the "Dec" column and its LHA at the top of the page. If the match occurs on the right-hand page and above the "C-S" (Contrary-Same) line, the declination is contrary in name to the latitude. If the match is below the C-S line, the declination and latitude have the same name but L.H.A. is read from the bottom of the page. In either case, the star's sidereal hour angle is given by:

$$\text{S.H.A. } ☆ = \text{L.H.A.} ☆ - \text{L.H.A. } ♈.$$

Example: Identify the star whose altitude is 50° and whose azimuth is 126° at a moment when L.H.A. ♈ is 122° and approximate latitude is 40° N.

Solution: This star is eastward of your meridian; so its L.H.A. must be greater that 180° and its azimuth (Zn) is equal to the tabulated azimuth angle (Z). For a star westward of your meridian, L.H.A. is less than 180° and Zn = 360° − Z.

Looking through the columns for latitude 40°, find (page 248) the nearest match between your data and the tabulated values of Hc and Z, and read declination (12° N) in the "Dec." column and its L.H.A. (328°) at the top of the page. Thus, the star's coordinates are dec. 12° N and S.H.A. ☆ 206°. (L.H.A. ☆ 328° − L.H.A. ♈ 122° = 206°.) Inspection of the star list in the almanac shows that with dec. 12° N and S.H.A. 206°, the star can only be Regulus.

2. *By formula:* Enter the H.O. 229 table with your latitude but call the observed azimuth "L.H.A." and the observed altitude "Dec." With these arguments, the tabulated "Hc" is the star's declination, and the tabulated "Z" is the body's Hour angle.

Example: Using the same observed data as before, (Lat. 40° N, L.H.A. ♈ 122°, Ho 50°, Zn 126°) rename Zn as "L.H.A. 126° and Ho as "Dec." 50°. Enter H.O. 229 with these values (page 293) and in the "Ho" column find the star's declination to be 12° N (same name), and in the "Z" column find 32°. The star is eastward of your meridian so its L.H.A. is 360° − 32° = 328°, and its S.H.A. is

$$\text{L.H.A. } ☆ \ 328° \ - \ \text{L.H.A. } ♈ \ 122° \ = \ 206°.$$

As before, with S.H.A. 206° and declination 12° N, the star can only be Regulus.

Stars can also be identified by the Star Identification Tables in H.O. 214 and by numerous other methods.

If a planet has been observed, proceed as described for a star to obtain the G.H.A. of the planet and its declination. With these, the planet can be identified on the daily almanac page opposite G.M.T. of sight.

3111. Star sights are simple enough when one has learned to identify the necessary stars and observe star altitudes. A timed altitude of a single star, like that of any other body, gives only a line of position. More often a round of sights is taken for a fix. This requires preparation

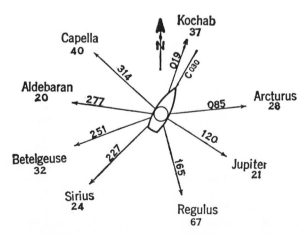

Fig. 3111. Twilight, Lat. 35° N, L.H.A. ♈ 145°.

and practice to assure rapid work in semi-darkness without interruptions which blind the eyes.

Observing stars has been discussed in Chapters 18 and 19, which describe three methods for taking star altitudes: (1) Bringing the star down to the horizon. (2) With the sextant upside down, bringing the horizon up to the star. (3) By setting the sextant to the star's approximate altitude, determined in advance. The method used will depend on circumstances and on the observer's preference. In any case, time should be allowed for the eyes to become accustomed to half-light or darkness, and exposure to bright light between sights should be avoided. If possible, have an assistant take the times and read the altitudes from the sextant.

When to take the sights and what bodies are to be observed should be considered in advance. This is instinctive with a skilled star man who recalls the conditions of the previous day and brings down his stars without reference to Almanacs. Visibility permitting, he will observe more or less the same stars night after night. To use a star chart or star finder one must predict the approximate time of the proposed observations. The best time for observing star altitudes, measured from the horizon as at sea, is during evening or morning twilight. These twilight periods begin or end at sunset or sunrise, and the times of these events are the bases for planning twilight observations. The duration of twilight, which increases in higher latitudes, also must be considered.

Evening twilight begins at the time of sunset as tabulated in the Almanacs, before the stars are visible, and continues for varying periods of time. In mid-latitudes the stars will begin to appear at about the time indicated in the *Nautical Almanac* column headed "Civil" at which time the sun is 6° below the horizon. About the time indicated in the "Naut" column, the sun is 12° below the horizon which is now too dark for best star sights. The *Air Almanac* gives the *duration* of civil twilight; that is, the interval during which the sun is between the horizon and 6° below it. At the end of evening civil twilight, found by *adding* the duration to the time of sunset, the brightest stars and planets can be expected to be visible. In the tropics the time is short and night falls suddenly. From 40° N or S the time is about 30 minutes and increases rapidly at greater latitudes until so-called twilight lasts all night. The exact time available when both stars and horizon are visible is uncertain. Beyond mid-latitudes it is prolonged; in the tropics the star observer must work rapidly.

At morning twilight the above procedure is similar but the duration from the A.A. is *subtracted*. In either case, plan to observe the less bright stars during the darker part of the available time. A very bright star or a brilliant planet may be visible at almost the time of sunset or sunrise.

What stars will be available and those best to observe for a fix may be known to an old hand, but observations will be facilitated by a sketch as in Fig. 3111. With altitude and azimuth taken from the star finder described in §3108, the sextant may be set and directed toward a star where it is hardly visible. Also remember that for Polaris one need only set the sextant to the D.R. latitude and turn to true north to find that most useful but sometimes elusive star.

3112. A star fix found at morning or evening twilight is an important event in a day's work of a navigator, because the intersecting lines of position usually provide a good position from which to carry forward the D.R. The method of obtaining an LOP from a star sight is essentially the same as for bodies in the solar system, the only differences being the method of computing G.H.A. (§2308) and the corrections applied to the sextant altitude (§1909). Fig. 3112a shows the plot of the following example in which the sights were computed by H.O. 211 and the lines are plotted from the D.R. position. In Fig. 3112b, the same sights are plotted from the A.P. used in the H.O. 214 solutions. The student should remember that any celestial line of position is plotted from the latitude and longitude used in the solution of *that* sight by whatever method.

Example: En route Los Angeles for Honolulu.

On June 1, about 2010 in D.R. 33° 30′ N, 124° 55′ W, the navigator observed Polaris, Arcturus, and Regulus for a Fix. Solution of the Polaris sight gave Lat. 33° 27′.0 N. Solution of the stars by H.O. 211 and H.O. 214 gave the following results

	By H.O. 211			By H.O. 214	
	Arcturus	Regulus		Arcturus	Regulus
D.R. Lat.	33° 30′ N	33° 30′ N	A.L.	34° 00′.0 N	34° 00′.0 N
D.R. Long.	124° 55′ W	124° 55′ W	A.λ	125° 21′.4 W	124° 34′.3 W
a	1′.3 T	1′.2 T		34′.0 T	28′.7 T
Zn	115°.3	246°.3		115°.4	245°.8

Req: Plot and record the 2010 Fix.
Ans: Fix at 2010, 33° 27′.0 N, 124° 55′ W.

The three sights as worked by H.O. 211 are plotted from the D.R. position for a fix in Fig. 3112a. In Fig. 3112b the same sights are plotted from assumed positions with the H.O. 214 solutions. The sights were taken within an interval of about 3 minutes, and the assumption of simultaneous observation is permissible unless high speeds be involved. The intersection of the various LOP at a point may rarely occur in practice, but it serves to illustrate the theory of a perfect fix. It is desirable to use stars approximately 120° apart in azimuth which tends to minimize the effect of any constant error in the observations.

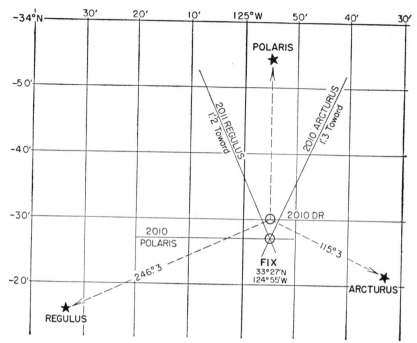

FIG. 3112a. FIX BY H.O. 211.

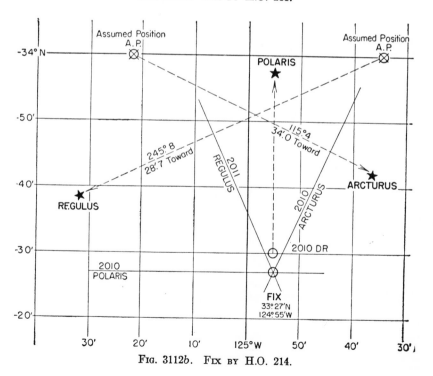

FIG. 3112b. FIX BY H.O. 214.

Note that the same fix is obtained despite the much longer altitude intercepts (*a*) obtained in the H.O. 214 solution. Query: Would shorter intercepts have resulted from using different assumed longitudes? A different assumed latitude? If an error in azimuth exists, is the accuracy of the fix affected more by the length of the intercept or by the length of the LOP from the azimuth line to the fix?

The triangle or "cocked hat," as in Fig. 3113*a*, is the usual result of three stars for a fix. Navigators commonly use the center of the triangle as the position of the fix and should continue to do so. Under certain conditions this is not the most likely position, but it is difficult to recognize when such conditions exist.

3113. Plotting a round of stars observed from a fast ship or from an airplane for a fix requires that all but one of the LOP be advanced, or moved back, to the time of the fix which is ordinarily that of the last sight. As pointed out in §1605 in the chapter on Sumner Lines, the easiest way to do this is to advance the points used as assumed positions. In practice, this process takes two forms:

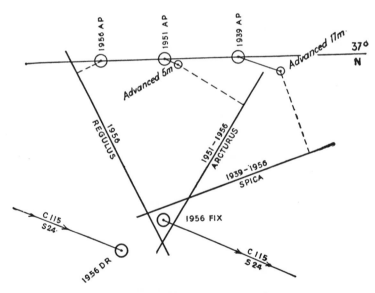

Fig. 3113*a*. From Advanced A.P.

(1) *Different assumed positions for each sight,* which must be used with H.O. 214 or any one of a dozen other methods, require that each of the earlier A.P. be advanced to the time of the last sight, assuming this to be the time of the fix. Fig. 3113*a* illustrates such a situation with the ship on C 115° true, S 24. The 1939 A.P. was advanced 17 minutes, 6.8

miles 115°, to 1956, and the Spica line was plotted from the A.P. so advanced. Similarly the 1951 A.P. was advanced 5 minutes to 1956, and the Arcturus line was plotted therefrom. The 1956 A.P. was not advanced, as Regulus, the last sight of the round, was observed at 1956, which was the time selected for the fix.

(2) *A single D.R. position as the assumed position for all sights* is the simplest plan when working with H.O. 211. Other than in exceptional cases, the time selected for the fix is that of the last sight. This also is the time when the navigator requires his D.R. for comparison with the fix. Thus, after taking a round of sights, to be computed from D.R. positions, it is customary to determine the D.R. at time of last sight and to use that D.R. as an assumed position from which all the sights are computed.

A case of the above procedure is shown in Fig. 3113*b*, ship on C 240° true, S 30. The Caph sight, last of the three, was taken at 0428, the D.R. at that time was determined and so labeled. With this point as an assumed position, the sight was computed and plotted from the 0428 D.R. as the 0428 Caph line. Next consider the Alpheratz sight, first of the round, and for the moment, label the 0428 D.R. as (A). The sight is then computed from (A) and the 0428 Alpheratz line, if plotted, would appear as that plotted by dotted lines in the sketch. But what is wanted for the fix at 0428 is the 0409-0428 line, and for that purpose the 0409

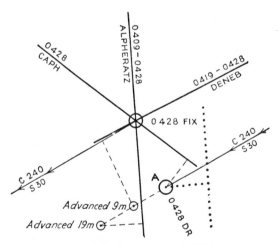

FIG. 3113*b*. FROM ADVANCED D.R.

line must be dragged ahead to 0428. The easiest way to do this is to advance (A) 19 minutes, 9.5 miles on C 240°, and from this advanced position plot the 0409-0428 Alpheratz line. Similarly the Deneb 0419 sight was computed from (A), and the 0419-0428 Deneb line was plotted from a point found by advancing (A) 9 minutes.

The student is often confused by the thought of pushing *ahead* the D.R. at the time of the last sight to locate the point from which to plot an earlier sight. Nevertheless, a review of the above will show that it is the easiest way, and the method should be mastered by plotting all of the problems at the close of this chapter.

3114. Problems in three star fixes as given below provide exercises in computing lines of position and in plotting this type of work. The first four problems are worked from a D.R. position by H.O. 211 as well as an A.P. position by H.O. 214. The last four have been worked only from an A.P. by H.O. 214.

P 1-31. En route Honolulu to San Diego.
June 2, about 1950 the navigator observed three stars in rapid succession as follows:

	(a) Regulus	(b) Arcturus	(c) Polaris
W.T.	19h 48m 35s	19h 49m 07s	19h 50m 17s
Hs	49° 44′.8	64° 54′.9	32° 09′.9

D.R. at 1950, 32° 50′ N, 134° 02′ W. W.E. on Z.T. 1m 27s slow, I.C. − 1′.5, Ht. Eye 35 ft.
Req: Solve (a) and (b) for LOP.

	(a) Regulus	(b) Arcturus
Ans:	A.P. 33° N, 134° 03′.9 W	33° N, 134° 18′.4 W
	a 5′.7 T	10′.8 T
	Zn 247°.8	116°.2

(c) Construct small plotting sheet, center lines 33° N, 134° W; use large scale. Plot results of (a) and (b) assuming sights taken simultaneously. Record longitude.
Ans: Longitude 134° 08′.0 W.

(d) Solve Polaris sight for latitude using longitude found in (c).
Ans: Lat. 32° 51′.8 N.

(e) Plot Polaris line and record fix.
Ans: 1950 Fix, 32° 52′.3 N, 134° 08′.5 W.

P 2-31. From north and west of Midway.
July 2, evening twilight, navigator observed three stars for a Fix:

	(a) Spica	(b) Dubhe	(c) Vega
W.T.	19h 39m 58s	19h 49m 58s	20h 09m 13s
Hs	40° 37′.1	49° 46′ 9	45° 37′.4

D.R. at 2010, time of last sight, 36° 42′ N, 179° 13′.0 E. Course 105° true, S 24.
W.E. on Z.T. 1m 03s slow, I.C. + 2′.5, Ht. Eye 27 ft.
Req: Solve all sights for LOP.

	(a) Spica	(b) Dubhe	(c) Vega
Ans: A.P.	37° N, 179° 42′.1 E	37° N, 178° 45′.2 E	37° N, 179° 28′.2 E
a	19′.0 T	24′.3 A	9′.2 A
Zn	198°.1	325°.3	069°.9

(d) Construct small plotting sheet, center lines 37° N, 179° E; use small scale. Plot problem without drawing 1941 and 1951 lines. Show only advanced Spica and Dubhe lines and 2010 Vega line. Plot and record 2010 Fix.
Ans: Fix at 2010, 36° 45′.0 N, 179° 23′.4 E.

P 3-31. Ship in Mid-North Atlantic.
July 2, shortly after 0400 Zone + 3 time, navigator observed a round of stars for a Fix:

	(a) Mirfak	(b) Fomalhaut	(c) Vega
W.T.	4h 07m 25s	4h 18m 24s	4h 27m 20s
Hs	41° 08′.6	25° 20′.2	34° 35′.2

D.R. at 0430, time of last sight, 34° 50′ N, 42° 27′ W. Course 140° true, S 30.
W.E. on Z.T. 2m 50s slow, I.C. + 1′.0, Ht. Eye 47 ft.
Req: Solve all sights for LOP.

		(a) Mirfak	(b) Fomalhaut	(c) Vega
Ans:	A.P.	35° N, 41° 58′.3 W	35° N, 42° 14′.6 W	35° N, 42° 28′.6 W
	a	22′.8 A	7′.2 T	4′.3 A
	Zn	051°.7	183°.8	296°.2

(d) Construct small plotting sheet, center lines 35° N, 42° W; use large scale. Plot problem without drawing 0410 and 0421 lines. Show only 0410-0430, 0421-0430, and 0430 lines, and record 0430 Fix.
Ans: Fix at 0430, 34° 51′.0 N, 42° 26′.8 W.

P 4-31. From east of Yokohama.
June 4, about 4 A.M., navigator observed three stars for a Fix.

	(a) Rasalhague	(b) Fomalhaut	(c) Schedar
W.T.	4h 12m 30s	4h 22m 25s	4h 32m 22s
Hs	44° 37′.1	17° 16′.7	46° 21′.5

D.R. at 0431, time of last sight, 35° 27′ N, 142° 20′ E. Course 250° true, S 30.
W.E. on (− 10) Z.T. 1m 15s fast, I.C. + 1′.4, Ht. Eye 26 ft.
Req: Solve all sights for LOP.

		(a) Rasalhague	(b) Fomalhaut	(c) Schedar
Ans:	A.P.	35° N, 142° 47′.3 E	35° N, 141° 54′.1 E	35° N, 142° 05′.9 E
	a	6′.8 T	7′.3 A	23′.7 T
	Zn	251°.6	148°.7	042°.2
ΔL correction		(−) 8′.5	(−) 23′.0	(+) 20′.0

(d) Construct plotting sheet, center lines 35° N, 142° E; use small scale. Advance Rasalhague and Fomalhaut lines to 0431, plot Schedar line, and record 0431 Fix.
Ans: Fix at 0431, 35° 22′.2 N, 142° 17′.7 E.

(e) Solve all sights from 0431 D.R. using H.O. 214 with Δd, Δt, and ΔL, or using H.O. 211 interpolating for Hc. (See §2904.)
Ans: (H.O. 211 solutions in parentheses)

	(a) Rasalhague		(b) Fomalhaut		(c) Schedar	
a	6′.0 A	(5′.8 A)	4′.5 T	(4′.6 T)	4′.1 A	(4′.1 A)
Zn	251°.6	(250°.9)	148°.7	(149°.0)	042°.2	(042°.8)

(f) Construct plotting sheet as before. Plot and record 0431 Fix.
Ans: 0431 Fix, 35° 22'.2 N, 142° 17'.7 E.

P 5-31. Ship south of the Azores, west of Madeira.
Mar. 7, about 6:45 p.m., navigator took a round of sights and obtained the following data:

	(a) Alphard	(b) Menkar	(c) Kochab
W.T.	18h 43m 00s	18h 51m 43s	19h 01m 23s
Hs	19° 28'.6	41° 08'.3	24° 42'.5

D.R. at 1900, time of the last sight, 36° 20' N, 32° 10' W. Course 054° true, S 36.
W.E. on Z.T. 1m 23s fast, I.C. — 1'.0, Ht. Eye 38 ft.
Req: Solve sights for LOP.

	(a) Alphard	(b) Menkar	(c) Kochab
Ans: A.P.	36° N, 32° 02'.0 W	36° N, 32° 34'.9 W	36° N, 32° 24'.9 W
a	22'.7 A	12'.5 A	17'.7 T
Zn	117°.0	238°.5	012°.0
ΔL correction	(—) 9'.1	(—) 10'.4	(+) 19'.6

(d) Construct small plotting sheet, center lines 36° N, 32° W; use large scale.
Plot LOP's and record 1900 Fix.
Ans: Fix at 1900, 36° 15'.0 N, 32° 17'.6 W.

(e) Solve all sights from 1900 D.R. using H.O. 214 with Δd, Δt, and ΔL, or H.O.
211 interpolating for Hc. (See §2904.)
Ans: (H.O. 211 solutions in parentheses)

	(a) Alphard		(b) Menkar		(c) Kochab	
a	7'.8 A	(7'.9 A)	15'.1 T	(15'.1 T)	4'.5 A	(4'.6 A)
Zn	117°.0	(117°.0)	238°.5	(238°.6)	012°.0	(012°.2)

(f) Construct plotting sheet as before. Plot and record 1900 Fix.
Ans: 1900 Fix, 36° 15'.0 N, 32° 17'.6 W.

P 6-31. Between Madeira and northwest coast of Africa.
Sept. 29, shortly after 0500, Zone + 1, navigator observed three stars for a
Fix:

	(a) Aldebaran	(b) Pollux	(c) Sirius
W.T.	5h 11m 00s	5h 21m 15s	5h 31m 20s
Hs	67° 21'.9	65° 34'.6	39° 14'.4

D.R. at 0531, time of last sight, 33° 13' N, 14° 51'.5 W. Course 237° true, S 30.
W.E. on Z.T. 48s fast, I.C. + 1'.2, Ht. Eye 20 ft.
Req: Solve sights for LOP.

	(a) Aldebaran	(b) Pollux	(c) Sirius
Ans: A.P.	33° N, 14° 36'.5 W	33° N, 14° 51'.8 W	33° N, 15° 17'.4 W
a	7'.3 A	2'.7 T	4'.0 A
Zn	227°.0	094°.3	166°.3

(d) Construct small plotting sheet, center lines 33° N, 15° W; use large scale.
Plot the LOP's, advancing the 0510 and 0520 A.P.'s. Record 0531 Fix.
Ans: Fix at 0531, 33° 09'.3 N, 14° 52'.0 W.

P 7-31. From about 13° west of San Francisco.
July 2, navigator took a round of sights and obtained the following data:

	(a) Polaris	(b) Altair	(c) Diphda
W.T.	3h 59m 45s	4h 09m 55s	4h 19m 50s
Hs	38° 27'.4	40° 00'.0	29° 13'.2

D.R. at 0420, time of last sight, 37° 55' N, 135° 08' W. Course 308° true, S 30.
W.E. on Z.T. 15s slow, I.C. + 1'.6, Ht. Eye 40 ft.
Req: Solve Polaris sight for Lat. Solve Altair and Deneb sights for LOP.

	(a) Polaris		(b) Altair	(c) Diphda
Ans:	Lat. at 0400	A.P.	38° N, 135° 22'.6 W	38° N, 134° 40'.6 W
	37° 47'.4 N	a	14'.0 A	0'.0
		Zn	246°.3	152°.6

(d) Construct small plotting sheet, center lines 38° N, 135° W; use large scale.
Plot 0400 latitude by Polaris and advance the parallel to 0420. Advance the 0410
A.P. and plot Altair line. Plot Diphda line and record 0420 Fix.
Ans: Fix at 0420, 37° 51'.3 N, 135° 02'.2 W.

P 8-31. July 30, south of Easter Island, Course 187°, speed 18. About 1800,
the navigator observed four stars for a fix; W.E. on Z.T. 1m 06s fast, I.C. − 2'.0,
Ht. Eye 30 ft., temperature 5° C, pressure 1033 mb., 1800 D.R. 37° 07' S, 108° 12' W:

	(a) Canopus	(b) Antares	(c) Regulus	(d) Achernar
W.T.	17s 41m 28s	17h 51m 12s	17h 52m 34s	18h 11m 17s
Hs	16° 26'.8	59° 13'.1	14° 31'.1	5° 37'.5

Req: Solve sights for LOP, correcting for temperature and pressure. Note: On
Achernar solution, determine sign of Δd from declination 59° 00'.

		(a) Canopus	(b) Antares
Ans:	A.P.	37° S, 108° 29'.6 W	37° S, 107° 53'.4 W
	a	5'.3 A	17'.1 A
	Zn	215°.4	079°.8

		(c) Regulus	(d) Achernar
	A.P.	37° S, 108° 25'.7 W	37° S, 108° 38'.5 W
	a	15'.9 A	18'.6 T
	Zn	297°.8	173°.0

(e) Construct small plotting sheet for *south* latitude, center lines 37° S, 108° W;
use scale for 2° of latitude. Advance or retire A.P.'s for all sights to 1800, plot and
record 1800 Fix.
Ans: Fix at 1800, 37° 11'.3 S, 108° 12'.0 W.

SPECIAL STAR CHARTS

Select the chart nearest to the L.H.A. ♈ of the intended date and time of observation as in §3106.

Measure azimuth on the compass rose.
Measure altitude on the altitude scale.

Each chart is correct for the indicated time and date (any year) at latitude 40° N. Approximate altitudes and azimuths at other latitudes between about 30° N and 50° N can be estimated by picturing the zenith (Z) at the new latitude.

NAVIGATIONAL STARS
For Latitude
40° North

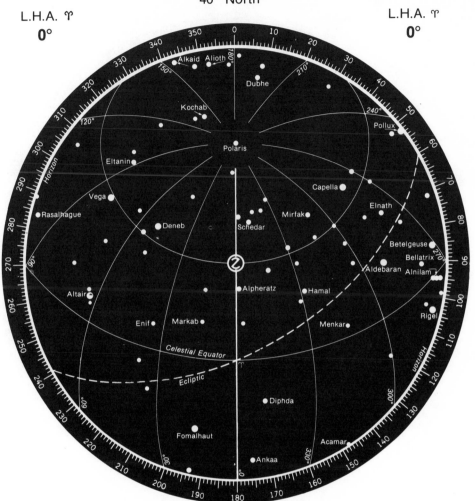

L.H.A. ♈
0°

L.H.A. ♈
0°

MERIDIANS INDICATE SIDEREAL HOUR ANGLE
Read Azimuth from Compass Rose
Read Altitude from Scale

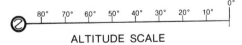

ALTITUDE SCALE

Local Mean Times of charted positions

Jan.	Feb.	Mar.	Apr.	May	June	July	Aug.	Sept.	Oct.	Nov.	Dec.
16h	14h	12h	10h	8h	6h	4h	2h	0h	22h	20h	18h

© Donald McClench 1978.   377

NAVIGATIONAL STARS
For Latitude
40° North

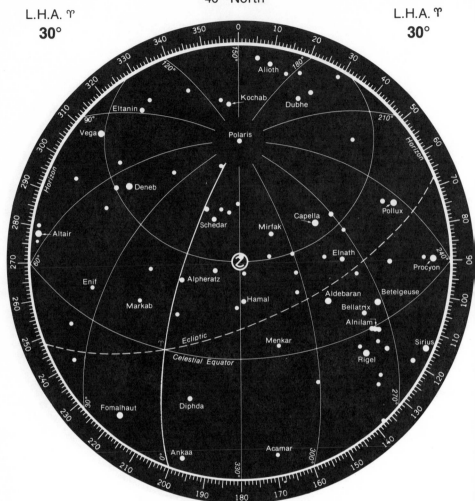

L.H.A. ♈
30°

L.H.A. ♈
30°

MERIDIANS INDICATE SIDEREAL HOUR ANGLE
Read Azimuth from Compass Rose
Read Altitude from Scale

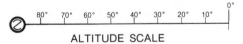

ALTITUDE SCALE

Local Mean Times of charted positions

Jan.	Feb.	Mar.	Apr.	May	June	July	Aug.	Sept.	Oct.	Nov.	Dec.
18h	16h	14h	12h	10h	8h	6h	4h	2h	0h	22h	20h

378

NAVIGATIONAL STARS
For Latitude
40° North

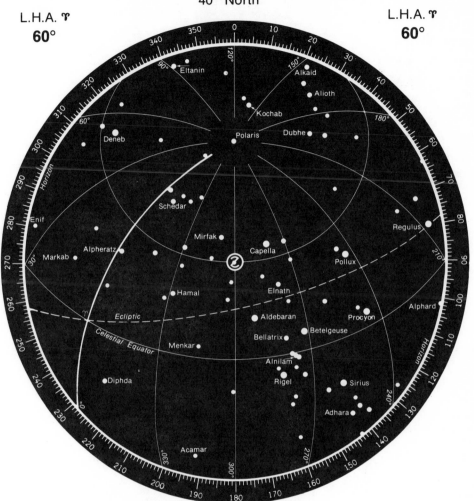

MERIDIANS INDICATE SIDEREAL HOUR ANGLE
Read Azimuth from Compass Rose
Read Altitude from Scale

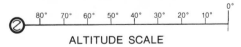

80° 70° 60° 50° 40° 30° 20° 10° 0°

ALTITUDE SCALE

Local Mean Times of charted positions

Jan.	Feb.	Mar.	Apr.	May	June	July	Aug.	Sept.	Oct.	Nov.	Dec.
20h	18h	16h	14h	12h	10h	8h	6h	4h	2h	0h	22h

© Donald McClench 1978.

379

NAVIGATIONAL STARS
For Latitude
40° North

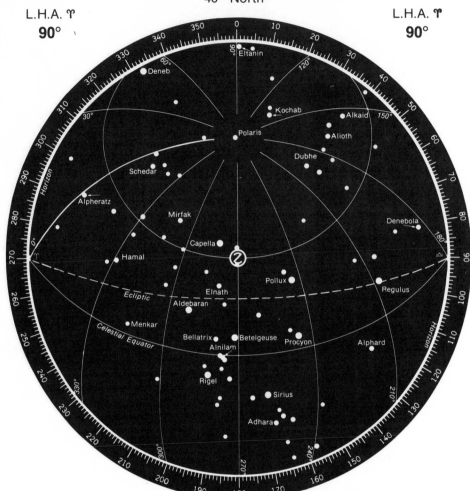

L.H.A. ♈
90°

L.H.A. ♈
90°

MERIDIANS INDICATE SIDEREAL HOUR ANGLE
Read Azimuth from Compass Rose
Read Altitude from Scale

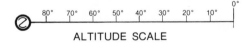

| | 80° | 70° | 60° | 50° | 40° | 30° | 20° | 10° | 0° |

ALTITUDE SCALE

Local Mean Times of charted positions

Jan.	Feb.	Mar.	Apr.	May	June	July	Aug.	Sept.	Oct.	Nov.	Dec.
22h	20h	18h	16h	14h	12h	10h	8h	6h	4h	2h	0h

© Donald McClench 1978.

NAVIGATIONAL STARS
For Latitude
40° North

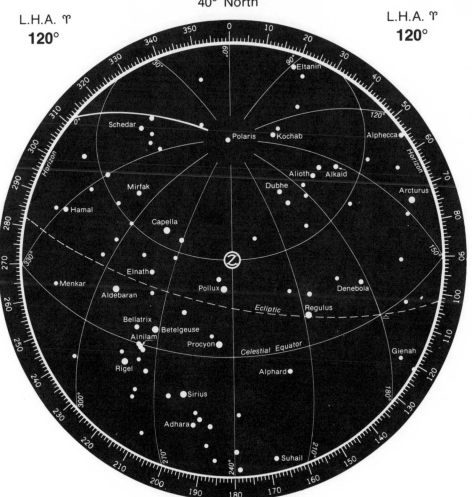

L.H.A. ♈
120°

L.H.A. ♈
120°

MERIDIANS INDICATE SIDEREAL HOUR ANGLE
Read Azimuth from Compass Rose
Read Altitude from Scale

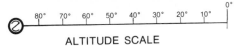

0°
80° 70° 60° 50° 40° 30° 20° 10°
ALTITUDE SCALE

Local Mean Times of charted positions

Jan.	Feb.	Mar.	Apr.	May	June	July	Aug.	Sept.	Oct.	Nov.	Dec.
0h	22h	20h	18h	16h	14h	12h	10h	8h	6h	4h	2h

© Donald McClench 1978.

381

NAVIGATIONAL STARS

For Latitude
40° North

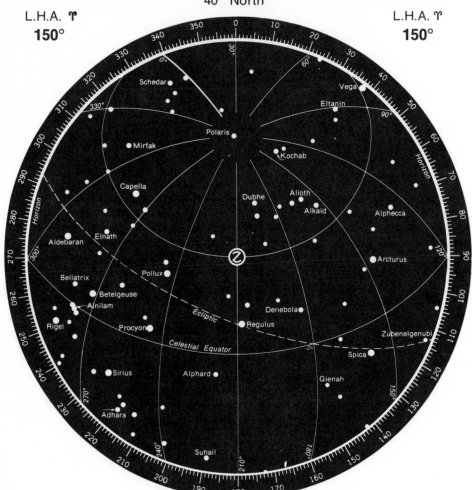

L.H.A. ♈
150°

L.H.A. ♈
150°

Schedar

Vega

Eltanin

Mirfak

Polaris

Kochab

Capella

Dubhe

Alioth

Alkaid

Alphecca

Elnath

Aldebaran

Bellatrix

Pollux

Arcturus

Betelgeuse

Anilam

Denebola

Rigel

Procyon

Regulus

Zubenelgenubi

Ecliptic

Celestial Equator

Spica

Sirius

Alphard

Gienah

Adhara

Suhail

Horizon

MERIDIANS INDICATE SIDEREAL HOUR ANGLE
Read Azimuth from Compass Rose
Read Altitude from Scale

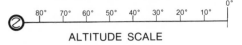

| 80° | 70° | 60° | 50° | 40° | 30° | 20° | 10° | 0° |

ALTITUDE SCALE

Local Mean Times of charted positions

Jan.	Feb.	Mar.	Apr.	May	June	July	Aug.	Sept.	Oct.	Nov.	Dec.
2h	0h	22h	20h	18h	16h	14h	12h	10h	8h	6h	4h

© Donald McClench 1978.

NAVIGATIONAL STARS
For Latitude
40° North

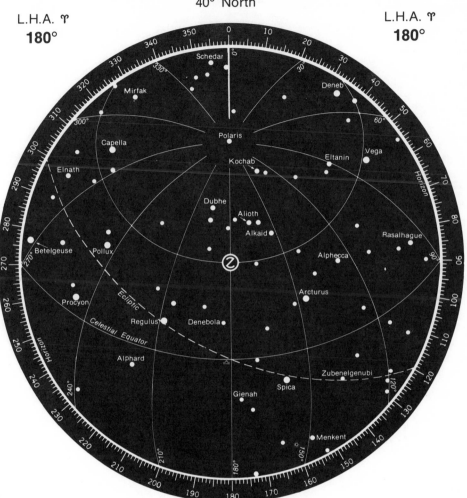

L.H.A. ♈
180°

L.H.A. ♈
180°

Schedar

Deneb

Mirfak

Polaris

Capella

Kochab

Eltanin

Vega

Elnath

Dubhe

Alioth

Betelgeuse

Pollux

Alkaid

Rasalhague

Ecliptic

Alphecca

Procyon

Arcturus

Celestial Equator

Regulus

Denebola

Alphard

Zubenelgenubi

Spica

Gienah

Menkent

Horizon

MERIDIANS INDICATE SIDEREAL HOUR ANGLE
Read Azimuth from Compass Rose
Read Altitude from Scale

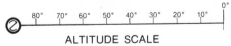

0°
80° 70° 60° 50° 40° 30° 20° 10°

ALTITUDE SCALE

Local Mean Times of charted positions

Jan.	Feb.	Mar.	Apr.	May	June	July	Aug.	Sept.	Oct.	Nov.	Dec.
4h	2h	0h	22h	20h	18h	16h	14h	12h	10h	8h	6h

ⓒ Donald McClench 1978.

383

NAVIGATIONAL STARS
For Latitude
40° North

L.H.A. ♈
210°

L.H.A. ♈
210°

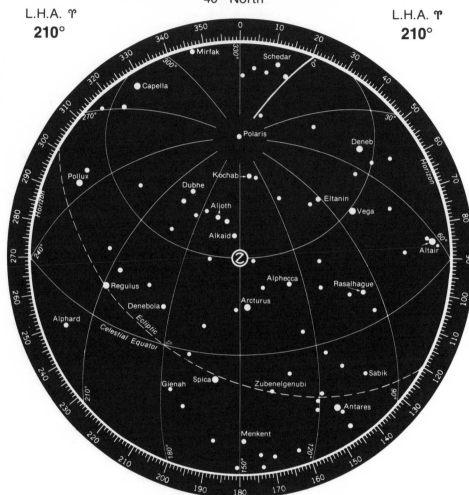

MERIDIANS INDICATE SIDEREAL HOUR ANGLE
Read Azimuth from Compass Rose
Read Altitude from Scale

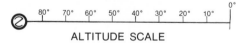

| 80° | 70° | 60° | 50° | 40° | 30° | 20° | 10° | 0° |

ALTITUDE SCALE

Local Mean Times of charted positions

Jan.	Feb.	Mar.	Apr.	May	June	July	Aug.	Sept.	Oct.	Nov.	Dec.
6h	4h	2h	0h	22h	20h	18h	16h	14h	12h	10h	8h

© Donald McClench 1978.

384

NAVIGATIONAL STARS
For Latitude
40° North

L.H.A. ♈
240°

L.H.A. ♈
240°

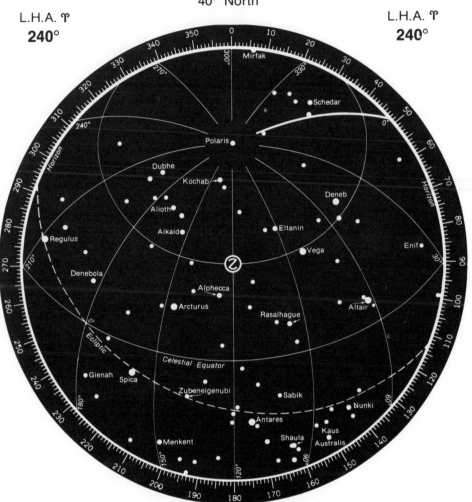

MERIDIANS INDICATE SIDEREAL HOUR ANGLE
Read Azimuth from Compass Rose
Read Altitude from Scale

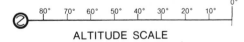

ALTITUDE SCALE

Local Mean Times of charted positions

Jan.	Feb.	Mar.	Apr.	May	June	July	Aug.	Sept.	Oct.	Nov.	Dec.
8h	6h	4h	2h	0h	22h	20h	18h	16h	14h	12h	10h

385

NAVIGATIONAL STARS
For Latitude
40° North

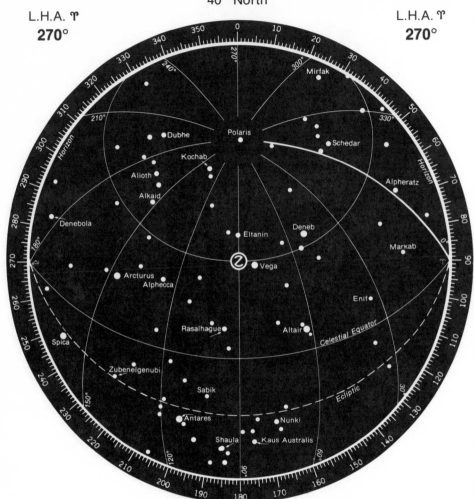

MERIDIANS INDICATE SIDEREAL HOUR ANGLE
Read Azimuth from Compass Rose
Read Altitude from Scale

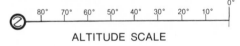

| | 80° | 70° | 60° | 50° | 40° | 30° | 20° | 10° | 0° |

ALTITUDE SCALE

Local Mean Times of charted positions

Jan.	Feb.	Mar.	Apr.	May	June	July	Aug.	Sept.	Oct.	Nov.	Dec.
10h	8h	6h	4h	2h	0h	22h	20h	18h	16h	14h	12h

© Donald McClench 1978.

NAVIGATIONAL STARS
For Latitude
40° North

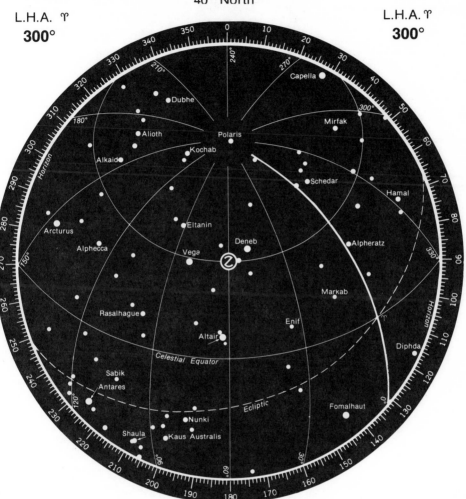

L.H.A. ♈
300°

L.H.A. ♈
300°

MERIDIANS INDICATE SIDEREAL HOUR ANGLE
Read Azimuth from Compass Rose
Read Altitude from Scale

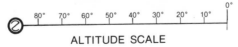

80°   70°   60°   50°   40°   30°   20°   10°   0°

ALTITUDE SCALE

Local Mean Times of charted positions

Jan.	Feb.	Mar.	Apr.	May	June	July	Aug.	Sept.	Oct.	Nov.	Dec.
12h	10h	8h	6h	4h	2h	0h	22h	20h	18h	16h	14h

387

NAVIGATIONAL STARS
For Latitude
40° North

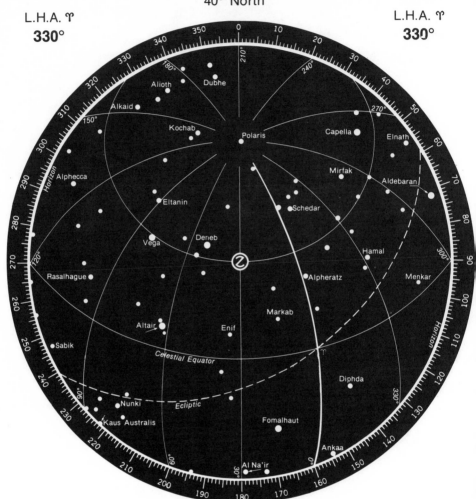

MERIDIANS INDICATE SIDEREAL HOUR ANGLE
Read Azimuth from Compass Rose
Read Altitude from Scale

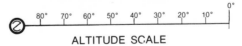

ALTITUDE SCALE

Local Mean Times of charted positions

Jan.	Feb.	Mar.	Apr.	May	June	July	Aug.	Sept.	Oct.	Nov.	Dec.
14h	12h	10h	8h	6h	4h	2h	0h	22h	20h	18h	16h

© Donald McClench 1978.

388

PLANETS, 1975

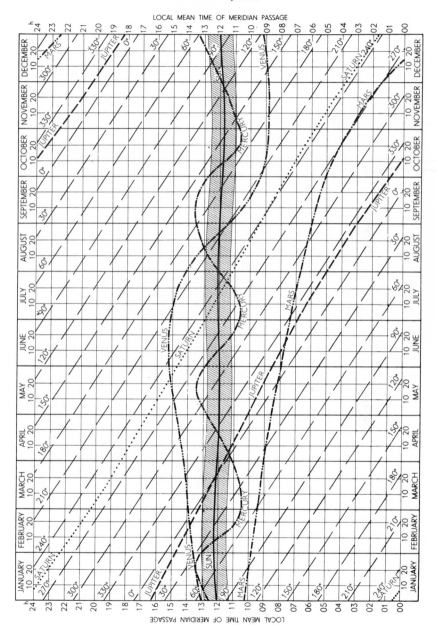

FIG. 3201. NAUTICAL ALMÁNAC DIAGRAM SHOWING SHA AND LMT OF LOCAL TRANSIT OF SUN
AND PLANETS

32. PLANETS AND THE MOON

THE brilliant planets are easy to observe and often afford the best lines of position to cross with star lines. The old prejudice against use of the moon, probably because of lack of convenient and accurate tabular data, is today unwarranted. It requires no identification, is easy to observe, and is often visible when the resulting line of position may be crossed with the sun for a fix. Use of both the moon and Venus in daytime is strongly recommended by Captain Dutton. With the simplified methods of obtaining data from both *Air* and *Nautical Almanacs* of today, moon and planet sights are worked practically like sun or star sights and, for his own convenience, the navigator should become accustomed to their use.

3201. Planets and planet sights. Stars twinkle; a planet shines with a steady light and often shows a perceptible disk. Jupiter, Venus, and Mars are brighter than any star, and are not easily forgotten. Saturn may be mistaken for a star.

All of the planets wander about and have no fixed position on a star chart, but, unlike the moon, may be seen for days or months on end in about the same position. Thus an experienced navigator, observing the heavens night after night, knows where he may find these wanderers. Venus changes its position among the stars most rapidly but never appears more than 47° from the sun. Jupiter and Saturn change their relative position less rapidly than Venus and Mars, and may be seen in almost the same position month after month.

Planet sights are generally taken at twilight in the same ways that stars are observed. Often they are visible before many stars are out while the horizon is a sharp line. Venus, and sometimes Jupiter, may be observed in daytime. The altitude of a planet is corrected as is that of a star. Given its declination and G.H.A. a planet sight may be worked for line of position by whatever method the navigator prefers for sun or stars, and the resulting LOP are plotted and used as are other Sumner Lines. Thus the navigator skilled with the stars may use the planets with equal facility. The G.H.A. and declination of the four planets, Venus,

Mars, Jupiter and Saturn are tabulated for each hour of the day in the *Nautical Almanac,* as is the Sun. The additional correction for minutes is very easy to determine with the correction code at the bottom of both G.H.A. column and declination column, the use of which was explained in §2306.

3202. Declination of planets is tabulated in the *Nautical Almanac* for every hour of G.M.T. each day of the year. The code d-value at the bottom of the declination column for each 3-day page represents the average hourly change in declination for the 3-day period. Exact declination for the minutes of a sight between the hourly tabulations, can be obtained by interpolating between the hourly listings. In order to obtain the exact declination at the time of sight without interpolating, the navigator enters the minute correction pages for the minutes of the sight and will find the correction for declination opposite the given "d" figure. *If the declination column is increasing in value, this correction is to be added; if it is decreasing in value, this correction should be subtracted.*

MAY 23

G.M.T. d h	ARIES G.H.A.	VENUS −3·6 G.H.A.	Dec.	MARS +0·7 G.H.A.	Dec.	MOON G.H.A.	v	Dec.	d	H.P.	Name	S.H.A.	Dec.
23 00	240 06·1	221 19·0 N 5 48·9		249 28·7 S 6 06·8		128 13·6	9·5	N16 43·5	5·4	57·1	Alphecca	126 45·7	N 26 51·3
01	255 08·5	236 18·8	49·9	264 29·4	06·1	142 42·1	9·5	16 38·1	5·6	57·1	Alpheratz	358 26·5	N 28 51·5
02	270 11·0	251 18·6	50·9	279 30·2	05·4	157 10·6	9·6	16 32·5	5·6	57·1	Altair	62 48·4	N 8 45·5
03	285 13·5	266 18·4 ·· 52·0		294 31·0 ·· 04·7		171 39·2	9·5	16 26·9	5·8	57·2	Ankaa	353 56·8	S 42 31·7
04	300 15·9	281 18·2	53·0	309 31·7	04·0	186 07·7	9·6	16 21·1	5·8	57·2	Antares	113 16·7	S 26 20·4
05	315 18·4	296 18·0	54·0	324 32·5	03·3	200 36·3	9·6	16 15·3	6·0	57·2			
06	330 20·8	311 17·8 N 5 55·0		339 33·3 S 6 02·7		215 04·9	9·6	N16 09·3	6·0	57·2	Arcturus	146 33·2	N 19 23·9
07	345 23·3	326 17·6	56·0	354 34·1	02·0	229 33·5	9·6	16 03·3	6·1	57·3	Atria	108 55·1	S 68 57·1
08	0 25·8	341 17·4	57·0	9 34·8	01·3	244 02·1	9·6	15 57·2	6·2	57·3	Canopus	264 15·0	S 52 40·7
F 09	15 28·2	356 17·2 ·· 58·0		24 35·6	6 00·6	258 30·7	9·6	15 51·0	6·3	57·3	Capella	281 36·1	N 45 57·4
R 10	30 30·7	11 17·0 5 59·0		39 36·4 ·5 59·9		272 59·3	9·6	15 44·7	6·4	57·3	Deneb	49 59·5	N 45 07·7
I 11	45 33·2	26 16·8 6 00·1		54 37·1	59·2	287 27·9	9·6	15 38·3	6·5	57·3	Pollux	244 18·5	N 28 07·6
D 12	60 35·6	41 16·6 N 6 01·1		69 37·9 S ·5 58·6		301 56·5	9·7	N15 31·8	6·6	57·4	Procyon	245 43·3	N 5 19·8
A 13	75 38·1	56 16·4	02·1	84 38·7	57·9	316 25·2	9·6	15 25·2	6·7	57·4	Rasalhague	96 44·6	N 12 35·4
Y 14	90 40·6	71 16·2	03·1	99 39·5	57·2	330 53·8	9·7	15 18·5	6·7	57·4	Regulus	208 27·5	N 12 10·2
15	105 43·0	86 16·0 ·· 04·1		114 40·2 ·· 56·5		345 22·5	9·7	15 11·8	6·9	57·4	Rigel	281 52·2	S 8 15·1
16	120 45·5	101 15·8	05·1	129 41·0	55·8	359 51·2	9·7	15 04·9	6·9	57·5	Spica	159 14·6	S 10 56·8
17	135 47·9	116 15·6	06·1	144 41·8	55·1	14 19·9	9·7	14 58·0	7·0	57·5	Suhail	223 23·0	S 43 16·2
18	150 50·4	131 15·4 N 6 07·1		159 42·5 S 5 54·5		28 48·6	9·7	N14 51·0	7·1	57·5	Vega	81 06·6	N 38 44·6
19	165 52·9	146 15·2	08·1	174 43·3	53·8	43 17·3	9·8	14 43·9	7·2	57·5	Zuben'ubi	137 50·9	S 15 52·2
20	180 55·3	161 15·0	09·2	189 44·1	53·1	57 46·1	9·7	14 36·7	7·3	57·5		S.H.A.	Mer. Pass.
21	195 57·8	176 14·8 ··· 10·2		204 44·9 ·· 52·4		72 14·8	9·8	14 29·4	7·4	57·6	Venus	341 12·9	9 15
22	211 00·3	191 14·6	11·2	219 45·6	51·7	86 43·6	9·7	14 22·0	7·4	57·6	Mars	9 22·6	7 22
23	226 02·7	206 14·4	12·2	234 46·4	51·0	101 12·3	9·8	14 14·6	7·6	57·6	Jupiter	158 19·9	21 22
Mer. Pass. 7 58·3		v −0·2 d 1·0		v 0·8 d 0·7		S.D. 15·5		15·6		15·8	Saturn	96 29·4	1 33

Fig. 3202. Excerpts from Daily Page, Nautical Almanac.

Example: Greenwich date May 23, G.M.T. 19h 41m 25s. Find the declination of Venus using Fig. 3202 and Apx. V.

Decl. at 19h	6° 08'.1 N (increasing) $d + 1.0$
Correction 41m (Apx. V)	+ 0'.7
Declination	6° 08'.8 N

Note: (1) No allowance is made in the correction table for seconds. (2) The d-value, 1.0 is the mean difference between tabulated values.

However, the actual difference between decl. for 19h and 20h is 1'.1. Hence, for most accurate results, the actual difference can be used. Thus,

$$\text{correction} = 41.4/60 \times 1'.1 = 0'.8$$

From the *Air Almanac*, the declination of a planet is taken from the daily sheet without correction.

3203. Planet's G.H.A. is tabulated like the declination for each hour G.M.T. of each day. The additional G.H.A. for minutes and seconds beyond this hourly tabulation is found on the minute page corresponding to time of sight, in the minute correction page section. Follow the Sun-Planets column under the minutes of sight to the seconds of sight, opposite which will be found the additional G.H.A. to be added to the hourly tabulation.

Inasmuch as the apparent speed of planets, because of their different orbits, is sometimes faster or slower than the tabulated speed of the sun, which is 15° per hour, the rate at which the Sun-Planets column is calculated, a small additional correction must be made for this variation. At the bottom of the G.H.A. column for planets is found a v-value which is used to enter the "d or v corr" column of the "Increments and Corrections" table at the back of the almanac (Appendix V of this book). The v correction, taken from the same page as the correction for minutes and seconds, is always to be *added* except occasionally for Venus when, as in Fig. 3202, it is marked − .

Example: Find G.H.A. for Mars and Venus for G.M.T. 10h 30m 18s using Fig. 3202.

	Mars	Venus
G.H.A. at 10h	39° 36'.4 $v + 0.8$	11° 17'.0 $v - 0.2$
Correction 30m 18s	7° 34'.5	7° 34'.5
v correction	(+) 0'.4	(−) 0'.1
G.H.A. at 10h 30m 18s	47° 11'.3	18° 51'.4

From the *Air Almanac*, take the G.H.A. of a planet from the daily sheet for the given date for the nearest tabulated time preceding sight, and add the necessary correction to exact G.M.T. of sight taken from Interpolation of G.H.A. Table by inspection. The left-hand column is entered with the minutes and seconds and the correction is found in the middle column.

3204. Venus by daylight. Even though Venus may be above the horizon during daylight, it is not always visible because of dust and water particles in the atmosphere which give the sky the milky appearance frequently observed near the north-eastern coast of the United States. A clear, deep-blue sky commonly found in the tropics provides the best background for observing Venus during daylight.

Perhaps the best method of forecasting where it will be located is to

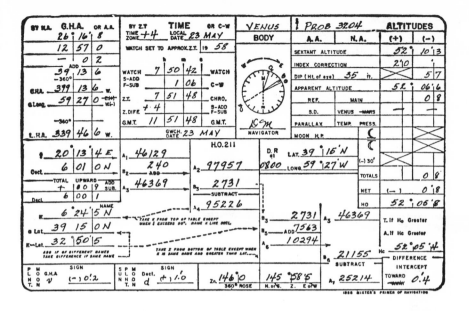

DECLINATION SAME NAME AS LATITUDE

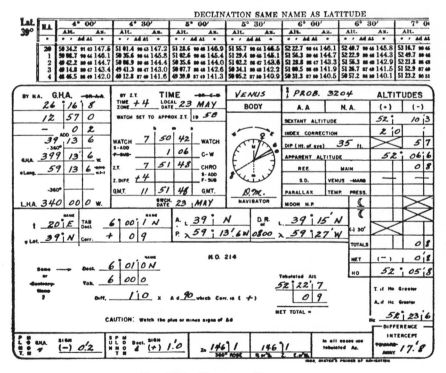

FIG. 3204. VENUS BY DAYLIGHT.

compute its altitude and azimuth for the approximate position and time of sight. This can be done either by H.O. 214 or by H.O. 211. The former method is more rapid and the coordinates found will be for the position assumed in the computation. Interpolation can be made for the D.R. position. The altitude should be within 1° of the true altitude if one's geographic position is known with fair accuracy. If the sextant is set to the computed altitude and pointed in the direction of the computed azimuth, the planet should be within the field of the sextant. A close approximation of the body's altitude and azimuth is also given by H.O. 2102–D (§3108).

Both the *Nautical Almanac* and the *Air Almanac* contain very useful diagrams showing graphically the locations of various celestial bodies in relation to the sun. The diagram for the *Nautical Almanac* for a typical year is shown in Fig. 3201. The horizontal lines indicate the 1st, 10th, and 20th day of each month; the vertical lines show the local mean times when the sun and five of the planets cross the local meridian. The solid, irregular line near 12h represents the sun whose time of crossing the meridian depends upon the equation of time (§2117). The shaded area is a band, 45m wide on each side of the sun; bodies within this band are too close to the sun for successful observation. The diagonal lines indicate S.H.A.

Bodies transiting the meridian earlier than the sun are westward, and those transiting later are eastward, of the sun. Thus on April 1, Venus rises before the sun (morning "star") followed by Saturn and Mercury. Mars and Jupiter follow the sun and will be above the horizon at sunset. Mars is too close to the sun to be seen on this date, but Jupiter (evening "star") is some five hours east of the sun, and in fact, is only about 15° west of the meridian at sunset. The star, Regulus, whose S.H.A. is 208°, will cross the meridian at about L.M.T. 21h 30m on April 1.

The diagram for the *Air Almanac* (Fig. 3209), provides similar information but, in addition, gives the relative positions of the moon, five of the first magnitude stars, and Aries.

Problem, §3204. May 23, shortly before 8:00 A.M. observed Venus from D.R. 39° 15′ N, 59° 27′ W, Hs 52° 10′.3, W.T. 7h 50m 42s, W.E. on Z.T. 1m 06s slow. I.C. + 2′.0, Ht. Eye 35 ft. Solve for LOP. See Fig. 3204 for solutions. Use Fig. 3202 and Apx. V.

3205. Moon sights. The moon may give a needed line of position at any time of day or night. It is easy to observe despite the common notion that it moves too fast to permit observing an accurate altitude. This is not true as the maximum rate of change of the moon's apparent position is less rapid than that of sun, stars, or planets. The young officer who has not used the moon is advised to take the moon when he needs it. Forget to worry about working the sight, which is simple enough with today's Almanacs.

When to observe the moon, provided it is visible at an altitude of 10°

or more, depends on when and whether it will give a line of position that is needed. Often the moon's upper limb must be observed; which limb to observe is determined by its visible shape. Before going further with the details of moon sights, review the causes of the moon's apparent motion as in §1718; also review §1809, §1907 and §1911 which discuss observing the moon's altitude. Working a moon sight for line of position differs from working any sight only in certain details of correcting the altitude and taking out the needed almanac data.

3206. Altitude corrections for the moon, as discussed in §1911 are unique in that the element of parallax is far greater than with other bodies and because both its H.P. and semidiameter vary rapidly.

The moon's altitude correction tables given on the inside back cover and facing page of the *Nautical Almanac* and this book include all of the corrections required. In previous almanacs, part of the altitude corrections were taken from the daily page. Corrections for I.C. and Dip (Ht. Eye) are, of course, always required as are the corrections first given in the 1958 almanac, for abnormal temperature and pressure.

In Tables of Altitude and Azimuth, such as H.O. 214, H.O. 211 and H.O. 208, published by the Oceanographic Office prior to 1950, there is a table to Correct The Observed Altitude of Moon, which is different from the moon altitude correction tables so far discussed. These old-type tables are similar to the Table D, "Correction To Observed Altitude of Moon" appearing in *Nautical Almanacs* issued prior to 1950. This kind of table requires a cumbersome 4-way interpolation. To use such tables it is necessary to obtain the horizontal parallax of the moon and semidiameter. The moon's horizontal parallax (H.P.) is given for each hour on the daily page. The moon's semidiameter (S.D.) is given at the bottom of the daily page successively for each of the three days.

The moon's altitude correction tables in the current almanacs are much easier to use as explained in §1911.

With the *Air Almanac*, altitudes of the moon may be corrected without interpolation. The correction for parallax and the S.D. are taken from the daily sheet for the given date by inspection. The correction for an altitude of the moon above the sea horizon is then the net total of I.C. ($\pm$), Refraction ($-$), Dip ($-$), Parallax ($+$), and S.D. ($\pm$).

3207. Declination of the moon is the same kind of quantity as is that of any other body but it behaves quite differently. Its variation per hour ranges from 0 to more than 16′, in contrast to the sun's maximum hourly difference in declination of about 1′. Furthermore, its variation per hour may change rapidly within a given day. For example, looking in the excerpts for July 2, 1966, the variation in declination between 0h and 1h is increasing 2′.2 for the first hour of the day whereas for the hour between 22h and 23h it is decreasing 1′.0.

Until recently, almanac tables for dealing with the erratic characteristics of the moon have been unsatisfactory. In the *Nautical Almanacs* from 1958 on, the daily tables for the moon are arranged as in Fig. 3202. Note the hourly differences (*d*) printed at the right of the declination column. The exact amount to correct the declination is obtained by entering the minute correction page corresponding to minutes of sight, where the correction will be found opposite the given *d* obtained from the daily page, for the hour of sight. *If the declination column is increasing in value, this correction is to be added; if it is decreasing in value, this correction should be subtracted.*

Example: Greenwich date May 23, observed moon at 5h 50m 47s G.M.T. Find declination at time of sight using Fig. 3202 and Apx. V.

Decl. at 5h	16° 15′.3 N (decreasing) *d* −6.0	
Correction for 51m	− 5′.2	
Decl. at sight	16° 10′.1 N	

In the *Air Almanac*, the moon's declination is listed for each 10m and can be taken without interpolation opposite the next *earlier* G.M.T. entry.

3208. Moon's G.H.A. is always increasing but its rate of increase varies from hour to hour and is always slower than for sun, stars, or planets. The *Nautical Almanac* tabulates the moon's G.H.A. for each hour of G.M.T. on the same line as its declination. To this figure there are two corrections necessary to obtain G.H.A. for exact time of sight.

First Correction. Enter the minute correction pages corresponding to minutes of sight. Follow the Moon column down to the seconds of sight. Opposite seconds of sight will be the first correction to G.H.A. for minutes and seconds over the tabulated hourly figure. Add to hourly figure. Be sure to take the correction out of the Moon column.

Second Correction. At the right of the tabulated G.H.A. for the hour of the sight is a *v* figure. Opposite this *v* figure, on the minute correction page corresponding to minutes of sight, will be found the 2nd correction to G.H.A. of moon. Always add both 1st and 2nd corrections to the tabulated G.H.A. for hour of sight.

The Moon columns on all minute correction pages tabulate a constant minimum speed of the moon at the rate of 14° 19′ per hour. The *v* value represents any increased speed over that rate, each hour, each day of the year.

The two following examples reflect the details of taking moon's G.H.A. from the *Nautical Almanac* using Fig. 3202 for first, and *Excerpts* for second, and all corrections.

Example: Find the G.H.A. of the moon at 6h 41m 47s on May 23 at Greenwich. Use Fig. 3202 and Apx. V.

G.H.A. at 6h	215° 04′.9 *v* + 9.6	
Correction for 41m 47s	9° 58′.2	
v correction	+ 6′.6	
G.H.A. at 6h 41m 47s	225° 09′.7	

PLANET LOCATION DIAGRAM

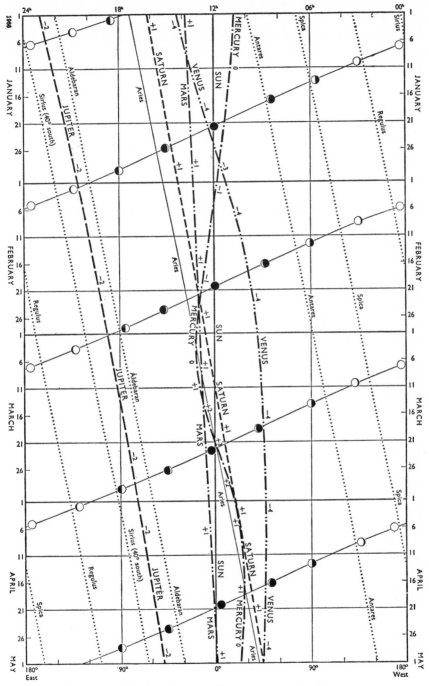

Fig. 3209. Planet Location Diagram from Air Almanac.

Example: Greenwich date March 7, 1966, observed moon at 0h 50m 38s G.M.T. Find G.H.A. at time of sight using Apx. V.

G.H.A. at 0h	356° 15′.6 $v + 8.2$
Correction for 50m 38s	12° 04′.9
v correction	6′.9
	368° 27′.4
Subtract 360°	360° 00′.0
G.H.A. at time of sight	8° 27′.4

From the *Air Almanac,* take moon's G.H.A. from daily sheet for the given date for the preceding 10m of G.M.T. before sight and add one correction from Interpolation of G.H.A. Table for minutes and seconds over the 10m listing. Be sure to use Moon side of Interpolation table.

3209. The moon at noon. We think of the moon as shining at night, as indeed it does. For navigators, however, the pale disks or crescents of the day are often the more important. When the moon is dimmed by the sun, turn the sextant upside down and bring the horizon to the moon, then right it and take the altitude. In most cases, the purpose of a daylight sight of the moon is a line of position for a fix with the sun.

The G.M.T. of upper transit, found on the daily pages of the *Nautical Almanac,* can be taken as approximate L.M.T. of local transit for planning purposes. The *Air Almanac* carries a series of diagrams giving for high latitudes the approximate L.M.T. of local transit (top scale) and the approximate interval (curved lines) between transit and either moonrise or moonset.

3210. Moonrise and moonset occur each day on an average of 50m later than on the previous day. This retardation varies from less than 15m to more than 90m in different latitudes and with differing declinations of the moon. All navigators at sea know about when to expect the moon and generally let it go at that, but when planning a specific mission, the minute of moonrise or moonset may be of importance.

The L.M.T. of Moonrise and Moonset in various latitudes is tabulated in both Almanacs for every day of the year *for the Meridian of Greenwich.* Unlike similar tabulated figures for the sun, those for the moon cannot be assumed as correct in other longitudes. The reasons for this fact and what to do about it will be developed by the solutions to the following examples using figures taken from Fig. 3210:

Example I (Long. W). Find L.M.T. and Z.T. of moonrise for an observer at 30° N, 125° W on July 25.
Ans: L.M.T. 1438, Z.T. 1458.

The times tabulated in the almanac are for the indicated latitudes at 0° longitude (Greenwich meridian). At Lat. 30° N, Long. 0° the L.M.T.

(G.M.T.) of moonrise is 1417 on July 25 and 1517 (60m later) on July 26. This means that in one trip around the earth, the moon has apparently lost 60m in 360° of travel. At longitude 90° W, it would have lost 15m, ¼ (= 90/360) of 60m and at that longitude would rise at L.M.T. 1417 plus 15m or 1432. Hence to find L.M.T. of moonrise at any longitude west of Greenwich, *increase* the tabulated time at 0° longitude for the given date by the time difference between the given date and the *following* date multiplied by the fraction $\lambda/360$. Thus:

		Moonrise
July 25 (λ 0°)	L.M.T. 1417	1417
July 26 (λ 0°)	L.M.T. 1517	
Difference	60m	
Corr. for λ (60 × 125/360)		+ 21m
L.M.T. at 125° W		1438
Corr. for 5° W of zone meridian		+ 20m
Z.T. at 125° W		1458

Example II (Long. E). Find L.M.T. and Z.T. of moonset for an observer at 40° N, 152° 12′ E on July 26.

   Ans: L.M.T. 0035, Z.T. 0026.

JULY 24, 25, 26

Lat.	Twilight Naut.	Twilight Civil	Sunrise	Moonrise 24	Moonrise 25	Moonrise 26	Moonrise 27
°	h m	h m	h m	h m	h m	h m	h m
N 72	□	□	□	16 30	19 02	■	■
N 70	□	□	□	15 55	17 45	19 24	20 25
68	////	////	01 32	15 30	17 08	18 31	19 31
66	////	////	02 15	15 11	16 41	17 59	18 58
64	////	00 36	02 44	14 55	16 21	17 35	18 34
62	////	01 43	03 06	14 42	16 04	17 16	18 15
60	.////	02 16	03 23	14 32	15 51	17 01	17 59
N 58	00 34	02 39	03 38	14 22	15 39	16 48	17 46
56	01 34	02 58	03 50	14 14	15 29	16 36	17 34
54	02 04	03 14	04 01	14 07	15 20	16 26	17 24
52	02 26	03 27	04 10	14 00	15 12	16 18	17 15
50	02 44	03 39	04 19	13 54	15 05	16 10	17 07
45	03 18	04 02	04 37	13 42	14 49	15 53	16 50
N 40	03 42	04 20	04 51	13 31	14 37	15 39	16 36
35	04 01	04 35	05 04	13 22	14 26	15 27	16 24
30	04 16	04 48	05 14	13 15	14 17	15 17	16 14
20	04 41	05 09	05 33	13 01	14 01	15 00	15 56
N 10	05 00	05 26	05 48	12 50	13 47	14 44	15 40
0	05 15	05 41	06 03	12 39	13 34	14 30	15 26
S 10	05 29	05 55	06 17	12 28	13 21	14 16	15 12
20	05 42	06 09	06 33	12 17	13 08	14 01	14 56
30	05 56	06 25	06 50	12 04	12 52	13 44	14 38
35	06 02	06 33	07 00	11 56	12 43	13 33	14 28
40	06 09	06 42	07 12	11 48	12 33	13 22	14 16
45	06 17	06 53	07 25	11 38	12 21	13 09	14 02
S 50	06 26	07 05	07 42	11 26	12 06	12 52	13 45
52	06 30	07 11	07 49	11 21	11 59	12 45	13 37
54	06 34	07 17	07 58	11 15	11 52	12 36	13 29
56	06 38	07 24	08 07	11 08	11 43	12 26	13 19
58	06 43	07 32	08 18	11 00	11 34	12 16	13 07
S 60	06 48	07 41	08 31	10 52	11 23	12 03	12 54

Lat.	Sunset	Twilight Civil	Twilight Naut.	Moonset 24	Moonset 25	Moonset 26	Moonset 27
°	h m	h m	h m	h m	h m	h m	h m
N 72	□	□	□	· 21 00	20 24	■	■
N 70	□	□	□	21 37	.21 42	22 00	22 56
68	22 35	////	////	22 03	22 20	22 53	23 50
66	21 54	////	////	22 23	22 47	23 26	24 23
64	21 26	23 24	////	22 39	23 08	23 50	24 47
62	21 05	22 26	////	22 52	23 25	24 08	00 08
60	20 48	21 55	////	23 03	23 39	24 24	00 24
N 58	20 34	21·31	23 28	23 13	23 51	24 37	00 37
56	20 22	21 13	22 36	23 22	·24 01	00 01	00 49
54	20 11	20 58	22 06	23 30	24 10	00 10	00 59
52	20 02	20 45	21 45	23 37	24 19	00 19	01 08
50	19 53	20 33	21 27	23 43	24 26	00 26	01 16
45	19 35	20 10	20 54	23 57	24 42	00 42	01 33
N 40	19 21	19 52	20 30	24 08	00 08	00 55	01 47
35	19 09	19 37	20 12	24 17	00 17·	01 06	01 59
30	·18 58	19 25	19 56	24 26	00 26	01 16	02 09
20	18 40	19 04	19 32	24 40	00 40	01 33	02 27
N 10	18 24	18 47	19 13	00 01	00 53	01 47	02 42
0	18 10	18 32	18 57	00 10	01 05	02 01	02 57
S 10	17 56	18 18	18 44	00 20	01 17	02 14	03 11
20	17 40	18 04	18 31	00 30	01 30	02 29	03 27
30	17 23	17 49	18 18	00 42	01 44	02 46	03 44

Day	Eqn. of Time 00ʰ	Eqn. of Time 12ʰ	Mer. Pass.	Mer. Pass. Upper	Mer. Pass. Lower	Age	Phase
	m s	m s	h m	h m	h m	d	
24	06 23	06 24	12 06	18 52	06 25	08	◖
25	06 25	06 25	12 06	19 47	07 19	09	
26	06 25	06 26	12 06	20 43	08 15	10	

FIG. 3210.   RISING, SETTING, AND TWILIGHT TABLES FROM *Nautical Almanac*.

At latitude 40° N, the time of moonset at 0° longitude is 0055 on July 26 and was 0008 on July 25, the previous day, a loss of 47m. At longitude 152° 12′ E, 152.2/360 of the whole loss at 0° longitude has not yet occurred. Hence, to find L.M.T. of moonset at any longitude east of Greenwich, *decrease* the tabulated time at 0° longitude for the given date by the time difference between the given date and the *preceding* date multiplied by the fraction λ/360. Thus for this example:

			Moonset
July 26 (λ 0°)	L.M.T.	0055	0055
July 25 (λ 0°)	L.M.T.	0008	
Difference		47m	
Corr. for λ (47 × 152.2/360)			− 20m
L.M.T. at 152° 12′ E			0035
Corr. for 2°.2 east of zone meridian			− 9m
Z.T. at 152° 12′ E			0026

Finding the time of moonrise and moonset by *Air Almanac* can be done in the same manner as by *Nautical Almanac*. However, the solution by *Air Almanac* has been simplified by including a "Diff." column giving the half-daily differences *to the following date*. A correction table in the back of the almanac is entered with the given longitude and the tabulated "diff." for the given date. The correction is added for west longitude and subtracted for east longitude unless "diff." carries a minus sign; in which case the operations are reversed.

Note also that the moon does not set on July 25 at 45° N, the 2442 tabulated indicating 0042 on July 26 as shown for that date. In such cases, the daily differences are found for the preceding (Long. E) or following (Long. W) event regardless of date. Note also in Fig. 3210 at 72° N the black rectangle indicating that the moon does not rise; the open rectangle showing that the sun is above the horizon all day; and the slanting lines at 60° N to 68° N meaning that twilight lasts all night.

In problems involving the rising and setting of the sun and moon, and the twilights; it is necessary to interpolate for latitude. Thus, in Example I, if the given latitude had been 32° 18′ N the times for 0° longitude would be respectively L.M.T. 1417 plus 9 × 2.3/5 = 1421; and L.M.T. 1517 plus 10 × 2.3/5 = 1522. Tables are given in the almanac (page XXXII) for performing this interpolation and that for longitude. However, some navigators prefer to work out the simple proportions numerically or by slide rule instead of using the tables which frequently require still another interpolation to be sure of obtaining the nearest minute of time.

The following shows a simplified form for solving problems such as Examples I and II by the *Nautical Almanac*.

July 25	1417	July 26	0055
July 26	1517	July 25	0008
Diff.	60m	Diff.	47m
Diff. × 125/360	+ 21m	Diff. × 152.2/360	− 20m
L.M.T.	1438	L.M.T.	0035
dλ	+ 20m	dλ	− 9m
Z.T.	1458	Z.T.	0026

3211. Tides and the transit of the moon have a more or less definite relation which is important to the mariner approaching a strange coast without tide tables. A review of §1720 will indicate that the time of high tide should be when the moon is on the upper or lower meridian of any given place.

The *Nautical Almanac* tabulates the G.M.T. of the moon's transit of the upper and lower meridian of Greenwich for each of the three days on every right-hand daily page. This is L.M.T. of transit, Long. 0°.

To obtain the exact time the moon will be on the ship's longitude an interpolation must be made for the ship's position in longitude east or west of Greenwich.

The time difference of transit from day to day can be easily found by subtracting the time for one date from the next.

As previously described in §3210 an interpolation is made for East or West longitude of ship similar to that done for Moonrise or Moonset.

The time of transit, however, is not the actual time of high water which, because of local conditions, is later, often several hours after transit. This interval, which is fairly constant for any given place, is termed the *luni-tidal interval*, the *establishment of the port* or the *vulgar establishment*. Or simply H.W.F. & C., which means High Water Full and Change (of the moon). Some charts of the coasts of the world give the H.W.F. & C. for the principal ports on the chart. The expected L.M.T. of high water in any such port is the L.M.T. of the moon's transit plus H.W.F. & C. for the port. This gives useful information, but H.W.F. & C. varies somewhat during a lunar month and as all mariners know, tides do not always obey the rules.

3212. Historic sights. In that fateful race to Norway in 1935, the yawl *Stormy Weather* took departure from Pollock Rip L.V. the morning of 9 June. Evening found her halfway to Cape Sable, but north of the course going strong on the starboard tack after a day of fog and raw rain. Skipper Rod Stephens needed a fix, and needed it badly, from which to make the Nova Scotia coast and to round Cape Sable. Flying clouds, black in patches, with moonlight all around, foretold bad luck with the stars. But sometimes the moon shone clear, as did Venus in the west, and Jupiter to south and east. This gave the navigator, Chick Larkin, his chance. Few men are better with a sextant, the fix plotted in Fig. 3212 resulted, and helped *Stormy* to win. The reader may see the night when planets and the moon are vital to the mission of his ship.

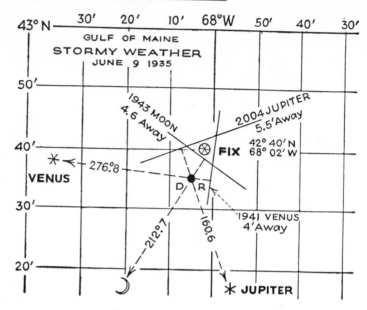

FIG. 3212. STORMY TO WIN!

3213. Questions and problems. The questions among the following problems afford special practice in detail peculiar to planet and moon sights. The problems may be solved by H.O. 214 or the Alternate solution may be worked from the D.R. by H.O. 211 or H.O. 214.

Q 1-32. *Declination of Planets.* With the excerpts from the *Nautical Almanac* given in Apx. V, find the declination of the following planets for the given dates and G.M.T.

		1966	G.M.T.			1966	G.M.T.
(a) Venus	Feb.	5	10h 41m 02s	(d) Saturn	Jan.	7	20h 51m 03s
(b) Saturn	Sept.	29	13h 50m 11s	(e) Venus	April	5	22h 40m 23s
(c) Jupiter	July	2	14h 51m 58s	(f) Mars	July	2	12h 21m 14s

Ans: (a) 12° 25′.5 S   (c) 22° 55′.0 N   (e) 10° 40′.0 S
       (b) 4° 03′.7 S   (d) 8° 27′.5 S   (f) 23° 47′.0 N

Q 2-32. *G.H.A. of Planets.* Compute G.H.A. of the planets listed below for the given dates and G.M.T.

		1966	G.M.T.			1966	G.M.T.
(a) Mars	Mar.	7	18h 20m 23s	(d) Saturn	Sept.	29	19h 21m 21s
(b) Venus	Mar.	7	1h 40m 19s	(e) Venus	Nov.	28	21h 50m 11s
(c) Jupiter	Dec.	27	7h 41m 08s	(f) Venus	Jan.	7	12h 50m 29s

Ans: (a) 81° 04′.9   (c) 85° 47′.7   (e) 145° 19′.2
       (b) 243° 39′.7   (d) 301° 35′.8   (f) 343° 47′.2

P 1-32. *Jupiter,* from ship in North Pacific, about 12° west of the date line. April 5, 1966, D.R. 35° 14′ N, 168° 11′ E, observed planet Jupiter. Hs 54° 33′.6 at W.T. 19h 11m 43s. W.E. on Z.T. 1m 42s fast, I.C. — 1′.5, Ht. Eye 30 ft. *Req:* Solve for LOP by H.O. 214.

Ans: A.P. 35° N, 167° 48′.0 E, *a* 12′.6 T, Zn 261°.1.

P 2-32. *Saturn,* from a ship in the South Atlantic, about 800 miles east of Montevideo.

Jan. 7, 1966, D.R. 34° 38′ S, 40° 15′ W, observed planet Saturn. Hs 34° 18′.3 at W.T. 19h 08m 26s. W.E. on Z.T. 1m 40s slow, I.C. + 1′.2, Ht. Eye 18 ft. *Req:* Solve for LOP.

Ans: A.P. 35° S, 40° 28′.4 W, *a* 8′.2 T, Zn 284°.9.

P 3-32. *Mars,* from about 150 miles north of Midway Island.

Sept. 29, 1966, D.R. 33° 15′ N, 176° 08′ W, observed planet Mars. Hs 43° 12′.5 at W.T. 5h 39m 06s, W.E. on Z.T. 56s slow, I.C. + 2′.5, Ht. Eye 30 ft. *Req:* Solve for LOP.

Ans: A.P. 33° N, 176° 11′.7 W, *a* 7′.3 A, Zn 100°.1.

P 4-32. *Venus,* from 38° east of the Cape of Good Hope.

June 3, 1966, D.R. 34° 15′ S, 56° 11′ E, observed planet Venus. Hs 25° 32′.8 at W.T. 6h 20m 18s, W.E. on Z.T. 1m 30s slow, I.C. + 1′.8, Ht. Eye 24 ft. *Req:* Solve for LOP.

Ans: A.P. 34° S, 55° 41′.6 E, *a* 14′.3 A, Zn 055°.4.

P 5-32. *Venus,* from a ship about 365 miles east of Savannah.

Jan. 7, 1966, D.R. 31° 55′ N, 74° 10′ W, observed planet Venus. Hs 20° 21′.2 at W.T. 17h 29m 56s. W.E. on Z.T. 1m 27s slow, I.C. − 1′.2, Ht. Eye 23 ft. *Req:* Solve for LOP.

Ans: A.P. 32° N, 74° 28′.3 W, *a* 13′.6 T, Zn 237°.8.

Q 3-32. *Moon's Altitude Correction.* With inside cover tables and excerpts from *Nautical Almanac* in Apx. V, find the true altitude of the moon for G.M.T. 5h 00m 00s on each of the following dates:

	1966		Limb	Hs	Temp.	Press.	I.C.	Ht. Eye	Ans.
(a)	March	7	Lower	42° 03′.4			− 1′.0	26 ft.	42° 58′.5
(b)	July	2	Upper	37° 33′.1			− 1′.0	26 ft.	37° 55′.0
(c)	April	5	Upper	78° 30′.0			+ 1′.2	38 ft.	78° 20′.6
(d)	Sept.	29	Lower	25° 01′.0			− 0′.8	30 ft.	25° 56′.4
(e)	Oct.	29	Lower	10° 17′.8	5° F	30.6 in.	+ 2′.0	18 ft.	11° 18′.5
(f)	June	3	Upper	4° 12′.0	90° F	29.3 in.	−1′.6	29 ft.	4° 36′.3

Q 4-32. *Declination of the Moon.* From the *Nautical Almanac* excerpts in Apx. V, find the declination of the moon in the following cases:

	1966	G.M.T.		1966	G.M.T.
(a)	April 5	0h 21m 10s	(d)	March 7	23h 20m 02s
(b)	April 5	1h 40m 39s	(e)	Aug. 1	6h 20m 37s
(c)	Feb. 5	3h 51m 20s	(f)	Sept. 29	19h 50m 18s

Ans: (a) 0° 06′.8 N (c) 22° 33′.4 N (e) 23° 07′.8 S
(b) 0° 15′.1 S (d) 4° 02′.6 N (f) 0° 01′.5 N

Q 5-32. *Moon's G.H.A.* From the *Nautical Almanac* excerpts in Apx. V, find G.H.A. of the moon in these cases:

	1966	G.M.T.		1966	G.M.T.
(a)	April 5	4h 20m 53s	(d)	Sept. 29	12h 31m 24s
(b)	March 7	18h 51m 20s	(e)	June 3	3h 11m 58s
(c)	July 2	4h 40m 25s	(f)	Nov. 28	1h 50m 21s

Ans: (a) 66° 43′.5 (c) 77° 01′.0 (e) 51° 10′.7
(b) 268° 58′.5 (d) 190° 37′.8 (f) 31° 25′.0

Q 6-32. *Moonrise and Moonset.* Find the Z.T. of moonrise and moonset, and the age of the moon for the following dates and positions:

	1966		Position	Moonrise	Moonset	Age
(a)	Oct.	29	38° 20′ N, 50° 17′ W	1738	0646	15d
(b)	May	11	22° 47′ S, 63° 10′ E	2301	1159	21d
(c)	July	2	31° 50′ N, 141° 06′ W	2002	0504	14d
(d)	Aug.	22	12° 22′ S, 43° 44′ E	1055	2355	6d

P 6-32. *Moon* from west and south of Juan Fernandez.
March 7, 1966, D.R. 36° 12′.8 S, 92° 14′.5 W, observed moon's lower limb. Hs 13° 13′.5 at W.T. 5h 09m 21s. W.E. on Z.T. 58s slow, I.C. − 1′.6, Ht. Eye 20 ft. *Req:* Solve for LOP.
Ans: A.P. 36° S, 91° 48′.1 W, *a* 11′.8 A, Zn 290°.7.

P 7-32. *Moon,* from north of St. Paul's Island in the Indian Ocean.
May 11, 1966, D.R. 34° 54′ S, 81° 38′ E, observed moon's *upper* limb. Hs 68° 04′.2 at W.T. 6h 22m 19s, W.E. on Z.T. 1m 18s fast, I.C. + 1′.2, Ht. Eye 28 ft. *Req:* Solve for LOP.
Ans: A.P. 35° S, 81° 15′.9 E, *a* 6′.9 T, Zn 294°.0.

P 8-32. *Moon,* from ship in North Pacific, almost due north from Wake Island.
November 28, 1966, D.R. 33° 52′ N, 164° 48′ E, during night observed lower limb of full moon above moonlit horizon. Hs 21° 56′.4 at W.T. 18h 51m 27s, W.E. on Z.T. 1m 12s fast. I.C. − 1′.0, Ht. Eye 32 ft. Temp. 42° F, Press. 30.80 in. *Req:* Solve for LOP.
Ans: A.P. 34° N, 164° 45′.1 E, *a* 20′.7 A, Zn 076°.5.

P 9-32. *Moon,* from 2° south of Flores Island of the Azores.
July 2, 1966, D.R. 37° 05′ N, 31° 16′ W, observed moon's *upper* limb. Hs 13° 49′.8 at W.T. 21h 20m 05s, W.E. on Z.T. 1m 10s slow, I.C. − 1′.5, Ht. Eye 36 ft. *Req:* Solve for LOP.
Ans: A.P. 37° N, 30° 57′.6 W, *a* 12′.1 T, Zn 140°.1.

P 10-32. *Moon,* from north and west of Midway Island, North Pacific.
August 22, 1966, D.R. 33° 21′ N, 171° 18′ E, observed moon's *upper* limb. Hs 39° 27′.4 at W.T. 16h 32m 18s, W.E. on Z.T. 1m 48s fast, I.C. − 1′.0, Ht. Eye 29 ft. *Req:* Solve for LOP.
Ans: A.P. 33° N, 171° 21′.6 E, *a* 20′.0 A, Zn 178°.8.

PLANETS AND THE MOON FOR A FIX

All courses and bearings are given in degrees true unless otherwise stated.

P 11-32. From Stormy Weather, in the Gulf of Maine, en route to win the race to Norway in 1935; Chick Larkin, navigator.

(a) June 9, 1935, evening twilight, about 1945, D.R. 42° 35′ N, 68° 05′ W, observed Venus. Corrected Ho 25° 46′.0 at 12h 37m 34s by Chro. which was 3m 30s slow. For 1935 Almanac data, assume Corr. Decl. as 21° 52′.8 N, and Corr. G.H.A. as 142° 29′.6, both at time of sight. *Req:* Solve for LOP from D.R.
Ans: *a* 4′.1 A, Zn 276°.7.
Alternate: Solve from A.P. (43° N, 68° 29′.6 W).
Ans: *a* 25′.0 A, Zn 276°.4.

(b) June 9, 1935, evening twilight, observed moon's *upper* limb. Corrected Ho 39° 04′.5 at 12h 39m 12s by Chro. which was 3m 30s slow. For 1935 Almanac data, use Corr. Decl. 3° 03′.5 S, Corr. G.H.A. 92° 52′.3, both at time of sight. *Req:* Solve for LOP from 1945 D.R.

Ans: a 4′.8 A, Zn 212°.7.
Alternate: Solve from A.P. (43° N, 67° 52′.3 W).
Ans: a 21′.4 T, Zn 212°.8.

(c) June 9, 1935, about 2004, observed Jupiter. Corrected Ho 29° 58′.5 at 1h 00m 42s by Chro. which was 3m 30s slow. For 1935 Almanac data, use Corr. Decl. 15° 11′.0 S, Corr. G.H.A. 50° 44′.2 at time of sight. *Req:* Solve for LOP from 1945 D.R.
Ans: a 5′.5 A, Zn 160°.6.
Alternate: Solve from A.P. (43° N, 67° 44′.2 W).
Ans: a 13′.0 T, Zn 161°.0.
Yacht making little headway and the navigator considered the three sights as taken simultaneously.

(d) Construct small plotting sheet, label center lines 42° 40′ N, 68° W; use large scale.
Req: Plot LOP from D.R. Record center of triangle formed at intersection of LOP as the Fix.
Ans: Fix, 42° 40′.4 N, 68° 00′.7 W.

(e) Construct small plotting sheet as in (d), and plot LOP from A.P. and record Fix.
Ans: Fix, 42° 40′.3 N, 68° 00′.7 W.

33. ALL IN A DAY

RESPONSIBILITY for the safe navigation of any vessel, be it dory or battleship, rests with the master. The work itself, the assignment of duties, and the records to be kept vary with ship, service, and circumstance. This chapter summarizes the important elements of the work, as if done by one man called the navigator, without attempting to enumerate all possible details, or to indicate those which at times may be omitted. Underlying principles and how to do the work have been discussed previously in this book.

Obviously, all of the work of the day is not carried on by the responsible navigating officer. Thus training the bridge personnel is important. After all, these are the men depended on in a pinch when their efficiency will reflect that of the navigator himself.

3301. First duties include checking, procuring, or putting in order the navigational equipment before sailing.

Compasses are of first importance. Inspect the magnetic compasses, test their electric and oil lighting, and see that the extra compensating magnets are properly stowed. Examine recent deviation cards and, if the ship swings at anchor, check the deviations of the standard compass on several headings and compare the steering compass. If the ship be new, or if structural changes have been made, or if the cargo be magnetic, swing ship at the first opportunity.

For the gyro system, consider if recent performance indicates the need of special attention. At least see that the oiling and cleaning schedules have been maintained and that copies of the makers' instruction book for each unit of the system are at hand. The navigator's degree of responsibility for the gyro system varies in different services.

Charts are second in importance only to the compass equipment, and should be supplemented with various lists and tables for the current year. A navigator about to make his first voyage on a strange ship should at least check the inventory of charts, light lists, tide and current tables, pilot guides and sailing directions. All should be up to date and corrected as complete for the proposed voyage as circumstance allows.

The radio direction finder should be tested and its latest calibration card examined. If possible, determine before sailing if recalibration is essential. Consider the probable limits of accuracy of this equipment.

Electronic navigational equipment assigned to the navigator should be tested as to proper adjustment and the calibration curves checked.

Other instruments and equipment for piloting and dead reckoning should be checked and inspected. This may include many items of which two are important on all vessels.

Sounding equipment, whether it be a single lead and line or includes the latest radio depth finding devices, should be in its proper place, ready for use.

Patent logs, if they are to be depended on for distance run, must be ready with any necessary gear. One complete outfit with spare runner *and spare line* is the very minimum for the smallest craft.

Sextants, of which not fewer than two should be on board if they can be had, should be in good adjustment and safely stowed.

Chronometers, or whatever the timekeeping equipment, if possible, should be on board several days in advance to permit checking their rates after delivery. Consider the time signals to be used and how the timekeepers are to be compared with time ticks. Aim at two independent sources of accurate time.

Two copies of the Nautical Almanac and a similar pair for next year, if that be imminent. *Air Almanacs* are a great convenience.

Tables for altitude and azimuth. If the ship be equipped with H.O. 214, some small book of tables with which the navigator is familiar also should be available for abandoning ship. Azimuth tables, preferably Burdwood's, otherwise H.O. 71, should be at hand, together with Bowditch for special information.

Plotting sheets and tools. Check the supply and see that the special charts or graphs required by the various recording instruments are in sufficient quantities.

Navigator's work book may be prescribed by the service or supplied by the navigator. Such a record book must be ready, together with what the idiosyncrasies of the navigator require for doing his work with accuracy, neatness and despatch.

Compass record book, either as officially prescribed or a suitable blankbook, will be needed.

3302. Sailing day. In practice, the preparations to be made by the navigator depend on whether or not a local pilot be engaged, and on the degree of responsibility to be placed on the pilot. Most of the following remarks and references assume that the navigator is to pilot the ship. Otherwise, notify the pilot's office in advance, and make such preparations as seem necessary.

In any case, the time of sailing must be considered. When so doing remember that tidal conditions somewhere along the route to the sea may be more important than at the time of leaving harbor. The sailing hour having been set, preparation must be made in advance. Start the gyro not less than 4 hours before sailing, see that it precesses to north, not south, and that the repeaters are in step. Meanwhile prepare as in §912 and see that every item of information which may be required is recorded either on the chart or in a note book before sailing.

Underway, with leadsmen at their stations and preparations for taking bearings completed, the business of piloting a ship to sea differs but little from the reverse process described in §913 and §915. One measure of the pilot's skill is the exactness with which he knows the ship's position at every instant.

Departure takes place from the point where the ship, clear of the coast, stands away on its course. The navigator should establish this point at once and with reasonable accuracy. It is even most important that the routine for keeping and plotting the D.R. be in effect from the moment of departure. A D.R. position may be of sudden importance before the first fix is obtained.

3303. The day's work, as the term is commonly used, includes the navigator's work at sea from dawn until dark, or from midnight to midnight, although the day's run and distance to go are reported as of noon.

In the days of sail, the record of courses in quarter-points steered by compass and the speeds by chip log were kept on a slate. The dead reckoning was worked up by the sailings and there was little or no plotting. A morning time sight for longitude and the noon sight for latitude gave the noon fix. This noon position was that of apparent noon, and at that time the ship's clocks were set to 12:00. An additional time sight might be taken in the afternoon to confirm the longitude. Star sights were neither required nor used as frequently as at present.

Today, methods are simpler but the work is more continuous because of high speeds and the importance of knowing the ship's position at any time. Various elements of a day's work are noted in the following paragraphs. Others to add or those to omit depend on circumstances.

Keeping and plotting the dead reckoning should be regarded as a continuous process which goes on all day, every day to the end that the D.R. position can be determined on a moment's notice.

Morning twilight fix by any combination of stars, planets or the moon. For Polaris, set sextant to D.R. latitude. Venus, Jupiter and the moon often may be observed shortly before dawn when the horizon is well defined.

Current is the difference between the last fix and the D.R. at that time. If excessive or unexpected, consider the possibility of some error hidden in log readings, compass corrections, or times of sight.

First sun sight, after the sun is more than 10° high and at the time its bearing best serves the navigator (§3004).

Azimuth of the sun by standard compass or gyro should be observed at the moment of the first sun sight or within the following hour. Check the deviation and make a general compass comparison to see that nothing has gone wrong.

A mid-morning sun sight may or may not be required, depending on how well the situation is in hand. Such a sight gives a running fix with the first sun sight, or assures a running fix at noon, or may give a fix when combined with a possible moon or Venus line. It is often good practice to take sights when they can be had, leaving them to be worked up if needed.

Time for the noon sight should be considered in advance. With the expected longitude at 1200, it may be taken from Tables 2 and 3, page iv.

Noon sight for latitude is a convenient tradition generally considered as a required element of the day's work. A sight for line of position taken shortly before or after noon serves the same purpose.

Reporting at noon the run for the last 24 hours, with distance to destination, is customary. Form and detail of the report vary with the service.

After noon the work is more or less the reverse of that for the morning, ending with a fix at evening twilight and the orders for the night.

3304. When routine fails. An established routine serves well so long as it can be carried on without serious interruption. But when for any reason the D.R. may be seriously in error, let the navigator forget routine and get some kind of a fix as quickly as possible. In daytime the sun with the moon or Venus may give the answer, or possibly the sun will give a running fix within an hour or two. When under the sun at noon a good fix may be had within a few minutes. In the middle of the night, contrary to book lore, it is often possible to get a fix, as must the submarine, sometimes with a bubble sextant. Or cross a single line with the bearing of a landmark, or with a radio bearing, if two radio bearings can't be had. If a fix be impossible, get any kind of a single line and think what it means. However accomplished, keep at it until the ship has found herself.

3305. Where routine helps. Certain elements of the day's work are best cared for by an exacting schedule carried out with almost the

same regularity as are recording course and distance or winding the
chronometers.

This advice is especially applicable to compass work wherein the
navigator may be lulled into a false sense of security by small deviations or the gyro's perfections. Responsibility for the compass equipment
rests with the navigator. Neglect of this duty may be avoided by including in the day's work a strict schedule for checking the compass or
compasses. The very minimum is a daily check on the deviation of all

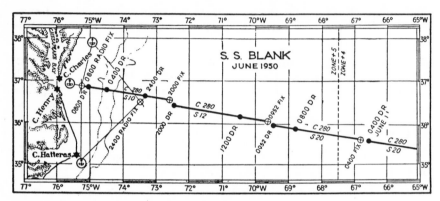

Fig. 3307. Landfall, Cruise C.

compasses while the ship heads on whatever the course may be. This
check is usually based on an azimuth of the morning sun. It should be
repeated in the afternoon. Even during the night it is sometimes possible to get a bearing of Polaris with a bright, clean azimuth mirror. It
is a fair guess that most disasters ascribed to "local magnetic disturbances" are due to careless compass control.

Deviation also should be checked whenever the course is materially
changed. Should repeated checks over a period of days indicate serious
uncertainties, ask permission to swing ship, but do not play with the adjusting magnets unless you are an old hand at that game, authorized by
superior authority. When a ship is gyro equipped it is regular practice to
compare gyro and standard compass at the beginning of every watch and
to record the comparison of the steering repeater and the magnetic steering compass every half hour.

3306. Records include the ship's log book, a pilot's note book, and
the navigator's work book. Almost equally essential on all vessels are
the chronometer and compass records. On large vessels report forms,
graphs, and other records become more numerous. When handling this
part of the work, points to remember include: (1) Avoid notes or figures

on odd bits of paper or scratch pads. (2) Your name or initials and date on every page, form, or card, at upper right corner, unless special space is provided. (3) Accuracy and speed require neatness. (4) Make notes and do all work in an orderly manner so arranged and labeled that it may be understood by your superior without explanation.

3307. Landfall. The time of landfall (Fig. 3307) must be considered before the navigator can complete his plans for that event. From a given distance at a given speed, the time is a matter of arithmetic, but time so found may not be best for making the land. What the navigator wants first is an exact position from which the ship may proceed into port or along the coast. An offshore lightship may be approached at any time. The line of a strange coast seen along the horizon in daytime most often shows no useful landmarks, but on a clear night one, or better two powerful lights simplify an accurate approach. For entering a harbor, daylight with proper tidal conditions is best. Or the weather, or the mission of the ship, may govern the whole situation.

* * *

3308. Problems in practical work. This final group of problems has been arranged in several series each of which includes various elements of the day's work at sea. Any one of the numerous sights may be considered as a separate problem. Or the time required for completing the work in any of the series may be reduced by omitting the solution of one or more of the sights and considering the series of events as a problem in plotting given data.

Solutions for LOP have been computed by H.O. 214 only. Attention is called to the necessity of using the stated A.P. to obtain answers in practical agreement with the given answers. If such positions be used, intercepts found by the student should be within 0'.5, azimuth within less than 0°.5, of the answers given in the text.

Fixes and R. Fixes, when plotted, should be within 1' of L or λ of the given answers, provided the same type of plotting sheet is used. Positions plotted from H.O. 211 solutions may differ slightly from those resulting from the H.O. 214 solutions.

All courses and bearings are given in degrees true from north unless otherwise stated. Always transfer the D.R. to a Fix but never to a R. Fix, unless so instructed in statement of problem.

CRUISE A

Bermuda for the Azores, from morning twilight until afternoon, Wednesday, May 11, 1966.

To conform best with key plotting of problem, use H.O. Position Plotting Sheet 3000-11z; Latitudes 33° to 37° and mark center meridian 46° W. Or construct small area plotting sheet for 2° latitude and 4° longitude; mark center lines 35° N and 46° W. Use large scale. Constants for all sights: W.E. on Z.T. 25s fast, I.C. + 1'.0, Ht. Eye 35 ft.

During the night, the navigator had estimated that morning twilight would make the horizon visible by 0420 and had projected the D.R. position at that time 34° 45′ N, 47° 10′ W, course 068°, speed 10.

Plot the 0420 D.R.

P A1-33. During morning twilight, the navigator observed two stars and obtained the following data:

	(a) Arcturus	(b) Polaris
W.T.	4h 11m 08s	4h 20m 32s
Hs	22° 30′.3	34° 40′.7

Req: (a) Solve Arcturus sight for LOP. (b) Solve Polaris sight for latitude.
Ans: (a) A.P., 35° N, 46° 46′.2 W; *a* 14′.1 T, Zn 278°.9.
  (b) Lat. at 0420, 34° 42′.5 N.
Req: (c) Plot 0411 Arcturus line advanced to 0420. Plot latitude by Polaris. Label and record 0420 Fix.
Ans: Fix at 0420, 34° 42′.5 N, 47° 05′.2 W.
Continue C 068°, S 10 from 0420 Fix.

P A2-33. Fix by sun and moon. About 0640 took advantage of the favorable positions of the sun and moon to observe both bodies, 0652 D.R. 34° 51′.9 N, 46° 36′.8 W, as follows:

	(a) Moon (Upper Limb)	(b) Sun (Lower Limb)
W.T	6h 40m 42s	6h 52m 04s
Hs	30° 01′.0	19° 45′.3

Req: Solve both sights for L.O.P., advance Moon LOP to 0652, and plot and record the 0652 Fix.

Moon (Upper Limb)
Ans: A.P. 35° N, 46° 27′.7 W
  a 11′.4 T, Zn 196°.0
  0652 Fix, 34° 51′.6 N, 46° 36′.7 W.

Sun (Lower Limb)
A.P. 35° N, 46° 50′.3 W
a 10′.0 T, Zn 081°.5

The 0652 fix confirmed the D.R. position and course 068°, S 10 was continued.

P A3-33. Morning sun. At about 0922 observed ☉; W.T. 9h 22m 13s, Hs 50° 40′.8.
Req: Plot 0922 D.R. (35° 01′.3 N, 46° 08′.4 W), solve sun sight for LOP.
Ans: A.P., 35° N, 46° 22′.6 W, *a* 13′.6 T, Zn 105°.1.

Deviation. At time of taking the above sight, bearing of sun per standard compass was 124°, variation per chart, 22° W.
Req: Deviation of standard compass.
Ans: Dev. 3°.1 E when on given course.

Course change. At 1030, course is changed to 115°, speed 10 knots.
Plot 1030 D.R. (35° 05′.5 N, 45° 55′.4 W) and change course line to 115°, S 10.
Plot 1200 D.R. (34° 59′.3 N, 45° 38′.6 W).

P A4-33. Noon sight. Lacking better information as to longitude, estimate the time of L.A.N. at the 1200 D.R. position, using Tables 2 and 3 in Apx. VIII.
Ans: 1159.
Alternate: Estimate W.T. of L.A.N. by G.H.A. method.
Ans: 11h 59m 17s.

Predict sextant altitude of sun at L.A.N.
Ans: Hs 72° 42′.

Observed ☉ at L.A.N., Hs 72° 47'.2.
Req: Latitude by meridian altitude method.
Ans: 1159 Lat., 34° 54'.0 N.

Plot latitude line and advance it and 0922 sun line to 1200. Record 1200 R. Fix.
(To advance an LOP around a "dog leg," see §3001.)
Ans: 1200 R. Fix, 34° 54'.0 N, 45° 37'.4 W.

At 1200, course was changed to 070°, S 12. Begin new D.R. course line from 1200 R. Fix.

P A5-33. Afternoon sun. About 1600, the navigator noticed clouds forming in the west and decided to observe the sun before it became obscured.
Req: Plot and record the 1600 D.R. position.
Ans: 1600 D.R., 35° 10'.4 N, 44° 42'.3 W.

Observed ☉ as follows:
W.T. 16h 00m 51s, Hs 33° 17'.5.
(Note: For the sun, 4m = 1° and 4s = 1'.)
Solve for LOP and plot the 1600 sun line.
Ans: A.P., 35° N, 45° 02'.2 W, *a* 12'.3 A, Zn 269°.2.
Is the ship making good more or less than 12 knots?
Ans: Approximately 1 knot less.

CRUISE B

U.S.S. Long Beach proceeding with a task force in the Western Pacific, Aug. 1, 1966.
To conform best with key plotting of problem, use Position Plotting Sheet H.O. 3000-10z, Latitudes 30° to 33°; label center meridian 170° E. Alternatively, construct small area plotting sheet for 2° of latitude and 4° of longitude; label center lines 32° N and 170° E; use small scale.
Constants for all sights: W.E. on Z.T. 20s fast, I.C. + 1'.0, Ht. Eye 65 ft. All sights taken with marine-type sextant.

The 0800 "posit," 32° 50' N, 171° 55' E, course 260°, 15 knots, sky overcast.

P B1-33. Ten o'clock sun. About 1000, the lower limb of the sun appeared long enough for the navigator to get an observation as follows:
W.T. 10h 00m 38s, Hs 63° 02'.9.
Solve for LOP and plot 1000 sun line. At 1000, the quartermaster recorded the reading of the dead reckoning tracer (DRT), 32° 44'.8 N, 171° 19'.8 E.
Ans: A.P., 33° N, 171° 30'.1 E, *a* 2'.7 T, Zn 117°.6.

Plot and record the 1000 E.P.
Ans: 1000 E.P., 32° 43'.9 N, 171° 23'.3 E.

P B2-33. Noon sight. The ship being outside the reliable daytime range of loran reception, the navigator prepared for his noon sights.
Plot and record the 1200 D.R.
Ans: 1200 D.R., 32° 39'.6 N, 170° 44'.7 E.

With Tables 2 and 3, Apx. VIII, find the Z.T. of L.A.N. at the 1200 D.R.
Ans: Z.T. of L.A.N., 1143.

Advance the 1000 E.P. for the time to L.A.N. and record its longitude.
Ans: 1143 longitude, 170° 53' E.

Using the G.H.A. method, estimate the W.T. of L.A.N. at the ship.
Ans: W.T. of L.A.N., 11h 43m 04s.

Predict sun's altitude at L.A.N., using latitude of 1200 D.R.
Ans: Predicted Hs, 75° 22′.7.

At L.A.N., the sun was obscured by clouds, but shortly afterward appeared long enough for the following observation of the lower limb:

W.T. 11h 50m 43s, Hs 75° 17′.6.

By usual method (H.O. 214, not meridian altitude), solve for L.O.P.
Ans: A.P., 33° N, 170° 58′.7 E, *a* 21′.9 T, Zn 187°.3.

Advance 1000 sun line to time of noon sight. Plot and record R. Fix.
Ans: 1150 R. Fix, 32° 38′.5 N, 170° 51′.0 E.

Run the 1150 R. Fix up to 1200 and record the 1200 position.
Ans: 1200 posit, 32° 38′.0 N, 170° 48′.0 E.

Since the navigator considered the 1200 posit to be the most probable position, a new D.R. track was started from there.

P B3-33. Afternoon sun. At 1420, the navigator took advantage of a clear spot in increasing cloudiness to observe the sun as follows:

W.T. 14h 20m 43s, Hs ☉ 52° 19′.2.

Advance 1200 posit to 1420 and plot 1420 D.R. Solve 1420 observation for LOP and plot sun line.
Ans: A.P., 33° N, 170° 28′.6 E, *a* 21′.8 T, Zn 256°.5.

P B4-33. At 1500, the DRT read L 32° 30′ N, λ 169° 56′ E, and the ship commenced maneuvering exercises at various courses and increased speeds. When maneuvers were completed at 1600, the DRT read L 32° 14′ N, λ 169° 32′ E, and the ship resumed C 260°, S 15.
Plot the D.R.'s at 1500 and 1600.

P B5-33. Evening position. Shortly after sunset, the quartermaster sighted a star low in the south through a break in the clouds. The navigator identified the star as Antares and succeeded in observing it as follows:

W.T. 19h 10m 35s, Hs 31° 24′.2.

Plot the 1910 D.R. (32° 05′.7 N, 168° 36′.6 E) and solve the Antares sight for LOP.
Ans: A.P., 32° N, 168° 47′.1 E, *a* 5′.7 A, Zn 173°.7.

No other stars appearing and the night skywave loran signals still being unsettled, the navigator advanced the 1420 sun line to 1910.
Plot and record the 1910 R. Fix.
Ans: 1910 R. Fix, 32° 05′.0 N, 168° 39′.4 E.
(Note: The advance of the 1420 sun line, despite intervening maneuvers, is the same in direction and distance as between the D.R.'s at 1420 and 1910. See §3001.)
At 2000, a loran fix was obtained; L 32° 03′.3 N, λ 168° 23′.5 E.

Cruise C

Electronic navigation to Bermuda. En route Newport, R.I. to St. George's Harbor, Bermuda; Monday, August 22, 1966.
To conform best to key plotting of this problem, use Position Plotting Sheet H.O. 3000 (31° to 38°). Label central meridian 66° W. All times are Eastern Daylight Saving Time (Zone + 4).

Plot the following Bermuda aids to navigation:

	Latitude (N)	Longitude (W)
Gibbs Hill Light Fl. ev. 10 sec. 354 ft. vis. 26 m.	32° 15′.0	64° 50′.0
North Rock Light Fl. ev. 6 sec. 60 ft. vis. 13 m.	32° 28′.5	64° 46′.0
Mount Hill (St. David's Island) Light F. 208 ft. vis. 20 m.	32° 21′.8	64° 39′.0
Kitchen Shoals Buoy Fl. ev. 3 sec.	32° 26′.0	64° 35′.8
Kindley Aeronautical Radiobeacon Frequency 375 kc. Identification **KB.**	32° 22′.0	64° 40′.6

The navigator desires to follow the rhumb line from Newport to Kitchen Shoals Buoy. Draw the rhumb line as a straight line connecting the following points:

Latitude	Longitude
36°	67° 11′.7
35°	66° 27′.3
34°	65° 43′.5
33°	65° 00′.1

and Kitchen Shoals Buoy.

P C1-33. Loran Fix. The 0500 D.R. is 34° 50′ N, 66° 20′ W; course 150°, speed 10 knots. At 0500, the navigator obtained two loran groundwave readings (T_G) in rapid succession as follows:

1H 3	T_G 3068
1H 4	T_G 4006

From the *Loran Table* excerpts in Apx. VII, find the appropriate coordinates of two points on each of these lines.

Ans:

	Latitude (N)	Longitude (W)
1H 3	35°	66° 14′.9
	34°	66° 02′.0
1H 4	35° 24′.0	67°
	34° 49′.1	66°

Plot and record the 0500 Loran Fix.
Ans: 0500 Loran Fix 34° 57′.5 N, 66° 14′.4 W.
Continue course 150°, speed 10 knots from the 0500 Fix. Plot and record the 1030 D.R.
Ans: 1030 D.R. 34° 10′ N, 65° 41′ W.

P C2-33. Loran Fix at noon. At about 1200 (approximate position 33° 55′ N, 65° 30′ W), the navigator obtained loran readings as follows:

(a) 1H 3	(b) 1H 4
Z.T. 1148	1200
T_G 3007	3834

From the *Loran Table* excerpts in Apx. VII, determine the appropriate chart coordinates of points on these lines. Plot the 1200 1H 4 line. Advance the 1148 1H 3 line to 1200. Plot and record the 1200 Loran Fix.

Ans:

		Latitude (N)	Longitude (W)
(a) 1H 3		34°	65° 33′.9
		33°	65° 18′.7
(b) 1H 4		34° 13′.2	66°
		33° 33′.0	65°

1200 Loran Fix, 33° 53′.8 N, 65° 31′.3 W.

Continue course 150°, speed 10 knots from the 1200 Fix. Plot and record the 1230 D.R.
Ans: 1230 D.R. 33° 50′ N, 65° 28′ W.

P C3-33. Preparation for landfall. (a) Plot and record the true course from the 1230 Fix to Kitchen Shoals Buoy.
Ans: True course 152°.

(b) If variation is 15° W and deviation is 2° E on this heading, what is the compass course?
Ans: Compass course 165°.

At 1230, alter course to 165° p.s.c.

(c) Using the *Nautical Almanac* excerpts in Apx. V, for August 22, 1966, compute the time of sunset and the end of nautical twilight.
Ans: Sunset 1859, Nautical twilight ends 1956.

(d) The height of the navigator's eye is 9 feet. Using Table 8 in Bowditch or the abbreviated Table 6 in Apx. VIII, compute the distance at which he should expect to sight the following lights:

	Answers	
Gibbs Hill Light	24.9	miles
North Rock Light	12.3	″
Mount Hill Light	19.9	″

P C4-33. Radio bearing. At 1930, a bearing was taken on Kindley radiobeacon. When the navigator had a good reading, 17° relative, he called "Mark," and the helmsman noted the compass heading at that instant to be 160° (5° off course). Compute the true bearing of Kindley Rbn.
Ans: Bearing to Kindley Rbn. 164° True.
Plot the 1930 radio bearing.

P C5-33. Landfall. Three lights were sighted almost simultaneously. At 2100, Gibbs Hill Light and North Rock Light were in range; and at the same time, the measured bearing of Mount Hill Light taken across the compass was 176° p.s.c. Compute the true bearing of Mount Hill Light, plot and record the 2100 Fix.
Ans: Mount Hill Light bearing 163° T.
    2100 Fix, 32° 34′.8 N, 64° 43′.8 W.

Find the course and distance to Kitchen Shoals Buoy from the 2100 Fix.
Ans: Course 143° T, distance approximately 10 miles.

Course was altered to 143° T; and at 2200, Kitchen Shoals Buoy was sighted dead ahead. Leaving it to starboard, the ship stood off and on the shore at St. David's Head awaiting daylight to enter the cut to St. George's Harbor.

CRUISE D

North and west of Midway Island, heading about ESE, Tuesday, April 5, 1966.
To conform best with key plotting of problem, use Position Plotting Sheet H.O. 3000-12z, Latitudes 35° to 38°. Orient the sheet for north latitude and label the central meridian 179° W.
(Note: From left to right, meridians should be labeled as follows: 179° E, 180°, 179° W, 178 W, 177° W.)
Constants for all sights; I.C. 0'.0, Ht. Eye 39 ft., W.E. on Z.T. 0s.
At 1900, zone time (—) 12 hours, D.R. position was 37° 36'.2 N, 179° 01'.3 E, course 105° true, speed 10 knots.

P D1-33. Planet and stars for a fix. About 1900, took evening sights and selected the following for reduction to lines of position.

	(a) Jupiter	(b) Regulus	(c) Polaris
Z.T.	18h 50m 07s	19h 10m 01s	19h 11m 56s
Hs	60° 35'.2	51° 51'.4	37° 45'.0

Solve Jupiter and Regulus sights for LOP. Advance or retire the A.P.'s to 1900 before plotting lines
Solve Polaris sight for latitude using 1900 longitude to obtain LHA ♈. Plot 1912 Polaris line and retire it to 1900.
Record 1900 Fix.
Ans: Fix at 1900, 37° 39'.0 N, 179° 00'.7 E.
Continue C 105°, S 10 knots from 1900 Fix.

P D2-33. Crossing the Date Line. Plot D.R. and record time of crossing the Date Line and latitude at crossing.

(a) What is the (—) 12 zone time at Date Line crossing? (b) What is the latitude? (c) What is the new date? (d) The new zone description? (e) How long will April 4 last at the ship? (f) By custom, ship's clocks are reset as directed by the Captain. Since a new time zone has been entered, what change should the navigator recommend be made in the ship's clocks?
Ans: (a) 2354 (—) 12 zone time. (b) Latitude of crossing, 37° 26'.3 N. (c) Monday, April 4, 1966. (d) New zone description, (+) 12 hours. (e) Remainder of April 4, 6m. (f) No change in clocks.

P D3-33. Next morning twilight, again April 5, 1966, the navigator observed three stars as follows:

	(a) Altair	(b) Arcturus	(c) Deneb
Z.T.	4h 51m 16s	5h 00m 00s	5h 10m 21s
Hs	50° 51'.9	38° 29'.0	60° 45'.6

Solve each sight for LOP, advance Altair and Arcturus LOP's to 0510, plot Deneb LOP, and record the 0510 Fix.
Ans: Fix at 0510, 37° 09'.4 N, 178° 59'.0 W.
Transfer course line to 0510 Fix position and continue on C 105°, S 10.

P D4-33. Planet and Sun for Fix. About 0840, the sky being clear and a deep blue, the navigator observed Venus by daylight followed by a sun observation as follows:

	(a) Venus	(b) Sun (Lower limb)
Z.T.	8h 40m 23s	8h 51m 23s
Hs	42° 08'.7	37° 48'.6

Solve each sight for LOP. Advance Venus line to 0851 and plot and record 0851 Fix.

Ans: 0851 Fix, 37° 00'.0 N, 178° 16'.4 W.

Continue C 105°, S 10.

P D5-33. Loran line. At 1100, the navigator found that he was receiving loran signals and obtained a corrected skywave reading of rate 2L 7; T$_G$ 5728. As in §1309, plot the 1100 loran line using Apx. VII.

Plot and record the 1100 E.P.

Ans: 1100 E.P., 36° 54'.6 N, 177° 51'.7 W.

Plot and record the 1200 D.R.

Ans: 36° 52'.0 N, 177° 38'.7 W.

P D6-33. Fix at L.A.N. Using tables 2 and 3, Apx. VIII, estimate LMT of L.A.N.

Ans: L.A.N., 1154.

Advance 1100 E.P. to estimated L.A.N. and record.

Ans: 36° 52'.2 N, 177° 40' W.

Using GHA method, estimate Z.T. of L.A.N.

Ans: Z.T. of L.A.N., 11h 53m 20s.

Using latitude of 1154 E.P., predict Hs 59° 10'.1.

At L.A.N., navigator observed ☉ Hs 59° 11'.8.

Compute latitude by meridian altitude method and record.

Ans: Lat. at L.A.N., 36° 50'.5 N.

Plot the L.A.N. latitude, advance the 1100 loran line, plot and record the R. Fix. at ·L.A.N.

Ans: 1153 R. Fix, 36° 50'.5 N, 177° 39'.0 W.

Ship continued on course C 105°, S 10.

CRUISE E

All solutions by *Air Almanac* and H.O. 214.

This problem in practical work is an exercise in the use of the *Air Almanac* for surface navigation, a practice which is frequently used at sea.

The sights are assumed to have been taken with a marine sextant with altitudes above the sea horizon. Solution for LOP and sextant altitude corrections are taken from the *Air Almanac* excerpts (Apx. VI), as explained in Chapter 24. As recommended on page A5 of the almanac, G.H.A. and Decl. of the sun and G.H.A. of Aries are rounded off before use. Values ending in 0'.5 are to be rounded to the nearest *even* whole minute.

New Zealand for Brisbane, Tuesday, April 12, 1966. **U.S.S. Transport** taking departure from Manakau Harbor.

Use Position Plotting Sheet H.O. 3000-12z, inverted for south latitude. Label central meridian 173° E. Constants for all sights; I.C. — 2'.0, Ht. Eye 36 ft., W.E. on Z.T. 1m 20s fast. Clocks keeping approximately Zone — 12 time and will be set to Zone — 11 time at the next hour following entry into that zone.

Departure. At 0800, April 12, 1966, took departure from 3 miles off Paratutai Light bearing 000° from ship. The position of Paratutai Light is L 37° 03' S, λ 174° 31' E.

Req: Point of departure.

Ans: L 37° 06' S, λ 174° 31' E.

P E1-33. Great circle course. Compute the initial great circle course and the great circle distance from 3 miles south of Paratutai Light to Brisbane (L 27° 28′ S, λ 153° 02′ E), (a) by H.O. 211 and/or (b) by H.O. 214.
Ans: (a) By H.O. 211, C 291°.7, 1229.4 miles.
     (b) By H.O. 214, C 291°.5, 1229.5 miles.

From 0800, ship on C 292°, S 10. Plot and record expected 1200 D.R.
Ans: Expected D.R. at 1200, 36° 51′.0 S, 173° 44′.5 E.

Using Tables 2 and 3 of the *Primer,* Apx. VIII, estimate the Z.T. of L.A.N. at the 1200 D.R. longitude.
Ans: Z.T. of L.A.N., 1226.

Plot and record the 1226 D.R.
Ans: 36° 49′.3 S, 173° 39′.3 E.

Using the 1226 longitude and G.H.A. method, compute W.T. of L.A.N. and predict Hs for 1225 latitude of 36° 49′ S.
Ans: W.T. of L.A.N., 12h 27m 43s, Hs, 44° 38′.

P E2-33. Noon sight. At L.A.N., observed ☉, Hs 44° 39′.5.
Req: Solve for Lat. as a meridian altitude sight.
Ans: Lat. at L.A.N., 36° 47′ S.

Radio bearing with sun line. To check E.P., observed radio bearing of Burgess Islet Light Station radiobeacon (35° 54′ S, 175° 07′ E) at time of noon sight. Corrected Mercator bearing was 120° *relative* to ship's head.
Req: True bearing of radiobeacon on C 292°.
Ans: True bearing, 052°.

Plot bearing. Is it consistent with D.R.?
Ans: D.R. is within area of reasonable bearing error.

Continued on C 292°, S 10.

P E3-33. Afternoon sun. April 12, 1966. D.R. 36° 36′.5 S, 173° 00′.0 E, observed ☉. Hs 24° 35′.4 at W.T. 15h 52m 15s.
Req: Solve for LOP.
Ans: A.P., 37° S, 172° 30′ E, *a* 4′.0 A, Zn 303°.5.

Note: Whenever the assumed longitude differs by exactly 30′.0 from the D.R. longitude, two A.P.'s are possible. Although either A.P. will yield essentially the same LOP, the usual preference is to use that A.P. having the shorter intercept (*a*).

Plot the 1551 sun line, advance the 1227 sun line to 1551, and record the 1551 R. Fix.
Ans: R. Fix at 1551, 36ʰ 34′.3 S, 172° 56′.8 E.

Continue C 292°, S 10 from 1551 R. Fix.

Preparation for a round of stars. Evening of April 12, 1966. Compute the times of (a) sunset and (b) civil twilight at the ship.
Ans: (−) 12 Zone time of (a) sunset, 1811, and (b) civil twilight, 1836.

Advance 1551 R. Fix to 1836, and plot and record 1836 D.R.
Ans: D.R. at 1836, 36° 24′.3 S, 172° 25′.2 E.

Compute LHA ♈ at civil twilight to nearest ½ degree.
Ans: LHA ♈, 111°.5 at 1836 Zone (−) 12.

With H.O. 2102-D (or equivalent) set for latitude 35° S and LHA ♈ 111°.5, select stars and/or planets (§3108) for a Fix. In this selection, consider both magnitude and distribution in azimuth. Record azimuth, altitude, and *t*.

Possible Ans:

Body	Azimuth	Altitude	t
Procyon	005°	49°	2° E
Regulus	046°	28°	40° E
Gienah	095°	24°	72° E
Acrux	146°	38°	75° E
Achernar	219°	31°	88° W
Rigel	305°	49°	34° W
Betelgeuse	329°	42°	23° W
Jupiter	333°	27°	26° W

P E4-33. Three body Fix. During evening twilight, observed three bodies for a fix. (Continue — 12 zone time until after the fix.)

	(a) Jupiter	(b) Achernar	(c) Gienah
W.T.	18h 36m 08s	18h 40m 23s	18h 45m 22s
Hs	25° 48'.2	31° 05'.5	26° 10'.1

Solve these sights for LOP's, advance and plot the lines, and record 1844 Fix.

Ans:	(a) Jupiter	(b) Achernar	(c) Gienah
A.P.	36° S, 172° 53' E	36° S, 172° 19' E	36° S, 172° 29' E
a	10'.2 A	13'.8 T	3'.8 A
Zn	333°.5	218°.7	093°.3

Fix at 1844, 36° 21'.7 S, 172° 23'.7 E.

Continue C 292°, S 10 from 1844 Fix.
The 1844 Fix shows that the ship entered a new time zone when it crossed longitude 172° 30' E. Set ship's clocks to new time.

(a) What is the new zone description?
Ans: (—) 11.

(b) How should ship's clocks be reset?
Ans: At 1900, set clocks to 1800; i.e., back one hour. (Note: G.M.T. 0700 is the same on both settings.)

Plot and record the 2000 D.R.
Ans: D.R. at 2000, 36° 13'.4 S, 171° 57'.3 E.

Orders for the night: Continue C 292°, S 10. Note: Students using the suggested H.O. 3000-12z plotting sheet will find it necessary to transfer the D.R. course line from the left-hand meridian to the right-hand meridian. A convenient method of doing this is to transfer a plotted position such as a fix or D.R. from one side of the plotting sheet to the other side. Be sure to label meridians correctly!

Plot and record the 0600 D.R., which is the approximate time of sunrise, from the Almanac.
Ans: D.R. at 0600, 35° 36'.0 S, 170° 03'.5 E.

P E5-33. Sights at dawn. Compute (a) Z.T. of beginning of civil twilight and (b) Z.T. of sunrise on Wednesday, April 13, 1966.
Ans: (a) Civil twilight, 0537. (b) Sunrise, 0604.

During dawn twilight, the navigator observed several bodies, selecting the following for plotting:

	(a) Rasalhague	(b) Venus	(c) Moon (Upper Limb)
W.T.	5h 37m 12s	5h 42m 15s	5h 51m 43s
Hs	35° 51'.6	39° 51'.7	80° 17'.7

Solve each sight for LOP, plot, and record 0550 Fix.

Ans:	(a) Rasalhague	(b) Venus	(c) Moon (Upper Limb)
A.P.	36° S, 169° 52′ E	36° S, 170° 00′ E	36° S, 170° 34′ E
a	8′.7 T	13′.5 T	16′.3 T
Zn	328°.2	069°.5	010°.3

Fix at 0550, 35° 39′.8 S, 170° 07′.0 E.

At 0550 Fix, change course to 294° to conform to great circle route; continue S 10.

34. ZERO HOUR

OVER the years run many stories of men who have taken to the boats and found their way over a trackless ocean to land. In these years of many missions, few of those who go down to the sea in ships are without personal knowledge of some brave man who likewise guided shipmates to safety. From such men of the seven seas a few suggestions have been gathered that may be useful to others who face the zero hour. The result is far from complete, but it is from the sea and of the sea, and not from books.

The value of whatever can be said depends on circumstances. To an experienced navigator, fully equipped, the problem is little different from that aboard ship, but many boats are lucky to have compass and chart, or may have nothing at all. An old quartermaster will know better what to do than a landlubber, but even the latter can learn to know the North Star. Thus the reader must judge when and to whom the following remarks apply. They relate to navigation with little reference to safety provisions or to seamanship.

3401. Personal preparation. This section is addressed to the individual with no knowledge of navigation who may find himself adrift alone or as the leader in an isolated boat without an experienced officer.

In any case, one or all of the following questions must be faced and answered as well as may be. (1) Your position when set adrift. (2) The course to steer. (3) How to steer that course. (4) Your position from day to day. (5) The indications of land before it can be seen.

How one may seek answers to these questions from a lifeboat is outlined in this chapter. Some of the methods require experience, the others may be followed by anyone who has or can develop a sense of direction. If time permits, read the chapters in this book on Tools of the Trade, The Magnetic Compass, Piloting, and Dead Reckoning before undertaking a detailed study of possibilities from a small boat.

The study of the first six sections of the chapter on Errors of The Compass is especially important for one inexperienced in such matters. Thereafter copy the Correcting and Uncorrecting forms from the top of the Compass Guide at the back of this book and keep them with you for guidance when confused. Without an understanding of its possible errors, a compass is of questionable value anywhere, and less in a steel lifeboat.

A review of the problems to be dealt with will indicate the wisdom of taking the following articles on your voyage if they can be procured. Remember that they are useless if they are not with you when you go over the side.

Pilot Charts of the waters likely to be traversed. If uncertain as to where bound take the set of six. The charts should be for the proper season of the year, but any chart is better than none.

These charts show the way to the nearest land, give the variation of the compass, and indicate the winds and currents to be expected during the period for which they are published. Charts of the North Atlantic, North Pacific, Indian Ocean, and Central American Waters are published for each month. Those for the South Atlantic and South Pacific Oceans are published for each quarter of the year. They are printed on conveniently thin paper and may be obtained from authorized chart dealers.

Pocket watch, or any watch which is running in good order is convenient and helpful in minor matters. Wrist watches, or small, thin or cheap pocket watches seldom keep accurate time. A first class watch, set to and keeping accurate time is an important contribution to the navigation of any craft adrift. If you have a good watch read Chapter 22 and set about making it keep time at a known rate. Then remember that the watch will probably be under water before you reach a boat or raft, and at all times keep it stowed or wrapped in a moistureproof, waterproof package.

Pocket compass may be useful when nothing better is at hand. To use such a compass in a steel lifeboat, stand on a thwart and keep the compass as far above the boat's magnetism as possible. This will reduce or eliminate the compass' deviation. If the compass is not graduated in degrees note that from N to E (8 points) is 90° and that 1 point equals 11¼°.

The position of the ship at the time of a disaster is of prime importance as a starting point for navigation when adrift. If it be posted or announced, record the position and see that you keep it with you.

3402. The ship's preparations vary with every ship. In part required by law or regulations, the details depend on the ship's officers. The law requires that a compass and a watertight tube containing properly selected Pilot Charts be stowed in each lifeboat. The preparations cited below reflect the practice of two well-known captains of torpedoed ships.

In each case conditions permitted carrying out the complete plan which worked well.

The problem of magnetic compasses in steel lifeboats was dealt with in advance. During harbor practice the ship's officers selected the practical position for each boat's compass where deviation seemed least. The ship's carpenter then fastened a small wooden platform for the compass box in the selected positions. With compass lashed in place, the deviations of each boat's compass were approximated by ranges and recorded before sailing. This plan was considered better than to depend only on checking the compass' errors after launching at sea.

In addition to the Pilot Chart tube, a watertight container, in which were small parallel rulers, 30°-60° triangle, small protractor, and pencils, was stowed in each lifeboat. On one ship an extra sextant was wrapped and stowed in the No. 1 boat.

Each officer kept a waterproof bag at hand which contained Bowditch's *Useful Tables* (H.O. 9-II), *Nautical Almanac* and the Red azimuth tables (H.O. 71). The Second Officer was responsible for taking the ship's chronometer into his lifeboat. Watches of all officers were regularly compared for error and rate.

At sea, the officers prepared and maintained large plotting sheets, kept in the Pilot Chart tube of each boat, which outlined the nearest coast with important data for the best landfall. Each watch, a slip was prepared giving the expected positions at half hour intervals, course and distance to best landfall, and the variation of the compass. Copies of this information were given to each boat officer. On another ship the same information at twelve hour intervals for the next three days was placed in the Pilot Chart tubes each day. An added suggestion is to include with the other data the bearing of sunrise and sunset for one or more days in advance.

3403. The best course to safety, as determined by ships' officers, involves various considerations which may be overlooked by the inexperienced.

Wind, not oars, must be depended on for distances beyond a few miles. A rubber life raft will drift straight before the wind. Likewise a lifeboat will sail before the wind, but a lifeboat sails best when the wind is just abaft the beam or on the quarter. A lifeboat under sail cannot make distance in the direction from which the wind blows.

Winds differ with the seasons, but shipmasters familiar with the waters know what winds to expect. Others must depend on what they know of the winds of the world or on a proper Pilot Chart. Such charts are seasonal and show conditions for the given month or quarter of the year, but any Pilot Chart is better than none. The arrows on the chart fly with the wind. The length of each arrow is the percentage of time the wind blows with the arrow. The number of feathers is the average force on the Beaufort scale. The more feathers, the stronger the wind. What must be considered is not necessarily the direction of the longest arrow, but the *average* direction of the wind. This average is almost self-evident on an examination of the wind centers on the chart.

At best, a lifeboat is a slow-moving thing, and ocean currents often must be considered. Chapter XXXII of Bowditch describes the ocean currents of the world in considerable detail, but the information on a Pilot Chart is more complete and convenient.

The relative possibility of being picked up is always a factor when deciding on the course to undertake. Steamer tracks, as in peacetime, are shown on all Pilot Charts.

Having reviewed the winds and the currents, consider the best landfall to seek. A small island may be difficult to find by approximate methods. A large island in a reasonably favorable direction is better. Or the course may be laid in a favorable direction toward the mainland. When completely ignorant of the lay of the land and without a chart, head true east (90°) or true west (270°).

If a landfall be selected which appears on the chart, a line from the boat's position to that point is the course. Having drawn the course line, lay a stick or any straight edge across the compass rose, parallel to the course line. Read the course in degrees from the compass rose in the direction of the proposed track.

3404. The direction to steer. A course, determined from a chart as in the preceding section, is a true course and must be corrected to find the course to steer by compass.

In a boat without a compass, the castaway must steer the true course guided only by the stars, the sun or the sea itself. Such true courses are plotted from the 360° rose on the chart without correction.

A navigator with his usual tables, knowing the local time, can find the azimuth of the sun or a star whenever they are visible. When such resources are not available, recourse must be had to one or another more or less approximate methods, among which are those given in the following paragraphs:

Polaris always bears within 1° of true north from wherever it can be seen, and may be easily identified as in Chapter **27**. Theoretically just visible from 1° N, it may be depended on at all times when stars are visible in latitudes above 10° N. No star marks the south pole.

The Belt of Orion, observed from any position, always rises true east and sets true west within an error unimportant when adrift. From a position on or near the equator, the Belt continues to bear true east until it passes the zenith and thereafter bears true west until it sets.

Spica, 7 hours after Orion, will rise and set approximately 10° south of true east and west when observed *from within the tropics.*

The sun does not usually rise true east, but the sun's approximate true bearing at sunrise and at sunset may be taken from H.O. 71 entered only with latitude and date.

Within the tropics the bearing of the rising or setting sun N or S of true east or west approximates the sun's declination N or S of the equator.

The sun at noon, local apparent time, always bears true south or true north as it reaches its maximum altitude. With a sextant the time of the sun's maximum altitude is marked with sufficient accuracy to approximate true north and south. Or any watch which will run, not necessarily set to exact time, will serve the same purpose. On the first day, time the interval from sunrise to sunset. At one-half of this interval after sunrise on the following day the sun will be approximately on the meridian. However, when and where the sun is very high at noon, it is difficult to judge its bearing by the eye and under such conditions this method of finding N or S becomes of little value.

The wind is another important indication of direction under certain conditions. Over large areas of the oceans the wind blows from the same general direction for long periods of time. The direction of these winds is shown on the Pilot Charts and is known to all mariners familiar with such regions. The long rolling swells run at right angles to the wind and these swells continue even when a temporary shift of wind kicks up other waves. Thus one often may steer by the direction of the swells when no other indication of direction is available. The method is least useful in the North Atlantic and North Pacific Oceans where the so-called circular storms of the meteorologist vary the direction of the wind and sea.

When the errors of the compass are seriously in question, the boat may be put on the desired true course by reference to a true bearing such as that of the sun. The reading of the compass is then the compass course to steer. However a compass course may have been determined, those familiar with small craft under sail know that you cannot keep your eyes on the compass. When the boat is properly headed, spot a far-distant cloud or a low-lying star and steer for it. Then from time to time check with the compass and if necessary pick a new mark.

3405. The dead reckoning must be kept up as well as may be. Captain Greenlaw, S.S. *Alaskan,* in the salvaged No. 3 lifeboat, without chart or compass, or much of anything to work with, kept his reckoning for 36 days, 1600 miles to a Brazilian landfall. Even a man alone on a rubber raft can keep a rough reckoning of where he is being blown. The uncertainties of course and distance are discussed in the following paragraphs as a meager substitute for small boat experience.

The course made good depends on several factors with which seamen from ships are not always familiar.

The average course actually steered, especially when close-hauled, is uncertain. The helmsman of a small boat under sail must meet the whims of wind, sea, and sail as he seeks to hold the given course. Even before the wind, he will probably keep her to port or starboard to avoid a jibe.

Leeway, even with a loaded boat, as shown by the angle the wake makes with the line of the keel, is far greater than that of a ship. When reefed and quartering to half a gale the boat will probably move sidewise as fast or faster than it moves ahead. Thus the course to plot is a matter of judgment.

Speed of lifeboats is often overestimated by men accustomed to watch the water from the decks or bridge of a ship. The water seems to slip by faster when nearer the eye. Many factors affect the speed. A lifeboat will sail fastest in smooth water, with a brisk breeze on the quarter. A loaded boat at sea in fair weather with a fair wind may make 3 knots, but averages 2 knots or less. With a strong fair wind and a fairly smooth sea, the speed may reach 5 knots.

Figures like the above are subject to all kinds of modifications, but dispel the 10-knot idea recently seen in print. With an improvised chip log and a watch, speed through the water may be measured with considerable accuracy. A modification of the same method, which also has been reported, is to note the time required for a chip to float a distance of 20 feet along the lee side. Then a few figures will show that a 12-second interval indicates about 1 knot speed, 6 seconds show 2 knots, etc. If without a watch and unaccustomed to counting seconds, a simple pendulum will serve. Tie a string to a small stone, or other weight. Hold the string between your fingers so that the bottom of the weight is 9¾ inches from the point of suspension; the pendulum will then beat seconds.

3406. Position by observation. Just what can be accomplished by observing the sun and the stars from a lifeboat depends on the skill and equipment available. A navigator with his sextant, an accurate source of time, an Almanac, and a small book of tables, may work as aboard ship although under more difficult conditions.

There are many ways by which an experienced navigator, thoroughly familiar with the stars, may use them to approximate both direction and latitude without instruments, tables, or time. Certain of these methods, including those noted in the following paragraphs, may be used by the novice without experience.

Latitude by Polaris when visible is the altitude of that star plus or minus a correction which varies from 0 to about 1°. Having observed a sextant altitude of Polaris, a correction estimated as in §2706 gives the latitude with better than lifeboat accuracy.

A thumb-nail altitude of the pole may be of some value if, perchance, your latitude is practically unknown. If and when the pointers of the Dipper are below Polaris, pointing up from the horizon, an altitude of the pole may be estimated by considering the positions of the pointers. Dubhe, the pointer nearest Polaris, is 28° from the pole; the other pointer is 5° from Dubhe or 33° from the pole. Thus, with one eye on the 5° between the pointers to estimate the distance from the horizon to the lower pointer, one may estimate the altitude of the pole. Without correction as for an altitude of Polaris, this is the latitude of the observer. The method is practical only from mid-northern latitudes, but under favorable conditions may give useful information.

Another thumb-nail method for latitude is based on the fact that the distance of any star from the pole is 90° minus its declination. Thus when from lower latitudes, as within the tropics, a star of known declination is seen to approach and skirt the horizon, an estimate of its minimum distance above the horizon plus its distance from the pole, gives the latitude. The uncertainties of such approximations are evident, but even so they may be of value.

The noon sight for latitude from the maximum altitude of the sun requires a sextant and an Almanac, but may be determined as in §2610 with little or no further knowledge of celestial navigation.

Longitude cannot be determined without accurate time. The result cannot be more accurate than the time used, 1 minute of time being equivalent to 15′ of longitude.

When taking a sight from a small craft, stand where there is the least motion, braced against some vertical support or a companion's shoulders, with arms and upper body flexible. Take the sights when near the top of a sea and avoid the top of a nearby wave as a horizon. When spray is flying use a plain sight tube, or no tube or telescope. Let an assistant take time and record the figures, and use the average of several sights like an airman.

To compute a sight, it is a fair guess that bulky tables like H.O. 214 will not be at hand. Young navigators trained only with H.O. 214 should learn how to work lifeboat sights with some one of the pocket tables.

3407. Signs of land. From the surface of the sea land is seldom visible from a distance of more than a few miles. There are numerous signs, however, which indicate unseen land, sometimes from a hundred miles or more offshore. Best known to mariners in areas where they are useful, these signs are equally available to strangers who observe and can interpret what they see, feel, hear and smell.

Reflection from the clouds marks the light of a great city from far at sea or warns the mariner of his approach to the low-lying Jersey beach with its endless seaside resorts. By day the light color of the shallow water in an atoll of the tropics may be seen in the sky when no clouds overhang the atoll. In arctic waters, bright areas in the sky indicate ice while shadows may indicate open water.

Clouds above Mauna Loa mark Hawaii from 150 miles. The clouds around a mountain peak may be seen long before the peak is visible. Such clouds are fixed and thus may be distinguished from the clouds which drift by.

In the tropics in early afternoon, small fleecy white clouds may often be seen from a distance of 20 miles or more suspended over a low island or an atoll or even over a coral reef.

The surface of the sea often gives indications of low-lying land before it can be seen. The long parallel rollers of the ocean bend and change their angle to the prevailing wind somewhat as in Fig. 3407. The sketch also suggests the confused area in the lee of an island and how the swells meet and again roll on before the wind. The bending of ocean swells is most often associated with the islands of the South Pacific but was first observed by the author when making for an island anchorage on the Maine coast.

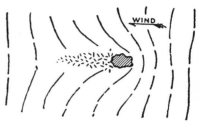

FIG. 3407. OCEAN SWELLS.

Seaweed is an indication of land to windward or in the direction from which a current flows. This is not true, however, of the floating weed of the Sargasso Sea, a relatively currentless area in the North Atlantic between 20°-35° N and 30°-70° W.

Sounds from the land with a favoring breeze may often be heard before land is sighted. Or at night or in fog the sound of the surf gives warning before the breakers are seen. Thus the fisherman in fog follows the beach around Cape Cod.

Smells and scents from unseen land to windward are far from a myth. The author's experience ranges from the stench of a Long Island fish factory to the smell of burning peat from the Falkland Islands when wandering the South Atlantic in December, 1900.

Birds, to one who knows them, give many indications. Land birds indicate nearby land, and even sea gulls, because of their feeding habits, are almost never found far at sea. A gull flying straight with a fish in its mouth is headed toward its family on some rock or another which at least is out of water. A bosun bird in straight flight near Bermuda is probably headed for that beautiful island.

*   *   *

The reader is again reminded that when and to whom the various remarks in this chapter apply depends on the circumstances of the situation. If a single suggestion saves a single life, the purpose of the chapter will have been accomplished.

APPENDIXES

I. STUDY AND TEACHING

SINCE the days of midshipmen in sail, the trend has been to separate the period of study from that of practice, day after day, coastwise and at sea, which together make the navigator. The following remarks relate to the study period and are addressed to students who seriously seek a practical knowledge of navigation, and to those first undertaking to teach the art.

I-1. Practical knowledge is the kind that is at a man's finger tips when required. If an unexpected can buoy be seen dead ahead in the mist, he must know which way to throw the wheel. Working a sight must be an incident, not a headache. Such knowledge is not gained by simply reading a book, or by listening to lectures. At each step one must learn to understand certain facts. Thereafter one must learn how to do things with the facts. This requires both study and practice with problems until the work can be done with ease and assurance.

I-2. To study the facts in a chapter, first read it and find out what it is all about. Then study each section. While so doing, write down the questions an instructor might ask, such as: What is - - - -? Define - - - -, etc. Having studied the section, answer the questions, preferably in writing, with minimum references to the text. Do this for each section of the chapter or assignment. Then close the book and repeat the whole process in the same way. Navigation is a subject which requires exact knowledge of each basic element before going on to the next.

I-3. The use of the facts is often illustrated by examples. Study each example and check its solution by checking (1) entries taken from the statement of the problem, (2) entries taken from tables, and (3) the arithmetic. Then solve the problem yourself without reference to the printed solution.

Answer all of the "Q" questions found at the end of a chapter. There are no trick questions. Each question requires only a numerical answer which, in many cases, may be computed mentally. In any case, the answers, with any necessary paper work, should be neatly arranged **in** the student's notebook before comparison with the given answers. From the beginning, the student should practice mental arithmetic, especially when taking out corrections and interpolating from tables, or when seeking the answer to a simple speed, time and distance question. *Use no scratch paper.* Do any odd bits of arithmetic at one side of the principal computation, so located or labeled that they may be identified by anyone.

Where problems are given, the student should solve not less than half of each type. Thereafter, let the student make up and solve his own problems. This is more difficult but far more instructive than solving a given problem. The persistence with which the student pursues problems will largely determine the practical knowledge acquired.

I-4. Note book and tools should be at hand from the start of serious study. These may be prescribed, but in any case must include the equivalent of the items presently discussed.

Note book or work book: A three ring loose-leaf binder for $8\frac{1}{2} \times 11$ sheets is convenient and takes the work forms listed in Appendix VIII. For general notes and computations, ruled sheets with a red margin line down the left side are best. Quad-ruled or other styles of ruling are readily available. Write or print the date, your name or initials, and the subject across the very top of the sheet and observe the principles of workmanship developed in Appendix II. Neatness is so important to the accuracy and speed of a navigator's work that the appearance of the student's notes is an excellent indication of his possibilities as a navigator.

Tools and other stationery include: (1) pencils, (2) erasers, (3) pencil sharpener, (4) dividers, (5) parallel rulers, and (6) protractor (4 inch). When desired or available, add (7) compass, (8) straightedge, (9) 45° and 30°-60° triangles, (10) small area plotting sheets and (11) work forms.

Tables and other data in this book suffice for the given examples, questions and problems. Other books are not essential, but the student would benefit by obtaining a Volume IV, H.O. 214 Tables which could be used for all problems herein, and would afford more practice in the use of those tables than the use of the *Primer Excerpts* provides. A copy of *Navigation Problems And Their Solutions*, as described in §1-7, is particularly helpful to self-students.

In addition to essentials, one or more charts, tide and current tables and almanacs for the current year, azimuth tables, and standard plotting sheets are helpful. Often books on navigation can be found in the ship's library, or in that of your school.

I-5. Selective study is essential to acquiring practical knowledge without delay.

The ramifications of navigation are endless both in the underlying sciences and in its practice at sea and in the air. What a student should study depends on his objective and on the time available. How quickly he can learn depends on the man and on how well he is taught how to do the right things in the simplest way.

Teachers face a grave responsibility in planning what to teach and how to teach it. The plan of this Primer is to teach modern surface navigation simply; references to air navigation are limited to a few matters of general interest. To meet the varying requirements of a textbook, two or more methods may be given for attaining the same end, and several chapters have been included which deal with subjects beyond the scope of junior courses. Footnotes suggest what to study and what to omit under various circumstances, but at best such advice is of a general nature.

I-6. Courses in navigation, present many problems to those responsible for their conception and conduct. The self-student, undertaking the subject without a teacher, faces many of the same problems.

A common mistake has been to attempt too much in the allotted time and thus teach little or nothing well enough to be of practical value. The type of student, time available for study and home work, and the time which the teaching personnel are able to devote to each student, largely determine what can be accomplished. Subjects and methods properly included depend on the objectives of the course. All this indicates the necessity of scheduling the details of a course in advance, especially when inexperienced instructors must be used.

The importance of what should or can be taught is evident. Omitted from this Primer, because they have little or no place in modern navigation, are the mathematical methods of piloting, the sailings, the old use of sidereal time and right ascension, and almost all of the older methods of working sights. All must agree that only one method for working sights for line position should be studied or taught until that method be mastered. Here again the choice is a matter of opinion, and depends somewhat on the work the student is likely to undertake.

When scheduling the lesson assignments for a course, the study requirements for each classroom period are equalized as well as may be. It is equally important to balance the problem and plotting work to be done between classes. The tendency is to underestimate by half the time a student requires for such work. Thus, inadvertently, assignments may be excessive, a condition which discourages the student and leads to carelessness.

The extent of the problems given at the close of each chapter is about three times that required of students in Naval Reserve training courses. All line of position problems may be solved from a D.R. position or from an assumed position. So here again instructors or self-students must select what fits their need. Many of the practical work problems may be shortened by not requiring the solution of all of the sights.

Whether the classroom period be fifty minutes or two hours, it should not be necessary to repeat in a lecture what the textbook has clearly explained. At Annapolis, it is customary to open a recitation period with a brief talk on the day's assignments and to close by pointing out important points in the new assignments. The intervening time is then available for contact with the students as they work the problems of the day. In laboratory or practical work periods all of the instructors' time is spent with the students.

Questions which require a written answer of more than a few words, in class, tests, or examinations, are burdensome to the instructor who must read the papers. On the other hand, such papers bring out a curious assortment of misconceptions and distorted ideas which otherwise would never be suspected. When returned corrected with explanations or, better yet, discussed with the student, they increase the personal contact which seems especially important in the teaching of navigation. Without an instructor, the student may obtain somewhat the same results by talking with experienced navigators. When so doing, allowance must be made for possible lack of familiarity with modern methods.

I-7. Work Forms and the Manual. The use of work forms when solving the problems of celestial navigation has a distinct educational value. The forerunners of those used in this book, which reflect the rules, were first devised for those who practice navigation intermittently. The distribution of a half-million forms of this type indicates their wide use by self-students and in connection with classroom instruction. In any case, some kind of simple form saves time and promotes neatness.

I-8. Mathematics, other than arithmetic, is not essential to the mastery of practical navigation. A knowledge of simple decimal arithmetic and ability to add and subtract time and arc are the prime necessities. An educational background with credits in mathematics, however, is of distinct value, especially when it has taught the use of tables, something of drafting, and a little algebra and plane geometry. The introduction of short courses in logarithms and trigonometry into courses in navigation means that much less time to teach the student how to navigate. There is no practical value in knowing that the "A" function in the H.O. 211 tables is 100,000 times the logarithm of the cosecant, unless, indeed, a bit of background gives confidence to the inquiring student.

*　　*　　*

This discussion has been written primarily for those who use the Primer. It also suggests how pride in the past and prejudice against the new, delay the training of surface navigators in days of dire need.

II. WORKMANSHIP

THE following discussions relate to those elements of workmanship which repeatedly enter into the study and practice of navigation. Good workmanship is not only essential to accuracy but saves time and trouble. It is a good habit, best acquired at the start.

II-1. Plotting is an important part of every navigator's work which the student must learn to do accurately, rapidly, and so that the work presents a clear picture to himself and to the captain or a Board of Inquiry.

Neatness in plotting is a first necessity for accuracy and clear reasoning. It is inherent with a good draftsman; it can be acquired by the inexperienced student. Lack of ability to plot neatly is a serious handicap.

Pencils of proper grade, kept sharp, are important. Avoid cheap, soft leads. Experiment for yourself and use a pencil that will make a fine sharp line that will not cut the chart or plotting sheet so that the line cannot be completely erased.

Erasing shield, such as used by draftsmen and typists, permits erasing lines, words, or figures, without injury to adjoining marks.

Other tools, necessary or convenient, include: dividers, parallel rulers, protractor, a pair of triangles (45° and 30°-60°), and a straightedge of about 18 inches. The universal drafting machine of a big chart room is a great convenience, and for aviators some form of course protractor is almost a necessity. Most of the plotting gadgets which attract students of surface navigation should be avoided until they have learned to do the work with the simple, old-fashioned tools.

Points may be accurately marked by the intersection of two fine lines. The prick of a pencil point or a divider tip, *exactly* at the intersection, may be helpful. For emphasis, draw a small circle around an important point such as a fix. Never use a big pencil daub to mark a point. Its center is probably not at the point and it is a poor mark from which to measure or through which to draw a line.

Lines. Too many lines, or too long lines, are confusing. Before drawing a line consider where it need begin and end. To draw a line through a point: Place pencil's point exactly on the point, slope the pencil slightly away from the ruler, which should be gently pushed against the tip of the lead. Press the ruler firmly on the paper and draw the line with the pencil point in the corner where the possibly vertical edge of the ruler meets the paper. There is no excuse for letting the ruler slip or drawing with pencil cocked across the top corner of a thick straightedge. Before drawing a line through two points, see that the pencil point, properly held, will pass through the second point.

Unbroken lines are generally used for all practical plotting, but dash lines may be used for special purposes. Many of the drawings in this book use dash lines only to better illustrate the problem.

II-2. At sea plotting includes various details relating especially to lines of position.

The azimuth or intercept line is drawn from the assumed position (D.R. or A.P.) *toward* or *away* from the body observed. Accuracy of direction is important, especially in case of long intercepts or long position lines. Lack of such accuracy more often results from careless plotting than from errors in finding the azimuth. If the azimuth angle is to be taken from a 360° true rose on the chart or plotting sheet, see that the edge of the parallel rulers is set along a line from the azimuth point on the graduated rose to an opposite point, 180° therefrom. Check this setting by noting that the line passes through the center of the rose. Or the azimuth may be measured from any meridian with the Field type of parallel rulers illustrated in Chapter 12.

The line of position may be plotted at right angles to the azimuth line without plotting that line. With parallel rulers set to the azimuth, prick off the intercept along the edge of the ruler. From that point draw the line of position with the 90° corner of a draftsman's triangle. A line of position to be used only when advanced may be omitted. Draw only the advanced line through the advanced point as in the right-hand sketch of Fig. 1605. The exact procedure for plotting a line of position is relatively unimportant. Establish your own routine and stick to it.

II-3. Labels. Immediately after plotting a point or drawing a line, it should be labeled. The label for a line should lie along that line. The label for a point should not lie along any line. A label across a chart or plotting sheet should read from the bottom of the sheet. Vertical labels should read from the right. When at an angle, top of label should be toward top of sheet.

Lettering of the style shown in Fig. II-3 is best. Anyone can learn to print this style of lettering neatly and rapidly. Exact forming of letters and figures is less important than that the bottom and top of the characters be in line and that they be properly spaced. Practice lettering between the edges of the long openings in an erasing shield. Then

A B C D E F G H I J K L M
N O P Q R S T U V W X Y Z
1 2 3 4 5 6 7 8 9 0

FIG. II-3. LETTERS FOR LABELS.

use only a beveled straightedge to stop the pencil's down strokes on a line. Good lettering contributes to that neatness and legibility which make for accurate and rapid plotting.

II-4. Legends arranged in Navy style are not only best but simplest in practice. No punctuation is required; signs for degrees (°), etc., are not used.

Time, an element of most labels, is always expressed by four figures, seconds being rounded off. Thus 7:15 A.M. is expressed as *0715.* At 5 minutes after 8 P.M. the label for the time is *2005.*

A point of position label prefixes the time to its name. Thus the dead reckoning position at 4:10 A.M. ship's time is labeled *0410 DR.* A fix at 4:23 P.M. is labeled *1623 FIX.*

Direction is shown by *three* figures of degrees true unless otherwise indicated. For example, 3° is labeled *003,* 26° is *026,* 321° is simply *321.*

C means course in degrees true.

S is for speed in knots which are nautical miles per hour.

The accepted arrangement of various legends is indicated by the following examples:

Course line, course 93°, speed 14 knots,

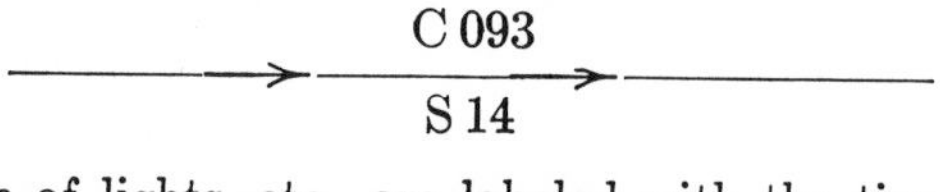

C 093
S 14

Bearing lines of lights, etc., are labeled with the time above the line and the bearing below the line. If Cape Cod light bore 273° true at 9:45 P.M. its bearing line would be labeled

2145
273

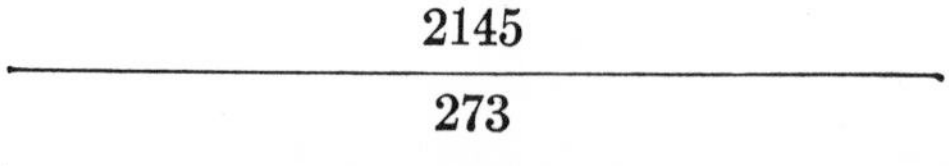

Lines of position from celestial bodies are labeled with the ship's time of sight above the line and the name of the body observed below the time figures. If the sun were observed at 8:15 A.M. the resulting line would be labeled

0815
<hr>
S U N

Advanced by course and distance to 11:20 A.M., label the line

0815—1120
<hr>
S U N

II-5. Arithmetic of navigation is simple enough, but, like that of any other business, requires special facility with certain items if blunders are to be avoided. In general, the best cure for blunders is to do the work in an orderly manner, with similar quantities accurately placed, the one under the other. Check additions, up or down, in a reverse direction to that of the first footing. Errors occur more often when subtracting. It is often necessary to take the difference when the lesser value is in the upper position. Check every subtraction by adding the difference to the lesser figure. Most of the following discussion relates to handling quantities representing time and arc.

Rounded figures. Although accurate enough for practical use, the last figure of the quantities used in navigation is seldom exactly correct. It is a *rounded* figure, the figure nearest to the exact value. Or if the value lie half way between two figures, it is customary to round to the higher figure. Thus 15′.4, 15′.5, 15′.6, when rounded to minutes, are written as 15′, 16′, and 16′, respectively.

Arc. The units of angular measure result from dividing any circle, whose center is at the intersection of the lines forming the angle, into 360°, each degree being divided into 60′, each of 60″. This results in the following well-known relations:

$$60'' \text{ (seconds)} = 1' \text{ (minute)}$$
$$60' \text{ (minutes)} = 1° \text{ (degree)}$$
$$360° \text{ (degrees)} = \text{Circumference of a circle}$$

In modern navigation, seconds of arc (″) are rounded to tenths of minutes (′), and seconds of arc (″) seldom appear except in the older books and tables.

Time. A limited but well-known table of time units is:

$$60s \text{ (seconds)} = 1m \text{ (minute)}$$
$$60m \text{ (minutes)} = 1h \text{ (hour)}$$
$$24h \text{ (hours)} = 1d \text{ (day)}$$

The minutes and seconds in the above table are quite different from arc units, but evidently the student who can add or subtract time, can deal with similar problems relating to angles with equal facility. In either case, the principal task is to acquire an automatic knowledge of how to carry or borrow 60.

Addition. Two examples of the addition of time are shown in the left half of Fig. II-5. The first is perfectly simple. In the next, the total of 78.5s requires the carrying of 60s as 1m to the minute column, etc. The light figures and the (−) and (+) signs show the mental process as you work from right to left. The principal trick in this kind of addition is to remember that,

WHEN THE TOTAL		WHEN THE TOTAL	
IS FROM	RECORD	IS FROM	RECORD
60 to 69	00 to 09	90 to 99	30 to 39
70 to 79	10 to 19	100 to 109	40 to 49
80 to 89	20 to 29	110 to 119	50 to 59
And carry (1)		*And carry* (1)	

Subtraction. The right-hand examples in Fig. II-5 illustrate subtraction of time. Again, the first is simple. The lower example is more complicated. The subtractions cannot be made without borrowing 60, 60, and 24. School days may have taught the student to subtract differently. For example, in the minute column he may add 1 to 52 and subtract 53 from 92, but the result will remain 39m.

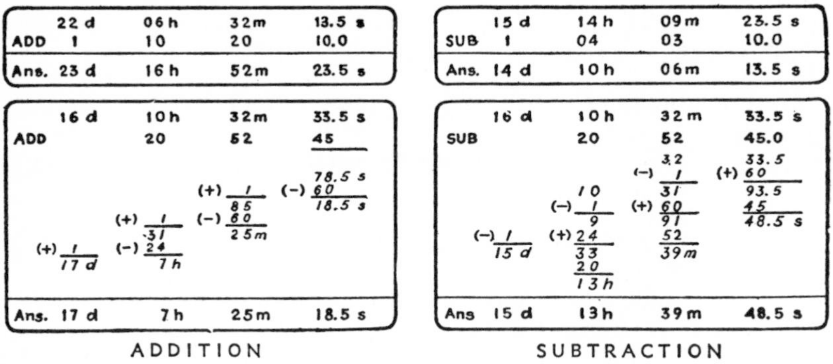

FIG. II-5. ARITHMETIC OF TIME.

Tenths of 60. The arithmetic of navigation often requires the conversion of seconds or minutes of time or arc into the nearest tenth of the next greater unit. For this purpose, remember that the tenths of sixty are:

0	6	12	18	24	30	36	42	48	54	60
0.0	0.1	0.2	0.3	0.4	0.5	0.6	0.7	0.8	0.9	1.0

When selecting the nearest tenth, it is customary to consider the halfway points, such as 3, 9, 15, etc., as representing the next higher tenth. For example, record 21 as 0.4 of the greater unit.

Add or subtract a correction? The plus (+) or minus (−) sign associated with a correction does not necessarily indicate whether it is to be added or subtracted. For example: a compass error marked (+) or East must be subtracted when converting true course to compass course. Beginners seldom understand why and when corrections related to timekeeping must be reversed, and often fail to recognize a situation where a (−) Equation of Time (Eq.T.) must be added. Even more often the novice fails to apply properly the correction required for finding the declination on an observed body from the figures given in the *Nautical Almanac*. Watch your textbook for specific discussions of these matters, and reason for yourself before you add or subtract.

II-6. Use of tables. When entering tables, a small celluloid protractor is an excellent horizontal guide. Hold the straight edge under the line on which the table is entered, and continue to hold it in that position while recording the desired figure. Again turn to the table, check the line and column where entered, and check the figure you have recorded with that in the table. This habit requires almost no time, and saves many a blunder. When entering the Almanac, watch the date. Be sure to use correct day's data out of the three-days listings on each page. With daily pages, it is helpful to cross off each day after it passes. With the *Air Almanac*, tear out the daily sheet after date has passed.

Interpolation, as the term is used in navigation, means finding a figure intermediate, or between, those given in a table. Modern tables have greatly reduced the necessity for difficult interpolations, and in most cases a single look should be sufficient without making any figures. A simple illustration of interpolation may be developed from the following short table:

SUN'S DECLINATION

| At 0h G.M.T. | −4° 25′.5 |
| At 1h G.M.T. | −4° 26′.5 |

The difference in declination is evidently 1′.0 per hour. How much must be added to the 0h figure to find the declination at 0h 36m (0.6h)? *Answer:* 0′.6. Or at 0h 48m (0.8h)? *Answer:* 0′.8. This is interpolation.

* * *

Train yourself to do minor calculations in your head. Seek out your own idiosyncrasies which produce blunders in longer computations. Such blunders are a burden to the study of navigation which must be eliminated. Until you can trust your own arithmetic, you cannot properly consider the real problems of the navigator.

III. RADAR PLOTTING

A S SUGGESTED in Chapter 13, the effective use of radar as an anti-collision device requires that the information available on the radar scope be properly interpreted. Such interpretation is mainly the application of well established principles of relative movement, here defined as the apparent movement of a distant object as seen from a moving vessel or displayed on its radar scope. The distant object may be moving or stationary. In either case, its relative movement with respect to your moving vessel will, when understood, provide much useful information.

The principles of relative movement have long been used to facilitate the tactical maneuvers of naval vessels in formation in which one vessel, often the flagship, is designated as "guide." Usually, the problem is to determine own ship's course and speed in order to change "station" with respect to the guide. In other words, the problem is to find a new course and a speed which will produce the desired relative movement between own ship and the guide whose course and speed are known beforehand.

III-1. The radar plot. It is recommended, if time, personnel, and plotting facilities permit, that the bearings and ranges read from the radar scope be transferred to a plotting sheet such as the *Radar Plotting Sheet,* WOXZP-5092 or the *Maneuvering Board,* WOXZP-5090 or 2665a (small), all published by DMAHC. This is particularly desirable for merchant vessels because a permanent record of an encounter is thus obtained.

It is recognized, however, that it is not always feasible for a hard-pressed watch officer to find the time to prepare a permanent plot. Consequently, the following discussion begins with a simple method of plotting directly on the radar scope, extracting the maximum amount of information in the shortest possible time; bearing in mind that some accuracy is sacrificed to convenience and that no permanent record will be retained. Later, instructions will be given for preparing a permanent record of an encounter on a separate plotting sheet.

III-2. Types of presentation. Radar scopes differ in the method of presenting ranges and bearings. Two types of presentation are briefly described in § 1318. In the "true presentation" (Fig. 1317b), the heading marker indicates the true course, and a manually-adjusted sighting line, often called a "cursor," indicates the true bearing. When the radar is set for "relative presentation" (Fig. 1317c) the heading marker remains at 0°, that is, dead ahead; and all bearings indicated by the cursor are relative. In Fig. 1317c, the bearing of the left tangent to Hoffman Island is 029° relative, that is, 29° to the right of dead ahead. A relative bearing can be converted to a true bearing by adding the true heading of own ship. Thus, if the ship is on true course 169°, the true bearing is 29° plus 169° or 198°. On true presentation, this bearing (198°) is directly indicated. See Fig. 1317b.

On many of the modern radar scopes, the presentation is always relative in the sense that the heading marker is always at 0°, but a second compass rose, concentric with the first, is provided. The second rose, often called the "true rose" or "true scale," can be rotated until the ship's true course is adjacent to both the heading marker and 0° on the "relative scale." Thus, if the relative scale shown in Fig. 1317c were enclosed by another scale with 169° set adjacent to the heading marker, it can be seen that the bearing of Hoffman Island would read 198°. If the true scale is automatically synchronized with the ship's gyro, courses and bearings read from it are true. If the true scale requires manual setting, one should be careful to note the true heading of the ship at the time the bearing is taken so as to allow for any yawing of the ship away from its normal course.

The methods for measuring range are described in §1319. The variable range circle is useful in determining the *speed* of another vessel in radar contact as described below. If a variable range circle is not provided, it may be found convenient to improvise a range scale by placing suitable marks along the edges of a narrow piece of flexible plastic.

More elaborate radars provide features other than those mentioned above. On "true motion" radar, provision is made for displaying the true motion of all contacts. The pip from a moving vessel exhibits a fuzzy tail astern of the vessel, while the pip from a stationary object appears without a tail. With this presentation, the electrical center (the point from which the trace originates) moves upward on the scope relative to the pips from stationary objects. The center must be reset periodically. Another refinement is provision for offsetting the center of the display so that a greater distance can be scanned ahead than astern. The reflection plotter or "plotting head" is almost indispensable if plotting is to be done directly on the radar scope. This device eliminates the objectionable parallax caused by the distance between the luminous screen of the scope and its transparent, protective cover.

III-3. Plotting on the scope is done by means of marks made on the plotting head with a china marking (grease) pencil. Bearings are measured by the cursor and, in the following explanation, are to be considered *relative* bearings unless specifically indicated to be otherwise. Ranges are measured by the movable range circle, if provided, otherwise by fixed range circles or a separate scale.

Plotting principles, and the information which can be obtained, are illustrated by two examples. Example I is a crossing situation in which the approaching vessel is on your port hand. Being the burdened vessel, it gives way to pass astern of you. Your radar is set on the 20-mile scale, relative presentation. The significance of each new bearing and range is discussed as it is plotted.

Example I: (See Fig. III-3 A.)

The following *relative* bearings and ranges are observed:

Time	Relative Bearing	Range (miles)
0900	278°	14.0
0906	278°	12.4
0912	278°	10.8
0918	274°	8.8

Required: (a) Analyze the situation at 0906.

Solution: The initial contact is marked and labeled "0900." This indicates that there is some object 8° forward of your port beam and 14 miles away. At 0906, the range has decreased to 12.4 miles on the same bearing. The pip is marked and labeled "06."

Discussion: The use of six-minute intervals is convenient because the distance traversed in that time interval is one-tenth of the speed. From 0900 to 0906, the object moved 1.6 miles relative to your ship. Thus the object's speed of relative movement is 16 knots. This is *relative* speed (RS), not actual speed. The direction of the 0906 position from the 0900 position is shown by the relative movement line joining these positions. This is the direction of *relative* movement (RM), not actual movement or course.

The direction of relative movement is important. If the object were stationary, as a vessel stopped or at anchor, the direction of relative movement would be parallel but opposite to your course *indicated by the heading marker on your radar*, and its relative speed would be the same as your speed. In this example, if your speed were 15 knots, in six minutes a stationary object would appear to move a relative distance of 1.5 miles to point *S* in Fig. III-3 A. The pip did not move to this point. Consequently, the object is not stationary and can be presumed to be a vessel making way through the water.

The direction of relative movement shows something else. Your radar scope is in fact a polar diagram with your ship at the center. The distance *from the center* to any point on a relative movement line measures the actual distance from your ship to that point. Consequently, the closest that a vessel, moving along a relative movement line, will get to your ship is measured by the shortest distance from the center to the relative movement line. In other words, the range at closest point of approach (CPA) is the length of a perpendicular dropped from the center to the relative movement line. In this example, the 0900-0906 relative movement line, extended, passes through the center and therefore the range at CPA is zero. In other words, the other vessel is on a collision course with you. Of course, this is also revealed by the constant radar bearings at 0900 and 0906 which have the same significance on the radar scope as a constant visual bearing.

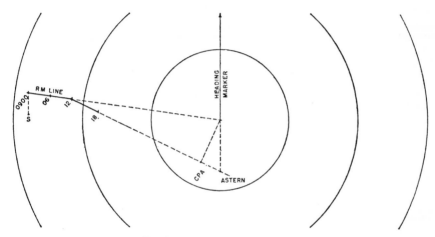

Fig. III-3 A. Radar Plotting.

Still more information can be obtained from the 0900 and 0906 positions. At 0906, the distance to the other vessel was 12.4 miles, which is also the relative distance since the relative movement line passes through the center. Since the vessel's *relative* speed is 16 knots, 46m will elapse before collision at 0952 (0906 + 46m).

Required: (b) Analyze the situation at 0912.
Solution: Plot the 0912 position and label it "12." This position falls on the extended relative movement line, 1.6 miles from the position 6m earlier. Both the direction and speed of relative movement are unchanged. Since *your* course and speed are constant, the 0912 position would not plot on the extended RM line if the other vessel had changed either its course or its speed. If *both* its course and its speed had been changed, the position might possibly plot on the RM line but the relative speed would be different. Since both RM and RS are unchanged from 0906, the vessel has not changed either course or speed. In general, pips which plot on the same straight line indicate no course change by either vessel.

Required: (c) Analyze the situation at 0918.
Solution: Plot the 0918 position and label it "18." The RM line has

taken a new direction. Since your course and speed are the same as
before, the new direction of the RM line means that the other vessel
has altered course or speed or both. Whatever was done, the collision
situation no longer exists because the 0912-0918 line extended no longer
passes through the center of the scope. In fact, if later pips follow
along the new RM line, the other vessel will pass astern of you, the
bow of your vessel being in the direction indicated by the heading
marker. Note that the relative distance between the 0912 and 0918
position is about 2.0 miles, indicating a relative speed of approximately
20 knots.

Required: (d) Find the distance and time at CPA.

Solution: Drop a perpendicular from the center to the 0912-0918 RM
line extended. This is done conveniently by sliding one side of any
right angle, such as the corner of a card or flexible plastic, along the
RM line until the other side is at the center of the scope. The foot of
the perpendicular is the CPA, 3.0 miles from the center and 8.4 miles
from the 0918 position. If the relative speed in the new direction is 20
knots, the other vessel will require 25m to arrive at CPA. At 0943
(0918 + 25m), it will be at its closest point, 3.0 miles from you.

Required: (e) Find the distance and time when the other vessel will
be astern of you.

Solution: The 0912-0918 RM line intersects the heading marker extended backwards at a point 3.3 miles from the center and 9.7 miles
from the 0918 position. This latter distance at 20 knots requires 29m,
and the other vessel will be astern of you at 0947 (0918 + 29m) at a
distance of 3.3 miles.

Discussion: It will doubtless have been observed that the distance
and time at CPA has been found without any knowledge of the course
or speed of either vessel, simply by noting the trend of pip marks across
the radar scope. On many occasions, this is all that is necessary. Risk
of collision is small if the distance at CPA is more than, say, six or eight
miles and there is no subsequent change in the trend of the successive
pips. However, the apparent simplicity should not lead to complacence.
The direction of relative movement is usually *not* the direction of the
other vessel's movement through the water.

For closer approaches, as in this example, the *actual* course and speed
of the other vessel should be determined for several reasons. First, it
will be easier for the Master or Watch Officer to visualize the situation
if he knows the course of the other vessel relative to his own. Second,
if it later becomes necessary for your vessel to increase the distance at
CPA, the proper action to take will be based upon sound knowledge instead of a guess. It is dangerous, even with experience, to attempt to
estimate the course and speed of an approaching vessel merely by watching the pips on the radar scope. The relative movement of a fast ship
on one course may be the same as that of a slow ship on another course.
Moreover, it is unnecessary to guess because the other vessel's course and
speed are easily obtained; as will now be explained.

Required: (f) Find the relative course and actual speed of the other
vessel between 0900 and 0912 if your speed is 15 knots.

Solution: **First method.** IF YOUR RADAR HAS A VARIABLE RANGE CIRCLE. (See Fig. III-3 B)

The time interval between the observations to be used is 12m. In this interval your ship moved 3 miles at 15 knots. Crank in the variable range circle to 3 miles, and mark its intersection with the heading marker (*r*). Transfer the 0900-0912 RM line parallel to itself and the same length, so that the earlier point falls on *r*. The direction of the later point (*m*) *from the center* is the relative course of the other vessel, that is, the *difference* between its course and yours. In this example the other vessel is steering 50° to the right of your course.

Crank the variable range circle to *m* and read the counter (4.0 miles).

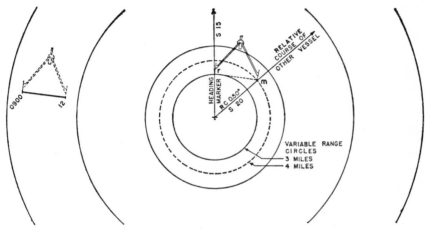

FIG. III-3 B. PLOTTING ON RADAR SCOPE WITH VARIABLE RANGE CIRCLE.

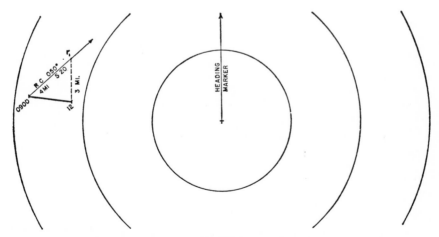

FIG. III-3 C. ALTERNATIVE METHOD OF PLOTTING ON RADAR SCOPE.

This is the distance actually traveled by the other vessel in 12m, so that its actual speed through the water is 20 knots.

Solution: **Second method.** IF A VARIABLE RANGE CIRCLE IS NOT AVAILABLE OR NOT USED. (See Fig. III-3 C)

This method is similar to the first method, but the pips marked on the scope are used directly instead of being transferred to the center.

Between 0900 and 0912 your ship moved 3 miles at 15 knots. From the 0912 position, lay off 3 miles parallel to the heading marker and mark this point r_1. The direction of r_1 from the 0900 position is the relative course (050°) of the other vessel and the distance is equivalent to that actually traveled by the other vessel, 4 miles in 12m or 20 knots.

Required: (g) Find the relative course and actual speed of the other vessel at 0918 if your speed remains at 15 knots.

Solution: **First method.** (See Fig. III-3 D) Since the time from 0912 to 0918 is only 6m, the distance to point r, is 1.5 miles at your speed (15 knots). By transferring the 0912-0918 RM line as before, it is seen that m indicates that the other ship is now on relative course 070°, speed 20 knots. That is, the other ship has changed course 20° to its right and maintained its speed.

Solution: **Second method.** (See Fig. III-3 E) For the six-minutes run of your ship between 0912 and 0918 at 15 knots, lay off from the 0918 position a distance of 1.5 miles parallel to the heading marker. The direction of this point (r_1) from the 0912 position is the relative course (070°) of the other vessel and the distance (2.0 miles) is equivalent to its actual speed (20 knots).

Discussion: It cannot be emphasized too strongly that the speed of the other vessel (20 knots) found by this method is its actual speed through the water, but the relative course is its direction relative to your ship's head *not relative to true north*. If the true course is desired it is only necessary to *add* your own course to the relative course of the other vessel. Thus:

Required: Find the true course of the other vessel whose relative course is 070°, (a) if your true course is 130°, and (b) if your true course is 322°.

Solution: (a) True course, 70° + 130° = 200°
(b) True course, 70° + 322° − 360° = 032°.

Example II is also a crossing situation, but a fast privileged vessel appears on your starboard bow on a course which involves risk of collision. You alter course to the right to increase CPA to a safer distance. Your radar is set on the 15-mile scale, relative presentation.

Example II: (See Fig. III-3 F.) Your speed is 12 knots, and the following *relative* bearings and ranges are observed:

Time	Relative Bearing	Range (miles)
2030	058°	14.0
2036	057½°	10.6

Required: (a) Analyze the situation at 2036.
Solution: Plot and label the 2030 and 2036 positions. A straight line

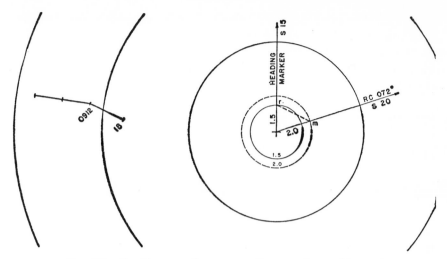

FIG. III-3 D. RELATIVE COURSE AND SPEED OF OTHER VESSEL, VARIABLE RANGE CIRCLE METHOD.

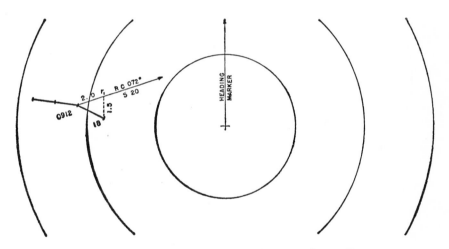

FIG. III-3 E. RELATIVE COURSE AND SPEED OF OTHER VESSEL, ALTERNATIVE METHOD.

joining the two positions and extending past the center indicates that the distance at CPA will be approximately one-half mile, too close for safety. The other vessel is privileged to the right of way, and your vessel is under the burden of keeping out of the way. Judging from the rapid movement of the pips (3.4 miles in 6 minutes), the other vessel is moving at high speed, and you should take action without delay.

Required: (b) Find the change of your course which will clear the other vessel by a distance of 2 miles at CPA if your speed of 12 knots is maintained and the course change is made at 2039. Use variable range circle.

Solution: 1. Find the relative course and speed of the other vessel by the method of Example I. Crank the variable range circle to the distance (1.2 miles) your ship will move in 6 minutes and mark its intersection (*r*) with the heading marker. Advance the 2030-2036 RM line parallel to itself until the earlier position is at *r*. The direction of the later position (*m*) from the center indicates the relative course of the other vessel to be 260°. Crank the variable range circle to *m* and read the distance (3.0 miles) on the counter. The other ship's speed is 30 knots.

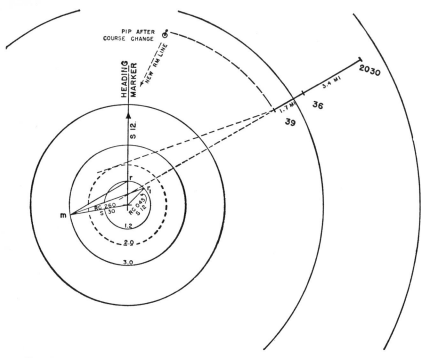

Fɪɢ. III-3 F. Fɪɴᴅɪɴɢ Cʜᴀɴɢᴇ ᴏғ Cᴏᴜʀsᴇ ᴛᴏ Iɴᴄʀᴇᴀsᴇ CPA Dɪsᴛᴀɴᴄᴇ.

2. Extend the RM line to 2039. The relative speed from 2030 to 2036 is 34 knots (3.4 miles in 6m). Advance the 2036 position for 3m at 34 knots (1.7 miles) and plot the 2039 position (bearing 057°, range 8.9 miles).

3. Find the new RM line. Crank the variable range circle to the desired CPA distance (2.0 miles) and draw a tangent to it from the 2039 position. Of the two possible tangents, the new RM line is the one which takes the other vessel across your bow (nearest the heading marker). (The student should study the result of choosing the other tangent.)

4. Find the change of your course. Crank the variable range circle to the distance you will move through the water in 6 minutes (1.2 miles).

From m, lay off m—r_1 parallel to the new RM line intersecting the variable range circle at r_1. The direction of r_1 (45°) from the center is the *change* in your course at 12 knots. The distance m—r_1 (4.0 miles) is the relative distance the other vessel will move in 6m after the course change, showing that the new relative speed will be 40 knots. Whatever true course you have been steering, your new course at 2039 is 45° to the right of it if you maintain 12 knots.

Discussion: Since your radar is set for relative presentation, the heading marker will remain at 000° when you change course. However, all pips will shift on the scope to new relative bearings. Thus, in the case represented by this example, each sweep of the electron beam will move the pip to the left on the scope until, when your 45° turn is completed, the echo of the other vessel will be approximately on bearing 012° (057° − 45°). The range will be somewhat less than at 2039 because the other ship is advancing during the time required to turn and also because of the normal reduction in your speed during the turn. The progress of the pips along the new RM line should be watched to see that the desired CPA is being attained.

III-4. Making a separate plot. The advantages of a separate plot are that it provides a permanent running record of an encounter between two or more vessels and that distances, courses, and speeds are obtained with greater accuracy than plotting on the scope. The disadvantages are that it is somewhat slower and requires a flat plotting surface with adequate lighting. The principles are the same as when plotting directly on the scope. They will be illustrated by means of the same situation as in Example II of the previous section. *All directions on a separate plot are true directions.*

Example III: (See Fig. III-4.) Your vessel is on course 030°, speed 12 knots. The following *true* bearings and ranges are observed on your radar:

Time	True Bearing	Range (miles)
2030	088°	14.0
2036	087½°	10.6

Required: (a) Find the distance and time at CPA.

Solution: 1. Plot the two positions and label them "$M_1/30$" and "$M_2/36$" respectively. Connect the two positions with a straight line and extend it past the center. M_1—M_2 is the relative movement line along which the other vessel will plot if *neither* vessel changes course or speed. CPA is at the foot of a perpendicular from the center to M_1—M_2 extended. Measure the distance from the center to CPA (0.4 mile).

2. The distance between M_1 and M_2 is the *relative distance* (3.4 miles) the other vessel moved in 6m; hence the *relative speed* is 34 knots.

3. The relative distance between M_2 and CPA is 10.6 miles. At a relative speed of 34 knots the other vessel will be at CPA in 19m, or at 2055 (2036 + 19m).

Required: (b) Find the course and speed of the other vessel.

Solution: Label the center *e* and draw *e—r* in the direction of your course (030°) and equal in length to your speed (12 knots) measured on the speed scale. From *r*, draw *r—m* parallel to M_1—M_2. This is the *relative speed* line. Since relative speed is 34 knots, plot *m*, 34 *speed* units from *r.* Draw *e—m*. The direction of *e—m* is the true course of the other vessel (290°), and the length of *e—m* in *speed* units is the speed of the other vessel (30 knots).

Discussion: It is highly desirable that the direction of all lines be indicated by arrow heads. Note that the relative speed line *always* extends from *r* in the same direction as M_1—M_2; that is, *r—m* is directed like the relative movement.

Required: (c) Predict the bearing and range of the other vessel at 2039.

Solution: The *relative* speed is 34 knots, so that at 2039 the other vessel will have moved 1.7 miles along M_1—M_2 *extended from M_2*. Plot this point ($M_3/39$) and measure its bearing (087°) and range (8.9 miles) from the center.

Required: (d) What course should you steer at 2039 in order to increase CPA to 2.0 miles if your speed is maintained at 12 knots?

Solution: 1. Draw a circle with *e* as a center and a radius of 2.0 miles by the *distance* scale. The new CPA will be on this circle.

2. Draw a new relative movement line from $M_3/39$ tangent to the 2-mile circle as shown in Fig. III-4. The new CPA will be at M_4.

3. From *m*, draw a line (r_1—*m*) parallel to M_3—M_4 until it intersects the 12-knot speed circle at r_1. This is the new relative speed line which is directed *toward* *m* although drawn backward.

4. The direction of *e*—r_1 (075°) is your new course at 12 knots.

Discussion: It will be seen that r_1—*m* intersects the 12-knot speed circle at two points, r_1 (course 075°) and r_2 (course 305½°). Either course will result in the desired CPA. Course 075° means a turn to the right of 45° from present course (030°). This is *toward* the other vessel. Course 305½° means a turn to the left of 84½° and *away* from the other vessel. The radar observer or student will find it helpful to visualize how the situation would appear from his bridge, assuming good visibility. At 2039, the other vessel would be seen bearing 057° relative (nearly on your starboard bow), and heading so as to cross your vessel from starboard to port. If darkness had set in, her range lights would be opened out to the left and her red side light would probably be seen. In this situation, a turn to the right results in a relative speed of over 40 knots (r_1—*m*) as compared with 18.6 knots (r_2—*m*) for the left turn. Hence, the deviation from the standard course will be considerably shorter. Also, a pronounced turn to the right, if seen by the other vessel, is a clear indication of your intention to pass astern of him. On the other hand, a turn to the left leaves the other vessel in doubt as to your intentions.

III-5. Relative bearings and the separate plot. When your vessel encounters another vessel and maneuvers are necessary to pass safely, it is the direction of the other vessel's motion through the water with respect to you that is important; not the direction with respect to true

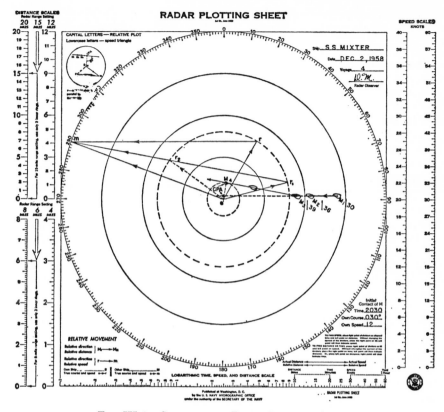

Fig. III-4. Solution by Radar Plotting Sheet.

north. No reference to true directions is made in the "Rules of the Road"; only such relative directions as "end on or nearly so," "on her own starboard side," "two points abaft her beam," etc. Hence, the interpretation of a maneuvering problem in terms of relative directions is not only more direct, but the transition from radar scope to bridge wing is made easier.

True directions are necessary if a separate plot is required or courses and bearings are to be plotted on a chart. However, any relative direction is easily converted to a true direction by the simple addition of own ship's true course. If plotting is done on the scope, the use of relative directions has much to recommend it.

Radars usually found on naval and merchant marine vessels are provided with means for reading true directions. On yachts and harbor craft, only relative presentation may be available. In any case, the ship's master will doubtless direct how he desires radar contacts to be plotted, reported, and recorded. It is appropriate that he should establish the conditions under which plots should or should not be prepared on his ship and whether true or relative directions are to be used. Thus, he could issue standing instructions that *all* radar contacts be marked on the scope and that a separate plot be made if it appears that the closest point of approach (CPA) of another vessel will be less than, say, five miles; or some other distance which he deems to be prudent. He could also direct that separate plots are not ordinarily required when well offshore, in the daytime, and in good visibility.

In deciding whether or not a record on a separate plotting sheet is necessary, he will doubtless consider the work load on his own bridge personnel and make up his mind whether the accuracy and permanence to be obtained by separate plot is more important than some navigational or other duties which must be foregone in order to obtain it.

It seems to be true that when navigational duties become more pressing, as when entering a harbor, the risk of collision also increases. Safety of the ship being the first consideration, time should be found at the very least to mark on the radar scope successive positions of an approaching ship with the time of the observation. The information obtainable from even a simple radar plot may mean the difference between safety and disaster.

III-6. The maneuvering board and tactical problems. The maneuvering board diagram shown in Fig. III-6 is a modification of H.O. 2665a used in the U.S. Navy and is similar to the diagram of the Coast Guard. The analysis of the relative movement between two vessels is simplified by selecting either of them as a "reference vessel" and attributing all movement to the other as the "maneuvering vessel." The center of the diagram always represents the reference vessel and is labeled R. The successive relative positions of the maneuvering vessel are labeled M_1, M_2, etc. The course-speed lines of the reference and maneuvering vessels are labeled e—r and e—m respectively. This standard labelling has been used in the preceding examples.

Since own vessel appears to be fixed at the center of one's radar scope while the pips of other vessels move relative to the center, it is logical in radar plotting to call own ship the reference vessel. However, in tactical maneuvers as between naval vessels, the flagship or other guide usually maintains a steady course and speed. Hence, it is convenient to let it be the reference vessel about which other units including own ship maneuver. The same principles of relative movement apply whichever vessel is selected as reference.

Fig. III-6 is a maneuvering board solution of the following tactical problem in which the guide is the reference vessel at the center.

Scale: 1 space = 1 mile; 2 knots.

Situation: Guide on course 020°, speed 16 knots. Your position is 7 miles on the starboard beam (110° true) of the guide.

Order: Take position 6 miles astern of the guide (bearing 200° true) using a speed of 18 knots.

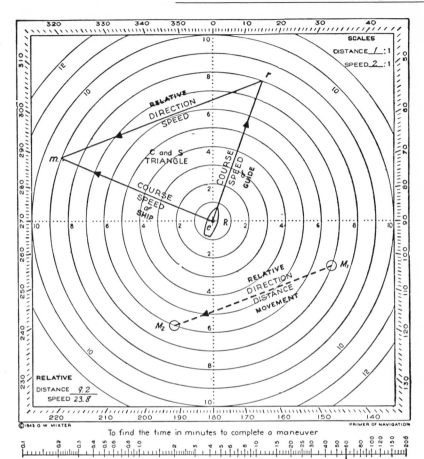

FIG. III-6. MANEUVERING BOARD.

Req: Your ship's course to new position. *Ans:* 292°.

Full explanations of tactical maneuvering principles are contained in Pub. 217, *Maneuvering Board Manual* and *Dutton's Navigation and Piloting*.

III-7. Practice plotting problems. Solution of the following problems will help to fix in the student's mind the principles of relative movement. It is recommended that as each problem is solved the student attempt to visualize an actual encounter between ships and try to picture the aspect of the other vessel as it approaches CPA. All problems should be plotted on a *Radar Plotting Sheet* or *Maneuvering Board*. If these are not available, the problems can be solved on a chart or plain paper with the aid of a protractor. Slight variations from the printed answers are to be expected due to minor differences in plotting.

DISTANCE AND TIME AT CPA

P 1-III. From the observations given, predict the distance and time at CPA and the time of crossing ahead or astern of you. Assume that neither ship changes course or speed.

	Time	Your True Course °	Relative Bearing °	Range Miles
(a)	0740	032	020	12.0
	0750	032	015	9.0
(b)	1117	183	050	14.3
	1121	183	051	12.5
(c)	2203	076	002	16.1
	2207	076	002	14.4
(d)	1414	240	213	13.2
	1429	240	214	11.5
(e)	0042	000	300	10.4
	0050	000	298	7.3

Answers to all of the preceding problems:

	(a)	(b)	(c)	(d)	(e)
Distance at CPA (Miles)	3.0	1.7	0	1.5	0.9
Time at CPA	0816	1149	2231	1608	0108.5
	Ahead	Astern		Ahead	Astern
Time of Crossing	0802.5	1153	Collision	1635	0110.5

COURSE AND SPEED OF OTHER VESSEL

P 2-III. For the problems in P 1-III, find the other vessel's relative course, true course, and actual speed if your actual speed is 12 knots.

Answers:	(a)	(b)	(c)	(d)	(e)
Relative course	251°	247.5°	184°	009.5°	094°
True course	283°	070.5°	260°	249.5°	094°
Actual speed (knots)	11.6	20.0	13.6	18.3	19.2

INTERPRETING A RADAR PLOT

P 3-III. Your ship is on course 000° true, speed 21.5 knots. The following radar bearings and ranges were observed:

Time	Bearing °	Range Miles
0250	006½	8.2
0254	007	6.0

Required: (a) If neither vessel changes course or speed, on which side of you will the other vessel pass?
(b) The distance at CPA.
(c) The time at CPA.

(d) The other vessel's course and speed.

(e) The two new courses which you can take at 21.5 knots to increase CPA to 2.0 miles. Assume no change by other vessel and that the change is made at 0257.

(f) At 0257, are you to starboard or port of the other vessel?

(g) Which of these courses avoids crossing ahead of the other vessel?

Answers:

(a) Starboard side of own ship (starboard-to-starboard)

(b) 0.2 mile

(c) 0305

(d) Course, 194°; Speed, 11.9 knots

(e) ′c/c 47° right, to T.C. 047°
    c/c 37½° left, to T.C. 322.5°

(f) Port

(g) 047°

TACTICAL MANEUVERS

P 4-III. *Scale:* 1 space = 1 mile; 2 knots.

Situation: Guide's course 205°, speed 15. You are 6 miles on guide's port beam.

Order: Take station 6 miles on starboard beam of guide.

Req: (a) Course, if you proceed at 18 knots. *Ans:* C 239°.

(b) Speed on C 230°. *Ans:* S 16.4.

(c) Course at S 20. *Ans:* C 246°.

(d) Speed on C 220°. *Ans:* S 15.4.

P 5-III. *Scale:* 1 space = 1 mile; 2 knots.

Situation: Guide on C 230, S 6. Own present position 5 miles bearing 185° from guide.

Order received at 1730: Take station 5 miles 045° on starboard bow of guide and arrive there at 1800.

Req: Course and speed required for maneuver. *Ans:* C 297°, S 15.3.

IV. OFFICIAL PUBLICATIONS

THE following is a partial list of navigational publications available from the government. Catalogs of charts and publications may be obtained free from the various issuing agencies.

The prefix initials to new charts and publications may appear unfamiliar due to recent reorganization of various government agencies. In 1963 the U. S. Naval Hydrographic Office (H.O.) became the U. S. Naval Oceanographic Office (NAVOCEANO). In 1973 the nautical chart and publication function of NAVOCEANO was transferred to the Defence Mapping Agency to become the Defence Mapping Agency Hydrographic Center (DMAHC). Similarly, in 1968 the U. S. Coast and Geodetic Survey (C&GS) was combined with the U. S. Lake Survey to form the National Ocean Survey (NOS) in the National Oceanic and Atmospheric Administration (NOAA).

Whenever possible, charts and publications should be purchased from sales agents listed in the catalogs; however, orders may be mailed directly to the agency. Catalogs and many of the publications may also be obtained from:

Superintendent of Documents
U.S. Government Printing Office
Washington, D. C. 20402

* * *

National Ocean Survey
Distribution Division (C44)
Riverdale, Maryland 20840

Catalogue of NOS charts, Coast Pilots, Tide and Current Tables, and Tidal Current Charts relating principally to the coasts of the United States and its possessions.

Charts of the coasts of the U. S. and its possessions as shown by the index charts and lists in the catalog.

Coast Pilots, and Intracoastal Waterways Pilots, for the coasts of the U. S. and its possessions, about 9 volumes. Each book furnishes information required by the navigator for the area indicated, which cannot be shown conveniently on charts.

458

Tide Tables, are issued in 4 volumes:
  Europe and West Coast of Africa
    (including the Mediterranean Sea)
  East Coast, North and South America
    (including Greenland)
  West Coast, North and South America
    (including Hawaiian Islands)
  Central and Western Pacific Ocean and Indian Ocean
  These tables include the predicted times and heights of low
water for a multitude of places throughout the world. Of necessity these are annual publications; therefore *use only the editions for the current year.*

Tidal Current Tables, are issued in 2 volumes:
  Tidal Current Tables, Atlantic Coast, North America
  Tidal Current Tables, Pacific Coast, North America and Asia
  These give the time, direction and strength of tidal currents
at numerous points; also brief discussions of the Gulf Stream
and other matters related to currents. *Use only the edition for
the current year.*

Tidal Current Charts:
  Boston Harbor
  Narragansett Bay
  Narragansett Bay to Nantucket Sound
  Long Island Sound and Block Island Sound
  New York Harbor
  Delaware Bay and River
  San Francisco Bay
  Puget Sound, Northern Part
  Puget Sound, Southern Part

  The above publications may be procured from agents. Direct orders should
be addressed to National Ocean Survey, Riverdale, Maryland 20840.

U. S. COAST GUARD
400 7th St. WASHINGTON, D.C. 20590

Light Lists issued in 5 volumes:
  I. Atlantic Coast; St. Croix River, Me. to Little River, S.C.
  II. Atlantic and Gulf Coasts; Little River, S.C. to Rio
      Grande River, Tex.
  III. Pacific Coast and Pacific Islands
  IV. Great Lakes
  V. Mississippi River System
  All aids to navigation maintained within and around the
United States are listed in the separate volumes shown above.
Included are data on radiobeacon and calibration stations, and
the Loran-A and Loran-C chains.

Aids to Marine Navigation of the United States
(C.G. Pub. No. 193)
   Describes basic principles underlying the marking of U.S.
coasts and waterways. Covers lighthouses, lightships, fog signals, buoys, radiobeacons, and loran.

Rules of the Road, International—Inland (C.G. Pub. No. 169)

Rules of the Road, Great Lakes, (C.G. Pub. No. 172)

Rules of the Road, Western Rivers, (C.G. Pub. No. 184)

Local Notices to Mariners. Issued as required by each Coast
   Guard District. Contain notices of changes to aids to navigation and other information of local interest only. Adequate for
   yachtsmen and other mariners operating locally.   *Free*

GREAT LAKES AND ST. LAWRENCE SEAWAY

   Information on aids to navigation in the St. Lawrence Seaway, the Great
Lakes, Lake Champlain, the New York Barge Canal system, and the Minnesota-
Ontario Border Lakes, available on request.
Catalog of Charts includes Great Lakes, Lake Champlain, New
   York Barge Canal System, Minnesota-Ontario Border Lakes.
   Write: National Ocean Survey, Riverdale, Maryland 20840.

Rules and Regulations, St. Lawrence Seaway. Write: Saint
   Lawrence Seaway Development Corp., Seaway Circle, Mas-
   sena, N.Y., 13662.

Nautical Charts and Related Publications. Write: Canadian
   Hydrographic Service, Chart Distribution Office, 615 Booth
   St., Ottawa, Ontario, Canada.

Defence Mapping Agency
Hydrographic Center
Washington, D.C. 20390

Charts and related publications obtainable from sales agents or as instructed in
catalog:

Catalog of Charts and Nautical Publications; issued in twelve
   sections:

Introduction, Part I; contains graphic index charts of world regions included in light lists, sailing directions, world and special charts, nautical and aeronautical charts and publications.

Introduction, Part II; contains index plates showing limits of
   loran charts; plotting, bottom-contour, great-circle, and other
   charts, including wall charts.

GENERAL AREA

REGION NO.

0	United States
1	Canada, Greenland, Iceland
2	Central and South America and Antarctica
3	Western Europe
4	Norway, Baltic and USSR
5	W. Africa and the Mediterranean
6	Indian Ocean
7	Australia and Indonesia
8	Oceania
9	East Asia

Maneuvering Board, large   (pad of 50)
      "   "   small   "

Radar Plotting Sheet, large   "
   "   "   "   small, green or black   "

Plotting Sheets, marine, four series:
  Large (920-936) 18 sheets, 35 × 46 inches, scale 1° Long. = 4 inches, for latitudes to 81° N or S. The sheets for higher latitudes than 64° N or S are at a scale of 1° Long. = 2 inches.
  Medium (900-910) Series, 11 sheets, 20 × 38 inches, scale 1° Long. = 4 inches, for latitudes to 65°. A helpful innovation on these sheets is that each degree line of latitude and longitude contains a ' scale. These sheets are especially recommended for yachtsmen.
  Small (960-975) 16 sheets, 17 × 22 inches, scale 1° Long. = 4 inches, for latitudes to 49°.
  Lifeboat size (940-953) 14 sheets 18 × 10 inches, scale 1° Long. = 2 inches, for latitudes to 74°.
  Universal, VP-OS, 1 sheet about 13 × 14 inches, scale same as Aircraft type, on which construction of the plotting sheet may be completed for any 4° of latitude.   (pad of 50)

Sailing Directions (Pilots), about 60 volumes relating to various areas of foreign waters and coasts. Each furnishes information for the navigator which cannot be shown on charts

List of Lights, six volumes covering the various coasts of the world except those of the United States and its possessions. Revised annually by new editions or supplements

RADIO AIDS

H.O. PUB. NO.

117A	*Radio Navigational Aids,* Atlantic and Mediterranean
117B	*Radio Navigational Aids,* Pacific and Indian Oceans

MISCELLANEOUS

220	*Navigation Dictionary*
2102-D	*Star Finder and Identifier*
249	*Sight Reduction Tables for Air Navigation;* Vol. I, altitude and azimuth of selected stars; Vol. II and Vol. III, altitude and azimuth angle of sun, moon, and planets.
229	*Sight Reduction Tables for Marine Navigation,* 6 Vol.
102	*International Code of Visual, Sound and Radio Signals.*

MANUALS

9	*American Practical Navigator,* Bowditch
217	*Maneuvering Board Manual*
226	*Handbook of Magnetic Compass Adjustment and Compensation*
1310	*Radar Navigation Manual—1975*

PILOT CHART ATLASES

106	*Atlas of Pilot Charts,* South Atlantic and Central American Waters
107	*Atlas of Pilot Charts,* South Pacific and Indian Oceans
108	*Atlas of Pilot Charts,* Northern North Atlantic Ocean

NAUTICAL PERIODICALS

Notice to Mariners. Published weekly; publicizes changes in aids to navigation throughout the world, and is official publication for correction of charts, sailing directions, light lists and other publications of the NOS, DMAHC and Coast Guard.

NOTE: A "Local" Notice to Mariners, containing similar information for each Coast Guard District is issued by each Coast Guard District Commandant. (See Coast Guard listings.)

U. S. NAVAL OBSERVATORY
NAUTICAL ALMANAC OFFICE, WASHINGTON, D.C., 20390

The Nautical Almanac, published annually in advance

The Air Almanac, published in advance for six-month period of each year.

V. NAUTICAL ALMANAC

EXCERPTS

THE following fourteen pages of excerpts from the daily pages of The American Nautical Almanac for the Year 1966 illustrates the present style of that publication. The excerpts are for the dates used in the examples and problems of this edition of the Primer. These pages include the principal data for the sun, moon and planets for these dates. Selected data for the stars used in the problems are also provided. The 1978 edition of the almanac has the same format and style as the 1966 edition.

The next seven pages provide excerpts from the increments and corrections and other tables needed in the problem solutions.

1966 JANUARY 7

G.M.T. d h	ARIES G.H.A.	VENUS −4.1 G.H.A.	Dec.	MARS +1.4 G.H.A.	Dec.	JUPITER −2.3 G.H.A.	Dec.	SATURN +1.3 G.H.A.	Dec.	STARS Name	S.H.A.	Dec.
7 00	106 06.5	150 33.8	S14 22.0	151 42.5	S18 24.2	22 56.8	N22 57.6	121 06.6	S 8 29.3			
01	121 09.0	165 36.6	21.4	166 43.0	23.7	37 59.5	57.6	136 08.9	29.2	Alphecca	126 41.7	N 26 49.5
02	136 11.5	180 39.4	20.9	181 43.5	23.1	53 02.3	57.5	151 11.1	29.1	Alpheratz	358 21.0	N 28 54.2
03	151 13.9	195 42.2	·· 20.3	196 44.0	·· 22.6	68 05.1	·· 57.5	166 13.4	·· 29.0	Altair	62 43.7	N 8 46.5
04	166 16.4	210 45.0	19.8	211 44.4	22.0	83 07.9	57.5	181 15.7	28.9	Ankaa	353 51.1	S 42 29.7
05	181 18.9	225 47.8	19.3	226 44.9	21.5	98 10.6	57.5	196 17.9	28.9	Antares	113 10.8	S 26 21.4
06	196 21.3	240 50.6	S14 18.7	241 45.4	S18 20.9	113 13.4	N22 57.5	211 20.2	S 8 28.8	Canopus	264 11.6	S 52 40.6
07	211 23.8	255 53.4	18.2	256 45.8	20.3	128 16.2	57.5	226 22.5	28.7	Capella	281 27.2	N 45 58.0
F 08	226 26.2	270 56.2	17.6	271 46.3	19.8	143 19.0	57.5	241 24.8	28.6	Deneb	49 56.5	N 45 09.4
09	241 28.7	285 59.0	·· 17.1	286 46.8	·· 19.2	158 21.8	·· 57.5	256 27.0	·· 28.5	Denebola	183 10.2	N 14 45.7
R 10	256 31.2	301 01.8	16.6	301 47.3	18.7	173 24.5	57.5	271 29.3	28.4	Diphda	349 31.9	S 18 10.6
I 11	271 33.6	316 04.7	16.0	316 47.7	18.1	188 27.3	57.5	286 31.6	28.3			
D 12	286 36.1	331 07.5	S14 15.5	331 48.2	S18 17.5	203 30.1	N22 57.5	301 33.8	S 8 28.3	Mirfak	309 31.8	N 49 44.7
A 13	301 38.6	346 10.3	15.0	346 48.7	17.0	218 32.9	57.5	316 36.1	28.2	Nunki	76 43.3	S 26 20.5
Y 14	316 41.0	1 13.2	14.4	1 49.2	16.4	233 35.6	57.5	331 38.3	28.1	Peacock	54 16.3	S 56 51.0
15	331 43.5	16 16.0	·· 13.9	16 49.6	·· 15.8	248 38.4	·· 57.5	346 40.6	·· 28.0	Pollux	244 11.3	N 28 06.6
16	346 46.0	31 18.8	13.4	31 50.1	15.3	263 41.2	57.5	1 42.9	27.9	Procyon	245 37.0	N 5 18.8
17	1 48.4	46 21.7	12.8	46 50.6	14.7	278 44.0	57.5	16 45.1	27.8			
18	16 50.9	61 24.6	S14 12.3	61 51.1	S18 14.2	293 46.7	N22 57.4	31 47.4	S 8 27.7	Rasalhague	96 40.2	N 12 34.9
19	31 53.4	76 27.4	11.8	76 51.6	13.6	308 49.5	57.4	46 49.7	27.6	Regulus	208 21.5	N 12 08.1
20	46 55.8	91 30.3	11.3	91 52.0	13.0	323 52.3	57.4	61 51.9	27.6	Sirius	259 05.1	S 16 40.1
21	61 58.3	106 33.1	·· 10.7	106 52.5	·· 12.5	338 55.1	·· 57.4	76 54.2	·· 27.5	Spica	159 09.3	S 10 59.0
22	77 00.7	121 36.0	10.2	121 53.0	11.9	353 57.8	57.4	91 56.5	27.4	Suhail	223 18.6	S 43 17.5
23	92 03.2	136 38.9	09.7	136 53.5	11.3	9 00.6	57.4	106 58.7	27.3			
8 00	107 05.7	151 41.8	S14 09.2	151 53.9	S18 10.8	24 03.4	N22·57.4	122 01.0	S 8 27.2	Vega	81 03.8	N 38 44.9
01	122 08.1	166 44.7	08.6	166 54.4	10.2	39 06.1	57.4	137 03.3	27.1	Zuben'ubl	137 45.5	S 15 54.0
02	137 10.6	181 47.6	08.1	181 54.9	09.6	54 08.9	57.4	152 05.5	27.0			
03	152 13.1	196 50.5	·· 07.6	196 55.4	·· 09.1	69 11.7	·· 57.4	167 07.8	·· 27.0		S.H.A.	Mer. Pass.
04	167 15.5	211 53.3	07.1	211 55.9	08.5	84 14.5	57.4	182 10.1	26.9	Venus	44 36.1	13 51
05	182 18.0	226 56.3	06.5	226 56.3	07.9	99 17.2	57.4	197 12.3	26.8	Mars	44 48.2	13 52
										Jupiter	276 57.7	22 20
Mer. Pass. 16 48.9		v 2.9 d 0.5		v 0.5 d 0.6		v 2.8 d 0.0		v 2.3 d 0.1		Saturn	14 55.3	15 50

1966 FEBRUARY 5

G.M.T. d h	ARIES G.H.A.	VENUS −3.7 G.H.A.	Dec.	MARS +1.4 G.H.A.	Dec.	JUPITER −2.1 G.H.A.	Dec.	SATURN +1.3 G.H.A.	Dec.	STARS Name	S.H.A.	Dec.
5 00	134 41.6	193 35.0	S12 23.7	157 57.4	S10 46.8	54 00.4	N22 55.0	147 00.7	S 7 19.8	Acamar	315 45.5	S 40 26.7
01	149 44.0	208 38.5	23.9	172 58.0	46.1	69 03.0	55.0	162 02.9	19.7	Achernar	335 53.4	S 57 24.9
02	164 46.5	223 42.0	24.1	187 58.6	45.3	84 05.5	55.0	177 05.1	19.6	Acrux	173 49.4	S 62 54.4
03	179 49.0	238 45.6	·· 24.2	202 59.2	·· 44.6	99 08.1	·· 55.0	192 07.3	·· 19.5	Adhara	255 40.5	S 28 55.6
04	194 51.4	253 49.1	24.4	217 59.8	43.8	114 10.6	55.0	207 09.5	19.4	Aldebaran	291 30.5	N 16 26.6
05	209 53.9	268 52.6	24.6	233 00.4	43.1	129 13.2	55.0	222 11.7	19.3			
06	224 56.4	283 56.2	S12 24.7	248 01.0	S10 42.4	144 15.8	N22 55.0	237 13.9	S 7 19.2	Alioth	166 51.7	N 56 08.4
07	239 58.8	298 59.7	24.9	263 01.6	41.6	159 18.3	55.0	252 16.2	19.1	Alkaid	153 26.9	N 49 28.7
S 08	255 01.3	314 03.2	25.1	278 02.2	40.9	174 20.9	55.0	267 18.4	19.0	Al Na'ir	28 29.1	S 47 07.8
A 09	270 03.8	329 06.7	·· 25.3	293 02.8	·· 40.2	189 23.4	·· 55.0	282 20.6	·· 18.8	Alnilam	276 22.6	S 1 13.4
T 10	285 06.2	344 10.2	25.4	308 03.4	39.4	204 26.0	55.0	297 22.8	18.7	Alphard	218 31.5	S 8 30.6
U 11	300 08.7	359 13.7	25.6	323 04.1	38.7	219 28.5	55.0	312 25.0	18.6			
R 12	315 11.1	14 17.2	S12 25.8	338 04.7	S10 37.9	234 31.1	N22 55.0	327 27.2	S 7 18.5	Alphecca	126 41.5	N 26 49.4
D 13	330 13.6	29 20.7	26.0	353 05.3	37.2	249 33.6	55.0	342 29.4	18.4	Alpheratz	358 21.0	N 28 54.1
A 14	345 16.1	44 24.2	26.1	8 05.9	36.5	264 36.2	55.0	357 31.6	18.3	Altair	62 43.6	N 8 46.4
Y 15	0 18.5	59 27.7	·· 26.3	23 06.5	·· 35.7	279 38.7	·· 55.0	12 33.8	·· 18.2	Ankaa	353 51.2	S 42 29.7
16	15 21.0	74 31.2	26.5	38 07.1	35.0	294 41.3	55.0	27 36.0	18.1	Antares	113 10.6	S 26 21.5
17	30 23.5	89 34.7	26.7	53 07.7	34.3	309 43.8	55.0	42 38.2	18.0			
18	45 25.9	104 38.2	S12 26.9	68 08.3	S10 33.5	324 46.4	N22 55.0	57 40.4	S 7 17.8	Arcturus	146 28.4	N 19 21.3
19	60 28.4	119 41.7	27.0	83 08.9	32.8	339 48.9	55.0	72 42.6	17.7	Atria	108 45.1	S 68 59.2
20	75 30.9	134 45.1	27.2	98 09.5	32.0	354 51.5	55.0	87 44.8	17.6	Avior	234 32.2	S 59 24.0
21	90 33.3	149 48.6	·· 27.4	113 10.1	·· 31.3	9 54.0	·· 55.0	102 47.0	·· 17.5	Bellatrix	279 10.3	N 6 19.2
22	105 35.8	164 52.1	27.6	128 10.7	30.6	24 56.6	55.0	117 49.2	17.4	Betelgeuse	271 40.0	N 7 24.1
23	120 38.2	179 55.5	27.8	143 11.3	29.8	39 59.1	55.0	132 51.4	17.3			
6 00	135 40.7	194 59.0	S12 27.9	158 11.9	S10 29.1	55 01.7	N22 55.0	147 53.6	S 7 17.2	Vega	81 03.7	N 38 44.8
01	150 43.2	210 02.4	28.1	173 12.5	28.3	70 04.2	55.0	162 55.8	17.1	Zuben'ubl	137 45.3	S 15 54.1
02	165 45.6	225 05.9	28.3	188 13.1	27.6	85 06.8	55.0	177 58.0	17.0			
03	180 48.1	240 09.3	·· 28.5	203 13.7	·· 26.9	100 09.3	·· 55.0	193 00.2	·· 16.8		S.H.A.	Mer. Pass.
04	195 50.6	255 12.8	28.7	218 14.3	26.1	115 11.9	55.1	208 02.4	16.7	Venus	58 26.3	11 09
05	210 53.0	270 16.2	28.8	233 15.0	25.4	130 14.4	55.1	223 04.6	16.6	Mars	24 00.6	13 29
										Jupiter	279 16.5	20 25
Mer. Pass. 15 02.7		v 3.6 d 0.2		v 0.6 d 0.7		v 2.6 d 0.0		v 2.2 d 0.1		Saturn	12 25.4	14 13

1966 JANUARY 7

G.M.T.	SUN		MOON					Lat.	Twilight		Sun-rise	Moonrise			
	G.H.A.	Dec.	G.H.A.	v	Dec.	d	H.P.		Naut.	Civil		7	8	9	10
d h	° '	° '	° '	'	° '	'	'	°	h m	h m	h m	h m	h m	h m	h m
7 00	178 29·9	S 22 27·4	1 26·5	1·9	N 26 01·9	1·2	60·7	N 40	06 18	06 52	07 22	17 07	18 23	19 42	20 59
01	193 29·6	27·1	15 47·4	1·8	26 00·7	1·5	60·8	35	06 09	06 41	07 08	17 24	18 38	19 53	21 06
02	208 29·3	26·8	30 08·2	1·9	25 59·2	1·7	60·8	30	06 01	06 31	06 57	17 38	18 50	20 03	21 12
03	223 29·0	·· 26·5	44 29·1	1·8	25 57·5	1·9	60·8	20	05 46	06 13	06 37	18 03	19 12	20 19	21 23
04	238 28·8	26·2	58 49·9	1·9	25 55·6	2·0	60·8	N 10	05 31	05 57	06 19	18 24	19 30	20 33	21 33
05	253 28·5	25·9	73 10·8	1·8	25 53·6	2·3	60·8	0	05 15	05 40	06 03	18 44	19 47	20 47	21 42
06	268 28·2	S 22 25·6	87 31·6	1·9	N 25 51·3	2·5	60·8	S 10	04 56	05 23	05 46	19 04	20 04	21 00	21 50
07	283 28·0	25·3	101 52·5	1·8	25 48·8	2·6	60·9	20	04 35	05 04	05 28	19 25	20 23	21 14	22 00
08	298 27·7	25·0	116 13·3	1·9	25 46·2	2·9	60·9	30	04 07	04 40	05 07	19 49	20 44	21 30	22 10
F 09	313 27·4	··· 24·7	130 34·2	1·9	25 43·3	3·1	60·9	35	03 50	04 26	04 55	20 04	20 56	21 39	22 16
R 10	328 27·2	24·3	144 55·1	1·9	25 40·2	3·2	60·9	40	03 28	04 09	04 41	20 20	21 10	21 50	22 23
I 11	343 26·9	24·0	159 16·0	1·9	25 37·0	3·5	60·9	Lat.	Sun-set	Twilight		Moonset			
D 12	358 26·6	S 22 23·7	173 36·9	2·0	N 25 33·5	3·7	60·9			Civil	Naut.	7	8	9	10
A 13	13 26·3	23·4	187 57·9	2·0	25 29·8	3·8	60·9	°	h m	h m	h m	h m	h m	h m	h m
Y 14	28 26·1	23·1	202 18·9	2·0	25 26·0	4·1	60·9	N 40	16 51	17 22	17 55	07 49	08 44	09 29	10 05
15	43 25·8	·· 22·8	216 39·9	2·1	25 21·9	4·2	61·0	35	17 05	17 32	18 04	07 32	08 29	09 16	09 57
16	58 25·5	22·4	231 01·0	2·1	25 17·7	4·5	61·0	30	17 16	17 42	18 12	07 18	08 16	09 06	09 49
17	73 25·3	22·1	245 22·1	2·1	25 13·2	4·6	61·0	20	17 36	18 00	18 27	06 52	07 53	08 48	09 36
18	88 25·0	S 22 21·8	259 43·2	2·2	N 25 08·6	4·8	61·0	N 10	17 54	18 16	18 43	06 30	07 33	08 31	09 24
19	103 24·7	21·5	274 04·4	2·2	25 03·8	5·0	61·0	0	18 10	18 33	18 59	06 10	07 14	08 16	09 13
20	118 24·5	21·2	288 25·6	2·2	24 58·8	5·3	61·0	S 10	18 27	18 50	19 17	05 49	06 56	08 01	09 02
21	133 24·2	·· 20·8	302 46·8	2·4	24 53·5	5·4	61·0	20	18 45	19 09	19 38	05 27	06 35	07 44	08 50
22	148 23·9	20·5	317 08·2	2·3	24 48·1	5·5	61·0	30	19 06	19 33	20 05	05 01	06 12	07 25	08 36
23	163 23·7	20·2	331 29·5	2·4	24 42·6	5·8	61·0	35	19 18	19 47	20 23	04 46	05 58	07 14	08 28
8 00	178 23·4	S 22 19·9	345 50·9	2·5	N 24 36·8	6·0	61·0	40	19 32	20 04	20 45	04 29	05 42	07 01	08 19
01	193 23·1	19·5	0 12·4	2·6	24 30·8	6·1	61·0								
02	208 22·9	19·2	14 34·0	2·6	24 24·7	6·4	61·0	Day	SUN			MOON			
03	223 22·6	·· 18·9	28 55·6	2·6	24 18·3	6·5	61·0		Eqn. of Time		Mer. Pass.	Mer. Pass.		Age	Phase
04	238 22·3	18·6	43 17·2	2·8	24 11·8	6·7	61·0		00h	12h		Upper	Lower		
05	253 22·1	18·2	57 39·0	2·8	24 05·1	6·8	61·1		m s	m s	h m	h m	h m	d	
	S.D. 16·3	d 0·3	S.D. 16·6		16·6		16·6	7	06 00	06 13	12 06	24 59	12 27	16	●
								8	06 26	06 39	12 07	00 59	13 31	17	
								9	06 51	07 04	12 07	02 02	14 32	18	

1966 FEBRUARY 5

G.M.T.	SUN		MOON					Lat.	Twilight		Sun-rise	Moonrise			
	G.H.A.	Dec.	G.H.A.	v	Dec.	d	H.P.		Naut.	Civil		3	4	5	6
d h	° '	° '	° '	'	° '	'	'	°	h m	h m	h m	h m	h m	h m	h m
5 00	176 29·8	S 16 07·4	4 53·0	3·1	N 23 06·9	8·5	61·3	N 40	06 05	06 38	07 06	14 39	15 52	17 12	18 32
01	191 29·8	06·7	19 15·1	3·1	22 58·4	8·6	61·4	35	06 00	06 30	06 57	14 56	16 08	17 25	18 41
02	206 29·7	05·9	33 37·2	3·2	22 49·8	8·8	61·4	30	05 55	06 24	06 49	15 11	16 22	17 36	18 49
03	221 29·7	·· 05·2	47 59·4	3·2	22 41·0	8·9	61·4	20	05 45	06 12	06 35	15 37	16 45	17 55	19 03
04	236 29·6	04·4	62 21·6	3·4	22 32·1	9·2	61·4	N 10	05 35	06 00	06 22	15 59	17 06	18 12	19 15
05	251 29·6	03·6	76 44·0	3·4	22 22·9	9·3	61·4	0	05 24	05 49	06 10	16 20	17 24	18 27	19 26
06	266 29·5	S 16 02·9	91 06·4	3·5	N 22 13·6	9·4	61·4	S 10	05 11	05 37	05 59	16 40	17 43	18 43	19 37
07	281 29·5	02·1	105 28·9	3·5	22 04·2	9·7	61·4	20	04 55	05 22	05 45	17 02	18 03	18 59	19 49
S 08	296 29·4	01·4	119 51·4	3·7	21 54·5	9·7	61·4	30	04 35	05 05	05 31	17 28	18 27	19 18	20 02
A 09	311 29·4	16 00·6	134 14·1	3·7	21 44·8	10·0	61·4	35	04 22	04 55	05 22	17 43	18 40	19 28	20 09
T 10	326 29·3	15 59·9	148 36·8	3·8	21 34·8	10·1	61·4	40	04 06	04 42	05 12	18 00	18 55	19 41	20 18
U 11	341 29·3	59·1	162 59·6	3·9	21 24·7	10·3	61·5	Lat.	Sun-set	Twilight		Moonset			
R 12	356 29·2	S 15 58·4	177 22·5	3·9	N 21 14·4	10·4	61·5			Civil	Naut.	3	4	5	6
D 13	11 29·2	·· 57·6	191 45·4	4·1	21 04·0	10·6	61·5	°	h m	h m	h m	h m	h m	h m	h m
A 14	26 29·1	56·8	206 08·5	4·1	20 53·4	10·7	61·5	N 40	17 22	17 58	18 23	06 27	07 17	07 58	
Y 15	41 29·1	·· 56·1	220 31·6	4·3	20 42·7	10·9	61·5	35	17 31	17 58	18 28	05 10	06 10	07 03	07 48
16	56 29·0	55·3	234 54·9	4·3	20 31·8	11·0	61·5	30	17 41	18 08	18 33	04 55	05 56	06 51	07 39
17	71 29·0	54·6	249 18·2	4·4	20 20·8	11·2	61·5	20	17 54	18 16	18 43	04 29	05 32	06 30	07 23
18	86 28·9	S 15 53·8	263 41·6	4·5	N 20 09·6	11·3	61·5	N 10	18 06	18 28	18 53	04 07	05 11	06 12	07 09
19	101 28·9	53·0	278 05·1	4·6	19 58·3	11·5	61·5	0	18 17	18 39	19 04	03 46	04 51	05 55	06 55
20	116 28·8	52·2	292 28·7	4·7	19 46·8	11·6	61·5	S 10	18 29	18 51	19 17	03 25	04 30	05 37	06 42
21	131 28·8	·· 51·5	306 52·4	4·7	19 35·2	11·8	61·5	20	18 42	19 05	19 32	03 03	04 08	05 18	06 27
22	146 28·7	50·8	321 16·1	4·9	19 23·4	11·8	61·5	30	18 57	19 22	19 53	02 36	03 44	04 57	06 11
23	161 28·7	50·0	335 40·0	5·0	19 11·6	12·0	61·5	35	19 05	19 33	20 05	02 21	03 29	04 44	06 01
6 00	176 28·6	S 15 49·2	350 04·0	5·0	N 18 59·6	12·2	61·5	40	19 15	19 45	20 21	02 04	03 12	04 29	05 50
01	191 28·6	48·5	4 28·0	5·2	18 47·4	12·3	61·5								
02	206 28·5	47·7	18 52·2	5·2	18 35·1	12·4	61·5	Day	SUN			MOON			
03	221 28·5	·· 47·0	33 16·4	5·4	18 22·7	12·5	61·5		Eqn. of Time		Mer. Pass.	Mer. Pass.		Age	Phase
04	236 28·5	46·2	47 40·8	5·4	18 10·2	12·7	61·5		00h	12h		Upper	Lower		
05	251 28·4	45·4	62 05·2	5·6	17 57·5	12·7	61·5		m s	m s	h m	h m	h m	d	
	S.D. 16·3	d 0·7	S.D. 16·5		16·7		16·7	3	13 49	13 52	12 14	22 35	10 03	13	◐
								4	13·55	13 58	12 14	23 40	11 08	14	
								5	14 01	14 03	12 14	24 41	12 11	15	

1966 MARCH 7

G.M.T.	ARIES G.H.A.	VENUS −4.3 G.H.A.	Dec.	MARS +1.4 G.H.A.	Dec.	JUPITER −1.9 G.H.A.	Dec.	SATURN +1.3 G.H.A.	Dec.	STARS Name	S.H.A.	Dec.
d h												
7 00	164 15.7	218 33.4	S14 17.1	165 46.5	S 1 28.1	83 04.9	N23 01.7	173 16.4	S 5 55.7	Acamar	315 45.6	S 40 26.7
01	179 18.2	233 34.3	17.1	180 47.2	27.3	98 07.2	01.7	188 18.6	55.6	Achernar	335 53.6	S 57 24.8
02	194 20.7	248 35.1	17.1	195 47.9	26.6	113 09.5	01.7	203 20.7	55.5	Acrux	173 49.1	S 62 54.6
03	209 23.1	263 36.0 ··	17.1	210 48.6 ··	25.8	128 11.8 ··	01.7	218 22.9 ··	55.4	Adhara	255 40.6	S 28 55.6
04	224 25.6	278 36.9	17.0	225 49.2	25.0	143 14.1	01.7	233 25.1	55.2	Aldebaran	291 30.6	N 16 26.6
05	239 28.1	293 37.8	17.0	240 49.9	24.2	158 16.3	01.8	248 27.5	55.1			
06	254 30.5	308 38.6	S14 17.0	255 50.6	S 1 23.4	173 18.6	N23 01.8	263 29.5	S 5 55.0	Alioth	166 51.4	N 56 08.4
07	269 33.0	323 39.5	17.0	270 51.3	22.6	188 20.9	01.8	278 31.6	54.9	Alkaid	153 26.6	N 49 28.7
08	284 35.4	338 40.4	17.0	285 52.0	21.8	203 23.2	01.8	293 33.8	54.8	Al Na'ir	28 29.0	S 47 07.7
M 09	299 37.9	353 41.2 ··	17.0	300 52.7 ··	21.0	218 25.5 ··	01.8	308 36.0 ··	54.6	Alnilam	276 22.7	S 1 13.4
O 10	314 40.4	8 42.1	17.0	315 53.4	20.2	233 27.8	01.8	323 38.2	54.5	Alphard	218 31.0	S 8 30.7
N 11	329 42.8	23 43.0	17.0	330 54.1	19.4	248 30.1	01.9	338 40.4	54.4			
D 12	344 45.3	38 43.8	S14 16.9	345 54.8	S 1 18.6	263 32.4	N23 01.9	353 42.5	S 5 54.3	Canopus	264 11.9	S 52 40.8
A 13	359 47.8	53 44.7	16.9	0 55.5	17.8	278 34.7	01.9	8 44.7	54.2	Capella	281 27.5	N 45 58.1
Y 14	14 50.2	68 45.5	16.9	15 56.1	17.0	293 36.9	01.9	23 46.9	54.0	Deneb	49 56.4	N 45 09.2
15	29 52.7	83 46.4 ··	16.9	30 56.8 ··	16.2	308 39.2 ··	01.9	38 49.1 ··	53.9	Denebola	183 09.9	N 14 45.6
16	44 55.2	98 47.2	16.9	45 57.5	15.4	323 41.5	01.9	53 51.3	53.8	Diphda	349 32.1	S 18 10.6
17	59 57.6	113 48.1	16.9	60 58.2	14.6	338 43.8	02.0	68 53.4	53.7			
18	75 00.1	128 48.9	S14 16.8	75 58.9	S 1 13.9	353 46.1	N23 02.0	83 55.6	S 5 53.6	Kochab	137 17.4	N 74 17.3
19	90 02.6	143 49.8	16.8	90 59.6	13.1	8 48.4	02.0	98 57.8	53.4	Markab	14 14.5	N 15 01.1
20	105 05.0	158 50.6	16.8	106 00.3	12.3	23 50.7	02.0	114 00.0	53.3	Menkar	314 52.8	N 3 57.4
21	120 07.5	173 51.4 ··	16.8	121 01.0 ··	11.5	38 52.9 ··	02.0	129 02.1 ··	53.2	Menkent	148 49.8	S 36 12.2
22	135 09.9	188 52.3	16.7	136 01.7	10.7	53 55.2	02.0	144 04.3	53.1	Miaplacidus	221 46.8	S 69 34.7
23	150 12.4	203 53.1	16.7	151 02.4	09.9	68 57.5	02.0	159 06.5	53.0			
8 00	165 14.9	218 53.9	S14 16.7	166 03.0	S 1 09.1	83 59.8	N23 02.1	174 08.7	S 5 52.8	Vega	81 03.4	N 38 44.7
01	180 17.3	233 54.8	16.7	181 03.7	08.3	99 02.1	02.1	189 10.9	52.7	Zuben'ubi	137 45.0	S 15 54.2
02	195 19.8	248 55.6	16.6	196 04.4	07.5	114 04.4	02.1	204 13.0	52.6			
03	210 22.3	263 56.4 ··	16.6	211 05.1 ··	06.7	129 06.6 ··	02.1	219 15.2 ··	52.5	Venus	S.H.A. 54 54.9	Mer.Pass. 9 27
04	225 24.7	278 57.2	16.6	226 05.8	05.9	144 08.9	02.1	234 17.4	52.4	Mars	2 13.4	12 57
05	240 27.2	293 58.0	16.6	241 06.5	05.1	159 11.2	02.1	249 19.6	52.2	Jupiter	278 53.2	18 29
Mer. Pass. 13 04.7		v 0.9	d 0.0	v 0.7	d 0.8	v 2.3	d 0.0	v 2.2	d 0.1	Saturn	9 07.5	12 29

1966 APRIL 5

G.M.T.	ARIES G.H.A.	VENUS −4.0 G.H.A.	Dec.	MARS +1.4 G.H.A.	Dec.	JUPITER −1.7 G.H.A.	Dec.	SATURN +1.4 G.H.A.	Dec.	STARS Name	S.H.A.	Dec.
d h												
5 00	192 50.7	222 44.6	S10 53.3	173 54.6	N 7 30.7	108 24.7	N23 14.7	198 35.4	S 4 34.0	Acamar	315 45.7	S 40 26.5
01	207 53.2	237 44.6	52.7	188 55.3	31.5	123 26.7	14.7	213 37.6	33.9	Achernar	335 53.7	S 57 24.6
02	222 55.7	252 44.7	52.1	203 56.0	32.2	138 28.8	14.7	228 39.8	33.8	Acrux	173 49.1	S 62 54.8
03	237 58.1	267 44.7 ··	51.6	218 56.7 ··	33.0	153 30.9 ··	14.7	243 42.0 ··	33.7	Altair	62 43.2	N 8 46.4
04	253 00.6	282 44.8	51.0	233 57.4	33.7	168 33.0	14.7	258 44.2	33.6	Arcturus	146 28.0	N 19 21.3
05	268 03.1	297 44.8	50.4	248 58.1	34.4	183 35.1	14.8	273 46.4	33.4			
06	283 05.5	312 44.9	S10 49.8	263 58.8	N 7 35.1	198 37.2	N23 14.8	288 48.6	S 4 33.3	Canopus	264 12.2	S 52 40.8
07	298 08.0	327 44.9	49.2	278 59.5	35.9	213 39.3	14.8	303 50.7	33.2	Capella	281 27.6	N 45 58.1
T 08	313 10.5	342 44.9	48.6	294 00.2	36.6	228 41.3	14.8	318 52.9	33.1	Deneb	49 56.4	N 45 09.1
U 09	328 12.9	357 45.0 ··	48.1	309 00.9 ··	37.3	243 43.4 ··	14.8	333 55.1 ··	33.0	Enif	34 22.5	N 9 42.9
E 10	343 15.4	12 45.0	47.5	324 01.6	38.1	258 45.5	14.9	348 57.3	32.9	Fomalhaut	16 03.7	S 29 48.2
S 11	358 17.8	27 45.1	46.9	339 02.3	38.8	273 47.6	14.9	3 59.5	32.8			
D 12	13 20.3	42 45.1	S10 46.3	354 03.1	N 7 39.6	288 49.7	N23 14.9	19 01.7	S 4 32.7			
A 13	28 22.8	57 45.2	45.7	9 03.8	40.3	303 51.8	14.9	34 03.9	32.5	Gacrux	172 40.6	S 56 55.5
Y 14	43 25.2	72 45.2	45.1	24 04.5	41.0	318 53.9	14.9	49 06.1	32.4	Gienah	176 28.9	S 17 21.3
15	58 27.7	87 45.2 ··	44.5	39 05.2 ··	41.8	333 55.9 ··	14.9	64 08.3 ··	32.3	Hadar	149 38.5	S 60 12.6
16	73 30.2	102 45.3	43.9	54 05.9	42.5	348 58.0	15.0	79 10.5	32.2	Hamal	328 41.6	N 23 18.1
17	88 32.6	117 45.3	43.4	69 06.6*	43.2	4 00.1	15.0	94 12.7	32.1	Kaus Aust.	84 31.2	S 34 24.2
18	103 35.1	132 45.4	S10 42.8	84 07.3	N 7 44.0	19 02.2	N23 15.0	109 14.9	S 4 32.0	Rasalhague	96 39.6	N 12 34.7
19	118 37.6	147 45.4	42.2	99 08.0	44.7	34 04.3	15.0	124 17.1	31.9	Regulus	208 21.3	N 12 08.0
20	133 40.0	162 45.4	41.6	114 08.7	45.4	49 06.4	15.0	139 19.2	31.8	Rigel	281 46.6	S 8 14.5
21	148 42.5	177 45.5 ··	41.0	129 09.4 ··	46.2	64 08.4 ··	15.1	154 21.4 ··	31.7	Rigil Kent.	140 40.3	S 60 41.7
22	163 44.9	192 45.5	40.4	144 10.1	46.9	79 10.5	15.1	169 23.6	31.5	Sabik	102 53.5	S 15 41.2
23	178 47.4	207 45.5	39.8	159 10.8	47.6	94 12.6	15.1	184 25.8	31.4			
6 00	193 49.9	222 45.6	S10 39.2	174 11.5	N 7 48.4	109 14.7	N23 15.1	199 28.0	S 4 31.3	Vega	81 03.2	N 38 44.7
01	208 52.3	237 45.6	38.6	189 12.2	49.1	124 16.8	15.1	214 30.2	31.2	Zuben'ubi	137 44.9	S 15 54.2
02	223 54.8	252 45.7	38.0	204 12.9	49.8	139 18.8	15.1	229 32.4	31.1			
03	238 57.3	267 45.7 ··	37.4	219 13.6 ··	50.6	154 20.9 ··	15.2	244 34.6 ··	31.0	Venus	S.H.A. 29 53.9	Mer.Pass. 9 09
04	253 59.7	282 45.7	36.8	234 14.3	51.3	169 23.0	15.2	259 36.8	30.9	Mars	341 03.9	12 24
05	269 02.2	297 45.8	36.2	249 15.0	52.0	184 25.1	15.2	274 39.0	30.8	Jupiter	275 34.0	16 44
Mer. Pass. 11 06.8		v 0.0	d 0.6	v 0.7	d 0.7	v 2.1	d 0.0	v 2.2	d 0.1	Saturn	5 44.7	10 44

1966 MARCH 7

G.M.T.	SUN G.H.A.	Dec.	MOON G.H.A.	v	Dec.	d	H.P.
d h	° ′	° ′	° ′	′	° ′	′	′
7 00	177 10·8	S 5 32·2	356 15·6	8·2	N10 22·4	15·8	61·3
01	192 11·0	31·3	10 42·8	8·3	10 06·6	15·8	61·3
02	207 11·1	30·3	25 10·1	8·4	9 50·8	15·9	61·3
03	222 11·3	·· 29·3	39 37·5	8·5	9 34·9	16·0	61·3
04	237 11·4	28·3	54 05·0	8·5	9 18·9	16·0	61·3
05	252 11·6	27·4	68 32·5	8·5	9 02·9	16·1	61·3
06	267 11·7	S 5 26·4	83 00·0	8·7	N 8 46·8	16·1	61·3
07	282 11·9	25·4	97 27·7	8·7	8 30·7	16·1	61·2
08	297 12·0	24·5	111 55·4	8·7	8 14·6	16·2	61·2
M 09	312 12·2	·· 23·5	126 23·1	8·9	7 58·4	16·2	61·2
O 10	327 12·3	22·5	140 51·0	8·8	7 42·2	16·3	61·2
N 11	342 12·5	21·5	155 18·8	9·0	7 25·9	16·3	61·2
D 12	357 12·6	S 5 20·6	169 46·8	9·0	N 7 09·6	16·4	61·2
A 13	12 12·8	19·6	184 14·8	9·0	6 53·2	16·4	61·2
Y 14	27 12·9	18·6	198 42·8	9·1	6 36·8	16·4	61·1
15	42 13·1	·· 17·7	213 10·9	9·2	6 20·4	16·4	61·1
16	57 13·2	16·7	227 39·1	9·2	6 04·0	16·5	61·1
17	72 13·4	15·7	242 07·3	9·3	5 47·5	16·5	61·1
18	87 13·5	S 5 14·7	256 35·6	9·3	N 5 31·0	16·5	61·1
19	102 13·7	13·8	271 03·9	9·4	5 14·5	16·5	61·1
20	117 13·8	12·8	285 32·3	9·4	4 58·0	16·6	61·0
21	132 14·0	·· 11·8	300 00·7	9·5	4 41·4	16·6	61·0
22	147 14·1	10·9	314 29·2	9·6	4 24·9	16·6	61·0
23	162 14·3	09·9	328 57·8	9·5	4 08·3	16·6	61·0
8 00	177 14·4	S 5 08·9	343 26·3	9·7	N 3 51·7	16·6	61·0
01	192 14·6	07·9	357 55·0	9·6	3 35·1	16·6	60·9
02	207 14·7	07·0	12 23·6	9·7	3 18·5	16·7	60·9
03	222 14·9	·· 06·0	26 52·3	9·8	3 01·8	16·6	60·9
04	237 15·0	05·0	41 21·1	9·8	2 45·2	16·6	60·9
05	252 15·2	04·0	55 49·9	9·8	2 28·6	16·7	60·9
	S.D. 16·1	d 1·0	S.D. 16·7		16·7		16·7

Lat.	Twilight Naut.	Civil	Sun-rise	Moonrise 5	6	7	8
°	h m	h m	h m	h m	h m	h m	h m
N 40	05 28	05 59	06 27	16 00	17 20	18 38	19 54
35	05 29	05 58	06 24	16 11	17 27	18 41	19 53
30	05 29	05 57	06 21	16 21	17 33	18 44	19 52
20	05 29	05 54	06 16	16 37	17 44	18 48	19 50
N 10	05 27	05 51	06 12	16 52	17 54	18 52	19 49
0	05 23	05 47	06 08	17 06	18 03	18 56	19 48
S 10	05 18	05 43	06 04	17 19	18 11	19 00	19 47
20	05 11	05 37	05 59	17 34	18 21	19 04	19 45
30	05 02	05 30	05 54	17 50	18 32	19 09	19 44
35	04 55	05 25	05 51	18 00	18 38	19 12	19 43
40	04 47	05 20	05 47	18 10	18 44	19 14	19 42

Lat.	Sun-set	Twilight Civil	Naut.	Moonset 5	6	7	8
°	h m	h m	h m	h m	h m	h m	h m
N 40	17 57	18 24	18 55	05 49	06 26	06 58	07 27
35	18 00	18 25	18 54	05 36	06 17	06 53	07 26
30	18 02	18 26	18 54	05 26	06 10	06 49	07 25
20	18 07	18 29	18 54	05 08	05 57	06 41	07 24
N 10	18 11	18 32	18 56	04 50	05 44	06 35	07 22
0	18 15	18 36	19 00	04 35	05 33	06 28	07 21
S 10	18 19	18 40	19 04	04 19	05 22	06 22	07 20
20	18 23	18 45	19 11	04 02	05 09	06 15	07 18
30	18 28	18 52	19 21	03 42	04 55	06 07	07 16
35	18 31	18 57	19 27	03 31	04 47	06 02	07 15
40	18 35	19 02	19 35	03 18	04 38	05 57	07 14

Day	SUN Eqn. of Time 00ʰ	12ʰ	Mer. Pass.	MOON Mer. Pass. Upper	Lower	Age	Phase
	m s	m s	h m	h m	h m		
5	11 45	11 38	12 12	23 20	10 50	13	○
6	11 31	11 24	12 11	24 16	11 48	14	
7	11 17	11 10	12 11	00 16	12 42	15	

1966 APRIL 5

G.M.T.	SUN G.H.A.	Dec.	MOON G.H.A.	v	Dec.	d	H.P.
d h	° ′	° ′	° ′	′	° ′	′	′
5 00	179 15·7	N 5 49·0	3 43·8	10·3	N 0 12·8	16·7	60·5
01	194 15·9	49·9	18 13·1	10·3	S 0 03·9	16·6	60·5
02	209 16·1	50·9	32 42·4	10·3	0 20·5	16·7	60·5
03	224 16·3	·· 51·9	47 11·7	10·3	0 37·2	16·6	60·5
04	239 16·5	52·8	61 41·0	10·3	0 53·8	16·6	60·5
05	254 16·6	53·8	76 10·3	10·3	1 10·4	16·6	60·5
06	269 16·8	N 5 54·7	90 39·6	10·4	S 1 27·0	16·6	60·4
07	284 17·0	55·7	105 09·0	10·3	1 43·6	16·6	60·4
T 08	299 17·2	56·6	119 38·3	10·4	2 00·2	16·5	60·4
U 09	314 17·4	·· 57·6	134 07·7	10·3	2 16·7	16·6	60·4
E 10	329 17·6	58·5	148 37·0	10·4	2 33·3	16·5	60·4
S 11	344 17·7	5 59·5	163 06·4	10·4	2 49·8	16·4	60·4
D 12	359 17·9	N 6 00·4	177 35·8	10·4	S 3 06·2	16·5	60·3
A 13	14 18·1	01·4	192 05·2	10·3	3 22·7	16·4	60·3
Y 14	29 18·3	02·3	206 34·5	10·4	3 39·1	16·4	60·3
15	44 18·5	·· 03·2	221 03·9	10·4	3 55·5	16·4	60·3
16	59 18·6	04·2	235 33·3	10·4	4 11·9	16·3	60·3
17	74 18·8	05·1	250 02·7	10·4	4 28·2	16·3	60·2
18	89 19·0	N 6 06·1	264 32·1	10·4	S 4 44·5	16·2	60·2
19	104 19·2	07·0	279 01·5	10·4	5 00·7	16·2	60·2
20	119 19·4	08·0	293 30·9	10·3	5 16·9	16·2	60·2
21	134 19·6	·· 08·9	308 00·2	10·4	5 33·1	16·1	60·1
22	149 19·7	09·9	322 29·6	10·4	5 49·2	16·1	60·1
23	164 19·9	10·8	336 59·0	10·4	6 05·3	16·0	60·1
6 00	179 20·1	N 6 11·8	351 28·4	10·3	S 6 21·3	16·0	60·1
01	194 20·3	12·7	5 57·7	10·4	6 37·3	16·0	60·1
02	209 20·5	13·7	20 27·1	10·3	6 53·3	15·8	60·0
03	224 20·6	·· 14·6	34 56·4	10·3	7 09·1	15·9	60·0
04	239 20·8	15·6	49 25·7	10·4	7 25·0	15·7	60·0
05	254 21·0	16·5	63 55·1	10·3	7 40·7	15·8	60·0
	S.D. 16·0	d 0·9	S.D. 16·5		16·4		16·3

Lat.	Twilight Naut.	Civil	Sun-rise	Moonrise 4	5	6	7
°	h m	h m	h m	h m	h m	h m	h m
N 40	04 39	05 11	05 39	17 25	18 41	19 55	21 08
35	04 47	05 17	05 42	17 27	18 38	19 48	20 58
30	04 53	05 21	05 45	17 29	18 35	19 42	20 49
20	05 03	05 29	05 51	17 29	18 31	19 32	20 33
N 10	05 10	05 34	05 55	17 31	18 27	19 23	20 19
0	05 15	05 39	06 00	17 32	18 23	19 14	20 06
S 10	05 18	05 43	06 04	17 34	18 20	19 06	19 53
20	05 20	05 46	06 08	17 36	18 16	18 57	19 39
30	05 21	05 49	06 13	17 37	18 12	18 47	19 24
35	05 21	05 50	06 16	17 38	18 09	18 41	19 15
40	05 20	05 51	06 19	17 39	18 07	18 35	19 05

Lat.	Sun-set	Twilight Civil	Naut.	Moonset 4	5	6	7
°	h m	h m	h m	h m	h m	h m	h m
N 40	18 28	18 56	19 28	05 24	05 51	06 19	06 48
35	18 24	18 50	19 20	05 21	05 52	06 24	06 57
30	18 21	18 45	19 13	05 18	05 53	06 28	07 04
20	18 15	18 37	19 03	05 14	05 54	06 35	07 17
N 10	18 10	18 32	18 56	05 09	05 56	06 41	07 28
0	18 06	18 27	18 51	05 05	05 57	06 47	07 39
S 10	18 02	18 23	18 47	05 01	05 58	06 53	07 49
20	17 58	18 19	18 45	04 57	05 59	07 00	08 01
30	17 53	18 16	18 44	04 52	06 00	07 07	08 14
35	17 50	18 15	18 44	04 49	06 01	07 11	08 21
40	17 47	18 14	18 45	04 46	06 01	07 16	08 30

Day	SUN Eqn. of Time 00ʰ	12ʰ	Mer. Pass.	MOON Mer. Pass. Upper	Lower	Age	Phase
	m s	m s	h m	h m	h m		
4	03 15	03 06	12 03	23 45	11 19	13	○
5	02 57	02 49	12 03	24 35	12 10	14	
6	02 40	02 31	12 03	00 35	13 01	15	

1966 MAY 11

G.M.T.	ARIES G.H.A.	VENUS −3.7 G.H.A.	Dec.	MARS +1.5 G.H.A.	Dec.	JUPITER −1.5 G.H.A.	Dec.	SATURN +1.4 G.H.A.	Dec.
11 00	228 19.7	221 47.2	N 1 06.4	183 41.2	N16 51.9	137 11.6	N23 24.5	230 32.6	S 3 08.6
01	243 22.2	236 47.0	· · 07.4	198 41.8	52.5	152 13.5	24.5	245 34.9	08.5
02	258 24.7	251 46.9	08.4	213 42.5	53.0	167 15.4	24.5	260 37.1	08.4
03	273 27.1	266 46.8	· · 09.4	228 43.1	· · 53.6	182 17.4	· · 24.5	275 39.4	· · 08.3
04	288 29.6	281 46.6	10.4	243 43.8	54.1	197 19.3	24.5	290 41.6	08.2
05	303 32.1	296 46.5	11.4	258 44.4	54.6	212 21.2	24.5	305 43.9	08.1
06	318 34.5	311 46.3	N 1 12.4	273 45.1	N16 55.2	227 23.1	N23 24.5	320 46.1	S 3 08.1
W 07	333 37.0	326 46.2	13.4	288 45.7	55.7	242 25.1	24.5	335 48.4	·08.0
E 08	348 39.5	341 46.0	14.4	303 46.4	56.3	257 27.0	24.5	350 50.6	07.9
D 09	3 41.9	356 45.9	· · 15.4	318 47.0	· · 56.8	272 28.9	· · 24.5	5 52.9	· · 07.8
N 10	18 44.4	11 45.8	16.4	333 47.7	57.3	287 30.8	24.5	20 55.2	07.7
E 11	33 46.8	26 45.6	17.4	348 48.3	57.9	302 32.8	24.5	35 57.4	07.7
S 12	48 49.3	41 45.5	N 1 18.4	3 48.9	N16 58.4	317 34.7	N23 24.5	50 59.7	S 3 07.6
D 13	63 51.8	56 45.3	19.4	18 49.6	58.9	332 36.6	24.5	66 01.9	07.5
A 14	78 54.2	71·45.2	20.5	33 50.2	·16 59.5	347 38.6	24.5	81 04.2	07.4
Y 15	93 56.7	·86 45.0	· · 21.5	48 50.9	17 00.0	2 40.5	· · 24.5	96 06.4	· · 07.3
16	108 59.2	101 44.9	22.5	63 51.5	00.6	17 42.4	24.5	111 08.7	07.2
17	124 01.6	116 44.7	23.5	78 52.2	01.1	32 44.3	24.5	126 10.9	07.2
18	139 04.1	131 44.6	N 1 24.5	93 52.8	N17 01.6	47 46.3	N23 24.5	141 13.2	S 3 07.1
19	154 06.6	146 44.5	25.5	108 53.5	02.2	62 48.2	24.5	156 15.5	07.0
20	169 09.0	161 44.3	26.5	123 54.1	02.7	77 50.1	24.5	171 17.7	06.9
21	184 11.5	176 44.2	· · 27.5	138 54.8	· · 03.2	92 52.0	· · 24.5	186 20.0	· · 06.8
22	199 13.9	191 44.0	28.5	153 55.4	03.8	107 54.0	24.5	201 22.2	06.8
23	214 16.4	206 43.9	29.5	168 56.1	04.3	122 55.9	24.5	216 24.5	06.7
12 00	229 18.9	221 43.7	N 1 30.5	183 56.7	N17 04.8	137 57.8	N23 24.5	231 26.7	S 3 06.6
01	244 21.3	236 43.6	31.5	198 57.3	05.4	152 59.7	24.5	246 29.0	06.5
02	259 23.8	251 43.4	32.5	213 58.0	05.9	168 01.7	24.5	261 31.3	06.4
03	274 26.3	266 43.3	· · 33.5	228 58.6	· · 06.4	183 03.6	· · 24.5	276 33.5	· · 06.4
04	289 28.7	281 43.1	34.5	243 59.3	07.0	198 05.5	24.5	291 35.8	06.3
05	304 31.2	296 43.0	35.5	258 59.9	07.5	213 07.4	24.5	306 38.0	06.2
Mer. Pass. 8 45.2		v −0.1 d 1.0		v 0.6 d 0.5		v 1.9 d 0.0		v 2.3 d 0.1	

STARS

Name	S.H.A.	Dec.
Alphecca	126 40.9	N 26 49.5
Alpheratz	358 20.9	N 28 54.0
Altair	62 43.0	N 8 46.4
Ankaa	353 51.1	S 42 29.3
Antares	113 09.8	S 26 21.6
Arcturus	146 28.0	N 19 21.4
Atria	108 43.4	S 68 58.1
Avior	234 33.0	S 59 24.2
Bellatrix	279 10.7	N 6 19.2
Betelgeuse	271 40.3	N 7 24.1
Canopus	264 12.4	S 52 40.7
Capella	281 27.7	N 45 58.0
Deneb	49 55.8	N 45 09.1
Denebola	183 09.8	N 14 45.7
Diphda	349 31.9	S 18 10.3
Schedar	350 22.0	N 56 20.9
Shaula	97 10.1	S 37 04.9
Sirius	259 05.5	S 16 40.2
Spica	159 08.7	S 10 59.2
Suhail	223 18.9	S 43 17.9
Vega	81 02.9	N 38 44.8
Zuben'ubi	137 44.7	S 15 54.3

	S.H.A.	Mer. Pass.
Venus	353 27.5	9 13
Mars	315 21.5	11 45
Jupiter	268 51.9	14 49
Saturn	2 12.9	8 37

1966 JUNE 3

G.M.T.	ARIES G.H.A.	VENUS −3.5 G.H.A.	Dec.	MARS +1.6 G.H.A.	Dec.	JUPITER −1.4 G.H.A.	Dec.	SATURN +1.3 G.H.A.	Dec.
3 00	250 59.9	219 52.1	N10 23.3	189 26.5	N21 02.6	154 39.3	N23 19.3	251 34.2	S 2 31.4
01	266 02.4	234 51.8	24.2	204 27.1	02.9	169 41.2	19.3	266 36.6	31.3
02	281 04.9	249 51.5	25.2	219 27.8	03.3	184 43.1	19.3	281 38.9	31.3
03	296 07.3	264 51.2	· · 26.2	234 28.4	· · 03.6	199 45.0	· · 19.3	296 41.2	· · 31.2
04	311 09.8	279 50.9	27.2	249 29.0	04.0	214 46.8	19.2	311 43.5	31.2
05	326 12.3	294 50.6	28.1	264 29.6	04.4	229 48.7	19.2	326 45.8	31.1
06	341 14.7	309 50.3	N10 29.1	279 30.2	N21 04.7	244 50.6	N23 19.2	341 48.2	S 2 31.0
07	356 17.2	324 50.0	30.1	294 30.8	05.1	259 52.5	19.2	356 50.5	31.0
08	11 19.7	339 49.7	31.1	309 31.4	05.4	274 54.3	19.2	11 52.8	30.9
F 09	26 22.1	354 49.4	· · 32.0	324 32.0	· · 05.8	289 56.2	· · 19.1	26 55.1	· · 30.9
R 10	41 24.6	9 49.1	33.0	339 32.6	06.2	304 58.1	19.1	41 57.5	30.8
I 11	56 27.0	24 48.8	34.0	354 33.2	06.5	320 00.0	19.1	57 00.0	30.8
D 12	71 29.5	39 48.5	N10 34.9	9 33.8	N21 06.9	335 01.8	N23 19.1	72 02.1	S 2 30.7
A 13	86 32.0	54 48.2	35.9	24 34.4	07.2	350 03.7	19.1	87 04.4	30.7
Y 14	101 34.4	69 47.9	36.9	39 35.0	07.6	5 05.6	19.0	102 06.7	30.6
15	116 36.9	84 47.6	· · 37.9	54 35.6	· · 07.9	20 07.5	· · 19.0	117 09.1	· · 30.6
16	131 39.4	99 47.3	38.8	69 36.2	08.3	35 09.3	19.0	132 11.4	30.5
17	146 41.8	114 47.0	39.8	84 36.8	08.7	50 11.2	19.0	147 13.7	30.5
18	161 44.3	129 46.7	N10 40.8	99 37.5	N21 09.0	65 13.1	N23 19.0	162 16.0	S 2 30.4
19	176 46.8	144 46.4	41.7	114 38.1	09.4	80 15.0	18.9	177 18.3	30.4
20	191 49.2	159 46.1	42.7	129 38.7	09.7	95 16.8	18.9	192 20.7	30.3
21	206 51.7	174 45.8	· · 43.7	144 39.3	· · 10.1	110 18.7	· · 18.9	207 23.0	· · 30.3
22	221 54.1	189 45.5	44.6	159 39.9	10.4	125 20.6	18.9	222 25.3	30.2
23	236 56.6	204 45.2	45.6	174 40.5	10.8	140 22.4	18.9	237 27.6	30.2
4 00	251 59.1	219 44.9	N10 46.6	189 41.1	N21 11.1	155 24.3	N23 18.8	252 30.0	S 2 30.1
01	267 01.5	234 44.6	47.6	204 41.7	11.5	170 26.2	18.8	267 32.3	30.1
02	282 04.0	249 44.3	48.5	219 42.3	11.8	185 28.1	18.8	282 34.6	30.0
03	297 06.5	264 44.0	· · 49.5	234 42.9	· · 12.2	200 29.9	· · 18.8	297 36.9	· · 30.0
04	312 08.9	279 43.7	50.5	249 43.5	12.5	215 31.8	18.8	312 39.3	29.9
05	327 11.4	294 43.4	51.4	264 44.1	12.9	230 33.7	18.7	327 41.6	29.9
Mer. Pass. 7 10.9		v −0.3 d 1.0		v 0.6 d 0.3		v 1.9 d 0.0		v 2.3 d 0.0	

STARS

Name	S.H.A.	Dec.
Arcturus	146 28.0	N 19 21.5
Atria	108 43.2	S 68 58.2
Avior	234 33.2	S 59 24.2
Bellatrix	279 10.6	N 6 19.3
Betelgeuse	271 40.3	N 7 24.2
Dubhe	194 35.1	N 61 56.4
Elnath	278 58.1	N 28 34.9
Eltanin	91 02.2	N 51 29.4
Enif	34 22.1	N 9 43.0
Fomalhaut	16 03.2	S 29 48.0
Rasalhague	96 39.2	N 12 34.9
Regulus	208 21.5	N 12 08.1
Rigel	281 46.7	S 8 14.3
Rigil Kent.	140 40.2	S 60 41.9
Sabik	102 53.2	S 15 41.2
Schedar	350 21.8	N 56 20.8
Shaula	97 10.0	S 37 04.9
Sirius	259 05.5	S 16 40.1
Spica	159 08.7	S 10 59.2
Suhail	223 19.0	S 43 17.9
Vega	81 02.8	N 38 44.9
Zuben'ubi	137 44.7	S 15 54.3

	S.H.A.	Mer. Pass.
Venus	327 45.8	9 21
Mars	297 42.0	11 21
Jupiter	263 25.2	13 37
Saturn	0 30.9	7 09

1966 MAY 11

G.M.T.	SUN G.H.A.	Dec.	MOON G.H.A.	v	Dec.	d	H.P.
d h	° '	° '	° '	'	° '	'	'
11 00	180 55.3	N17 42.4	281 09.0	11.2	S24 07.0	6.4	54.8
01	195 55.3	43.0	295 39.2	11.2	24 00.6	6.4	54.8
02	210 55.4	43.7	310 09.4	11.3	23 54.2	6.6	54.7
03	225 55.4	·· 44.3	324 39.7	11.4	23 47.6	6.6	54.7
04	240 55.4	45.0	339 10.1	11.4	23 41.0	6.8	54.7
05	255 55.4	45.6	353 40.5	11.5	23 34.2	6.9	54.7
06	270 55.5	N17 46.3	8 11.0	11.6	S23 27.3	7.0	54.7
W 07	285 55.5	46.9	22 41.6	11.7	23 20.3	7.0	54.7
E 08	300 55.5	47.6	37 12.3	11.7	23 13.3	7.2	54.6
D 09	315 55.5	·· 48.2	51 43.0	11.9	23 06.1	7.3	54.6
N 10	330 55.5	48.8	66 13.9	11.9	22 58.8	7.4	54.6
E 11	345 55.6	49.5	80 44.8	11.9	22 51.4	7.5	54.6
S 12	0 55.6	N17 50.1	95 15.7	12.1	S22 43.9	7.5	54.6
D 13	15 55.6	50.8	109 46.8	12.1	22 36.4	7.7	54.6
A 14	30 55.6	51.4	124 17.9	12.2	22 28.7	7.8	54.6
Y 15	45 55.6	·· 52.1	138 49.1	12.3	22 20.9	7.9	54.5
16	60 55.7	52.7	153 20.4	12.3	22 13.0	7.9	54.5
17	75 55.7	53.4	167 51.7	12.5	22 05.1	8.1	54.5
18	90 55.7	N17 54.0	182 23.2	12.5	S21 57.0	8.1	54.5
19	105 55.7	54.6	196 54.7	12.5	21 48.9	8.3	54.5
20	120 55.7	55.3	211 26.2	12.7	21 40.6	8.3	54.5
21	135 55.7	·· 55.9	225 57.9	12.7	21 32.3	8.4	54.5
22	150 55.8	56.6	240 29.6	12.8	21 23.9	8.5	54.5
23	165 55.8	57.2	255 01.4	12.9	21 15.4	8.6	54.4
12 00	180 55.8	N17 57.8	269 33.3	12.9	S21 06.8	8.7	54.4
01	195 55.8	58.5	284 05.2	13.0	20 58.1	8.8	54.4
02	210 55.8	59.1	298 37.2	13.1	20 49.3	8.9	54.4
03	225 55.8	17 59.7	313 09.3	13.2	20 40.4	8.9	54.4
04	240 55.9	18 00.4	327 41.5	13.2	20 31.5	9.0	54.4
05	255 55.9	01.0	342 13.7	13.3	20 22.5	9.1	54.4
	S.D. 15.9	d 0.6	S.D. 15.0		14.9		14.8

Lat.	Twilight Naut.	Civil	Sun-rise	Moonrise 10	11	12	13
°	h m	h m	h m	h m	h m	h m	h m
N 40	03 42	04 19	04 49	00 04	00 45	01 19	01 48
35	03 59	04 32	05 00	24 30	00 30	01 06	01 38
30	04 13	04 44	05 10	24 17	00 17	00 55	01 29
20	04 35	05 02	05 26	23 53	24 36	00 36	01 14
N 10	04 52	05 18	05 40	23 33	24 18	00 18	01 00
0	05 06	05 31	05 53	23 14	24 02	00 02	00 47
S 10	05 18	05 44	06 06	22 55	23 46	24 34	00 34
20	05 30	05 56	06 19	22 35	23 28	24 20	00 20
30	05 41	06 10	06 35	22 12	23 09	24 05	00 05
35	05 47	06 17	06 44	21 58	22 57	23 55	24 53
40	05 53	06 25	06 54	21 42	22 44	23 45	24 45

Lat.	Sun-set	Twilight Civil	Naut.	Moonset 10	11	12	13
°	h m	h m	h m	h m	h m	h m	h m
N 40	19 04	19 34	20 12	09 10	10 12	11 13	12 14
35	18 53	19 21	19 55	09 27	10 26	11 25	12 23
30	18 43	19 09	19 40	09 42	10 39	11 36	12 31
20	18 27	18 51	19 18	10 07	11 01	11 54	12 45
N 10	18 13	18 35	19 01	10 28	11 20	12 10	12 57
0	18 00	18 22	18 47	10 48	11 38	12 24	13 08
S 10	17 47	18 09	18 34	11 08	11 55	12 39	13 19
20	17 33	17 56	18 23	11 30	12 14	12 54	13 31
30	17 18	17 43	18 11	11 54	12 36	13 12	13 44
35	17 08	17 35	18 06	12 08	12 48	13 22	13 52
40	16 58	17 27	18 00	12 24	13 02	13 33	14 00

Day	SUN Eqn. of Time 00h	12h	Mer. Pass.	MOON Mer. Pass. Upper	Lower	Age	Phase
	m s	m s	h m	h m	h m		
10	03 39	03 40	11 56	04 36	17 01	20	
11	03 41	03 42	11 56	05 26	17 50	21	◗
12	03 43	03 44	11 56	06 13	18 36	22	

1966 JUNE 3

G.M.T.	SUN G.H.A.	Dec.	MOON G.H.A.	v	Dec.	d	H.P.
d h	° '	° '	° '	'	° '	'	'
3 00	180 31.5	N22 13.9	4 56.2	8.2	S22 47.7	8.3	57.4
01	195 31.4	14.2	19 23.4	8.3	22 56.0	8.1	57.4
02	210 31.4	14.5	33 50.7	8.1	23 04.1	8.0	57.4
03	225 31.3	·· 14.8	48 17.8	8.2	23 12.1	7.8	57.3
04	240 31.2	15.1	62 45.0	8.1	23 19.9	7.6	57.3
05	255 31.1	15.5	77 12.1	8.0	23 27.7	7.6	57.3
06	270 31.0	N22 15.8	91 39.1	8.0	S23 35.3	7.4	57.3
07	285 30.9	16.1	106 06.1	8.0	23 42.7	7.3	57.3
08	300 30.8	16.4	120 33.1	8.0	23 50.0	7.1	57.3
F 09	315 30.7	·· 16.7	135 00.1	7.9	23 57.1	7.1	57.2
R 10	330 30.6	17.0	149 27.0	7.9	24 04.2	6.9	57.2
I 11	345 30.4	17.3	163 53.9	7.8	24 11.0	6.8	57.2
D 12	0 30.4	N22 17.6	178 20.7	7.8	S24 17.8	6.5	57.1
A 13	15 30.2	17.9	192 47.5	7.8	24 24.3	6.5	57.1
Y 14	30 30.1	18.3	207 14.3	7.8	24 30.8	6.3	57.1
15	45 30.0	·· 18.6	221 41.1	7.7	24 37.1	6.1	57.1
16	60 29.9	18.9	236 07.8	7.7	24 43.2	6.0	57.0
17	75 29.8	19.2	250 34.5	7.7	24 49.2	5.9	57.0
18	90 29.7	N22 19.5	265 01.2	7.6	S24 55.1	5.7	57.0
19	105 29.6	19.8	279 27.8	7.6	25 00.8	5.5	57.0
20	120 29.5	20.1	293 54.4	7.7	25 06.3	5.4	56.9
21	135 29.4	·· 20.4	308 21.1	7.5	25 11.7	5.3	56.9
22	150 29.3	20.7	322 47.6	7.6	25 17.0	5.1	56.9
23	165 29.2	21.0	337 14.2	7.6	25 22.1	5.0	56.9
4 00	180 29.1	N22 21.3	351 40.8	7.5	S25 27.1	4.8	56.8
01	195 29.0	21.6	6 07.3	7.5	25 31.9	4.6	56.8
02	210 28.9	21.9	20 33.8	7.5	25 36.5	4.5	56.8
03	225 28.8	·· 22.2	35 00.3	7.5	25 41.0	4.4	56.8
04	240 28.7	22.5	49 26.8	7.5	25 45.4	4.2	56.7
05	255 28.6	22.8	63 53.3	7.5	25 49.6	4.1	56.7
	S.D. 15.8	d 0.3	S.D. 15.6		15.4		15.2

Lat.	Twilight Naut.	Civil	Sun-rise	Moonrise 3	4	5	6
°	h m	h m	h m	h m	h m	h m	h m
N 40	03 19	04 00	04 32	19 58	21 00	21 55	22 40
35	03 41	04 17	04 46	19 41	20 42	21 37	22 24
30	03 59	04 32	04 59	19 27	20 27	21 22	22 10
20	04 26	04 55	05 20	19 02	20 01	20 56	21 46
N 10	04 52	05 15	05 38	18 41	19 38	20 33	21 25
0	05 06	05 32	05 55	18 21	19 17	20 12	21 05
S 10	05 22	05 48	06 11	18 02	18 56	19 51	20 45
20	05 38	06 05	06 29	17 41	18 33	19 28	20 24
30	05 53	06 23	06 49	17 17	18 07	19 02	19 59
35	06 01	06 33	07 01	17 04	17 52	18 47	19 45
40	06 10	06 44	07 14	16 47	17 34	18 29	19 28

Lat.	Sun-set	Twilight Civil	Naut.	Moonset 3	4	5	6
°	h m	h m	h m	h m	h m	h m	h m
N 40	19 24	19 57	20 37	04 24	05 08	05 59	06 57
35	19 09	19 39	20 15	04 39	05 25	06 17	07 14
30	18 58	19 25	19 58	04 52	05 40	06 33	07 29
20	18 38	19 03	19 32	05 15	06 05	07 00	07 55
N 10	18 19	18 41	19 08	05 34	06 27	07 22	08 17
0	18 02	18 24	18 50	05 53	06 48	07 44	08 38
S 10	17 45	18 08	18 34	06 11	07 09	08 05	08 58
20	17 28	17 51	18 19	06 31	07 31	08 28	09 20
30	17 07	17 33	18 03	06 54	07 56	08 54	09 46
35	16 56	17 24	17 55	07 07	08 11	09 09	10 00
40	16 42	17 12	17 46	07 22	08 28	09 27	10 17

Day	SUN Eqn. of Time 00h	12h	Mer. Pass.	MOON Mer. Pass. Upper	Lower	Age	Phase
	m s	m s	h m	h m	h m		
3	02 06	02 02	11 58	24 35	12 07	14	○
4	01 57	01 52	11 58	00 35	13 02	15	
5	01 47	01 41	11 58	01 30	13 58	16	

1966 JULY 2

G.M.T.	ARIES G.H.A.	VENUS −3.4 G.H.A.	Dec.	MARS +1.8 G.H.A.	Dec.	JUPITER −1.4 G.H.A.	Dec.	SATURN +1.2 G.H.A.	Dec.	STARS Name	S.H.A.	Dec.
d h	° '	° '	° '	° '	° '	° '	° '	° '	° '		° '	° '
2 00	279 35.0	214 38.3	N19 48.2	196 22.4	N23 45.8	176 13.7	N22 55.7	279 03.6	S 2 11.1	Alphecca	126 40.9	N 26 49.7
01	294 37.5	229 37.7	48.8	211 23.0	45.9	191 15.6	55.7	294 06.0	11.1	Alpheratz	358 20.4	N 28 54.1
02	309 39.9	244 37.1	49.4	226 23.6	46.0	206 17.4	55.6	309 08.4	11.1	Altair	62 42.7	N 8 46.6
03	324 42.4	259 36.5	•• 50.0	241 24.2	•• 46.1	221 19.3	•• 55.6	324 10.8	•• 11.1	Ankaa	353 50.6	S 42 29.1
04	339 44.8	274 35.9	50.5	256 24.8	46.2	236 21.2	55.5	339 13.2	11.1	Antares	113 09.7	S 26 21.6
05	354 47.3	289 35.2	51.1	271 25.4	46.3	251 23.0	55.5	354 15.7	11.1			
06	9 49.8	304 34.6	N19 51.7	286 26.0	N23 46.4	266 24.9	N22 55.4	9 18.1	S 2 11.1	Canopus	264 12.5	S 52 40.5
S 07	24 52.2	319 34.0	52.3	301 26.6	46.5	281 26.7	55.4	24 20.5	11.0	Capella	281 27.6	N 45 57.9
08	39 54.7	334 33.4	52.9	316 27.2	46.6	296 28.6	55.3	39 22.9	11.0	Deneb	49 55.4	N 45 09.4
A 09	54 57.2	349 32.7	•• 53.4	331 27.8	•• 46.7	311 30.4	•• 55.3	54 25.4	•• 11.0	Denebola	183 10.0	N 14 45.8
T 10	69 59.6	4 32.1	54.0	346 28.4	46.8	326 32.3	55.2	69 27.8	11.0	Diphda	349 31.5	S 18 10.2
U 11	85 02.1	19 31.5	54.6	1 29.0	46.9	341 34.1	55.2	84 30.2	11.0			
R 12	100 04.6	34 30.9	N19 55.1	16 29.6	N23 47.0	356 36.0	N22 55.1	99 32.6	S .2 11.0	Dubhe	194 35.3	N 61 56.3
D 13	115 07.0	49 30.3	55.7	31 30.2	47.1	11 37.8	. 55.1	114 35.1	11.0	Elnath	278 58.0	N 28 34.9
A 14	130 09.5	64 29.6	56.3	46 30.8	47.2	26 39.7	55.0	129 37.5	11.0	Eltanin	91 02.2	N 51 29.5
-Y 15	145 12.0	79 29.0	•• 56.9	61 31.4	•• 47.3	41 41.5	•• 55.0	144 39.9	•• 11.0	Enif	34 21.9	N 9 43.1
16	160 14.4	94 28.4	57.4	76 32.0	47.4	56 43.4	54.9	159 42.3	11.0	Fomalhaut	16 03.0	S 29 48.0
17	175 16.9	109 27.8	58.0	91 32.6	47.5	71 45.2	54.9	174 44.8	11.0			
18	190 19.3	124 27.1	N19 58.6	106 33.2	N23 47.6	86 47.1	N22 54.9	189 47.2	S 2 11.0	Mirfak	309 31.9	N 49 44.4
19	205 21.8	139 26.5	59.1	121 33.8	47.7	101 49.0	54.8	204 49.6	11.0	Shaula	97 09.9	S 37 05.0
20	220 24.3	154 25.9	19 59.7	136 34.4	47.8	116 50.8	54.8	219 52.0	11.0	Sirius	259 05.5	S 16 40.0
21	235 26.7	169 25.2	20 00.3	151 35.0	•• 47.9	131 52.7	•• 54.7	234 54.5	•• 11.0	Spica	159 08.8	S 10 59.2
22	250 29.2	184 24.6	00.8	166 35.6	48.0	146 54.5	54.7	249 56.9	11.0	Suhail	223 19.1	S 43 17.8
23	265 31.7	199 24.0	01.4	181 36.2	48.1	161 56.4	54.6	264 59.3	11.0			
3 00	280 34.1	214 23.4	N20 01.9	196 36.8	N23 48.2	176 58.2	N22 54.6	280 01.8	S 2 11.0	Vega	81 02.7	N 38 45.0
01	295 36.6	229 22.7	02.5	211 37.4	48.3	192 00.1	54.5	295 04.2	11.0	Zuben'ubl	137 44.7	S 15 54.3
02	310 39.1	244 22.1	03.1	226 38.0	48.4	207 01.9	54.5	310 06.6	11.0			
03	325 41.5	259 21.5	•• 03.6	241 38.6	•• 48.5	222 03.8	•• 54.4	325 09.0	•• 11.0		S.H.A.	Mer. Pass.
04	340 44.0	274 20.8	04.2	256 39.2	48.6	237 05.6	54.4	340 11.5	11.0		° '	h m
05	355 46.4	289 20.2	04.7	271 39.8	48.7	252 07.5	54.3	355 13.9	11.0	Venus	296 17.2	9 41
										Mars	277 32.2	10 55
										Jupiter	256 53.5	12 17
Mer. Pass. 5 24.7		v −0.6	d 0.6	v 0.6	d 0.1	v 1.9	d 0.0	v 2.4	d 0.0	Saturn	359 29.6	5 27

1966 JULY 31

G.M.T.	ARIES G.H.A.	VENUS −3.3 G.H.A.	Dec.	MARS +1.8 G.H.A.	Dec.	JUPITER −1.4 G.H.A.	Dec.	SATURN +1.0 G.H.A.	Dec.	STARS Name	S.H.A.	Dec.
d h	°	° '	° '	° '	° '	° '	° '	° '	° '		° '	° '
31 00	308 10.0	206 03.6	N22 35.2	203 39.4	N23 31.3	197 49.2	N22 13.6	307 48.6	S 2 23.8	Acamar	315 45.2	S 40 26.0
01	323 12.5	221 02.8	35.1	218 40.1	31.1	212 51.1	13.5	322 51.2	23.9	Achernar	335 52.8	S 57 24.1
02	338 15.0	236 02.0	34.9	233 40.7	31.0	227 52.9	13.5	337 53.7	23.9	Acrux	173 49.8	S 62 55.0
03	353 17.4	251 01.2	•• 34.8	248 41.4	•• 30.9	242 54.8	•• 13.4	352 56.2	•• 23.9	Adhara	255 40.8	S 28 55.3
04	8 19.9	266 00.4	34.7	263 42.1	30.7	257 56.7	13.3	7 58.8	24.0	Aldebaran	291 30.4	N 16 26.7
05	23 22.3	280 59.6	34.5	278 42.7	30.6	272 58.6	13.2	23 01.3	24.0			
06	38 24.8	295 58.8	N22 34.4	293 43.4	N23 30.4	288 00.5	N22 13.2	38 03.8	S 2 24.1	Alphecca	126 41.0	N 26 49.8
07	53 27.3	310 58.0	. 34.2	308 44.1	30.3	303 02.3	13.1	53 06.4	24.1	Alpheratz	358 20.2	N 28 54.2
08	68 29.7	325 57.2	34.1	323 44.8	30.1	318 04.2	13.0	68 08.9	24.2	Altair	62 42.6	N 8 46.7
S 09	83 32.2	340 56.4	•• 33.9	338 45.4	•• 30.0	333 06.1	•• 13.0	83 11.4	•• 24.2	Ankaa	353 50.3	S 42 29.0
U 10	98 34.7	355 55.6	33.8	353 46.1	29.8	348 08.0	12.9	98 14.0	24.2	Antares	113 09.8	S 26 21.7
N 11	113 37.1	10 54.8	33.7	8 46.8	29.7	3 09.8	12.8	113 16.5	24.3			
D 12	128 39.6	25 54.0	N22 33.5	23 47.4	N23 29.5	18 11.7	N22 12.7	128 19.0	S 2 24.3	Canopus	264 12.4	S 52 40.3
A 13	143 42.1	40 53.2	33.4	38 48.1	29.4	33 13.6	12.7	143 21.6	24.4	Capella	281 27.3	N 45 57.9
Y 14	158 44.5	55 52.4	33.2	53 48.8	29.3	48 15.5	12.6	158 24.1	24.4	Deneb	49 55.3	N 45 09.5
15	173 47.0	70 51.6	•• 33.1	68 49.4	•• 29.1	63 17.4	•• 12.5	173 26.6	•• 24.4	Denebola	183 10.0	N 14 45.8
16	188 49.5	85 50.8	32.9	83 50.1	29.0	78 19.2	12.4	188 29.2	24.5	Diphda	349 31.3	S 18 10.1
17	203 51.9	100 50.0	32.7	98 50.8	28.8	93 21.1	12.4	203 31.7	24.5			
18	218 54.4	115 49.2	N22 32.6	113 51.5	N23 28.7	108 23.0	N22 12.3	218 34.3	S 2 24.6	Rasalhague	96 39.2	N 12 35.0
19	233 56.8	130 48.4	32.4	128 52.1	28.5	123 24.9	12.2	233 36.8	24.6	Regulus	208 21.6	N 12 08.1
20	248 59.3	145 47.6	32.3	143 52.8	28.4	138 26.8	12.2	248 39.3	24.7	Rigel	281 46.4	S 8 14.1
21	264 01.8	160 46.8	•• 32.1	158 53.5	•• 28.2	153 28.6	•• 12.1	263 41.9	•• 24.7	Rigil Kent.	140 40.5	S 60 42.0
22	279 04.2	175 46.0	32.0	173 54.1	28.1	168 30.5	12.0	278 44.4	24.7	Sabik	102 53.1	S 15 41.2
23	294 06.7	190 45.2	31.8	188 54.8	27.9	183 32.4	11.9	293 46.9	24.8			
1 00	309 09.2	205 44.4	N22 31.6	203 55.5	N23 27.8	198 34.3	N22 11.9	308 49.5	S 2 24.8	Vega	81 02.7	N 38 45.2
01	324 11.6	220 43.6	31.5	218 56.2	27.6	213 36.1	11.8	323 52.0	24.9	Zuben'ubl	137 44.8	S 15 54.3
02	339 14.1	235 42.8	31.3	233 56.8	27.5	228 38.0	11.7	338 54.5	24.9			
03	354 16.6	250 42.0	•• 31.2	248 57.5	•• 27.3	243 39.9	•• 11.6	353 57.1	•• 24.9		S.H.A.	Mer. Pass.
04	9 19.0	265 41.2	31.0	263 58.2	27.2	258 41.8	11.6	8 59.6	25.0		° '	h m
05	24 21.5	280 40.4	30.8	278 58.9	27.0	273 43.7	11.5	24 02.2	25.0	Venus	257 53.6	10 16
										Mars	255 29.4	10 25
										Jupiter	249 39.2	10 47
Mer. Pass. 3 26.8		v −0.8	d 0.1	v 0.7	d 0.1	v 1.9	d 0.1	v 2.5	d 0.0	Saturn	359 38.6	3 28

1966 JULY 2

G.M.T.	SUN G.H.A.	SUN Dec.	MOON G.H.A.	MOON v	MOON Dec.	MOON d	MOON H.P.	Lat.	Twilight Naut.	Twilight Civil	Sun- rise	Moonrise 29	Moonrise 30	Moonrise 31	Moonrise 1
d h	° ′	° ′	° ′	′	° ′	′	′	°	h m	h m	h m	h m	h m	h m	h m
2 00	179 03·4	N23 05·5	9 29·8	7·8	S 26 25·7	2·2	56·1	N 40	03 20	04 02	04 34	17 45	18 49	19 46	20 35
01	194 03·3	05·4	23 56·6	7·8	26 27·9	2·1	56·1	35	03 43	04 20	04 49	17 29	18 31	19 28	20 18
02	209 03·2	05·2	38 23·4	7·9	26 30·0	1·9	56·1	30	04 02	04 35	05 02	17 15	18 16	19 13	20 03
03	224 03·0	•• 05·0	52 50·3	7·8	26 31·9	1·8	56·1	20	04 30	04 59	05 24	16 52	17 50	18 46	19 38
04	239 02·9	04·8	67 17·1	7·9	26 33·7	1·7	56·0	N 10	04 53	05 20	05 43	16 32	17 28	18 24	19 16
05	254 02·8	04·7	81 44·0	7·8	26 35·4	1·4	56·0	0	05 11	05 38	06 00	16 13	17 07	18 02	18 56
06	269 02·7	N23 04·5	96 10·8	7·9	S 26 36·8	1·4	56·0	S 10	05 28	05 54	06 17	15 54	16 47	17 41	18 35
07	284 02·6	04·3	110 37·7	7·9	26 38·2	1·2	56·0	20	05 44	06 11	06 35	15 34	16 24	17 18	18 14
S 08	299 02·5	04·1	125 04·6	7·9	26 39·4	1·0	56·0	30	06 00	06 30	06 56	15 11	15 59	16 52	17 48
A 09	314 02·3	•• 03·9	139 31·5	7·9	26 40·4	0·9	55·9	35	06 09	06 41	07 08	14 58	15 44	16 37	17 34
T 10	329 02·2	03·8	153 58·4	8·0	26 41·3	0·8	55·9	40	06 18	06 52	07 23	14 43	15 27	16 19	17 16
U 11	344 02·1	03·6	168 25·4	7·9	26 42·1	0·6	55·9	Lat.	Sun- set	Twilight Civil	Twilight Naut.	Moonset 30	Moonset 1	Moonset 2	Moonset 3
R 12	359 02·0	N23 03·4	182 52·3	8·0	S 26 42·7	0·4	55·9	°	h m	h m	h m	h m	h m	h m	h m
D 13	14 01·9	03·2	197 19·3	8·0	26 43·1	0·3	55·9	N 40	19 33	20 05	20 47	02 22	03 03	03 51	04 45
A 14	29 01·7	03·0	211 46·3	8·0	26 43·4	0·2	55·8	35	19 18	19 47	20 23	02 36	03 19	04 08	05 03
Y 15	44 01·6	•• 02·8	226 13·3	8·0	26 43·6	0·0	55·8	30	19 05	19 32	20 06	02 48	03 33	04 23	05 18
16	59 01·5	02·7	240 40·3	8·1	26 43·6	0·1	55·8	20	18 43	19 08	19 37	03 09	03 58	04 50	05 45
17	74 01·4	02·5	255 07·4	8·1	26 43·5	0·3	55·8	N 10	18 25	18 48	19 15	03 27	04 19	05 13	06 07
18	89 01·3	N23 02·3	269 34·5	8·1	S 26 43·2	0·4	55·8	0	18 07	18 30	18 56	03 45	04 39	05 34	06 28
19	104 01·2	02·1	284 01·6	8·2	26 42·8	0·6	55·7	S 10	17 50	18 13	18 39	04 02	04 59	05 55	06 49
20	119 01·0	01·9	298 28·8	8·2	26 42·2	0·7	55·7	20	17 32	17 56	18 23	04 21	05 20	06 18	07 12
21	134 00·9	•• 01·7	312 56·0	8·2	26 41·5	0·9	55·7	30	17 11	17 37	18 07	04 42	05 45	06 44	07 38
22	149 00·8	01·5	327 23·2	8·2	26 40·6	1·0	55·7	35	16 59	17 27	17 59	04 55	05 59	06 59	07 53
23	164 00·7	01·4	341 50·4	8·3	26 39·6	1·2	55·7	40	16 45	17 15	17 49	05 09	06 16	07 17	08 10
3 00	179 00·6	N23 01·2	356 17·7	8·4	S 26 38·4	1·3	55·6		SUN	SUN	SUN	MOON	MOON	MOON	MOON
01	194 00·5	01·0	10 45·1	8·3	26 37·1	1·4	55·6	Day	Eqn. of Time 00ʰ	Eqn. of Time 12ʰ	Mer. Pass.	Mer. Pass. Upper	Mer. Pass. Lower	Age	Phase
02	209 00·3	00·8	25 12·4	8·5	26 35·7	1·6	55·6		m s	m s	h m	h m	h m	d	
03	224 00·2	•• 00·6	39 39·9	8·4	26 34·1	1·7	55·6	30	03 23	03 29	12 03	22 26	09 59	12	
04	239 00·1	00·4	54 07·3	8·5	26 32·4	1·9	55·6	1	03 35	03 40	12 04	23 21	10 53	13	
05	254 00·0	00·2	68 34·8	8·6	26 30·5	2·0	55·5	2	03 46	03 52	12 04	24 15	11 48	14	
	S.D. 15·8	d 0·2	S.D. 15·5		15·4		15·2								

1966 JULY 31

G.M.T.	SUN G.H.A.	SUN Dec.	MOON G.H.A.	MOON v	MOON Dec.	MOON d	MOON H.P.	Lat.	Twilight Naut.	Twilight Civil	Sun- rise	Moonrise 30	Moonrise 31	Moonrise 1	Moonrise 2
d h	° ′	° ′	° ′	′	° ′	′	′	°	h m	h m	h m	h m	h m	h m	h m
31 00	178 24·7	N18 26·3	13 51·4	9·5	S 25 56·5	3·8	55·1	N 40	03 49	04 26	04 57	18 31	19 14	19 50	20 19
01	193 24·7	25·7	28 19·9	9·6	25 52·7	3·9	55·0	35	04 06	04 40	05 08	18 14	18 58	19 36	20 09
02	208 24·8	25·1	42 48·5	9·6	25 48·8	4·0	55·0	30	04 21	04 52	05 18	17 59	18 45	19 25	19 59
03	223 24·8	•• 24·5	57 17·1	9·7	25 44·8	4·2	55·0	20	04 43	05 11	05 35	17 33	18 21	19 04	19 44
04	238 24·8	23·9	71 45·8	9·7	25 40·6	4·2	55·0	N 10	05 01	05 27	05 49	17 11	18 01	18 47	19 29
05	253 24·9	23·3	86 14·5	9·8	25 36·4	4·5	55·0	0	05 16	05 41	06 03	16 50	17 42	18 30	19 16
06	268 24·9	N18 22·6	100 43·3	9·8	S 25 31·9	4·5	55·0	S 10	05 29	05 54	06 16	16 29	17 22	18 14	19 03
07	283 24·9	22·0	115 12·1	10·0	25 27·4	4·6	54·9	20	05 41	06 07	06 30	16 07	17 02	17 56	18 49
08	298 24·9	21·4	129 41·1	9·9	25 22·8	4·8	54·9	30	05 52	06 21	06 46	15 40	16 38	17 35	18 32
S 09	313 24·9	•• 20·8	144 10·0	10·1	25 18·0	4·9	54·9	35	05 58	06 29	06 56	15 26	16 24	17 24	18 23
U 10	328 25·0	20·2	158 39·1	10·1	25 13·1	5·1	54·9	40	06 05	06 37	07 06	15 08	16 08	17 10	18 12
N 11	343 25·0	19·6	173 08·2	10·1	25 08·0	5·1	54·9	Lat.	Sun- set	Twilight Civil	Twilight Naut.	Moonset 30	Moonset 31	Moonset 1	Moonset 2
D 12	358 25·1	N18 19·0	187 37·3	10·3	S 25 02·9	5·3	54·9	°	h m	h m	h m	h m	h m	h m	h m
A 13	13 25·1	18·4	202 06·6	10·2	24 57·6	5·4	54·9	N 40	19 15	19 46	20 23	02 38	03 36	04 37	05 40
Y 14	28 25·1	17·7	216 35·8	10·4	24 52·2	5·5	54·8	35	19 04	19 32	20 06	02 56	03 53	04 53	05 52
15	43 25·2	•• 17·1	231 05·2	10·4	24 46·7	5·6	54·8	30	18 54	19 19	19 52	03 12	04 08	05 06	06 03
16	58 25·2	16·5	245 34·6	10·5	24 41·1	5·8	54·8	20	18 38	19 01	19 29	03 38	04 33	05 28	06 22
17	73 25·2	15·9	260 04·1	10·6	24 35·3	5·8	54·8	N 10	18 23	18 45	19 11	04 01	04 55	05 47	06 38
18	88 25·3	N18 15·3	274 33·7	10·6	S 24 29·5	6·0	54·8	0	18 10	18 32	18 57	04 22	05 15	06 06	06 53
19	103 25·3	14·7	289 03·3	10·7	24 23·5	6·1	54·8	S 10	17 56	18 19	18 44	04 43	05 35	06 23	07 08
20	118 25·3	14·0	303 33·0	10·8	24 17·4	6·2	54·8	20	17 43	18 06	18 32	05 06	05 57	06 43	07 24
21	133 25·4	•• 13·4	318 02·8	10·8	24 11·2	6·3	54·7	30	17 27	17 52	18 21	05 33	06 22	07 04	07 42
22	148 25·4	12·8	332 32·6	10·9	24 04·9	6·5	54·7	35	17 17	17 44	18 15	05 48	06 36	07 17	07 52
23	163 25·4	12·2	347 02·5	11·0	23 58·4	6·5	54·7	40	17 07	17 36	18 08	06 05	06 53	07 31	08 04
1 00	178 25·5	N18 11·6	1 32·5	11·1	S 23 51·9	6·7	54·7		SUN	SUN	SUN	MOON	MOON	MOON	MOON
01	193 25·5	10·9	16 02·6	11·1	23 45·2	6·7	54·7	Day	Eqn. of Time 00ʰ	Eqn. of Time 12ʰ	Mer. Pass.	Mer. Pass. Upper	Mer. Pass. Lower	Age	Phase
02	208 25·5	10·3	30 32·7	11·2	23 38·5	6·9	54·7		m s	m s	h m	h m	h m	d	
03	223 25·6	•• 09·7	45 02·9	11·2	23 31·6	7·0	54·7	30	06 23	06 22	12 06	23 03	10 36	12	
04	238 25·6	09·1	59 33·1	11·4	23 24·6	7·1	54·6	31	06 21	06 20	12 06	23 54	11 28	13	
05	253 25·6	08·4	74 03·5	11·4	23 17·5	7·2	54·6	1	06 18	06 17	12 06	24 42	12 18	14	
	S.D. 15·8	d 0·6	S.D. 15·1		15·0		14·9								

1966 AUG. 1

G.M.T.	ARIES G.H.A.	VENUS −3.3 G.H.A.	Dec.	MARS +1.8 G.H.A.	Dec.	JUPITER −1.4 G.H.A.	Dec.	SATURN +1.0 G.H.A.	Dec.
d 1 00	309 09.2	205 44.4	N22 31.6	203 55.5	N23 27.8	198 34.3	N22 11.9	308 49.5	S 2 24.8
01	324 11.6	220 43.6	31.5	218 56.2	27.6	213 36.1	11.8	323 52.0	24.9
02	339 14.1	235 42.8	31.3	233 56.8	27.5	228 38.0	11.7	338 54.5	24.9
03	354 16.6	250 42.0 ··	31.2	248 57.5 ··	27.3	243 39.9 ··	11.6	353 57.1 ··	24.9
04	9 19.0	265 41.2	31.0	263 58.2	27.2	258 41.8	11.6	8 59.6	25.0
05	24 21.5	280 40.4	30.8	278 58.9	27.0	273 43.7	11.5	24 02.2	25.0
06	39 24.0	295 39.6	N22 30.6	293 59.5	N23 26.9	288 45.5	N22 11.4	39 04.7	S 2 25.1
07	54 26.4	310 38.8	30.5	309 00.2	26.7	303 47.4	11.4	54 07.2	25.1
M 08	69 28.9	325 38.0	30.3	324 00.9	26.6	318 49.3	11.3	69 09.8	25.2
O 09	84 31.3	340 37.2 ··	30.1	339 01.5 ··	26.4	333 51.2 ··	11.2	84 12.3 ··	25.2
N 10	99 33.8	355 36.4	30.0	354 02.2	26.3	348 53.1	11.1	99 14.8	25.3
N 11	114 36.3	10 35.6	29.8	9 02.9	26.1	3 54.9	11.1	114 17.4	25.3
D 12	129 38.7	25 34.8	N22 29.6	24 03.6	N23 26.0	18 56.8	N22 11.0	129 19.9	S 2 25.3
A 13	144 41.2	40 34.0	29.4	39 04.2	25.8	33 58.7	10.9	144 22.5	25.4
Y 14	159 43.7	55 33.2	29.3	54 04.9	25.7	49 00.6	10.8	159 25.0	25.4
15	174 46.1	70 32.4 ··	29.1	69 05.6 ··	25.5	64 02.5 ··	10.8	174 27.5 ··	25.5
16	189 48.6	85 31.6	28.9	84 06.3	25.3	79 04.3	10.7	189 30.1	25.5
17	204 51.1	100 30.8	28.7	99 06.9	25.2	94 06.2	10.6	204 32.6	25.6
18	219 53.5	115 30.0	N22 28.5	114 07.6	N23 25.0	109 08.1	N22 10.6	219 35.2	S 2 25.6
19	234 56.0	130 29.2	28.3	129 08.3	24.9	124 10.0	10.5	234 37.7	25.6
20	249 58.5	145 28.4	28.2	144 09.0	24.7	139 11.9	10.4	249 40.2	25.7
21	265 00.9	160 27.6 ··	28.0	159 09.6 ··	24.6	154 13.7 ··	10.3	264 42.8 ··	25.7
22	280 03.4	175 26.8	27.8	174 10.3	24.4	169 15.6	10.3	279 45.3	25.8
23	295 05.8	190 26.0	27.6	189 11.0	24.2	184 17.5	10.2	294 47.8	25.8
2 00	310 08.3	205 25.2	N22 27.4	204 11.7	N23 24.1	199 19.4	N22 10.1	309 50.4	S 2 25.9
01	325 10.8	220 24.4	27.2	219 12.4	23.9	214 21.3	10.0	324 52.9	25.9
02	340 13.2	235 23.6	27.0	234 13.0	23.8	229 23.1	10.0	339 55.5	26.0
03	355 15.7	250 22.8 ··	26.8	249 13.7 ··	23.6	244 25.0 ··	09.9	354 58.0 ··	26.0
04	10 18.2	265 22.0	26.6	264 14.4	23.5	259 26.9	09.8	10 00.6	26.0
05	25 20.6	280 21.2	26.5	279 15.1	23.3	274 28.8	09.8	25 03.1	26.1
Mer. Pass. 3 26.8		v −0.8	d 0.1	v 0.7	d 0.1	v 1.9	d 0.1	v 2.5	d 0.0

STARS (1966 AUG. 1)

Name	S.H.A.	Dec.
Acamar	315 45.2	S 40 26.0
Achernar	335 52.8	S 57 24.1
Acrux	173 49.8	S 62 55.0
Adhara	255 40.8	S 28 55.3
Aldebaran	291 30.4	N 16 26.7
Alphecca	126 41.0	N 26 49.8
Alpheratz	358 20.2	N 28 54.2
Altair	62 42.6	N 8 46.7
Ankaa	353 50.3	S 42 29.0
Antares	113 09.8	S 26 21.7
Canopus	264 12.4	S 52 40.3
Capella	281 27.3	N 45 57.9
Deneb	49 55.3	N 45 09.5
Denebola	183 10.0	N 14 45.8
Diphda	349 31.3	S 18 10.1
Rasalhague	96 39.2	N 12 35.0
Regulus	208 21.6	N 12 08.1
Rigel	281 46.4	S 8 14.1
Rigil Kent.	140 40.5	S 60 42.0
Sabik	102 53.1	S 15 41.2
Vega	81 02.7	N 38 45.2
Zuben'ubi	137 44.8	S 15 54.3

	S.H.A.	Mer. Pass.
Venus	257 53.6	10 16
Mars	255 29.4	10 25
Jupiter	249 39.2	10 47
Saturn	359 38.6	3 28

1966 AUGUST 22

G.M.T.	ARIES G.H.A.	VENUS −3.3 G.H.A.	Dec.	MARS +1.9 G.H.A.	Dec.	JUPITER −1.5 G.H.A.	Dec.	SATURN +0.9 G.H.A.	Dec.
d 22 00	329 51.1	199 23.0	N18 51.6	209 55.7	N21 33.6	214 31.9	N21 32.7	330 25.3	S 2 53.1
01	344 53.5	214 22.3	50.9	224 56.5	33.3	229 33.8	32.6	345 27.9	53.2
02	359 56.0	229 21.6	50.2	239 57.3	33.0	244 35.8	32.5	0 30.5	53.3
03	14 58.5	244 21.0 ··	49.5	254 58.0 ··	32.7	259 37.7 ··	32.4	15 33.1 ··	53.3
04	30 00.9	259 20.3	48.8	269 58.8	32.4	274 39.6	32.4	30 35.7	53.4
05	45 03.4	274 19.6	48.1	284 59.5	32.1	289 41.6	32.3	45 38.3	53.5
06	60 05.9	289 18.9	N18 47.4	300 00.3	N21 31.8	304 43.5	N21 32.2	60 40.9	S 2 53.5
07	75 08.3	304 18.2	46.7	315 01.1	31.5	319 45.4	32.1	75 43.5	53.6
M 08	90 10.8	319 17.6	46.0	330 01.8	31.2	334 47.3	32.0	90 46.1	53.7
O 09	105 13.3	334 16.9 ··	45.3	345 02.6 ··	30.9	349 49.3 ··	32.0	105 48.7 ··	53.7
N 10	120 15.7	349 16.2	44.6	0 03.4	30.6	4 51.2	31.9	120 51.3	53.8
N 11	135 18.2	4 15.5	43.9	15 04.1	30.3	19 53.1	31.8	135 53.9	53.9
D 12	150 20.6	19 14.8	N18 43.2	30 04.9	N21 30.0	34 55.0	N21 31.7	150 56.5	S 2 54.0
A 13	165 23.1	34 14.2	42.5	45 05.7	29.7	49 57.0	31.6	165 59.1	54.0
Y 14	180 25.6	49 13.5	41.8	60 06.4	29.4	64 58.9	31.5	181 01.7	54.1
15	195 28.0	64 12.8 ··	41.1	75 07.2 ··	29.1	80 00.8 ··	31.5	196 04.3 ··	54.2
16	210 30.5	79 12.1	40.3	90 07.9	28.8	95 02.8	31.4	211 06.9	54.2
17	225 33.0	94 11.4	39.6	105 08.7	28.5	110 04.7	31.3	226 09.5	54.3
18	240 35.4	109 10.8	N18 38.9	120 09.5	N21 28.2	125 06.6	N21 31.2	241 12.1	S 2 54.4
19	255 37.9	124 10.1	38.2	135 10.2	27.9	140 08.5	31.1	256 14.7	54.4
20	270 40.4	139 09.4	37.5	150 11.0	27.6	155 10.5	31.1	271 17.4	54.5
21	285 42.8	154 08.7 ··	36.8	165 11.8 ··	27.3	170 12.4 ··	31.0	286 20.0 ··	54.6
22	300 45.3	169 08.1	36.1	180 12.5	27.0	185 14.3	30.9	301 22.6	54.6
23	315 47.8	184 07.4	35.3	195 13.3	26.7	200 16.2	30.8	316 25.2	54.7
23 00	330 50.2	199 06.7	N18 34.6	210 14.1	N21 26.4	215 18.2	N21 30.7	331 27.8	S 2 54.8
01	345 52.7	214 06.0	33.9	225 14.8	26.1	230 20.1	30.6	346 30.4	54.8
02	0 55.1	229 05.4	33.2	240 15.6	25.8	245 22.0	30.6	1 33.0	54.9
03	15 57.6	244 04.7 ··	32.5	255 16.4 ··	25.5	260 24.0 ··	30.5	16 35.6 ··	55.0
04	31 00.1	259 04.0	31.8	270 17.1	25.1	275 25.9	30.4	31 38.2	55.0
05	46 02.5	274 03.3	31.0	285 17.9	24.8	290 27.8	30.3	46 40.8	55.1
Mer. Pass. 2 04.2		v −0.7	d 0.7	v 0.8	d 0.3	v 1.9	d 0.1	v 2.6	d 0.1

STARS (1966 AUGUST 22)

Name	S.H.A.	Dec.
Acamar	315 45.1	S 40 25.9
Achernar	335 52.6	S 57 24.1
Acrux	173 49.9	S 62 54.9
Adhara	255 40.7	S 28 55.2
Aldebaran	291 30.3	N 16 26.7
Arcturus	146 28.2	N 19 21.5
Atria	108 43.5	S 68 58.5
Avior	234 33.3	S 59 23.8
Bellatrix	279 10.2	N 6 19.4
Betelgeuse	271 39.9	N 7 24.3
Canopus	264 12.3	S 52 40.2
Capella	281 27.1	N 45 57.9
Deneb	49 55.3	N 45 09.6
Denebola	183 10.1	N 14 45.7
Diphda	349 31.2	S 18 10.0
Schedar	350 20.9	N 56 21.1
Shaula	97 10.0	S 37 05.0
Sirius	259 05.3	S 16 39.9
Spica	159 08.9	S 10 59.2
Suhail	223 19.1	S 43 17.6
Vega	81 02.7	N 38 45.2
Zuben'ubi	137 44.9	S 15 54.2

	S.H.A.	Mer. Pass.
Venus	230 47.6	10 42
Mars	240 45.6	10 01
Jupiter	244 53.8	9 44
Saturn	0 31.0	2 02

1966 AUG. 1

G.M.T.	SUN G.H.A.	Dec.	MOON G.H.A.	v	Dec.	d	H.P.
d h	° '	° '	° '	'	° '	'	'
1 00	178 25·5	N18 11·6	1 32·5	11·1	S23 51·9	6·7	54·7
01	193 25·5	10·9	16 02·6	11·1	23 45·2	6·7	54·7
02	208 25·5	·10·3	30 32·7	11·2	23 38·5	6·9	54·7
03	223 25·6	· · 09·7	45 02·9	11·2	23 31·6	7·0	54·7
04	238 25·6	09·1	59 33·1	11·4	23 24·6	7·1	54·6
05	253 25·6	08·4	74 03·5	11·4	23 17·5	7·2	54·6
06	268 25·7	N18 07·8	88 33·9	11·5	S23 10·3	7·3	54·6
07	283 25·7	07·2	103 04·4	11·5	23 03·0	7·4	54·6
08	298 25·7	06·6	117 34·9	11·7	22 55·6	7·5	54·6
M 09	313 25·8	· · 05·9	132 05·6	11·7	22 48·1	7·6	54·6
O 10	328 25·8	05·3	146 36·3	11·8	22 40·5	7·7	54·6
N 11	343 25·8	04·7	161 07·1	11·8	22 32·8	7·8	54·6
D 12	358 25·9	N18 04·1	175 37·9	11·9	S22 25·0	7·9	54·5
A 13	13 25·9	03·4	190 08·8	12·0	22 17·1	8·0	54·5
Y 14	28 26·0	02·8	204 39·8	12·1	22 09·1	8·1	54·5
15	43 26·0	· · 02·2	219 10·9	12·2	22 01·0	8·2	54·5
16	58 26·0	01·6	233 42·1	12·2	21 52·8	8·3	54·5
17	73 26·1	00·9	248 13·3	12·3	21 44·5	8·4	54·5
18	88 26·1	N18 00·3	262 44·6	12·4	S21 36·1	8·5	54·5
19	103 26·2	17 59·7	277 16·0	12·4	21 27·6	8·6	54·5
20	118 26·2	59·0	291 47·4	12·5	21 19·0	8·6	54·5
21	133 26·2	· · 58·4	306 18·9	12·6	21 10·4	8·8	54·4
22	148 26·3	57·8	320 50·5	12·7	21 01·6	8·8	54·4
23	163 26·3	57·1	335 22·2	12·7	20 52·8	9·0	54·4
2 00	178 26·3	N17 56·5	349 53·9	12·9	S20 43·8	9·0	54·4
01	193 26·4	55·9	4 25·8	12·8	20 34·8	9·1	54·4
02	208 26·4	55·2	18 57·6	13·0	20 25·7	9·2	54·4
03	223 26·5	· · 54·6	33 29·6	13·0	20 16·5	9·3	54·4
04	238 26·5	54·0	48 01·6	13·2	20 07·2	9·3	54·4
05	253 26·6	53·3	62 33·8	13·1	19 57·9	9·5	54·4
	S.D. 15·8	d 0·6	S.D. 15·1		15·0		14·9

Lat.	Twilight Naut.	Civil	Sun-rise	Moonrise 30	31	1	2
°	h m	h m	h m	h m	h m	h m	h m
N 40	03 49	04 26	04 57	18 31	19 14	19 50	20 19
35	04 06	04 40	05 08	18 14	18 58	19 36	20 09
30	04 21	04 52	05 18	17 59	18 45	19 25	19 59
20	04 43	05 11	05 35	17 33	18 21	19 04	19 44
N 10	05 01	05 27	05 49	17 11	18 01	18 47	19 29
0	05 16	05 41	06 03	16 50	17 42	18 30	19 16
S 10	05 29	05 54	06 16	16 29	17 22	18 14	19 03
20	05 41	06 07	06 30	16 07	17 02	17 56	18 49
30	05 52	06 21	06 46	15 40	16 38	17 35	18 32
35	05 58	06 29	06 56	15 26	16 24	17 24	18 23
40	06 05	06 37	07 06	15 08	16 08	17 10	18 12

Lat.	Sun-set	Twilight Civil	Naut.	Moonset 30	31	1	2
°	h m	h m	h m	h m	h m	h m	h m
N 40	19 15	19 46	20 23	02 38	03 36	04 37	05 40
35	19 04	19 32	20 06	02 56	03 53	04 53	05 52
30	18 54	19 20	19 52	03 12	04 08	05 06	06 03
20	18 38	19 01	19 29	03 38	04 33	05 28	06 22
N 10	18 23	18 45	19 11	04 01	04 55	05 47	06 38
0	18 10	18 32	18 57	04 22	05 15	06 06	06 53
S 10	17 56	18 19	18 44	04 43	05 35	06 23	07 08
20	17 43	18 06	18 32	05 06	05 57	06 43	07 24
30	17 27	17 52	18 21	05 33	06 22	07 04	07 42
35	17 17	17 44	18 15	05 48	06 36	07 17	07 52
40	17 07	17 36	18 08	06 05	06 53	07 31	08 04

Day	SUN Eqn. of Time 00h	12h	Mer. Pass.	MOON Mer. Pass. Upper	Lower	Age	Phase
	m s	m s	h m	h m	h m	d	
30	06 23	06 22	12 06	23 03	10 36	12	○
31	06 21	06 20	12 06	23 54	11 28	13	
1	06 18	06 17	12 06	24 42	12 18	14	

1966 AUGUST 22

G.M.T.	SUN G.H.A.	Dec.	MOON G.H.A.	v	Dec.	d	H.P.
d h	° '	° '	° '	'	° '	'	'
22 00	179 14·0	N12 00·7	107 50·5	10·3	S15 39·9	13·0	58·5
01	194 14·2	11 59·9	122 19·8	10·2	15 52·9	12·9	58·5
02	209 14·3	59·0	136 49·0	10·2	16 05·8	12·8	58·5
03	224 14·5	· · 58·2	151 18·2	10·2	16 18·6	12·7	58·4
04	239 14·7	57·4	165 47·4	10·2	16 31·3	12·5	58·4
05	254 14·8	56·5	180 16·6	10·1	16 43·8	12·5	58·4
06	269 15·0	N11 55·7	194 45·7	10·1	S16 56·3	12·4	58·3
07	284 15·1	54·9	209 14·8	10·0	17 08·7	12·3	58·3
08	299 15·3	54·0	223 43·8	10·0	17 21·0	12·1	58·3
M 09	314 15·4	· · 53·2	238 12·8	10·0	17 33·1	12·1	58·2
O 10	329 15·6	52·3	252 41·8	10·0	17 45·2	11·9	58·2
N 11	344 15·7	51·5	267 10·8	9·9	17 57·1	11·9	58·2
D 12	359 15·9	N11 50·7	281 39·7	9·9	S18 09·0	11·7	58·1
A 13	14 16·1	49·8	296 08·6	9·9	18 20·7	11·6	58·1
Y 14	29 16·2	49·0	310 37·5	9·8	18 32·3	11·5	58·1
15	44 16·4	· · 48·1	325 06·3	9·8	18 43·8	11·4	58·0
16	59 16·5	47·3	339 35·1	9·7	18 55·2	11·2	58·0
17	74 16·7	46·5	354 03·8	9·7	19 06·4	11·2	57·9
18	89 16·9	N11 45·6	8 32·5	9·7	S19 17·6	11·0	57·9
19	104 17·0	44·8	23 01·2	9·6	19 28·6	10·9	57·9
20	119 17·2	43·9	37 29·8	9·7	19 39·5	10·8	57·8
21	134 17·3	· · 43·1	51 58·5	9·5	19 50·3	10·7	57·8
22	149 17·5	42·3	66 27·0	9·6	20 01·0	10·6	57·8
23	164 17·6	41·4	80 55·6	9·5	20 11·6	10·4	57·7
23 00	179 17·8	N11 40·6	95 24·1	9·5	S20 22·0	10·3	57·7
01	194 18·0	39·7	109 52·6	9·4	20 32·3	10·2	57·7
02	209 18·1	38·9	124 21·0	9·4	20 42·5	10·1	57·6
03	224 18·3	· · 38·0	138 49·4	9·4	20 52·6	9·9	57·6
04	239 18·4	37·2	153 17·8	9·3	21 02·5	9·8	57·6
05	254 18·6	36·4	167 46·1	9·3	21 12·3	9·7	57·5
	S.D. 15·8	d 0·8	S.D. 16·3		16·1		15·8

Lat.	Twilight Naut.	Civil	Sun-rise	Moonrise 20	21	22	23
°	h m	h m	h m	h m	h m	h m	h m
N 40	04 14	04 48	05 17	09 54	11 07	12 19	13 29
35	04 26	04 58	05 24	09 50	10 59	12 07	13 14
30	04 36	05 06	05 30	09 47	10 53	11 58	13 02
20	04 52	05 19	05 41	09 41	10 41	11 41	12 41
N 10	05 04	05 29	05 51	09 36	10 31	11 26	12 22
0	05 14	05 39	06 00	09 31	10 21	11 12	12 04
S 10	05 22	05 47	06 09	09 27	10 12	10 59	11 47
20	05 29	05 55	06 18	09 22	10 02	10 44	11 29
30	05 36	06 04	06 28	09 17	09 51	10 28	11 08
35	05 39	06 08	06 34	09 14	09 45	10 18	10 56
40	05 41	06 13	06 41	09 10	09 38	10 08	10 42

Lat.	Sun-set	Twilight Civil	Naut.	Moonset 20	21	22	23
°	h m	h m	h m	h m	h m	h m	h m
N 40	18 49	19 18	19 52	21 22	21 51	22 23	23 00
35	18 42	19 08	19 40	21 27	22 00	22 35	23 15
30	18 35	19 00	19 30	21 32	22 08	22 46	23 28
20	18 25	18 47	19 14	21 41	22 22	23 05	23 51
N 10	18 15	18 37	19 02	21 48	22 34	23 21	24 11
0	18 06	18 28	18 52	21 55	22 46	23 37	24 30
S 10	17 58	18 19	18 44	22 02	22 57	23 53	24 49
20	17 49	18 11	18 37	22 10	23 10	24 09	00 09
30	17 39	18 03	18 31	22 18	23 24	24 29	00 29
35	17 33	17 59	18 28	22 23	23 32	24 40	00 40
40	17 26	17 54	18 26	22 29	23 41	24 53	00 53

Day	SUN Eqn. of Time 00h	12h	Mer. Pass.	MOON Mer. Pass. Upper	Lower	Age	Phase
	m s	m s	h m	h m	h m	d	
20	03 33	03 26	12 03	15 43	03 18	04	☽
21	03 19	03 12	12 03	16 33	04 08	05	
22	03 04	02 57	12 03	17 25	04 59	06	

1966 SEPTEMBER 29

G.M.T.	ARIES	VENUS −3·4		MARS +1·8		JUPITER −1·6		SATURN +0·9		STARS		
	G.H.A.	G.H.A.	Dec.	G.H.A.	Dec.	G.H.A.	Dec.	G.H.A.	Dec.	Name	S.H.A.	Dec.
d h	° ′	° ′	° ′	° ′	° ′	° ′	° ′	° ′	° ′		° ′	° ′
29 00	7 18·3	191 29·1 N	3 23·0	222 54·5 N15 30·3		244 51·1 N20 19·2		10 24·5 S 4 02·6		Acamar	315 44·8	S 40 26·0
01	22 20·8	206 28·7	21·7	237 55·4	29·8	259 53·2	19·1	25 27·1	02·7	Achernar	335 52·3	S 57 24·2
02	37 23·3	221 28·3	20·5	252 56·4	29·3	274 55·2	19·0	40 29·8	02·8	Acrux	173 50·0	S 62 54·8
03	52 25·7	236 27·9 · · 19·3		267 57·3 · ·	28·8	289 57·3 · ·	19·0	55 32·4 · · 02·8		Adhara	255 40·4	S 28 55·2
04	67 28·2	251 27·5	18·1	282 58·3	28·4	304 59·4	18·9	70 35·0	02·9	Aldebaran	291 30·0	N 16 26·8
05	82 30·7	266 27·1	16·8	297 59·2	27·9	320 01·5	18·8	85 37·7	03·0			
06	97 33·1	281 26·7 N	3 15·6	313 00·2 N15 27·4		335 03·6 N20 18·7		100 40·3 S 4 03·1		Alphecca	126 41·2	N 26 49·7
T 07	112 35·6	296 26·3	14·4	328 01·1	26·9	350 05·6	18·7	115 43·0	03·1	Alpheratz	358 19·9	N 28 54·5
08	127 38·1	311 25·9	13·1	343 02·1	26·4	5 07·7	18·6	130 45·6	03·2	Altair	62 42·7	N 8 46·8
H 09	142 40·5	326 25·5 · ·	11·9	358 03·0 · ·	26·0	20 09·8 · ·	18·5	145 48·2 · · 03·3		Ankaa	353 50·0	S 42 29·1
U 10	157 43·0	341 25·1	10·7	13 04·0	25·5	35 11·9	18·4	160 50·9	03·4	Antares	113 10·0	S 26 21·6
R 11	172 45·5	356 24·7	09·5	28 04·9	25·0	50 14·0	18·4	175 53·5	03·4			
S 12	187 47·9	11 24·3 N	3 08·2	43 05·9 N15 24·5		65 16·0 N20 18·3		190 56·1 S 4 03·5		Mirfak	309 31·0	N 49 44·6
D 13	202 50·4	26 23·9	07·0	58 06·8	24·0	80 18·1	18·2	205 58·8	03·6	Nunki	76 42·1	S 26 20·5
A 14	217 52·8	41 23·5	05·8	73 07·8	23·6	95 20·2	18·2	221 01·4	03·7	Peacock	54 14·5	S 56 50·9
Y 15	232 55·3	56 23·1 · · 04·5		88 08·7 · ·	23·1	110 22·3 ⁚ ·	18·1	236 04·1 · · 03·7		Pollux	244 11·1	N 28 06·6
16	247 57·8	71 22·7	03·3	103 09·7	22·6	125 24·4	18·0	251 06·7	03·8	Procyon	245 36·9	N 5 18·9
17	263 00·2	86 22·3	02·1	118 10·6	22·1	140 26·5	17·9	266 09·3	03·9			
18	278 02·7	101 21·9 N	3 00·8	133 11·6 N15 21·6		155 28·5 N20 17·9		281 12·0 S 4 04·0		Schedar.	350 20·7	N 56 21·3
19	293 05·2	116 21·5	2 59·6	148 12·5	21·2	170 30·6	17·8	296 14·6	04·0	Shaula	97 10·2	S 37 05·0
20	308 07·6	131 21·1	58·4	163 13·5	20·7	185 32·7	17·7	311 17·2	04·1	Sirius	259 05·0	S 16 39·8
21	323 10·1	146 20·7 · ·	57·1	178 14·4 · ·	20·2	200 34·8 · ·	17·6	326 19·9 · · 04·2		Spica	159 09·0	S 10 59·1
22	338 12·6	161 20·3	55·9	193 15·4	19·7	215 36·9	17·6	341 22·5	04·3	Suhail	223 18·9	S 43 17·5
23	353 15·0	176 19·9	54·7	208 16·3	19·2	230 39·0	17·5	356 25·2	04·3			
30 00	8 17·5	191 19·5 N	2 53·5	223 17·3 N15 18·8		245 41·0 N20 17·4		11 27·8 S 4 04·4		Vega	81 03·0	N 38 45·3
01	23 20·0	206 19·1	52·2	238 18·2	18·3	260 43·1	17·4	26 30·4	04·5	Zuben'ubi	137 45·0	S 15 54·2
02	38 22·4	221 18·7	51·0	253 19·2	17·8	275 45·2	17·3	41 33·1	04·6		S.H.A.	Mer. Pass.
03	53 24·9	236 18·3 · ·	49·8	268 20·1 · ·	17·3	290 47·3 · ·	17·2	56 35·7 · · 04·6			° ′	h m
04	68 27·3	251 17·9	48·5	283 21·1	16·8	305 49·4	17·1	71 38·3	04·7	Venus	184 10·8	11 14
05	83 29·8	266 17·5	47·3	298 22·0	16·3	320 51·5	17·1	86 41·0	04·8	Mars	215 36·2	9 08
	h m									Jupiter	237 32·8	7 40
Mer. Pass. 23 26·9		v −0·4	d 1·2	v 0·9	d 0·5	v 2·1	d 0·1	v 2·6	d 0·1	Saturn	3 06·2	23 14

1966 OCTOBER 29

G.M.T.	ARIES	VENUS −3·5		MARS +1·7		JUPITER −1·8		SATURN +1·1		STARS		
	G.H.A.	G.H.A.	Dec.	G.H.A.	Dec.	G.H.A.	Dec.	G.H.A.	Dec.	Name	S.H.A.	Dec.
d h	° ′	° ′	° ′	° ′	° ′	° ′	° ′	° ′	° ′		° ′	° ′
29 00	36 52·5	186 21·9 S11 17·2		235 04·6 N 9 20·6		270 53·7 N19 38·2		41 45·9 S 4 46·2		Acamar	315 44·6	S 40 26·1
01	51 55·0	201 21·4	18·3	250 05·7	20·1	285 55·9	38·2	56 48·5	46·3	Achernar	335 52·2	S 57 24·2
02	66 57·4	216 20·9	19·4	265 06·8	19·6	300 58·2	38·1	71 51·1	46·3	Acrux	173 49·9	S 62 54·6
03	81 59·9	231 20·4 · ·	20·6	280 07·8 · ·	19·0	316 00·5 · ·	38·1	86 53·6 · · 46·3		Adhara	255 40·2	S 28 55·2
04	97 02·3	246 19·8	21·7	295 08·9	18·5	331 02·8	38·1	101 56·2	46·4	Aldebaran	291 29·8	N 16 26·8
05	112 04·8	261 19·3	22·9	310 10·0	18·0	346 05·0	38·0	116 58·8	46·4			
06	127 07·3	276 18·8 S11 24·0		325 11·1 N 9 17·4		1 07·3 N19 38·0		132 01·4 S 4 46·5		Alioth	166 51·9	N 56 08·4
07	142 09·7	291 18·3	25·1	340 12·2	16·9	16 09·6	37·9	147 03·9	46·5	Alkaid	153 27·0	N 49 28·8
S 08	157 12·2	306 17·8	26·3	355 13·2	16·4	31 11·8	37·9	162 06·5	46·6	Al Na'ir	28 27·7	S 47 07·6
A 09	172 14·7	321 17·3 · ·	27·4	10 14·3 · ·	15·8	46 14·1 · ·	37·9	177 09·1 · · 46·6		Alnilam	276 22·1	S 1 13·1
T 10	187 17·1	336 16·7	28·5	25 15·4	15·3	61 16·4	37·8	192 11·7	46·6	Alphard	218 30·9	S 8 30·6
U 11	202 19·6	351 16·2	29·7	40 16·5	14·7	76 18·7	37·8	207 14·2	46·7			
R 12	217 22·1	6 15·7 S11 30·8		55 17·6 N 9 14·2		91 20·9 N19 37·8		222 16·8 S 4 46·7		Alphecca	126 41·3	N 26 49·6
D 13	232 24·5	21 15·2	31·9	70 18·6	13·7	106 23·2	37·7	237 19·4	46·8	Alpheratz	358 19·9	N 28 54·5
A 14	247 27·0	36 14·7	33·0	85 19·7	13·1	121 25·5	37·7	252 22·0	46·8	Altair	62 42·8	N 8 46·8
Y 15	262 29·5	51 14·1 · ·	34·2	100 20·8 · ·	12·6	136 27·8 · ·	37·7	267 24·5 · · 46·8		Ankaa	353 50·0	S 42 29·3
16	277 31·9	66 13·6	35·3	115 21·9	12·1	151 30·1	37·6	282 27·1	46·9	Antares	113 10·1	S 26 21·6
17	292 34·4	81 13·1	36·4	130 23·0	11·5	166 32·3	37·6	297 29·7	46·9			
18	307 36·8	96 12·6 S11 37·6		145 24·0 N 9 11·0		181 34·6 N19 37·6		312 32·3 S 4 47·0		Schedar	350 20·7	N 56 21·5
19	322 39·3	111 12·1	38·7	160 25·1	10·4	196 36·9	37·5	327 34·8	47·0	Shaula	97 10·3	S 37 05·0
20	337 41·8	126 11·5	39·8	175 26·2	09·9	211 39·2	37·5	342 37·4	47·0	Sirius	259 04·8	S 16 39·9
21	352 44·2	141 11·0 · ·	40·9	190 27·3 · ·	09·4	226 41·4 · ·	37·5	357 40·0 · · 47·1		Spica	159 08·9	S 10 59·1
22	7 46·7	156 10·5	42·1	205 28·4	08·8	241 43·7	37·4	12 42·5	47·1	Suhail	223 18·7	S 43 17·4
23	22 49·2	171 10·0	43·2	220 29·5	08·3	256 46·0	37·4	27 45·1	47·2			
30 00	37 51·6	186 09·5 S11 44·3		235 30·5 N 9 07·8		271 48·3 N19 37·3		42 47·7 S 4 47·2		Vega	81 03·2	N 38 45·3
01	52 54·1	201 08·9	45·5	250 31·6	07·2	286 50·6	37·3	57 50·3	47·2	Zuben'ubi	137 45·0	S 15 54·2
02	67 56·6	216 08·4	46·6	265 32·7	06·7	301 52·8	37·3	72 52·8	47·3		S.H.A.	Mer. Pass.
03	82 59·0	231 07·9 · ·	47·7	280 33·8 · ·	06·1	316 55·1 · ·	37·2	87 55·4 · · 47·3			° ′	h m
04	98 01·5	246 07·4	48·8	295 34·9	05·6	331 57·4	37·2	102 58·0	47·3	Venus	149 29·4	11 35
05	113 04·0	261 06·8	50·0	310 36·0	05·1	346 59·7	37·2	118 00·5	47·4	Mars	198 12·1	8 19
	h m									Jupiter	234 01·2	5 56
Mer. Pass. 21 29·0		v −0·5	d 1·1	v 1·1	d 0·5	v 2·3	d 0·0	v 2·6	d 0·0	Saturn	4 53·4	21 09

1966 SEPTEMBER 29

G.M.T.	SUN G.H.A.	SUN Dec.	MOON G.H.A.	v	Dec.	d	H.P.
d h	° ′	° ′	° ′	′	° ′	′	′
29 00	182 20·9	S 2 08·8	7 47·5	17·0	S 4 27·1	13·4	54·0
01	197 21·1	09·8	22 23·5	16·9	4 13·7	13·5	54·0
02	212 21·3	10·8	36 59·4	17·0	4 00·2	13·4	54·0
03	227 21·5	·· 11·7	51 35·4	17·0	3 46·8	13·5	54·0
04	242 21·8	12·7	66 11·4	16·9	3 33·3	13·5	54·0
05	257 22·0	13·7	80 47·3	17·0	3 19·8	13·5	54·0
06	272 22·2	S 2 14·7	95 23·3	17·0	S 3 06·3	13·5	54·0
T 07	287 22·4	15·6	109 59·3	17·0	2 52·8	13·5	54·1
H 08	302 22·6	16·6	124 35·3	17·0	2 39·3	13·5	54·1
U 09	317 22·8	·· 17·6	139 11·3	17·0	2 25·8	13·6	54·1
R 10	332 23·0	18·5	153 47·3	17·0	2 12·2	13·5	54·1
S 11	347 23·2	19·5	168 23·3	17·0	1 58·7	13·6	54·1
D 12	2 23·4	S 2 20·5	182 59·3	17·1	S 1 45·1	13·6	54·1
A 13	17 23·6	21·5	197 35·4	17·0	1 31·5	13·5	54·1
Y 14	32 23·8	22·4	212 11·4	17·0	1 18·0	13·6	54·1
15	47 24·0	·· 23·4	226 47·4	17·0	1 04·4	13·5	54·1
16	62 24·3	24·4	241 23·4	17·0	0 50·8	13·6	54·1
17	77 24·5	25·4	255 59·4	17·0	0 37·2	13·7	54·1
18	92 24·7	S 2 26·3	270 35·4	17·0	S 0 23·5	13·6	54·1
19	107 24·9	27·3	285 11·4	17·0	S 0 09·9	13·6	54·1
20	122 25·1	28·3	299 47·4	17·0	N 0 03·7	13·6	54·1
21	137 25·3	·· 29·2	314 23·4	17·0	0 17·3	13·6	54·1
22	152 25·5	30·2	328 59·4	16·9	0 30·9	13·7	54·1
23	167 25·7	31·2	343 35·3	17·0	0 44·6	13·6	54·1
30 00	182 25·9	S 2 32·2	358 11·3	17·0	N 0 58·2	13·6	54·1
01	197 26·1	33·1	12 47·3	16·9	1 11·8	13·6	54·2
02	212 26·3	34·1	27 23·2	16·9	1 25·4	13·7	54·2
03	227 26·5	·· 35·1	41 59·1	16·9	1 39·1	13·6	54·2
04	242 26·7	36·0	56 35·0	16·9	1 52·7	13·6	54·2
05	257 26·9	37·0	71 10·9	16·9	2 06·3	13·6	54·2
	S.D. 16·0	d 1·0	S.D. 14·7		14·7		14·8

Lat.	Twilight Naut.	Civil	Sunrise	Moonrise 28	29	30	1
°	h m	h m	h m	h m	h m	h m	h m
N 40	04 55	05 27	05 54	17 39	17 59	18 20	18 42
35	04 58	05 27	05 53	17 35	17 59	18 23	18 48
30	05 00	05 28	05 52	17 33	17 59	18 25	18 53
20	05 03	05 28	05 50	17 27	17 59	18 30	19 02
N 10	05 03	05 28	05 49	17 23	17 58	18 34	19 11
0	05 03	05 27	05 47	17 18	17 58	18 38	19 19
S 10	05 00	05 25	05 46	17 14	17 58	18 41	19 26
20	04 56	05 22	05 44	17 09	17 57	18 46	19 35
30	04 50	05 18	05 42	17 04	17 57	18 50	19 45
35	04 45	05 15	05 40	17 01	17 57	18 53	19 50
40	04 40	05 12	05 39	16 58	17 57	18 56	19 56

Lat.	Sunset	Twilight Civil	Naut.	Moonset 28	29	30	1
°	h m	h m	h m	h m	h m	h m	h m
N 40	17 47	18 13	18 45	04 27	05 26	06 25	07 25
35	17 48	18 13	18 42	04 32	05 28	06 24	07 20
30	17 49	18 13	18 40	04 37	05 30	06 23	07 16
20	17 50	18 12	18 38	04 45	05 33	06 21	07 09
N 10	17 52	18 13	18 37	04 51	05 35	06 19	07 03
0	17 54	18 14	18 38	04 58	05 37	06 17	06 57
S 10	17 55	18 17	18 41	05 04	05 40	06 15	06 51
20	17 57	18 20	18 45	05 11	05 42	06 13	06 45
30	17 57	18 24	18 52	05 18	05 45	06 11	06 38
35	18 01	18 27	18 56	05 22	05 46	06 10	06 34
40	18 03	18 30	19 02	05 27	05 48	06 09	06 30

Day	SUN Eqn. of Time 00h	12h	Mer. Pass.	MOON Mer. Pass. Upper	Lower	Age	Phase
	m s	m s	h m	h m	h m	d	
28	09 03	09 13	11 51	23 28	11 08	14	●
29	09 23	09 33	11 50	24 07	11 48	15	
30	09 43	09 53	11 50	00 07	12 27	16	

1966 OCTOBER 29

G.M.T.	SUN G.H.A.	SUN Dec.	MOON G.H.A.	v	Dec.	d	H.P.
d h	° ′	° ′	° ′	′	° ′	′	′
29 00	184 02·8	S 13 13·8	8 01·0	15·5	N 10 17·8	13·1	54·8
01	199 02·8	14·7	22 35·5	15·4	10 30·9	13·0	54·8
02	214 02·9	15·5	37 09·9	15·4	10 43·9	13·0	54·8
03	229 02·9	·· 16·3	51 44·3	15·3	10 56·9	13·0	54·8
04	244 03·0	17·2	66 18·6	15·3	11 09·9	12·9	54·8
05	259 03·0	18·0	80 52·9	15·2	11 22·9	12·9	54·8
06	274 03·0	S 13 18·8	95 27·1	15·1	N 11 35·8	12·9	54·8
07	289 03·1	19·7	110 01·2	15·1	11 48·7	12·8	54·9
S 08	304 03·1	20·5	124 35·3	15·0	12 01·5	12·8	54·9
A 09	319 03·2	·· 21·3	139 09·3	15·0	12 14·3	12·7	54·9
T 10	334 03·2	22·2	153 43·3	14·9	12 27·0	12·7	54·9
U 11	349 03·3	23·0	168 17·2	14·8	12 39·7	12·7	54·9
R 12	4 03·3	S 13 23·8	182 51·0	14·8	N 12 52·4	12·6	54·9
D 13	19 03·4	24·7	197 24·8	14·7	13 05·0	12·6	54·9
A 14	34 03·4	25·5	211 58·5	14·6	13 17·6	12·5	55·0
Y 15	49 03·4	·· 26·3	226 32·1	14·6	13 30·1	12·5	55·0
16	64 03·5	27·2	241 05·7	14·5	13 42·6	12·4	55·0
17	79 03·5	28·0	255 39·2	14·4	13 55·0	12·4	55·0
18	94 03·6	S 13 28·8	270 12·6	14·4	N 14 07·4	12·3	55·0
19	109 03·6	29·6	284 46·0	14·3	14 19·7	12·3	55·0
20	124 03·7	30·5	299 19·3	14·2	14 32·0	12·2	55·1
21	139 03·7	·· 31·3	313 52·5	14·2	14 44·2	12·2	55·1
22	154 03·7	32·1	328 25·7	14·1	14 56·4	12·1	55·1
23	169 03·8	32·9	342 58·8	14·0	15 08·5	12·1	55·1
30 00	184 03·8	S 13 33·8	357 31·8	13·9	N 15 20·6	12·0	55·1
01	199 03·9	34·6	12 04·7	13·9	15 32·6	11·9	55·1
02	214 03·9	35·4	26 37·6	13·8	15 44·5	11·9	55·1
03	229 03·9	·· 36·2	41 10·4	13·7	15 56·4	11·8	55·2
04	244 04·0	37·1	55 43·1	13·6	16 08·2	11·8	55·2
05	259 04·0	37·9	70 15·7	13·6	16 20·0	11·7	55·2
	S.D. 16·1	d 0·8	S.D. 14·9		15·0		15·1

Lat.	Twilight Naut.	Civil	Sunrise	Moonrise 28	29	30	31
°	h m	h m	h m	h m	h m	h m	h m
N 40	05 25	05 57	06 25	16 47	17 10	17 37	18 09
35	05 22	05 52	06 18	16 52	17 18	17 48	18 23
30	05 18	05 47	06 11	16 56	17 25	17 58	18 36
20	05 11	05 37	06 00	17 04	17 38	18 15	18 58
N 10	05 03	05 28	05 50	17 11	17 49	18 31	19 16
0	04 55	05 19	05 40	17 17	18 00	18 45	19 34
S 10	04 44	05 09	05 31	17 23	18 10	18 59	19 52
20	04 31	04 58	05 20	17 30	18 22	19 15	20 11
30	04 14	04 43	05 08	17 39	18 35	19 33	20 33
35	04 03	04 35	05 01	17 43	18 42	19 43	20 46
40	03 50	04 25	04 54	17 48	18 51	19 55	21 01

Lat.	Sunset	Twilight Civil	Naut.	Moonset 28	29	30	31
°	h m	h m	h m	h m	h m	h m	h m
N 40	17 02	17 30	18 02	05 17	06 18	07 21	08 27
35	17 09	17 35	18 05	05 13	06 11	07 11	08 13
30	17 16	17 41	18 09	05 10	06 05	07 02	08 02
20	17 28	17 50	18 16	05 05	05 55	06 47	07 42
N 10	17 38	17 59	18 24	05 00	05 46	06 34	07 24
0	17 47	18 09	18 33	04 56	05 37	06 21	07 08
S 10	17 57	18 19	18 44	04 51	05 29	06 09	06 52
20	18 07	18 30	18 57	04 47	05 20	05 55	06 35
30	18 20	18 45	19 14	04 41	05 09	05 40	06 15
35	18 27	18 53	19 25	04 38	05 04	05 32	06 04
40	18 35	19 04	19 39	04 35	04 57	05 22	05 51

Day	SUN Eqn. of Time 00h	12h	Mer. Pass.	MOON Mer. Pass. Upper	Lower	Age	Phase
	m s	m s	h m	h m	h m	d	
28	16 06	16 09	11 44	23 27	11 02	14	●
29	16 11	16 13	11 44	24 10	11 48	15	
30	16 15	16 17	11 44	00 10	12 33	16	

1966 NOVEMBER 28

G.M.T.	ARIES G.H.A.	VENUS −3.5 G.H.A.	Dec.	MARS +1.5 G.H.A.	Dec.	JUPITER −2.0 G.H.A.	Dec.	SATURN +1.2 G.H.A.	Dec.	STARS Name	S.H.A.	Dec.
28 00	66 26.7	178 05.6	S21 57.2	248 44.9	N 2 54.8	299 36.1	N19 31.9	72 01.2	S 4 57.9	Acamar	315 44.6	S40 26.2
01	81 29.1	193 04.7	57.8	263 46.1	54.3	314 38.6	31.9	87 03.7	57.9	Achernar	335 52.3	S 57 24.5
02	96 31.6	208 03.9	58.3	278 47.3	53.8	329 41.2	31.9	102 06.2	57.9	Acrux	173 49.6	S 62 54.6
03	111 34.1	223 03.0 ··	58.9	293 48.5 ··	53.2	344 43.7 ··	31.9	117 08.6 ··	57.9	Adhara	255 40.0	S 28 55.3
04	126 36.5	238 02.1	21 59.5	308 49.7	52.7	359 46.2	32.0	132 11.1	57.9	Aldebaran	291 29.6	N 16 26.8
05	141 39.0	253 01.2	22 00.0	323 50.9	52.2	14 48.7	32.0	147 13.5	57.8			
06	156 41.5	268 00.4	S22 00.6	338 52.1	N 2 51.7	29 51.2	N19 32.0	162 16.0	S 4 57.8	Alioth	166 51.7	N 56 08.2
07	171 43.9	282 59.5	01.1	353 53.3	51.1	44 53.8	32.0	177 18.5	57.8	Alkaid	153 26.9	N 49 28.6
08	186 46.4	297 58.6	01.7	8 54.5	50.6	59 56.3	32.0	192 20.9	57.8	Al Na'ir	28 27.9	S 47 07.7
M 09	201 48.9	312 57.8 ··	02.2	23 55.7 ··	50.1	74 58.8 ··	32.1	207 23.4 ··	57.8	Alnilam	276 21.9	S 1 13.1
O 10	216 51.3	327 56.9	02.8	38 56.9	49.6	90 01.3	32.1	222 25.8	57.8	Alphard	218 30.7	S 8 30.6
N 11	231 53.8	342 56.0	03.3	53 58.1	49.1	105 03.8	32.1	237 28.3	57.8			
D 12	246 56.2	357 55.1	S22 03.9	68 59.3	N 2 48.5	120 06.4	N19 32.1	252 30.8	S 4 57.8	Rasalhague	96 39.6	N 12 34.9
A 13	261 58.7	12 54.3	04.4	84 00.5	48.0	135 08.9	32.1	267 33.2	57.8	Regulus	208 21.0	N 12 07.9
Y 14	277 01.2	27 53.4	05.0	99 01.7	47.5	150 11.4	32.2	282 35.7	57.7	Rigel	281 45.7	S 8 14.2
15	292 03.6	42 52.5 ··	05.5	114 02.9 ··	47.0	165 13.9 ··	32.2	297 38.1 ··	57.7	Rigil Kent.	140 40.8	S 60 41.7
16	307 06.1	57 51.6	06.0	129 04.1	46.4	180 16.5	32.2	312 40.6	57.7	Sabik	102 53.4	S 15 41.2
17	322 08.6	72 50.7	06.6	144 05.3	45.9	195 19.0	32.2	327 43.1	57.7			
18	337 11.0	87 49.9	S22 07.1	159 06.5	N 2 45.4	210 21.5	N19 32.3	342 45.5	S 4 57.7	Schedar	350 20.8	N 56 21.6
19	352 13.5	102 49.0	07.7	174 07.7	44.9	225 24.0	32.3	357 48.0	57.7	Shaula	97 10.3	S 37 05.0
20	7 16.0	117 48.1	08.2	189 08.9	44.3	240 26.5	32.3	12 50.4	57.7	Sirius	259 04.6	S 16 40.0
21	22 18.4	132 47.2 ··	08.7	204 10.1 ··	43.8	255 29.1 ··	32.3	27 52.9 ··	57.7	Spica	159 08.8	S 10 59.2
22	37 20.9	147 46.4	09.3	219 11.3	43.3	270 31.6	32.3	42 55.4	57.7	Suhail	223 18.4	S 43 17.5
23	52 23.4	162 45.5	09.8	234 12.5	42.8	285 34.1	32.4	57 57.8	57.6			
29 00	67 25.8	177 44.6	S22 10.3	249 13.7	N 2 42.2	300 36.7	N19 32.4	73 00.3	S 4 57.6	Vega	81 03.3	N 38 45.2
01	82 28.3	192 43.7	10.9	264 14.9	41.7	315 39.2	32.4	88 02.7	57.6	Zuben'ubi	137 44.9	S 15 54.2
02	97 30.7	207 42.8	11.4	279 16.1	41.2	330 41.7	32.4	103 05.2	57.6		S.H.A.	Mer. Pass.
03	112 33.2	222 42.0 ··	11.9	294 17.3 ··	40.7	345 44.2 ··	32.5	118 07.6 ··	57.6		° ′	h m
04	127 35.7	237 41.1	12.5	309 18.5	40.2	0 46.8	32.5	133 10.1	57.6	Venus	111 38.9	12 08
05	142 38.1	252 40.2	13.0	324 19.7	39.6	15 49.3	32.5	148 12.6	57.6	Mars	182 18.2	7 24
										Jupiter	233 09.4	4 01
Mer. Pass. 19 31.0		v −0.9	d 0.5	v 1.2	d 0.5	v 2.5	d 0.0	v 2.5	d 0.0	Saturn	5 34.5	19 09

1966 DECEMBER 27

G.M.T.	ARIES G.H.A.	VENUS −3.4 G.H.A.	Dec.	MARS +1.2 G.H.A.	Dec.	JUPITER −2.1 G.H.A.	Dec.	SATURN +1.3 G.H.A.	Dec.	STARS Name	S.H.A.	Dec.
27 00	95 01.7	167 04.4	S23 29.7	263 26.8	S 2 47.6	330 09.7	N20 04.1	99 53.8	S 4 33.1	Acamar	315 44.7	S40 26.3
01	110 04.2	182 03.4	29.3	278 28.2	48.0	345 12.4	04.2	114 56.1	33.0	Achernar	335 52.5	S 57 24.6
02	125 06.7	197 02.5	29.0	293 29.5	48.5	0 15.1	04.3	129 58.5	32.9	Acrux	173 49.1	S 62 54.6
03	140 09.1	212 01.5 ··	28.7	308 30.9 ··	48.9	15 17.9 ··	04.3	145 00.8 ··	32.9	Adhara	255 39.9	S 28 55.4
04	155 11.6	227 00.6	28.4	323 32.2	49.4	30 20.6	04.4	160 03.1	32.8	Aldebaran	291 29.6	N 16 26.8
05	170 14.0	241 59.7	28.1	338 33.5	49.8	45 23.4	04.5	175 05.5	32.8			
06	185 16.5	256 58.7	S23 27.8	353 34.9	S 2 50.3	60 26.1	N20 04.5	190 07.8	S 4 32.7	Alioth	166 51.4	N 56 08.1
07	200 19.0	271 57.8	27.5	8 36.2	50.7	75 28.8	04.6	205 10.2	32.6	Alkaid	153 26.6	N 49 28.4
T 08	215 21.4	286 56.8	27.1	23 37.6	51.1	90 31.6	04.7	220 12.5	32.6	Al Na'ir	28 28.0	S 47 07.6
U 09	230 23.9	301 55.9 ··	26.8	38 38.9 ··	51.6	105 34.3 ··	04.7	235 14.9 ··	32.5	Alnilam	276 21.6	S 1 13.2
E 10	245 26.4	316 55.0	26.5	53 40.3	52.0	120 37.1	04.8	250 17.2	32.5	Alphard	218 30.5	S 8 30.7
S 11	260 28.8	331 54.0	26.2	68 41.6	52.5	135 39.8	04.9	265 19.6	32.4			
D 12	275 31.3	346 53.1	S23 25.8	83 43.0	S 2 52.9	150 42.5	N20 04.9	280 21.9	S 4 32.3	Rasalhague	96 39.5	N 12 34.8
A 13	290 33.8	1 52.2	25.5	98 44.3	53.4	165 45.3	05.0	295 24.3	32.3	Regulus	208 20.7	N 12 07.8
Y 14	305 36.2	16 51.2	25.2	113 45.7	53.8	180 48.0	05.0	310 26.6	32.2	Rigel	281 45.6	S 8 14.3
15	320 38.7	31 50.3 ··	24.9	128 47.0 ··	54.3	195 50.8 ··	05.1	325 28.9 ··	32.2	Rigil Kent.	140 40.5	S 60 41.7
16	335 41.2	46 49.3	24.5	143 48.3	54.7	210 53.5	05.2	340 31.3	32.1	Sabik	102 53.3	S 15 41.2
17	350 43.6	61 48.4	24.2	158 49.7	55.2	225 56.2	05.2	355 33.6	32.0			
18	5 46.1	76 47.5	S23 23.9	173 51.1	S 2 55.6	240 59.0	N20 05.4	10 36.0	S 4 32.0	Schedar	350 21.0	N 56 21.6
19	20 48.5	91 46.5	23.5	188 52.4	56.1	256 01.7	05.4	25 38.3	31.9	Shaula	97 10.2	S 37 04.9
20	35 51.0	106 45.6	23.2	203 53.7	56.5	271 04.5	05.5	40 40.7	31.9	Sirius	259 04.5	S 16 40.1
21	50 53.5	121 44.7 ··	22.8	218 55.1 ··	57.0	286 07.2 ··	05.6	55 43.0 ··	31.8	Spica	159 08.5	S 10 59.3
22	65 55.9	136 43.7	22.5	233 56.4	57.4	301 10.0	05.6	70 45.3	31.7	Suhail	223 18.2	S 43 17.7
23	80 58.4	151 42.8	22.2	248 57.8	57.9	316 12.7	05.7	85 47.7	31.7			
28 00	96 00.9	166 41.9	S23 21.8	263 59.1	S 2 58.3	331 15.4	N20 05.8	100 50.0	S 4 31.6	Vega	81 03.3	N 38 45.0
01	111 03.3	181 40.9	21.5	279 00.5	58.7	346 18.2	05.8	115 52.4	31.5	Zuben'ubi	137 44.7	S 15 54.3
02	126 05.8	196 40.0	21.1	294 01.8	59.2	1 20.9	05.9	130 54.7	31.5		S.H.A.	Mer. Pass.
03	141 08.3	211 39.1 ··	20.8	309 03.2	2 59.6	16 23.7 ··	06.0	145 57.1 ··	31.4		° ′	h m
04	156 10.7	226 38.1	20.5	324 04.5	3 00.1	31 26.4	06.0	160 59.4	31.4	Venus	70 41.0	12 54
05	171 13.2	241 37.2	20.1	339 05.9	00.5	46 29.2	06.1	176 01.7	31.3	Mars	167 58.2	6 23
										Jupiter	235 14.5	1 55
Mer. Pass. 17 33.1		v −0.9	d 0.4	v 1.4	d 0.4	v 2.7	d 0.1	v 2.3	d 0.1	Saturn	4 49.1	17 14

1966 NOVEMBER 28

G.M.T.	SUN G.H.A.	Dec.	MOON G.H.A.	v	Dec.	d	H.P.
28 00	183 04·2	S 21 11·4	4 47·0	9·9	N 22 31·8	8·7	56·2
01	198 04·0	11·9	19 15·9	9·9	22 40·5	8·7	56·2
02	213 03·8	12·3	33 44·8	9·8	22 49·2	8·5	56·3
03	228 03·6	·· 12·8	48 13·6	9·7	22 57·7	8·4	56·3
04	243 03·4	13·2	62 42·3	9·5	23 06·1	8·3	56·3
05	258 03·2	13·7	77 10·8	9·5	23 14·4	8·2	56·3
06	273 03·0	S 21 14·1	91 39·3	9·4	N 23 22·6	8·0	56·3
07	288 02·8	14·6	106 07·7	9·3	23 30·6	8·0	56·4
08	303 02·6	15·0	120 36·0	9·2	23 38·6	7·8	56·4
M 09	318 02·4	·· 15·5	135 04·2	9·1	23 46·4	7·7	56·4
O 10	333 02·2	15·9	149 32·3	9·0	23 54·1	7·6	56·4
N 11	348 01·9	·16·3	164 00·3	8·9	24 01·7	7·4	56·5
D 12	3 01·7	S 21 16·8	178 28·2	8·9	N 24 09·1	7·4	56·5
A 13	18 01·5	17·2	192 56·1	8·7	24 16·5	7·2	56·5
Y 14	33 01·3	17·7	207 23·8	8·6	24 23·7	7·1	56·5
15	48 01·1	·· 18·1	221 51·4	8·6	24 30·8	6·9	56·5
16	63 00·9	18·6	236 19·0	8·4	24 37·7	6·8	56·6
17	78 00·7	19·0	250 46·4	8·4	24 44·5	6·7	56·6
18	93 00·5	S 21 19·4	265 13·8	8·3	N 24 51·2	6·6	56·6
19	108 00·3	19·9	279 41·1	8·2	24 57·8	6·4	56·6
20	123 00·0	20·3	294 08·3	8·1	25 04·2	6·3	56·6
21	137 59·8	·· 20·7	308 35·4	8·0	25 10·5	6·2	56·7
22	152 59·6	21·2	323 02·4	7·9	25 16·7	6·0	56·7
23	167 59·4	21·6	337 29·3	7·9	25 22·7	5·9	56·7
29 00	182 59·2	S 21 22·1	351 56·2	7·7	N 25 28·6	5·7	56·7
01	197 59·0	22·5	6 22·9	7·7	25 34·3	5·6	56·8
02	212 58·8	22·9	20 49·6	7·6	25 39·9	5·5	56·8
03	227 58·6	·· 23·3	35 16·2	7·5	25 45·4	5·3	56·8
04	242 58·3	23·8	49 42·7	7·5	25 50·7	5·2	56·8
05	257 58·1	·24·2	64 09·2	7·3	25 55·9	5·0	56·8
	S.D. 16·2	d 0·4	S.D. 15·2		15·4		15·5

Lat.	Twilight Naut.	Civil	Sun- rise	Moonrise 27	28	29	30
°	h m	h m	h m	h m	h m	h m	h m
N 40	05 56	06 29	06 59	16 09	16 46	17 32	18 28
35	05 48	06 19	06 46	16 22	17 02	17 50	18 47
30	05 40	06 10	06 35	16 34	17 16	18 06	19 03
20	05 26	05 53	06 16	16 54	17 40	18 32	19 29
N 10	05 11	05 37	06 00	17 11	18 01	18 55	19 53
0	04 56	05 22	05 44	17 28	18 20	19·16	20 15
S 10	04 39	05 06	05 28	17 45	18 40	19 38	20 37
20	04 19	04 47	05 11	18 02	19 01	20 01	21 00
30	03 53	04 25	04 52	18 23	19 26	20 28	21 27
35	03 36	04 11	04 40	18 35	19 40	20 43	21 43
40	03 15	03 55	04 27	18 49	19 56	21 02	22 01

Lat.	Sun- set	Twilight Civil	Naut.	Moonset 27	28	29	30
°	h m	h m	h m	h. m	h m	h m	h m
N 40	16 37	17 06	17 40	06 14	07 21	08 28	09 31
35	16 49	17 17	17 48	06 02	07 06	08 10	09 12
30	17 00	17 26	17 55	05 52	06 53	07 55	08 56
20	17 19	17 43	18 10	05 33	06 31	07 30	08 30
N 10	17 36	17 58	18 24	05 17	06 11	07 08	08 06
0	17 52	18 14	18 40	05 02	05 53	06 47	07 44
S 10	18 07	18 30	18 57	04 48	05 34	06 26	07 22
20	18 25	18 49	19 17	04 32	05 15	06 04	06 59
30	18 44	19 11	19 44	04 14	04 53	05 38	06 31
35	18 56	19 25	20 00	04 04	04 40	05 24	06 16
40	19 09	19 41	20 21	03 52	04 25	05 06	05 57

Day	Eqn. of Time 00h	12h	Mer. Pass.	Mer. Pass. Upper	Lower	Age	Phase
	m s	m s	h m	h m	h m	d	
27	12 37	12 27	11 48	23 40	11 15	15	○
28	12 17	12 07	11 48	24 33	12 06	16	
29	11 57	11 47	11 48	00 33	13 02	17	

1966 DECEMBER 28

G.M.T.	SUN G.H.A.	Dec.	MOON G.H.A.	v	Dec.	d	H.P.
27 00	179 49·4	S 23 21·5	10 02·0	6·0	N 26 40·9	·4	57·5
01	194 49·1	21·4	24 27·0	6·0	26 44·3	3·2	57·5
02	209 48·8	21·4	38 52·0	5·9	26 47·5	3·0	57·6
03	224 48·5	·· 21·3	53 16·9	5·8	26 50·5	2·9	57·6
04	239 48·2	21·2	67 41·7	5·7	26 53·4	2·7	57·6
05	254 47·9	21·1	82 06·4	5·7	26 56·1	2·6	57·7
06	269 47·6	S 23 21·0	96 31·1	5·6	N 26 58·7	2·4	57·7
07	284 47·3	20·9	110 55·7	5·6	27 01·1	2·2	57·7
T 08	299 46·9	20·8	125 20·3	5·5	27 03·3	2·0	57·7
U 09	314 46·6	·· 20·7	139 44·8	5·4	27 05·3	1·9	57·8
E 10	329 46·3	20·6	154 09·2	5·4	27 07·2	1·7	57·8
S 11	344 46·0	20·5	168 33·6	5·3	27 08·9	1·5	57·8
D 12	359 45·8	S 23 20·4	182 57·9	5·3	N 27 10·4	1·4	57·8
A 13	14 45·4	20·3	197 22·2	5·2	27 11·8	1·2	57·9
Y 14	29 45·1	20·2	211 46·4	5·2	27 13·0	1·0	57·9
15	44 44·8	·· 20·1	226 10·6	5·1	27 14·0	0·9	57·9
16	59 44·5	20·0	240 34·7	5·1	27 14·9	0·7	57·9
17	74 44·2	19·9	254 58·8	5·1	27 15·6	0·5	58·0
18	89 43·9	S 23 19·7	269 22·9	5·0	N 27 16·1	0·3	58·0
19	104 43·6	19·6	283 46·9	5·0	27 16·4	0·2	58·0
20	119 43·3	19·5	298 10·9	4·9	27 16·6	0·1	58·0
21	134 43·0	·· 19·4	312 34·8	5·0	27 16·5	0·2	58·1
22	149 42·7	19·3	326 58·8	4·9	27 16·3	0·3	58·1
23	164 42·3	19·2	341 22·7	4·8	27 16·0	0·6	58·1
28 00	179 42·0	S 23 19·1	355 46·5	4·9	N 27 15·4	0·7	58·1
01	194 41·7	19·0	10 10·4	4·8	27 14·7	0·9	58·2
02	209 41·4	18·9	24 34·2	4·8	27 13·8	1·1	58·2
03	224 41·1	·· 18·8	38 58·0	4·8	27 12·7	1·3	58·2
04	239 40·8	18·6	53 21·8	4·8	27 11·4	1·4	58·2
05	254 40·5	18·5	67 45·6	4·7	27 10·0	1·6	58·2
	S.D. 16·3	d 0·1	S.D. 15·8		15·9		16·0

Lat.	Twilight Naut.	Civil	Sun- rise	Moonrise 27	28	29	30
°	h m	h m	h m	h m	h m	h m	h m
N 40	06 16	06 50	07 21	16 17	17 20	18 31	19 46
35	06 07	06 39	07 07	16 35	17 38	18 47	19 59
30	05 58	06 28	06 54	16 51	17 53	19 01	20 10
20	05 42	06 09	06 33	17 18	18 20	19 24	20 28
N 10	05 26	05 52	06 15	17 41	18 42	19 44	20 45
0	05 09	05 35	05 58	18 03	19 04	20 03	21 00
S 10	04 50	05 17	05 40	18 25	19 25	20 22	21 15
20	04 28	04 57	05 21	18 49	19 47	20 42	21 31
30	03 59	04 32	04 59	19 16	20 14	21 05	21 50
35	03 40	04 17	04 46	19 31	20 28	21 18	22 00
40	03 17	03 59	04 31	19 50	20 46	21 33	22 12

Lat.	Sun- set	Twilight Civil	Naut.	Moonset 27	28	29	30
°	h m	h m	h m	h m	h m	h m	h m
N 40	16 42	17 13	17 46	07 17	08 17	09 09	09 52
35	16 56	17.24	17 56	06 59	07 59	08 53	09 38
30	17 09	17 35	18 05	06 44	07 44	08 39	09 27
20	17 29	17 53	18 21	06 17	07 17	08 14	09 06
N 10	17 48	18 11	18 37	05 54	06 54	07 52	08 48
0	18 05	18 28	18 54	05 32	06 32	07 32	08 31
S 10	18 23	18 46	19 13	05 11	06 10	07 12	08 13
20	18 41	19 06	19 35	04 48	05 47	06 50	07 55
30	19 03	19 31	20 04	04 21	05 20	06 25	07 33
35	19 16	19 46	20 23	04 05	05 04	06 10	07 21
40	19 31	20 04	20 46	03 47	04 45	05 53	07 07

Day	Eqn. of Time 00h	12h	Mer. Pass.	Mer. Pass. Upper	Lower	Age	Phase
	m s	m s	h m	h m	h m	d	
27	00 42	00 56	12 01	24 18	11 48	15	○
28	01 11	01 26	12 01	00 18	12 48	16	
29	01 41	01 55	12 02	01 18	13 48	17	

10ᵐ INCREMENTS AND CORRECTIONS 11ᵐ

10	SUN PLANETS	ARIES	MOON	v or Corrn d	v or Corrn d	v or Corrn d
	° ′	° ′	° ′	′ ′	′ ′	′ ′
00	2 30·0	2 30·4	2 23·2	0·0 0·0	6·0 1·1	12·0 2·1
01	2 30·3	2 30·7	2 23·4	0·1 0·0	6·1 1·1	12·1 2·1
02	2 30·5	2 30·9	2 23·6	0·2 0·0	6·2 1·1	12·2 2·1
03	2 30·8	2 31·2	2 23·9	0·3 0·1	6·3 1·1	12·3 2·2
04	2 31·0	2 31·4	2 24·1	0·4 0·1	6·4 1·1	12·4 2·2
05	2 31·3	2 31·7	2 24·4	0·5 0·1	6·5 1·1	12·5 2·2
06	2 31·5	2 31·9	2 24·6	0·6 0·1	6·6 1·2	12·6 2·2
07	2 31·8	2 32·2	2 24·8	0·7 0·1	6·7 1·2	12·7 2·2
08	2 32·0	2 32·4	2 25·1	0·8 0·1	6·8 1·2	12·8 2·2
09	2 32·3	2 32·7	2 25·3	0·9 0·2	6·9 1·2	12·9 2·3
10	2 32·5	2 32·9	2 25·6	1·0 0·2	7·0 1·2	13·0 2·3
11	2 32·8	2 33·2	2 25·8	1·1 0·2	7·1 1·2	13·1 2·3
12	2 33·0	2 33·4	2 26·0	1·2 0·2	7·2 1·3	13·2 2·3
13	2 33·3	2 33·7	2 26·3	1·3 0·2	7·3 1·3	13·3 2·3
14	2 33·5	2 33·9	2 26·5	1·4 0·2	7·4 1·3	13·4 2·3
15	2 33·8	2 34·2	2 26·7	1·5 0·3	7·5 1·3	13·5 2·4
16	2 34·0	2 34·4	2 27·0	1·6 0·3	7·6 1·3	13·6 2·4
17	2 34·3	2 34·7	2 27·2	1·7 0·3	7·7 1·3	13·7 2·4
18	2 34·5	2 34·9	2 27·5	1·8 0·3	7·8 1·4	13·8 2·4
19	2 34·8	2 35·2	2 27·7	1·9 0·3	7·9 1·4	13·9 2·4
20	2 35·0	2 35·4	2 27·9	2·0 0·4	8·0 1·4	14·0 2·5
21	2 35·3	2 35·7	2 28·2	2·1 0·4	8·1 1·4	14·1 2·5
22	2 35·5	2 35·9	2 28·4	2·2 0·4	8·2 1·4	14·2 2·5
23	2 35·8	2 36·2	2 28·7	2·3 0·4	8·3 1·5	14·3 2·5
·24	2 36·0	2 36·4	2 28·9	2·4 0·4	8·4 1·5	14·4 2·5
25	2 36·3	2 36·7	2 29·1	2·5 0·4	8·5 1·5	14·5 2·5
26	2 36·5	2 36·9	2 29·4	2·6 0·5	8·6 1·5	14·6 2·6
27	2 36·8	2 37·2	2 29·6	2·7 0·5	8·7 1·5	14·7 2·6
28	2 37·0	2 37·4	2 29·8	2·8 0·5	8·8 1·5	14·8 2·6
29	2 37·3	2 37·7	2 30·1	2·9 0·5	8·9 1·6	14·9 2·6
30	2 37·5	2 37·9	2 30·3	3·0 0·5	9·0 1·6	15·0 2·6
31	2 37·8	2 38·2	2 30·6	3·1 0·5	9·1 1·6	15·1 2·6
32	2 38·0	2 38·4	2 30·8	3·2 0·6	9·2 1·6	15·2 2·7
33	2 38·3	2 38·7	2 31·0	3·3 0·6	9·3 1·6	15·3 2·7
34	2 38·5	2 38·9	2 31·3	3·4 0·6	9·4 1·6	15·4 2·7
35	2 38·8	2 39·2	2 31·5	3·5 0·6	9·5 1·7	15·5 2·7
36	2 39·0	2 39·4	2 31·8	3·6 0·6	9·6 1·7	15·6 2·7
37	2 39·2	2 39·7	2 32·0	3·7 0·6	9·7 1·7	15·7 2·7
38	2 39·5	2 39·9	2 32·2	3·8 0·7	9·8 1·7	15·8 2·8
39	2 39·8	2 40·2	2 32·5	3·9 0·7	9·9 1·7	15·9 2·8
40	2 40·0	2 40·4	2 32·7	4·0 0·7	10·0 1·8	16·0 2·8
41	2 40·3	2 40·7	2 32·9	4·1 0·7	10·1 1·8	16·1 2·8
42	2 40·5	2 40·9	2 33·2	4·2 0·7	10·2 1·8	16·2 2·8
43	2 40·8	2 41·2	2 33·4	4·3 0·8	10·3 1·8	16·3 2·9
44	2 41·0	2 41·4	2 33·7	4·4 0·8	10·4 1·8	16·4 2·9
45	2 41·3	2 41·7	2 33·9	4·5 0·8	10·5 1·8	16·5 2·9
46	2 41·5	2 41·9	2 34·1	4·6 0·8	10·6 1·9	16·6 2·9
47	2 41·8	2 42·2	2 34·4	4·7 0·8	10·7 1·9	16·7 2·9
48	2 42·0	2 42·4	2 34·6	4·8 0·8	10·8 1·9	16·8 2·9
49	2 42·3	2 42·7	2 34·9	4·9 0·9	10·9 1·9	16·9 3·0
50	2 42·5	2 42·9	2 35·1	5·0 0·9	11·0 1·9	17·0 3·0
51	2 42·8	2 43·2	2 35·3	5·1 0·9	11·1 1·9	17·1 3·0
52	2 43·0	2 43·4	2 35·6	5·2 0·9	11·2 2·0	17·2 3·0
53	2 43·3	2 43·7	2 35·8	5·3 0·9	11·3 2·0	17·3 3·0
54	2 43·5	2 43·9	2 36·1	5·4 0·9	11·4 2·0	17·4 3·0
55	2 43·8	2 44·2	2 36·3	5·5 1·0	11·5 2·0	17·5 3·1
56	2 44·0	2 44·4	2 36·5	5·6 1·0	11·6 2·0	17·6 3·1
57	2 44·3	2 44·7	2 36·8	5·7 1·0	11·7 2·0	17·7 3·1
58	2 44·5	2 45·0	2 37·0	5·8 1·0	11·8 2·1	17·8 3·1
59	2 44·8	2 45·2	2 37·2	5·9 1·0	11·9 2·1	17·9 3·1
60	2 45·0	2 45·5	2 37·5	6·0 1·1	12·0 2·1	18·0 3·2

11	SUN PLANETS	ARIES	MOON	v or Corrn d	v or Corrn d	v or Corrn d
	° ′	° ′	° ′	′ ′	′ ′	′ ′
00	2 45·0	2 45·5	2 37·5	0·0 0·0	6·0 1·2	12·0 2·3
01	2 45·3	2 45·7	2 37·7	0·1 0·0	6·1 1·2	12·1 2·3
02	2 45·5	2 46·0	2 38·0	0·2 0·0	6·2 1·2	12·2 2·3
03	2 45·8	2 46·2	2 38·2	0·3 0·1	6·3 1·2	12·3 2·4
04	2 46·0	2 46·5	2 38·4	0·4 0·1	6·4 1·2	12·4 2·4
05	2 46·3	2 46·7	2 38·7	0·5 0·1	6·5 1·2	12·5 2·4
06	2 46·5	2 47·0	2 38·9	0·6 0·1	6·6 1·3	12·6 2·4
07	2 46·8	2 47·2	2 39·2	0·7 0·1	6·7 1·3	12·7 2·4
08	2 47·0	2 47·5	2 39·4	0·8 0·2	6·8 1·3	12·8 2·5
09	2 47·3	2 47·7	2 39·6	0·9 0·2	6·9 1·3	12·9 2·5
10	2 47·5	2 48·0	2 39·9	1·0 0·2	7·0 1·3	13·0 2·5
11	2 47·8	2 48·2	2 40·1	1·1 0·2	7·1 1·4	13·1 2·5
12	2 48·0	2 48·5	2 40·3	1·2 0·2	7·2 1·4	13·2 2·5
13	2 48·3	2 48·7	2 40·6	1·3 0·2	7·3 1·4	13·3 2·5
14	2 48·5	2 49·0	2 40·8	1·4 0·3	7·4 1·4	13·4 2·6
15	2 48·8	2 49·2	2 41·1	1·5 0·3	7·5 1·4	13·5 2·6
16	2 49·0	2 49·5	2 41·3	1·6 0·3	7·6 1·5	13·6 2·6
17	2 49·3	2 49·7	2 41·5	1·7 0·3	7·7 1·5	13·7 2·6
18	2 49·5	2 50·0	2 41·8	1·8 0·3	7·8 1·5	13·8 2·6
19	2 49·8	2 50·2	2 42·0	1·9 0·4	7·9 1·5	13·9 2·7
20	2 50·0	2 50·5	2 42·3	2·0 0·4	8·0 1·5	14·0 2·7
21	2 50·3	2 50·7	2 42·5	2·1 0·4	8·1 1·6	14·1 2·7
22	2 50·5	2 51·0	2 42·7	2·2 0·4	8·2 1·6	14·2 2·7
23	2 50·8	2 51·2	2 43·0	2·3 0·4	8·3 1·6	14·3 2·7
24	2 51·0	2 51·5	2 43·2	2·4 0·5	8·4 1·6	14·4 2·8
25	2 51·3	2 51·7	2 43·4	2·5 0·5	8·5 1·6	14·5 2·8
26	2 51·5	2 52·0	2 43·7	2·6 0·5	8·6 1·6	14·6 2·8
27	2 51·8	2 52·2	2 43·9	2·7 0·5	8·7 1·7	14·7 2·8
28	2 52·0	2 52·5	2 44·2	2·8 0·5	8·8 1·7	14·8 2·8
29	2 52·3	2 52·7	2 44·4	2·9 0·6	8·9 1·7	14·9 2·9
30	2 52·5	2 53·0	2 44·6	3·0 0·6	9·0 1·7	15·0 2·9
31	2 52·8	2 53·2	2 44·9	3·1 0·6	9·1 1·7	15·1 2·9
32	2 53·0	2 53·5	2 45·1	3·2 0·6	9·2 1·8	15·2 2·9
33	2 53·3	2 53·7	2 45·4	3·3 0·6	9·3 1·8	15·3 2·9
34	2 53·5	2 54·0	2 45·6	3·4 0·7	9·4 1·8	15·4 3·0
35	2 53·8	2 54·2	2 45·8	3·5 0·7	9·5 1·8	15·5 3·0
36	2 54·0	2 54·5	2 46·1	3·6 0·7	9·6 1·8	15·6 3·0
37	2 54·3	2 54·7	2 46·3	3·7 0·7	9·7 1·9	15·7 3·0
38	2 54·5	2 55·0	2 46·6	3·8 0·7	9·8 1·9	15·8 3·0
39	2 54·8	2 55·2	2 46·8	3·9 0·7	9·9 1·9	15·9 3·0
40	2 55·0	2 55·5	2 47·0	4·0 0·8	10·0 1·9	16·0 3·1
41	2 55·3	2 55·7	2 47·3	4·1 0·8	10·1 1·9	16·1 3·1
42	2 55·5	2 56·0	2 47·5	4·2 0·8	10·2 2·0	16·2 3·1
43	2 55·8	2 56·2	2 47·7	4·3 0·8	10·3 2·0	16·3 3·1
44	2 56·0	2 56·5	2 48·0	4·4 0·8	10·4 2·0	16·4 3·1
45	2 56·3	2 56·7	2 48·2	4·5 0·9	10·5 2·0	16·5 3·2
46	2 56·5	2 57·0	2 48·5	4·6 0·9	10·6 2·0	16·6 3·2
47	2 56·8	2 57·2	2 48·7	4·7 0·9	10·7 2·1	16·7 3·2
48	2 57·0	2 57·5	2 48·9	4·8 0·9	10·8 2·1	16·8 3·2
49	2 57·3	2 57·7	2 49·2	4·9 0·9	10·9 2·1	16·9 3·2
50	2 57·5	2 58·0	2 49·4	5·0 1·0	11·0 2·1	17·0 3·3
51	2 57·8	2 58·2	2 49·7	5·1 1·0	11·1 2·1	17·1 3·3
52	2 58·0	2 58·5	2 49·9	5·2 1·0	11·2 2·1	17·2 3·3
53	2 58·3	2 58·7	2 50·1	5·3 1·0	11·3 2·2	17·3 3·3
54	2 58·5	2 59·0	2 50·4	5·4 1·0	11·4 2·2	17·4 3·3
55	2 58·8	2 59·2	2 50·6	5·5 1·1	11·5 2·2	17·5 3·4
56	2 59·0	2 59·5	2 50·8	5·6 1·1	11·6 2·2	17·6 3·4
57	2 59·3	2 59·7	2 51·1	5·7 1·1	11·7 2·2	17·7 3·4
58	2 59·5	3 00·0	2 51·3	5·8 1·1	11·8 2·3	17·8 3·4
59	2 59·8	3 00·2	2 51·6	5·9 1·1	11·9 2·3	17·9 3·4
60	3 00·0	3 00·5	2 51·8	6·0 1·2	12·0 2·3	18·0 3·5

INCREMENTS AND CORRECTIONS

20ᵐ

20	SUN PLANETS	ARIES	MOON	v or Corr d	v or Corr d	v or Corr d
00	5 00·0	5 00·8	4 46·3	0·0 0·0	6·0 2·1	12·0 4·1
01	5 00·3	5 01·1	4 46·6	0·1 0·0	6·1 2·1	12·1 4·1
02	5 00·5	5 01·3	4 46·8	0·2 0·1	6·2 2·1	12·2 4·2
03	5 00·8	5 01·6	4 47·0	0·3 0·1	6·3 2·2	12·3 4·2
04	5 01·0	5 01·8	4 47·3	0·4 0·1	6·4 2·2	12·4 4·2
05	5 01·3	5 02·1	4 47·5	0·5 0·2	6·5 2·2	12·5 4·3
06	5 01·5	5 02·3	4 47·8	0·6 0·2	6·6 2·3	12·6 4·3
07	5 01·8	5 02·6	4 48·0	0·7 0·2	6·7 2·3	12·7 4·3
08	5 02·0	5 02·8	4 48·2	0·8 0·3	6·8 2·3	12·8 4·4
09	5 02·3	5 03·1	4 48·5	0·9 0·3	6·9 2·4	12·9 4·4
10	5 02·5	5 03·3	4 48·7	1·0 0·3	7·0 2·4	13·0 4·4
11	5 02·8	5 03·6	4 49·0	1·1 0·4	7·1 2·4	13·1 4·5
12	5 03·0	5 03·8	4 49·2	1·2 0·4	7·2 2·5	13·2 4·5
13	5 03·3	5 04·1	4 49·4	1·3 0·4	7·3 2·5	13·3 4·5
14	5 03·5	5 04·3	4 49·7	1·4 0·5	7·4 2·5	13·4 4·6
15	5 03·8	5 04·6	4 49·9	1·5 0·5	7·5 2·6	13·5 4·6
16	5 04·0	5 04·8	4 50·2	1·6 0·5	7·6 2·6	13·6 4·6
17	5 04·3	5 05·1	4 50·4	1·7 0·6	7·7 2·6	13·7 4·7
18	5 04·5	5 05·3	4 50·6	1·8 0·6	7·8 2·7	13·8 4·7
19	5 04·8	5 05·6	4 50·9	1·9 0·6	7·9 2·7	13·9 4·7
20	5 05·0	5 05·8	4 51·1	2·0 0·7	8·0 2·7	14·0 4·8
21	5 05·3	5 06·1	4 51·3	2·1 0·7	8·1 2·8	14·1 4·8
22	5 05·5	5 06·3	4 51·6	2·2 0·8	8·2 2·8	14·2 4·9
23	5 05·8	5 06·6	4 51·8	2·3 0·8	8·3 2·8	14·3 4·9
24	5 06·0	5 06·8	4 52·1	2·4 0·8	8·4 2·9	14·4 4·9
25	5 06·3	5 07·1	4 52·3	2·5 0·9	8·5 2·9	14·5 5·0
26	5 06·5	5 07·3	4 52·5	2·6 0·9	8·6 2·9	14·6 5·0
27	5 06·8	5 07·6	4 52·8	2·7 0·9	8·7 3·0	14·7 5·0
28	5 07·0	5 07·8	4 53·0	2·8 1·0	8·8 3·0	14·8 5·1
29	5 07·3	5 08·1	4 53·3	2·9 1·0	8·9 3·0	14·9 5·1
30	5 07·5	5 08·3	4 53·5	3·0 1·0	9·0 3·1	15·0 5·1
31	5 07·8	5 08·6	4 53·7	3·1 1·1	9·1 3·1	15·1 5·2
32	5 08·0	5 08·8	4 54·0	3·2 1·1	9·2 3·1	15·2 5·2
33	5 08·3	5 09·1	4 54·2	3·3 1·1	9·3 3·2	15·3 5·2
34	5 08·5	5 09·3	4 54·4	3·4 1·2	9·4 3·2	15·4 5·3
35	5 08·8	5 09·6	4 54·7	3·5 1·2	9·5 3·2	15·5 5·3
36	5 09·0	5 09·8	4 54·9	3·6 1·2	9·6 3·3	15·6 5·3
37	5 09·3	5 10·1	4 55·2	3·7 1·3	9·7 3·3	15·7 5·4
38	5 09·5	5 10·3	4 55·4	3·8 1·3	9·8 3·3	15·8 5·4
39	5 09·8	5 10·6	4 55·6	3·9 1·3	9·9 3·4	15·9 5·4
40	5 10·0	5 10·8	4 55·9	4·0 1·4	10·0 3·4	16·0 5·5
41	5 10·3	5 11·1	4 56·1	4·1 1·4	10·1 3·5	16·1 5·5
42	5 10·5	5 11·4	4 56·4	4·2 1·4	10·2 3·5	16·2 5·5
43	5 10·8	5 11·6	4 56·6	4·3 1·5	10·3 3·5	16·3 5·6
44	5 11·0	5 11·9	4 56·8	4·4 1·5	10·4 3·6	16·4 5·6
45	5 11·3	5 12·1	4 57·1	4·5 1·5	10·5 3·6	16·5 5·6
46	5 11·5	5 12·4	4 57·3	4·6 1·6	10·6 3·6	16·6 5·7
47	5 11·8	5 12·6	4 57·5	4·7 1·6	10·7 3·7	16·7 5·7
48	5 12·0	5 12·9	4 57·8	4·8 1·6	10·8 3·7	16·8 5·7
49	5 12·3	5 13·1	4 58·0	4·9 1·7	10·9 3·7	16·9 5·8
50	5 12·5	5 13·4	4 58·3	5·0 1·7	11·0 3·8	17·0 5·8
51	5 12·8	5 13·6	4 58·5	5·1 1·7	11·1 3·8	17·1 5·8
52	5 13·0	5 13·9	4 58·7	5·2 1·8	11·2 3·8	17·2 5·9
53	5 13·3	5 14·1	4 59·0	5·3 1·8	11·3 3·9	17·3 5·9
54	5 13·5	5 14·4	4 59·2	5·4 1·8	11·4 3·9	17·4 5·9
55	5 13·8	5 14·6	4 59·5	5·5 1·9	11·5 3·9	17·5 6·0
56	5 14·0	5 14·9	4 59·7	5·6 1·9	11·6 4·0	17·6 6·0
57	5 14·3	5 15·1	4 59·9	5·7 1·9	11·7 4·0	17·7 6·0
58	5 14·5	5 15·4	5 00·2	5·8 2·0	11·8 4·0	17·8 6·1
59	5 14·8	5 15·6	5 00·4	5·9 2·0	11·9 4·1	17·9 6·1
60	5 15·0	5 15·9	5 00·7	6·0 2·1	12·0 4·1	18·0 6·2

21ᵐ

21	SUN PLANETS	ARIES	MOON	v or Corr d	v or Corr d	v or Corr d
00	5 15·0	5 15·9	5 00·7	0·0 0·0	6·0 2·2	12·0 4·3
01	5 15·3	5 16·1	5 00·9	0·1 0·0	6·1 2·2	12·1 4·3
02	5 15·5	5 16·4	5 01·1	0·2 0·1	6·2 2·2	12·2 4·4
03	5 15·8	5 16·6	5 01·4	0·3 0·1	6·3 2·3	12·3 4·4
04	5 16·0	5 16·9	5 01·6	0·4 0·1	6·4 2·3	12·4 4·4
05	5 16·3	5 17·1	5 01·8	0·5 0·2	6·5 2·3	12·5 4·5
06	5 16·5	5 17·4	5 02·1	0·6 0·2	6·6 2·4	12·6 4·5
07	5 16·8	5 17·6	5 02·3	0·7 0·3	6·7 2·4	12·7 4·6
08	5 17·0	5 17·9	5 02·6	0·8 0·3	6·8 2·4	12·8 4·6
09	5 17·3	5 18·1	5 02·8	0·9 0·3	6·9 2·5	12·9 4·6
10	5 17·5	5 18·4	5 03·0	1·0 0·4	7·0 2·5	13·0 4·7
11	5 17·8	5 18·6	5 03·3	1·1 0·4	7·1 2·5	13·1 4·7
12	5 18·0	5 18·9	5 03·5	1·2 0·4	7·2 2·6	13·2 4·7
13	5 18·3	5 19·1	5 03·8	1·3 0·5	7·3 2·6	13·3 4·8
14	5 18·5	5 19·4	5 04·0	1·4 0·5	7·4 2·7	13·4 4·8
15	5 18·8	5 19·6	5 04·2	1·5 0·5	7·5 2·7	13·5 4·8
16	5 19·0	5 19·9	5 04·5	1·6 0·6	7·6 2·7	13·6 4·9
17	5 19·3	5 20·1	5 04·7	1·7 0·6	7·7 2·8	13·7 4·9
18	5 19·5	5 20·4	5 04·9	1·8 0·6	7·8 2·8	13·8 4·9
19	5 19·8	5 20·6	5 05·2	1·9 0·7	7·9 2·8	13·9 5·0
20	5 20·0	5 20·9	5 05·4	2·0 0·7	8·0 2·9	14·0 5·0
21	5 20·3	5 21·1	5 05·7	2·1 0·8	8·1 2·9	14·1 5·1
22	5 20·5	5 21·4	5 05·9	2·2 0·8	8·2 2·9	14·2 5·1
23	5 20·8	5 21·6	5 06·1	2·3 0·8	8·3 3·0	14·3 5·1
24	5 21·0	5 21·9	5 06·4	2·4 0·9	8·4 3·0	14·4 5·2
25	5 21·3	5 22·1	5 06·6	2·5 0·9	8·5 3·0	14·5 5·2
26	5 21·5	5 22·4	5 06·9	2·6 0·9	8·6 3·1	14·6 5·2
27	5 21·8	5 22·6	5 07·1	2·7 1·0	8·7 3·1	14·7 5·3
28	5 22·0	5 22·9	5 07·3	2·8 1·0	8·8 3·2	14·8 5·3
29	5 22·3	5 23·1	5 07·6	2·9 1·0	8·9 3·2	14·9 5·3
30	5 22·5	5 23·4	5 07·8	3·0 1·1	9·0 3·2	15·0 5·4
31	5 22·8	5 23·6	5 08·0	3·1 1·1	9·1 3·3	15·1 5·4
32	5 23·0	5 23·9	5 08·3	3·2 1·1	9·2 3·3	15·2 5·4
33	5 23·3	5 24·1	5 08·5	3·3 1·2	9·3 3·3	15·3 5·5
34	5 23·5	5 24·4	5 08·8	3·4 1·2	9·4 3·4	15·4 5·5
35	5 23·8	5 24·6	5 09·0	3·5 1·3	9·5 3·4	15·5 5·6
36	5 24·0	5 24·9	5 09·2	3·6 1·3	9·6 3·4	15·6 5·6
37	5 24·3	5 25·1	5 09·5	3·7 1·3	9·7 3·5	15·7 5·6
38	5 24·5	5 25·4	5 09·7	3·8 1·4	9·8 3·5	15·8 5·7
39	5 24·8	5 25·6	5 10·0	3·9 1·4	9·9 3·5	15·9 5·7
40	5 25·0	5 25·9	5 10·2	4·0 1·4	10·0 3·6	16·0 5·7
41	5 25·3	5 26·1	5 10·4	4·1 1·5	10·1 3·6	16·1 5·8
42	5 25·5	5 26·4	5 10·7	4·2 1·5	10·2 3·7	16·2 5·8
43	5 25·8	5 26·6	5 10·9	4·3 1·5	10·3 3·7	16·3 5·8
44	5 26·0	5 26·9	5 11·1	4·4 1·6	10·4 3·7	16·4 5·9
45	5 26·3	5 27·1	5 11·4	4·5 1·6	10·5 3·8	16·5 5·9
46	5 26·5	5 27·4	5 11·6	4·6 1·6	10·6 3·8	16·6 5·9
47	5 26·8	5 27·6	5 11·9	4·7 1·7	10·7 3·8	16·7 6·0
48	5 27·0	5 27·9	5 12·1	4·8 1·7	10·8 3·9	16·8 6·0
49	5 27·3	5 28·1	5 12·3	4·9 1·8	10·9 3·9	16·9 6·1
50	5 27·5	5 28·4	5 12·6	5·0 1·8	11·0 3·9	17·0 6·1
51	5 27·8	5 28·6	5 12·8	5·1 1·8	11·1 4·0	17·1 6·1
52	5 28·0	5 28·9	5 13·1	5·2 1·9	11·2 4·0	17·2 6·2
53	5 28·3	5 29·1	5 13·3	5·3 1·9	11·3 4·0	17·3 6·2
54	5 28·5	5 29·4	5 13·5	5·4 1·9	11·4 4·1	17·4 6·2
55	5 28·8	5 29·7	5 13·8	5·5 2·0	11·5 4·1	17·5 6·3
56	5 29·0	5 29·9	5 14·0	5·6 2·0	11·6 4·2	17·6 6·3
57	5 29·3	5 30·2	5 14·3	5·7 2·0	11·7 4·2	17·7 6·3
58	5 29·5	5 30·4	5 14·5	5·8 2·1	11·8 4·2	17·8 6·4
59	5 29·8	5 30·7	5 14·7	5·9 2·1	11·9 4·3	17·9 6·4
60	5 30·0	5 30·9	5 15·0	6·0 2·2	12·0 4·3	18·0 6·5

30ᵐ — INCREMENTS AND CORRECTIONS — 31ᵐ

30	SUN PLANETS	ARIES	MOON	v or Corrⁿ (d)	v or Corrⁿ (d)	v or Corrⁿ (d)
00	7 30·0	7 31·2	7 09·5	0·0 0·0	6·0 3·1	12·0 6·1
01	7 30·3	7 31·5	7 09·7	0·1 0·1	6·1 3·1	12·1 6·2
02	7 30·5	7 31·7	7 10·0	0·2 0·1	6·2 3·2	12·2 6·2
03	7 30·8	7 32·0	7 10·2	0·3 0·2	6·3 3·2	12·3 6·3
04	7 31·0	7 32·2	7 10·5	0·4 0·2	6·4 3·3	12·4 6·3
05	7 31·3	7 32·5	7 10·7	0·5 0·3	6·5 3·3	12·5 6·4
06	7 31·5	7 32·7	7 10·9	0·6 0·3	6·6 3·4	12·6 6·4
07	7 31·8	7 33·0	7 11·2	0·7 0·4	6·7 3·4	12·7 6·5
08	7 32·0	7 33·2	7 11·4	0·8 0·4	6·8 3·5	12·8 6·5
09	7 32·3	7 33·5	7 11·6	0·9 0·5	6·9 3·5	12·9 6·6
10	7 32·5	7 33·7	7 11·9	1·0 0·5	7·0 3·6	13·0 6·6
11	7 32·8	7 34·0	7 12·1	1·1 0·6	7·1 3·6	13·1 6·7
12	7 33·0	7 34·2	7 12·4	1·2 0·6	7·2 3·7	13·2 6·7
13	7 33·3	7 34·5	7 12·6	1·3 0·7	7·3 3·7	13·3 6·8
14	7 33·5	7 34·7	7 12·8	1·4 0·7	7·4 3·8	13·4 6·8
15	7 33·8	7 35·0	7 13·1	1·5 0·8	7·5 3·8	13·5 6·9
16	7 34·0	7 35·2	7 13·3	1·6 0·8	7·6 3·9	13·6 6·9
17	7 34·3	7 35·5	7 13·6	1·7 0·9	7·7 3·9	13·7 7·0
18	7 34·5	7 35·7	7 13·8	1·8 0·9	7·8 4·0	13·8 7·0
19	7 34·8	7 36·0	7 14·0	1·9 1·0	7·9 4·0	13·9 7·1
20	7 35·0	7 36·2	7 14·3	2·0 1·0	8·0 4·1	14·0 7·1
21	7 35·3	7 36·5	7 14·5	2·1 1·1	8·1 4·1	14·1 7·2
22	7 35·5	7 36·7	7 14·7	2·2 1·1	8·2 4·2	14·2 7·2
23	7 35·8	7 37·0	7 15·0	2·3 1·2	8·3 4·2	14·3 7·3
24	7 36·0	7 37·2	7 15·2	2·4 1·2	8·4 4·3	14·4 7·3
25	7 36·3	7 37·5	7 15·5	2·5 1·3	8·5 4·3	14·5 7·4
26	7 36·5	7 37·7	7 15·7	2·6 1·3	8·6 4·4	14·6 7·4
27	7 36·8	7 38·0	7 15·9	2·7 1·4	8·7 4·4	14·7 7·5
28	7 37·0	7 38·3	7 16·2	2·8 1·4	8·8 4·5	14·8 7·5
29	7 37·3	7 38·5	7 16·4	2·9 1·5	8·9 4·5	14·9 7·6
30	7 37·5	7 38·8	7 16·7	3·0 1·5	9·0 4·6	15·0 7·6
31	7 37·8	7 39·0	7 16·9	3·1 1·6	9·1 4·6	15·1 7·7
32	7 38·0	7 39·3	7 17·1	3·2 1·6	9·2 4·7	15·2 7·7
33	7 38·3	7 39·5	7 17·4	3·3 1·7	9·3 4·7	15·3 7·8
34	7 38·5	7 39·8	7 17·6	3·4 1·7	9·4 4·8	15·4 7·8
35	7 38·8	7 40·0	7 17·9	3·5 1·8	9·5 4·8	15·5 7·9
36	7 39·0	7 40·3	7 18·1	3·6 1·8	9·6 4·9	15·6 7·9
37	7 39·3	7 40·5	7 18·3	3·7 1·9	9·7 4·9	15·7 8·0
38	7 39·5	7 40·8	7 18·6	3·8 1·9	9·8 5·0	15·8 8·0
39	7 39·8	7 41·0	7 18·8	3·9 2·0	9·9 5·0	15·9 8·1
40	7 40·0	7 41·3	7 19·0	4·0 2·0	10·0 5·1	16·0 8·1
41	7 40·3	7 41·5	7 19·3	4·1 2·1	10·1 5·1	16·1 8·2
42	7 40·5	7 41·8	7 19·5	4·2 2·1	10·2 5·2	16·2 8·2
43	7 40·8	7 42·0	7 19·8	4·3 2·2	10·3 5·2	16·3 8·3
44	7 41·0	7 42·3	7 20·0	4·4 2·2	10·4 5·3	16·4 8·3
45	7 41·3	7 42·5	7 20·2	4·5 2·3	10·5 5·3	16·5 8·4
46	7 41·5	7 42·8	7 20·5	4·6 2·3	10·6 5·4	16·6 8·4
47	7 41·8	7 43·0	7 20·7	4·7 2·4	10·7 5·4	16·7 8·5
48	7 42·0	7 43·3	7 21·0	4·8 2·4	10·8 5·5	16·8 8·5
49	7 42·3	7 43·5	7 21·2	4·9 2·5	10·9 5·5	16·9 8·6
50	7 42·5	7 43·8	7 21·4	5·0 2·5	11·0 5·6	17·0 8·6
51	7 42·8	7 44·0	7 21·6	5·1 2·6	11·1 5·6	17·1 8·7
52	7 43·0	7 44·3	7 21·9	5·2 2·6	11·2 5·7	17·2 8·7
53	7 43·3	7 44·5	7 22·1	5·3 2·7	11·3 5·7	17·3 8·8
54	7 43·5	7 44·8	7 22·4	5·4 2·7	11·4 5·8	17·4 8·8
55	7 43·8	7 45·0	7 22·6	5·5 2·8	11·5 5·8	17·5 8·9
56	7 44·0	7 45·3	7 22·9	5·6 2·8	11·6 5·9	17·6 8·9
57	7 44·3	7 45·5	7 23·1	5·7 2·9	11·7 5·9	17·7 9·0
58	7 44·5	7 45·8	7 23·3	5·8 2·9	11·8 6·0	17·8 9·0
59	7 44·8	7 46·0	7 23·6	5·9 3·0	11·9 6·0	17·9 9·1
60	7 45·0	7 46·3	7 23·8	6·0 3·1	12·0 6·1	18·0 9·2

31	SUN PLANETS	ARIES	MOON	v or Corrⁿ (d)	v or Corrⁿ (d)	v or Corrⁿ (d)
00	7 45·0	7 46·3	7 23·8	0·0 0·0	6·0 3·2	12·0 6·3
01	7 45·3	7 46·5	7 24·1	0·1 0·1	6·1 3·2	12·1 6·4
02	7 45·5	7 46·8	7 24·3	0·2 0·1	6·2 3·3	12·2 6·4
03	7 45·8	7 47·0	7 24·5	0·3 0·2	6·3 3·3	12·3 6·5
04	7 46·0	7 47·3	7 24·8	0·4 0·2	6·4 3·4	12·4 6·5
05	7 46·3	7 47·5	7 25·0	0·5 0·3	6·5 3·4	12·5 6·6
06	7 46·5	7 47·8	7 25·2	0·6 0·3	6·6 3·5	12·6 6·6
07	7 46·8	7 48·0	7 25·5	0·7 0·4	6·7 3·5	12·7 6·7
08	7 47·0	7 48·3	7 25·7	0·8 0·4	6·8 3·6	12·8 6·7
09	7 47·3	7 48·5	7 26·0	0·9 0·5	6·9 3·6	12·9 6·8
10	7 47·5	7 48·8	7 26·2	1·0 0·5	7·0 3·7	13·0 6·8
11	7 47·8	7 49·0	7 26·4	1·1 0·6	7·1 3·7	13·1 6·9
12	7 48·0	7 49·3	7 26·7	1·2 0·6	7·2 3·8	13·2 6·9
13	7 48·3	7 49·5	7 26·9	1·3 0·7	7·3 3·8	13·3 7·0
14	7 48·5	7 49·8	7 27·2	1·4 0·7	7·4 3·9	13·4 7·0
15	7 48·8	7 50·0	7 27·4	1·5 0·8	7·5 3·9	13·5 7·1
16	7 49·0	7 50·3	7 27·6	1·6 0·8	7·6 4·0	13·6 7·1
17	7 49·3	7 50·5	7 27·9	1·7 0·9	7·7 4·0	13·7 7·2
18	7 49·5	7 50·8	7 28·1	1·8 0·9	7·8 4·1	13·8 7·2
19	7 49·8	7 51·0	7 28·4	1·9 1·0	7·9 4·1	13·9 7·3
20	7 50·0	7 51·3	7 28·6	2·0 1·1	8·0 4·2	14·0 7·4
21	7 50·3	7 51·5	7 28·8	2·1 1·1	8·1 4·3	14·1 7·4
22	7 50·5	7 51·8	7 29·1	2·2 1·2	8·2 4·3	14·2 7·5
23	7 50·8	7 52·0	7 29·3	2·3 1·2	8·3 4·4	14·3 7·5
24	7 51·0	7 52·3	7 29·5	2·4 1·3	8·4 4·4	14·4 7·6
25	7 51·3	7 52·5	7 29·8	2·5 1·3	8·5 4·5	14·5 7·6
26	7 51·5	7 52·8	7 30·0	2·6 1·4	8·6 4·5	14·6 7·7
27	7 51·8	7 53·0	7 30·3	2·7 1·4	8·7 4·6	14·7 7·7
28	7 52·0	7 53·3	7 30·5	2·8 1·5	8·8 4·6	14·8 7·8
29	7 52·3	7 53·5	7 30·7	2·9 1·5	8·9 4·7	14·9 7·8
30	7 52·5	7 53·8	7 31·0	3·0 1·6	9·0 4·7	15·0 7·9
31	7 52·8	7 54·0	7 31·2	3·1 1·6	9·1 4·8	15·1 7·9
32	7 53·0	7 54·3	7 31·5	3·2 1·7	9·2 4·8	15·2 8·0
33	7 53·3	7 54·5	7 31·7	3·3 1·7	9·3 4·9	15·3 8·0
34	7 53·5	7 54·8	7 31·9	3·4 1·8	9·4 4·9	15·4 8·1
35	7 53·8	7 55·0	7 32·2	3·5 1·8	9·5 5·0	15·5 8·1
36	7 54·0	7 55·3	7 32·4	3·6 1·9	9·6 5·0	15·6 8·2
37	7 54·3	7 55·5	7 32·6	3·7 1·9	9·7 5·1	15·7 8·2
38	7 54·5	7 55·8	7 32·9	3·8 2·0	9·8 5·1	15·8 8·3
39	7 54·8	7 56·0	7 33·1	3·9 2·0	9·9 5·2	15·9 8·3
40	7 55·0	7 56·3	7 33·4	4·0 2·1	10·0 5·3	16·0 8·4
41	7 55·3	7 56·6	7 33·6	4·1 2·1	10·1 5·3	16·1 8·5
42	7 55·5	7 56·8	7 33·8	4·2 2·2	10·2 5·4	16·2 8·5
43	7 55·8	7 57·1	7 34·1	4·3 2·3	10·3 5·4	16·3 8·6
44	7 56·0	7 57·3	7 34·3	4·4 2·3	10·4 5·5	16·4 8·6
45	7 56·3	7 57·6	7 34·6	4·5 2·4	10·5 5·5	16·5 8·7
46	7 56·5	7 57·8	7 34·8	4·6 2·4	10·6 5·6	16·6 8·7
47	7 56·8	7 58·1	7 35·0	4·7 2·5	10·7 5·6	16·7 8·8
48	7 57·0	7 58·3	7 35·3	4·8 2·5	10·8 5·7	16·8 8·8
49	7 57·3	7 58·6	7 35·5	4·9 2·6	10·9 5·7	16·9 8·9
50	7 57·5	7 58·8	7 35·7	5·0 2·6	11·0 5·8	17·0 8·9
51	7 57·8	7 59·1	7 36·0	5·1 2·7	11·1 5·8	17·1 9·0
52	7 58·0	7 59·3	7 36·2	5·2 2·7	11·2 5·9	17·2 9·0
53	7 58·3	7 59·6	7 36·5	5·3 2·8	11·3 5·9	17·3 9·1
54	7 58·5	7 59·8	7 36·7	5·4 2·8	11·4 6·0	17·4 9·1
55	7 58·8	8 00·1	7 36·9	5·5 2·9	11·5 6·0	17·5 9·2
56	7 59·0	8 00·3	7 37·2	5·6 2·9	11·6 6·1	17·6 9·2
57	7 59·3	8 00·6	7 37·4	5·7 3·0	11·7 6·1	17·7 9·3
58	7 59·5	8 00·8	7 37·7	5·8 3·0	11·8 6·2	17·8 9·3
59	7 59·8	8 01·1	7 37·9	5·9 3·1	11·9 6·2	17·9 9·4
60	8 00·0	8 01·3	7 38·1	6·0 3·2	12·0 6·3	18·0 9·5

40ᵐ INCREMENTS AND CORRECTIONS 41ᵐ

40ᵐ	SUN PLANETS	ARIES	MOON	v or Corrⁿ / d	v or Corrⁿ / d	v or Corrⁿ / d
s	° ′	° ′	° ′	′ ′	′ ′	′ ′
00	10 00·0	10 01·6	9 32·7	0·0 0·0	6·0 4·1	12·0 8·1
01	10 00·3	10 01·9	9 32·9	0·1 0·1	6·1 4·1	12·1 8·2
02	10 00·5	10 02·1	9 33·1	0·2 0·1	6·2 4·2	12·2 8·2
03	10 00·8	10 02·4	9 33·4	0·3 0·2	6·3 4·3	12·3 8·3
04	10 01·0	10 02·6	9 33·6	0·4 0·3	6·4 4·3	12·4 8·4
05	10 01·3	10 02·9	9 33·9	0·5 0·4	6·5 4·4	12·5 8·4
06	10 01·5	10 03·1	9 34·1	0·6 0·4	6·6 4·5	12·6 8·5
07	10 01·8	10 03·4	9 34·3	0·7 0·5	6·7 4·5	12·7 8·6
08	10 02·0	10 03·6	9 34·6	0·8 0·5	6·8 4·6	12·8 8·6
09	10 02·3	10 03·9	9 34·8	0·9 0·6	6·9 4·7	12·9 8·7
10	10 02·5	10 04·1	9 35·1	1·0 0·7	7·0 4·7	13·0 8·8
11	10 02·8	10 04·4	9 35·3	1·1 0·7	7·1 4·8	13·1 8·8
12	10 03·0	10 04·7	9 35·5	1·2 0·8	7·2 4·9	13·2 8·9
13	10 03·3	10 04·9	9 35·8	1·3 0·9	7·3 4·9	13·3 9·0
14	10 03·5	10 05·2	9 36·0	1·4 0·9	7·4 5·0	13·4 9·0
15	10 03·8	10 05·4	9 36·2	1·5 1·0	7·5 5·1	13·5 9·1
16	10 04·0	10 05·7	9 36·5	1·6 1·1	7·6 5·1	13·6 9·2
17	10 04·3	10 05·9	9 36·7	1·7 1·1	7·7 5·2	13·7 9·2
18	10 04·5	10 06·2	9 37·0	1·8 1·2	7·8 5·3	13·8 9·3
19	10 04·8	10 06·4	9 37·2	1·9 1·3	7·9 5·3	13·9 9·4
20	10 05·0	10 06·7	9 37·4	2·0 1·4	8·0 5·4	14·0 9·5
21	10 05·3	10 06·9	9 37·7	2·1 1·4	8·1 5·5	14·1 9·5
22	10 05·5	10 07·2	9 37·9	2·2 1·5	8·2 5·5	14·2 9·6
23	10 05·8	10 07·4	9 38·2	2·3 1·6	8·3 5·6	14·3 9·7
24	10 06·0	10 07·7	9 38·4	2·4 1·6	8·4 5·7	14·4 9·7
25	10 06·3	10 07·9	9 38·6	2·5 1·7	8·5 5·7	14·5 9·8
26	10 06·5	10 08·2	9 38·9	2·6 1·8	8·6 5·8	14·6 9·9
27	10 06·8	10 08·4	9 39·1	2·7 1·8	8·7 5·9	14·7 9·9
28	10 07·0	10 08·7	9 39·3	2·8 1·9	8·8 5·9	14·8 10·0
29	10 07·3	10 08·9	9 39·6	2·9 2·0	8·9 6·0	14·9 10·1
30	10 07·5	10 09·2	9 39·8	3·0 2·0	9·0 6·1	15·0 10·1
31	10 07·8	10 09·4	9 40·1	3·1 2·1	9·1 6·1	15·1 10·2
32	10 08·0	10 09·7	9 40·3	3·2 2·2	9·2 6·2	15·2 10·3
33	10 08·3	10 09·9	9 40·5	3·3 2·2	9·3 6·3	15·3 10·3
34	10 08·5	10 10·2	9 40·8	3·4 2·3	9·4 6·3	15·4 10·4
35	10 08·8	10 10·4	9 41·0	3·5 2·4	9·5 6·4	15·5 10·5
36	10 09·0	10 10·7	9 41·3	3·6 2·4	9·6 6·5	15·6 10·5
37	10 09·3	10 10·9	9 41·5	3·7 2·5	9·7 6·5	15·7 10·6
38	10 09·5	10 11·2	9 41·7	3·8 2·6	9·8 6·6	15·8 10·7
39	10 09·8	10 11·4	9 42·0	3·9 2·7	9·9 6·7	15·9 10·7
40	10 10·0	10 11·7	9 42·2	4·0 2·7	10·0 6·8	16·0 10·8
41	10 10·3	10 11·9	9 42·4	4·1 2·8	10·1 6·8	16·1 10·9
42	10 10·5	10 12·2	9 42·7	4·2 2·8	10·2 6·9	16·2 10·9
43	10 10·8	10 12·4	9 42·9	4·3 2·9	10·3 7·0	16·3 11·0
44	10 11·0	10 12·7	9 43·2	4·4 3·0	10·4 7·0	16·4 11·1
45	10 11·3	10 12·9	9 43·4	4·5 3·0	10·5 7·1	16·5 11·1
46	10 11·5	10 13·2	9 43·6	4·6 3·1	10·6 7·2	16·6 11·2
47	10 11·8	10 13·4	9 43·9	4·7 3·2	10·7 7·2	16·7 11·3
48	10 12·0	10 13·7	9 44·1	4·8 3·2	10·8 7·3	16·8 11·4
49	10 12·3	10 13·9	9 44·4	4·9 3·3	10·9 7·4	16·9 11·4
50	10 12·5	10 14·2	9 44·6	5·0 3·4	11·0 7·4	17·0 11·5
51	10 12·8	10 14·4	9 44·8	5·1 3·4	11·1 7·5	17·1 11·5
52	10 13·0	10 14·7	9 45·1	5·2 3·5	11·2 7·6	17·2 11·6
53	10 13·3	10 14·9	9 45·3	5·3 3·6	11·3 7·6	17·3 11·7
54	10 13·5	10 15·2	9 45·6	5·4 3·6	11·4 7·7	17·4 11·7
55	10 13·8	10 15·4	9 45·8	5·5 3·7	11·5 7·8	17·5 11·8
56	10 14·0	10 15·7	9 46·0	5·6 3·8	11·6 7·8	17·6 11·9
57	10 14·3	10 15·9	9 46·3	5·7 3·8	11·7 7·9	17·7 11·9
58	10 14·5	10 16·2	9 46·5	5·8 3·9	11·8 8·0	17·8 12·0
59	10 14·8	10 16·4	9 46·7	5·9 4·0	11·9 8·0	17·9 12·1
60	10 15·0	10 16·7	9 47·0	6·0 4·1	12·0 8·1	18·0 12·2

41ᵐ	SUN PLANETS	ARIES	MOON	v or Corrⁿ / d	v or Corrⁿ / d	v or Corrⁿ / d
s	° ′	° ′	° ′	′ ′	′ ′	′ ′
00	10 15·0	10 16·7	9 47·0	0·0 0·0	6·0 4·2	12·0 8·3
01	10 15·3	10 16·9	9 47·2	0·1 0·1	6·1 4·2	12·1 8·4
02	10 15·5	10 17·2	9 47·5	0·2 0·1	6·2 4·3	12·2 8·4
03	10 15·8	10 17·4	9 47·7	0·3 0·2	6·3 4·4	12·3 8·5
04	10 16·0	10 17·7	9 47·9	0·4 0·3	6·4 4·4	12·4 8·6
05	10 16·3	10 17·9	9 48·2	0·5 0·3	6·5 4·5	12·5 8·6
06	10 16·5	10 18·2	9 48·4	0·6 0·4	6·6 4·6	12·6 8·7
07	10 16·8	10 18·4	9 48·7	0·7 0·5	6·7 4·6	12·7 8·8
08	10 17·0	10 18·7	9 48·9	0·8 0·6	6·8 4·7	12·8 8·9
09	10 17·3	10 18·9	9 49·1	0·9 0·6	6·9 4·8	12·9 8·9
10	10 17·5	10 19·2	9 49·4	1·0 0·7	7·0 4·8	13·0 9·0
11	10 17·8	10 19·4	9 49·6	1·1 0·8	7·1 4·9	13·1 9·1
12	10 18·0	10 19·7	9 49·8	1·2 0·8	7·2 5·0	13·2 9·1
13	10 18·3	10 19·9	9 50·1	1·3 0·9	7·3 5·0	13·3 9·2
14	10 18·5	10 20·2	9 50·3	1·4 1·0	7·4 5·1	13·4 9·3
15	10 18·8	10 20·4	9 50·6	1·5 1·0	7·5 5·2	13·5 9·3
16	10 19·0	10 20·7	9 50·8	1·6 1·1	7·6 5·3	13·6 9·4
17	10 19·3	10 20·9	9 51·0	1·7 1·2	7·7 5·3	13·7 9·5
18	10 19·5	10 21·2	9 51·3	1·8 1·2	7·8 5·4	13·8 9·5
19	10 19·8	10 21·4	9 51·5	1·9 1·3	7·9 5·5	13·9 9·6
20	10 20·0	10 21·7	9 51·8	2·0 1·4	8·0 5·5	14·0 9·7
21	10 20·3	10 21·9	9 52·0	2·1 1·5	8·1 5·6	14·1 9·8
22	10 20·5	10 22·2	9 52·2	2·2 1·5	8·2 5·7	14·2 9·8
23	10 20·8	10 22·4	9 52·5	2·3 1·6	8·3 5·7	14·3 9·9
24	10 21·0	10 22·7	9 52·7	2·4 1·7	8·4 5·8	14·4 10·0
25	10 21·3	10 23·0	9 52·9	2·5 1·7	8·5 5·9	14·5 10·0
26	10 21·5	10 23·2	9 53·2	2·6 1·8	8·6 5·9	14·6 10·1
27	10 21·8	10 23·5	9 53·4	2·7 1·9	8·7 6·0	14·7 10·2
28	10 22·0	10 23·7	9 53·7	2·8 1·9	8·8 6·1	14·8 10·2
29	10 22·3	10 24·0	9 53·9	2·9 2·0	8·9 6·2	14·9 10·3
30	10 22·5	10 24·2	9 54·1	3·0 2·1	9·0 6·2	15·0 10·4
31	10 22·8	10 24·5	9 54·4	3·1 2·1	9·1 6·3	15·1 10·4
32	10 23·0	10 24·7	9 54·6	3·2 2·2	9·2 6·4	15·2 10·5
33	10 23·3	10 25·0	9 54·9	3·3 2·3	9·3 6·4	15·3 10·6
34	10 23·5	10 25·2	9 55·1	3·4 2·4	9·4 6·5	15·4 10·7
35	10 23·8	10 25·5	9 55·3	3·5 2·4	9·5 6·6	15·5 10·7
36	10 24·0	10 25·7	9 55·6	3·6 2·5	9·6 6·6	15·6 10·8
37	10 24·3	10 26·0	9 55·8	3·7 2·6	9·7 6·7	15·7 10·9
38	10 24·5	10 26·2	9 56·1	3·8 2·6	9·8 6·8	15·8 10·9
39	10 24·8	10 26·5	9 56·3	3·9 2·7	9·9 6·8	15·9 11·0
40	10 25·0	10 26·7	9 56·5	4·0 2·8	10·0 6·9	16·0 11·1
41	10 25·3	10 27·0	9 56·8	4·1 2·8	10·1 7·0	16·1 11·1
42	10 25·5	10 27·2	9 57·0	4·2 2·9	10·2 7·1	16·2 11·2
43	10 25·8	10 27·5	9 57·2	4·3 3·0	10·3 7·1	16·3 11·3
44	10 26·0	10 27·7	9 57·5	4·4 3·0	10·4 7·2	16·4 11·3
45	10 26·3	10 28·0	9 57·7	4·5 3·1	10·5 7·3	16·5 11·4
46	10 26·5	10 28·2	9 58·0	4·6 3·2	10·6 7·3	16·6 11·5
47	10 26·8	10 28·5	9 58·2	4·7 3·3	10·7 7·4	16·7 11·6
48	10 27·0	10 28·7	9 58·4	4·8 3·3	10·8 7·5	16·8 11·6
49	10 27·3	10 29·0	9 58·7	4·9 3·4	10·9 7·5	16·9 11·7
50	10 27·5	10 29·2	9 58·9	5·0 3·5	11·0 7·6	17·0 11·8
51	10 27·8	10 29·5	9 59·2	5·1 3·5	11·1 7·7	17·1 11·8
52	10 28·0	10 29·7	9 59·4	5·2 3·6	11·2 7·7	17·2 11·9
53	10 28·3	10 30·0	9 59·6	5·3 3·7	11·3 7·8	17·3 12·0
54	10 28·5	10 30·2	9 59·9	5·4 3·7	11·4 7·9	17·4 12·0
55	10 28·8	10 30·5	10 00·1	5·5 3·8	11·5 8·0	17·5 12·1
56	10 29·0	10 30·7	10 00·3	5·6 3·9	11·6 8·0	17·6 12·2
57	10 29·3	10 31·0	10 00·6	5·7 3·9	11·7 8·1	17·7 12·2
58	10 29·5	10 31·2	10 00·8	5·8 4·0	11·8 8·1	17·8 12·3
59	10 29·8	10 31·5	10 01·1	5·9 4·1	11·9 8·2	17·9 12·4
60	10 30·0	10 31·7	10 01·3	6·0 4·2	12·0 8·3	18·0 12·5

50ᵐ — INCREMENTS AND CORRECTIONS

50	SUN PLANETS	ARIES	MOON	v or Corrn d	v or Corrn d	v or Corrn d
00	12 30·0	12 32·1	11 55·8	0·0 0·0	6·0 5·1	12·0 10·1
01	12 30·3	12 32·3	11 56·1	0·1 0·1	6·1 5·1	12·1 10·2
02	12 30·5	12 32·6	11 56·3	0·2 0·2	6·2 5·2	12·2 10·3
03	12 30·8	12 32·8	11 56·5	0·3 0·3	6·3 5·3	12·3 10·4
04	12 31·0	12 33·1	11 56·8	0·4 0·3	6·4 5·4	12·4 10·4
05	12 31·3	12 33·3	11 57·0	0·5 0·4	6·5 5·5	12·5 10·5
06	12 31·5	12 33·6	11 57·3	0·6 0·5	6·6 5·6	12·6 10·6
07	12 31·8	12 33·8	11 57·5	0·7 0·6	6·7 5·6	12·7 10·7
08	12 32·0	12 34·1	11 57·7	0·8 0·7	6·8 5·7	12·8 10·8
09	12 32·3	12 34·3	11 58·0	0·9 0·8	6·9 5·8	12·9 10·9
10	12 32·5	12 34·6	11 58·2	1·0 0·8	7·0 5·9	13·0 10·9
11	12 32·8	12 34·8	11 58·5	1·1 0·9	7·1 6·0	13·1 11·0
12	12 33·0	12 35·1	11 58·7	1·2 1·0	7·2 6·1	13·2 11·1
13	12 33·3	12 35·3	11 58·9	1·3 1·1	7·3 6·1	13·3 11·2
14	12 33·5	12 35·6	11 59·2	1·4 1·2	7·4 6·2	13·4 11·3
15	12 33·8	12 35·8	11 59·4	1·5 1·3	7·5 6·3	13·5 11·4
16	12 34·0	12 36·1	11 59·7	1·6 1·3	7·6 6·4	13·6 11·4
17	12 34·3	12 36·3	11 59·9	1·7 1·4	7·7 6·5	13·7 11·5
18	12 34·5	12 36·6	12 00·1	1·8 1·5	7·8 6·6	13·8 11·6
19	12 34·8	12 36·8	12 00·4	1·9 1·6	7·9 6·6	13·9 11·7
20	12 35·0	12 37·1	12 00·6	2·0 1·7	8·0 6·7	14·0 11·8
21	12 35·3	12 37·3	12 00·8	2·1 1·8	8·1 6·8	14·1 11·9
22	12 35·5	12 37·6	12 01·1	2·2 1·9	8·2 6·9	14·2 12·0
23	12 35·8	12 37·8	12 01·3	2·3 1·9	8·3 7·0	14·3 12·0
24	12 36·0	12 38·1	12 01·6	2·4 2·0	8·4 7·1	14·4 12·1
25	12 36·3	12 38·3	12 01·8	2·5 2·1	8·5 7·2	14·5 12·2
26	12 36·5	12 38·6	12 02·0	2·6 2·2	8·6 7·2	14·6 12·3
27	12 36·8	12 38·8	12 02·3	2·7 2·3	8·7 7·3	14·7 12·4
28	12 37·0	12 39·1	12 02·5	2·8 2·4	8·8 7·4	14·8 12·5
29	12 37·3	12 39·3	12 02·8	2·9 2·4	8·9 7·5	14·9 12·5
30	12 37·5	12 39·6	12 03·0	3·0 2·5	9·0 7·6	15·0 12·6
31	12 37·8	12 39·8	12 03·2	3·1 2·6	9·1 7·7	15·1 12·7
32	12 38·0	12 40·1	12 03·5	3·2 2·7	9·2 7·7	15·2 12·8
33	12 38·3	12 40·3	12 03·7	3·3 2·8	9·3 7·8	15·3 12·9
34	12 38·5	12 40·6	12 03·9	3·4 2·9	9·4 7·9	15·4 13·0
35	12 38·8	12 40·8	12 04·2	3·5 2·9	9·5 8·0	15·5 13·0
36	12 39·0	12 41·1	12 04·4	3·6 3·0	9·6 8·1	15·6 13·1
37	12 39·3	12 41·3	12 04·7	3·7 3·1	9·7 8·2	15·7 13·2
38	12 39·5	12 41·6	12 04·9	3·8 3·2	9·8 8·2	15·8 13·3
39	12 39·8	12 41·8	12 05·1	3·9 3·3	9·9 8·3	15·9 13·4
40	12 40·0	12 42·1	12 05·4	4·0 3·4	10·0 8·4	16·0 13·5
41	12 40·3	12 42·3	12 05·6	4·1 3·5	10·1 8·5	16·1 13·6
42	12 40·5	12 42·6	12 05·9	4·2 3·6	10·2 8·6	16·2 13·6
43	12 40·8	12 42·8	12 06·1	4·3 3·6	10·3 8·7	16·3 13·7
44	12 41·0	12 43·1	12 06·3	4·4 3·7	10·4 8·8	16·4 13·8
45	12 41·3	12 43·3	12 06·6	4·5 3·8	10·5 8·8	16·5 13·9
46	12 41·5	12 43·6	12 06·8	4·6 3·9	10·6 8·9	16·6 14·0
47	12 41·8	12 43·8	12 07·0	4·7 4·0	10·7 9·0	16·7 14·1
48	12 42·0	12 44·1	12 07·3	4·8 4·0	10·8 9·1	16·8 14·1
49	12 42·3	12 44·3	12 07·5	4·9 4·1	10·9 9·2	16·9 14·2
50	12 42·5	12 44·6	12 07·8	5·0 4·2	11·0 9·3	17·0 14·3
51	12 42·8	12 44·8	12 08·0	5·1 4·3	11·1 9·3	17·1 14·4
52	12 43·0	12 45·1	12 08·2	5·2 4·4	11·2 9·4	17·2 14·5
53	12 43·3	12 45·3	12 08·5	5·3 4·5	11·3 9·5	17·3 14·6
54	12 43·5	12 45·6	12 08·7	5·4 4·5	11·4 9·6	17·4 14·6
55	12 43·8	12 45·8	12 09·0	5·5 4·6	11·5 9·7	17·5 14·7
56	12 44·0	12 46·1	12 09·2	5·6 4·7	11·6 9·8	17·6 14·8
57	12 44·3	12 46·3	12 09·4	5·7 4·8	11·7 9·8	17·7 14·9
58	12 44·5	12 46·6	12 09·7	5·8 4·9	11·8 9·9	17·8 15·0
59	12 44·8	12 46·8	12 09·9	5·9 5·0	11·9 10·0	17·9 15·1
60	12 45·0	12 47·1	12 10·2	6·0 5·1	12·0 10·1	18·0 15·2

51ᵐ — INCREMENTS AND CORRECTIONS

51	SUN PLANETS	ARIES	MOON	v or Corrn d	v or Corrn d	v or Corrn d
00	12 45·0	12 47·1	12 10·2	0·0 0·0	6·0 5·2	12·0 10·3
01	12 45·3	12 47·3	12 10·4	0·1 0·1	6·1 5·2	12·1 10·4
02	12 45·5	12 47·6	12 10·6	0·2 0·2	6·2 5·3	12·2 10·5
03	12 45·8	12 47·8	12 10·9	0·3 0·3	6·3 5·4	12·3 10·6
04	12 46·0	12 48·1	12 11·1	0·4 0·3	6·4 5·5	12·4 10·6
05	12 46·3	12 48·3	12 11·3	0·5 0·4	6·5 5·6	12·5 10·7
06	12 46·5	12 48·6	12 11·6	0·6 0·5	6·6 5·7	12·6 10·8
07	12 46·8	12 48·8	12 11·8	0·7 0·6	6·7 5·8	12·7 10·9
08	12 47·0	12 49·1	12 12·1	0·8 0·7	6·8 5·8	12·8 11·0
09	12 47·3	12 49·4	12 12·3	0·9 0·8	6·9 5·9	12·9 11·1
10	12 47·5	12 49·6	12 12·5	1·0 0·9	7·0 6·0	13·0 11·2
11	12 47·8	12 49·9	12 12·8	1·1 0·9	7·1 6·1	13·1 11·2
12	12 48·0	12 50·1	12 13·0	1·2 1·0	7·2 6·2	13·2 11·3
13	12 48·3	12 50·4	12 13·3	1·3 1·1	7·3 6·3	13·3 11·4
14	12 48·5	12 50·6	12 13·5	1·4 1·2	7·4 6·4	13·4 11·5
15	12 48·8	12 50·9	12 13·7	1·5 1·3	7·5 6·4	13·5 11·6
16	12 49·0	12 51·1	12 14·0	1·6 1·4	7·6 6·5	13·6 11·7
17	12 49·3	12 51·4	12 14·2	1·7 1·5	7·7 6·6	13·7 11·8
18	12 49·5	12 51·6	12 14·4	1·8 1·5	7·8 6·7	13·8 11·8
19	12 49·8	12 51·9	12 14·7	1·9 1·6	7·9 6·8	13·9 11·9
20	12 50·0	12 52·1	12 14·9	2·0 1·7	8·0 6·9	14·0 12·0
21	12 50·3	12 52·4	12 15·2	2·1 1·8	8·1 7·0	14·1 12·1
22	12 50·5	12 52·6	12 15·4	2·2 1·9	8·2 7·0	14·2 12·2
23	12 50·8	12 52·9	12 15·6	2·3 2·0	8·3 7·1	14·3 12·3
24	12 51·0	12 53·1	12 15·9	2·4 2·1	8·4 7·2	14·4 12·4
25	12 51·3	12 53·4	12 16·1	2·5 2·1	8·5 7·3	14·5 12·4
26	12 51·5	12 53·6	12 16·4	2·6 2·2	8·6 7·4	14·6 12·5
27	12 51·8	12 53·9	12 16·6	2·7 2·3	8·7 7·5	14·7 12·6
28	12 52·0	12 54·1	12 16·8	2·8 2·4	8·8 7·6	14·8 12·7
29	12 52·3	12 54·4	12 17·1	2·9 2·5	8·9 7·6	14·9 12·8
30	12 52·5	12 54·6	12 17·3	3·0 2·6	9·0 7·7	15·0 12·9
31	12 52·8	12 54·9	12 17·5	3·1 2·7	9·1 7·8	15·1 13·0
32	12 53·0	12 55·1	12 17·8	3·2 2·7	9·2 7·9	15·2 13·0
33	12 53·3	12 55·4	12 18·0	3·3 2·8	9·3 8·0	15·3 13·1
34	12 53·5	12 55·6	12 18·3	3·4 2·9	9·4 8·1	15·4 13·2
35	12 53·8	12 55·9	12 18·5	3·5 3·0	9·5 8·2	15·5 13·3
36	12 54·0	12 56·1	12 18·7	3·6 3·1	9·6 8·2	15·6 13·4
37	12 54·3	12 56·4	12 19·0	3·7 3·2	9·7 8·3	15·7 13·5
38	12 54·5	12 56·6	12 19·2	3·8 3·3	9·8 8·4	15·8 13·6
39	12 54·8	12 56·9	12 19·5	3·9 3·3	9·9 8·5	15·9 13·6
40	12 55·0	12 57·1	12 19·7	4·0 3·4	10·0 8·6	16·0 13·7
41	12 55·3	12 57·4	12 19·9	4·1 3·5	10·1 8·7	16·1 13·8
42	12 55·5	12 57·6	12 20·2	4·2 3·6	10·2 8·8	16·2 13·9
43	12 55·8	12 57·9	12 20·4	4·3 3·7	10·3 8·8	16·3 14·0
44	12 56·0	12 58·1	12 20·6	4·4 3·8	10·4 8·9	16·4 14·1
45	12 56·3	12 58·4	12 20·9	4·5 3·9	10·5 9·0	16·5 14·2
46	12 56·5	12 58·6	12 21·1	4·6 3·9	10·6 9·1	16·6 14·3
47	12 56·8	12 58·9	12 21·4	4·7 4·0	10·7 9·2	16·7 14·3
48	12 57·0	12 59·1	12 21·6	4·8 4·1	10·8 9·3	16·8 14·4
49	12 57·3	12 59·4	12 21·8	4·9 4·2	10·9 9·4	16·9 14·5
50	12 57·5	12 59·6	12 22·1	5·0 4·3	11·0 9·4	17·0 14·6
51	12 57·8	12 59·9	12 22·3	5·1 4·4	11·1 9·5	17·1 14·7
52	12 58·0	13 00·1	12 22·6	5·2 4·5	11·2 9·6	17·2 14·8
53	12 58·3	13 00·4	12 22·8	5·3 4·5	11·3 9·7	17·3 14·8
54	12 58·5	13 00·6	12 23·0	5·4 4·6	11·4 9·8	17·4 14·9
55	12 58·8	13 00·9	12 23·3	5·5 4·7	11·5 9·9	17·5 15·0
56	12 59·0	13 01·1	12 23·5	5·6 4·8	11·6 10·0	17·6 15·1
57	12 59·3	13 01·4	12 23·8	5·7 4·9	11·7 10·0	17·7 15·2
58	12 59·5	13 01·6	12 24·0	5·8 5·0	11·8 10·1	17·8 15·3
59	12 59·8	13 01·9	12 24·2	5·9 5·1	11·9 10·2	17·9 15·4
60	13 00·0	13 02·1	12 24·5	6·0 5·2	12·0 10·3	18·0 15·5

POLARIS (POLE STAR) TABLES, 1966
FOR DETERMINING LATITUDE FROM SEXTANT ALTITUDE AND FOR AZIMUTH

L.H.A. ARIES	50°–59°	80°–89°	110°–119°	120°–129°	140°–149°	180°–189°	190°–199°	200°–209°	240°–249°	260°–269°	290°–299°	330°–339°
	a_0	a_0	a_0	a_0	a_0	a_0	a_0	a_0	a_0	a_0	a_0	a_0
0	0 08·7	0 24·8	0 50·0	0 59·3	1 17·5	1 45·2	1 49·0	1 51·4	1 45·2	1 33·4	1 08·5	0 32·5
1	09·0	25·5	50·9	1 00·2	18·4	45·6	49·3	51·6	44·7	32·7	07·6	31·7
2	09·4	26·2	51·9	01·2	19·2	46·1	49·6	51·7	44·2	32·0	06·7	30·8
3	09·7	27·0	52·8	02·1	20·1	46·5	49·9	51·8	43·7	31·3	05·8	30·1
4	10·1	27·7	53·7	03·0	20·9	46·9	50·2	51·9	43·2	30·5	04·9	29·3
5	0 10·5	0 28·5	0 54·6	1 04·0	1 21·8	1 47·3	1 50·4	1 52·0	1 42·7	1 29·8	1 03·9	0 28·5
6	10·9	29·3	55·6	04·9	22·6	47·7	50·6	52·1	42·2	29·0	03·0	27·7
7	11·3	30·1	56·5	05·8	23·4	48·0	50·9	52·1	41·6	28·2	02·1	27·0
8	11·8	30·9	57·4	06·7	24·3	48·4	51·1	52·2	41·1	27·4	01·1	26·2
9	12·2	31·7	58·4	07·6	25·1	48·7	51·2	52·2	40·5	26·7	1 00·2	25·5
10	0 12·7	0 32·5	0 59·3	1 08·6	1 25·9	1 49·0	1 51·4	1 52·2	1 39·9	1 25·9	0 59·3	0 24·8

Lat.	a_1	a_1	a_1	a_1	a_1	a_1	a_1	a_1	a_1	a_1	a_1	a_1
0	0·5	0·3	0·1	0·1	0·2	0·5	0·6	0·6	0·4	0·3	0·1	0·3
10	·5	·3	·2	·2	·3	·5	·6	·6	·5	·3	·2	·3
20	·5	·4	·3	·3	·3	·5	·6	·6	·5	·4	·3	·4
30	·6	·4	·4	·4	·4	·6	·6	·6	·5	·4	·4	·4
40	0·6	0·5	0·5	0·5	0·5	0·6	0·6	0·6	0·6	0·5	0·5	0·5
45	·6	·5	·5	·5	·5	·6	·6	·6	·6	·5	·5	·5
50	·6	·6	·6	·6	·6	·6	·6	·6	·6	·6	·6	·6
55	·6	·7	·7	·7	·7	·6	·6	·6	·6	·7	·7	·7
60	·6	·7	·8	·8	·8	·6	·6	·6	·7	·7	·8	·7
62	0·7	0·8	0·9	0·9	0·8	0·7	0·6	0·6	0·7	0·8	0·9	0·8
64	·7	·8	0·9	0·9	0·9	·7	·6	·6	·7	·8	0·9	·8
66	·7	0·9	1·0	1·0	1·0	·7	·6	·6	·7	0·9	1·0	0·9
68	0·7	1·0	1·1	1·1	1·0	0·7	0·6	0·6	0·8	1·0	1·1	1·0

Month	a_2	a_2	a_2	a_2	a_2	a_2	a_2	a_2	a_2	a_2	a_2	a_2
Jan.	0·7	0·7	0·6	0·6	0·6	0·5	0·5	0·5	0·5	0·5	0·6	0·6
Feb.	·8	·8	·8	·8	·7	·6	·6	·5	·4	·4	·4	·5
Mar.	·7	·8	·9	0·9	0·9	·7	·7	·6	·4	·4	·3	·4
Apr.	0·6	0·8	0·9	1·0	1·0	0·9	0·8	0·8	0·5	0·4	0·3	0·2
May	·5	·7	·9	0·9	1·0	1·0	0·9	0·9	·6	·5	·3	·2
June	·4	·5	·8	·8	0·9	1·0	1·0	1·0	·8	·7	·4	·2
July	0·3	0·4	0·6	0·7	0·8	1·0	1·0	1·0	0·9	0·8	0·6	0·4
Aug.	·3	·3	·4	·5	·6	0·8	0·9	0·9	·9	·9	·8	·5
Sept,	·3	·3	·3	·4	·4	·6	·7	·8	·9	·9	·9	·7
Oct.	0·4	0·3	0·3	0·3	0·3	0·4	0·5	0·6	0·8	0·9	0·9	0·9
Nov.	·6	·4	·3	·2	·2	·3	·3	·4	·6	·8	·9	1·0
Dec.	0·8	0·6	0·4	0·3	0·2	0·2	0·2	0·2	0·5	0·6	0·8	1·0

Lat.	AZIMUTH											
0	359·6	359·3	359·1	359·1	359·2	359·6	359·8	359·9	0·5	0·7	0·9	0·7
20	359·6	359·2	359·1	359·1	359·1	359·6	359·8	359·9	0·5	0·8	0·9	0·8
40	359·5	359·0	358·8	358·8	359·0	359·5	359·7	359·9	0·6	0·9	1·2	1·0
50	359·4	358·8	358·6	358·6	358·7	359·4	359·6	359·9	0·8	1·1	1·4	1·2
55	359·3	358·7	358·5	358·5	358·6	359·4	359·6	359·9	0·9	1·3	1·5	1·3
60	359·2	358·5	358·2	358·2	358·4	359·3	359·6	359·8	1·0	1·4	1·8	1·5
65	359·1	358·2	357·9	357·9	358·1	359·1	359·5	359·8	1·2	1·7	2·1	1·8

Latitude = corrected sextant altitude − 1° + a_0 + a_1 + a_2

The table is entered with L.H.A. Aries to determine the column to be used; each column refers to a range of 10°. a_0 is taken, with mental interpolation, from the upper table with the units of L.H.A. Aries in degrees as argument; a_1, a_2 are taken, without interpolation, from the second and third tables with arguments latitude and month respectively. a_0, a_1, a_2 are always positive. The final table gives the azimuth of *Polaris*.

CONVERSION OF ARC TO TIME

0°-59°	h m	60°-119°	h m	120°-179°	h m	180°-239°	h m	240°-299°	h m	300°-359°	h m	′	0′.00 m s	0′.25 m s	0′.50 m s	0′.75 m s
0	0 00	60	4 00	120	8 00	180	12 00	240	16 00	300	20 00	0	0 00	0 01	0 02	0 03
1	0 04	61	4 04	121	8 04	181	12 04	241	16 04	301	20 04	1	0 04	0 05	0 06	0 07
2	0 08	62	4 08	122	8 08	182	12 08	242	16 08	302	20 08	2	0 08	0 09	0 10	0 11
3	0 12	63	4 12	123	8 12	183	12 12	243	16 12	303	20 12	3	0 12	0 13	0 14	0 15
4	0 16	64	4 16	124	8 16	184	12 16	244	16 16	304	20 16	4	0 16	0 17	0 18	0 19
5	0 20	65	4 20	125	8 20	185	12 20	245	16 20	305	20 20	5	0 20	0 21	0 22	0 23
6	0 24	66	4 24	126	8 24	186	12 24	246	16 24	306	20 24	6	0 24	0 25	0 26	0 27
7	0 28	67	4 28	127	8 28	187	12 28	247	16 28	307	20 28	7	0 28	0 29	0 30	0 31
8	0 32	68	4 32	128	8 32	188	12 32	248	16 32	308	20 32	8	0 32	0 33	0 34	0 35
9	0 36	69	4 36	129	8 36	189	12 36	249	16 36	309	20 36	9	0 36	0 37	0 38	0 39
10	0 40	70	4 40	130	8 40	190	12 40	250	16 40	310	20 40	10	0 40	0 41	0 42	0 43
11	0 44	71	4 44	131	8 44	191	12 44	251	16 44	311	20 44	11	0 44	0 45	0 46	0 47
12	0 48	72	4 48	132	8 48	192	12 48	252	16 48	312	20 48	12	0 48	0 49	0 50	0 51
13	0 52	73	4 52	133	8 52	193	12 52	253	16 52	313	20 52	13	0 52	0 53	0 54	0 55
14	0 56	74	4 56	134	8 56	194	12 56	254	16 56	314	20 56	14	0 56	0 57	0 58	0 59
15	1 00	75	5 00	135	9 00	195	13 00	255	17 00	315	21 00	15	1 00	1 01	1 02	1 03
16	1 04	76	5 04	136	9 04	196	13 04	256	17 04	316	21 04	16	1 04	1 05	1 06	1 07
17	1 08	77	5 08	137	9 08	197	13 08	257	17 08	317	21 08	17	1 08	1 09	1 10	1 11
18	1 12	78	5 12	138	9 12	198	13 12	258	17 12	318	21 12	18	1 12	1 13	1 14	1 15
19	1 16	79	5 16	139	9 16	199	13 16	259	17 16	319	21 16	19	1 16	1 17	1 18	1 19
20	1 20	80	5 20	140	9 20	200	13 20	260	17 20	320	21 20	20	1 20	1 21	1 22	1 23
21	1 24	81	5 24	141	9 24	201	13 24	261	17 24	321	21 24	21	1 24	1 25	1 26	1 27
22	1 28	82	5 28	142	9 28	202	13 28	262	17 28	322	21 28	22	1 28	1 29	1 30	1 31
23	1 32	83	5 32	143	9 32	203	13 32	263	17 32	323	21 32	23	1 32	1 33	1 34	1 35
24	1 36	84	5 36	144	9 36	204	13 36	264	17 36	324	21 36	24	1 36	1 37	1 38	1 39
25	1 40	85	5 40	145	9 40	205	13 40	265	17 40	325	21 40	25	1 40	1 41	1 42	1 43
26	1 44	86	5 44	146	9 44	206	13 44	266	17 44	326	21 44	26	1 44	1 45	1 46	1 47
27	1 48	87	5 48	147	9 48	207	13 48	267	17 48	327	21 48	27	1 48	1 49	1 50	1 51
28	1 52	88	5 52	148	9 52	208	13 52	268	17 52	328	21 52	28	1 52	1 53	1 54	1 55
29	1 56	89	5 56	149	9 56	209	13 56	269	17 56	329	21 56	29	1 56	1 57	1 58	1 59
30	2 00	90	6 00	150	10 00	210	14 00	270	18 00	330	22 00	30	2 00	2 01	2 02	2 03
31	2 04	91	6 04	151	10 04	211	14 04	271	18 04	331	22 04	31	2 04	2 05	2 06	2 07
32	2 08	92	6 08	152	10 08	212	14 08	272	18 08	332	22 08	32	2 08	2 09	2 10	2 11
33	2 12	93	6 12	153	10 12	213	14 12	273	18 12	333	22 12	33	2 12	2 13	2 14	2 15
34	2 16	94	6 16	154	10 16	214	14 16	274	18 16	334	22 16	34	2 16	2 17	2 18	2 19
35	2 20	95	6 20	155	10 20	215	14 20	275	18 20	335	22 20	35	2 20	2 21	2 22	2 23
36	2 24	96	6 24	156	10 24	216	14 24	276	18 24	336	22 24	36	2 24	2 25	2 26	2 27
37	2 28	97	6 28	157	10 28	217	14 28	277	18 28	337	22 28	37	2 28	2 29	2 30	2 31
38	2 32	98	6 32	158	10 32	218	14 32	278	18 32	338	22 32	38	2 32	2 33	2 34	2 35
39	2 36	99	6 36	159	10 36	219	14 36	279	18 36	339	22 36	39	2 36	2 37	2 38	2 39
40	2 40	100	6 40	160	10 40	220	14 40	280	18 40	340	22 40	40	2 40	2 41	2 42	2 43
41	2 44	101	6 44	161	10 44	221	14 44	281	18 44	341	22 44	41	2 44	2 45	2 46	2 47
42	2 48	102	6 48	162	10 48	222	14 48	282	18 48	342	22 48	42	2 48	2 49	2 50	2 51
43	2 52	103	6 52	163	10 52	223	14 52	283	18 52	343	22 52	43	2 52	2 53	2 54	2 55
44	2 56	104	6 56	164	10 56	224	14 56	284	18 56	344	22 56	44	2 56	2 57	2 58	2 59
45	3 00	105	7 00	165	11 00	225	15 00	285	19 00	345	23 00	45	3 00	3 01	3 02	3 03
46	3 04	106	7 04	166	11 04	226	15 04	286	19 04	346	23 04	46	3 04	3 05	3 06	3 07
47	3 08	107	7 08	167	11 08	227	15 08	287	19 08	347	23 08	47	3 08	3 09	3 10	3 11
48	3 12	108	7 12	168	11 12	228	15 12	288	19 12	348	23 12	48	3 12	3 13	3 14	3 15
49	3 16	109	7 16	169	11 16	229	15 16	289	19 16	349	23 16	49	3 16	3 17	3 18	3 19
50	3 20	110	7 20	170	11 20	230	15 20	290	19 20	350	23 20	50	3 20	3 21	3 22	3 23
51	3 24	111	7 24	171	11 24	231	15 24	291	19 24	351	23 24	51	3 24	3 25	3 26	3 27
52	3 28	112	7 28	172	11 28	232	15 28	292	19 28	352	23 28	52	3 28	3 29	3 30	3 31
53	3 32	113	7 32	173	11 32	233	15 32	293	19 32	353	23 32	53	3 32	3 33	3 34	3 35
54	3 36	114	7 36	174	11 36	234	15 36	294	19 36	354	23 36	54	3 36	3 37	3 38	3 39
55	3 40	115	7 40	175	11 40	235	15 40	295	19 40	355	23 40	55	3 40	3 41	3 42	3 43
56	3 44	116	7 44	176	11 44	236	15 44	296	19 44	356	23 44	56	3 44	3 45	3 46	3 47
57	3 48	117	7 48	177	11 48	237	15 48	297	19 48	357	23 48	57	3 48	3 49	3 50	3 51
58	3 52	118	7 52	178	11 52	238	15 52	298	19 52	358	23 52	58	3 52	3 53	3 54	3 55
59	3 56	119	7 56	179	11 56	239	15 56	299	19 56	359	23 56	59	3 56	3 57	3 58	3 59

The above table is for converting expressions in arc to their equivalent in time ; its main use in this Almanac is for the conversion of longitude for application to L.M.T. (*added* if *west*, *subtracted* if *east*) to give G.M.T. or vice versa, particularly in the case of sunrise, sunset, etc.

VI. AIR ALMANAC

EXCERPTS

THE following four pages of excerpts are taken from The Air Almanac for January-April 1966. They illustrate the present style of that publication. The Air Almanac for 1978 has the same style and format but covers a six month interval.

These excerpts provide data for the solution of all Air Almanac examples and problems in this edition of the Primer.

STARS, JAN.—APR., 1966

No.	Name	Mag.	S.H.A.	Dec.
7*	Acamar	3·1	315 46	S.40 27
5*	Achernar	0·6	335 54	S.57 25
30*	Acrux	1·1	173 49	S.62 55
19	Adhara †	1·6	255 41	S.28 56
10*	Aldebaran †	1·1	291 31	N.16 27
32*	Alioth	1·7	166 52	N.56 08
34*	Alkaid	1·9	153 27	N.49 29
55	Al Na'ir	2·2	28 29	S.47 08
15	Alnilam	1·8	276 23	S. 1 13
25*	Alphard †	2·2	218 31	S. 8 31
41*	Alphecca †	2·3	126 41	N.26 49
1*	Alpheratz †	2·2	358 21	N.28 54
51*	Altair †	0·9	62 43	N. 8 46
2	Ankaa	2·4	353 51	S.42 30
42*	Antares †	1·2	113 10	S.26 22
37*	Arcturus †	0·2	146 28	N.19 21
43	Atria	1·9	108 45	S.68 58
22	Avior	1·7	234 32	S.59 24
13	Bellatrix	1·7	279 10	N. 6 19
16*	Betelgeuse †	0·1-1·2	271 40	N. 7 24
17*	Canopus	-0·9	264 12	S.52 41
12*	Capella	0·2	281 27	N.45 58
53*	Deneb	1·3	49 56	N.45 09
28*	Denebola †	2·2	183 10	N.14 46
4*	Diphda †	2·2	349 32	S.18 11
27*	Dubhe	2·0	194 35	N.61 56
14	Elnath †	1·8	278 58	N.28 35
47	Eltanin	2·4	91 03	N.51 29
54*	Enif †	2·5	34 23	N. 9 43
56*	Fomalhaut †	1·3	16 04	S.29 48
31	Gacrux	1·6	172 41	S.56 55
29*	Gienah· †	2·8	176 29	S.17 21
35	Hadar	0·9	149 39	S.60 12
6*	Hamal †	2·2	328 42	N.23 18
48	Kaus Aust.	2·0	84 32	S.34 24
40*	Kochab	2·2	137 18	N.74 17
57	Markab †	2·6	14 14	N.15 01
8*	Menkar ·†	2·8	314 53	N. 3 57
36	Menkent	2·3	148 50	S.36 12
24*	Miaplacidus	1·8	221 47	S.69 35
9*	Mirfak	1·9	309 32	N.49 45
50*	Nunki †·	2·1	76 43	S.26 21
52*	Peacock	2·1	54 16	S.56 51
21*	Pollux †	1·2	244 11	N.28 07
20*	Procyon †	0·5	245 37	N. 5 19
46*	Rasalhague †	2·1	96 40	N.12 35
26*	Regulus †	1·3	208 21	N.12 08
11*	Rigel †	0·3	281 47	S. 8 14
38*	Rigil Kent.	0·1	140 41	S.60 42
44	Sabik †	2·6	102 54	S.15 41
3*	Schedar	2·5	350 22	N.56 21
45*	Shaula	1·7	97 11	S.37 05
18*	Sirius †	-1·6	259 05	S.16 40
33*	Spica †	1·2	159 09	S.10 59
23*	Suhail	2·2	223 19	S.43 18
49*	Vega	0·1	81 03	N.38 45
39	Zuben'ubi †	2·9	137 45	S.15 54

INTERPOLATION OF G.H.A.

Increment to be added for intervals of G.M.T. to G.H.A. of: Sun, Aries (♈) and planets ; Moon

SUN, etc.		MOON	SUN, etc.		MOON	SUN, etc.		MOON
00 00	0 00	00 00	03 17	0 50	03 25	06 37	1 40	06 52
01	0 01	00 02	21	0 51	03 29	41	1 41	06 56
05	0 02	00 06	25	0 52	03 33	45	1 42	07 00
09	0 03	00 10	29	0 53	03 37	49	1 43	07 04
13	0 04	00 14	33	0 54	03 41	53	1 44	07 08
17	0 05	00 18	37	0 55	03 45	06 57	1 45	07 13
21	0 06	00 22	41	0 56	03 49	07 01	1 46	07 17
25	0 07	00 26	45	0 57	03 54	05	1 47	07 21
29	0 08	00 31	49	0 58	03 58	09	1 48	07 25
33	0 09	00 35	53	0 59	04 02	13	1 49	07 29
37	0 10	00 39	03 57	1 00	04 06	17	1 50	07 33
41	0 11	00 43	04 01	1 01	04 10	21	1 51	07 37
45	0 12	00 47	05	1 02	04 14	25	1 52	07 42
49	0 13	00 51	09	1 03	04 19	29	1 53	07 46
53	0 14	00 55	13	1 04	04 23	33	1 54	07 50
00 57	0 15	01 00	17	1 05	04 27	37	1 55	07 54
01 01	0 16	01 04	21	1 06	04 31	41	1 56	07 58
05	0 17	01 08	25	1 07	04 35	45	1 57	08 02
09	0 18	01 12	29	1 08	04 39	49	1 58	08 06
13	0 19	01 16	33	1 09	04 43	53	1 59	08 11
17	0 20	01 20	37	1 10	04 48	07 57	2 00	08 15
21	0 21	01 24	41	1 11	04 52	08 01	2 01	08 19
25	0 22	01 29	45	1 12	04 56	05	2 02	08 23
29	0 23	01 33	49	1 13	05 00	09	2 03	08 27
33	0 24	01 37	53	1 14	05 04	13	2 04	08 31
37	0 25	01 41	04 57	1 15	05 08	17	2 05	08 35
41	0 26	01 45	05 01	1 16	05 13	21	2 06	08 40
45	0 27	01 49	05	1 17	05 17	25	2 07	08 44
49	0 28	01 53	09	1 18	05 21	29	2 08	08 48
53	0 29	01 58	13	1 19	05 25	33	2 09	08 52
01 57	0 30	02 02	17	1 20	05 29	37	2 10	08 56
02 01	0 31	02 06	21	1 21	05 33	41	2 11	09 00
05	0 32	02 10	25	1 22	05 37	45	2 12	09 04
09	0 33	02 14	29	1 23	05 41	49	2 13	09 09
13	0 34	02 18	33	1 24	05 46	53	2 14	09 13
17	0 35	02 22	37	1 25	05 50	08 57	2 15	09 17
21	0 36	02 27	41	1 26	05 54	09 01	2 16	09 21
25	0 37	02 31	45	1 27	05 58	05	2 17	09 25
29	0 38	02 35	49	1 28	06 02	09	2 18	09 29
33	0 39	02 39	53	1 29	06 06	13	2 19	09 33
37	0 40	02 43	05 57	1 30	06 10	17	2 20	09 38
41	0 41	02 47	06 01	1 31	06 15	21	2 21	09 42
45	0 42	02 51	05	1 32	06 19	25	2 22	09 46
49	0 43	02 56	09	1 33	06 23	29	2 23	09 50
53	0 44	03 00	13	1 34	06 27	33	2 24	09 54
02 57	0 45	03 04	17	1 35	06 31	37	2 25	09 58
03 01	0 46	03 08	21	1 36	06 35	41	2 26	10 00
05	0 47	03 12	25	1 37	06 39	45	2 27	
09	0 48	03 16	29	1 38	06 44	49	2 28	
13	0 49	03 20	33	1 39	06 48	53	2 29	
17	0 50	03 25	37	1 40	06 52	09 57	2 30	
03 21		03 29	06 41		06 56	10 00		

* Stars used in H.O. 249 (A.P. 3270) Vol. I.
† Stars that may be used with Vols. 2 and 3.

GREENWICH A. M. 1966 APRIL 12 (TUESDAY)

GMT	⊙ SUN GHA	Dec.	ARIES GHA ♈	VENUS −4.0 GHA	Dec.	JUPITER −1.7 GHA	Dec.	SATURN 1.4 GHA	Dec.	☽ MOON GHA	Dec.	Lat.	Moon-rise	Diff.
h m	° '	° '	° '	° '	° '	° '	° '	° '	° '	° '	° '	N	h m	m
00 00	179 45,1	N 8 26,1	199 44,7	222 47	S 9 05	114 12	N23 18	204 44	S 4 15	274 41	S26 35	•	h m	m
10	182 15,1	26,2	202 15,1	225 17		116 42		207 15		277 06	35	72	■	*
20	184 45,1	26,4	204 45,5	227 47		119 13		209 45		279 30	35	70	■	*
30	187 15,1	• 26,5	207 15,9	230 17 •		121 43 •		212 15 •		281 55 •	35	68	■	*
40	189 45,2	26,7	209 46,4	232 47		124 13		214 46		284 20	34	66	■	*
50	192 15,2	26,8	212 16,8	235 17		126 44		217 16		286 45	34	64	■	*
01 00	194 45,2	N 8 27,0	214 47,2	237 47	S 9 05	129 14	N23 18	219 47	S 4 15	289 09	S26 34	62	04 31	17
10	197 15,2	27,1	217 17,6	240 17		131 44		222 17		291 34	34	60	03 50	20
20	199 45,3	27,3	219 48,0	242 47		134 15		224 47		293 59	33	58	03 21	22
30	202 15,3	27,4	222 18,4	245 17 •		136 45 •		227 18 •		296 23 •	33	56	03 00	23
40	204 45,3	27,6	224 48,8	247 47		139 15		229 48		298 48	33	54	02 41	23
50	207 15,4	27,8	227 19,2	250 17		141 46		232 18		301 13	33	52	02 26	24
02 00	209 45,4	N 8 27,9	229 49,6	252 47	S 9 04	144 16	N23 18	234 49	S 4 15	303 37	S26 32	50	02 13	24
10	212 15,4	28,1	232 20,1	255 17		146 46		237 19		306 02	32	45	01 46	24
20	214 45,4	28,2	234 50,5	257 47		149 17		239 49		308 27	32	40	01 24	25
30	217 15,5	28,4	237 20,9	260 17 •		151 47 •		242 20 •		310 52 •	32	35	01 06	25
40	219 45,5	28,5	239 51,3	262 47		154 17		244 50		313 16	31	30	00 51	26
50	222 15,5	28,7	242 21,7	265 17		156 48		247 21		315 41	31	30	00 25	26
03 00	224 45,5	N 8 28,8	244 52,1	267 47	S 9 03	159 18	N23 18	249 51	S 4 15	318 06	S26 31	20	00 02	26
10	227 15,6	29,0	247 22,5	270 17		161 48		252 21		320 30	30	10	24 33	25
20	229 45,6	29,1	249 52,9	272 47		164 19		254 52		322 55	30	0	24 13	26
30	232 15,6	• 29,3	252 23,3	275 17 •		166 49 •		257 22 •		325 20 •	30	10	24 13	26
40	234 45,7	29,4	254 53,7	277 47		169 19		259 52		327 45	29	20	23 51	27
50	237 15,7	29,6	257 24,2	280 17		171 50		262 23 •		330 09	29	30	23 26	28
04 00	239 45,7	N 8 29,7	259 54,6	282 47	S 9 03	174 20	N23 18	264 53	S 4 15	332 34	S26 29	35	23 12	29
10	242 15,7	29,9	262 25,0	285 17		176 50		267 23		334 59	29	40	22 55	29
20	244 45,8	30,0	264 55,4	287 47		179 21		269 54		337 24	28	45	22 35	30
30	247 15,8	• 30,2	267 25,8	290 17 •		181 51 •		272 24 •		339 48 •	28	50	22 09	32
40	249 45,8	30,3	269 56,2	292 47		184 22		274 55		342 13	28			
50	252 15,8	30,5	272 26,6	295 17		186 52		277 25		344 38	27	52	21 57	32
05 00	254 45,9	N 8 30,7	274 57,0	297 47	S 9 02	189 22	N23 18	279 55	S 4 15	347 02	S26 27	54	21 42	33
10	257 15,9	30,8	277 27,4	300 17		191 53		282 26		349 27	27	56	21 26	34
20	259 45,9	31,0	279 57,9	302 47		194 23		284 56		351 52	26	58	21 06	36
30	262 16,0	• 31,1	282 28,3	305 17 •		196 53 •		287 26 •		354 17 •	26	60	20 40	38
40	264 46,0	31,3	284 58,7	307 47		199 24		289 57		356 41	26	S		
50	267 16,0	31,4	287 29,1	310 17		201 54		292 27		359 06	25	Moon's P. in A.		
06 00	269 46,0	N 8 31,6	289 59,5	312 47	S 9 01	204 24	N23 18	294 58	S 4 15	1 31	S26 25			
10	272 16,1	31,7	292 29,9	315 17		206 55		297 28		3 56	25			
20	274 46,1	31,9	295 00,3	317 47		209 25		299 58		6 20	24			
30	277 16,1	• 32,0	297 30,7	320 17 •		211 55 •		302 29 •		8 45 •	24	Alt.	Corr.	Alt.	Corr.
40	279 46,2	32,2	300 01,1	322 47		214 26		304 59		11 10	23	•	+	•	+
50	282 16,2	32,3	302 31,6	325 17		216 56		307 29		13 35	23	0	55	56	30
07 00	284 46,2	N 8 32,5	305 02,0	327 47	S 9 01	219 26	N23 18	310 00	S 4 15	15 59	S26 23	8	54	57	29
10	287 16,2	32,6	307 32,4	330 17		221 57		312 30		18 24	22	13	53	58	28
20	289 46,3	32,8	310 02,8	332 47		224 27		315 00		20 49	22	17	52	60	27
30	292 16,3	• 32,9	312 33,2	335 17 •		226 57 •		317 31 •		23 14 •	22	20	51	61	26
40	294 46,3	33,1	315 03,6	337 47		229 28		320 01		25 38	21	23	50	62	25
50	297 16,3	33,2	317 34,0	340 17		231 58		322 32		28 03	21	26	49	63	24
08 00	299 46,4	N 8 33,4	320 04,4	342 47	S 9 00	234 28	N23 18	325 02	S 4 15	30 28	S26 20	28	48	64	23
10	302 16,4	33,5	322 34,8	345 17		236 59		327 32		32 53	20	30	47	65	22
20	304 46,4	33,7	325 05,2	347 47		239 29		330 03		35 17	20	32	46	67	21
30	307 16,5	• 33,9	327 35,7	350 17 •		241 59 •		332 33 •		37 42 •	19	34	45	68	20
40	309 46,5	34,0	330 06,1	352 47		244 30		335 03		40 07	19	36	44	69	19
50	312 16,5	34,2	332 36,5	355 17		247 00		337 34		42 32	18	37	43	70	18
09 00	314 46,5	N 8 34,3	335 06,9	357 47	S 8 59	249 30	N23 18	340 04	S 4 14	44 56	S26 18	39	42	71	17
10	317 16,6	34,5	337 37,3	0 17		252 01		342 34		47 21	17	41	41	72	16
20	319 46,6	34,6	340 07,7	2 47		254 31		345 05		49 46	17	42	40	73	15
30	322 16,6	• 34,8	342 38,1	5 17 •		257 01 •		347 35 •		52 11 •	17	43	39	74	14
40	324 46,6	34,9	345 08,5	7 47		259 32		350 06		54 36	16	45	38	75	13
50	327 16,7	35,1	347 38,9	10 17		262 02		352 36		57 00	16	47	37	76	12
10 00	329 46,7	N 8 35,2	350 09,4	12 47	S 8 58	264 32	N23 18	355 06	S 4 14	59 25	S26 15	48	36	77	11
10	332 16,7	35,4	352 39,8	15 17		267 03		357 37		61 50	15	49	35	79	10
20	334 46,8	35,5	355 10,2	17 47		269 33		0 07		64 15	14	50	34	80	
30	337 16,8	• 35,7	357 40,6	20 17 •		272 03 •		2 37 •		66 39 •	14	52	33		
40	339 46,8	35,8	0 11,0	22 47		274 34		5 08		69 04	14	53	32		
50	342 16,8	36,0	2 41,4	25 17		277 04		7 38		71 29	13	54	31		
11 00	344 46,9	N 8 36,1	5 11,8	27 47	S 8 58	279 34	N23 18	10 09	S 4 14	73 54	S26 13	56	30		
10	347 16,9	36,3	7 42,2	30 17		282 05		12 39		76 19	12	57			
20	349 46,9	36,4	10 12,6	32 47		284 35		15 09		78 43	12	⊙Sun SD 16'·0		
30	352 16,9	• 36,6	12 43,1	35 17 •		287 05 •		17 40 •		81 08 •	11	Moon SD 15'		
40	354 47,0	36,7	15 13,5	37 47		289 36		20 10		83 33	11	Age 21 ◄		
50	357 17,0	36,9	17 43,9	40 17		292 06		22 40		85 58	10			

GREENWICH P. M. 1966 APRIL 12 (TUESDAY)

GMT	☉ SUN GHA	Dec.	ARIES GHA ♈	VENUS −4.0 GHA	Dec.	JUPITER −1.7 GHA	Dec.	SATURN 1.4 GHA	Dec.	☽ MOON GHA	Dec.
h m	° ′	° ′	° ′	° ′	° ′	° ′	° ′	° ′	° ′	° ′	° ′
12 00	359 47.0	N 8 37.1	20 14.3	42 47	S 8 57	294 37	N23 18	25 11	S 4 14	88 23	S26 10
10	2 17.1	37.2	22 44.7	45 16		297 07		27 41		90 47	09
20	4 47.1	37.4	25 15.1	47 46		299 37		30 11		93 12	09
30	7 17.1 •	37.5	27 45.5	50 16 •		302 08 •	•	32 42 •	•	95 37 •	08
40	9 47.1	37.7	30 15.9	52 46		304 38		35 12		98 02	08
50	12 17.2	37.8	32 46.3	55 16		307 08		37 43		100 27	07
13 00	14 47.2	N 8 38.0	35 16.7	57 46	S 8 56	309 39	N23 18	40 13	S.4 14	102 51	S26 07
10	17 17.2	38.1	37 47.2	60 16		312 09		42 43		105 16	06
20	19 47.2	38.3	40 17.6	62 46		314 39		45 14		107 41	06
30	22 17.3 •	38.4	42 48.0	65 16 •		317 10 •		47 44 •	•	110 06 •	05
40	24 47.3	38.6	45 18.4	67 46		319 40		50 14		112 31	05
50	27 17.3	38.7	47 48.8	70 16		322 10		52 45		114 55	04
14 00	29 47.4	N 8 38.9	50 19.2	72 46	S 8 56	324 41	N23 18	55 15	S 4 14	117 20	S26 04
10	32 17.4	39.0	52 49.6	75 16		327 11		57 45		119 45	03
20	34 47.4	39.2	55 20.0	77 46		329 41		60 16		122 10	03
30	37 17.4 •	39.3	57 50.4	80 16 •		332 12 •	•	62.46 •	•	124 35 •	02
40	39 47.5	39.5	60 20.9	82 46		334 42		65 17		126 59	02
50	42 17.5	39.6	62 51.3	85 16		337 12		67 47		129 24	01
15 00	44 47.5	N 8 39.8	65 21.7	87 46	S 8 55	339 43	N23 18	70 17	S 4 14	131 49	S26 01
10	47 17.5	39.9	67 52.1	90 16		342 13		72 48		134 14	26 00
20	49 47.6	40.1	70 22.5	92 46		344 43		75 18		136 39	25 59
30	52 17.6 •	40.2	72 52.9	95 16 •		347 14 •	•	77 48 •	•	139 04 •	59
40	54 47.6	40.4	75 23.3	97 46		349 44		80 19		141 28	58
50	57 17.7	40.6	77 53.7	100 16		352 14		82 49		143 53	58
16 00	59 47.7	N 8 40.7	80 24.1	102 46	S 8 54	354 45	N23 18	85 20	S 4 14	146 18	S25 57
10	62 17.7	40.9	82 54.6	105 16		357 15		87 50		148 43	57
20	64 47.7	41.0	85 25.0	107 46		359 45		90 20		151 08	56
30	67 17.8 •	41.2	87 55.4	110 16 •		2 16 •		92 51 •	•	153 33 •	55
40	69 47.8	41.3	90 25.8	112 46		4 46		95 21		155 57	55
50	72 17.8	41.5	92 56.2	115 16		7 16		97 51		158 22	54
17 00	74 47.8	N 8 41.6	95 26.6	117 46	S 8 53	9 47	N23 18	100 22	S 4 14	160 47	S25 54
10	77 17.9	41.8	97 57.0	120 16		12 17		102 52		163 12	53
20	79 47.9	41.9	100 27.4	122 46		14 47		105 22		165 37	53
30	82 17.9 •	42.1	102 57.8	125 16 •		17 18 •	•	107 53 •	•	168 02 •	52
40	84 48.0	42.2	105 28.2	127 46		19 48		110 23		170 26	51
50	87 18.0	42.4	107 58.7	130 16		22 18		112 54		172 51	51
18 00	89 48.0	N 8 42.5	110 29.1	132 46	S 8 53	24 49	N23 18	115 24	S 4 13	175 16	S25 50
10	92 18.0	42.7	112 59.5	135 16		27 19		117 54		177 41	49
20	94 48.1	42.8	115 29.9	137 46		29 49		120 25		180 06	49
30	97 18.1 •	43.0	118 00.3	140 16 •		32 20 •	•	122 55 •	•	182 31 •	48
40	99 48.1	43.1	120 30.7	142 46		34 50		125 25		184 56	48
50	102 18.1	43.3	123 01.1	145 16		37 20		127 56		187 20	47
19 00	104 48.2	N 8 43.4	125 31.5	147 46	S 8 52	39 51	N23 18	130 26	S 4 13	189 45	S25 46
10	107 18.2	43.6	128 01.9	150 16		42 21		132 56		192 10	46
20	109 48.2	43.7	130 32.4	152 46		44 51		135 27		194 35	45
30	112 18.2 •	43.9	133 02.8	155 16 •		47 22 •	•	137 57 •	•	197 00 •	44
40	114 48.3	44.1	135 33.2	157 46		49 52		140 28		199 25	44
50	117 18.3	44.2	138 03.6	160 16		52 22		142 58		201 50	43
20 00	119 48.3	N 8 44.4	140 34.0	162 46	S 8 51	54 53	N23 18	145 28	S 4 13	204 15	S25 42
10	122 18.4	44.5	143 04.4	165 16		57 23		147 59		206 39	42
20	124 48.4	44.7	145 34.8	167 46		59 54		150 29		209 04	41
30	127 18.4 •	44.8	148 05.2	170 16 •		62 24	•	152 59 •	•	211 29 •	41
40	129 48.5	45.0	150 35.6	172 46		64 54		155 30		213 54	40
50	132 18.5	45.1	153 06.0	175 16		67 25		158 00		216 19	39
21 00	134 48.5	N 8 45.3	155 36.5	177 46	S 8 51	69 55	N23 18	160 31	S 4 13	218 44	S25 39
10	137 18.5	45.4	158 06.9	180 16		72 25		163 01		221 09	38
20	139-48.5	45.6	160 37.3	182 46		74 56		165 31		223 34	37
30	142 18.6 •	45.7	163 07.7	185 16 •		77 26 •	•	168 02 •	•	225 59 •	37
40	144 48.6	45.9	165 38.1	187 46		79 56		170 32		228 23	36
50	147 18.6	46.0	168 08.5	190 16		82 27		173 02		230 48	35
22 00	149 48.7	N 8 46.2	170 38.9	192 46	S 8 50	84 57	N23 18	175 33	S 4 13	233 13	S25 34
10	152 18.7	46.3	173 09.3	195 16		87 27		178 03		235 38	34
20	154 48.7	46.5	175 39.7	197 46		89 58		180 33		238 03	33
30	157 18.7 •	46.6	178 10.2	200 16 •		92 28 •	•	183 04 •	•	240 28 •	32
40	159 48.8	46.8	180 40.6	202 46		94 58		185 34		242 53	32
50	162 18.8	46.9	183 11.0	205 16		97 29		188 05		245 18	31
23 00	164 48.8	N 8 47.1	185 41.4	207 46	S 8 49	99 59	N23 18	190 35	S 4.13	247 43	S25 30
10	167 18.8	47.2	188 11.8	210 16		102 29		193 05		250 07	30
20	169 48.9	47.4	190 42.2	212 46		105 00		195 36		252 32	29
30	172 18.9 •	47.5	193 12.6	215 16 •		107 30 •	•	198 06 •	•	254 57 •	28
40	174 48.9	47.7	195 43.0	217 46		110 00		200 36		257 22	27
50	177 19.0	47.8	198 13.4	220 16		112 31		203 07		259 47	27

Moonset / Diff panel

Lat.	Moon-set h m	Diff. m
N		
72	■	*
70	■	*
68	■	*
66	■	*
64	■	*
62	07 19	37
60	08 00	34
58	08 28	33
56	08 50	32
54	09 08	31
52	09 23	30
50	09 36	30
45	10 03	29
40	10 25	29
35	10 42	28
30	10 58	28
20	11 23	27
10	11 46	27
0	12 06	26
10	12 27	25
20	12 49	25
30	13 15	24
35	13 29	23
40	13 46	23
45	14 07	22
50	14 33	21
52	14 46	21
54	15 01	20
56	15 17	19
58	15 38	17
60	16 03	15
S		

Moon's P. in A.

Alt.	Corr. +	Alt.	Corr. +
0	55	56	30
6	54	57	29
12	53	58	29
16	52	59	27
20	51	61	26
22	50	62	25
25	49	63	24
27	48	64	23
29	47	65	22
31	46	66	21
33	45	68	20
35	44	69	19
37	43	70	18
39	42	71	17
40	41	72	16
42	40	73	15
43	39	74	14
45	38	75	13
46	37	76	12
48	36	77	11
49	35	78	10
50	34	80	
52	33		
53	32		
54	31		
56	30		
57			

☉Sun SD 16·0
Moon SD 15
Age 22⁴

SUNRISE

Lat.	April					
	5	8	11	14	17	20
°	h m	h m	h m	h m	h m	h m
N 50	05 29	05 23	05 17	05 10	05 04	04 58
45	34	29	23	18	13	05 08
40	39	34	29	25	20	16
35	42	38	34	30	26	22
30	45	42	38	35	32	28
N 20	05 51	05 48	05 46	05 43	05 41	05 38
N 10	05 55	54	52	50	49	47
0	06 00	05 59	05 58	05 57	05 56	05 56
S 10	04	06 04	06 04	06 04	06 04	06 04
20	08	09	09	10	11	12
S 30	06 13	06 14	06 16	06 18	06 20	06 22
35	16	18	20	23	25	27
40	19	22	25	28	30	33
45	22	26	29	33	37	41
50	26	31	35	40	45	49

MORNING CIVIL TWILIGHT

Lat.	April					
	5	8	11	14	17	20
°	h m	h m	h m	h m	h m	h m
N 50	04 56	04 50	04 43	04 36	04 30	04 23
45	05 05	04 59	04 53	48	42	37
40	11	05 06	05 01	04 57	04 52	47
35	17	12	08	05 04	05 00	04 56
30	21	18	14	10	07	05 04
N 20	05 29	05 26	05 23	05 21	05 18	05 16
N 10	34	32	31	29	27	26
0	39	38	37	36	35	34
S 10	43	43	42	42	42	42
20	46	47	47	48	49	50
S 30	05 49	05 51	05 52	05 54	05 56	05 57
35	50	52	55	05 57	05 59	06 01
40	51	54	05 57	06 00	06 03	06
45	52	56	06 00	03	07	11
50	54	58	03	07	12	16

SUNSET

Lat.	April					
	5	8	11	14	17	20
°	h m	h m	h m	h m	h m	h m
N 50	18 37	18 42	18 47	18 51	18 56	19 01
45	32	36	40	44	47	18 51
40	28	31	34	37	40	43
35	24	27	29	31	34	36
30	21	23	24	26	28	30
N 20	18 15	18 16	18 17	18 18	18 19	18 20
N 10	10	10	10	10	11	11
0	06	05	18 04	18 04	18 03	18 02
S 10	18 02	18 00	17 59	17 57	17 56	17 54
20	17 58	17 55	53	50	48	46
S 30	17 53	17 49	17 46	17 42	17 39	17 36
35	50	46	42	38	34	30
40	47	42	37	33	28	24
45	43	38	32	27	22	17
50	39	32	26	20	14	08

EVENING CIVIL TWILIGHT

Lat.	April					
	5	8	11	14	17	20
°	h m	h m	h m	h m	h m	h m
N 50	19 10	19 15	19 20	19 26	19 31	19 36
45	19 02	19 06	10	14	18	22
40	18 56	18 59	19 02	19 05	08	11
35	50	52	18 55	18 57	19 00	19 02
30	45	47	49	51	18 53	18 55
N 20	18 37	18 38	18 39	18 40	18 41	18 42
N 10	32	32	32	32	32	32
0	27	26	25	25	24	23
S 10	23	21	20	18	17	16
20	19	17	15	12	10	08
S 30	18 16	18 13	18 10	18 06	18 03	18 00
35	15	11	07	03	18 00	17 56
40	14	09	04	18 00	17 56	52
45	12	07	18 02	17 56	52	47
50	11	05	17 59	53	47	41

POLARIS (POLE STAR) TABLE, 1966
FOR DETERMINING THE LATITUDE FROM A SEXTANT ALTITUDE

L.H.A.♈	Q	L.H.A.♈	Q	L.H.A.♈	Q	L.H.A.♈	Q	L.H.A.♈	Q	L.H.A.♈	Q	L.H.A.♈	Q	L.H.A.♈	Q
358 40	−46	80 47	−33	112 33	− 6	142 10	+21	182 36	+48	264 12	+31	295 36	+ 4	325 19	−23
0 46	−47	82 09	−32	113 38	− 5	143 20	+22	185 04	+49	265 31	+30	296 40	+ 3	326 30	−24
3 01	−48	83 29	−31	114 42	− 4	144 31	+23	187 48	+50	266 49	+29	297 45	+ 2	327 42	−25
5 27	−49	84 47	−30	115 47	− 3	145 42	+24	190 53	+51	268 06	+28	298 49	+ 1	328 55	−26
8 08	−50	86 05	−29	116 51	− 2	146 55	+25	194 33	+52	269 22	+27	299 54	0	330 08	−27
11 10	−51	87 21	−28	117 56	− 1	148 08	+26	199 23	+53	270 37	+26	300 59	− 1	331 22	−28
14 47	−52	88 37	−27	119 00	0	149 22	+27	220 36	+52	271 51	+25	302 03	− 2	332 38	−29
19 33	−53	89 51	−26	120 05	+ 1	150 37	+28	225 26	+51	273 04	+24	303 08	− 3	333 54	−30
40 26	−52	91 04	−25	121 10	+ 2	151 53	+29	229 06	+50	274 17	+23	304 12	− 4	335 12	−31
45 12	−51	92 17	−24	122 14	+ 3	153 10	+30	232 11	+49	275 28	+22	305 17	− 5	336 30	−32
48 49	−50	93 29	−23	123 19	+ 4	154 28	+31	234 55	+48	276 39	+21	306 21	− 6	337 50	−33
51 51	−49	94 40	−22	124 23	+ 5	155 47	+32	237 23	+47	277 49	+20	307 26	− 7	339 12	−34
54 32	−48	95 50	−21	125 28	+ 6	157 08	+33	239 39	+46	278 59	+19	308 31	− 8	340 35	−35
56 58	−47	97 00	−20	126 33	+ 7	158 30	+34	241 47	+45	280 08	+18	309 36	− 9	342 00	−36
59 13	−46	98 09	−19	127 38	+ 8	159 54	+35	243 47	+44	281 17	+17	310 41	−10	343 26	−37
61 19	−45	99 18	−18	128 43	+ 9	161 20	+36	245 42	+43	282 25	+16	311 47	−11	344 55	−38
63 18	−44	100 26	−17	129 49	+10	162 48	+37	247 31	+42	283 32	+15	312 52	−12	346 26	−39
65 11	−43	101 34	−16	130 54	+11	164 17	+38	249 16	+41	284 39	+14	313 58	−13	348 00	−40
66 59	−42	102 41	−15	132 00	+12	165 49	+39	250 57	+40	285 46	+13	315 04	−14	349 37	−41
68 42	−41	103 48	−14	133 06	+13	167 24	+40	252 35	+39	286 53	+12	316 11	−15	351 17	−42
70 22	−40	104 55	−13	134 13	+14	169 02	+41	254 10	+38	287 59	+11	317 18	−16	353 00	−43
71 59	−39	106 01	−12	135 20	+15	170 43	+42	255 42	+37	289 05	+10	318 25	−17	354 48	−44
73 33	−38	107 07	−11	136 27	+16	172 28	+43	257 11	+36	290 10	+ 9	319 33	−18	356 41	−45
75 04	−37	108 12	−10	137 34	+17	174 17	+44	258 39	+35	291 16	+ 8	320 41	−19	358 40	−46
76 33	−36	109 18	− 9	138 42	+18	176 12	+45	260 05	+34	292 21	+ 7	321 50	−20	0 46	−47
77 59	−35	110 23	− 8	139 51	+19	178 12	+46	261 29	+33	293 26	+ 6	322 59	−21	3 01	−48
79 24	−34	111 28	− 7	141 00	+20	180 20	+47	262 51	+32	294 31	+ 5	324 09	−22	5 27	−49
80 47		112 33		142 10		182 36		264 12		295 36		325 19		8 08	

Q, which does not include refraction, is to be applied to the corrected sextant altitude of Polaris.
Polaris: Mag. 2·1, S.H.A. 330°00' ; Dec. N. 89°06'·6

REFRACTION					
Height above sea level in units of 1,000 ft.					
R.	0	5	10	15	20	25
Sextant Altitude						
0	90	90	90	90	90	90
1	63	59	55	51	46	41
2	33	29	26	22	19	16
3	21	19	16	14	12	10
4	16	14	12	10	8	7
5	12	11	9	8	7	5
6	10	9	7	5 50	4 50	3 50
7	8 10	6 50	5 50	4 50	4 00	3 00
8	6 50	5 50	.5 00	4 00	3 10	2 30
9	6 00	5 10	4 10	3 20	2 40	2 00

To be subtracted from sextant altitude

CORRECTION FOR DIP OF THE HORIZON									
To be subtracted from sextant altitude.									
Ht.	Dip	Ht.	Dip	Ht.	Dip	Ht.	Dip	Ht.	Dip
Ft.		Ft.		Ft.		Ft		Ft	
0		114		437		968		1,707	
2	1	137	11	481	21	1,033	31	1,792	41
6	2	162	12	527	22	1,099	32	1,880	42
12	3	189	13	575	23	1,168	33	1,970	43
21	4	218	14	625	24	1,239	34	2,061	44
31	5	250	15	677	25	1,311	35	2,155	45
43	6	283	16	731	26	1,386	36	2,251	46
58	7	318	17	787	27	1,463	37	2,349	47
75	8	356	18	845	28	1,543	38	2,449	48
93	9	395	19	906	29	1,624	39	2,551	49
114	10	437	20	968	30	1,707	40	2,655	50

VII. TABLES AND EXCERPTS FOR LOP

THE tables and excerpts on the following pages suffice for finding the solutions of the astronomical triangle required by the Primer's problems, by two different methods.

H.O. No. 211, COMPLETE

Reproduced by permission of the Oceanographic Office of the United States Navy, these are the complete tables as published by that office. They provide for the solution of the astronomical triangle under all circumstances.

The author of this Primer is solely responsible for the slight rearrangement of the tables, the principal difference from their original form being the deletion of certain figures in the interest of legibility. In most cases, on the intermediate or 0′.5 lines, two or more initial figures have been omitted and the complete figure to be used consists of the printed figures preceded by the omitted digits which appear in the line below.

When using these tables take out nearest printed function and do not interpolate except when taking out Hc. When halfway between, take out as the answer the nearest rounded minute of arc.

The "When L.H.A. (E or W)—" at the top of the left-hand pages, as in the official Third Edition of H.O. No. 211, has the same meaning as "When t (E or W)—."

Also note that the official tables are prefixed by these words of caution: "When the hour angle approaches 90°, a significant error of 1 or 2 miles may occur when computing the altitude of celestial bodies, unless attention is paid to interpolation. It is a good plan to discard those sights where the value of K is found to lie between the limits of 87° 30′ and 92° 30′."

H.O. No. 214, EXCERPT ONLY.

Two pages of data taken from Vol. IV of H.O. No. 214 provide for finding the altitudes and azimuths required by the Primer problems for line of position. The principal columns are arranged like the official tables. To permit condensing the data, the Decl. headings are at right and left.

Use Δ d method only. Take care to assume nearest whole degree of latitude, i.e., when in 39° 29′ N assume 39° not 40°. Use declination column nearest to declination of body and correct forward or backward. Select assumed position longitude that is nearest the D.R. longitude which, when applied to G.H.A., will produce L.H.A. in full degrees only. Do not interpolate for Z.

492 Primer of Navigation

When L.H.A. (E or W) is GREATER

′	A (0°)	B	A (0° 30′)	B	A (1°)	B	A (1° 30′)	B	A (2°)	B	′
0	-------	0.0	205916	1.7	175814	6.6	158208	14.9	145718	26.5	30
	383730	0.0	198	1.7	454	6.7	7967	15.1	538	26.7	
1	353627	0.0	204492	1.8	175097	6.8	157728	15.2	145358	26.9	29
	336018	0.0	3797	1.8	4742	7.0	490	15.4	179	27.1	
2	323524	0.0	203113	1.9	174391	7.1	157254	15.6	145000	27.3	28
	313833	0.0	2440	1.9	042	7.2	019	15.7	4823	27.6	
3	305915	0.0	201777	2.0	173696	7.3	156784	15.9	144646	27.8	27
	299221	0.0	124	2.1	352	7.4	552	16.1	470	28.0	
4	293421	0.0	200480	2.1	173012	7.5	156320	16.2	144295	28.3	26
	288306	0.0	199846	2.2	2674	7.6	090	16.4	120	28.5	
5	283730	0.0	199221	2.3	172339	7.8	155861	16.6	143946	28.7	25
	279591	0.1	8605	2.3	006	7.9	633	16.8	773	28.9	
6	275812	0.1	197993	2.4	171676	8.0	155406	16.9	143600	29.2	24
	2336	0.1	.399	2.4	348	8.1	180	17.1	428	29.4	
7	269118	0.1	196808	2.5	171023	8.2	154956	17.3	143257	29.6	23
	6121	0.1	225	2.6	0700	8.4	733	17.5	086	29.9	
8	263318	0.1	195650	2.7	170379	8.5	154511	17.6	142916	30.1	22
	0685	0.1	082	2.7	0061	8.6	290	17.8	747	30.4	
9	258203	0.1	194522	2.8	169745	8.7	154070	18.0	142579	30.6	21
	5855	0.2	3969	2.9	432	8.9	3851	18.2	411	30.8	
10	253627	0.2	193422	2.9	169121	9.0	153633	18.4	142243	31.1	20
	1508	0.2	2883	3.0	8811	9.1	417	18.6	077	31.3	
11	249488	0.2	192350	3.1	168505	9.3	153201	18.7	141911	31.5	19
	7558	0.2	1824	3.2	200	9.4	2987	18.9	745	31.8	
12	245709	0.3	191303	3.2	167897	9.5	152774	19.1	141581	32,0	18
	3936	0.3	0790	3.3	597	9.7	561	19.3	417	32.3	
13	242233	0.3	190282	3.4	167298	9.8	152350	19.5	141253	32.5	17
	0594	0.3	189780	3.5	002	9.9	140	19.7	090	32.8	
14	239015	0.4	189283	3.6	166708	10.1	151931	19.9	140928	33.0	16
	7491	0.4	8793	3.6	415	10.2	722	20.1	766	33.3	
15	236018	0.4	188307	3.7	166125	10.3	151515	20.3	140605	33.5	15
	4594	0.4	7827	3.8	5836	10.5	309	20.5	445	33.7	
16	233215	0.5	187353	3.9	165550	10.6	151104	20.6	140285	34.0	14
	1879	0.5	6883	4.0	265	10.8	0899	20.8	125	34.2	
17	230583	0.5	186419	4.1	164982	10.9	150696	21.0	139967	34.5	13
	229324	0.6	5959	4.1	701	11.0	494	21.2	809	34.7	
18	228100	0.6	185505	4.2	164422	11.2	150292	21.4	139651	35.0	12
	6910	0.6	055	4.3	144	11.3	092	21.6	494	35.3	
19	225752	0.7	184609	4.4	163868	11.5	149892	21.8	139338	35.5	11
	4621	0.7	168	4.5	594	11.6	693	22.0	182	35.8	
20	223525	0.7	183732	4.6	163322	11.8	149495	22.2	139027	36.0	10
	2452	0.8	300	4.7	052	11.9	299	22.4	8872	36.3	
21	221406	0.8	182872	4.8	162783	12.1	149103	22.6	138718	36.5	9
	0384	0.9	448	4.9	516	12.2	8907	22.9	564	36.8	
22	219385	0.9	182029	5.0	162250	12.4	148713	23.1	138411	37.1	8
	8409	0.9	1613	5.1	1986	12.5	520	23.3	258	37.3	
23	217455	1.0	181201	5.2	161724	12.7	148327	23.5	138106	37.6	7
	6521	1.0	0794	5.3	463	12.8	135	23.7	7955	37.9	
24	215607	1.1	180390	5.4	161204	13.0	147945	23.9	137804	38.1	6
	4711	1.1	179990	5.5	0946	13.1	755	24.1	653	38.4	
25	213834	1.1	179593	5.6	160690	13.3	147566	24.3	137504	38.6	5
	2974	1.2	200	5.7	435	13.4	377	24.5	354	38.9	
26	212130	1.2	178810	5.8	160182	13.6	147190	24.7	137205	39.2	4
	1303	1.3	424	5.9	159930	13.8	003	24.9	057	39.4	
27	210491	1.3	178042	6.0	159680	13.9	146817	25.2	136909	39.7	3
	209695	1.4	7663	6.1	431	14.1	632	25.4	761	40.0	
28	208912	1.4	177287	6.2	159184	14.2	146448	25.6	136615	40.3	2
	143	1.5	6914	6.3	8938	14.4	264	25.8	468	40.5	
29	207388	1.5	176544	6.4	158693	14.6	146081	26.0	136322	40.8	1
	6646	1.6	178	6.5	450	14.7	5899	26.2	177	41.1	
30	205916	1.7	175814	6.6	158208	14.9	145718	26.5	136032	41.4	0
	A	B	A	B	A	B	A	B	A	B	
′	179° 30′		179°		178° 30′		178° 0		177° 30′		′

Always take "Z" from Bottom of Table, except when "K" is SAME Name

than 90°, take "K" from BOTTOM of Table

'	2° 30'		3°		3° 30'		4°		4° 30'		'
	A	B	A	B	A	B	A	B	A	B	
0	136032	41.4	128120	59.6	121432	81.1	115641	105.9	110536	134.1	30
	5888	41.6	000	59.9	329	81.5	551	106.4	455	134.6	
1	135744	41.9	127880	60.2	121226	81.9	115461	106.8	110375	135.1	29
	600	42.2	760	60.6	124	82.2	371	107.3	296	135.6	
2	135457	42.5	127640	60.9	121021	82.6	115282	107.7	110216	136.1	28
	315	42.7	521	61.2	0919	83.0	192	108.1	136	136.6	
3	135173	43.0	127403	61.6	120817	83.4	115103	108.6	110057	137.1	27
	031	43.3	284	61.9	715	83.8	014	109.0	109977	137.6	
4	134890	43.6	127166	62.2	120614	84.2	114925	109.5	109898	138.1	26
	749	43.9	049	62.6	513	84.6	836	109.9	819	138.6	
5	134609	44.2	126931	62.9	120412	85.0	114747	110.4	109740	139.1	25
	469	44.4	814	63.3	311	85.4	659	110.8	662	139.6	
6	134330	44.7	126697	63.6	120211	85.8	114571	111.3	109583	140.1	24
	191	45.0	581	63.9	110	86.2	483	111.7	505	140.6	
7	134052	45.3	126465	64.3	120010	86.6	114395	112.2	109426	141.1	23
	3914	45.6	349	64.6	119910	87.0	307	112.7	348	141.7	
8	133777	45.9	126233	65.0	119811	87.4	114220	113.1	109270	142.2	22
	640	46.2	118	65.3	711	87.8	133	113.6	192	142.7	
9	133503	46.5	126003	65.7	119612	88.2	114045	114.0	109115	143.2	21
	367	46.8	5888	66.0	513	88.6	3958	114.5	037	143.7	
10	133231	47.1	125774	66.4	119415	89.0	113872	114.9	108960	144.2	20
	096	47.4	660	66.7	316	89.4	785	115.4	882	144.7	
11	132961	47.6	125546	67.1	119218	89.8	113699	115.9	108805	145.2	19
	826	47.9	433	67.4	120	90.2	612	116.3	728	145.8	
12	132692	48.2	125320	67.8	119022	90.6	113526	116.8	108651	146.3	18
	558	48.5	207	68.1	8925	91.0	440	117.3	574	146.8	
13	132425	48.8	125094	68.5	118827	91.4	113354	117.7	108498	147.3	17
	292	49.1	4982	68.8	730	91.8	269	118.2	421	147.8	
14	132159	49.4	124870	69.2	118633	92.3	113183	118.7	108345	148.4	16
	027	49.7	759	69.6	537	92.7	098	119.1	269	148.9	
15	131896	50.0	124647	69.9	118440	93.1	113013	119.6	108193	149.4	15
	764	50.3	536	70.3	344	93.5	2928	120.1	117	149.9	
16	131633	50.7	124425	70.6	118248	93.9	112843	120.5	108041	150.5	14
	503	51.0	315	71.0	152	94.3	759	121.0	7965	151.0	
17	131373	51.3	124204	71.3	118056	94.7	112674	121.5	107890	151.5	13
	243	51.6	095	71.7	7961	95.2	590	121.9	814	152.1	
18	131114	51.9	123985	72.1	117866	95.6	112506	122.4	107739	152.6	12
	0985	52.2	875	72.4	771	96.0	422	122.9	664	153.1	
19	130856	52.5	123766	72.8	117676	96.4	112338	123.4	107589	153.6	11
	728	52.8	657	73.2	581	96.9	255	123.9	514	154.2	
20	130600	53.1	123549	73.5	117487	97.3	112171	124.3	107439	154.7	10
	473	53.4	441	73.9	393	97.7	088	124.8	364	155.2	
21	130346	53.7	123332	74.3	117299	98.1	112005	125.3	107290	155.8	9
	219	54.1	225	74.6	205	98.5	1922	125.8	216	156.3	
22	130093	54.4	123117	75.0	117112	99.0	111839	126.2	107141	156.9	8
	129967	54.7	010	75.4	018	99.4	757	126.7	067	157.4	
23	129841	55.0	122903	75.8	116925	99.8	111674	127.2	106993	157.9	7
	716	55.3	796	76.1	832	100.3	592	127.7	919	158.5	
24	129591	55.7	122690	76.5	116739	100.7	111510	128.2	106846	159.0	6
	466	56.0	584	76.9	647	101.1	428	128.7	772	159.6	
25	129342	56.3	122478	77.3	116554	101.6	111346	129.2	106698	160.1	5
	218	56.6	372	77.6	462	102.0	264	129.7	625	160.6	
26	129095	56.9	122267	78.0	116370	102.4	111183	130.1	106552	161.2	4
	8972	57.3	161	78.4	278	102.9	101	130.6	479	161.7	
27	128849	57.6	122057	78.8	116187	103.3	111020	131.1	106406	162.3	3
	727	57.9	1952	79.2	096	103.7	0939	131.6	333	162.8	
28	128605	58.2	121848	79.5	116004	104.2	110858	132.1	106260	163.4	2
	483	58.6	743	79.9	5913	104.6	777	132.6	187	163.9	
29	128362	58.9	121639	80.3	115823	105.0	110696	133.1	106115	164.5	1
	240	59.2	536	80.7	732	105.5	616	133.6	043	165.0	
30	128120	59.6	121432	81.1	115641	105.9	110536	134.1	105970	165.6	0
	A	B	A	B	A	B	A	B	A	B	
	177°		176° 30'		176°		175° 30'		175°		'

and GREATER than Latitude, in which case take "Z" from TOP of Table

When L.H.A. (E or W) is GREATER

′	5°		5° 30′		6°		6° 30′		7°		′
	A	B	A	B	A	B	A	B	A	B	
0	105970	**165.6**	101843	**200.4**	98076	**239**	94614	**280**	91411	**325**	30
	898	**166.1**	777	**201.0**	017	**239**	559	**281**	359	**326**	
1	105826	**166.7**	101712	**201.6**	97957	**240**	94503	**281**	91308	**326**	29
	754	**167.2**	646	**202.2**	897	**241**	448	**282**	257	**327**	
2	105683	**167.8**	101581	**202.8**	97837	**241**	94393	**283**	91205	**328**	28
	611	**168.4**	516	**203.5**	777	**242**	338	**284**	154	**329**	
3	105539	**168.9**	101451	**204.1**	97717	**243**	94283	**284**	91103	**330**	27
	468	**169.4**	386	**204.7**	658	**243**	228	**285**	052	**330**	
4	105397	**170.0**	101321	**205.3**	97598	**244**	94173	**286**	91001	**331**	26
	325	**170.6**	256	**205.9**	539	**245**	118	**287**	90950	**332**	
5	105254	**171.1**	101192	**206.5**	97480	**245**	94063	**287**	90899	**333**	25
	183	**171.7**	127	**207.1**	420	**246**	009	**288**	848	**333**	
6	105113	**172.3**	101063	**207.8**	97361	**247**	93954	**289**	90798	**334**	24
	042	**172.8**	0998	**208.4**	302	**247**	899	**289**	747	**335**	
7	104971	**173.4**	100934	**209.0**	97243	**248**	93845	**290**	90696	**336**	23
	901	**174.0**	870	**209.6**	184	**249**	790	**291**	646	**337**	
8	104830	**174.5**	100806	**210.3**	97126	**249**	93736	**292**	90595	**337**	22
	760	**175.1**	742	**210.9**	067	**250**	682	**292**	545	**338**	
9	104690	**175.7**	100678	**211.5**	97008	**251**	93628	**293**	90494	**339**	21
	620	**176.2**	614	**212.1**	96950	**251**	573	**294**	444	**340**	
10	104550	**176.8**	100550	**212.8**	96891	**252**	93519	**295**	90394	**341**	20
	480	**177.4**	487	**213.4**	833	**253**	465	**295**	344	**341**	
11	104411	**178.0**	100423	**214.0**	96774	**253**	93411	**296**	90293	**342**	19
	341	**178.5**	360	**214.6**	716	**254**	358	**297**	243	**343**	
12	104272	**179.1**	100296	**215.3**	96658	**255**	93304	**298**	90193	**344**	18
	202	**179.7**	233	**215.9**	600	**255**	250	**298**	143	**345**	
13	104133	**180.3**	100170	**216.5**	96542	**256**	93196	**299**	90093	**345**	17
	064	**180.8**	107	**217.2**	484	**257**	143	**300**	044	**346**	
14	103995	**181.4**	100044	**217.8**	96426	**257**	93089	**301**	89994	**347**	16
	926	**182.0**	99981	**218.4**	368	**258**	036	**301**	944	**348**	
15	103857	**182.6**	99918	**219.1**	96310	**259**	92982	**302**	89894	**349**	15
	788	**183.2**	856	**219.7**	253	**260**	929	**303**	845	**349**	
16	103720	**183.7**	99793	**220.3**	96195	**260**	92876	**304**	89795	**350**	14
	651	**184.3**	731	**221.0**	138	**261**	823	**304**	746	**351**	
17	103583	**184.9**	99668	**221.6**	96080	**262**	92769	**305**	89696	**352**	13
	515	**185.5**	606	**222.3**	023	**262**	716	**306**	647	**353**	
18	103447	**186.1**	99544	**222.9**	95966	**263**	92663	**307**	89597	**353**	12
	379	**186.7**	481	**223.5**	909	**264**	610	**307**	548	**354**	
19	103311	**187.2**	99420	**224.2**	95851	**264**	92558	**308**	89499	**355**	11
	243	**187.8**	357	**224.8**	795	**265**	505	**309**	450	**356**	
20	103175	**188.4**	99296	**225.5**	95737	**266**	92452	**310**	89401	**357**	10
	107	**189.0**	234	**226.1**	681	**267**	399	**310**	352	**357**	
21	103040	**189.6**	99172	**226.8**	95624	**267**	92347	**311**	89303	**358**	9
	2973	**190.2**	110	**227.4**	567	**268**	294	**312**	254	**359**	
22	102905	**190.8**	99049	**228.1**	95510	**269**	92242	**313**	89205	**360**	8
	838	**191.4**	98988	**228.7**	454	**269**	189	**313**	156	**361**	
23	102771	**192.0**	98926	**229.4**	95397	**270**	92137	**314**	89107	**362**	7
	704	**192.6**	865	**230.0**	341	**271**	085	**315**	059	**362**	
24	102637	**193.2**	98804	**230.7**	95285	**271**	92032	**316**	89010	**363**	6
	570	**193.8**	743	**231.3**	228	**272**	91980	**316**	88961	**364**	
25	102504	**194.4**	98682	**232.0**	95172	**273**	91928	**317**	88913	**365**	5
	437	**195.0**	621	**232.6**	116	**274**	876	**318**	864	**366**	
26	102371	**195.6**	98560	**233.3**	95060	**274**	91824	**319**	88816	**366**	4
	304	**196.2**	499	**233.9**	004	**275**	772	**319**	767	**367**	
27	102238	**196.8**	98439	**234.6**	94948	**276**	91720	**320**	88719	**368**	3
	172	**197.4**	378	**235.3**	892	**276**	668	**321**	671	**369**	
28	102106	**198.0**	98318	**235.9**	94836	**277**	91617	**322**	88623	**370**	2
	040	**198.6**	257	**236.6**	781	**278**	565	**323**	574	**371**	
29	101974	**199.2**	98197	**237.2**	94725	**279**	91514	**323**	88526	**371**	1
	908	**199.8**	137	**237.9**	670	**279**	462	**324**	478	**372**	
30	101843	200.4	98076	238.6	94614	280	91411	325	88430	373	0
	A	B	A	B	A	B	A	B	A	B	
′	174° 30′		174°		173° 30′		173°		172° 30′		

Always take "Z" from Bottom of Table, except when "K" is SAME Name

than 90°, take "K" from BOTTOM of Table

′	7° 30′ A	B	8° A	B	8° 30′ A	B	9° A	B	9° 30′ A	B	′
0	88430	373	85644	425	83030	480	80567	538	78239	600	30
	382	374	599	426	82987	481	527	539	201	601	
1	88334	375	85555	426	82945	482	80487	540	78164	602	29
	286	376	510	427	903	482	447	541	126	603	
2	88239	376	85465	428	861	483	80407	542	78088	604	28
	191	377	420	429	819	484	368	543	051	605	
3	88143	378	85376	430	82777	485	80328	544	78013	606	27
	096	379	331	431	735	486	288	545	77976	607	
4	88048	380	85286	432	82693	487	80249	546	77938	608	26
	001	381	242	433	651	488	209	547	901	609	
5	87953	381	85197	434	82609	489	80170	548	77863	610	25
	906	382	153	434	567	490	130	549	826	611	
6	87858	383	85108	435	82526	491	80091	550	77788	612	24
	811	384	064	436	484	492	051	551	751	614	
7	87764	385	85020	437	82442	493	80012	552	77714	615	23
	716	386	84976	438	400	494	79973	553	677	616	
8	87669	387	84931	439	82359	495	79933	554	77639	617	22
	622	387	887	440	317	496	894	555	602	618	
9	87575	388	84843	441	82276	497	79855	556	77565	619	21
	528	389	799	442	234	498	816	557	528	620	
10	87481	390	84755	443	82193	499	79777	558	77491	621	20
	434	391	711	444	151	500	737	559	454	622	
11	87387	392	84667	444	82110	501	79698	560	77417	623	19
	341	392	623	445	069	502	659	561	380	624	
12	87294	393	84579	446	82027	503	79620	562	77343	625	18
	247	394	535	447	81986	504	581	563	306	626	
13	87201	395	84492	448	81945	504	79542	564	77269	627	17
	154	396	448	449	904	505	503	565	232	629	
14	87107	397	84404	450	81863	506	79465	566	77195	630	16
	061	398	361	451	821	507	426	567	158	631	
15	87015	399	84317	452	81780	508	79387	568	77122	632	15
	86968	399	273	453	739	509	348	569	085	633	
16	86922	400	84230	454	81698	510	79309	570	77048	634	14
	876	401	186	454	657	511	271	571	011	635	
17	86829	402	84143	455	81617	512	79232	573	76975	636	13
	783	403	100	456	576	513	193	574	938	637	
18	86737	404	84056	457	81535	514	79155	575	76902	638	12
	691	405	013	458	494	515	116	576	865	639	
19	86645	405	83970	459	81453	516	79078	577	76828	641	11
	599	406	927	460	413	517	039	578	792	642	
20	86553	407	83884	461	81372	518	79001	579	76756	643	10
	507	408	840	462	331	519	78962	580	719	644	
21	86461	409	83797	463	81291	520	78924	581	76683	645	9
	415	410	754	464	250	521	886	582	646	646	
22	86370	411	83711	465	81210	522	78847	583	76610	647	8
	324	411	668	466	169	523	809	584	574	648	
23	86278	412	83626	467	81129	524	78771	585	76537	649	7
	233	413	583	467	088	525	733	586	501	650	
24	86187	414	83540	468	81048	526	78694	587	76465	652	6
	142	415	497	469	008	527	656	588	429	653	
25	86096	416	83455	470	80967	528	78618	589	76393	654	5
	051	417	412	471	927	529	580	590	357	655	
26	86006	418	83369	472	80887	530	78542	591	76320	656	4
	85960	418	327	473	847	531	504	592	284	657	
27	85915	419	83284	474	80807	532	78466	593	76248	658	3
	870	420	242	475	767	533	428	594	212	659	
28	85825	421	83199	476	80727	534	78390	595	76176	660	2
	779	422	157	477	687	535	352	597	141	661	
29	85734	423	83114	478	80647	536	78315	598	76105	663	1
	689	424	072	479	607	537	277	599	069	664	
30	85644	425	83030	480	80567	538	78239	600	76033	665	0
	A	B	A	B	A	B	A	B	A	B	′
′	172°		171° 30′		171°		170° 30′		170°		

and GREATER than Latitude, in which case take "Z" from TOP of Table

When L.H.A. (E or W) is GREATER

r	10° A	B	10° 30′ A	B	11° A	B	11° 30′ A	B	12° A	B	r
0	76033	665	73937	733	71940	805	70034	881	68212	960	30
	75997	666	03	735	08	807	03	882	182	961	
1	75961	667	73869	736	71875	808	69972	883	68153	962	29
	26	668	35	737	43	809	41	885	23	964	
2	75890	669	73801	738	71810	810	69910	886	68093	965	28
	54	670	767	739	778	811	879	887	64	966	
3	75819	672	73733	740	71746	813	69849	888	68034	968	27
	783	673	699	742	13	814	18	890	05	969	
4	75747	674	73665	743	71681	815	69787	891	67975	970	26
	12	675	31	744	49	816	56	892	45	972	
5	75676	676	73597	745	71616	818	69725	894	67916	973	25
	41	677	63	746	584	819	694	895	886	974	
6	75605	678	73530	747	71552	820	69664	896	67857	976	24
	570	679	496	749	20	821	33	897	28	977	
7	75534	680	73462	750	71488	823	69602	899	67798	978	23
	499	682	29	751	55	824	571	900	69	980	
8	75464	683	73395	752	71423	825	69541	901	67739	981	22
	28	684	61	753	391	826	10	903	10	982	
9	75393	685	73328	755	71359	828	69479	904	67681	984	21
	58	686	294	756	27	829	49	905	51	985	
10	75322	687	73260	757	71295	830	69418	907	67622	987	20
	287	688	27	758	63	831	387	908	593	988	
11	75252	690	73193	759	71231	833	69357	909	67563	989	19
	17	691	60	761	199	834	26	910	34	991	
12	75182	692	73127	762	71167	835	69296	912	67505	992	18
	47	693	093	763	35	836	65	913	476	993	
13	75112	694	73060	764	71104	838	69235	914	67447	995	17
	077	695	26	765	072	839	04	916	17	996	
14	75042	696	72993	766	71040	840	69174	917	67388	997	16
	07	698	60	768	08	841	44	918	59	999	
15	74972	699	72926	769	70976	843	69113	920	67330	1000	15
	37	700	893	770	45	844	083	921	01	1002	
16	74902	701	72860	771	70913	845	69053	922	67272	1003	14
	867	702	27	772	881	846	22	924	43	1004	
17	74832	703	72794	774	70850	848	68992	925	67214	1006	13
	797	704	60	775	18	849	62	926	185	1007	
18	74763	706	72727	776	70786	850	68931	928	67156	1008	12
	28	707	694	777	55	851	01	929	27	1010	
19	74693	708	72661	779	70723	853	68871	930	67098	1011	11
	59	709	28	780	692	854	41	932	69	1013	
20	74624	710	72595	781	70660	855	68811	933	67040	1014	10
	589	711	62	782	29	856	781	934	11	1015	
21	74555	712	72529	783	70597	858	68750	935	66982	1017	9
	20	714	496	785	66	859	20	937	53	1018	
22	74486	715	72463	786	70534	860	68690	938	66925	1020	8
	51	716	30	787	03	862	60	939	896	1021	
23	74417	717	72397	788	70471	863	68630	941	66867	1022	7
	382	718	65	790	40	864	00	942	38	1024	
24	74348	719	72332	791	70409	865	68570	943	66810	1025	6
	13	721	299	792	377	867	40	945	781	1026	
25	74279	722	72266	793	70346	868	68510	946	66752	1028	5
	45	723	34	794	15	869	480	947	24	1029	
26	74210	724	72201	796	70284	870	68450	949	66695	1031	4
	176	725	168	797	52	872	21	950	66	1032	
27	74142	726	72135	798	70221	873	68391	951	66638	1033	3
	07	728	03	799	190	874	61	953	09	1035	
28	74073	729	72070	800	70159	876	68331	954	66580	1036	2
	39	730	38	802	28	877	01	955	52	1038	
29	74005	731	72005	803	70097	878	68272	957	66523	1039	1
	73971	732	71973	804	65	879	42	958	495	1040	
30	73937	733	71940	805	70034	881	68212	960	66466	1042	0
	A	B	A	B	A	B	A	B	A	B	
	169° 30′		169°		168° 30′		168°		167° 30′		

Always take "Z" from Bottom of Table, except when "K" is SAME Name

than 90°, take "K" from BOTTOM of Table

′	12° 30′ A	B	13° A	B	13° 30′ A	B	14° A	B	14° 30′ A	B	′
0	66466	1042	64791	1128	63181	1217	61632	1310	60140	1406	30
	38	43	64	29	55	18	07	11	16	07	
1	66409	1045	64736	1130	63129	1220	61582	1313	60091	1409	29
	381	46	09	32	03	21	56	14	67	11	
2	66352	1047	64682	1133	63076	1223	61531	1316	60042	1412	28
	24	49	55	35	50	24	06	17	18	14	
3	66296	1050	64627	1136	63024	1226	61481	1319	59994	1416	27
	67	52	00	38	62998	27	55	21	69	17	
4	66239	1053	64573	1139	62971	1229	61430	1322	59945	1419	26
	11	54	46	41	45	30	05	24	21	21	
5	66182	1056	64518	1142	62919	1232	61380	1325	59896	1422	25
	54	57	491	44	893	34	55	27	72	24	
6	66126	1059	64464	1145	62867	1235	61330	1329	59848	1425	24
	098	60	37	47	41	37	04	30	24	27	
7	66069	1061	64410	1148	62815	1238	61279	1332	59800	1429	23
	41	63	383	50	789	40	54	33	775	30	
8	66013	1064	64356	1151	62763	1241	61229	1335	59751	1432	22
	65985	66	29	52	37	43	04	36	27	34	
9	65957	1067	64302	1154	62711	1244	61179	1338	59703	1435	21
	28	69	275	55	685	46	54	40	679	37	
10	65900	1070	64248	1157	62659	1247	61129	1341	59654	1439	20
	872	71	21	58	33	49	04	43	30	40	
11	65844	1073	64194	1160	62607	1250	61079	1344	59606	1442	19
	16	74	67	61	581	52	54	46	582	44	
12	65788	1076	64140	1163	62555	1253	61029	1348	59558	1445	18
	60	77	13	64	29	55	04	49	34	47	
13	65732	1079	64086	1166	62503	1257	60979	1351	59510	1449	17
	04	80	59	67	477	58	54	52	486	50	
14	65676	1081	64032	1169	62451	1260	60929	1354	59462	1452	16
	48	83	05	70	25	-61	04	56	38	54	
15	65620	1084	63978	1172	62400	1263	60879	1357	59414	1455	15
	592	86	52	73	374	64	55	59	390	57	
16	65564	1087	63925	1175	62348	1266	60830	1360	59366	1459	14
	37	89	898	76	22	67	05	62	42	60	
17	65509	1090	63871	1178	62296	1269	60780	1364	59318	1462	13
	481	91	45	79	71	70	55	65	294	64	
18	65453	1093	63818	1181	62245	1272	60730	1367	59270	1465	12
	25	94	791	82	19	74	06	68	46	67	
19	65398	1096	63764	1184	62194	1275	60681	1370	59222	1469	11
	70	97	38	85	68	77	56	72	198	70	
20	65342	1099	63711	1187	62142	1278	60631	1373	59175	1472	10
	14	1100	684	88	17	80	07	75	51	74	
21	65287	1101	63658	1190	62091	1281	60582	1377	59127	1475	9
	59	03	31	91	65	83	57	78	03	77	
22	65231	1104	63605	1193	62040	1284	60533	1380	59079	1479	8
	04	06	578	94	14	86	08	81	55	80	
23	65176	1107	63551	1196	61989	1288	60483	1383	59032	1482	7
	48	09	25	97	63	89	59	85	08	84	
24	65121	1110	63498	1199	61938	1291	60434	1386	58984	1485	6
	093	12	72	1200	12	92	10	88	60	87	
25	65066	1113	63445	1202	61887	1294	60385	1390	58937	1489	5
	38	14	19	03	61	95	60	91	13	90	
26	65011	1116	63392	1205	61836	1297	60336	1393	58889	1492	4
	64983	17	66	06	10	99	11	94	66	94	
27	64956	1119	63340	1208	61785	1300	60287	1396	58842	1495	3
	28	20	13	09	59	01	62	98	18	97	
28	64901	1122	63287	1211	61734	1303	60238	1399	58795	1499	2
	873	23	60	12	09	05	13	1401	71	1500	
29	64846	1125	63234	1214	61683	1306	60189	1403	58748	1502	1
	19	26	08	15	58	08	64	04	24	04	
30	64791	1128	63181	1217	61632	1310	60140	1406	58700	1506	0
	A	B	A	B	A	B	A	B	A	B	′
	167°		166° 30′		166°		165° 30′		165°		

and GREATER than Latitude, in which case take "Z" from TOP of Table

When L.H.A. (E or W) is GREATER

′	15° A	15° B	15° 30′ A	15° 30′ B	16° A	16° B	16° 30′ A	16° 30′ B	17° A	17° B	′
0	58700	1506	57310	1609	55966	1716	54666	1826	53406	1940	30
	677	07	287	11	44	18	44	28	386	42	
1	58653	1509	57265	1612	55922	1719	54623	1830	53365	1944	29
	30	11	42	14	00	21	02	32	44	46	
2	58606	1512	57219	1616	55878	1723	54581	1834	53324	1948	28
	583	14	196	18	56	25	59	36	03	50	
3	58559	1516	57174	1619	55834	1727	54538	1837	53283	1952	27
	36	17	51	21	12	28	17	39	62	54	
4	58512	1519	57128	1623	55790	1730	54496	1841	53241	1956	26
	489	21	06	25	68	32	74	43	21	58	
5	58465	1523	57083	1627	55746	1734	54453	1845	53200	1960	25
	42	24	60	28	25	36	32	47	180	62	
6	58418	1526	57038	1630	55703	1738	54411	1849	53159	1964	24
	395	28	15	32	681	39	390	51	39	66	
7	58372	1529	56992	1634	55659	1741	54368	1853	53118	1967	23
	48	31	70	35	37	43	47	54	098	69	
8	58325	1533	56947	1637	55615	1745	54326	1856	53077	1971	22
	02	34	25	39	593	47	05	58	57	73	
9	58278	1536	56902	1641	55572	1749	54284	1860	53036	1975	21
	55	38	880	42	50	50	63	62	16	77	
10	58232	1540	56857	1644	55528	1752	54242	1864	52995	1979	20
	08	41	35	46	06	54	20	66	75	81	
11	58185	1543	56812	1648	55484	1756	54199	1868	52954	1983	19
	62	45	790	49	63	58	78	70	34	85	
12	58138	1546	56767	1651	55441	1760	54157	1871	52914	1987	18
	15	48	45	53	19	61	36	73	893	89	
13	58092	1550	56722	1655	55397	1763	54115	1875	52873	1991	17
	69	52	00	57	76	65	094	77	52	93	
14	58046	1553	56677	1658	55354	1767	54073	1879	52832	1995	16
	22	55	55	60	32	69	52	81	12	97	
15	57999	1557	56632	1662	55311	1771	54031	1883	52791	1999	15
	76	59	10	64	289	72	10	85	71	2001	
16	57953	1560	56588	1665	55267	1774	53989	1887	52751	2003	14
	30	62	65	67	46	76	68	89	30	05	
17	57907	1564	56543	1669	55224	1778	53947	1890	52710	2007	13
	884	65	21	71	02	80	26	92	690	09	
18	57860	1567	56498	1673	55181	1782	53905	1894	52670	2010	12
	37	69	76	74	59	83	884	96	49	12	
19	57814	1571	56454	1676	55138	1785	53864	1898	52629	2014	11
	791	72	31	78	16	87	43	1900	09	16	
20	57768	1574	56409	1680	55095	1789	53822	1902	52588	2018	10
	45	76	387	82	73	91	01	04	68	20	
21	57722	1578	56365	1683	55051	1793	53780	1906	52548	2022	9
	609	79	42	85	30	95	59	08	28	24	
22	57676	1581	56320	1687	55008	1796	53738	1910	52508	2026	8
	53	83	298	89	54987	98	18	11	487	28	
23	57630	1584	56276	1691	54965	1800	53697	1913	52467	2030	7
	07	86	54	92	44	02	76	15	47	32	
24	57584	1588	56231	1694	54922	1804	53655	1917	52427	2034	6
	61	90	09	96	01	06	34	19	07	36	
25	57538	1591	56187	1698	54880	1808	53614	1921	52387	2038	5
	16	93	65	1700	58	09	593	23	66	40	
26	57493	1595	56143	1701	54837	1811	53572	1925	52346	2042	4
	70	97	21	03	15	13	51	27	26	44	
27	57447	1598	56099	1705	54794	1815	53531	1929	52306	2046	3
	24	1600	76	07	73	17	10	31	286	48	
28	57401	1602	56054	1709	54751	1819	53489	1933	52266	2050	2
	378	04	32	10	30	21	68	35	46	52	
29	57356	1605	56010	1712	54708	1823	53448	1936	52226	2054	1
	33	07	55988	14	687	24	27	38	06	56	
30	57310	1609	55966	1716	54666	1826	53406	1940	52186	2058	0
	A	B	A	B	A	B	A	B	A	B	
′	164° 30′		164°		163° 30′		163°		162° 30′		′

Always take "Z" from Bottom of Table, except when "K" is SAME Name

than 90°, take "K" from BOTTOM of Table

′	17° 30′ A	17° 30′ B	18° A	18° B	18° 30′ A	18° 30′ B	19° A	19° B	19° 30′ A	19° 30′ B	′
0	52186	2058	51002	2179	49852	2304	48736	2433	47650	2565	30
	66	60	50982	81	33	06	17	35	33	68	
1	52146	2062	50963	2183	49815	2309	48699	2437	47615	2570	29
	26	64	43	85	796	11	81	39	597	72	
2	52106	2066	50924	2188	49777	2313	48662	2442	47579	2574	28
	086	68	05	90	58	15	44	44	61	76	
3	52066	2070	50885	2192	49739	2317	48626	2446	47544	2579	27
	46	72	66	94	20	19	08	48	26	81	
4	52026	2074	50846	2196	49702	2321	48589	2450	47508	2583	26
	06	76	27	98	683	23	71	53	490	85	
5	51986	2078	50808	2200	49664	2325	48553	2455	47472	2588	25
	66	80	788	02	45	28	34	57	55	90	
6	51946	2082	50769	2204	49626	2330	48516	2459	47437	2592	24
	26	84	50	06	08	32	498	61	19	94	
7	51906	2086	50730	2208	49589	2334	48480	2463	47402	2597	23
	886	88	11	10	70	36	62	66	384	99	
8	51867	2090	50692	2212	49551	2338	48443	2468	47366	2601	22
	47	92	73	14	33	40	25	70	48	03	
9	51827	2094	50653	2216	49514	2343	48407	2472	47331	2606	21
	07	96	34	18	495	45	389	74	13	08	
10	51787	2098	50615	2221	49477	2347	48371	2477	47295	2610	20
	67	2100	596	23	58	49	52	79	78	13	
11	51747	2102	50576	2225	49439	2351	48334	2481	47260	2615	19
	28	04	57	27	21	53	16	83	42	17	
12	51708	2106	50538	2229	49402	2355	48298	2485	47225	2619	18
	688	08	19	31	383	57	80	88	07	22	
13	51668	2110	50499	2233	49365	2360	48262	2490	47189	2624	17
	49	12	80	35	46	62	44	92	72	26	
14	51629	2114	50461	2237	49327	2364	48225	2494	47154	2628	16
	09	16	42	39	09	66	07	96	37	31	
15	51589	2118	50423	2241	49290	2368	48189	2499	47119	2633	15
	70	20	04	43	71	70	71	2501	01	35	
16	51550	2122	50385	2246	49253	2372	48153	2503	47084	2637	14
	30	24	65	48	34	75	35	05	66	40	
17	51510	2126	50346	2250	49216	2377	48117	2507	47049	2642	13
	491	28	27	52	197	79	099	10	31	44	
18	51471	2130	50308	2254	49179	2381	48081	2512	47014	2646	12
	51	32	289	56	60	83	63	14	46996	49	
19	51432	2134	50270	2258	49141	2385	48045	2516	46978	2651	11
	12	36	51	60	23	87	27	19	61	53	
20	51392	2138	50232	2262	49104	2390	48009	2521	46943	2656	10
	73	41	13	64	086	92	47991	23	26	58	
21	51353	2143	50194	2266	49067	2394	47973	2525	46908	2660	9
	34	45	75	69	49	96	55	27	891	62	
22	51314	2147	50156	2271	49030	2398	47937	2530	46873	2665	8
	294	49	37	73	12	2400	19	32	56	67	
23	51275	2151	50117	2275	48993	2403	47901	2534	46839	2669	7
	55	53	098	77	75	05	883	36	21	72	
24	51236	2155	50080	2279	48957	2407	47865	2539	46804	2674	6
	16	57	61	81	38	09	47	41	786	76	
25	51197	2159	50042	2283	48920	2411	47829	2543	46769	2678	5
	77	61	23	85	01	13	11	45	51	81	
26	51158	2163	50004	2287	48883	2416	47793	2547	46734	2683	4
	38	65	49985	90	64	18	75	50	16	85	
27	51119	2167	49966	2292	48846	2420	47758	2552	46699	2688	3
	099	69	47	94	28	22	40	54	82	90	
28	51080	2171	49928	2296	48809	2424	47722	2556	46664	2692	2
	60	73	09	98	791	26	04	59	47	94	
29	51041	2175	49890	2300	48772	2429	47686	2561	46630	2697	1
	21	77	71	02	54	31	68	63	12	99	
30	51002	2179	49852	2304	48736	2433	47650	2565	46595	2701	0
	A	B	A	B	A	B	A	B	A	B	
′	162°		161° 30′		161°		160° 30′		160°		′

and GREATER than Latitude, in which case take "Z" from TOP of Table

When L.H.A. (E or W) is GREATER

′	20° A	20° B	20° 30′ A	20° 30′ B	21° A	21° B	21° 30′ A	21° 30′ B	22° A	22° B	′
0	46595	2701	45567	2841	44567	2985	43592	3132	42642	3283	30
	77	04	51	44	51	88	76	35	27	86	
1	46560	2706	45534	2846	44534	2990	43560	3137	42611	3288	29
	43	08	17	48	18	92	44	40	596	91	
2	46525	2711	45500	2851	44501	2994	43528	3142	42580	3294	28
	08	13	483	53	485	97	12	45	64	96	
3	46491	2715	45466	2855	44468	2999	43496	3147	42549	3299	27
	73	17	49	58	52	3002	80	50	33	3301	
4	46456	2720	45433	2860	44436	3004	43464	3152	42518	3304	26
	39	22	16	62	19	07	48	55	02	06	
5	46422	2724	45399	2865	44403	3009	43432	3157	42486	3309	25
	04	27	82	67	386	12	16	60	71	12	
6	46387	2729	45365	2870	44370	3014	43400	3162	42455	3314	24
	70	31	48	72	54	16	385	65	40	17	
7	46353	2734	45332	2874	44337	3019	43369	3167	42424	3319	23
	35	36	15	77	21	21	53	70	09	22	
8	46318	2738	45298	2879	44305	3024	43337	3172	42393	3324	22
	01	41	81	81	288	26	21	75	78	27	
9	46284	2743	45265	2884	44272	3029	43305	3177	42362	3329	21
	66	45	48	86	56	31	289	80	47	32	
10	46249	2748	45231	2889	44239	3033	43273	3182	42331	3335	20
	32	50	14	91	23	36	57	85	16	37	
11	46215	2752	45198	2893	44207	3038	43241	3187	42300	3340	19
	198	55	81	96	190	41	25	90	285	42	
12	46181	2757	45164	2898	44174	3043	43210	3192	42269	3345	18
	63	59	47	2901	58	46	194	95	54	47	
13	46146	2761	45131	2903	44142	3048	43178	3197	42238	3350	17
	29	64	14	05	25	51	62	3200	23	53	
14	46112	2766	45097	2908	44109	3053	43146	3202	42207	3355	16
	095	68	81	10	093	56	30	05	192	58	
15	46078	2771	45064	2913	44077	3058	43114	3207	42176	3360	15
	61	73	47	15	60	60	099	10	61	63	
16	46043	2775	45031	2917	44044	3063	43083	3212	42145	3366	14
	26	78	14	20	28	65	67	15	30	68	
17	46009	2780	44997	2922	44012	3068	43051	3217	42115	3371	13
	45992	82	81	24	43995	70	35	20	099	73	
18	45975	2785	44964	2927	43979	3073	43020	3222	42084	3376	12
	58	87	47	29	63	75	04	25	68	79	
19	45941	2789	44937	2932	43947	3078	42988	3227	42053	3381	11
	24	92	14	34	31	80	72	30	38	84	
20	45907	2794	44898	2936	43914	3083	42956	3233	42022	3386	10
	890	97	81	39	898	85	41	35	07	89	
21	45873	2799	44864	2941	43882	3088	42925	3238	41991	3391	9
	56	2801	48	44	66	90	09	40	76	94	
22	45839	2804	44831	2946	43850	3092	42893	3243	41961	3597	8
	22	06	15	49	34	95	78	45	45	99	
23	45805	2808	44798	2951	43818	3097	42862	3248	41930	3402	7
	788	11	82	53	01	3100	46	50	15	04	
24	45771	2813	44765	2956	43785	3102	42830	3253	41899	3407	6
	54	15	48	58	69	05	15	55	84	10	
25	45737	2818	44732	2961	43753	3107	42799	3258	41869	3412	5
	20	20	15	63	37	10	83	60	53	15	
26	45703	2822	44699	2965	43721	3112	42768	3263	41838	3418	4
	686	25	82	68	05	15	52	66	23	20	
27	45669	2827	44666	2970	43689	3117	42736	3268	41808	3423	3
	52	29	49	73	73	20	21	71	792	25	
28	45635	2832	44633	2975	43657	3122	42705	3273	41777	3428	2
	18	34	16	78	41	25	689	76	62	31	
29	45601	2836	44600	2980	43624	3127	42674	3278	41746	3433	1
	584	39	583	82	08	30	58	81	31	36	
30	45567	2841	44567	2985	43592	3132	42642	3283	41716	3438	0
	A	B	A	B	A	B	A	B	A	B	
′	159° 30′		159°		158° 30′		158°		157° 30′		′

Always take "Z" from Bottom of Table, except when "K" is SAME Name

than 90°, take "K" from BOTTOM of Table

′	22° 30′ A	B	23° A	B	23° 30′ A	B	24° A	B	24° 30′ A	B	′
0	41716	3438	40812	3597	39930	3760	39069	3927	38227	4098	30
	01	41	797	3600	15	63	54	30	13	4101	
1	41685	3444	40782	3603	39901	3766	39040	3932	38200	4103	29
	70	46	68	05	886	68	26	35	186	06	
2	41655	3449	40753	3608	39872	3771	39012	3938	38172	4109	28
	40	52	38	11	57	74	38998	41	58	12	
3	41625	3454	40723	3613	39843	3777	38984	3944	38144	4115	27
	09	57	08	16	28	79	69	47	30	18	
4	41594	3459	40693	3619	39814	3782	38955	3949	38117	4121	26
	79	62	78	22	799	85	41	52	03	24	
5	41564	3465	40664	3624	39785	3788	38927	3955	38089	4127	25
	49	67	49	27	71	90	13	58	75	29	
6	41533	3470	40634	3630	39756	3793	38899	3961	38061	4132	24
	18	73	19	32	42	96	85	64	48	35	
7	41503	3475	40604	3635	39727	3799	38871	3966	38034	4138	23
	488	78	590	38	13	3801	56	69	20	41	
8	41473	3480	40575	3640	39698	3804	38842	3972	38006	4144	22
	58	83	60	43	84	07	28	75	37992	47	
9	41443	3486	40545	3646	39669	3810	38814	3978	37979	4150	21
	27	88	30	48	55	13	00	81	65	53	
10	41412	3491	40516	3651	39641	3815	38786	3983	37951	4155	20
	397	94	01	54	26	18	72	86	37	58	
11	41382	3496	40486	3657	39612	3821	38758	3989	37924	4161	19
	67	99	71	59	597	24	44	92	10	64	
12	41352	3502	40457	3662	39583	3826	38730	3995	37896	4167	18
	37	04	42	65	69	29	16	98	82	70	
13	41322	3507	40427	3667	39554	3832	38702	4000	37869	4173	17
	07	09	13	70	40	35	688	03	55	76	
14	41291	3512	40398	3673	39525	3838	38674	4006	37841	4179	16
	76	15	83	76	11	40	60	09	28	82	
15	41261	3517	40368	3678	39497	3843	38645	4012	37814	4185	15
	46	20	54	81	82	46	31	15	00	87	
16	41231	3523	40339	3684	39468	3849	38617	4017	37786	4190	14
	16	25	24	86	54	51	03	20	73	93	
17	41201	3528	40310	3689	39439	3854	38589	4023	37759	4196	13
	186	31	295	92	25	57	75	26	45	99	
18	41171	3533	40280	3695	39411	3860	38561	4029	37732	4202	12
	56	36	66	97	396	63	47	32	18	05	
19	41141	3539	40251	3700	39382	3865	38533	4035	37704	4208	11
	26	41	36	03	68	68	20	37	691	11	
20	41111	3544	40222	3705	39353	3871	38506	4040	37677	4214	10
	096	47	07	08	39	74	492	43	63	17	
21	41081	3549	·40192	3711	39325	3876	38478	4046	37650	4220	9
	66	52	78	14	11	79	64	49	36	22	
22	41051	3555	40163	3716	39296	3882	38450	4052	37623	4225	8
	36	57	49	19	82	85	36	55	09	28	
23	41021	3560	40134	3722	39268	3888	38422	4057	37595	4231	7
	06	63	19	25	54	90	08	60	82	34	
24	40991	3565	40105	3727	39239	3893	38394	4063	37568	4237	6
	76	68	090	30	25	96	80	66	54	40	
25	40961	3571	40076	3733	39211	3899	38366	4069	37541	4243	5
	46	73	61	35	197	3902	52	72	27	46	
26	40931	3576	40046	3738	39182	3904	38338	4075	37514	4249	4
	16	79	32	41	68	07	24	78	00	52	
27	40902	3581	40017	3744	39154	3910	38311	4080	37486	4255	3
	887	84	03	46	40	13	297	83	73	58	
28	40872	3587	39988	3749	39125	3916	38283	4086	37459	4261	2
	57	89	74	52	11	18	69	89	46	64	
29	40842	3592	39959	3755	39097	3921	38255	4092	37432	4266	1
	27	95	45	57	83	24	41	95	19	69	
30	40812	3597	39930	3760	39069	3927	38227	4098	37405	4272	0
	A	B	A	B	A	B	A	B	A	B	
′	157°		156° 30′		156°		155° 30′		155°		′

and GREATER than Latitude, in which case take "Z" from TOP of Table

When L.H.A. (E or W) is GREATER

′	25° A	25° B	25° 30′ A	25° 30′ B	26° A	26° B	26° 30′ A	26° 30′ B	27° A	27° B	′
0	37405	4272	36602	4451	35816	4634	35047	4821	34295	5012	30
	392	75	588	54	03	37	35	24	83	15	
1	37378	4278	36575	4457	35790	4640	35022	4827	34270	5018	29
	65	81	62	60	77	43	09	30	58	22	
2	37351	4284	36549	4463	35764	4646	34997	4833	34246	5025	28
	37	87	35	66	51	49	84	37	33	28	
3	37324	4290	36522	4469	35738	4651	34971	4840	34221	5031	27
	10	93	09	72	25	56	59	43	09	34	
4	37297	4296	36496	4475	35712	4659	34946	4846	34196	5038	26
	83	99	83	78	699	62	33	49	84	41	
5	37270	4302	36469	4481	35686	4665	34921	4852	34172	5044	25
	56	05	56	84	74	68	08	56	59	47	
6	37243	4308	36443	4487	35661	4671	34896	4859	34147	5051	24
	29	11	30	90	48	74	83	62	34	54	
7	37216	4314	36417	4493	35635	4677	34870	4865	34122	5057	23
	03	17	03	96	22	80	58	68	10	60	
8	37189	4320	36390	4499	35609	4683	34845	4871	34097	5064	22
	76	23	77	4503	596	86	32	75	85	67	
9	37162	4326	36364	4506	35583	4690	34820	4878	34073	5070	21
	49	29	51	09	71	93	07	81	61	73	
10	37135	4332	36338	4512	35558	4696	34795	4884	34048	5076	20
	22	34	25	15	45	99	82	87	36	80	
11	37108	4337	36311	4518	35532	4702	34770	4890	34024	5083	19
	095	40	298	21	19	05	57	94	11	86	
12	37081	4343	36285	4524	35506	4708	34744	4897	33999	5089	18
	68	.46	72	27	493	11	32	4900	87	93	
13	37055	4349	36259	4530	35481	4714	34719	4903	33974	5096	17
	41	52	46	33	68	18	07	06	62	99	
14	37028	4355	36233	4536	35455	4721	34694	4910	33950	5102	16
	14	58	20	39	42	24	82	13	38	06	
15	37001	4361	36206	4542	35429	4727	34669	4916	33925	5109	15
	36988	64	193	45	17	30	57	19	13	12	
16	36974	4367	36180	4548	35404	4733	34644	4922	33901	5115	14
	61	70	67	51	391	36	32	25	889	19	
17	36948	4373	36154	4554	35378	4739	34619	4929	33876	5122	13
	34	76	41	57	65	42	07	32	64	25	
18	36921	4379	36128	4560	35353	4746	34594	4935	33852	5128	12
	07	82	15	63	40	49	82	38	40	32	
19	36894	4385	36102	4566	35327	4752	34569	4941	33827	5135	11
	81	88	089	69	14	55	57	45	15	38	
20	36867	4391	36076	4573	35302	4758	34544	4948	33803	5142	10
	54	94	63	76	289	61	32	51	791	45	
21	36841	4397	36050	4579	35276	4764	34519	4954	33779	5148	9
	27	4400	37	82	63	69	07	57	66	51	
22	36814	4403	36024	4585	35251	4771	34494	4961	33754	5155	8
	01	06	11	88	38	74	82	64	42	58	
23	36787	4409	35998	4591	35225	4777	34469	4967	33730	5161	7
	74	12	85	94	12	80	57	70	17	64	
24	36761	4415	35972	4597	35200	4783	34445	4973	33705	5168	6
	47	18	59	4600	187	86	32	77	693	71	
25	36734	4421	35946	4603	35174	4789	34420	4980	33681	5174	5
	21	24	33	06	61	93	07	83	69	78	
26	36708	4427	35920	4609	35149	4796	34395	4986	33657	5181	4
	694	30	07	12	36	99	82	89	44	84	
27	36681	4433	35894	4615	35123	4802	34370	4993	33632	5187	3
	68	36	81	19	11	05	57	96	20	91	
28	36655	4439	35868	4622	35098	4808	34345	4999	33608	5194	2
	41	42	55	25	85	11	32	5002	596	97	
29	36628	4445	35842	4628	35073	4815	34320	5005	33584	5200	1
	15	48	29	31	60	18	08	09	72	04	
30	36602	4451	35816	4634	35047	4821	34295	5012	33559	5207	0
	A	B	A	B	A	B	A	B	A	B	
	154° 30′		154°		153° 30′		153°		152° 30′		′

Always take "Z" from Bottom of Table, except when "K" is SAME Name

than 90°, take "K" from BOTTOM of Table

′	27° 30′ A	27° 30′ B	28° A	28° B	28° 30′ A	28° 30′ B	29° A	29° B	29° 30′ A	29° 30′ B	′
0	33559	5207	32839	5406	32134	5610	31443	5818	30766	6030	30
	47	10	27	10	22	14	31	22	55	34	
1	33535	5214	32815	5413	32110	5617	31420	5825	30744	6038	29
	23	17	03	17	099	20	09	29	33	41	
2	33511	5220	32792	5420	32087	5624	31397	5832	30721	6045	28
	499	24	80	23	76	27	86	36	10	48	
3	33487	5227	32768	5426	32064	5631	31375	5839	30699	6052	27
	75	30	56	30	52	34	63	43	88	55	
4	33462	5233	32744	5433	32041	5638	31352	5846	30677	6059	26
	50	37	32	37	29	41	40	50	66	62	
5	33438	5240	32720	5440	32018	5645	31329	5853	30655	6066	25
	26	43	09	43	06	48	18	57	43	70	
6	33414	5247	32697	5447	31994	5651	31306	5860	30632	6073	24
	02	50	85	50	83	55	295	64	21	77	
7	33390	5253	32673	5454	31971	5658	31284	5867	30610	6080	23
	78	57	61	57	60	62	72	71	599	84	
8	33366	5260	32649	5460	31948	5665	31261	5874	30588	6088	22
	54	63	38	64	36	69	50	78	77	91	
9	33342	5266	32625	5467	31925	5672	31238	5881	30566	6095	21
	30	70	14	70	13	75	27	85	55	98	
10	33318	5275	32602	5474	31902	5679	31216	5888	30544	6102	20
	06	77	590	77	890	82	04	92	32	06	
11	33293	5280	32579	5481	31879	5686	31193	5895	30521	6109	19
	81	83	67	84	67	89	82	99	10	13	
12	33269	5287	32555	5487	31856	5693	31170	5902	30499	6116	18
	57	90	43	91	44	96	59	06	88	20	
13	33245	5293	32532	5494	31833	5700	31148	5909	30477	6124	17
	33	96	20	98	21	03	37	13	66	27	
14	33221	5300	32508	5501	31809	5707	31125	5917	30455	6131	16
	09	03	496	04	798	10	14	20	44	34	
15	33197	5306	32484	5508	31786	5714	31103	5924	30433	6138	15
	85	10	73	11	75	17	091	27	22	42	
16	33173	5313	32461	5515	31763	5720	31080	5931	30411	6145	14
	61	16	49	18	52	24	69	34	00	49	
17	33149	5320	32438	5521	31740	5727	31058	5938	30389	6153	13
	37	23	26	25	29	31	46	41	78	56	
18	33125	5326	32414	5528	31717	5734	31035	5945	30367	6160	12
	13	30	02	32	06	38	24	48	56	63	
19	33101	5333	32391	5535	31694	5741	31013	5952	30345	6167	11
	089	36	79	38	83	45	01	55	34	71	
20	33077	5340	32367	5542	31672	5748	30990	5959	30322	6174	10
	65	43	55	45	60	52	79	63	11	78	
21	33054	5346	32344	5549	31648	5755	30968	5966	30300	6181	9
	42	50	32	52	37	59	56	70	289	85	
22	33030	5353	32320	5555	31626	5762	30945	5973	30278	6189	8
	18	56	09	59	14	66	34	77	67	92	
23	33006	5360	32297	5562	31603	5769	30923	5980	30256	6196	7
	32994	63	85	66	591	73	12	84	45	6200	
24	32982	5366	32274	5569	31580	5776	30900	5988	30235	6203	6
	70	70	62	72	69	80	889	91	24	07	
25	32958	5373	32250	5576	31557	5783	30878	5995	30213	6210	5
	46	76	39	79	46	87	67	98	02	14	
26	32934	5380	32227	5583	31534	5790	30856	6002	30191	6218	4
	22	83	15	86	23	94	44	05	80	21	
27	32910	5386	32204	5590	31511	5797	30833	6009	30169	6225	3
	898	90	192	93	00	5801	22	12	58	29	
28	32887	5393	32180	5596	31488	5804	30811	6016	30147	6232	2
	75	96	69	5600	77	08	00	20	36	36	
29	32863	5400	32157	5603	31466	5811	30788	6023	30125	6240	1
	51	03	45	07	54	15	77	27	14	43	
30	32839	5406	32134	5610	31443	5818	30766	6030	30103	6247	0
	A	B	A	B	A	B	A	B	A	B	
	152°		151° 30′		151°		150° 30′		150°		′

and GREATER than Latitude, in which case take "Z" from TOP of Table

When L.H.A. (E or W) is GREATER

′	30° A	30° B	30° 30′ A	30° 30′ B	31° A	31° B	31° 30′ A	31° 30′ B	32° A	32° B	′
0	30103	6247	29453	6468	28816	6693	28191	6923	27579	7158	30
	·092	51	42	72	06	97	81	27	69	62	
1	30081	6254	29432	6475	28795	6701	28171	6931	27559	7166	29
	70	58	21	79	85	05	61	35	49	70	
2	30059	6262	29410	6483	28774	6709	28150	6939	27539	7174	28
	48	65	399	87	63	12	40	43	28	78	
3	30037	6269	29389	6490	28753	6716	28130	6947	27518	7182	27
	26	73	78	94	43	20	19	51	08	86	
4	30016	6276	29367	6498	28732	6724	28109	6954	27498	7190	26
	05	80	57	6501	22	28	099	58	88	93	
5	29994	6284	29346	6505	28711	6731	28089	6962	27478	7197	25
	83	87	35	09	01	35	78	66	68	7201	
6	29972	6291	29325	6513	28690	6739	28068	6970	27458	7205	24
	61	94	14	16	80	43	58	74	48	09	
7	29950	6298	29303	6520	28669	6747	28047	6978	27438	7213	23
	39	6302	293	24	59	50	37	82	28	17	
8	29928	6305	29282	6528	28648	6754	28027	6985	27418	7221	22
	17	09	71	31	38	58	17	89	08	25	
9	29907	6313	29261	6535	28627	6762	28006	6993	27398	7229	21
	896	16	50	39	17	66	27996	97	87	33	
10	29885	6320	29239	6543	28606	6770	27986	7001	27377	7237	20
	74	24	29	46	596	73	76	05	67	41	
11	29863	6328	29218	6550	28586	6777	27965	7009	27357	7245	19
	52	31	07	54	75	81	55	13	47	49	
12	29841	6335	29197	6558	28565	6785	27945	7017	27337	7253	18
	31	39	86	61	54	89	35	21	27	57	
13	29820	6342	29175	6565	28544	6791	27925	7024	27317	7261	17
	09	46	65	69	33	96	14	28	07	65	
14	29798	6350	29154	6573	28523	6800	27904	7032	27297	7269	16
	87	53	44	76	13	04	894	36	87	73	
15	29776	6357	29133	6580	28502	6808	27884	7040	27277	7277	15
	66	61	22	84	492	12	74	44	67	81	
16	29755	6364	29112	6588	28481	6815	27863	7048	27257	7285	14
	44	68	01	91	71	19	53	52	47	89	
17	29733	6372	29091	6595	28461	6823	27843	7056	27237	7293	13
	22	75	80	99	50	27	33	60	27	97	
18	29711	6379	29069	6603	28440	6831	27823	7064	27217	7301	12
	01	83	59	06	29	35	12	67	07	05	
19	29690	6386	29048	6610	28419	6839	27802	7071	27197	7309	11
	79	90	38	14	09	42	792	75	87	13	
20	29668	6394	29027	6618	28398	6846	27782	7079	27177	7317	10
	57	98	16	22	88	50	72	83	67	21	
21	29647	6401	29006	6625	28378	6854	27761	7087	27157	7325	9
	36	05	28995	29	67	58	51	91	47	29	
22	29625	6409	28985	6633	28357	6862	27741	7095	27137	7333	8
	14	12	74	37	46	65	31	99	27	37	
23	29604	6416	28964	6640	28336	6869	27721	7103	27117	7341	7
	593	20	53	44	26	75	11	07	07	45	
24	29582	6423	28942	6648	28315	6877	27701	7111	27098	7349	6
	71	27	32	52	05	81	690	15	88	53	
25	29560	6431	28921	6655	28295	6885	27680	7118	27078	7357	5
	50	35	11	59	84	89	70	22	68	61	
26	29539	6438	28900	6663	28274	6893	27660	7126	27058	7365	4
	28	42	890	67	64	96	50	30	48	69	
27	29517	6446	28879	6671	28253	6900	27640	7134	27038	7373	3
	07	49	69	74	43	04	30	38	28	77	
28	29496	6453	28858	6678	28233	6908	27619	7142	27018	7381	2
	85	57	48	82	22	12	09	46	08	85	
29	29475	6461	28837	6686	28212	6916	27599	7150	26998	7389	1
	64	64	27	90	02	20	89	54	88	93	
30	29453	6468	28816	6693	28191	6923	27579	7158	26978	7397	0
	A	B	A	B	A	B	A	B	A	B	
′	149° 30′		149°		148° 30′		148°		147° 30′		′

Always take "Z" from Bottom of Table, except when "K" is SAME Name

than 90°, take "K" from BOTTOM of Table

′	32° 30′ A	B	33° A	B	33° 30′ A	B	34° A	B	34° 30′ A	B	′
0	26978	7397	26389	7641	25811	7889	25244	8143	24687	8401	30
	68	7401	79	45	01	93	35	47	78	05	
1	26958	7405	26370	7649	25792	7898	25225	8151	24669	8409	29
	49	09	60	53	82	7902	16	55	60	14	
2	26939	7413	26350	7657	25773	7906	25206	8160	24650	8418	28
	29	17	40	61	63	10	197	64	41	22	
3	26919	7421	26331	7665	25754	7914	25188	8168	24632	8427	27
	09	25	21	70	44	19	78	72	23	31	
4	26899	7429	26311	7674	25735	7923	25169	8177	24614	8435	26
	89	33	02	78	25	27	60	81	05	40	
5	26879	7437	26292	7682	25716	7931	25150	8185	24595	8444	25
	69	41	82	86	06	35	41	89	86	48	
6	26860	7445	26273	7690	25697	7940	25132	8194	24577	8453	24
	50	49	63	94	87	44	22	98	68	57	
7	26840	7453	26253	7698	25678	7948	25113	8202	24559	8461	23
	30	58	44	7702	68	52	04	07	50	66	
8	26820	7462	26234	7707	25659	7956	25094	8211	24540	8470	22
	10	66	24	11	49	61	85	15	31	75	
9	26800	7470	26214	7715	25640	7965	25076	8219	24522	8479	21
	790	74	05	19	30	69	66	24	13	83	
10	26781	7478	26195	7723	25621	7973	25057	8228	24504	8488	20
	71	82	85	27	11	77	48	32	495	92	
11	26761	7486	26176	7731	25602	7982	25038	8237	24486	8496	19
	51	90	66	36	592	86	29	41	77	8501	
12	26741	7494	26157	7740	25583	7990	25020	8245	24467	8505	18
	31	98	47	44	73	94	11	49	58	10	
13	26722	7502	26137	7748	25564	7998	25001	8254	24449	8514	17
	12	06	28	52	54	8003	24992	58	40	18	
14	26702	7510	26118	7756	25545	8007	24983	8262	24431	8523	16
	692	14	08	60	36	11	73	67	22	27	
15	26682	7518	26099	7764	25526	8015	24964	8271	24413	8531	15
	72	22	89	69	17	20	55	75	04	36	
16	26663	7526	26079	7773	25507	8024	24946	8280	24395	8540	14
	53	31	70	77	498	28	36	84	85	45	
17	26643	7535	26060	7781	25488	8032	24927	8288	24376	8549	13
	33	39	51	85	79	37	18	92	67	53	
18	26623	7543	26041	7789	25469	8041	24909	8297	24358	8558	12
	14	47	31	93	60	45	899	8301	49	62	
19	26604	7551	26022	7798	25451	8049	24890	8305	24340	8567	11
	594	55	12	7802	41	53	81	10	31	71	
20	26584	7559	26002	7806	25432	8058	24872	8314	24322	8575	10
	74	63	25993	10	22	62	62	18	13	80	
21	26565	7567	25983	7814	25413	8066	24853	8323	24304	8584	9
	55	71	74	18	03	70	44	27	295	89	
22	26545	7575	25964	7823	25394	8075	24835	8331	24286	8593	8
	35	79	54	27	85	79	25	36	76	97	
23	26526	7584	25945	7831	25375	8083	24816	8340	24267	8602	7
	16	88	35	35	66	87	07	44	58	06	
24	26506	7592	25926	7839	25356	8091	24798	8349	24249	8611	6
	496	96	16	43	47	96	88	53	40	15	
25	26486	7600	25907	7848	25338	8100	24779	8357	24231	8619	5
	77	04	897	52	28	04	70	62	22	24	
26	26467	7608	25887	7856	25319	8108	24761	8366	24213	8628	4
	57	12	78	60	09	13	52	70	04	33	
27	26447	7616	25868	7864	25300	8117	24742	8375	24195	8637	3
	38	20	59	68	291	21	33	79	86	41	
28	26428	7625	25849	7873	25281	8125	24724	8383	24177	8646	2
	18	29	40	77	72	30	15	88	68	50	
29	26409	7633	25830	7881	25263	8134	24706	8392	24159	8655	1
	399	37	21	85	53	38	696	96	50	59	
30	26389	7641	25811	7889	25244	8143	24687	8401	24141	8663	0
	A	B	A	B	A	B	A	B	A	B	
′	147°		146° 30′		146°		145° 30′		145°		′

and GREATER than Latitude, in which case take "Z" from TOP of Table

When L.H.A. (E or W) is GREATER

′	35° A	35° B	35° 30′ A	35° 30′ B	36° A	36° B	36° 30′ A	36° 30′ B	37° A	37° B	′
0	24141	8663	23605	8931	23078	9204	22561	9482	22054	9765	30
	32	68	596	36	69	09	53	87	45	70	
1	24123	8672	23587	8940	23061	9213	22544	9492	22037	9775	29
	14	77	78	45	52	18	36	96	29	79	
2	24105	8681	23569	8949	23043	9223	22527	9501	22020	9784	28
	096	86	60	54	35	27	19	05	12	89	
3	24087	8690	23551	8958	23026	9232	22510	9510	22003	9794	27
	78	94	43	63	17	36	0	15	21995	98	
4	24069	8699	23534	8967	23009	9241	22493	9520	21987	9803	26
	60	8703	25	72	00	46	84	24	78	08	
5	24051	8708	23516	8976	22991	9250	22476	9529	21970	9813	25
	42	12	07	81	83	55	67	34	62	18	
6	24033	8717	23498	8986	22974	9259	22459	9538	21953	9822	24
	24	21	90	90	65	64	50	43	45	27	
7	24015	8726	23481	8995	22957	9269	22442	9548	21937	9832	23
	06	30	72	99	48	73	33	52	28	37	
8	23997	8734	23463	9004	22939	9278	22425	9557	21920	9843	22
	88	39	54	08	31	82	16	62	12	46	
9	23979	8743	23446	9013	22922	9287	22408	9566	21903	9851	21
	70	48	37	17	13	92	399	71	895	56	
10	23961	8752	23428	9022	22905	9296	22391	9576	21887	9861	20
	52	57	19	26	896	9301	82	81	78	65	
11	23943	8761	23410	9031	22887	9305	22374	9585	21870	9870	19
	34	66	02	35	79	10	66	90	62	75	
12	23925	8770	23393	9040	22870	9315	22357	9595	21853	9880	18
	16	75	84	44	62	19	49	99	45	85	
13	23907	8779	23375	9049	22853	9324	22340	9604	21837	9889	17
	898	83	66	54	44	29	32	09	28	94	
14	23889	8788	23358	9058	22836	9333	22323	9614	21820	9899	16
	80	92	49	63	27	38	15	18	12	9904	
15	23871	8797	23340	9067	22818	9342	22306	9623	21803	9909	15
	63	8801	31	72	10	47	298	28	795	13	
16	23854	8806	23323	9076	22801	9352	22289	9632	21787	9918	14
	45	10	14	81	793	56	81	37	78	23	
17	23836	8815	23305	9085	22784	9361	22272	9642	21770	9928	13
	27	19	296	90	75	66	64	47	62	33	
18	23818	8824	23288	9094	22767	9370	22256	9651	21754	9937	12
	09	28	79	99	58	75	47	56	45	42	
19	23800	8833	23270	9104	22750	9380	22239	9661	21737	9947	11
	791	37	61	08	41	84	30	65	29	52	
20	23782	8842	23252	9113	22732	9389	22222	9670	21720	9957	10
	73	46	44	17	24	94	13	75	12	62	
21	23764	8850	23235	9122	22715	9398	22205	9680	21704	9966	9
	55	55	26	26	07	9403	197	84	696	71	
22	23747	8859	23218	9131	22698	9407	22188	9689	21687	9976	8
	38	64	09	36	90	12	80	94	79	81	
23	23729	8868	23200	9140	22681	9417	22171	9699	21671	9986	7
	20	73	191	45	72	21	63	9703	62	90	
24	23711	8877	23183	9149	22664	9426	22154	9708	21654	9995	6
	02	82	74	54	55	31	46	13	46	10000	
25	23693	8886	23165	9158	22647	9435	22138	9718	21638	10005	5
	84	91	56	63	38	40	29	22	29	10	
26	23675	8895	23148	9168	22630	9445	22121	9727	21621	10015	4
	67	8900	39	72	21	49	12	32	13	19	
27	23658	8904	23130	9177	22612	9454	22104	9737	21605	10024	3
	49	09	22	81	04	59	096	41	596	29	
28	23640	8913	23113	9186	22595	9463	22087	9746	21588	10034	2
	31	18	04	90	87	68	79	51	80	39	
29	23622	8922	23095	9195	22578	9473	22070	9756	21572	10044	1
	13	27	87	9200	70	77	62	60	63	49	
30	23605	8931	23078	9204	22561	9482	22054	9765	21555	10053	0
	A	B	A	B	A	B	A	B	A	B	
′	144° 30′		144°		143° 30′		143°		142° 30′		′

Always take "Z" from Bottom of Table, except when "K" is SAME Name;

than 90°, take "K" from BOTTOM of Table

	37° 30'		38°		38° 30'		39°		39° 30'		
′	A	B	A	B	A	B	A	B	A	B	′
0	21555	10053	21066	10347	20585	10646	20113	10950	19649	11259	30
	47	58	58	52	77	51	05	55	41	65	
1	21539	10063	21050	10357	20569	10656	20097	10960	19634	11270	29
	31	68	42	62	61	61	89	65	26	75	
2	21522	10073	21033	10367	20553	10666	20082	10970	19618	11280	28
	14	78	25	72	45	71	74	75	11	85	
3	21506	10082	21017	10376	20537	10676	20066	10980	19603	11291	27
	498	87	09	81	29	81	58	86	595	96	
4	21489	10092	21001	10386	20522	10686	20050	10991	19588	11301	26
	81	97	20993	91	14	91	43	96	80	06	
5	21473	10102	20985	10396	20506	10696	20035	11001	19572	11311	25
	65	07	77	401	498	701	27	06	65	17	
6	21457	10112	20969	10406	20490	10706	20019	11011	19557	11322	24
	48	16	61	11	82	11	12	16	49	27	
7	21440	10121	20953	10416	20474	10716	20004	11021	19541	11332	23
	32	26	45	21	66	21	19996	27	34	38	
8	21424	10131	20937	10426	20458	10726	19988	11032	19527	11343	22
	16	36	29	31	50	31	80	37	19	48	
9	21407	10141	20921	10436	20442	10736	19973	11042	19511	11353	21
	399	46	13	41	35	41	65	47	04	59	
10	21391	10151	20905	10446	20427	10746	19957	11052	19496	11364	20
	83	55	897	51	19	51	49	57	88	69	
11	21375	10160	20888	10456	20411	10756	19942	11063	19481	11374	19
	67	65	80	61	03	61	34	68	73	80	
12	21358	10170	20872	10466	20395	10767	19926	11073	19466	11385	18
	50	75	64	71	87	72	19	78	58	90	
13	21342	10180	20856	10476	20379	10777	19911	11083	19450	11395	17
	34	85	48	81	71	82	03	88	43	400	
14	21326	10190	20840	10486	20364	10787	19895	11094	19435	11406	16
	18	95	32	91	56	92	88	99	28	11	
15	21309	10199	20824	10496	20348	10797	19880	11104	19420	11416	15
	01	204	16	500	40	802	72	09	12	22	
16	21293	10209	20808	10505	20332	10807	19864	11114	19405	11427	14
	85	14	00	10	24	12	57	19	397	32	
17	21277	10219	20792	10515	20316	10817	19849	11124	19390	11437	13
	69	24	84	20	09	22	41	30	82	43	
18	21260	10229	20776	10525	20301	10827	19834	11135	19375	11448	12
	52	34	68	30	293	32	26	40	67	53	
19	21244	10239	20760	10535	20285	10838	19818	11145	19359	11458	11
	36	43	52	40	77	43	10	50	52	64	
20	21228	10248	20744	10545	20269	10848	19803	11156	19344	11469	10
	20	53	36	50	61	53	795	61	37	74	
21	21212	10258	20728	10555	20254	10858	19787	11166	19329	11479	9
	04	63	20	60	46	58	79	71	21	85	
22	21195	10268	20712	10565	20238	10868	19772	11176	19314	11490	8
	87	73	04	70	30	73	64	81	06	95	
23	21179	10278	20696	10575	20222	10878	19756	11187	19299	11501	7
	71	83	88	80	14	83	49	92	91	06	
24	21163	10288	20680	10585	20207	10888	19741	11197	19284	11511	6
	55	93	72	90	199	94	33	202	76	16	
25	21147	10298	20665	10595	20191	10899	19726	11207	19269	11522	5
	39	302	57	600	83	904	18	13	61	27	
26	21131	10307	20649	10605	20175	10909	19710	11218	19253	11532	4
	22	12	41	10	67	14	03	23	46	37	
27	21114	10317	20633	10615	20160	10919	19695	11228	19238	11543	3
	06	22	25	20	52	24	87	33	31	48	
28	21098	10327	20617	10625	20144	10929	19680	11239	19223	11553	2
	90	32	09	30	36	34	72	44	16	59	
29	21082	10337	20601	10635	20128	10939	19664	11249	19208	11564	1
	74	42	593	40	21	45	57	54	01	69	
30	21066	10347	20585	10646	20113	10950	19649	11259	19193	11575	0
	A	B	A	B	A	B	A	B	A	B	
	142°		141° 30'		141°		140° 30'		140°		′

and GREATER than Latitude, in which case take "Z" from TOP of Table

When L.H.A, (E or W) is GREATER

′	40° A	40° B	40° 30′ A	40° 30′ B	41° A	41° B	41° 30′ A	41° 30′ B	42° A	42° B	′
0	19193	11575	18746	11895	18306	12222	17873	12554	17449	12893	30
	86	80	38	901	298	28	66	60	42	98	
1	19178	11585	18731	11906	18291	12233	17859	12566	17435	12904	29
	71	90	23	12	84	38	52	71	28	10	
2	19163	11596	18716	11917	18277	12244	17845	12577	17421	12915	28
	56	601	09	22	69	49	38	82	14	21	
3	19148	11606	18701	11928	18262	12255	17831	12588	17407	12927	27
	41	12	694	33	55	60	24	93	00	32	
4	19133	11617	18686	11939	18248	12266	17816	12599	17393	12938	26
	26	22	79	44	40	71	09	605	86	44	
5	19118	11628	18672	11949	18233	12277	17802	12610	17379	12950	25
	11	33	64	55	26	82	795	16	72	55	
6	19103	11638	18657	11960	18219	12288	17788	12622	17365	12961	24
	096	44	50	66	11	93	81	27	58	67	
7	19088	11649	18642	11971	18204	12299	17774	12633	17351	12972	23
	81	54	35	77	197	305	66	38	44	78	
8	19073	11660	18627	11982	18190	12310	17760	12644	17337	12984	22
	66	65	20	87	82	16	52	50	30	90	
9	19058	11670	18613	11993	18175	12321	17745	12655	17323	12995	21
	51	76	05	98	68	27	38	61	16	13001	
10	19043	11681	18598	12004	18161	12332	17731	12667	17309	13007	20
	36	86	91	09	54	38	24	72	02	12	
11	19028	11692	18583	12014	18146	12343	17717	12678	17295	13018	19
	21	97	76	20	39	49	10	83	88	24	
12	19013	11702	18569	12025	18132	12354	17703	12689	17281	13030	18
	06	08	61	31	25	60	696	95	74	35	
13	18998	11713	18554	12036	18117	12365	17689	12700	17267	13041	17
	91	18	47	42	10	71	81	06	60	47	
14	18983	11724	18539	12047	18103	12376	17674	12711	17253	13053	16
	76	29	32	53	096	82	67	17	46	58	
15	18968	11734	18525	12058	18089	12387	17660	12723	17239	13064	15
	61	40	17	63	81	93	53	28	32	70	
16	18953	11745	18510	12069	18074	12398	17646	12734	17225	13075	14
	46	50	03	74	67	404	39	40	18	81	
17	18939	11756	18495	12080	18060	12410	17632	12745	17212	13087	13
	31	61	88	85	53	15	25	51	05	93	
18	18924	11766	18481	12091	18045	12421	17618	12757	17198	13098	12
	16	72	73	96	38	26	11	62	91	104	
19	18909	11777	18466	12102	18031	12432	17604	12768	17184	13110	11
	01	82	59	07	24	37	597	74	77	16	
20	18894	11788	18451	12112	18017	12443	17590	12779	17170	13121	10
	86	93	44	18	10	48	83	85	63	27	
21	18879	11799	18437	12123	18002	12454	17575	12790	17156	13133	9
	72	804	29	29	17995	60	68	96	49	39	
22	18864	11809	18422	12134	17988	12465	17561	12802	17142	13144	8
	57	15	15	40	81	71	54	07	35	50	
23	18849	11820	18408	12145	17974	12476	17547	12813	17128	13156	7
	42	25	00	51	66	82	40	19	21	62	
24	18834	11831	18393	12156	17959	12487	17533	12824	17114	13168	6
	27	36	86	62	52	93	26	30	08	73	
25	18820	11842	18378	12167	17945	12499	17519	12836	17101	13179	5
	12	47	71	73	38	504	12	41	094	85	
26	18805	11852	18364	12178	17931	12510	17505	12847	17087	13191	4
	797	58	57	84	24	15	498	53	80	96	
27	18790	11863	18349	12189	17916	12521	17491	12859	17073	13202	3
	83	68	42	95	09	26	84	64	66	08	
28	18775	11874	18335	12200	17902	12532	17477	12870	17059	13214	2
	68	79	27	05	895	38	70	76	52	20	
29	18760	11885	18320	12211	17888	12543	17463	12881	17046	13225	1
	53	90	13	16	81	49	56	87	39	31	
30	18746	11895	18306	12222	17873	12554	17449	12893	17032	13237	0
	B	A	B	A	B	A	B	A	B	A	
	139° 30′		139°		138° 30′		138°		137° 30′		′

Always take "Z" from Bottom of Table, except when "K" is SAME Name

than 90°, take "K" from BOTTOM of Table

′	42° 30′ A	42° 30′ B	43° A	43° B	43° 30′ A	43° 30′ B	44° A	44° B	44° 30′ A	44° 30′ B	′
0	17032	13237	16622	13587	16219	13944	15823	14307	15434	14676	30
	25	43	15	93	12	50	16	13	27	82	
1	17018	13248	16608	13599	16205	13956	15810	14319	15421	14688	29
	11	54	01	6C5	199	62	03	25	14	94	
2	17004	13260	16595	13611	16192	13968	15797	14331	15408	14701	28
	16997	66	88	17	86	74	90	37	02	07	
3	16990	13272	16581	13623	16179	13980	15784	14343	15395	14713	27
	83	77	74	28	72	86	77	49	89	19	
4	16977	13283	16567	13634	16166	13992	15771	14355	15382	14726	26
	70	89	61	40	59	98	64	62	76	32	
5	16963	13295	16554	13646	16152	14004	15758	14368	15370	14738	25
	56	301	47	52	46	10	51	74	63	44	
6	16949	13306	16540	13658	16139	14016	15744	14380	15357	14750	24
	42	12	34	64	32	22	38	86	50	57	
7	16935	13318	16527	13670	16126	14028	15731	14392	15344	14763	23
	28	24	20	76	19	34	25	98	38	69	
8	16922	13330	16513	13682	16112	14040	15718	14404	15331	14775	22
	15	36	07	88	06	46	12	11	25	82	
9	16908	13341	16500	13694	16099	14052	15705	14417	15318	14788	21
	01	47	493	700	93	58	699	23	12	94	
10	16894	13353	16487	13705	16086	14064	15692	14429	15306	14800	20
	87	59	80	11	79	70	86	35	.299	07	
11	16880	13365	16473	13717	16073	14076	15679	14441	15293	14813	19
	74	70	66	23	66	82	73	47	86	19	
12	16867	13376	16460	13729	16060	14088	15666	14453	15280	14825	18
	60	82	53	35	53	94	60	60	74	31	
13	16853	13388	16446	13741	16046	14100	15653	14466	15267	14838	17
	46	94	39	47	40	06	47	72	61	44	
14	16839	13400	16433	13753	16033	14112	15640	14478	15255	14850	16
	33	05	26	59	27	18	34	84	48	57	
15	16826	13411	16419	13765	16020	14124	15627	14490	15242	14863	15
	19	17	13	71	13	30	21	96	35	69	
16	16812	13423	16406	13777	16007	14136	15614	14503	15229	14875	14
	05	29	399	83	00	42	08	09	23	82	
17	16798	13435	16392	13789	15994	14149	15602	14515	15216	14888	13
	92	40	86	94	87	55	595	21	10	94	
18	16785	13446	16379	13800	15980	14161	15589	14527	15204	14900	12
	78	52	72	06	74	67	82	33	197	07	
19	16771	13458	16366	13812	15967	14173	15576	14540	15191	14913	11
	64	64	59	18	61	79	69	46	84	19	
20	16757	13470	16352	13824	15954	14185	15563	14552	15178	14925	10
	51	76	46	30	47	91	56	58	72	32	
21	16744	13481	16339	13836	15941	14197	15550	14564	15165	14938	9
	37	87	32	42	34	203	43	70	59	44	
22	16730	13493	16325	13848	15928	14209	15537	14577	15153	14951	8
	23	99	19	54	21	15	30	83	46	57	
23	16717	13505	16312	13860	15915	14221	15524	14589	15140	14963	7
	10	11	05	66	08	27	17	95	34	69	
24	16703	13517	16299	13872	15901	14233	15511	14601	15127	14976	6
	696	23	92	78	895	40	05	08	21	82	
25	16689	13528	16285	13884	15888	14246	15498	14614	15115	14988	5
	83	34	79	90	82	52	92	20	08	95	
26	16676	13540	16272	13896	15875	14258	15485	14626	15102	15001	4
	69	46	65	902	69	64	79	32	096	07	
27	16662	13552	16259	13908	15862	14270	15472	14639	15089	15014	3
	56	58	52	14	56	76	66	45	83	20	
28	16649	13564	16245	13920	15849	14282	15459	14651	15077	15026	2
	42	70	39	26	42	88	53	57	70	33	
29	16635	13575	16232	13932	15836	14294	15447	14663	15064	15039	1
	28	81	25	38	29	300	40	70	58	45	
30	16622	13587	16219	13944	15823	14307	15434	14676	15051	15051	0
	A	B	A	B	A	B	A	B	A	B	
′	137°		136° 30′		136°		135° 30′		135°		′

and GREATER than Latitude, in which case take "Z" from TOP of Table

When L.H.A. (E or W) is GREATER

´	45° A	45° B	45° 30' A	45° 30' B	46° A	46° B	46° 30' A	46° 30' B	47° A	47° B	´
0	15051	15051	14676	15434	14307	15823	13944	16219	13587	16622	30
	45	58	70	40	00	29	38	25	81	28	
1	15039	15064	14663	15447	14294	15836	13932	16232	13575	16635	29
	33	70	57	53	88	42	26	39	70	42	
2	15026	15077	14651	15459	14282	15849	13920	16245	13564	16649	28
	20	83	45	66	76	56	·14	52	58	56	
3	15014	15089	14639	15472	14270	15862	13908	16259	13552	16662	27
	07	96	32	79	64	69	02	65	46	69	
4	15001	15102	14626	15485	14258	15875	13896	16272	13540	16676	26
	14995	08	20	92	52	32	90	79	34	83	
5	14988	15115	14614	15498	14246	15888	13884	16285	13528	16689	25
	82	21	08	505	40	95	78	92	23	96	
6	14976	15127	14601	15511	14233	15901	13872	16299	13517	16703	24
	69	34	595	17	27	08	66	305	11	10	
7	14963	15140	14589	15524	14221	15915	13860	16312	13505	16717	23
	57	46	83	30	15	21	54	19	499	23	
8	14951	15153	14577	15537	14209	15928	13848	16325	13493	16730	22
	44	59	70	43	03	34	42	32	87	37	
9	14938	15165	14564	15550	14197	15941	13836	16339	13481	16744	21
	32	72	58	56	91	47	30	46	76	51	
10	14925	15178	14552	15563	14185	15954	13824	16352	13470	16757	20
	19	84	46	69	79	61	18	59	64	64	
11	14913	15191	14540	15576	14173	15967	13812	16366	13458	16771	19
	07	97	33	82	67	74	06	72	52	78	
12	14900	15204	14527	15589	14161	15980	13800	16379	13446	16785	18
	894	10	21	95	55	87	794	86	40	92	
13	14888	15216	14515	15602	14149	15994	13788	16392	13435	16798	17
	82	23	09	08	42	16000	83	99	29	805	
14	14875	15229	14503	15614	14136	16007	13777	16406	13423	16812	16
	69	35	496	21	30	13	71	13	17	19	
15	14863	15242	14490	15627	14124	16020	13765	16419	13411	16826	15
	57	48	84	34	18	27	59	26	05	33	
16	14850	15255	14478	15640	14112	16033	13753	16433	13400	16839	14
	44	61	72	47	06	40	47	39	394	46	
17	14838	15267	14466	15653	14100	16046	13741	16446	13388	16853	13
	31	74	60	60	094	53	35	53	82	60	
18	14825	15280	14453	15666	14088	16060	13729	16460	13376	16867	12
	19	86	47	73	82	66	23	66	70	74	
19	14813	15293	14441	15679	14076	16073	13717	16473	13365	16880	11
	07	99	35	86	70	79	11	80	59	87	
20	14800	15306	14429	15692	14064	16086	13705	16487	13353	16894	10
	794	12	23	99	58	93	699	93	47	901	
21	14788	15318	14417	15705	14052	16099	13694	16500	13341	16908	9
	82	25	11	12	46	105	88	07	36	15	
22	14775	15331	14404	15718	14040	16112	13682	16513	13330	16922	8
	69	38	398	25	34	19	76	20	24	28	
23	14763	15344	14392	15731	14028	16126	13670	16527	13318	16935	7
	57	50	86	38	22	32	64	34	12	42	
24	14750	15357	14380	15744	14016	16139	13658	16540	13306	16949	6
	44	63	74	51	10	46	52	47	01	56	
25	14738	15370	14368	15758	14004	16152	13646	16554	13295	16963	5
	32	76	62	64	13998	59	40	61	89	70	
26	14725	15382	14355	15771	13992	16166	13634	16567	13283	16977	4
	19	89	49	77	86	72	28	74	77	83	
27	14713	15395	14343	15784	13980	16179	13623	16581	13272	16990	3
	07	402	37	90	74	85	17	88	66	97	
28	14701	15408	14331	15797	13968	16192	13611	16595	13260	17004	2
	694	14	25	803	62	99	05	601	54	11	
29	14688	15421	14319	15810	13956	16205	13599	16608	13248	17018	1
	82	27	13	16	50	12	93	15	43	25	
30	14676	15434	14307	15823	13944	16219	13587	16622	13237	17032	0
	A	B	A	B	A	B	A	B	A	B	
	134° 30'		134°		133° 30'		133°		132° 30'		

Always take "Z" from Bottom of Table, except when "K" is SAME Name

than 90°, take "K" from BOTTOM of Table

'	47° 30' A	47° 30' B	48° A	48° B	48° 30' A	48° 30' B	49° A	49° B	49° 30' A	49° 30' B	'
0	13237	17032	12893	17449	12554	17873	12222	18306	11895	18746	30
	31	39	87	56	49	81	16	13	90	53	
1	13225	17045	12881	17463	12543	17888	12211	18320	11885	18760	29
	20	52	76	70	38	95	05	27	79	68	
2	13214	17059	12870	17477	12532	17902	12200	18335	11874	18775	28
	08	66	64	84	26	09	195	42	68	83	
3	13202	17073	12859	17491	12521	17916	12189	18349	11863	18790	27
	196	80	53	98	15	24	84	57	58	97	
4	13191	17087	12847	17505	12510	17931	12178	18364	11852	18805	26
	85	94	41	12	04	38	73	71	47	12	
5	13179	17101	12836	17519	12499	17945	12167	18378	11842	18820	25
	73	08	30	26	93	52	62	86	36	27	
6	13168	17114	12824	17533	12487	17959	12156	18393	11831	18834	24
	62	21	19	40	82	66	51	400	25	42	
7	13156	17128	12813	17547	12476	17974	12145	18408	11820	18849	23
	50	35	07	54	71	81	40	15	15	57	
8	13144	17142	12802	17561	12465	17988	12134	18422	11809	18864	22
	39	49	796	68	60	95	29	29	04	72	
9	13133	17156	12790	17576	12454	18002	12123	18437	11799	18879	21
	27	63	85	83	48	10	18	44	93	86	
10	13121	17170	12779	17590	12443	18017	12112	18451	11788	18894	20
	16	77	74	97	37	24	07	59	82	901	
11	13110	17184	12768	17604	12432	18031	12102	18466	11777	18909	19
	04	91	62	11	26	38	096	73	72	16	
12	13098	17198	12757	17618	12421	18045	12091	18481	11766	18924	18
	93	205	51	25	15	53	85	88	61	31	
13	13087	17212	12745	17632	12410	18060	12080	18495	11756	18939	17
	81	18	40	39	04	67	74	503	50	46	
14	13075	17225	12734	17646	12398	18074	12069	18510	11745	18953	16
	70	32	28	53	93	81	63	17	40	61	
15	13064	17239	12723	17660	12387	18089	12058	18525	11734	18968	15
	58	46	17	67	82	96	53	32	29	76	
16	13053	17253	12711	17674	12376	18103	12047	18539	11724	18983	14
	47	60	06	81	71	10	42	47	18	91	
17	13041	17267	12700	17689	12365	18117	12036	18554	11713	18998	13
	35	74	695	96	60	25	31	61	08	19006	
18	13030	17281	12689	17703	12354	18132	12025	18569	11702	19013	12
	24	88	83	10	49	39	20	76	697	21	
19	13018	17295	12678	17717	12343	18146	12014	18583	11692	19028	11
	12	302	72	24	38	54	09	91	86	36	
20	13007	17309	12666	17731	12332	18161	12004	18598	11681	19043	10
	01	16	61	38	27	68	11998	605	76	51	
21	12995	17323	12655	17745	12321	18175	11993	18613	11670	19058	9
	90	30	50	52	16	82	87	20	65	66	
22	12984	17337	12644	17760	12310	18190	11982	18627	11660	19073	8
	78	44	38	67	05	97	76	35	54	81	
23	12972	17351	12633	17774	12299	18204	11971	18642	11649	19088	7
	67	58	27	81	93	11	66	50	44	96	
24	12961	17365	12622	17788	12288	18219	11960	18657	11638	19103	6
	55	72	16	95	82	26	55	64	33	11	
25	12950	17379	12610	17802	12277	18233	11949	18672	11628	19118	5
	44	86	05	09	71	40	44	79	22	26	
26	12938	17393	12599	17816	12266	18248	11939	18686	11617	19133	4
	32	400	93	24	60	55	33	94	12	41	
27	12927	17407	12588	17831	12255	18262	11928	18701	11606	19148	3
	21	14	82	38	49	69	22	09	01	56	
28	12915	17421	12577	17845	12244	18277	11917	18716	11596	19163	2
	10	28	71	52	38	84	12	23	90	71	
29	12904	17435	12566	17859	12233	18291	11906	18731	11585	19178	1
	898	42	60	66	27	98	01	38	80	86	
30	12893	17449	12554	17873	12222	18306	11895	18746	11575	19193	0
	A	B	A	B	A	B	A	B	A	B	
'	132°		131° 30'		131°		130° 30'		130°		'

and GREATER than Latitude, in which case take "Z" from TOP of Table

When L.H.A. (E or W) is GREATER

′	50° A	50° B	50° 30′ A	50° 30′ B	51° A	51° B	51° 30′ A	51° 30′ B	52° A	52° B	′
0	11575	19193	11259	19649	10950	20113	10646	20585	10347	21066	30
	69	201	54	57	45	21	40	93	42	74	
1	11564	19208	11249	19664	10939	20128	10635	20601	10337	21082	29
	59	16	44	72	34	36	30	09	32	90	
2	11553	19223	11239	19680	10929	20144	10625	20617	10327	21098	28
	48	31	33	87	24	52	20	25	22	106	
3	11543	19238	11228	19695	10919	20160	10615	20633	10317	21114	27
	37	46	23	703	14	67	10	41	12	22	
4	11532	19253	11218	19710	10909	20175	10605	20649	10307	21131	26
	27	61	13	18	04	83	00	57	02	39	
5	11522	19269	11207	19726	10899	20191	10595	20665	10298	21147	25
	16	76	02	33	94	99	90	72	93	55	
6	11511	19284	11197	19741	10888	20207	10585	20680	10288	21163	24
	06	91	92	49	83	14	80	88	83	71	
7	11501	19299	11187	19756	10878	20222	10575	20696	10278	21179	23
	495	306	81	64	73	30	70	704	73	87	
8	11490	19314	11176	19772	10868	20238	10565	20712	10268	21195	22
	85	21	71	79	63	46	60	20	63	204	
9	11479	19329	11166	19787	10858	20254	10555	20728	10258	21212	21
	74	37	61	95	53	61	50	36	53	20	
10	11469	19344	11156	19803	10848	20269	10545	20744	10248	21228	20
	64	52	50	10	43	77	40	52	43	36	
11	11458	19359	11145	19818	10838	20285	10535	20760	10239	21244	19
	53	67	40	26	32	93	30	68	34	52	
12	11448	19375	11135	19834	10827	20301	10525	20776	10229	21260	18
	43	82	30	41	22	08	20	84	24	69	
13	11437	19390	11124	19849	10817	20316	10515	20792	10219	21277	17
	32	97	19	57	12	24	10	800	14	85	
14	11427	19405	11114	19864	10807	20332	10505	20808	10209	21293	16
	21	12	09	72	02	40	00	16	04	301	
15	11416	19420	11104	19880	10797	20348	10496	20824	10199	21309	15
	11	28	099	88	92	56	91	32	95	18	
16	11406	19435	11094	19895	10787	20364	10486	20840	10190	21326	14
	00	43	88	903	82	71	81	48	85	34	
17	11395	19450	11083	19911	10777	20379	10476	20856	10180	21342	13
	90	58	78	18	72	87	71	64	75	50	
18	11385	19466	11073	19926	10767	20395	10466	20872	10170	21358	12
	80	73	68	34	61	403	61	80	65	67	
19	11374	19481	11063	19942	10756	20411	10456	20888	10160	21375	11
	69	88	57	49	51	19	51	97	55	83	
20	11364	19496	11052	19957	10746	20427	10446	20905	10151	21391	10
	59	504	47	65	41	35	41	13	46	99	
21	11353	19511	11042	19973	10736	20442	10436	20921	10141	21407	9
	48	19	37	80	31	50	31	29	36	16	
22	11343	19527	11032	19988	10726	20458	10426	20937	10131	21424	8
	38	34	27	96	21	66	21	45	26	32	
23	11332	19542	11021	20004	10716	20474	10416	20953	10121	21440	7
	27	49	16	12	11	82	11	61	16	48	
24	11322	19557	11011	20019	10706	20490	10406	20969	10112	21457	6
	17	65	06	27	01	98	01	77	07	65	
25	11311	19572	11001	20035	10696	20506	10396	20985	10102	21473	5
	06	80	10996	43	91	16	91	93	097	81	
26	11301	19588	10991	20050	10686	20522	10386	21001	10092	21489	4
	296	95	86	58	81	29	81	09	87	98	
27	11291	19603	10980	20066	10676	20537	10376	21017	10082	21506	3
	85	11	75	74	71	45	72	25	78	14	
28	11280	19618	10970	20082	10666	20553	10367	21033	10073	21522	2
	75	26	65	89	61	61	62	42	68	31	
29	11270	19634	10960	20097	10656	20569	10357	21050	10063	21539	1
	65	41	55	105	51	77	52	58	58	47	
30	11259	19649	10950	20113	10646	20585	10347	21066	10053	21555	0
	A	B	A	B	A	B	A	B	A	B	
	129° 30′		129°		128° 30′		128°		127° 30′		

Always take "Z" from Bottom of Table, except when "K" is SAME Name

than 90°, take "K" from BOTTOM of Table

	52° 30'		53°		53° 30'		54°		54° 30'		
'	**A**	**B**	**A**	**B**	**A**	**B**	**A**	**B**	**A**	**B**	**'**
0	10053	21555	9765	22054	9482	22561	9204	23078	8931	23605	30
	49	63	60	62	77	70	00	87	27	13	
1	10044	21572	9756	22070	9473	22578	9195	23095	8922	23622	29
	39	80	51	79	68	87	90	104	18	31	
2	10034	21588	9746	22087	9463	22595	9186	23113	8913	23640	28
	29	96	41	96	59	604	81	22	09	49	
3	10024	21605	9737	22104	9454	22612	9177	23130	8904	23658	27
	19	13	32	12	49	21	72	39	00	67	
4	10015	21621	9727	22121	9445	22630	9168	23148	8895	23675	26
	10	29	22	29	40	38	63	56	91	84	
5	10005	21638	9718	22138	9435	22647	9158	23165	8886	23693	25
	00	46	13	46	31	55	54	74	82	702	
6	9995	21654	9708	22154	9426	22664	9149	23183	8877	23711	24
	90	62	03	63	21	72	45	91	73	20	
7	9986	21671	9699	22171	9417	22681	9140	23200	8868	23729	23
	81	79	94	80	12	90	36	09	·64	38	
8	9976	21687	9689	22188	9407	22698	9131	23218	8859	23747	22
	71	96	84	97	03	707	26	26	55	55	
9	9966	21704	9680	22205	9398	22715	9122	23235	8850	23764	21
	62	12	75	13	94	24	17	44	46	73	
10	9957	21720	9670	22222	9389	22732	9113	23252	8842	23782	20
	52	29	65	30	84	41	08	61	37	91	
11	9947	21737	9661	22239	9380	22750	9104	23270	8833	23800	19
	42	45	56	47	75	58	9099	79	28	09	
12	9937	21754	9651	22256	9370	22767	9094	23288	8824	23818	18
	.33	62	47	64	66	75	90	96	19	27	
13	9928	21770	9642	22272	9361	22784	9085	23305	8815	23836	17
	23	78	·37	81	56	93	81	14	10	45	
14	9918	21787	9632	22289	9352	22801	9076	23323	8806	23854	16
	13	95	28	98	47	10	72	31	01	63	
15	9909	21803	9623	22306	9342	22818	9067	23340	8797	23871	15
	04	12	18	15	38	27	63	49	92	80	
16	9899	21820	9614	22323	9333	22836	9058	23358	8788	23889	14
	94	28	09	32	29	44	54	66	83	98	
17	9889	21837	9604	22340	9324	22853	9049	23375	8779	23907	13
	85	45	9599	49	19	62	44	84	75	16	
18	9880	21853	9595	22357	9315	22870	9040	23393	8770	23925	12
	75	62	90	66	10	79	35	402	66	34	
19	9870	21870	9585	22374	9305	22887	9031	23410	8761	23943	11
	65	78	81	82	01	96	26	19	57	52	
20	9861	21887	9576	22391	9296	22905	9022	23428	8752	23961	10
	56	95	71	99	92	13	17	37	48	70	
21	9851	21903	9566	22408	9287	22922	9013	23446	8743	23979	9
	46	12	62	16	82	31	08	54	39	88	
22	9841	21920	9557	22425	9278	22939	9004	23463	8734	23997	8
	37	28	52	33	73	48	8999	72	30	24006	
23	9832	21937	9548	22442	9269	22957	8995	23481	8726	24015	7
	27	45	43	50	64	65	90	90	21	24	
24	9822	21953	9538	22459	9259	22974	8985	23498	8717	24033	6
	18	62	34	67	55	83	81	507	12	42	
25	9813	21970	9529	22476	9250	22991	8976	23516	8708	24051	5
	08	78	24	84	46	23000	72	25	03	60	
26	9803	21987	9520	22493	9241	23009	8967	23534	8699	24069	4
	9798	95	15	501	36	17	63	43	94	78	
27	9794	22003	9510	22510	9232	23026	8958	23551	8690	24087	3
	89	12	05	19	27	35	54	60	86	96	
28	9784	22020	9501	22527	9223	23043	8949	23569	8681	24105	2
	79	29	9496	36	18	52	45	78	77	14	
29	9775	22037	9491	22544	9213	23061	8940	23587	8672	24123	1
	70	45	87	53	09	69	36	96	68	32	
30	9765	22054	9482	22561	9204	23078	8931	23605	8663	24141	0
	A	**B**	**A**	**B**	**A**	**B**	**A**	**B**	**A**	**B**	
'	127°		126° 30'		126°		125° 30'		125°		**'**

and GREATER than Latitude, in which case take "Z" from TOP of Table

When L.H.A. (E or W) is GREATER

′	55° A	55° B	55° 30′ A	55° 30′ B	56° A	56° B	56° 30′ A	56° 30′ B	57° A	57° B	′
0	8663	24141	8401	24687	8143	25244	7889	25811	7641	26389	30
	59	50	8396	96	38	53	85	21	37	99	
1	8655	24159	8392	24706	8134	25263	7881	25830	7633	26409	29
	50	68	·88	15	30	72	77	40	29	18	
2	8646	24177	8383	24724	8125	25281	7873	25849	7624	26428	28
	41	86	79	33	21	91	68	59	20	38	
3	8637	24195	8375	24742	8117	25300	7864	25868	7616	26447	27
	33	204	70	52	13	09	60	78	12	57	
4	8628	24213	8366	24761	8108	25319	7856	25887	7608	26467	26
	24	22	62	70	04	28	52	97	04	77	
5	8619	24231	8357	24779	8100	25338	7848	25907	7600	26486	25
	15	40	53	88	8096	47	43	16	7596	96	
6	8611	24249	8349	24798	8092	25356	7839	25926	7592	26506	24
	06	58	44	807	87	66	35	35	88	16	
7	8602	24267	8340	24816	8083	25375	7831	25945	7584	26526	23
	8597	76	36	25	79	85	27	54	79	35	
8	8593	24286	8331	24835	8075	25394	7823	25964	7575	26545	22
	89	95	27	44	70	403	18	74	71	55	
9	8584	24304	8323	24853	8066	25413	7814	25983	7567	26565	21
	80	13	18	62	62	22	10	93	63	74	
10	8575	24322	8314	24872	8058	25432	7806	26002	7559	26584	20
	71	31	10	81	53	41	02	12	55	94	
11	8567	24340	8305	24890	8049	25451	7798	26022	7551	26604	19
	62	49	01	99	45	60	93	31	47	14	
12	8558	24358	8297	24909	8041	25469	7789	26041	7543	26623	18
	53	67	92	18	36	79	85	51	39	33	
13	8549	24376	8288	24927	8032	25488	7781	26060	7535	26643	17
	45	85	84	36	28	98	77	70	31	53	
14	8540	24395	8280	24946	8024	25507	7773	26079	7526	26663	16
	36	404	75	55	20	17	69	89	22	72	
15	8531	24413	8271	24964	8015	25526	7764	26099	7518	26682	15
	27	22	67	73	11	36	60	108	14	92	
16	8523	24431	8262	24983	8007	25545	7756	26118	7510	26702	14
	18	40	58	92	03	54	52	28	06	12	
17	8514	24449	8254	25001	7998	25564	7748	26137	7502	26722	13
	10	58	49	11	94	73	44	47	7498	31	
18	8505	24467	8245	25020	7990	25583	7740	26157	7494	26741	12
	01	77	41	29	86	92	36	66	90	51	
19	8496	24486	8237	25038	7982	25602	7731	26176	7486	26761	11
	92	95	32	48	77	11	27	85	82	71	
20	8488	24504	8228	25057	7973	25621	7723	26195	7478	26781	10
	83	13	24	66	69	30	19	205	74	90	
21	8479	24522	8219	25076	7965	25640	7715	26214	7470	26800	9
	75	31	15	85	61	49	11	24	66	10	
22	8470	24540	8211	25094	7956	25659	7707	26234	7462	26820	8
	66	50	07	104	52	68	02	44	58	30	
23	8461	24559	8202	25113	7948	25678	7698	26253	7453	26840	7
	57	68	8198	22	44	87	94	63	49	50	
24	8453	24577	8194	25132	7940	25697	7690	26273	7445	26860	6
	48	86	89	41	35	706	86	82	41	69	
25	8444	24595	8185	25150	7931	25716	7682	26292	7437	26879	5
	40	605	81	60	27	25	78	302	33	89	
26	8435	24614	8177	25169	7923	25735	7674	26311	7429	26899	4
	31	23	72	78	19	44	70	21	25	909	
27	8427	24632	8168	25188	7914	25754	7665	26331	7421	26919	3
	22	41	64	97	10	63	61	40	17	29	
28	8418	24650	8160	25206	7906	25773	7657	26350	7413	26939	2
	14	60	55	16	02	82	53	60	09	49	
29	8409	24669	8151	25225	7898	25792	7649	26370	7405	26958	1
	05	78	47	34	93	801	45	79	01	68	
30	8401	24687	8143	25244	7889	25811	7641	26389	7397	26978	0
	A	B	A	B	A	B	A	B	A	B	
′	124° 30′		124°		123° 30′		123°		122° 30′		′

Always take "Z" from Bottom of Table, except when "K" is SAME Name

than 90°, take "K" from BOTTOM of Table.

'	57° 30' A	B	58° A	B	58° 30' A	B	59° A	B	59° 30' A	B	'
0	7397	26978	7158	27579	6923	28191	6693	28816	6468	29453	30
	93	88	54	89	20	202	90	27	64	64	
1	7389	26998	7150	27599	6916	28212	6686	28837	6460	29475	29
	85	27008	46	609	12	22	82	48	57	85	
2	7381	27018	7142	27619	6908	28233	6678	28858	6453	29496	28
	77	28	38	30	04	43	74	69	49	507	
3	7373	27038	7134	27640	6900	28253	6671	28879	6446	29517	27
	69	48	30		6896	64	67	90	42	28	
4	7365	27058	7126	27660	6892	28274	6663	28900	6438	29539	26
	61	68	22	70	89	84	59	11	34	50	
5	7357	27078	7118	27680	6885	28295	6655	28921	6431	29560	25
	53	88	15	90	81	305	52	32	27	71	
6	7349	27098	7111	27701	6877	28315	6648	28942	6423	29582	24
	45	107	07	11	73	26	44	53	20	93	
7	7341	27117	7103	27721	6869	28336	6640	28964	6416	29604	23
	37	27	7099	31	65	46	37	74	12	14	
8	7333	27137	7095	27741	6862	28357	6633	28985	6409	29625	22
	29	47	91	51	58	67	29	95	05	36	
9	7325	27157	7087	27761	6854	28378	6625	29006	6401	29647	21
	21	67	83	72	50	88	22	16	6397	57	
10	7317	27177	7079	27782	6846	28398	6618	29027	6394	29668	20
	13	87	75	92	42	409	14	38	90	79	
11	7309	27197	7071	27802	6839	28419	6610	29048	6386	29690	19
	05	207	68	12	35	29	07	59	83	701	
12	7301	27217	7064	27823	6831	28440	6603	29069	6379	29711	18
	7297	27	60	33	27	50	6599	80	75	22	
13	7293	27237	7056	27843	6823	28461	6595	29091	6372	29733	17
	89	47	52	53	19	71	91	101	68	44	
14	7285	27257	7048	27863	6815	28481	6588	29112	6364	29755	16
	81	67	44	74	12	92	84	22	61	66	
15	7277	27277	7040	27884	6808	28502	6580	29133	6357	29776	15
	73	87	36	94	04	13	76	44	53	87	
16	7269	27297	7032	27904	6800	28523	6573	29154	6349	29798	14
	65	307	28	34	6796	33	69	65	46	809	
17	7261	27317	7024	27925	6792	28544	6565	29175	6342	29820	13
	57	27	21	35	89	54	61	86	38	31	
18	7253	27337	7017	27945	6785	28565	6558	29197	6335	29841	12
	49	47	13	55	81	75	54	207	31	52	
19	7245	27357	7009	27965	6777	28586	6550	29218	6327	29863	11
	41	67	05	76	73	96	46	29	24	74	
20	7237	27377	7001	27986	6770	28607	6543	29239	6320	29885	10
	33	87	6997	96	66	17	39	50	16	96	
21	7229	27398	6993	28006	6762	28627	6535	29261	6313	29907	9
	25	408	89	17	58	38	31	71	09	17	
22	7221	27418	6985	28027	6754	28648	6528	29282	6305	29929	8
	17	28	82	37	50	59	24	93	02	39	
23	7213	27438	6978	28047	6747	28669	6520	29303	6298	29950	7
	09	48	74	58	43	80	16	14	94	61	
24	7205	27458	6970	28068	6739	28690	6513	29325	6291	29972	6
	01	68	66	78	35	701	09	35	87	83	
25	7197	27478	6962	28089	6731	28711	6505	29346	6283	29994	5
	93	88	58	99	28	22	02	57	80	30005	
26	7190	27498	6954	28109	6724	28732	6498	29367	6276	30015	4
	86	508	51	19	20	43	94	78	72	26	
27	7182	27518	6947	28130	6716	28753	6490	29389	6269	30037	3
	78	28	43	40	12	63	87	99	65	48	
28	7174	27539	6939	28150	6709	28774	6483	29410	6261	30059	2
	70	49	35	61	05	84	79	21	58	70	
29	7166	27559	6931	28171	6701	28795	6475	29432	6254	30081	1
	62	69	27	81	6697	806	72	42	51	92	
30	7158	27579	6923	28191	6693	28816	6468	29453	6247	30103	0
	A	B	A	B	A	B	A	B	A	B	
'	122°		121° 30'		121°		120° 30'		120°		'

and GREATER than Latitude, in which case take "Z" from TOP of Table

When L.H.A. (E or W) is GREATER

′	60° A	60° B	60° 30′ A	60° 30′ B	61° A	61° B	61° 30′ A	61° 30′ B	62° A	62° B	′
0	6247	30103	6030	30766	5818	31443	5610	32134	5406	32839	30
	43	14	27	77	15	54	07	45	03	51	
1	6240	30125	6023	30788	5811	31466	5603	32157	5400	32863	29
	36	36	20	800	08	77	00	69	5396	75	
2	6232	30147	6016	30811	5804	31488	5596	32180	5393	32887	28
	29	58	12	.22	01	500	93	92	90	98	
3	6225	30169	6009	30833	5797	31511	5590	32204	5386	32910	27
	21	80	05	44	94	23	86	15	83	22	
4	6218	30191	6002	30856	5790	31534	5583	32227	5380	32934	26
	14	202	5998	67	87	46	79	39	76	46	
5	6210	30213	5995	30878	5783	31557	5575	32250	5373	32958	25
	07	24	91	89	80	69	72	62	70	70	
6	6203	30235	5987	30900	5776	31580	5569	32274	5366	32982	24
	00	45	84	12	73	91	66	85	63	94	
7	6196	30256	5980	30923	5769	31603	5562	32297	5360	33006	23
	92	67	77	34	66	14	59	309	56	18	
8	6189	30278	5973	30945	5762	31626	5555	32320	5353	33030	22
	85	89	70	56	59	37	52	32	50	42	
9	6181	30300	5966	30968	5755	31649	5549	32344	5346	33054	21
	78	11	63	79	52	60	45	55	43	65	
10	6174	30322	5959	30990	5748	31672	5542	32367	5340	33077	20
	71	34	55	31001	45	83	38	79	36	89	
11	6167	30345	5952	31013	5741	31694	5535	32391	5333	33101	19
	63	55	48	24	38	706	32	402	30	13	
12	6160	30367	5945	31035	5734	31717	5528	32414	5326	33125	18
	56	78	41	46	31	29	25	26	23	37	
13	6152	30389	5938	31058	5727	31740	5521	32438	5320	33149	17
	49	400	34	69	24	52	18	49	16	61	
14	6145	30411	5931	31080	5720	31763	5515	32461	5313	33173	16
	42	22	27	91	17	75	11	73	10	85	
15	6138	30433	5924	31103	5714	31786	5508	32484	5306	33197	15
	34	44	20	14	10	98	04	96	03	209	
16	6131	30455	5917	31125	5707	31809	5501	32508	5300	33221	14
	27	66	13	37	03	21	5498	20	5296	33	
17	6124	30477	5909	31148	5700	31833	5494	32532	5293	33245	13
	20	88	06	59	5696	44	91	43	90	57	
18	6116	30499	5902	31170	5693	31856	5487	32555	5286	33269	12
	13	510	5899	82	89	67	84	67	83	81	
19	6109	30521	5895	31193	5686	31879	5481	32579	5280	33293	11
	06	32	92	204	′82	90	77	90	76	306	
20	6102	30544	5888	31216	5679	31902	5474	32602	5273	33318	10
	6098	55	85	27	75	13	70	14	70	30	
21	6095	30566	5881	31238	5672	31925	5467	32625	5266	33342	9
	91	77	78	50	69	36	64	38	63	54	
22	6088	30588	5874	31261	5665	31948	5460	32649	5260	33366	8
	84	99	71	72	62	60	57	61	57	78	
23	6080	30610	5867	31284	5658	31971	5454	32673	5253	33390	7
	77	21	64	95	55	83	50	85	50	402	
24	6073	30632	5860	31306	5651	31994	5447	32697	5247	33414	6
	70	43	57	18	48	32006	43	709	43	26	
25	6066	30655	5853	31329	5644	32018	5440	32720	5240	33438	5
	62	66	50	40	41	29	37	32	37	50	
26	6059	30677	5846	31352	5638	32041	5433	32744	5233	33462	4
	55	88	43	63	34	52	30	56	30	75	
27	6052	30699	5839	31375	5631	32064	5427	32768	5227	33487	3
	48	710	36	86	27	76	23	80	24	99	
28	6045	30721	5832	31397	5624	32087	5420	32792	5220	33511	2
	41	33	29	409	20	99	17	803	17	23	
29	6037	30744	5825	31420	5617	32110	5413	32815	5214	33535	1
	34	55	22	31	14	22	10	27	10	47	
30	6030	30766	5818	31443	5610	32134	5406	32839	5207	33559	0
	A	B	A	B	A	B	A	B	A	B	
′	119° 30′		119°		118° 30′		118°		117° 30′		′

Always take "Z" from Bottom of Table, except when "K" is SAME Name

than 90°, take "K" from BOTTOM of Table

'	62° 30' A	62° 30' B	63° A	63° B	63° 30' A	63° 30' B	64° A	64° B	64° 30' A	64° 30' B	'
0	5207	33559	5012	34295	4821	35047	4634	35816	4451	36602	30
	04	72	09	308	18	60	31	29	48	15	
1	5200	33584	5005	34320	4815	35073	4628	35842	4445	36628	29
	5197	96	02	32	11	85	25	55	42	41	
2	5194	33608	4999	34345	4808	35098	4622	35868	4439	36655	28
	91	20	96	57	05	111	19	81	36	68	
3	5187	33632	4993	34370	4802	35123	4615	35894	4433	36681	27
	84	44	89	82	4799	36	12	907	30	94	
4	5181	33657	4986	34395	4796	35149	4609	35920	4427	36708	26
	78	69	83	407	93	61	06	33	24	21	
5	5174	33681	4980	34420	4789	35174	4603	35946	4421	36734	25
	71	93	77	32	86	87	00	59	18	47	
6	5168	33705	4973	34444	4783	35200	4597	35972	4415	36761	24
	64	17	70	57	80	12	94	85	12	74	
7	5161	33730	4967	34469	4777	35225	4591	35998	4409	36787	23
	58	42	64	82	74	38	88	36011	06	801	
8	5155	33754	4961	34494	4771	35251	4585	36024	4403	36814	22
	51	66	57	507	67	63	82	37	00	27	
9	5148	33779	4954	34519	4764	35276	4579	36050	4397	36841	21
	45	91	51	32	61	89	76	63	94	54	
10	5142	33803	4948	34544	4758	35302	4573	36076	4391	36867	20
	38	15	45	57	55	14	69	89	88	81	
11	5135	33827	4941	34569	4752	35327	4566	36102	4385	36894	19
	32	40	38	82	49	40	63	15	82	907	
12	5128	33852	4935	34594	4746	35353	4560	36128	4379	36921	18
	25	64	32	607	42	65	57	41	76	34	
13	5122	33876	4929	34619	4739	35378	4554	36154	4373	36948	17
	19	89	25	32	36	91	51	67	70	61	
14	5115	33901	4922	34644	4733	35404	4548	36180	4367	36974	16
	12	13	19	57	30	17	45	93	64	88	
15	5109	33925	4916	34669	4727	35429	4542	36206	4361	37001	15
	06	38	13	82	24	42	39	20	58	14	
16	5102	33950	4910	34694	4721	35455	4536	36233	4355	37028	14
	5099	62	06	707	18	68	33	46	52	41	
17	5096	33974	4903	34719	4714	35481	4530	36259	4349	37055	13
	93	87	00	32	11	93	27	72	46	68	
18	5089	33999	4897	34744	4708	35506	4524	36285	4343	37081	12
	86	34011	94	57	05	19	21	98	40	95	
19	5083	34024	4890	34770	4702	35532	4518	36311	4337	37108	11
	80	36	87	82	4699	45	15	25	34	22	
20	5076	34048	4884	34795	4696	35558	4512	36338	4332	37135	10
	73	61	81	807	93	71	09	51	29	49	
21	5070	34073	4878	34820	4690	35583	4506	36364	4326	37162	9
	67	85	75	32	86	96	03	77	23	76	
22	5064	34097	4871	34845	4683	35609	4500	36390	4320	37189	8
	60	110	68	58	80	22	4497	403	17	203	
23	5057	34122	4865	34870	4677	35635	4493	36417	4314	37216	7
	54	34	62	83	74	48	90	30	11	29	
24	5051	34147	4859	34896	4671	35661	4487	36443	4308	37243	6
	47	59	56	908	68	74	84	56	05	56	
25	5044	34172	4852	34921	4665	35686	4481	36469	4302	37270	5
	41	84	49	33	62	99	78	83	4299	83	
26	5038	34196	4846	34946	4659	35712	4475	36496	4296	37297	4
	34	209	43	59	56	25	72	509	93	310	
27	5031	34221	4840	34971	4652	35738	4469	36522	4290	37324	3
	28	33	37	84	49	51	66	35	87	37	
28	5025	34246	4833	34997	4646	35764	4463	36549	4284	37351	2
	22	58	30	35009	43	77	60	62	81	65	
29	5018	34270	4827	35022	4640	35790	4457	36575	4278	37378	1
	15	83	24	35	37	803	54	88	75	92	
30	5012	34295	4821	35047	4634	35816	4451	36602	4272	37405	0
	A	B	A	B	A	B	A	B	A	B	
'	117°		116° 30'		116°		115° 30'		115°		'

and GREATER than Latitude, in which case take "Z" from TOP of Table

When L.H.A. (E or W) is GREATER

'	65° A	65° B	65° 30' A	65° 30' B	66° A	66° B	66° 30' A	66° 30' B	67° 00' A	67° 00' B	'
0	4272	37405	4098	38227	3927	39069	3760	39930	3597	40812	30
	69	19	95	41	24	83	57	45	95	27	
1	4266	37432	4092	38255	3921	39097	3755	39959	3592	40842	29
	64	46	89	69	18	111	52	74	89	57	
2	4261	37459	4086	38283	3916	39125	3749	39988	3587	40872	28
	58	73	83	97	13	40	46	40003	84	87	
3	4255	37487	4080	38311	3910	39154	3744	40017	3581	40902	27
	52	500	78	24	07	68	41	32	79	16	
4	4249	37514	4075	38338	3904	39182	3738	40046	3576	40931	26
	46	27	72	52	02	97	35	61	73	46	
5	4243	37541	4069	38366	3899	39211	3733	40076	3571	40961	25
	40	54	66	80	96	25	30	90	68	76	
6	4237	37568	4063	38394	3893	39239	3727	40105	3565	40991	24
	34	82	60	408	90	54	25	19	63	41006	
7	4231	37595	4057	38422	3888	39268	3722	40134	3560	41021	23
	28	609	55	36	85	82	19	49	57	36	
8	4225	37623	4052	38450	3882	39296	3716	40163	3555	41051	22
	22	36	49	64	79	311	14	78	52	66	
9	4220	37650	4046	38478	3876	39325	3711	40192	3549	41081	21
	17	63	43	92	74	39	08	207	47	96	
10	4214	37677	4040	38506	3871	39353	3705	40222	3544	41111	20
	11	91	37	20	68	68	03	36	41	26	
11	4208	37704	4035	38533	3865	39382	3700	40251	3539	41141	19
	05	18	32	47	63	96	3697	66	36	56	
12	4202	37732	4029	38561	3860	39411	3695	40280	3533	41171	18
	4199	45	26	75	57	25	92	95	31	86	
13	4196	37759	4023	38589	3854	39439	3689	40310	3528	41201	17
	93	73	20	603	51	54	86	24	25	16	
14	4190	37786	4017	38617	3849	39468	3684	40339	3523	41231	16
	87	800	15	31	46	82	81	54	20	46	
15	4185	37814	4012	38645	3843	39497	3678	40368	3517	41261	15
	82	28	09	60	40	511	76	83	15	76	
16	4179	37841	4006	38674	3838	39525	3673	40398	3512	41291	14
	76	55	03	88	35	40	70	413	09	307	
17	4173	37869	4000	38702	3832	39554	3667	40427	3507	41322	13
	70	82	3998	16	29	69	65	42	04	37	
18	4167	37896	3995	38730	3826	39583	3662	40457	3502	41352	12
	64	910	92	44	24	97	59	71	3499	67	
19	4161	37924	3989	38758	3821	39612	3657	40486	3496	41382	11
	58	37	86	72	18	26	54	501	94	97	
20	4155	37951	3983	38786	3815	39641	3651	40516	3491	41412	10
	53	65	81	800	13	55	48	30	88	27	
21	4150	37979	3978	38814	3810	39669	3646	40545	3486	41443	9
	47	92	75	28	07	84	43	60	83	58	
22	4144	38006	3972	38842	3804	39698	3640	40575	3480	41473	8
	41	20	69	56	01	713	38	90	78	88	
23	4138	38034	3966	38871	3799	39727	3635	40604	3475	41503	7
	35	48	64	85	96	42	32	19	73	18	
24	4132	38061	3961	38899	3793	39756	3630	40634	3470	41533	6
	29	75	58	913	90	71	27	49	67	49	
25	4127	38089	3955	38927	3788	39785	3624	40664	3465	41564	5
	24	103	52	41	85	99	22	78	62	79	
26	4121	38117	3949	38955	3782	39814	3619	40693	3459	41594	4
	18	30	47	69	79	28	16	708	57	609	
27	4115	38144	3944	38984	3777	39843	3613	40723	3454	41625	3
	12	58	41	98	74	57	11	38	52	40	
28	4109	38172	3938	39012	3771	39872	3608	40753	3449	41655	2
	06	86	35	26	68	86	05	68	46	70	
29	4103	38200	3933	39040	3766	39901	3603	40782	3444	41685	1
	01	13	30	54	63	15	00	97	41	701	
30	4098	38227	3927	39069	3760	39930	3597	40812	3438	41716	0
	A	B	A	B	A	B	A	B	A	B	
'	114° 30'		114°		113° 30'		113°		112° 30'		'

Always take "Z" from Bottom of Table, except when "K" is SAME Name

'than 90°, take "K" from BOTTOM of Table

'	67° 30' A	B	68° A	B	68° 30' A	B	69° A	B	69° 30' A	B	'
0	3438	41716	3283	42642	3132	43592	2985	44567	2841	45567	30
	36	31	81	58	30	608	82	83	39	84	
1	3433	41746	3278	42674	3127	43624	2980	44600	2836	45601	29
	31	62	76	89	25	41	78	16	34	18	
2	3428	41777	3273	42705	3122	43657	2975	44633	2832	45635	28
	25	92	71	21	20	73	73	49	29	52	
3	3423	41808	3268	42736	3117	43689	2970	44666	2827	45669	27
	20	23	66	52	15	705	68	82	25	86	
4	3418	41838	3263	42768	3112	43721	2965	44699	2822	45703	26
	15	53	60	83	10	37	63	715	20	20	
5	3412	41869	3258	42799	3107	43753	2961	44732	2818	45737	25
	10	84	55	815	05	69	58	48	15	54	
6	3407	41899	3253	42830	3102	43785	2956	44765	2813	45771	24
	04	915	50	46	00	801	53	82	11	88	
7	3402	41930	3248	42862	3097	43818	2951	44798	2808	45805	23
	3399	45	45	78	95	34	49	815	06	22	
8	3397	41961	3243	42893	3092	43850	2946	44831	2804	45839	22
	94	76	40	909	90	66	44	48	01	56	
9	3391	41991	3237	42925	3088	43882	2941	44864	2799	45873	21
	89	42007	35	41	85	98	39	81	97	90	
10	3386	42022	3233	42956	3083	43914	2936	44898	2794	45907	20
	84	38	30	72	80	31	34	914	92	24	
11	3381	42053	3227	42988	3078	43947	2932	44931	2789	45941	19
	79	68	25	43004	75	63	29	47	87	58	
12	3376	42084	3222	43020	3073	43979	2927	44964	2785	45975	18
	73	99	20	35	70	95	24	81	82	92	
13	3371	42115	3217	43051	3068	44012	2922	44997	2780	46009	17
	68	30	15	67	65	'28	20	45014	78	26	
14	3366	42145	3212	43083	3063	44044	2917	45031	2775	46043	16
	63	61	10	99	60	60	15	47	73	61	
15	3360	42176	3207	43114	3058	44077	2913	45064	2771	46078	15
	58	92	05	30	56	93	10	81	68	95	
16	3355	42207	3202	43146	3053	44109	2908	45097	2766	46112	14
	53	23	00	62	51	25	05	114	64	29	
17	3350	42238	3197	43178	3048	44142	2903	45131	2761	46146	13
	48	54	95	94	46	58	01	47	59	63	
18	3345	42269	3192	43210	3043	44174	2898	45164	2757	46181	12
	42	85	90	25	41	90	96	81	55	98	
19	3340	42300	3187	43241	3038	44207	2893	45198	2752	46215	11
	37	16	85	57	36	23	91	214	50	32	
20	3335	42331	3182	43273	3033	44239	2889	45231	2748	46249	10
	32	47	80	89	31	56	86	48	45	66	
21	3329	42362	3177	43305	3029	44272	2884	45265	2743	46284	9
	27	78	75	21	26	88	81	81	41	301	
22	3324	42393	3172	43337	3024	44305	2879	45298	2738	46318	8
	22	409	70	53	21	21	77	315	36	35	
23	3319	42424	3167	43369	3019	44337	2874	45332	2734	46353	7
	17	40	65	85	16	54	72	48	31	70	
24	3314	42455	3162	43400	3014	44370	2870	45365	2729	46387	6
	12	71	60	16	12	86	67	82	27	404	
25	3309	42486	3157	43432	3009	44403	2865	45399	2724	46422	5
	06	502	55	48	07	19	62	416	22	39	
26	3304	42518	3152	43464	3004	44436	2860	45433	2720	46456	4
	01	33	50	80	02	52	58	49	17	73	
27	3299	42549	3147	43496	2999	44468	2855	45466	2715	46491	3
	96	64	45	512	97	85	53	83	13	508	
28	3294	42580	3142	43528	2994	44501	2851	45500	2711	46525	2
	91	96	40	44	92	18	48	17	08	43	
29	3289	42611	3137	43560	2990	44534	2846	45534	2706	46560	1
	86	27	35	76	87	51	44	51	04	77	
30	3283	42642	3132	43592	2985	44567	2841	45567	2701	46595	0
	A	B	A	B	A	B	A	B	A	B	
'	112°		111° 30'		111°		110° 30'		110°		'

and GREATER than Latitude, in which case take "Z" from TOP of Table

When L.H.A. (E or W) is GREATER

'	70° A	70° B	70° 30' A	70° 30' B	71° A	71° B	71° 30' A	71° 30' B	72° 00' A	72° 00' B	'
0	2701	46595	2565	47650	2433	48736	2304	49852	2179	51002	30
	2699	612	63	68	31	54	02	71	77	21	
1	2697	46630	2561	47686	2429	48772	2300	49890	2175	51041	29
	94	47	59	704	27	91	2298	909	73	60	
2	2692	46664	2556	47722	2424	48809	2296	49928	2171	51080	28
	'90	82	54	40	22	28	94	47	69	99	
3	2688	46699	2552	47758	2420	48846	2292	49966	2167	51119	27
	85	716	50	75	18	64	90	85	65	38	
4	2683	46734	2547	47793	2416	48883	2287	50004	2163	51158	26
	81	51	45	811	13	901	85	23	61	77	
5	2678	46769	2543	47829	2411	48920	2283	50042	2159	51197	25
	76	86	41	47	09	38	81	61	57	216	
6	2674	46804	2539	47865	2407	48957	2279	50080	2155	51236	24
	72	21	36	83	05	75	77	98	53	55	
7	2669	46839	2534	47901	2403	48993	2275	50117	2151	51275	23
	67	56	32	19	00	49012	73	37	49	94	
8	2665	46873	2530	47937	2398	49030	2271	50156	2147	51314	22
	62	91	28	55	96	49	69	75	45	34	
9	2660	46908	2525	47973	2394	49067	2266	50194	2143	51353	21
	58	26	23	91	92	86	64	213	41	73	
10	2656	46943	2521	48009	2390	49104	2262	50232	2138	51392	20
	53	61	19	27	87	23	60	51	36	412	
11	2651	46978	2516	48045	2385	49141	2258	50270	2134	51432	19
	49	96	14	63	83	60	56	89	32	51	
12	2646	47014	2512	48081	2381	49179	2254	50308	2130	51471	18
	44	31	10	99	79	97	52	27	28	91	
13	2642	47049	2507	48117	2377	49216	2250	50346	2126	51510	17
	40	66	05	35	75	34	48	65	24	30	
14	2637	47084	2503	48153	2372	49253	2246	50385	2122	51550	16
	35	101	01	71	70	71	43	404	20	70	
15	2633	47119	2499	48189	2368	49290	2241	50423	2118	51589	15
	31	37	96	207	66	309	39	42	16	609	
16	2628	47154	2494	48226	2364	49327	2237	50461	2114	51629	14
	26	72	92	44	62	46	35	80	12	49	
17	2624	47189	2490	48262	2360	49365	2233	50499	2110	51668	13
	22	207	88	80	58	83	31	519	08	88	
18	2619	47225	2485	48298	2355	49402	2229	50538	2106	51708	12
	17	42	83	316	53	21	27	57	04	28	
19	2615	47260	2481	48334	2351	49439	2225	50576	2102	51747	11
	13	78	79	52	49	58	23	96	00	67	
20	2610	47295	2477	48371	2347	49477	2221	50615	2098	51787	10
	08	313	74	89	45	95	18	34	96	807	
21	2606	47331	2472	48407	2343	49514	2216	50653	2094	51827	9
	04	48	70	25	40	33	14	73	92	47	
22	2601	47366	2468	48443	2338	49551	2212	50692	2090	51867	8
	2599	84	66	62	36	70	10	711	88	86	
23	2597	47402	2463	48480	2334	49589	2208	50730	2086	51906	7
	94	19	61	98	32	608	06	50	84	26	
24	2592	47437	2459	48516	2330	49626	2204	50769	2082	51946	6
	90	55	57	34	28	45	02	88	80	66	
25	2588	47472	2455	48553	2325	49664	2200	50808	2078	51986	5
	85	90	53	71	23	83	2198	27	76	52006	
26	2583	47508	2450	48589	2321	49702	2196	50846	2074	52026	4
	81	26	48	608	19	20	94	66	72	46	
27	2579	47544	2446	48626	2317	49739	2192	50885	2070	52066	3
	76	61	44	44	15	58	90	905	68	86	
28	2574	47579	2442	48662	2313	49777	2188	50924	2066	52106	2
	72	97	39	81	11	96	85	43	64	26	
29	2570	47615	2437	48699	2309	49815	2183	50963	2062	52146	1
	68	33	35	717	06	33	81	82	60	66	
30	2565	47650	2433	48736	2304	49852	2179	51002	2058	52186	0
	A	B	A	B	A	B	A	B	A	B	
•	109° 30'		109°		108° 30'		108°		107° 30'		'

Always take "Z" from Bottom of Table, except when "K" is SAME Name

than 90°, take "K" from BOTTOM of Table

′	72° 30′ A	72° 30′ B	73° A	73° B	73° 30′ A	73° 30′ B	74° A	74° B	74° 30′ A	74° 30′ B	
0	2058	52186	1940	53406	1826	54666	1716	55966	1609	57310	30
	56	206	38	27	24	87	14	88	07	33	
1	2054	52226	1936	53448	1823	54708	1712	56010	1605	57356	29
	52	46	35	68	21	30	10	32	04	78	
2	2050	52266	1933	53489	1819	54751	1709	56054	1602	57401	28
	48	86	31	510	17	73	07	76	00	24	
3	2046	52306	1929	53531	1815	54794	1705	56099	1598	57447	27
	44	26	27	51	13	815	03	121	97	70	
4	2042	52346	1925	53572	1811	54837	1701	56143	1595	57493	26
	40	66	23	93	09	58	00	65	93	516	
5	2038	52387	1921	53614	1808	54880	1698	56187	1591	57538	25
	36	407	19	34	06	901	96	209	90	61	
6	2034	52427	1917	53655	1804	54922	1694	56231	1588	57584	24
	32	47	15	76	02	44	92	54	86	607	
7	2030	52467	1913	53697	1800	54965	1691	56276	1584	57630	23
	28	87	11	718	1798	87	89	98	83	53	
8	2026	52508	1910	53738	1796	55008	1687	56320	1581	57676	22
	24	28	08	59	95	30	85	42	79	99	
9	2022	52548	1906	53780	1793	55051	1683	56365	1578	57722	21
	20	68	04	801	91	73	82	87	76	45	
10	2018	52588	1902	53822	1789	55095	1680	56409	1574	57768	20
	16	609	00	43	87	116	78	31	72	91	
11	2014	52629	1898	53864	1785	55138	1676	56454	1571	57814	19
	12	49	96	84	83	59	74	76	69	37	
12	2010	52670	1894	53905	1782	55181	1673	56498	1567	57860	18
	09	90	92	26	80	202	71	521	65	84	
13	2007	52710	1890	53947	1778	55224	1669	56543	1564	57907	17
	05	30	89	68	76	46	67	65	62	30	
14	2003	52751	1887	53989	1774	55267	1665	56588	1560	57953	16
	01	71	85	54010	72	89	64	610	59	76	
15	1999	52791	1883	54031	1771	55311	1662	56632	1557	57999	15
	97	812	81	52	69	32	60	55	55	58022	
16	1995	52832	1879	54073	1767	55354	1658	56677	1553	58046	14
	93	52	77	94	65	76	57	700	52	69	
17	1991	52873	1875	54115	1763	55397	1655	56722	1550	58092	13
	89	93	73	36	61	419	53	45	48	115	
18	1987	52914	1871	54157	1760	55441	1651	56767	1546	58138	12
	85	34	70	78	58	63	50	90	45	62	
19	1983	52954	1868	54199	1756	55484	1648	56812	1543	58185	11
	81	75	66	220	54	506	46	35	41	208	
20	1979	52995	1864	54242	1752	55528	1644	56857	1540	58232	10
	77	53016	62	63	50	50	42	80	38	55	
21	1975	53036	1860	54284	1749	55572	1641	56902	1536	58278	9
	73	57	58	305	47	93	39	25	34	302	
22	1971	53077	1856	54326	1745	55615	1637	56947	1533	58325	8
	69	98	54	47	43	37	35	70	31	48	
23	1967	53118	1853	54368	1741	55659	1634	56992	1529	58372	7
	66	39	51	90	39	81	32	57015	28	95	
24	1964	53159	1849	54411	1738	55703	1630	57038	1526	58418	6
	62	80	47	32	36	25	28	60	24	42	
25	1960	53200	1845	54453	1734	55746	1627	57083	1523	58465	5
	58	21	43	74	32	68	25	106	21	89	
26	1956	53241	1841	54496	1730	55790	1623	57128	1519	58512	4
	54	62	39	517	28	812	21	51	17	36	
27	1952	53283	1837	54538	1727	55834	1619	57174	1516	58559	3
	50	303	36	59	25	56	18	96	14	83	
28	1948	53324	1834	54581	1723	55878	1616	57219	1512	58606	2
	46	44	32	602	21	900	14	42	11	30	
29	1944	53365	1830	54623	1719	55922	1612	57265	1509	58653	1
	42	86	28	44	18	44	11	87	07	77	
30	1940	53406	1826	54666	1716	55966	1609	57310	1506	58700	0
	A	B	A	B	A	B	A	B	A	B	
	107°		106° 30′		106°		105° 30′		105°		′

and GREATER than Latitude, in which case take "Z" from TOP of Table

When L.H.A. (E or W) is GREATER

'	75° A	75° B	75° 30' A	75° 30' B	76° A	76° B	76° 30' A	76° 30' B	77° A	77° B	'
0	1506	58700	1406	60140	1310	61632	1217	63181	1128	64791	30
	04	24	04	64	08	58	15	208	26	819	
1	1502	58748	1403	60189	1306	61683	1214	63234	1125	64846	29
	00	71	01	213	05	709	12	60	23	73	
2	1499	58795	1399	60238	1303	61734	1211	63287	1122	64901	28
	97	818	98	62	01	59	09	313	20	28	
3	1495	58842	1396	60287	1300	61785	1208	63340	1119	64956	27
	94	66	94	311	1299	810	06	66	17	83	
4	1492	58889	1393	60336	1297	61836	1205	63392	1116	65011	26
	90	913	91	60	95	61	03	419	14	38	
5	1489	58937	1390	60385	1294	61887	1202	63445	1113	65066	25
	87	60	88	410	92	912	00	72	12	93	
6	1485	58984	1386	60434	1291	61938	1199	63498	1110	65121	24
	84	59008	85	59	89	63	97	525	09	48	
7	1482	59032	1383	60483	1288	61989	1196	63551	1107	65176	23
	80	55	81	508	86	62014	94	78	06	204	
8	1479	59079	1380	60533	1284	62040	1193	63605	1104	65231	22
	77	103	78	57	83	65	91	31	03	59	
9	1475	59127	1377	60582	1281	62091	1190	63658	1101	65287	21
	74	51	75	607	80	117	88	84	00	314	
10	1472	59175	1373	60631	1278	62142	1187	63711	1099	65342	20
	70	98	72	56	77	68	85	38	97	70	
11	1469	59222	1370	60681	1275	62194	1184	63764	1096	65398	19
	67	46	68	706	74	219	82	91	94	425	
12	1465	59270	1367	60730	1272	62245	1181	63818	1093	65453	18
	64	94	65	55	70	71	79	45	91	81	
13	1462	59318	1364	60780	1269	62296	1178	63871	1090	65509	17
	60	42	62	805	67	322	76	98	89	37	
14	1459	59366	1360	60830	1266	62348	1175	63925	1087	65564	16
	57	90	59	55	64	74	73	52	86	92	
15	1455	59414	1357	60879	1263	62400	1172	63978	1084	65620	15
	54	38	56	904	61	25	70	64005	83	48	
16	1452	59462	1354	60929	1260	62451	1169	64032	1081	65676	14
	50	86	52	54	58	77	67	59	80	704	
17	1449	59510	1351	60979	1257	62503	1166	64086	1079	65732	13
	47	34	49	61004	55	29	64	113	77	60	
18	1445	59558	1348	61029	1253	62555	1163	64140	1076	65788	12
	44	82	46	54	52	81	61	67	74	816	
19	1442	59606	1344	61079	1250	62607	1160	64194	1073	65844	11
	40	30	43	104	49	33	58	221	71	72	
20	1439	59654	1341	61129	1247	62659	1157	64248	1070	65900	10
	37	79	40	54	46	85	55	75	69	28	
21	1435	59703	1338	61179	1244	62711	1154	64302	1067	65957	9
	34	27	36	204	43	37	52	29	66	85	
22	1432	59751	1335	61229	1241	62763	1151	64356	1064	66013	8
	30	75	33	54	40	89	50	83	63	41	
23	1429	59800	1332	61279	1238	62815	1148	64410	1061	66069	7
	27	24	30	304	37	41	47	37	60	98	
24	1425	59848	1329	61330	1235	62867	1145	64464	1059	66126	6
	24	72	27	55	34	93	44	91	57	54	
25	1422	59896	1325	61380	1232	62919	1142	64518	1056	66182	5
	21	921	24	405	30	45	41	46	54	211	
26	1419	59945	1322	61430	1229	62971	1139	64573	1053	66239	4
	17	69	21	56	27	98	38	600	52	67	
27	1416	59994	1319	61481	1226	63024	1136	64627	1050	66296	3
	14	60018	17	506	24	50	35	55	49	324	
28	1412	60042	1316	61531	1223	63076	1133	64682	1047	66352	2
	11	67	14	56	21	103	32	709	46	81	
29	1409	60091	1313	61582	1220	63129	1130	64736	1045	66409	1
	07	116	11	607	18	55	29	64	43	38	
30	1406	60140	1310	61632	1217	63181	1128	64791	1042	66466	0
	A	B	A	B	A	B	A	B	A	B	
'	104° 30'		104°		103° 30'		103°		102° 30'		'

Always take "Z" from Bottom of Table, except when "K" is SAME Name

than 90°, take "K" from BOTTOM of Table

′	77° 30′		78°		78° 30′		79°		79° 30′		′
	A	B	A	B	A	B	A	B	A	B	
0	1042	66466	960	68212	881	70034	805	71940	733	73937	30
	40	95	958	42	879	65	804	73	732	71	
1	1039	66523	957	68272	878	70097	803	72005	731	74005	29
	38	52	955	301	877	128	802	38	730	39	
2	1036	66580	954	68331	876	70159	800	72070	729	74073	28
	35	609	953	61	874	90	799	103	728	107	
3	1033	66638	951	68391	873	70221	798	72136	726	74142	27
	32	66	950	421	872	52	797	68	725	76	
4	1031	66695	949	68450	870	70284	796	72201	724	74210	26
	29	724	947	80	869	315	794	34	723	45	
5	1028	66752	946	68510	868	70346	793	72266	722	74279	25
	26	81	945	40	867	77	792	99	721	313	
6	1025	66810	943	68570	865	70409	791	72332	719	74348	24
	24	38	942	600	864	40	790	65	718	82	
7	1022	66867	941	68630	863	70471	788	72397	717	74417	23
	21	96	939	60	862	503	787	430	716	51	
8	1020	66925	938	68690	860	70534	786	72463	715	74486	22
	18	53	937	720	859	66	785	96	714	520	
9	1017	66982	935	68750	858	70597	783	72529	712	74555	21
	15	67011	934	81	856	629	782	62	711	89	
10	1014	67040	933	68811	855	70660	781	72595	710	74624	20
	13	69	932	41	854	92	780	628	709	59	
11	1011	67098	930	68871	853	70723	779	72661	708	74693	19
	10	127	929	901	851	55	777	94	707	728	
12	1008	67156	928	68931	850	70786	776	72727	706	74763	18
	07	85	926	62	849	818	775	60	704	97	
13	1006	67214	925	68992	848	70850	774	72794	703	74832	17
	04	43	924	69022	846	81	772	827	702	67	
14	1003	67272	922	69053	845	70913	771	72860	701	74902	16
	02	301	921	83	844	45	770	93	700	37	
15	1000	67330	920	69113	843	70976	769	72926	699	74972	15
	999	59	918	44	841	71008	768	60	698	75007	
16	997	67388	917	69174	840	71040	767	72993	696	75042	14
	996	417	916	204	839	72	765	73026	695	77	
17	995	67447	914	69235	838	71104	764	73060	694	75112	13
	993	76	913	65	836	35	763	93	693	47	
18	992	67505	912	69296	835	71167	762	73127	692	75182	12
	991	34	910	326	834	99	761	60	691	217	
19	989	67563	909	69357	833	71231	759	73193	690	75252	11
	988	93	908	87	831	63	758	227	688	87	
20	987	67622	907	69418	830	71295	757	73260	687	75322	10
	985	51	905	49	829	327	756	94	686	58	
21	984	67681	904	69479	828	71359	755	73328	685	75393	9
	982	710	903	510	826	91	753	61	684	428	
22	981	67739	901	69541	825	71423	752	73395	683	75464	8
	980	69	900	71	824	55	751	429	682	99	
23	978	67798	899	69602	823	71488	750	73462	680	75534	7
	977	828	897	33	821	520	749	96	679	70	
24	976	67857	896	69664	820	71552	747	73530	678	75605	6
	974	86	895	94	819	84	746	63	677	41	
25	973	67916	894	69725	818	71616	745	73597	676	75676	5
	972	45	892	56	816	49	744	631	675	712	
26	970	67975	891	69787	815	71681	743	73665	674	75747	4
	969	68005	890	818	814	713	742	99	673	83	
27	968	68034	888	69849	813	71746	740	73733	672	75819	3
	966	64	887	79	811	78	739	67	670	54	
28	965	68093	886	69910	810	71810	738	73801	669	75890	2
	964	123	885	41	809	43	737	35	668	926	
29	962	68153	883	69972	808	71875	736	73869	667	75961	1
	961	82	882	70003	807	908	735	903	666	97	
30	960	68212	881	70034	805	71940	733	73937	665	76033	0
	A	B	A	B	A	B	A	B	A	B	
′	102°		101° 30′		101°		100° 30′		100°		′

and GREATER than Latitude, in which case take "Z" from TOP of Table

When L.H.A. (E or W) is **GREATER**

′	80° A	80° B	80° 30′ A	80° 30′ B	81° A	81° B	81° 30′ A	81° 30′ B	82° A	82° B	′
0	665	76033	600	78239	538	80567	480	83030	425	85644	30
	664	069	599	277	537	607	479	072	424	689	
1	663	76105	598	78315	536	80647	478	83114	423	85734	29
	661	141	597	352	535	687	477	157	422	779	
2	660	76176	595	78390	534	80727	476	83199	421	85825	28
	659	212	594	428	533	767	475	242	420	870	
3	658	76248	593	78466	532	80807	474	83284	419	85915	27
	657	284	592	504	531	847	473	327	418	960	
4	656	76320	591	78542	530	80887	472	83369	418	86006	26
	655	357	590	580	529	927	471	412	417	051	
5	654	76393	589	78618	528	80967	470	83455	416	86096	25
	653	429	588	656	527	81008	469	497	415	142	
6	652	76465	587	78694	526	81048	468	83540	414	86187	24
	650	501	586	733	525	088	467	583	413	233	
7	649	76537	585	78771	524	81129	467	83626	412	86278	23
	648	574	584	809	523	169	466	668	411	324	
8	647	76610	583	78847	522	81210	465	83711	411	86370	22
	646	646	582	886	521	250	464	754	410	415	
9	645	76683	581	78924	520	81291	463	83797	409	86461	21
	644	719	580	962	519	331	462	840	408	507	
10	643	76756	579	79001	518	81372	461	83884	407	86553	20
	642	792	578	039	517	413	460	927	406	599	
11	641	76828	577	79078	516	81453	459	83970	405	86645	19
	639	865	576	116	515	494	458	84013	405	691	
12	638	76902	575	79155	514	81535	457	84056	404	86737	18
	637	938	574	193	513	576	456	100	403	783	
13	636	76975	573	79232	512	81617	455	84143	402	86829	17
	635	77011	571	271	511	657	454	186	401	876	
14	634	77048	570	79309	510	81698	454	84230	400	86922	16
	633	085	569	348	509	739	453	273	399	968	
15	632	77122	568	79387	508	81780	452	84317	399	87015	15
	631	158	567	426	507	821	451	361	398	061	
16	630	77195	566	79465	506	81863	450	84404	397	87107	14
	629	232	565	503	505	904	449	448	396	154	
17	627	77269	564	79542	504	81945	448	84492	395	87201	13
	626	306	563	581	504	986	447	535	394	247	
18	625	77343	562	79620	503	82027	446	84579	393	87294	12
	624	380	561	659	502	069	445	623	392	341	
19	623	77417	560	79698	501	82110	444	84667	392	87387	11
	622	454	559	737	500	151	444	711	391	434	
20	621	77491	558	79777	499	82193	443	84755	390	87481	10
	620	528	557	816	498	234	442	799	389	528	
21	619	77565	556	79855	497	82276	441	84843	388	87575	9
	618	602	555	894	496	317	440	887	387	622	
22	617	77639	554	79933	495	82359	439	84931	387	87669	8
	616	677	553	973	494	400	438	976	386	716	
23	615	77714	552	80012	493	82442	437	85020	385	87764	7
	614	751	551	051	492	484	436	064	384	811	
24	612	77788	550	80091	491	82526	435	85100	383	87858	6
	611	826	549	130	490	567	434	143	382	906	
25	610	77863	548	80170	489	82609	434	85197	381	87953	5
	609	901	547	209	488	651	433	242	381	88001	
26	608	77938	546	80249	487	82693	432	85286	380	88048	4
	607	976	545	288	486	735	431	331	379	096	
27	606	78013	544	80328	485	82777	430	85376	378	88143	3
	605	051	543	368	484	819	429	420	377	191	
28	604	78088	542	80407	483	82861	428	85465	376	88239	2
	603	126	541	447	482	903	427	510	376	286	
29	602	78164	540	80487	482	82945	426	85555	375	88334	1
	601	201	539	527	481	987	426	599	374	382	
30	600	78239	538	80567	480	83030	425	85644	373	88430	0
	A	B	A	B	A	B	A	B	A	B	
′	99° 30′		99°		98° 30′		98°		97° 30′		′

Always take "Z" from Bottom of Table, except when "K" is SAME Name

than 90°, take "K" from BOTTOM of Table

′	82° 30′ A	82° 30′ B	83° A	83° B	83° 30′ A	83° 30′ B	84° A	84° B	84° 30′ A	84° 30′ B	′
0	373	88430	325	91411	280	94614	238.6	98076	200.4	101843	30
	372	478	324	462	279	670	237.9	137	199.8	908	
1	371	88526	323	91514	279	94725	237.2	98197	199.2	101974	29
	371	574	323	565	278	781	236.6	257	198.6	2040	
2	370	88623	322	91617	277	94836	235.9	98318	198.0	102106	28
	369	671	321	668	276	892	235.3	378	197.4	172	
3	368	88719	320	91720	276	94948	234.6	98439	196.8	102238	27
	367	767	319	772	275	95004	233.9	499	196.2	304	
4	366	88816	319	91824	274	95060	233.3	98560	195.6	102371	26
	366	864	318	876	274	116	232.6	621	195.0	437	
5	365	88913	317	91928	273	95172	232.0	98682	194.4	102504	25
	364	961	316	980	272	228	231.3	743	193.8	570	
6	363	89010	316	92032	271	95285	230.7	98804	193.2	102637	24
	362	059	315	085	271	341	230.0	865	192.6	704	
7	362	89107	314	92137	270	95397	229.4	98926	192.0	102771	23
	361	156	313	189	269	454	228.7	988	191.4	838	
8	360	89205	313	92242	269	95510	228.1	99049	190.8	102905	22
	359	254	312	294	268	567	227.4	111	190.2	973	
9	358	89303	311	92347	267	95624	226.8	99172	189.6	103040	21
	357	352	310	399	267	681	226.1	234	189.0	107	
10	357	89401	310	92452	266	95737	225.5	99296	188.4	103175	20
	356	450	309	505	265	795	224.8	357	187.8	243	
11	355	89499	308	92558	264	95851	224.2	99419	187.2	103311	19
	354	548	307	610	264	909	223.5	487	186.7	379	
12	353	89597	307	92663	263	95966	222.9	99544	186.1	103447	18
	353	647	306	716	262	96023	222.3	606	185.5	515	
13	352	89696	305	92769	262	96080	221.6	99668	184.9	103583	17
	351	746	304	823	261	138	221.0	731	184.3	651	
14	350	89795	304	92876	260	96195	220.3	99793	183.7	103720	16
	349	845	303	929	260	253	219.7	856	183.2	788	
15	349	89894	302	92982	259	96310	219.1	99918	182.6	103857	15
	348	944	301	93036	258	368	218.4	981	182.0	926	
16	347	89994	301	93089	257	96426	217.8	100044	181.4	103995	14
	346	90044	300	143	257	484	217.2	107	180.8	4064	
17	345	90093	299	93196	256	96542	216.5	100170	180.3	104133	13
	345	143	298	250	255	600	215.9	233	179.7	202	
18	344	90193	298	93304	255	96658	215.3	100296	179.1	104272	12
	343	243	297	358	254	716	214.6	360	178.5	341	
19	342	90293	296	93411	253	96774	214.0	100423	178.0	104411	11
	341	344	295	465	253	833	213.4	487	177.4	480	
20	341	90394	295	93519	252	96891	212.8	100550	176.8	104550	10
	340	444	294	573	251	950	212.1	614	176.2	620	
21	339	90494	293	93628	251	97008	211.5	100678	175.7	104690	9
	338	545	292	682	250	067	210.9	742	175.1	760	
22	337	90595	292	93736	249	97126	210.3	100806	174.5	104830	8
	337	646	291	790	249	184	209.6	870	174.0	901	
23	336	90696	290	93845	248	97243	209.0	100934	173.4	104971	7
	335	747	289	899	247	302	208.4	998	172.8	5042	
24	334	90798	289	93954	247	97361	207.8	101063	172.3	105113	6
	333	848	288	94009	246	420	207.1	127	171.7	183	
25	333	90899	287	94063	245	97480	206.5	101192	171.1	105254	5
	332	950	287	118	245	539	205.9	256	170.6	325	
26	331	91001	286	94173	244	97598	205.3	101321	170.0	105397	4
	330	052	285	228	243	658	204.7	386	169.5	468	
27	330	91103	284	94283	243	97717	204.1	101451	168.9	105539	3
	329	154	284	338	242	777	203.5	516	168.4	611	
28	328	91205	283	94393	241	97837	202.8	101581	167.8	105683	2
	327	257	282	448	241	897	202.2	646	167.2	754	
29	326	91308	281	94503	240	97957	201.6	101712	166.7	105826	1
	326	359	281	559	239	98017	201.0	777	166.0	898	
30	325	91411	280	94614	239	98076	200.4	101843	165.6	105970	0
′	A	B	A	B	A	B	A	B	A	B	′
	97°		96° 30′		96°		95° 30′		95°		

and GREATER than Latitude, in which case take "Z" from TOP of Table

When L.H.A. (E or W) is GREATER

,	85° A	85° B	85° 30' A	85° 30' B	86° A	86° B	86° 30' A	86° 30' B	87° A	87° B	,
0	165.6	105970	134.1	110536	105.9	115641	81.1	121432	59.6	128120	30
	165.0	6043	133.6	616	105.5	732	80.7	536	59.2	241	
1	164.5	106115	133.1	110696	105.0	115823	80.3	121639	58.9	128362	29
	163.9	187	132.6	777	104.6	913	79.9	743	58.6	483	
2	163.4	106260	132.1	110858	104.2	116004	79.5	121848	58.2	128605	28
	162.8	333	131.6	939	103.7	096	79.2	952	57.9	727	
3	162.3	106406	131.1	111020	103.3	116187	78.8	122057	57.6	128849	27
	161.7	479	130.6	101	102.9	278	78.4	161	57.3	972	
4	161.2	106552	130.1	111183	102.4	116370	78.0	122267	56.9	129095	26
	160.6	625	129.6	264	102.0	462	77.6	372	56.6	218	
5	160.1	106698	129.2	111346	101.6	116554	77.3	122478	56.3	129342	25
	159.6	772	128.7	428	101.1	647	76.9	584	56.0	466	
6	159.0	106846	128.2	111510	100.7	116739	76.5	122690	55.7	129591	24
	158.5	919	127.7	592	100.3	832	76.1	796	55.3	716	
7	157.9	106993	127.2	111674	99.8	116925	75.8	122903	55.0	129841	23
	157.4	7067	126.7	757	99.4	7018	75.4	3010	54.7	967	
8	156.9	107141	126.2	111839	99.0	117112	75.0	123117	54.4	130093	22
	156.3	216	125.8	922	98.5	205	74.6	225	54.1	219	
9	155.8	107290	125.3	112005	98.1	117299	74.3	123332	53.7	130346	21
	155.2	364	124.8	088	97.7	393	73.9	441	53.4	473	
10	154.7	107439	124.3	112171	97.3	117487	73.5	123549	53.1	130600	20
	154.2	514	123.8	255	96.8	581	73.2	657	52.8	728	
11	153.6	107589	123.4	112338	96.4	117676	72.8	123766	52.5	130856	19
	153.1	664	122.9	422	96.0	771	72.4	875	52.2	985	
12	152.6	107739	122.4	112506	95.6	117866	72.1	123985	51.9	131114	18
	152.1	814	121.9	590	95.2	961	71.7	4095	51.6	243	
13	151.5	107890	121.5	112674	94.7	118056	71.3	124204	51.3	131373	17
	151.0	965	121.0	759	94.3	152	71.0	315	51.0	503	
14	150.5	108041	120.5	112843	93.9	118248	70.6	124425	50.7	131633	16
	149.9	117	120.1	928	93.5	344	70.3	536	50.3	764	
15	149.4	108193	119.6	113013	93.1	118440	69.9	124647	50.0	131896	15
	148.9	269	119.1	098	92.7	537	69.5	759	49.7	2027	
16	148.4	108345	118.7	113183	92.3	118633	69.2	124870	49.4	132159	14
	147.8	421	118.2	269	91.8	730	68.8	982	49.1	292	
17	147.3	108498	117.7	113354	91.4	118827	68.5	125094	48.8	132425	13
	146.8	574	117.3	440	91.0	925	68.1	207	48.5	558	
18	146.3	108651	116.8	113526	90.6	119022	67.8	125320	48.2	132692	12
	145.8	728	116.3	612	90.2	120	67.4	433	47.9	826	
19	145.2	108805	115.9	113699	89.8	119218	67.1	125546	47.6	132961	11
	144.7	882	115.4	785	89.4	316	66.7	660	47.3	3096	
20	144.2	108960	114.9	113872	89.0	119415	66.4	125774	47.1	133231	10
	143.7	9037	114.5	958	88.6	513	66.0	888	46.8	367	
21	143.2	109115	114.0	114045	88.2	119612	65.7	126003	46.5	133503	9
	142.7	192	113.6	133	87.8	711	65.3	118	46.2	640	
22	142.2	109270	113.1	114220	87.4	119811	65.0	126233	45.9	133777	8
	141.6	348	112.7	307	87.0	910	64.6	349	45.6	914	
23	141.1	109426	112.2	114395	86.6	120010	64.3	126465	45.3	134052	7
	140.6	505	111.7	483	86.2	110	63.9	581	45.0	191	
24	140.1	109583	111.3	114571	85.8	120211	63.6	126697	44.7	134330	6
	139.6	662	110.8	659	85.4	311	63.3	814	44.4	469	
25	139.1	109740	110.4	114747	85.0	120412	62.9	126931	44.2	134609	5
	138.6	819	109.9	836	84.6	513	62.6	7049	43.9	749	
26	138.1	109898	109.5	114925	84.2	120614	62.2	127166	43.6	134890	4
	137.6	978	109.0	5014	83.8	715	61.9	284	43.3	5031	
27	137.1	110057	108.6	115103	83.4	120817	61.6	127403	43.0	135173	3
	136.6	136	108.1	192	83.0	919	61.2	521	42.7	315	
28	136.1	110216	107.7	115282	82.6	121021	60.9	127640	42.5	135457	2
	135.6	296	107.3	371	82.2	124	60.6	760	42.2	600	
29	135.1	110375	106.8	115461	81.9	121226	60.2	127880	41.9	135744	1
	134.6	455	106.4	551	81.5	329	59.9	8000	41.6	888	
30	134.1	110536	105.9	115641	81.1	121432	59.6	128120	41.4	136032	0
	A	B	A	B	A	B	A	B	A	B	
,	94° 30'		94°		93° 30'		93°		92° 30'		,

Always take "Z" from Bottom of Table, except when "K" is SAME Name

than 90°, take "K" from BOTTOM of Table

′	87° 30′ A	B	88° A	B	88° 30′ A	B	89° A	B	89° 30′ A	B	r
0	41.4	136032	26.5	145718	14.9	158208	6.6	175814	1.7	205916	30
	41.1	177	26.2	899	14.7	450	6.5	6178	1.6	6646	
1	40.8	136322	26.0	146031	14.6	158693	6.4	176544	1.5	207388	29
	40.5	468	25.8	264	14.4	938	6.3	914	1.5	8143	
2	40.3	136615	25.6	146448	14.2	159184	6.2	177287	1.4	208912	28
	40.0	761	25.4	632	14.1	431	6.1	663	1.4	9695	
3	39.7	136909	25.2	146817	13.9	159680	6.0	178042	1.3	210491	27
	39.4	7057	24.9	7003	13.7	930	5.9	424	1.3	1303	
4	39.2	137205	24.7	147190	13.6	160182	5.8	178810	1.2	212130	26
	38.9	354	24.5	377	13.4	435	5.7	9200	1.2	2974	
5	38.6	137503	24.3	147566	13.3	160690	5.6	179593	1.1	213834	25
	38.4	653	24.1	755	13.1	946	5.5	990	1.1	4711	
6	38.1	137804	23.9	147945	13.0	161204	5.4	180390	1.1	215607	24
	37.8	955	23.7	8135	12.8	463	5.3	794	1.0	6521	
7	37.6	138106	23.5	148327	12.7	161724	5.2	181201	1.0	217455	23
	37.3	258	23.3	520	12.5	966	5.1	613	0.9	8409	
8	37.1	138411	23.1	148713	12.4	162250	5.0	182029	0.9	219385	22
	36.8	564	22.8	907	12.2	516	4.9	448	0.9	220384	
9	36.5	138718	22.6	149103	12.1	162783	4.8	182872	0.8	221406	21
	36.3	872	22.4	299	11.9	3052	4.7	3300	0.8	2452	
10	36.0	139027	22.2	149495	11.8	163322	4.6	183732	0.7	223525	20
	35.8	182	22.0	693	11.6	594	4.5	4168	0.7	4624	
11	35.5	139338	21.8	149892	11.5	163868	4.4	184609	0.7	225752	19
	35.3	494	21.6	150092	11.3	4144	4.3	5055	0.6	6910	
12	35.0	139651	21.4	150292	11.2	164422	4.2	185505	0.6	228100	18
	34.7	809	21.2	494	11.0	701	4.1	959	0.6	9324	
13	34.5	139967	21.0	150696	10.9	164982	4.1	186419	0.5	230583	17
	34.2	140125	20.8	899	10.8	5265	4.0	883	0.5	1879	
14	34.0	140285	20.6	151104	10.6	165550	3.9	187353	0.5	233215	16
	33.7	445	20.5	309	10.5	836	3.8	827	0.4	4594	
15	33.5	140605	20.3	151515	10.3	166125	3.7	188307	0.4	236018	15
	33.2	766	20.1	722	10.2	415	3.6	793	0.4	7491	
16	33.0	140928	19.9	151931	10.1	166708	3.6	189283	0.4	239015	14
	32.8	1090	19.7	2149	9.9	7002	3.5	780	0.3	240594	
17	32.5	141253	19.5	152350	9.8	167293	3.4	190282	0.3	242233	13
	32.3	417	19.3	561	9.7	597	3.3	790	0.3	3936	
18	32.0	141581	19.1	152774	9.5	167897	3.2	191303	0.3	245709	12
	31.8	745	18.9	987	9.4	8300	3.2	824	0.2	7558	
19	31.5	141911	18.7	153201	9.3	168505	3.1	192350	0.2	249488	11
	31.3	2077	18.6	417	9.1	811	3.0	883	0.2	251508	
20	31.1	142243	18.4	153633	9.0	169121	2.9	193422	0.2	253627	10
	30.8	411	18.2	851	8.9	432	2.9	969	0.2	5855	
21	30.6	142579	18.0	154070	8.7	169745	2.8	194522	0.1	258203	9
	30.4	747	17.8	290	8.6	170061	2.7	5082	0.1	269685	
22	30.1	142916	17.6	154511	8.5	170379	2.7	195650	0.1	263318	8
	29.9	3086	17.5	733	8.4	760	2.6	6225	0.1	6121	
23	29.6	143257	17.3	154956	8.2	171023	2.5	196808	0.1	269118	7
	29.4	428	17.1	5180	8.1	348	2.4	7399	0.1	272336	
24	29.2	143600	16.9	155406	8.0	171676	2.4	197998	0.1	275812	6
	28.9	773	16.8	633	7.9	2006	2.3	8605	0.1	9591	
25	28.7	143946	16.6	155861	7.8	172339	2.3	199221	0.0	283304	5
	28.5	4120	16.4	6090	7.6	674	2.2	846	0.0	8306	
26	28.3	144295	16.2	156320	7.5	173012	2.1	200480	0.0	293421	4
	28.0	470	16.1	552	7.4	352	2.1	1124	0.0	9221	
27	27.8	144646	15.9	156784	7.3	173696	2.0	201777	0.0	305915	3
	27.6	823	15.7	7019	7.2	4042	1.9	2440	0.0	313833	
28	27.4	145000	15.6	157254	7.1	174391	1.9	203113	0.0	323524	2
	27.1	179	15.4	490	6.9	742	1.8	797	0.0	336018	
29	26.9	145358	15.2	157728	6.8	175097	1.8	204492	0.0	353627	1
	26.7	538	15.1	967	6.7	454	1.7	5198	0.0	383730	
30	26.5	145718	14.9	158208	6.6	175814	1.7	205916	0.0	--------	0
′	A	B	A	B	A	B	A	B	A	B	′
	92°		91° 30′		91°		90° 30′		90°		

and GREATER than Latitude. in which case take "Z" from TOP of Table

DECLINATION **SAME** NAME AS LATITUDE

Lat.°	H.A.° '	Decl.° '	Alt.° '	Δd	Δt	Az.°	Alt.° '	Δd	Δt	Az.°	Decl.° '
31	2	8 30	67 25.4	1.0	10	174.8	67 55.3	1.0	10	174.7	9 00
	21	23 00	69 41.7	47	82	108.1	69 55.4	45	82	106.8	23 30
33	38	12 00	49 26.1	61	78	112.2	49 44.3	60	78	111.6	12 30
	48	15 00	43 04.8	52	83	100.6	43 20.4	52	83	100.1	15 30
	17	16 00	67 05.1	78	61	133.8	67 28.2	77	62	133.0	16 30
	2	18 00	74 53.6	99	13	172.7	75 23.4	99	14	172.5	18 30
	25	18 00	63 01.4	62	75	117.6	63 20.0	61	75	116.7	18 30
	39	18 00	52 00.9	51	82	103.5	52 16.2	51	82	102.8	18 30
	24	19 00	64 23.3	61	75	117.2	64 41.5	60	76	116.2	19 30
	28	28 00	65 26.3	32	84	94.3	65 35.7	30	84	93.1	28 30
34	59	15 30	34 07.1	51	83	93.9	34 22.4	51	83	93.4	16 00
	27	16 00	59 47.5	66	72	119.8	60 07.3	66	73	119.1	16 30
	66	16 00	28 34.4	51	83	89.4	28 49.5	50	83	88.9	16 30
	77	23 30	23 12.2	48	81	76.5	23 26.5	47	80	76.0	24 00
	45	52 30	53 10.7	21	60	45.9	52 50.5	24	57	43.5	54 00
35	54	58 00	33 49.4	60	79	105.3	34 07.4	60	79	104.9	8 30
	44	12 30	44 22.9	61	78	108.4	44 40.9	60	78	107.8	13 00
	40	17 30	50 26.3	56	79	105.7	50 43.1	56	79	105.1	18 00
	61	17 30	33 27.1	51	82	91.3	33 42.4	51	82	90.8	18 00
	78	17 30	19 34.0	53	81	81.9	19 49.8	52	81	81.5	18 00
	76	19 00	21 58.2	52	81	81.6	22 13.6	51	81	81.1	19 30
	66	22 00	31 35.2	48	81	83.9	31 49.5	47	81	83.4	22 30
	39	23 00	54 06.4	48	81	98.9	54 20.5	47	81	98.1	23 30
	22	23 30	67 42.1	59	75	115.1	67 59.6	57	75	114.0	24 00
	71	38 30	34 27.4	34	73	63.8	34 57.5	33	72	62.1	40 00
	30	45 00	65 07.3	23	69	57.2	64 52.6	26	67	54.9	46 00
	65	49 30	41 22.5	15	64	51.7	41 30.8	13	63	50.3	50 30
	58	56 00	45 54.6	06	56	43.0	45 52.8	07	55	42.2	56 30
36	40	3 30	40 52.8	73	69	121.9	41 14.5	72	69	121.5	4 00
	47	8 30	39 14.4	65	76	110.9	39 33.7	64	76	110.5	9 00
	70	17 00	25 52.7	53	81	87.2	26 08.7	53	81	86.7	17 30
	45	19 00	47 04.6	54	80	101.0	47 20.7	54	80	100.3	19 30
	45	22 00	48 38.5	50	80	97.2	48 53.4	49	80	96.5	22 30
	27	23 00	63 16.7	58	76	111.7	63 33.8	57	76	110.7	23 30
	2	26 00	79 51.3	99	18	169.7	80 20.9	99	19	169.3	26 30
	54	45 00	48 45.2	12	70	60.2	48 51.8	10	69	58.7	46 00
	88	57 00	30 33.2	34	51	39.2	30 43.4	34	50	38.7	57 30
	135	69 30	20 30.1	79	21	15.3	24 25.6	78	17	12.0	74 30
37	46	6 00	37 55.6	69	73	114.9	38 16.1	68	73	114.4	6 30
	30	8 30	50 37.4	78	63	128.8	51 00.7	77	63	128.3	9 00
	50	11 30	38 32.3	62	77	106.3	38 50.9	62	77	105.8	12 00
	56	19 00	38 11.1	54	80	94.2	38 27.1	53	80	93.7	19 30
	62	21 30	34 42.6	51	80	87.9	34 57.9	51	80	87.4	22 00
	55	23 00	41 03.4	50	80	90.4	41 18.3	49	80	89.9	23 30
	34	26 00	59 11.7	49	78	101.1	59 26.2	48	79	100.2	26 30
	57	38 30	45 38.8	29	75	69.9	46 03.5	26	74	67.8	40 00
	38	45 00	60 31.4	04	71	62.2	60 28.1	07	69	60.2	46 00
	90	45 00	25 11.1	47	62	51.4	25 39.1	46	61	50.4	46 00
	114	52 30	16 14.6	65	46	35.4	17 12.9	65	45	34.2	54 00
	167	57 30	5 07.9	98	09	07.0	6 36.5	98	09	06.7	59 00
	51	60 30	50 28.2	22	48	37.0	50 06.9	25	46	34.7	62 00
38	45	8 30	39 56.9	69	72	114.2	40 17.4	68	72	113.7	9 00
	32	12 00	51 24.8	74	66	123.8	51 47.0	74	66	123.2	12 30
	30	23 00	60 18.8	61	74	111.7	60 36.8	00	74	110.9	23 30

DECLINATION **SAME** NAME TO LATITUDE

Lat.°	H.A.° '	Decl.° '	Alt.° '	△d	△t	Az.°	Alt.° '	△d	△t	Az.°	Decl.° '
39	49	17 30	42 29.6	61	76	102.5	42 47.7	60	76	102.0	18 00
	36	23 00	55 33.1	59	75	107.0	55 50.7	58	75	106.2	23 30

DECLINATION **CONTRARY** NAME TO LATITUDE

Lat.°	H.A.° '	Decl.°	Alt.° '	△d	△t	Az.°	Alt.° '	△d	△t	Az.°	Decl.° '
31	58	5 00	24 03.3	61	80	112.3	23 45.1	61	79	112.7	5 30
32	39	5 00	37 36.9	74	68	127.7	37 14.7	74	67	128.1	5 30
	55	14 00	20 06.4	67	72	122.2	19 46.2	67	72	122.6	14 30
	6	26 00	31 43.1	99	10	173.7	31 13.3	99	10	173.7	26 30
33	1	16 30	40 29.4	1.0	03	178.7	39 59.5	1.0	03	178.8	17 00
	11	16 30	39 23.7	98	21	166.3	38 54.4	98	21	166.4	17 00
34	49	10 00	26 00.6	72	69	124.2	25 39.0	72	69	124.6	10 30
35	45	10 30	27 42.6	76	65	128.2	27 19.9	76	64	128.6	11 00
	41	19 30	23 26.5	81	56	137.5	23 02.1	81	55	137.8	19 30
	15	23 00	30 16.8	97	23	164.0	29 47.7	97	23	164.1	23 30
	4	29 00	25 53.3	1.0	06	176.1	24 53.4	1.0	06	176.2	30 00
	35	29 00	17 59.2	87	44	148.2	17 07.0	87	43	148.7	30 00
36	66	7 00	14 46.3	64	76	110.3	14 26.9	65	76	110.7	7 30
	58	8 30	19 42.1	68	72	117.0	19 21.5	69	72	117.4	9 00
	26	12 30	35 38.4	90	43	148.2	35 11.4	90	43	148.5	13 00
	3	19 30	34 25.6	1.0	06	176.6	33 55.7	1.0	06	176.6	20 00
	16	20 00	31 59.3	96	25	162.2	31 30.3	97	25	162.4	20 30
	26	23 00	26 05.0	92	37	153.3	25 37.4	92	37	153.5	23 30
37	51	8 30	24 05.2	73	68	122.7	23 43.2	74	67	123.0	9 00
	5	10 30	42 16.1	1.0	10	173.4	41 46.2	1.0	10	173.4	11 00
	14	10 30	40 42.8	97	26	161.7	40 13.7	97	26	161.9	11 00
	61	12 00	14 41.4	69	71	117.8	14 20.7	69	71	118.2	12 30
	44	26 30	14 13.0	82	52	140.1	13 48.4	82	51	140.4	27 00
38	25	18 00	29 16.4	92	37	152.6	28 48.7	92	37	152.8	18 30
39	40	5 00	32 33.7	81	59	130.6	32 09.5	81	59	130.9	5 30
	50	9 30	22 52.9	76	64	124.9	22 30.0	76	64	125.3	10 00

MULTIPLICATION TABLE

DEC. DIFF. OR H. A. DIFF. (minutes of arc)

Δ	1'	2'	3'	4'	5'	6'	7'	8'	9'	10'	11'	12'	13'	14'	15'
01	0.0	0.0	0.0	0.0	0.1	0.1	0.1	0.1	0.1	0.1	0.1	0.1	0.1	0.1	0.2
02	.0	.0	.1	.1	.1	.1	.1	.2	.2	.2	.2	.2	.3	.3	.3
03	.0	.1	.1	.1	.2	.2	.2	.2	.3	.3	.3	.4	.4	.4	.5
04	.0	.1	.1	.2	.2	.2	.3	.3	.4	.4	.4	.5	.5	.6	.6
05	0.1	0.1	0.2	0.2	0.3	0.3	0.4	0.4	0.5	0.5	0.6	0.6	0.7	0.7	0.8
06	.1	.1	.2	.2	.3	.4	.4	.5	.5	.6	.7	.7	.8	.8	.9
07	.1	.2	.2	.3	.4	.4	.5	.6	.6	.7	.8	.8	.9	.9	1.0
08	.1	.2	.2	.3	.4	.5	.6	.6	.7	.8	.9	1.0	1.0	1.1	1.2
09	.1	.2	.3	.4	.5	.5	.6	.7	.8	.9	1.0	1.1	1.1	1.2	1.4
10	0.1	0.2	0.3	0.4	0.5	0.6	0.7	0.8	0.9	1.0	1.1	1.2	1.3	1.4	1.5
11	.1	.2	.3	.4	.6	.7	.8	.9	1.0	1.1	1.2	1.3	1.4	1.5	1.7
12	.1	.2	.4	.5	.6	.7	.8	1.0	1.1	1.2	1.3	1.4	1.6	1.7	1.8
13	.1	.3	.4	.5	.7	.8	.9	1.0	1.2	1.3	1.4	1.6	1.7	1.8	2.0
14	.1	.3	.4	.6	.7	.8	1.0	1.1	1.3	1.4	1.5	1.7	1.8	2.0	2.1
15	0.2	0.3	0.5	0.6	0.8	0.9	1.1	1.2	1.4	1.5	1.7	1.8	2.0	2.1	2.3
16	.2	.3	.5	.6	.8	1.0	1.1	1.3	1.4	1.6	1.8	1.9	2.1	2.2	2.4
17	.2	.3	.5	.7	.9	1.0	1.2	1.4	1.5	1.7	1.9	2.0	2.2	2.4	2.6
18	.2	.4	.5	.7	.9	1.1	1.3	1.4	1.6	1.8	2.0	2.2	2.3	2.5	2.7
19	.2	.4	.6	.8	1.0	1.1	1.3	1.5	1.7	1.9	2.1	2.3	2.5	2.7	2.9
20	0.2	0.4	0.6	0.8	1.0	1.2	1.4	1.6	1.8	2.0	2.2	2.4	2.6	2.8	3.0
21	.2	.4	.6	.8	1.1	1.3	1.5	1.7	1.9	2.1	2.3	2.5	2.7	2.9	3.2
22	.2	.4	.7	.9	1.1	1.3	1.5	1.8	2.0	2.2	2.4	2.6	2.9	3.1	3.3
23	.2	.5	.7	.9	1.2	1.4	1.6	1.8	2.1	2.3	2.5	2.8	3.0	3.2	3.5
24	.2	.5	.7	1.0	1.2	1.4	1.7	1.9	2.2	2.4	2.6	2.9	3.1	3.4	3.6
25	0.3	0.5	0.8	1.0	1.3	1.5	1.8	2.0	2.3	2.5	2.8	3.0	3.3	3.5	3.8
26	.3	.5	.8	1.0	1.3	1.6	1.8	2.1	2.3	2.6	2.9	3.1	3.4	3.6	3.9
27	.3	.5	.8	1.1	1.4	1.6	1.9	2.2	2.4	2.7	3.0	3.2	3.5	3.8	4.1
28	.3	.6	.8	1.1	1.4	1.7	2.0	2.2	2.5	2.8	3.1	3.4	3.6	3.9	4.2
29	.3	.6	.9	1.2	1.5	1.7	2.0	2.3	2.6	2.9	3.2	3.5	3.8	4.1	4.4
30	0.3	0.6	0.9	1.2	1.5	1.8	2.1	2.4	2.7	3.0	3.3	3.6	3.9	4.2	4.5
31	.3	.6	.9	1.2	1.6	1.9	2.2	2.5	2.8	3.1	3.4	3.7	4.0	4.3	4.7
32	.3	.6	1.0	1.3	1.6	1.9	2.2	2.6	2.9	3.2	3.5	3.8	4.2	4.5	4.8
33	.3	.7	1.0	1.3	1.7	2.0	2.3	2.6	3.0	3.3	3.6	4.0	4.3	4.6	5.0
34	.3	.7	1.0	1.4	1.7	2.0	2.4	2.7	3.1	3.4	3.7	4.1	4.4	4.8	5.1
35	0.4	0.7	1.1	1.4	1.8	2.1	2.5	2.8	3.2	3.5	3.9	4.2	4.6	4.9	5.3
36	.4	.7	1.1	1.4	1.8	2.2	2.5	2.9	3.2	3.6	4.0	4.3	4.7	5.0	5.4
37	.4	.7	1.1	1.5	1.9	2.2	2.6	3.0	3.3	3.7	4.1	4.4	4.8	5.2	5.6
38	.4	.8	1.1	1.5	1.9	2.3	2.7	3.0	3.4	3.8	4.2	4.6	4.9	5.3	5.7
39	.4	.8	1.2	1.6	2.0	2.3	2.7	3.1	3.5	3.9	4.3	4.7	5.1	5.5	5.9
40	0.4	0.8	1.2	1.6	2.0	2.4	2.8	3.2	3.6	4.0	4.4	4.8	5.2	5.6	6.0
41	.4	.8	1.2	1.6	2.1	2.5	2.9	3.3	3.7	4.1	4.5	4.9	5.3	5.7	6.2
42	.4	.8	1.3	1.7	2.1	2.5	2.9	3.4	3.8	4.2	4.6	5.0	5.5	5.9	6.3
43	.4	.9	1.3	1.7	2.2	2.6	3.0	3.4	3.9	4.3	4.7	5.2	5.6	6.0	6.5
44	.4	.9	1.3	1.8	2.2	2.6	3.1	3.5	4.0	4.4	4.8	5.3	5.7	6.2	6.6
45	0.5	0.9	1.4	1.8	2.3	2.7	3.2	3.6	4.1	4.5	5.0	5.4	5.9	6.3	6.8
46	.5	.9	1.4	1.8	2.3	2.8	3.2	3.7	4.1	4.6	5.1	5.5	6.0	6.4	6.9
47	.5	.9	1.4	1.9	2.4	2.8	3.3	3.8	4.2	4.7	5.2	5.6	6.1	6.6	7.1
48	.5	1.0	1.4	1.9	2.4	2.9	3.4	3.8	4.3	4.8	5.3	5.8	6.2	6.7	7.2
49	.5	1.0	1.5	2.0	2.5	2.9	3.4	3.9	4.4	4.9	5.4	5.9	6.4	6.9	7.4
50	0.5	1.0	1.5	2.0	2.5	3.0	3.5	4.0	4.5	5.0	5.5	6.0	6.5	7.0	7.5
51	.5	1.0	1.5	2.0	2.6	3.1	3.6	4.1	4.6	5.1	5.6	6.1	6.6	7.1	7.7
52	.5	1.0	1.6	2.1	2.6	3.1	3.6	4.2	4.7	5.2	5.7	6.2	6.8	7.3	7.8
53	.5	1.1	1.6	2.1	2.7	3.2	3.7	4.2	4.8	5.3	5.8	6.4	6.9	7.4	8.0
54	.5	1.1	1.6	2.2	2.7	3.2	3.8	4.3	4.9	5.4	5.9	6.5	7.0	7.6	8.1
55	0.6	1.1	1.7	2.2	2.8	3.3	3.9	4.4	5.0	5.5	6.1	6.6	7.2	7.7	8.3
56	.6	1.1	1.7	2.2	2.8	3.4	3.9	4.5	5.0	5.6	6.2	6.7	7.3	7.8	8.4
57	.6	1.1	1.7	2.3	2.9	3.4	4.0	4.6	5.1	5.7	6.3	6.8	7.4	8.0	8.6
58	.6	1.2	1.7	2.3	2.9	3.5	4.1	4.6	5.2	5.8	6.4	7.0	7.5	8.1	8.7
59	.6	1.2	1.8	2.4	3.0	3.5	4.1	4.7	5.3	5.9	6.5	7.1	7.7	8.3	8.9
60	0.6	1.2	1.8	2.4	3.0	3.6	4.2	4.8	5.4	6.0	6.6	7.2	7.8	8.4	9.0
61	.6	1.2	1.8	2.4	3.1	3.7	4.3	4.9	5.5	6.1	6.7	7.3	7.9	8.5	9.2
62	.6	1.2	1.9	2.5	3.1	3.7	4.3	5.0	5.6	6.2	6.8	7.4	8.1	8.7	9.3
63	.6	1.3	1.9	2.5	3.2	3.8	4.4	5.0	5.7	6.3	6.9	7.6	8.2	8.8	9.4
64	.6	1.3	1.9	2.6	3.2	3.8	4.5	5.1	5.8	6.4	7.0	7.7	8.3	9.0	9.6
65	0.7	1.3	2.0	2.6	3.3	3.9	4.6	5.2	5.9	6.5	7.2	7.8	8.5	9.1	9.8
66	.7	1.3	2.0	2.6	3.3	4.0	4.6	5.3	5.9	6.6	7.3	7.9	8.6	9.2	9.9
67	.7	1.3	2.0	2.7	3.4	4.0	4.7	5.4	6.0	6.7	7.4	8.0	8.7	9.4	10.0
68	.7	1.4	2.0	2.7	3.4	4.1	4.8	5.4	6.1	6.8	7.5	8.2	8.8	9.5	10.2
69	.7	1.4	2.1	2.8	3.5	4.1	4.8	5.5	6.2	6.9	7.6	8.3	9.0	9.7	10.4
70	0.7	1.4	2.1	2.8	3.5	4.2	4.9	5.6	6.3	7.0	7.7	8.4	9.1	9.8	10.5
71	.7	1.4	2.1	2.8	3.6	4.3	5.0	5.7	6.4	7.1	7.8	8.5	9.2	9.9	10.6
72	.7	1.4	2.2	2.9	3.6	4.3	5.0	5.8	6.5	7.2	7.9	8.6	9.4	10.1	10.8
73	.7	1.5	2.2	2.9	3.7	4.4	5.1	5.8	6.6	7.3	8.0	8.8	9.5	10.2	11.0
74	.7	1.5	2.2	3.0	3.7	4.4	5.2	5.9	6.7	7.4	8.1	8.9	9.6	10.4	11.1
75	0.8	1.5	2.3	3.0	3.8	4.5	5.3	6.0	6.8	7.5	8.3	9.0	9.8	10.5	11.3
76	.8	1.5	2.3	3.0	3.8	4.6	5.3	6.1	6.8	7.6	8.4	9.1	9.9	10.6	11.4
77	.8	1.5	2.3	3.1	3.9	4.6	5.4	6.2	6.9	7.7	8.5	9.2	10.0	10.8	11.6
78	.8	1.6	2.3	3.1	3.9	4.7	5.5	6.2	7.0	7.8	8.6	9.4	10.1	10.9	11.7
79	.8	1.6	2.4	3.2	4.0	4.7	5.5	6.3	7.1	7.9	8.7	9.5	10.3	11.1	11.9
80	0.8	1.6	2.4	3.2	4.0	4.8	5.6	6.4	7.2	8.0	8.8	9.6	10.4	11.2	12.0
81	.8	1.6	2.4	3.2	4.1	4.9	5.7	6.5	7.3	8.1	8.9	9.7	10.5	11.3	12.2
82	.8	1.6	2.5	3.3	4.1	4.9	5.7	6.6	7.4	8.2	9.0	9.8	10.7	11.5	12.3
83	.8	1.7	2.5	3.3	4.2	5.0	5.8	6.6	7.5	8.3	9.1	10.0	10.8	11.6	12.5
84	.8	1.7	2.5	3.4	4.2	5.0	5.9	6.7	7.6	8.4	9.2	10.1	10.9	11.8	12.6
85	0.9	1.7	2.6	3.4	4.3	5.1	6.0	6.8	7.7	8.5	9.4	10.2	11.1	11.9	12.8
86	.9	1.7	2.6	3.4	4.3	5.2	6.0	6.9	7.7	8.6	9.5	10.3	11.2	12.0	12.9
87	.9	1.7	2.6	3.5	4.4	5.2	6.1	7.0	7.8	8.7	9.6	10.4	11.3	12.2	13.1
88	.9	1.8	2.6	3.5	4.4	5.3	6.2	7.0	7.9	8.8	9.7	10.6	11.4	12.3	13.2
89	.9	1.8	2.7	3.6	4.5	5.3	6.2	7.1	8.0	8.9	9.8	10.7	11.6	12.5	13.4
90	0.9	1.8	2.7	3.6	4.5	5.4	6.3	7.2	8.1	9.0	9.9	10.8	11.7	12.6	13.5
91	.9	1.8	2.7	3.6	4.6	5.5	6.4	7.3	8.2	9.1	10.0	10.9	11.8	12.7	13.7
92	.9	1.8	2.8	3.7	4.6	5.5	6.4	7.4	8.3	9.2	10.1	11.0	12.0	12.9	13.8
93	.9	1.9	2.8	3.7	4.7	5.6	6.5	7.4	8.4	9.3	10.2	11.2	12.1	13.0	14.0
94	.9	1.9	2.8	3.8	4.7	5.6	6.6	7.5	8.5	9.4	10.3	11.3	12.2	13.2	14.1
95	1.0	1.9	2.9	3.8	4.8	5.7	6.7	7.6	8.6	9.5	10.5	11.4	12.4	13.3	14.3
96	1.0	1.9	2.9	3.8	4.8	5.8	6.7	7.7	8.6	9.6	10.6	11.5	12.5	13.4	14.4
97	1.0	1.9	2.9	3.9	4.8	5.8	6.8	7.8	8.7	9.7	10.7	11.6	12.6	13.6	14.6
98	1.0	2.0	2.9	3.9	4.9	5.9	6.8	7.8	8.8	9.8	10.8	11.8	12.7	13.7	14.7
99	1.0	2.0	3.0	4.0	4.9	5.9	6.9	7.9	8.9	9.9	10.9	11.9	12.9	13.9	14.9

DEC. DIFF. OR H. A. DIFF. (tenths of minutes)

Δ	0.1'	0.2'	0.3'	0.4'	0.5'	0.6'	0.7'	0.8'	0.9'
01	0.0	0.0	0.0	0.0	0.0	0.0	0.0	0.0	0.0
05	0.0	0.0	0.0	0.0	0.0	0.0	0.0	0.0	0.0
10	0.0	0.0	0.0	0.0	0.0	0.1	0.1	0.1	0.1
15	0.0	0.0	0.0	0.1	0.1	0.1	0.1	0.1	0.1
20	0.0	0.0	0.1	0.1	0.1	0.1	0.1	0.2	0.2
25	0.0	0.1	0.1	0.1	0.1	0.2	0.2	0.2	0.2
30	0.0	0.1	0.1	0.1	0.2	0.2	0.2	0.2	0.3
35	0.0	0.1	0.1	0.1	0.2	0.2	0.2	0.3	0.3
40	0.0	0.1	0.1	0.2	0.2	0.2	0.3	0.3	0.4
45	0.0	0.1	0.1	0.2	0.2	0.3	0.3	0.4	0.4
50	0.1	0.1	0.2	0.2	0.3	0.3	0.4	0.4	0.5
55	0.1	0.1	0.2	0.2	0.3	0.3	0.4	0.4	0.5
60	0.1	0.1	0.2	0.2	0.3	0.4	0.4	0.5	0.5
65	0.1	0.1	0.2	0.3	0.3	0.4	0.5	0.5	0.6
70	0.1	0.1	0.2	0.3	0.4	0.4	0.5	0.6	0.6
75	0.1	0.2	0.2	0.3	0.4	0.5	0.5	0.6	0.7
80	0.1	0.2	0.2	0.3	0.4	0.5	0.6	0.6	0.7
85	0.1	0.2	0.3	0.3	0.4	0.5	0.6	0.7	0.8
90	0.1	0.2	0.3	0.4	0.5	0.5	0.6	0.7	0.8
95	0.1	0.2	0.3	0.4	0.5	0.6	0.7	0.8	0.9

Bottom row repeats the column headers: Δ | 1' | 2' | 3' | 4' | 5' | 6' | 7' | 8' | 9' | 10' | 11' | 12' | 13' | 14' | 15' | Δ | 0.1' | 0.2' | 0.3' | 0.4' | 0.5' | 0.6' | 0.7' | 0.8' | 0.9' | Δ

ALTITUDE CORRECTION FOR D. R. LATITUDE

LATITUDE DIFFERENCE (minutes of arc)

Az.	16'	17'	18'	19'	20'	21'	22'	23'	24'	25'	26'	27'	28'	29'	30'	Az.
10 / 170	15.8	16.7	17.7	18.7	19.7	20.7	21.7	22.7	23.6	24.6	25.6	26.6	27.6	28.6	29.5	10 / 170
11 / 169	15.7	16.7	17.7	18.7	19.6	20.6	21.6	22.6	23.6	24.5	25.5	26.5	27.5	28.5	29.4	11 / 169
12 / 168	15.7	16.6	17.6	18.6	19.6	20.5	21.5	22.5	23.5	24.5	25.4	26.4	27.4	28.4	29.3	12 / 168
13 / 167	15.6	16.6	17.6	18.5	19.5	20.5	21.4	22.4	23.4	24.4	25.3	26.3	27.3	28.3	29.2	13 / 167
14 / 166	15.5	16.5	17.5	18.4	19.4	20.4	21.3	22.3	23.3	24.3	25.2	26.2	27.2	28.1	29.1	14 / 166
30 / 150	13.9	14.7	15.6	16.5	17.3	18.2	19.1	19.9	20.8	21.7	22.5	23.4	24.2	25.1	26.0	30 / 150
31 / 149	13.7	14.6	15.4	16.3	17.1	18.0	18.9	19.7	20.6	21.4	22.3	23.1	24.0	24.9	25.7	31 / 149
32 / 148	13.6	14.4	15.3	16.1	17.0	17.8	18.7	19.5	20.4	21.2	22.0	22.9	23.7	24.6	25.4	32 / 148
33 / 147	13.4	14.3	15.1	15.9	16.8	17.6	18.5	19.3	20.1	21.0	21.8	22.6	23.5	24.3	25.2	33 / 147
34 / 146	13.3	14.1	14.9	15.8	16.6	17.4	18.2	19.1	19.9	20.7	21.6	22.4	23.2	24.0	24.9	34 / 146
40 / 140	12.3	13.0	13.8	14.6	15.3	16.1	16.9	17.6	18.4	19.2	19.9	20.7	21.4	22.2	23.0	40 / 140
41 / 139	12.1	12.8	13.6	14.3	15.1	15.8	16.6	17.4	18.1	18.9	19.6	20.4	21.1	21.9	22.6	41 / 139
42 / 138	11.9	12.6	13.4	14.1	14.9	15.6	16.3	17.1	17.8	18.6	19.3	20.1	20.8	21.6	22.3	42 / 138
43 / 137	11.7	12.4	13.2	13.9	14.6	15.4	16.1	16.8	17.6	18.3	19.0	19.7	20.5	21.2	21.9	43 / 137
44 / 136	11.5	12.2	13.0	13.7	14.4	15.1	15.8	16.5	17.3	18.0	18.7	19.4	20.1	20.9	21.6	44 / 136
55 / 125	9.2	9.8	10.3	10.9	11.5	12.0	12.6	13.2	13.8	14.3	14.9	15.5	16.1	16.6	17.2	55 / 125
56 / 124	8.9	9.5	10.1	10.6	11.2	11.7	12.3	12.9	13.4	14.0	14.5	15.1	15.7	16.2	16.8	56 / 124
57 / 123	8.7	9.3	9.8	10.3	10.9	11.4	12.0	12.5	13.1	13.6	14.2	14.7	15.2	15.8	16.3	57 / 123
58 / 122	8.5	9.0	9.5	10.1	10.6	11.1	11.7	12.2	12.7	13.3	13.8	14.3	14.8	15.4	15.9	58 / 122
59 / 121	8.2	8.8	9.3	9.8	10.3	10.8	11.3	11.8	12.4	12.9	13.4	13.9	14.4	14.9	15.5	59 / 121
60 / 120	8.0	8.5	9.0	9.5	10.0	10.5	11.0	11.5	12.0	12.5	13.0	13.5	14.0	14.5	15.0	60 / 120
61 / 119	7.8	8.2	8.7	9.2	9.7	10.2	10.7	11.2	11.6	12.1	12.6	13.1	13.6	14.1	14.6	61 / 119
62 / 118	7.5	8.0	8.5	8.9	9.4	9.9	10.3	10.8	11.3	11.7	12.2	12.7	13.1	13.6	14.1	62 / 118
63 / 117	7.3	7.7	8.2	8.6	9.1	9.5	10.0	10.4	10.9	11.3	11.8	12.3	12.7	13.2	13.6	63 / 117
64 / 116	7.0	7.5	7.9	8.3	8.8	9.2	9.6	10.1	10.5	11.0	11.4	11.8	12.3	12.7	13.2	64 / 116
65 / 115	6.8	7.2	7.6	8.0	8.5	8.9	9.3	9.7	10.1	10.6	11.0	11.4	11.8	12.3	12.7	65 / 115
66 / 114	6.5	6.9	7.3	7.7	8.1	8.5	8.9	9.4	9.8	10.2	10.6	11.0	11.4	11.8	12.2	66 / 114
67 / 113	6.3	6.6	7.0	7.4	7.8	8.2	8.6	9.0	9.4	9.8	10.2	10.5	10.9	11.3	11.7	67 / 113
68 / 112	6.0	6.4	6.7	7.1	7.5	7.9	8.2	8.6	9.0	9.4	9.7	10.1	10.5	10.9	11.2	68 / 112
69 / 111	5.7	6.1	6.5	6.8	7.2	7.5	7.9	8.2	8.6	9.0	9.3	9.7	10.0	10.4	10.8	69 / 111
70 / 110	5.5	5.8	6.2	6.5	6.8	7.2	7.5	7.9	8.2	8.6	8.9	9.2	9.6	9.9	10.3	70 / 110
71 / 109	5.2	5.5	5.9	6.2	6.5	6.8	7.2	7.5	7.8	8.1	8.5	8.8	9.1	9.4	9.8	71 / 109
72 / 108	4.9	5.3	5.6	5.9	6.2	6.5	6.8	7.1	7.4	7.7	8.0	8.3	8.7	9.0	9.3	72 / 108
73 / 107	4.7	5.0	5.3	5.6	5.8	6.1	6.4	6.7	7.0	7.3	7.6	7.9	8.2	8.5	8.8	73 / 107
74 / 106	4.4	4.7	5.0	5.2	5.5	5.8	6.1	6.3	6.6	6.9	7.2	7.4	7.7	8.0	8.3	74 / 106

LAT. DIFF. (tenths of minutes of arc)

Az.	0.1'	0.2'	0.3'	0.4'	0.5'	0.6'	0.7'	0.8'	0.9'	Az.
10 / 170	0.1	0.2	0.3	0.4	0.5	0.6	0.7	0.8	0.9	10 / 170
11 / 169										11 / 169
12 / 168										12 / 168
13 / 167										13 / 167
14 / 166										14 / 166
30 / 150	0.1	0.2	0.3	0.3	0.4	0.5	0.6	0.7	0.8	30 / 150
31 / 149										31 / 149
32 / 148										32 / 148
33 / 147										33 / 147
34 / 146			0.2						0.7	34 / 146
40 / 140	0.1	0.2	0.2	0.3	0.4	0.5	0.5	0.6	0.7	40 / 140
41 / 139										41 / 139
42 / 138		0.1				0.4				42 / 138
43 / 137										43 / 137
44 / 136									0.6	44 / 136
55 / 125	0.1	0.1	0.2	0.2	0.3	0.3	0.4	0.5	0.5	55 / 125
56 / 124								0.4		56 / 124
57 / 123										57 / 123
58 / 122										58 / 122
59 / 121										59 / 121
60 / 120	0.0	0.1	0.2	0.2	0.3	0.3	0.4	0.4	0.5	60 / 120
61 / 119			0.1		0.2		0.3		0.4	61 / 119
62 / 118										62 / 118
63 / 117										63 / 117
64 / 116										64 / 116
65 / 115	0.0	0.1	0.1	0.2	0.2	0.3	0.3	0.3	0.4	65 / 115
66 / 114						0.2				66 / 114
67 / 113										67 / 113
68 / 112									0.3	68 / 112
69 / 111				0.1						69 / 111
70 / 110	0.0	0.1	0.1	0.1	0.2	0.2	0.2	0.3	0.3	70 / 110
71 / 109										71 / 109
72 / 108								0.2		72 / 108
73 / 107					0.1					73 / 107
74 / 106									0.2	74 / 106

Azimuth angle greater than 90°:
If DR latitude is greater than selected tabulated latitude, the correction is *minus*; but for DR latitude less than selected tabulated latitude, the correction is *plus*.
Azimuth angle less than 90°:
If DR latitude is greater than selected tabulated latitude, ΔL correction is *plus*; but for DR latitude less than selected tabulated latitude, the correction is *minus*.

T	1H 3-3000		1H 3-3020		1H 3-3040		1H 3-3060		1H 3-3080		T
Lat	Lo	Δ	Lo	Δ	Lo	Δ	Lo	Δ	Lo	Δ	Long
37 N	66 20.7W	+32	66 27.0W	+32	66 33.3W	+32	66 39.7W	+32	66 46.0W	+32	
36	66 03.2	37	66 10.6	37	66 17.9	37	66 25.2	37	66 32.5	37	
35 N	65 46.6W	42	65 54.9W	42	66 03.2W	42	66 11.5W	42	66 19.8W	42	
34 N	65 30.7W	+46	65 39.9W	+46	65 49.1W	+46	65 58.3W	+46	66 07.6W	+46	
33	65 15.2	51	65 25.4	51	65 35.5	51	65 45.7	51	65 55.8	51	
32	65 00.2	55	65 11.3	55	65 22.3	55	65 33.4	56	65 44.5	56	
31	64 45.7	60	64 57.6	60	65 09.6	60	65 21.5	60	65 33.5	60	
30	64 31.5	64	64 44.3	64	64 57.1	64	65 09.9	64	65 22.8	65	

Rate 1H 4

T	1H 4-3800		1H 4-3820		1H 4-3840		1H 4-4000		1H 4-4020		T	
Lat	L	Δ	L	Δ	L	Δ	L	Δ	L	Δ	Long	
	36 02.9N	+15	36 05.8N	+15	36 08.7N	+15	36 31.1N	+14	36 33.9N	+14	69	W
	35 24.9	17	35 28.3	17	35 31.6	17	35 57.3	16	36 00.4	16	68	
	34 45.8	20	34 49.7	19	34 53.5	19	35 22.9	18	35 26.5	18	67	
	34 05.7	22	34 10.1	22	34 14.5	22	34 47.9	20	34 51.9	20	66	
	33 24.5	25	33 29.5	25	33 34.4	24	34 12.1	23	34 16.6	23	65	
	32 42.1N	+28	32 47.7N	+28	32 53.2N	+28	33 35.4N	+26	33 40.5N	+25	64	W
	31 58.6	31	32 04.8	31	32 11.0	31	32 57.8	28	33 03.4	28	63	
	31 14.0	35	31 20.9	34	31 27.6	34	32 19.4	31	32 25.5	31	62	
	30 28.2	38	30 35.7	38	30 43.2	37	31 39.9	34	31 46.7	34	61	
	29 41.2	42	29 49.4	41	29 57.5	41	30 59.5	37	31 06.8	37	60	

Rate 2L 7

T	2L7-5700		2L7-5720		2L7-5740		2L7-5760		2L7-5780		T	
Lat	L	Δ	L	Δ	L	Δ	L	Δ	L	Δ	Long	
	22 39.0N	+ 9	22 40.8N	+ 9	22 42.6N	+ 9	22 44.4N	+ 9	22 46.3N	+ 9	167	W
	23 15.7	12	23 18.2	12	23 20.7	12	23 23.2	13	23 25.7	13	168	W
	24 13.7N	+ 19	24 17.5N	+ 19	24 21.4N	+ 20	24 25.5N	+ 21	24 29.7N	+ 21	169	W
	L		L		L		L		L			
	LO		LO		LO		LO		LO			
35 N	176 44.1W	- 64	176 31.2W	- 64	176 18.4W	- 64	176 05.6W	- 64	175 52.9W	- 63		
36	177 29.7	70	177 15.8	70	177 01.9	69	176 48.1	69	176 34.3	69		
37	178 16.7	76	178 01.6	75	177 46.5	75	177 31.6	75	177 16.7	74		
38	179 05.0	82	178 48.7	81	178 32.5	81	178 16.4	81	178 00.3	80		
39	179 54.8	88	179 37.2	87	179 19.8	87	179 02.5	87	178 45.2	86		
40 N	179 13.8E	+ 94	179 32.6E	+ 94	179 51.4E	+ 93	179 50.0W	- 93	179 31.5W	- 93		

VIII. HANDY TABLES AND FORMS

TABLES

Day	Jan	Feb	Mar	Apr	May	June	July	Aug	Sep	Oct	Nov	Dec	Day
	°	°	°	°	°	°	°	°	°	°	°	°	
1	100	131	158	189	218	249	278	309	340	9	40	69	1
2	101	132	159	190	219	250	279	310	341	10	41	70	2
3	102	133	160	191	220	251	280	311	342	11	42	71	3
4	103	134	161	192	221	252	281	312	343	12	43	72	4
5	104	135	162	193	222	253	282	313	344	13	44	73	5
6	105	136	163	194	223	254	283	314	345	14	45	74	6
7	106	136½	164	195	224	255	284	315	346	15	46	75	7
8	107	137	165	196	225	256	285	316	347	16	47	76	8
9	108	138	166	197	226	257	286	317	348	17	48	77	9
10	109	139	167	198	227	258	287	318	349	18	49	78	10
11	110	140	168	199	228	259	288	319	350	19	50	79	11
12	111	141	169	200	229	260	289	320	350½	20	51	80	12
13	112	142	170	201	230	261	290	321	351	21	52	81	13
14	113	143	171	202	231	262	291	322	352	22	53	82	14
15	114	144	172	203	232	263	292	323	353	23	54	83	15
16	115	145	173	204	233	264	293	324	354	24	55	84	16
17	116	146	174	204½	234	265	294	325	355	25	56	85	17
18	117	147	175	205	235	266	295	326	356	26	57	86	18
19	118	148	176	206	236	267	296	327	357	27	58	87	19
20	119	149	177	207	237	268	297	328	358	28	59	88	20
21	120	150	178	208	238	269	298	329	359	29	60	89	21
22	121	151	179	209	239	270	299	330	0	30	61	90	22
23	122	152	180	210	240	271	300	331	1	31	62	91	23
24	123	153	181	211	241	272	301	332	2	32	63	92	24
25	124	154	182	212	242	273	302	333	3	33	63½	93	25
26	125	155	183	213	243	274	303	334	4	34	64	94	26
27	126	156	184	214	244	275	304	335	5	35	65	95	27
28	127	157	185	215	245	276	305	336	6	36	66	96	28
29	128	157½	186	216	246	277	306	337	7	37	67	97	29
30	129	158	187	217	247	277½	307	338	8	38	68	98	30
31	130	159	188	218	248	278	308	339	9	39	69	99	31
Day	Jan	Feb	Mar	Apr	May	June	July	Aug	Sep	Oct	Nov	Dec	Day

To correct for any L.M.T. after 0h, **ADD** correction from following table. If necessary, subtract 360°.

Min.	0	4	8	12	16	20	24	28	32	36	40	44	48	52	56	60	Min.
Hrs.	°	°	°	°	°	°	°	°	°	°	°	°	°	°	°	°	Hrs.
0	0	1	2	3	4	5	6	7	8	9	10	11	12	13	14	15	0
1	15	16	17	18	19	20	21	22	23	24	25	26	27	28	29	30	1
2	30	31	32	33	34	35	36	37	38	39	40	41	42	43	44	45	2
3	45	46	47	48	49	50	51	52	53	54	55	56	57	58	59	60	3
4	60	61	62	63	64	65	66	67	68	69	70	71	72	73	74	75	4
5	75	76	77	78	79	80	81	82	83	84	85	86	87	88	89	90	5
6	90	91	92	93	94	95	96	97	98	99	100	101	102	103	104	105	6
7	105	106	107	108	109	110	111	112	113	114	115	116	117	118	119	120	7
8	120	121	122	123	124	125	126	127	128	129	130	131	132	133	134	135	8
9	135	136	137	138	139	140	141	142	143	144	145	146	147	148	149	150	9
10	150	151	152	153	154	155	156	157	158	159	160	161	162	163	164	165	10
11	165	166	167	168	169	170	171	172	173	174	175	176	177	178	179	180	11
12	180	181	182	184	185	186	187	188	189	190	191	192	193	194	195	196	12
13	196	197	198	199	200	201	202	203	204	205	206	207	208	209	210	211	13
14	211	212	213	214	215	216	217	218	219	220	221	222	223	224	225	226	14
15	226	227	228	229	230	231	232	233	234	235	236	237	238	239	240	241	15
16	241	242	243	244	245	246	247	248	249	250	251	252	253	254	255	256	16
17	256	257	258	259	260	261	262	263	264	265	266	267	268	269	270	271	17
18	271	272	273	274	275	276	277	278	279	280	281	282	283	284	285	286	18
19	286	287	288	289	290	291	292	293	294	295	296	297	298	299	300	301	19
20	301	302	303	304	305	306	307	308	309	310	311	312	313	314	315	316	20
21	316	317	318	319	320	321	322	323	324	325	326	327	328	329	330	331	21
22	331	332	333	334	335	336	337	338	339	340	341	342	343	344	345	346	22
23	346	347	348	349	350	351	352	353	354	355	356	357	358	359	0	1	23

G. W. MIXTER 1943

TABLE 2 — L.M.T. OF NOON 12h L.A.T. — ANY YEAR

Day	Jan	Feb	Mar	Apr	May	June	July	Aug	Sep	Oct	Nov	Dec	Day
1	1204	1214	1213	1204	1157	1158	1204	1206	1200	1150	1144	1149	1
2	04	14	12	04	57	58	04	06	00	49	44	49	2
3	05	14	12	03	57	58	04	06	1159	49	44	50	3
4	05	14	12	03	57	58	04	06	59	49	44	50	4
5	05	14	12	03	57	58	04	06	59	49	44	51	5
6	06	14	11	03	57	58	05	06	58	48	44	51	6
7	06	14	11	02	56	59	05	06	58	48	44	51	7
8	07	14	11	02	56	59	05	06	58	48	44	52	8
9	07	14	11	02	56	59	05	05	57	47	44	52	9
10	08	14	10	01	56	59	05	05	57	47	44	53	10
11	08	14	10	01	56	59	05	05	57	47	44	53	11
12	08	14	10	01	56	1200	05	05	56	47	44	54	12
13	09	14	10	01	56	00	06	05	56	46	44	54	13
14	09	14	09	00	56	00	06	05	56	46	44	55	14
15	09	14	09	00	56	00	06	04	55	46	45	55	15
16	10	14	09	00	56	00	06	04	55	46	45	56	16
17	10	14	09	00	56	01	06	04	55	45	45	56	17
18	11	14	08	1159	55	01	06	04	54	45	45	57	18
19	11	14	08	59	56	01	06	04	54	45	45	57	19
20	11	14	08	59	56	01	06	03	54	45	46	58	20
21	11	14	07	59	56	02	06	03	53	45	46	58	21
22	12	14	07	59	57	02	06	03	53	45	46	59	22
23	12	14	07	58	57	02	06	03	52	44	46	59	23
24	12	13	06	58	57	02	06	02	52	44	47	1200	24
25	12	13	06	58	57	02	06	02	52	44	47	00	25
26	13	13	06	58	57	03	06	02	51	44	47	01	26
27	13	13	06	58	57	03	06	02	51	44	47	01	27
28	13	13	05	57	57	03	06	01	51	44	48	02	28
29	13	13	05	57	57	03	06	01	50	44	48	02	29
30	13	12	05	57	57	03	06	01	50	44	49	03	30
31	1214	1212	1204	1157	1157	1204	1206	1200	1150	1144	1149	1203	31
	Jan	Feb	Mar	Apr	May	June	July	Aug	Sep	Oct	Nov	Dec	

TABLE 3 — To convert L.M.T. to Z.T. Corr. in minutes

ADD — For Long Diff. **WEST** of Zone Center | SUBTRACT — For Long Diff. **EAST** of Zone Center

	8°	7°	6°	5°	4°	3°	2°	1°	0°		0°	1°	2°	3°	4°	5°	6°	7°	8°	
0'	32	28	24	20	16	12	8	4	0	0'	0	4	8	12	16	20	24	28	32	0'
15'	33	29	25	21	17	13	9	5	1	15'	1	5	9	13	17	21	25	29	33	15'
30'	34	30	26	22	18	14	10	6	2	30'	2	6	10	14	18	22	26	30	34	30'
45'	35	31	27	23	19	15	11	7	3	45'	3	7	11	15	19	23	27	31	35	45'
60'	36	32	28	24	20	16	12	8	4	60'	4	8	12	16	20	24	28	32	36	60'

SUBTRACT | ADD
To convert Z. T. to L. M. T. Corr. in minutes

TABLE 4 — Centers of TIME ZONES and Zone Descriptions

LONGITUDES EAST →

0	15°	30°	45°	60°	75°	90°	105°	120°	135°	150°	165°	180°
0	−1	−2	−3	−4	−5	−6	−7	−8	−9	−10	−11	−12+

← WEST LONGITUDES

180°	165°	150°	135°	120°	105°	90°	75°	60°	45°	30°	15°	0
−12+	+11	+10	+9	+8	+7	+6	+5	+4	+3	+2	+1	0

G. W. MIXTER 1942

HANDY TABLES

TABLE 5

LENGTH OF A DEGREE OF LONG.

Lat.	Mi.	Lat.	Mi.	Lat.	Mi.	Lat.	Mi.
4	59.9	24	54.9	44	43.3	64	26.4
5	59.8	25	54.5	45	42.5	65	25.5
6	59.7	26	54.0	46	41.8	66	24.5
7	59.6	27	53.6	47	41.0	67	23.5
8	59.5	28	53.1	48	40.3	68	22.6
9	59.3	29	52.6	49	39.5	69	21.6
10	59.2	30	52.1	50	38.7	70	20.6
11	59.0	31	51.5	51	37.9	71	19.6
12	58.8	32	51.0	52	37.1	72	18.6
13	58.5	33	50.4	53	36.2	73	17.6
14	58.3	34	49.9	54	35.4	74	16.6
15	58.0	35	49.3	55	34.5	75	15.6
16	57.8	36	48.7	56	33.7	76	14.6
17	57.5	37	48.0	57	32.8	77	13.6
18	57.1	38	47.4	58	31.9	78	12.5
19	56.8	39	46.7	59	31.0	79	11.5
20	56.5	40	46.1	60	30.1	80	10.5
21	56.1	41	45.4	61	29.2	81	9.4
22	55.7	42	44.7	62	28.3	82	8.4
23	55.3	43	44.0	63	27.3	83	7.3

TABLE 6

VISIBILITY AT SEA

Ht. E.	Mi.	Ht. E.	Mi.	Ht. E.	Mi.
2	1.7	100	12	1,000	36
4	2.3	120	13	1,100	38
6	2.8	140	14	1,200	40
8	3.1	160	15	1,300	41
10	3.6	180	15	1,400	43
12	4.0	200	16	1,500	44
14	4.3	250	18	1,600	46
16	4.6	300	20	1,800	49
18	4.9	350	22	2,000	51
20	5.1	400	23	2,500	57
25	5.7	450	24	3,000	63
30	6.3	500	26	3,500	68
35	6.8	550	27	4,000	73
40	7.2	600	28	4,500	77
45	7.7	650	29	5,000	81
50	8.1	700	30	6,000	89
60	8.9	750	31	7,000	96
70	9.6	800	32	8,000	103
80	10.3	850	33	9,000	109
90	10.9	900	34	10,000	115

TIME, SPEED, DISTANCE — TABLE 7

Min.	5	½	6	½	7	½	8	½	9	½	10	½	11	½	12	½	13	½	14	½	15	Min.
1	0.1	0.1	0.1	0.1	0.1	0.1	0.1	0.1	0.2	0.2	0.2	0.2	0.2	0.2	0.2	0.2	0.2	0.2	0.2	0.2	0.3	1
2	.2	.2	.2	.2	.2	.3	.3	.3	.3	.3	.3	.3	.4	.4	.4	.4	.4	.5	.5	.5	.5	2
4	.3	.4	.4	.4	.5	.5	.5	.6	.6	.6	.7	.7	.7	.8	.8	.8	.9	.9	.9	1.0	1.0	4
6	.5	.6	.6	.7	.7	.8	.8	.9	.9	1.0	1.0	1.1	1.1	1.2	1.2	1.3	1.3	1.4	1.4	1.5	1.5	6
8	.7	.7	.8	.9	.9	1.0	1.1	1.1	1.2	1.3	1.3	1.4	1.5	1.5	1.6	1.7	1.7	1.8	1.9	1.9	2.0	8
10	.8	.9	1.0	1.1	1.2	1.3	1.3	1.4	1.5	1.6	1.7	1.8	1.8	1.9	2.0	2.1	2.2	2.3	2.3	2.4	2.5	10
12	1.0	1.1	1.2	1.3	1.4	1.5	1.6	1.7	1.8	1.9	2.0	2.1	2.2	2.3	2.4	2.5	2.6	2.7	2.8	2.9	3.0	12
14	1.2	1.3	1.4	1.5	1.6	1.8	1.9	2.0	2.1	2.2	2.3	2.5	2.6	2.7	2.8	2.9	3.0	3.2	3.3	3.4	3.5	14
16	1.3	1.5	1.6	1.7	1.9	2.0	2.1	2.3	2.4	2.5	2.7	2.8	2.9	3.1	3.2	3.3	3.5	3.6	3.7	3.9	4.0	16
18	1.5	1.7	1.8	2.0	2.1	2.3	2.4	2.6	2.7	2.9	3.0	3.2	3.3	3.5	3.6	3.8	3.9	4.1	4.2	4.4	4.5	18
20	1.7	1.8	2.0	2.2	2.3	2.5	2.7	2.8	3.0	3.2	3.3	3.5	3.7	3.8	4.0	4.2	4.3	4.5	4.7	4.8	5.0	20
22	1.8	2.0	2.2	2.4	2.6	2.8	2.9	3.1	3.3	3.5	3.7	3.9	4.0	4.2	4.4	4.6	4.8	5.0	5.1	5.3	5.5	22
24	2.0	2.2	2.4	2.6	2.8	3.0	3.2	3.4	3.6	3.8	4.0	4.2	4.4	4.6	4.8	5.0	5.2	5.4	5.6	5.8	6.0	24
26	2.2	2.4	2.6	2.8	3.0	3.3	3.5	3.7	3.9	4.1	4.3	4.6	4.8	5.0	5.2	5.4	5.6	5.9	6.1	6.3	6.5	26
28	2.3	2.6	2.8	3.0	3.3	3.5	3.7	4.0	4.2	4.4	4.7	4.9	5.1	5.4	5.6	5.8	6.1	6.3	6.5	6.8	7.0	28
30	2.5	2.8	3.0	3.3	3.5	3.8	4.0	4.3	4.5	4.8	5.0	5.3	5.5	5.8	6.0	6.3	6.5	6.8	7.0	7.3	7.5	30
32	2.7	2.9	3.2	3.5	3.7	4.0	4.3	4.5	4.8	5.1	5.3	5.6	5.9	6.1	6.4	6.7	6.9	7.2	7.5	7.7	8.0	32
34	2.8	3.1	3.4	3.7	4.0	4.3	4.5	4.8	5.1	5.4	5.7	6.0	6.2	6.5	6.8	7.1	7.4	7.7	7.9	8.2	8.5	34
36	3.0	3.3	3.6	3.9	4.2	4.5	4.8	5.1	5.4	5.7	6.0	6.3	6.6	6.9	7.2	7.5	7.8	8.1	8.4	8.7	9.0	36
38	3.2	3.5	3.8	4.1	4.4	4.8	5.1	5.4	5.7	6.0	6.3	6.7	7.0	7.3	7.6	7.9	8.2	8.6	8.9	9.2	9.5	38
40	3.3	3.7	4.0	4.3	4.7	5.0	5.3	5.7	6.0	6.3	6.7	7.0	7.3	7.7	8.0	8.3	8.7	9.0	9.3	9.7	10.0	40
42	3.5	3.9	4.2	4.6	4.9	5.3	5.6	6.0	6.3	6.7	7.0	7.4	7.7	8.1	8.4	8.8	9.1	9.5	9.8	10.2	10.5	42
44	3.7	4.0	4.4	4.8	5.1	5.5	5.9	6.2	6.6	7.0	7.3	7.7	8.1	8.4	8.8	9.2	9.5	9.9	10.3	10.6	11.0	44
46	3.8	4.2	4.6	5.0	5.4	5.8	6.1	6.5	6.9	7.3	7.7	8.1	8.4	8.8	9.2	9.6	10.0	10.4	10.7	11.1	11.5	46
48	4.0	4.4	4.8	5.2	5.6	6.0	6.4	6.8	7.2	7.6	8.0	8.4	8.8	9.2	9.6	10.0	10.4	10.8	11.2	11.6	12.0	48
50	4.2	4.6	5.0	5.4	5.8	6.3	6.7	7.1	7.5	7.9	8.3	8.8	9.2	9.6	10.0	10.4	10.8	11.3	11.7	12.1	12.5	50
52	4.3	4.8	5.2	5.6	6.1	6.5	6.9	7.4	7.8	8.2	8.7	9.1	9.5	10.0	10.4	10.8	11.3	11.7	12.1	12.6	13.0	52
54	4.5	5.0	5.4	5.9	6.3	6.8	7.2	7.7	8.1	8.6	9.0	9.5	9.9	10.4	10.8	11.3	11.7	12.2	12.6	13.1	13.5	54
56	4.7	5.1	5.6	6.1	6.5	7.0	7.5	7.9	8.4	8.9	9.3	9.8	10.3	10.7	11.2	11.7	12.1	12.6	13.1	13.5	14.0	56
58	4.8	5.3	5.8	6.3	6.8	7.3	7.7	8.2	8.7	9.2	9.7	10.2	10.6	11.1	11.6	12.1	12.6	13.1	13.5	14.0	14.5	58
60	5	½	6	½	7	½	8	½	9	½	10	½	11	½	12	½	13	½	14	½	15	60

G. W. MIXTER 1943

Day	Jan	Feb	Mar	Apr	May	June	July	Aug	Sep	Oct	Nov	Dec	Day
	°	°	°	°	°	°	°	°	°	°	°	°	
1	260	229	202	171	142	111	82	51	20	351	320	291	1
2	259	228	201	170	141	110	81	50	19	350	319	290	2
3	258	227	200	169	140	109	80	49	18	349	318	289	3
4	257	226	199	168	139	108	79	48	17	348	317	288	4
5	256	225	198	167	138	107	78	47	16	347	316	287	5
6	255	224	197	166	137	106	77	46	15	346	315	286	6
7	254	223½	196	165	136	105	76	45	14	345	314	285	7
8	253	223	195	164	135	104	75	44	13	344	313	284	8
9	252	222	194	163	134	103	74	43	12	343	312	283	9
10	251	221	193	162	133	102	73	42	11	342	311	282	10
11	250	220	192	161	132	101	72	41	10	341	310	281	11
12	249	219	191	160	131	100	71	40	9½	340	309	280	12
13	248	218	190	159	130	99	70	39	9	339	308	279	13
14	247	217	189	158	129	98	69	38	8	338	307	278	14
15	246	216	188	157	128	97	68	37	7	337	306	277	15
16	245	215	187	156	127	96	67	36	6	336	305	276	16
17	244	214	186	155½	126	95	66	35	5	335	304	275	17
18	243	213	185	155	125	94	65	34	4	334	303	274	18
19	242	212	184	154	124	93	64	33	3	333	302	273	19
20	241	211	183	153	123	92	63	32	2	332	301	272	20
21	240	210	182	152	122	91	62	31	1	331	300	271	21
22	239	209	181	151	121	90	61	30	360	330	299	270	22
23	238	208	180	150	120	89	60	29	359	329	298	269	23
24	237	207	179	149	119	88	59	28	358	328	297	268	24
25	236	206	178	148	118	87	58	27	357	327	296½	267	25
26	235	205	177	147	117	86	57	26	356	326	296	266	26
27	234	204	176	146	116	85	56	25	355	325	295	265	27
28	233	203	175	145	115	84	55	24	354	324	294	264	28
29	232	202½	174	144	114	83	54	23	353	323	293	263	29
30	231	202	173	143	113	82½	53	22	352	322	292	262	30
31	230	201	172	142	112	82	52	21	351	321	291	261	31
Day	Jan	Feb	Mar	Apr	May	June	July	Aug	Sep	Oct	Nov	Dec	Day

To correct for any L.M.T. after 0h, **SUBTRACT** correction from following table. If necessary, add 360°

Min.	0	4	8	12	16	20	24	28	32	36	40	44	48	52	56	60	Min.
Hrs.	°	°	°	°	°	°	°	°	°	°	°	°	°	°	°	°	Hrs.
0	0	1	2	3	4	5	6	7	8	9	10	11	12	13	14	15	0
1	15	16	17	18	19	20	21	22	23	24	25	26	27	28	29	30	1
2	30	31	32	33	34	35	36	37	38	39	40	41	42	43	44	45	2
3	45	46	47	48	49	50	51	52	53	54	55	56	57	58	59	60	3
4	60	61	62	63	64	65	66	67	68	69	70	71	72	73	74	75	4
5	75	76	77	78	79	80	81	82	83	84	85	86	87	88	89	90	5
6	90	91	92	93	94	95	96	97	98	99	100	101	102	103	104	105	6
7	105	106	107	108	109	110	111	112	113	114	115	116	117	118	119	120	7
8	120	121	122	123	124	125	126	127	128	129	130	131	132	133	134	135	8
9	135	136	137	138	139	140	141	142	143	144	145	146	147	148	149	150	9
10	150	151	152	153	154	155	156	157	158	159	160	161	162	163	164	165	10
11	165	166	167	168	169	170	171	172	173	174	175	176	177	178	179	180	11
12	180	181	182	184	185	186	187	188	189	190	191	192	193	194	195	196	12
13	196	197	198	199	200	201	202	203	204	205	206	207	208	209	210	211	13
14	211	212	213	214	215	216	217	218	219	220	221	222	223	224	225	226	14
15	226	227	228	229	230	231	232	233	234	235	236	237	238	239	240	241	15
16	241	242	243	244	245	246	247	248	249	250	251	252	253	254	255	256	16
17	256	257	258	259	260	261	262	263	264	265	266	267	268	269	270	271	17
18	271	272	273	274	275	276	277	278	279	280	281	282	283	284	285	286	18
19	286	287	288	289	290	291	292	293	294	295	296	297	298	299	300	301	19
20	391	302	303	304	305	306	307	308	309	310	311	312	313	314	315	316	20
21	316	317	318	319	320	321	322	323	324	325	326	327	328	329	330	331	21
22	331	332	333	334	335	336	337	338	339	340	341	342	343	344	345	346	22
23	346	347	348	349	350	351	352	353	354	355	356	357	358	359	0	1	23

G. W. MIXTER 1943

Day	Dec (S)	Nov (S)	Oct (S)	Sep	Aug (N)	July (N)	June (N)	May (N)	Apr (N)	Mar	Feb (S)	Jan (S)	Day
1	21 47	14 23	3 08	8 21 N	18 04	23 08	22 02	15 02	4 29	7 38 S	17 08	23 01	1
2	21 57	14 43	3 31	7 59	17 49	23 03	22 10	15 20	4 53	7 15	16 51	22 56	2
3	22 05	15 01	3 54	7 37	17 33	22 59	22 18	15 38	5 16	6 52	16 33	22 50	3
4	22 14	15 20	4 18	7 15	17 18	22 54	22 25	15 56	5 38	6 29	16 16	22 44	4
5	22 22	15 39	4 41	6 53	17 01	22 49	22 32	16 13	6 01	6 06	15 58	22 38	5
6	22 29	15 57	5 04	6 30	16 45	22 43	22 38	16 30	6 24	5 43	15 39	22 31	6
7	22 36	16 15	5 27	6 08	16 29	22 37	22 45	16 47	6 47	5 20	15 21	22 24	7
8	22 43	16 32	5 50	5 45	16 12	22 30	22 50	17 03	7 09	4 56	15 02	22 16	8
9	22 49	16 50	6 13	5 23	15 54	22 23	22 55	17 19	7 32	4 33	14 43	22 07	9
10	22 54	17 07	6 35	5 00	15 37	22 16	23 00	17 35	7 54	4 09	14 23	21 59	10
11	23 00	17 23	6 58	4 37	15 19	22 08	23 05	17 51	8 16	3 46	14 04	21 50	11
12	23 04	17 40	7 21	4 14	15 02	22 00	23 09	18 06	8 38	3 22	13 44	21 40	12
13	23 09	17 56	7 43	3 51	14 43	21 52	23 12	18 21	9 00	2 59	13 24	21 30	13
14	23 13	18 12	8 06	3 28	14 25	21 43	23 16	18 36	9 22	2 35	13 04	21 20	14
15	23 16	18 27	8 28	3 05	14 07	21 34	23 19	18 50	9 43	2 11	12 43	21 09	15
16	23 19	18 43	8 50	2 42	13 48	21 24	23 21	19 04	10 05	1 48	12 22	20 58	16
17	23 21	18 57	9 12	2 19	13 29	21 14	23 23	19 18	10 26	1 24	12 01	20 46	17
18	23 23	19 12	9 34	1 56	13 09	21 04	23 25	19 31	10 47	1 00	11 40	20 34	18
19	23 25	19 26	9 56	1 33	12 50	20 53	23 26	19 44	11 08	0 36	11 19	20 22	19
20	23 26	19 40	10 18	1 09	12 30	20 42	23 26	19 57	11 28	0 13 S	10 58	20 09	20
21	23 27	19 53	10 39	0 46	12 11	20 31	23 27	20 09	11 49	0 11 N	10 36	19 56	21
22	23 27	20 07	11 00	0 23	11 50	20 19	23 27	20 22	12 09	0 35	10 14	19 42	22
23	23 26	20 19	11 21	0 01 N	11 30	20 07	23 26	20 33	12 29	0 58	9 52	19 28	23
24	23 26	20 32	11 42	0 24 S	11 10	19 55	23 25	20 45	12 49	1 22	9 30	19 14	24
25	23 24	20 44	12 03	0 48	10 49	19 42	23 24	20 56	13 09	1 46	9 08	19 00	25
26	23 23	20 55	12 24	1 11	10 28	19 29	23 22	21 06	13 28	2 09	8 46	18 45	26
27	23 20	21 07	12 44	1 34	10 08	19 16	23 20	21 16	13 47	2 33	8 23	18 29	27
28	23 18	21 17	13 05	1 58	9 46	19 02	23 18	21 26	14 06	2 56	8 01	18 14	28
29	23 15	21 28	13 25	2 21	9 25	18 48	23 15	21 36	14 25	3 20	7 38	17 58	29
30	23 11	21 38	13 44	2 44	9 04	18 34	23 11	21 45	14 44	3 43	7 15	17 42	30
31	23 07	21 47	14 04	3 08	8 42	18 19	23 08	21 54	15 02	4 06	6 52	17 25	31

Maximum error from the use of this table for any year will be about 12′
The possible error reduces to zero about June 21 and Dec. 21.

Day	Dec (m s)	Nov (m s)	Oct (m s)	Sep (m s)	Aug (m s)	July (m s)	June (m s)	May (m s)	Apr (m s)	Mar (m s)	Feb (m s)	Jan (m s)	Day
1	+10 59	+16 21	+10 15	−0 02	−6 12	−3 36	+2 24	+2 56	−4 01	−12 31	−13 42	−3 35	1
2	+10 37	+16 22	+10 34	+0 17	−6 08	−3 47	+2 14	+3 03	−3 43	−12 19	−13 50	−4 03	2
3	+10 13	+16 23	+10 52	+0 37	−6 04	−3 59	+2 05	+3 10	−3 25	−12 07	−13 57	−4 31	3
4	+9 49	+16 22	+11 11	+0 56	−5 59	−4 10	+1 55	+3 16	−3 07	−11 54	−14 03	−4 59	4
5	+9 25	+16 21	+11 29	+1 16	−5 54	−4 20	+1 45	+3 22	−2 50	−11 41	−14 08	−5 26	5
6	+8 59	+16 19	+11 47	+1 36	−5 47	−4 31	+1 34	+3 27	−2 32	−11 27	−14 12	−5 52	6
7	+8 34	+16 16	+12 04	+1 56	−5 41	−4 41	+1 23	+3 31	−2 15	−11 13	−14 16	−6 19	7
8	+8 08	+16 12	+12 21	+2 16	−5 34	−4 51	+1 12	+3 35	−1 58	−10 58	−14 19	−6 44	8
9	+7 41	+16 07	+12 38	+2 37	−5 26	−5 00	+1 00	+3 38	−1 41	−10 43	−14 21	−7 10	9
10	+7 14	+16 02	+12 54	+2 57	−5 17	−5 09	+0 48	+3 41	−1 25	−10 28	−14 22	−7 34	10
11	+6 47	+15 56	+13 09	+3 18	−5 08	−5 17	+0 36	+3 43	−1 09	−10 12	−14 23	−7 59	11
12	+6 19	+15 49	+13 24	+3 39	−4 59	−5 25	+0 24	+3 45	−0 53	−9 57	−14 23	−8 22	12
13	+5 51	+15 41	+13 39	+4 00	−4 48	−5 33	+0 12	+3 46	−0 38	−9 40	−14 22	−8 45	13
14	+5 22	+15 32	+13 53	+4 21	−4 38	−5 40	−0 01	+3 46	−0 22	−9 24	−14 20	−9 08	14
15	+4 54	+15 23	+14 07	+4 43	−4 26	−5 46	−0 14	+3 46	−0 07	−9 07	−14 18	−9 29	15
16	+4 25	+15 12	+14 20	+5 04	−4 14	−5 52	−0 27	+3 45	+0 07	−8 50	−14 14	−9 50	16
17	+3 55	+15 01	+14 33	+5 25	−4 02	−5 58	−0 39	+3 44	+0 21	−8 33	−14 11	−10 11	17
18	+3 26	+14 49	+14 45	+5 47	−3 49	−6 03	−0 52	+3 42	+0 35	−8 15	−14 06	−10 30	18
19	+2 57	+14 36	+14 56	+6 08	−3 36	−6 07	−1 05	+3 40	+0 49	−7 58	−14 00	−10 49	19
20	+2 27	+14 22	+15 07	+6 29	−3 22	−6 11	−1 18	+3 37	+1 02	−7 40	−13 54	−11 07	20
21	+1 57	+14 08	+15 17	+6 51	−3 07	−6 14	−1 31	+3 34	+1 15	−7 22	−13 48	−11 24	21
22	+1 27	+13 52	+15 27	+7 12	−2 52	−6 17	−1 44	+3 30	+1 27	−7 04	−13 40	−11 41	22
23	+0 57	+13 36	+15 35	+7 33	−2 37	−6 19	−1 57	+3 25	+1 39	−6 46	−13 32	−11 57	23
24	+0 27	+13 19	+15 43	+7 54	−2 21	−6 21	−2 10	+3 20	+1 50	−6 27	−13 23	−12 12	24
25	−0 03	+13 02	+15 51	+8 14	−2 05	−6 21	−2 23	+3 15	+2 01	−6 09	−13 14	−12 26	25
26	−0 32	+12 43	+15 57	+8 35	−1 49	−6 22	−2 35	+3 09	+2 11	−5 51	−13 04	−12 39	26
27	−1 02	+12 24	+16 03	+8 55	−1 32	−6 22	−2 48	+3 03	+2 21	−5 32	−12 54	−12 51	27
28	−1 32	+12 04	+16 08	+9 16	−1 14	−6 21	−3 00	+2 56	+2 31	−5 14	−12 43	−13 03	28
29	−2 01	+11 43	+16 13	+9 36	−0 57	−6 20	−3 12	+2 48	+2 40	−4 55	−12 31	−13 14	29
30	−2 30	+11 21	+16 16	+9 55	−0 39	−6 18	−3 24	+2 41	+2 48	−4 37	−12 19	−13 24	30
31	−2 59	+10 59	+16 19	+10 15	−0 20	−6 15	−3 36	+2 32	+2 56	−4 19	−12 07	−13 33	31

Maximum error from the use of this table for any year will be about 20 sec. The possible error reduces to 2 sec. or less four times each year.

COMPASS GUIDE

Computations may begin or end with any item
Use Eq. T. or Decl. of Sun for any Year from Tables X or Y

CORRECTING	UNCORRECTING
COURSE, points _____	TRUE _____
COMPASS _____	Variation E− / W+ _____
Deviation E+ / W− _____	MAGNETIC _____
MAGNETIC _____	Deviation E− / W+ _____
Variation E+ / W− _____	COMPASS _____
TRUE _____	Set Stbd − / Port + _____
Set Stbd + / Port − _____	COMPASS _____
PLOT, true _____	COURSE, points _____

To set the L.A.T. on hack watch

Date _____	TIME ZONE _____
Long. _____	
Set to Z. T. ____ h ____ m	
Long Diff. E+ / W− _____	
L. M. T. ____ h ____ m	
Eq. T ( ) _____	
L.A.T. ____ h ____ m	
H. A.(t) _____	
G'wich Date _____	
G.M.T. ____ h ____ m	

DEVIATION

SHIP HEADS _____ Lat. _____

True BEARING or AZIMUTH _____	
Variation E− / W+ _____	
MAGNETIC _____	
COMPASS _____	E / W
DEVIATION _____	

Magnetic greater Dev. E
Compass " Dev. W

East Dev. takes Ship to Right of Course
West Dev. takes Ship to Left of Course

ADJUSTMENT

Start with Correctors where found

(1) Head EAST, cut Dev. to 0

W Dev. FORENAFT MAGNETS Dev. E	
Place Blue Fw'd	Place Blue Aft.
If Blue is Fw'd, Raise	If Blue is Fw'd, Lower
If Blue is Aft, Lower	If Blue is Aft. Raise

or (1) Head WEST, cut Dev. to 0

W Dev. FORENAFT MAGNETS Dev. E	
Place Blue Aft.	Place Blue Fw'd.
If Blue is Aft. Raise	If Blue is Fw'd, Raise
If Blue is Fw'd Lower	If Blue is Aft, Lower

(2) Head SOUTH, cut Dev. to 0

W Dev. THWARTSHIP MAGNETS Dev. E	
Place Blue to Port	Place Blue to Stbd
If Blue is Port, Raise	If Blue is Stbd, Raise
If Blue is Stbd, Lower	If Blue is Port, Lower

or (2) Head NORTH, cut Dev. to 0

W Dev. THWARTSHIP MAGNETS Dev. E	
Place Blue to Stbd.	Place Blue to Port
If Blue is Stbd, Raise	If Blue is Port, Raise
If Blue is Port, Lower	If Blue is Stbd, Lower

(3) Head on Adjacent Intercardinal Point

Move SPHERES, cut Dev. to 0

Head	NE		SE		SW		NW	
Dev.	W	E	W	E	W	E	W	E
Move	Out	In	In	Out	Out	In	In	Out

Swing on each 45°, record Deviations
If any exceed 3°, consult Chap. 5

Courtesy of
WILFRED O. WHITE & SONS, INC.

COMPASS POINTS AND DEGREES
The quarter points are named according to Merchant Marine practice

	°		°		°		°
NORTH	0.	**EAST**	90.	**SOUTH**	180.	**WEST**	270.
N¼E	2.8	E¼S	92.8	S¼W	182.8	W¼N	272.8
N½E	5.6	E½S	95.6	S½W	185.6	W½N	275.6
N¾E	8.4	E¾S	98.4	S¾W	188.4	W¾N	278.4
NxE	11.3	ExS	101.3	SxW	191.3	WxN	281.3
NxE¼E	14.1	ExS¼S	104.1	SxW¼W	194.1	WxN¼N	284.1
NxE½E	16.9	ExS½S	106.9	SxW½W	196.9	WxN½N	286.9
NxE¾E	19.7	ExS¾S	109.7	SxW¾W	199.7	WxN¾N	289.7
NNE	22.5	ESE	112.5	SSW	202.5	WNW	292.5
NExN¾N	25.3	SExE¾E	115.3	SWxS¾S	205.3	NWxW¾W	295.3
NExN½N	28.1	SExE½E	118.1	SWxS½S	208.1	NWxW½W	298.1
NExN¼N	30.9	SExE¼E	120.9	SWxS¼S	210.9	NWxW¼W	300.9
NExN	33.8	SExE	123.8	SWxS	213.8	NWxW	303.8
NE¾N	36.6	SE¾E	126.6	SW¾S	216.6	NW¾W	306.6
NE½N	39.4	SE½E	129.4	SW½S	219.4	NW½W	309.4
NE¼N	42.2	SE¼E	132.2	SW¼S	222.2	NW¼W	312.2
NE	45.	SE	135.	SW	225.	NW	315.
NE¼E	47.8	SE¼S	137.8	SW¼W	227.8	NW¼N	317.8
NE½E	50.6	SE½S	140.6	SW½W	230.6	NW½N	320.6
NE¾E	53.4	SE¾S	143.4	SW¾W	233.4	NW¾N	323.4
NExE	56.3	SExS	146.3	SWxW	236.3	NWxN	326.3
NExE¼E	59.1	SExS¼S	149.1	SWxW¼W	239.1	NWxN¼N	329.1
NExE½E	61.9	SExS½S	151.9	SWxW½W	241.9	NWxN½N	331.9
NExE¾E	64.7	SExS¾S	154.7	SWxW¾W	244.7	NWxN¾N	334.7
ENE	67.5	SSE	157.5	WSW	247.5	NNW	337.5
ExN¾N	70.3	SxE¾E	160.3	WxS¾S	250.3	NxW¾W	340.3
ExN½N	73.1	SxE½E	163.1	WxS½S	253.1	NxW½W	343.1
ExN¼N	75.9	SxE¼E	165.9	WxS¼S	255.9	NxW¼W	345.9
ExN	78.8	SxE	168.8	WxS	258.8	NxW	348.8
E¾N	81.6	S¾E	171.6	W¾S	261.6	N¾W	351.6
E½N	84.4	S½E	174.4	W½S	264.4	N½W	354.4
E¼N	87.2	S¼E	177.2	W¼S	267.2	N¼W	357.2
EAST	90.	**SOUTH**	180.	**WEST**	270.	**NORTH**	360.

Ⓒ 1932, G. W. MIXTER

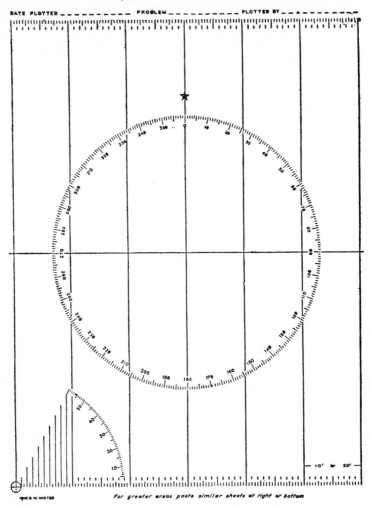

The above drawing is a one-half size reproduction of the Problem Plotting Sheet suitable for sample problems. It provides for an area 1° x 1°. or 2° x 2° in a latitude of 40° or larger by joining two or more sheets. When used for 2° x 2° the scale is approximately the same as that of a standard plotting sheet. See §1108 for the method of locating the parallels of latitude.

INDEX

All references are to page numbers.

543

HAPPY VOYAGE

ALTITUDE CORRECTION TABLES 0°–35°—MOON

App. Alt.	0°–4° Corrⁿ	5°–9° Corrⁿ	10°–14° Corrⁿ	15°–19° Corrⁿ	20°–24° Corrⁿ	25°–29° Corrⁿ	30°–34° Corrⁿ	App. Alt.
00	⁰ 33.8	⁵ 58.2	¹⁰ 62.1	¹⁵ 62.8	²⁰ 62.2	²⁵ 60.8	³⁰ 58.9	00
10	35.9	58.5	62.2	62.8	62.1	60.8	58.8	10
20	37.8	58.7	62.2	62.8	62.1	60.7	58.8	20
30	39.6	58.9	62.3	62.8	62.1	60.7	58.7	30
40	41.2	59.1	62.3	62.8	62.0	60.6	58.6	40
50	42.6	59.3	62.4	62.7	62.0	60.6	58.5	50
00	¹ 44.0	⁶ 59.5	¹¹ 62.4	¹⁶ 62.7	²¹ 62.0	²⁶ 60.5	³¹ 58.5	00
10	45.2	59.7	62.4	62.7	61.9	60.4	58.4	10
20	46.3	59.9	62.5	62.7	61.9	60.4	58.3	20
30	47.3	60.0	62.5	62.7	61.9	60.3	58.2	30
40	48.3	60.2	62.5	62.7	61.8	60.3	58.2	40
50	49.2	60.3	62.6	62.6	61.8	60.2	58.1	50
00	² 50.0	⁷ 60.5	¹² 62.6	¹⁷ 62.7	²² 61.7	²⁷ 60.1	³² 58.0	00
10	50.8	60.6	62.6	62.6	61.7	60.1	57.9	10
20	51.4	60.7	62.6	62.6	61.6	60.0	57.8	20
30	52.1	60.9	62.7	62.6	61.6	59.9	57.8	30
40	52.7	61.0	62.7	62.6	61.5	59.9	57.7	40
50	53.3	61.1	62.7	62.6	61.5	59.8	57.6	50
00	³ 53.8	⁸ 61.2	¹³ 62.7	¹⁸ 62.5	²³ 61.5	²⁸ 59.7	³³ 57.5	00
10	54.3	61.3	62.7	62.5	61.4	59.7	57.4	10
20	54.8	61.4	62.7	62.5	61.4	59.6	57.4	20
30	55.2	61.5	62.8	62.5	61.3	59.6	57.3	30
40	55.6	61.6	62.8	62.4	61.3	59.5	57.2	40
50	56.0	61.6	62.8	62.4	61.2	59.4	57.1	50
00	⁴ 56.4	⁹ 61.7	¹⁴ 62.8	¹⁹ 62.4	²⁴ 61.2	²⁹ 59.3	³⁴ 57.0	00
10	56.7	61.8	62.8	62.3	61.1	59.3	56.9	10
20	57.1	61.9	62.8	62.3	61.1	59.2	56.9	20
30	57.4	61.9	62.8	62.3	61.0	59.1	56.8	30
40	57.7	62.0	62.8	62.2	60.9	59.1	56.7	40
50	57.9	62.1	62.8	62.2	60.9	59.0	56.6	50

H.P.	L U	L U	L U	L U	L U	L U	L U	H.P.
54.0	0.3 0.9	0.3 0.9	0.4 1.0	0.5 1.1	0.6 1.2	0.7 1.3	0.9 1.5	54.0
54.3	0.7 1.1	0.7 1.2	0.7 1.2	0.8 1.3	0.9 1.4	1.1 1.5	1.2 1.7	54.3
54.6	1.1 1.4	1.1 1.4	1.1 1.4	1.2 1.5	1.3 1.6	1.4 1.7	1.5 1.8	54.6
54.9	1.4 1.6	1.5 1.6	1.5 1.6	1.6 1.7	1.6 1.8	1.8 1.9	1.9 2.0	54.9
55.2	1.8 1.8	1.8 1.8	1.9 1.9	1.9 1.9	2.0 2.0	2.1 2.1	2.2 2.2	55.2
55.5	2.2 2.0	2.2 2.0	2.3 2.1	2.3 2.1	2.4 2.2	2.4 2.3	2.5 2.4	55.5
55.8	2.6 2.2	2.6 2.2	2.6 2.3	2.7 2.3	2.7 2.4	2.8 2.4	2.9 2.5	55.8
56.1	3.0 2.4	3.0 2.5	3.0 2.5	3.0 2.5	3.1 2.6	3.1 2.6	3.2 2.7	56.1
56.4	3.4 2.7	3.4 2.7	3.4 2.7	3.4 2.7	3.4 2.8	3.5 2.8	3.5 2.9	56.4
56.7	3.7 2.9	3.7 2.9	3.8 2.9	3.8 2.9	3.8 3.0	3.8 3.0	3.9 3.0	56.7
57.0	4.1 3.1	4.1 3.1	4.1 3.1	4.1 3.1	4.2 3.1	4.2 3.2	4.2 3.2	57.0
57.3	4.5 3.3	4.5 3.3	4.5 3.3	4.5 3.3	4.5 3.3	4.6 3.4	4.6 3.4	57.3
57.6	4.9 3.5	4.9 3.5	4.9 3.5	4.9 3.5	4.9 3.5	4.9 3.5	4.9 3.6	57.6
57.9	5.3 3.8	5.3 3.8	5.2 3.8	5.2 3.7	5.2 3.7	5.2 3.7	5.2 3.7	57.9
58.2	5.6 4.0	5.6 4.0	5.6 4.0	5.6 4.0	5.6 3.9	5.6 3.9	5.6 3.9	58.2
58.5	6.0 4.2	6.0 4.2	6.0 4.2	6.0 4.2	6.0 4.1	5.9 4.1	5.9 4.1	58.5
58.8	6.4 4.4	6.4 4.4	6.4 4.4	6.3 4.4	6.3 4.3	6.3 4.3	6.2 4.2	58.8
59.1	6.8 4.6	6.8 4.6	6.7 4.6	6.7 4.6	6.7 4.5	6.6 4.5	6.6 4.4	59.1
59.4	7.2 4.8	7.1 4.8	7.1 4.8	7.1 4.8	7.0 4.7	7.0 4.7	6.9 4.6	59.4
59.7	7.5 5.1	7.5 5.0	7.5 5.0	7.5 5.0	7.4 4.9	7.3 4.8	7.2 4.7	59.7
60.0	7.9 5.3	7.9 5.3	7.9 5.2	7.8 5.2	7.8 5.1	7.7 5.0	7.6 4.9	60.0
60.3	8.3 5.5	8.3 5.5	8.2 5.4	8.2 5.4	8.1 5.3	8.0 5.2	7.9 5.1	60.3
60.6	8.7 5.7	8.7 5.7	8.6 5.7	8.6 5.6	8.5 5.5	8.4 5.4	8.2 5.3	60.6
60.9	9.1 5.9	9.0 5.9	9.0 5.9	8.9 5.8	8.8 5.7	8.7 5.6	8.6 5.4	60.9
61.2	9.5 6.2	9.4 6.1	9.4 6.1	9.3 6.0	9.2 5.9	9.1 5.8	8.9 5.6	61.2
61.5	9.8 6.4	9.8 6.3	9.7 6.3	9.7 6.2	9.5 6.1	9.4 5.9	9.2 5.8	61.5

DIP

Ht. of Eye	Corrⁿ	Ht. of Eye	Ht. of Eye	Corrⁿ	Ht. of Eye
m		ft.	m		ft.
2.4	-2.8	8.0	9.5	-5.5	31.5
2.6	-2.9	8.6	9.9	-5.6	32.7
2.8	-3.0	9.2	10.3	-5.7	33.9
3.0	-3.1	9.8	10.6	-5.8	35.1
3.2	-3.2	10.5	11.0	-5.9	36.3
3.4	-3.3	11.2	11.4	-6.0	37.6
3.6	-3.4	11.9	11.8	-6.1	38.9
3.8	-3.5	12.6	12.2	-6.2	40.1
4.0	-3.6	13.3	12.6	-6.3	41.5
4.3	-3.7	14.1	13.0	-6.4	42.8
4.5	-3.8	14.9	13.4	-6.5	44.2
4.7	-3.9	15.7	13.8	-6.6	45.5
5.0	-4.0	16.5	14.2	-6.7	46.9
5.2	-4.1	17.4	14.7	-6.8	48.4
5.5	-4.2	18.3	15.1	-6.9	49.8
5.8	-4.3	19.1	15.5	-7.0	51.3
6.1	-4.4	20.1	16.0	-7.1	52.8
6.3	-4.5	21.0	16.5	-7.2	54.3
6.6	-4.6	22.0	16.9	-7.3	55.8
6.9	-4.7	22.9	17.4	-7.4	57.4
7.2	-4.8	23.9	17.9	-7.5	58.9
7.5	-4.9	24.9	18.4	-7.6	60.5
7.9	-5.0	26.0	18.8	-7.7	62.1
8.2	-5.1	27.1	19.3	-7.8	63.8
8.5	-5.2	28.1	19.8	-7.9	65.4
8.8	-5.3	29.2	20.4	-8.0	67.1
9.2	-5.4	30.4	20.9	-8.1	68.8
9.5		31.5	21.4		70.5

MOON CORRECTION TABLE

The correction is in two parts; the first correction is taken from the upper part of the table with argument apparent altitude, and the second from the lower part, with argument H.P., in the same column as that from which the first correction was taken. Separate corrections are given in the lower part for lower (L) and upper (U) limbs. All corrections are to be **added** to apparent altitude, *but 30' is to be subtracted from the altitude of the upper limb.*

For corrections for pressure and temperature see page A4.

For bubble sextant observations ignore dip, take the mean of upper and lower limb corrections and subtract 15' from the altitude.

App. Alt. = Apparent altitude = Sextant altitude corrected for index error and dip.